AF394809

2024

2024

The Election
That Surprised India

Rajdeep
Sardesai

HarperCollins *Publishers* India

First published in India by HarperCollins *Publishers* 2024
4th Floor, Tower A, Building No. 10, DLF Cyber City,
DLF Phase II, Gurugram, Haryana – 122002
www.harpercollins.co.in

2 4 6 8 10 9 7 5 3 1

P-ISBN: 978-93-6213-529-2
E-ISBN: 978-93-6213-112-6

Typeset in 11.5/16 Dante MT Std at
HarperCollins *Publishers* India

Printed and bound at
Thomson Press (India) Ltd

To the Indian voter for their remarkable capacity to surprise

Contents

Contents

INTRODUCTION

2024: The Election That Surprised India

Frequently asked question: So how did all you high-flying journalists and know-it-all pollsters get the 2024 election outcome so wrong?

THERE is no city quite like Varanasi. The chaos and cacophony of narrow streets blend with the silence of the soul. The presence of the river—mighty, sacred and slow—lifts this ancient place to a transcendence that is both otherworldly and intensely human. It was perhaps only appropriate that my travels across the country for the 2024 general election were ending in this unique city of antiquity by the banks of the Ganga. Varanasi, after all, is now the flagship city for Narendra Modi and the Bharatiya Janata Party's (BJP's) long-term project to dominate India in every sphere, politically, culturally and ideologically. It was here, by the riverbank, that Modi began his unstoppable streak to the top in 2014, a lead position he solidified in the last decade. Strongman. Personality cult. Media myth. The fastest-growing large economy in the world. A Ram temple finally consecrated in Ayodhya amidst public euphoria. A larger-than-life global leader—a 'vishwaguru'. The narrative around the rise of Modi suggested that the 2024 general elections were a 'done deal', that the BJP's claim to win 'char sau paar' (400-plus) seats was not just bravado but inevitable; a fractured Opposition was only in the contest as unelectable faces in the crowd. 'Aayega toh Modi hi! (Only Modi will come!),' screamed his army of cheerleaders. Even the stars were firmly aligned.

Or so it seemed.

It took an unlikely voice in Varanasi for the bubble to burst. I was recording for a show by the ghats that gently sloped into the holy river's waters. Dusk was falling in shades of magenta. The shimmering lights of the Ganga aarti were fading in the distance. My guest was popular stand-up comedian Shyam Rangeela, whose mimicry of India's top political figures, especially Prime Minister Modi, had made him a viral sensation. During the elections, however, the skinny figure of Rangeela had made the headlines not as a comic artiste but because his nomination to fight against Modi from Varanasi was rejected by the presiding officer on highly specious grounds. I asked him if he had chosen to contest only as an attention-seeking gimmick. 'Are you telling me that I cannot contest against Modi ji? Am I not a citizen of India?' he countered. I pointed out that a token fight in Varanasi against India's neta No. 1 was hardly going to alter the course of a national election. 'Dekho, sir, yeh India ka election hai; yahan kuch bhi ho sakta hai (This is an Indian election; anything can happen)!' was his punchline.

Like the eternal charm of the sacred city around us, a stand-up comedian's words were simple yet profound. Rangeela's Varanasi election bid was largely symbolic, but surely those of us who called the 2024 election even before the campaign kicked off were guilty of forgetting a cardinal principle of life and politics: the future is unpredictable. Especially in a country of 1.4 billion (140 crore) people, where the 970 million (97 crore)-strong electorate is spread across a subcontinental-sized landmass with multiple languages, castes, religious faiths and ethnicities. How then could a handful of news anchors and pundits smugly sitting in an air-conditioned studio predict the fate of the nation with such utter confidence?

When the election results were declared, I recalled my conversation with Rangeela. Is there something that stand-up comics, with their distinctive ability to cut the crap and sense the public pulse, can see that grey-haired journalists and cocky pollsters cannot? Forget 'char sau paar', in 2024, the Modi-led BJP could not even cross the magic halfway mark of 272 seats. Having been unable to secure a majority, the Prime Minister must now rely on unpredictable allies to ensure a stable government. I have to confess that I too was among those who were relatively sure that the BJP would get a majority by itself. While I was never a part of the 'char sau paar' club, I was still expecting a comfortable win (280-plus was my number for the BJP). In fact, when I started working on this book in the summer of 2023, my original title was 'Hat-Trick', a term indelibly associated with a unique achievement in cricket. Like so many others, I too was swayed by the 'Modi ki guarantee' drumbeat and the event-driven 'spectacle' of his politics, convinced that the resource-rich BJP's election machine would overwhelm all else.

On the election road, we encountered many voices that conflicted with our Mood of the Nation surveys, ordinary men and women who complained about 'mehngai' (inflation) and 'berozgaari' (unemployment), paper leaks in recruitment exams, local corruption and 'ahankari' (arrogant) leaders. In Varanasi itself, where Modi's supporters were loudly proclaiming a record-breaking victory, we spent time with the wonderfully skilled 'bunkars' (weavers) of Peeli Kothi, famed for their fine Banarasi sari–weaving skills. In this Muslim-dominated area, the weavers recounted their post-Covid struggles and how incomes had fallen sharply. In sheer desperation, some of them had opened paan shops in the vicinity to make ends meet. While most journalists were reporting on the beautification of the ghats, the construction of the Kashi–Vishwanath Corridor, the massive influx of tourists, very few cared about the plight of Varanasi's weavers. The prime ministerial roadshow did not wend its way through Peeli Kothi's paan-stained by-lanes. As a Varanasi-based writer once said, Varanasi is like Cleopatra: her identity and beauty lie in her ancientness. Yet Varanasi, which should be a heritage site, is being turned into a cheap imitation of a present-day municipality. In trying to introduce rapid infrastructural change, many traditional occupations in the region have been sacrificed. Yes, parts of the city are cleaner, but they have been made somehow faceless as well. Locals say Varanasi is no longer the magical city of Kabir, India's great fourteenth-century mystic poet who was born here.

In Ayodhya, we saw the rush of pilgrims heading for the Ram temple, but we also heard stories of shady real-estate deals being struck by a neta–bureaucrat–builder nexus and of old homes and small ancient shrines being razed to accommodate road-widening projects. We heard murmurs of dissent and bouts of rage in different corners of the country as well, especially among youth and farmers, but were they truly representative of the much wider electorate?

The danger of whistle-stop election journalism is that it doesn't allow you the luxury of reflection and measured analysis; you simply hurtle, camera crew in tow, from one state to the next. Maybe we should have listened more intently to the counter-narratives being thrown up, to those who weren't getting carried away with the well-spun feel-good factor. Perhaps I was spending too much time on social media and in WhatsApp echo chambers, where the lines between news and noise rapidly evaporate.

'Janata Janardhan' is a frequently used Hindi aphorism that roughly translates to 'the public is god'. If political demigods were brought down to earth in this election, it is probably because they took the public—their voters—for granted. More often than not, power-hungry politicians and 'infallible' pollsters with 'exact numbers' get disconnected from the people and their concerns. Likewise, celebrity journalists who spend much of their time in TV studios and in courting access to influential politicians lose touch with the common public.

And so, I say here: Mea culpa. Mea maxima culpa.

The need of the hour seems to be an urgent return to the drawing board and real-time course correction. A little less arrogance from all stakeholders could hopefully lead to new beginnings. And ensure that, unlike in 2024, we aren't so surprised by the voter next time.

═

Frequently asked question: What really changed between 2019 and 2024 for Team Modi–Shah?

The projected Modi 'hat-trick' did happen eventually. Well, sort of. After a hard-fought election, in June 2024, Narendra Modi was sworn in as India's Prime Minister for a third consecutive term, the first since Jawaharlal Nehru to do so. It is undoubtedly a creditable achievement at a time when many governments globally are biting the dust. Only this time, there was none of the delirious fanfare that normally accompanies a Modi triumph. In a strange way, Modi had formed the government and yet, paradoxically, he had also lost. He had survived anti-incumbency but also become a victim of it, losing as many as 63 seats compared to 2019. The Opposition, and the Congress party in particular, lost but in a strange twist won too, almost doubling their seat tally and substantially increasing their vote share. In the country's three electorally largest states—Uttar Pradesh, Maharashtra, West Bengal—the BJP lost ground, but it gained unexpectedly in states like Odisha and Telangana, even winning its first-ever seat in Kerala. The Congress gained where it had strong regional alliances but also made a dent in direct fights with the BJP in states like Rajasthan and Haryana. Gujarat and Madhya Pradesh saw a BJP sweep, but the party's southern push met with mixed fortunes: Tamil Nadu, especially, proving to be a bridge too far. Not for the first time, Uttar Pradesh, whose sheer size and complex caste arithmetic is designed to make it unfathomable, proved to be the unexpected game-changer. The Centre for the Study of Developing Societies (CSDS) post-poll survey (see annexure) provides illuminating micro-details of some of these shifting strands.

What does this all add up to? The Indian voter in 2024 mirrored what India is, or was meant to be: a land of incredible diversity where the idea of 'One Nation, One Leader, One Religion' was always going to be challenged. The 2014 and 2019 elections are best described as 'wave' elections, where the people's decisive mandate was determined by emotion as much as reality. In 2014, an angry voter wanted to get rid of the Congress-led government, and a Modi-inspired BJP was in the right place at the right time to capitalize on this demand for change. In 2019, a Pakistan-sponsored terror attack on election eve spurred a wave of aggressive nationalism that submerged all else. In contrast, 2024 marked the return to 'normalcy', a state-by-state electoral contest, wherein local anti-incumbency became a key factor in shaping and swinging voter choices. For example, the onion farmers of north Maharashtra were angry over the Centre's onion export restrictions, while in Marathwada, Maratha reservations were a major talking point. In a sense, the 'localized' nature of the election made it a far more competitive, state-level, seat-by-seat battle. The BJP's overall national vote share only declined marginally, but the 'hawa' (wind) changed in major battleground states.

In a fascinating review of the 2024 elections in ThePrint, political scientist Yogendra Yadav and researchers Shreyas Sardesai and Rahul Shastri examined the sociology of the verdict and found that the BJP's social coalition remains largely intact. Affluent and urban middle-class Hindus, Other Backward Classes (OBCs), Economically Backward Classes (EBCs) and Adivasis still helped create a political advantage for the BJP. Modi's welfarist programmes—be it cash handouts to farmers or free rations for the poor—still impacted millions of 'labharthis' (beneficiaries) and enabled the BJP to offset the anti-incumbency effect. While Muslim voters consolidated behind the Congress and its allies, the biggest shift compared to 2019 took place among Dalit voters, where the BJP-led National Democratic Alliance (NDA) suffered a significant 5 per cent loss in vote share, which switched to the Opposition. This Dalit–Muslim tactical alliance had a major effect on the election outcome, especially in Uttar Pradesh, the biggest electoral battleground. From a bulldozer mandate in 2022 to a 'Mandalized' caste-conscious verdict two years later, Uttar Pradesh is the turnaround story of 2024: the NDA vote share dropped by nearly 10 percentage points here.

The familiar explanation is that the Congress's 'Samvidhan khatre mein hai' (The Constitution is in danger) slogan struck a chord among the people. Dalits and non-dominant OBCs, in particular, feared that reservation benefits would be lost if the BJP got another big majority. But it is my belief that the Dalit vote erosion took place also because of the economic dislocation of marginalized groups. In the past ten years, many at the bottom of the pyramid, especially those who work in the informal sector, have lost jobs with their lives being uprooted. A report prepared by India Ratings and Research—a leading research services agency—says that 6.3 million (63 lakh) informal sector establishments and 16 million (1.6 crore) jobs were lost between 2015–16 and 2022–23. For Indian Muslims too the past decade has been psychologically scarring; their religious identity and livelihoods have been systematically assaulted. From beef bans to 'love jihad' campaigns, Muslims have often borne the brunt of executive diktats. The dreaded yellow machine 'bulldozer' in particular has become symbolic of the unconstitutional manner in which a number of Muslim-owned homes have been demolished in BJP-ruled states under the guise of 'instant justice'. With negligible political representation in the BJP, the feeling amongst Muslims of being targeted and pushed into second-class citizenship is inescapable.

Which is why the 2024 general election verdict must be viewed, as this book attempts to, through the rear-view mirror of everything that preceded it: the deadly Covid-19 pandemic, an economically ruinous lockdown, the abrogation of Article 370 in Jammu and Kashmir, contentious legislation like the Citizenship Amendment Act (CAA), the impunity with which hate speech has been unleashed, the year-long farmer protests, ethnic violence in Manipur and the fierce power tussles in states like Maharashtra, West Bengal and Uttar Pradesh. After a bruising, polarized decade, the nation needed some relief, some breathing space from what columnist Pratap Bhanu Mehta calls 'the suffocating shadow of authoritarianism and the nauseous winds of communalism'.

Between 2014 and 2019, the Modi government sought to consolidate its majority at the Centre, still tentative, still careful not to browbeat both allies and adversaries. Unilateral moves like demonetization in 2016 did suggest a growing disregard for consensus-building, but there were still some checks and balances left in the system. But the overwhelming mandate of 2019 birthed a very different kind of governance model, where creeping autocratic tendencies created an overpowering 'supremo cult' and a single individual's dominance led to an excessive and brutal centralization of power. More accurately, all control rested firmly in the hands of a hard-nosed political executive driven by one and a half persons, if we add the intimidating presence of Union Home Minister Amit Shah to the Modi cult. In fact, the growing clout of Shah is one of the striking aspects of the new power game in town, which is why I often refer to the ruling arrangement as Team Modi–Shah. A word which often crept into street-corner debates and chai shop chatter in north India in 2024 was 'tanashahi' (dictatorship)—used to describe the larger-than-life figure who was out to crush all dissent and threaten India's democratic values, the form of 'zabardasti' (force) that was emanating from New Delhi and riding roughshod over all personal freedoms.

The impact of this overbearing executive, with its ruthless, heavy-handed edge on Indian politics, is what this book seeks to capture. In the space of five years India was forced to transition to a quasi-autocracy in which the Modi–Shah duo bulldozed their way through every sector of life. From the rise of unapologetic Hindutva to abrupt Covid lockdowns, from the misuse of enforcement agencies to squeezing the media, the backstory of Team Modi–Shah's decision-making reveals just how much changed in a relatively short period. It is my belief that the Indian voter in 2024 sought a breather—let's call it an intermission—from a phase of intensely bruising, excoriating, liberty-squashing, one-sided politics. A cut-to-size cult figure and a robust Opposition suggest a pause button has been pressed on damagingly disruptive politics. Verdict 2024 has raised hopes of greater calm and a more democratic order before the battle is resumed.

=

Frequently asked question: Was 2024 a free and fair election? Did the media play fair?

The short answer to both questions is a resounding 'No'. Structurally, Indian elections have always been weighted in favour of the ruling party. The Congress in its heyday often had a massive starting-point advantage over its rivals. Even so, the 2024 elections must be seen as arguably the most unfair election in the history of Indian electoral politics. There was no level playing field. The scale of monetary asymmetry, media inequality and central agency power created a staggeringly imbalanced contest where one side held all the lethal weapons required to demolish its rivals. Even Indira Gandhi, in 1977, ensured a fairer post-Emergency election compared to the manner in which Team Modi–Shah sought to crush, indeed extinguish, the Opposition all through the election campaign.

A 'level playing field' is part of the basic structure of the Constitution, argues lawyer-politician Dr Abhishek Manu Singhvi. The senior Supreme Court lawyer should know. In the last decade, the former member of Parliament (MP) from the Congress has become one of the 'go-to' lawyers for Opposition politicians desperately trying to protect themselves against action from the enforcement agencies. As the book details, the central agencies, especially the Enforcement Directorate (ED), used their coercive powers to bully the Opposition into submission, creating a skewed election system. Law enforcement agencies were used as political campaigners by Modi–Shah. Nor are these actions of a piece with the usual power games played by crooked politicians from different parties, all of whom have a history of misusing enforcement agencies at one time or another. No, the current pattern is something altogether different, disturbing for its sheer brazenness and scale. Cases were closed or slowed down against those who switched sides and joined the BJP-led alliance, while those who refused to bend were targeted.

The 'washing machine' has become an effective metaphor for this misuse of agencies. When a case was closed against a prominent politician who had just joined hands with the BJP, Congress spokesperson Pawan Khera displayed an actual washing machine at a party press meet. Khera held up a 'dirty' T-shirt with 'corruption, fraud, scam' written on it and loaded it into the machine. Once it had been 'washed', Khera extracted a miraculously clean T-shirt with 'BJP Modi wash' written on it.

Symbolically, this 'washing machine' represents the change in political India. In 2014, Modi was the so-called anti-corruption crusader out to transform the country. Now, he is part of the ruling establishment, desperate to retain power at all costs. In the multimedia age, with the proliferation of video content on mobile phones, terms like 'washing machine' quickly became part of everyday usage. On a visit to Nashik to deliver a lecture in May 2023, I was surprised by just how many people instantly responded to my 'washing machine' comment. 'Khoke chi sarkar, khoke chi sarkar,' they screamed out. In Mumbai's underworld lingo, 'khoka' means one crore rupees. The audience was referring to the alleged payout of Rs 50 crore for each member of the Legislative Assembly (MLA) to topple the Maharashtra government in 2022. The dealmaking shenanigans have made Maharashtra the country's most volatile state in this period.

The harsh Prevention of Money Laundering Act (PMLA), in particular, has become a weapon for the Modi government to keep the Opposition in check. In a move unheard of in a democracy, and reviving dark memories of Indira Gandhi's 1975 Emergency, two Opposition chief ministers were arrested in the lead-up to the 2024 election campaign under the PMLA. The PMLA provisions make it virtually impossible to get bail, which has only aided in the weaponization of the ED, labelled the 'Extortion Department' by Shiv Sena (Uddhav Balasaheb Thackeray [UBT]) leaders in Maharashtra.

Did the Election Commission of India (ECI) do enough to curb these shocking moves by the Modi regime, which can certainly be described as an abuse of power? Sadly not. Never before, not even in the pre-

T.N. Seshan era, when the ECI was a relatively unknown entity, has the election umpire been so feeble, opaque and biased in its functioning. The reluctance to flash a red card when Modi delivered one of his most viciously abusive communal speeches in Rajasthan's Banswara has severely dented the reputation of the ECI. Its unwillingness to hold regular press meetings and share information with the public was just as troubling. Why the Opposition's demand for a complete count of a Voter-Verified Paper Audit Trail (VVPAT) was treated so casually is also mystifying. Even the election schedule seemed designed to favour the ruling party: for example, a four-phase election in a peaceful state like Maharashtra was inexplicable. The ECI's inordinate delay in declaring final turnout figures for each phase led to wild conspiracy theories that only expose the wider trust deficit faced by an institution which is at the heart of India's democratic order. As per an Association of Democratic Reforms report, the number of votes officially polled in the electronic voting machines and the number of votes counted do not match in as many as 537 of the 543 constituencies. The average discrepancy is more than 1,000 votes in these seats and while it might not have influenced the final outcome, surely the tallying errors demand a convincing explanation. In the 1980s, it was almost impossible to defeat the Pakistan cricket team on their home ground because the Pak umpires were believed to function as the team's twelfth men. In 2024, India's ECI faced, and continues to face, a similar credibility crisis.

Beyond counting mechanisms, there are even deeper questions of electoral and democratic reform at stake. The ECI's failure to check monetary imbalances skewed the 2024 election even further. Election finances are a dark and murky area. No one is quite sure how much money was actually spent by parties and candidates, but what is certain is that the BJP as the dominant party in power had a huge advantage over the competition. When the Supreme Court finally forced the disclosure of electoral bonds in February 2024, it turned out that the BJP had redeemed nearly 50 per cent of the total bonds sold, way more than any other party. In my travels across the country, the financial inequity was striking. While

BJP posters and hoardings glared down from every pillar and corner, in some places, particularly in the Hindi heartland, the Opposition was all but invisible. Regional parties with their clout in specific geographies were better off monetarily, but overall, the picture was hardly reassuring. The manner in which the Income Tax department served a string of notices to the Congress party just ahead of the elections is a prime example of how easy it is to use state power to financially choke the Opposition.

Yet even a cash-strapped Opposition might have had half a chance if only the media had been fair in its news coverage. As a senior journalist in mainstream media, I wasn't sure just how far to go in critiquing my own tribe in this book. Maybe a separate book is needed to document the fall from grace of many media outlets that lined up to become obsequious cheerleaders of those in power rather than fearlessly speak truth to power. Fear is the operative word here. In the book, I recount the story of New Delhi Television (NDTV), one of the earliest private news networks in the country, and how it became the target of a hostile takeover by the Adani Group, a corporate behemoth close to the government. There was little vigorous media debate on the NDTV takeover, revealing the chilling influence that an all-powerful government–big business nexus can exert on the entire news industry. Everyone is petrified and everyone is self-censoring. I realized this when I was invited to a lunch with a news broadcaster who suggested that I don't bring my phone into the room. 'Who knows who is tapping which phone and how,' he warned.

Unrelenting government pressure to toe the line has only worsened the credibility crisis confronting the media. I recall covering the farm protests in 2020–21 and being surrounded by a group of heavily built protestors trying to snatch my mic away. 'You are part of the godi media,' they hollered. I tried to reason with them that I was only trying to report their side of the story but to little avail. Like with 'washing machine' and 'khoke', 'godi media' is now a commonly used term, referring to a media that has become the government's lapdog. It's a term that discomfits me because it means a blanket condemnation of an entire profession, not too dissimilar from the 'sab neta chor hai' (all politicians are thieves) slogan.

That the term 'godi media' is being echoed by ordinary folk is deeply worrying. More so because the public anger is not unfounded. Large sections of the media have abandoned even the pretence of objectivity in their craven, sycophantic fawning before the Modi-led regime. The media has been turned into a Uriah Heep, the Dickensian character with a perpetually bent backbone and a grovelling manner. In fact, had it not been for the disrupting influence of spirited and daring YouTubers and digital and social media 'revolutionaries', the Opposition story might have got almost totally lost.

Which begs the inconvenient question: Would the Opposition have fared much better, possibly even won the elections, with a fairer media? As a democratic pillar, can the media be allowed to get away so easily with its complete failure to hold the government accountable for its actions and omissions over a long decade in power? Think about just one fact. Modi did over eighty interviews in the 2024 election campaign, but not a single interviewer questioned him on falsified Covid death figures, the plight of small and micro enterprises, Manipur's travails or the Chinese border aggression, or chose to cross-question him in a remotely journalistic manner. Instead, the Indian media chooses to constantly interrogate, mock and deride only the Opposition, almost as if asking questions of the government is not part of our job profile any longer.

A level playing field in 2024? Hardly.

＝

Frequently asked question: So who really won the 2024 elections?

The 2024 election verdict is extraordinary in so many ways, more specifically because no one quite won this election. It is an election nobody won. The Modi-led BJP 'lost' because they couldn't achieve their stated goal. 'Char sau paar' may have been a catchy headline, but not even getting past the halfway mark on their own and being forced into a coalition arrangement is a rejection of what was effectively a referendum on ten years of Modi raj. The Opposition certainly didn't win it, because it couldn't collectively cross the halfway mark. Its performance was far better than expected but not nearly good enough for it to be a serious contender for power. Had the Indian National Developmental Inclusive Alliance (INDIA) managed to retain Bihar Chief Minister Nitish Kumar within its fold, it might have proved to be a game-changer. If the Congress hadn't been stuck in a defeatist mindset at the very outset, it might have fought harder in a few key states. Or if Naveen Patnaik had not badly miscalculated in Odisha, the BJP numbers could have been even lower than 240.

But beyond the 'what-if' counterfactuals, here is the conundrum: If Modi lost and the Opposition did not win, then who scored in 2024? The answer lies with the silent but omnipresent Indian voter. It is quite astonishing how the voter was able to see through the fog of the media's mythmaking, humble imperious leaders and, in the end, protect democracy. In a political milieu where there was no level playing field, 2024 became a David versus Goliath fight between the janata and the netas, and amazingly, the janata fought back to put the netas on notice— an exceptional achievement for the Indian voter.

India is a traditional society divided by fault lines of caste and religious identities, but it is also energized by the boundless aspirations of its people. Money power, media control and charismatic leaders do influence election outcomes but so does a genuine public connect. In chapter 13, I explore ten stories that might restore our collective faith in democratic values. These are inspirational tales of a diverse range of individuals who overcame heavy odds to win some pretty incredible victories. Where but in India would a twenty-six-year-old Dalit mother of two from a low-income family defeat an entire party machine? Or a young Muslim woman give up her academic career only to successfully win votes across communities? Or a tribal leader raise a youthful volunteer force by crowd-sourcing funds? Or a septuagenarian politician triumph in the home of Ram against a saffron army? Or an academic from Manipur provide a healing touch to a scarred and wounded people? Or indeed an unknown political worker, derisively referred to as a family 'clerk', defeat an over-confident star minister?

This is why the 2024 election that 'surprised' India with all its twists and turns is a special story that needs to be told. As with my earlier election books, I do not aim to sit in judgement. This is a book written by a newsman who is still passionate about observing Indian politics from a privileged vantage point. I remain a cheery optimist, which is perhaps the chief reason why I have been reporting on Indian elections for thirty-five years and may often appear overenthusiastic in the TV studio on counting day. This is the tenth general election I have reported on, and I am convinced that every election in this incredible country is distinct from the other.

Undeniably, 2024 too is in a league of its own. It produced a mandate that revealed both the strengths and the limitations of Indian democracy. In a sense, this was the year when humility trumped hubris, when conceit surrendered to courage, when cynicism was eclipsed by hope, when a diversity dividend scored over homogeneity. Which is why the real winner of this election is the unheralded Indian voter, the people who are able to make their voice heard only once every five years. Millions of anonymous voters bear the brunt of a grossly unequal society in silence, but they know how and when to strike back in their own quiet, dignified way.

The great Indian voter has shown that the power of the inked finger isn't dead. Neither is Indian electoral democracy.

ONE

'Abki Baar Char Sau Paar': The Gods That Failed

TUESDAY, 4 June 2024: 5 a.m. The alarm rang shrilly. Outside, it was still dark. Dawn had not yet broken. My thoughts were racing. What would the day bring? Today, the clamour of a long election campaign was finally ending, and at last we would hear that silent entity who is at the centre of every Indian general election: the voter.

I arrived at the India Today studios to find, as always, the place already abuzz. Camerapersons, assistants, graphic designers and make-up artists were rushing around, ensuring that everything was as perfect as it could be. After all, there is no bigger occasion in TV news than the day of the general election result.

Just forty-eight hours ago exit pollsters had taken centre stage. All polls pointed to a clear majority and a historic hat-trick for Narendra Modi and the BJP. Some pollsters even predicted a record-breaking 400-plus seats for the ruling alliance. Throughout this election there had been an echoing battle cry, led by none other than the Prime Minister himself: 'Abki baar char sau paar.' Now the pollsters added to this all-round heraldry, projecting a massive majority for the BJP.

Among exit pollsters, there is no bigger star than Pradeep Gupta, a printing technology graduate from Jabalpur. Unknown until a decade

1

ago, the fifty-five-year-old is considered the Nostradamus of elections, a man with a reputation for getting it right almost every time. What Gupta says is almost gospel for pundits, journalists and politicians. His numbers are believed to always point in the right direction. The sample sizes of his surveys—he claims to cover each of the 543 constituencies—are simply too big not to be more or less accurate.

Gupta has notched up an impressive CV, claiming to have got 65 out of 69 poll verdicts bang on in the last ten years. His polling methods have even been the subject of a case study at Harvard Business School. He has contributed analysis to a variety of global organizations and worked on a major consumer-driven project for the Gates Foundation. Starting off as a first-generation entrepreneur with a small printing unit in 1998, then transitioning into market research and consumer surveys in 2005, he now presides over a team of several hundred on-ground researchers and backroom staff from a plush office in Andheri, one of Mumbai's busy suburbs. Gupta is the 'it' man of election surveys, the hero of exit polls, always ready to break into a jig when he gets it right. Ahead of the general elections, he was wooed by several news channels offering him multi-crore contracts. But he remained for now with the TV Today network.

Interestingly, I had a small role in making Gupta a 'star' pollster on TV. In 2015, he was contracted by a rival news network for the Bihar assembly polls. He predicted 180-plus seats for the Nitish Kumar–Lalu Prasad Yadav–Congress 'Mahagathbandhan' or Grand Alliance in the 234-member Bihar assembly. Most other polls were predicting a tight contest or a BJP win. The channel's editorial team and the owners, a leading industrial group, panicked on seeing Pradeep's prediction and, fearing a backlash from the Modi government, decided not to telecast the polls. I agreed to show his numbers as part of a 'poll of polls' feature on India Today. As it turned out, the alliance did win big; Gupta had been spot on. From the next election, he was part of Team TV Today.

On Saturday, 1 June, around 10 p.m., Gupta revealed his final tally: 361–401 for the NDA, with the BJP set to get 322–340 seats on its own, he claimed. His tone was typically confident. When I suggested that he may have under-polled women in West Bengal or perhaps hastily analysed the final rounds of a seven-phase election, he was dismissive of my concerns. 'Don't worry, we will be right once again,' he said. It isn't easy to quarrel with a pollster whose sample size is more than 0.5 million (5 lakh) respondents in face-to-face interviews across each of the 543 constituencies. Although many reporters (including myself) had noticed a less-than-euphoric response to the 'Modi ki guarantee' catchline while travelling across the country, Gupta was unfazed. 'The election is more competitive in some parts, but the winner is clear. There will be no major ulat-pher (change),' he insisted. In fact, he later told me that his raw data had put the NDA at an even higher number—420 seats—which he later scaled down after political assessment. Meanwhile, 'Modi magic again,' screeched the news channels, each one trying to outdo the other in pumping up the volume.

On Sunday, 2 June, the banner headlines on the exit polls in popular newspapers reflected the buoyant mood in TV studios: 'PM Modi set to storm back to power,' said one; 'Mount 400 no longer a dream,' said another. Ah, 400! A magical number achieved only once before in Indian elections—in 1984, when Rajiv Gandhi swept to power within weeks of the assassination of his mother, Indira Gandhi. Could Modi now go a step further with a hat-trick of wins, beating back any signs of anti-incumbency? Not surprisingly, the exit poll numbers had the Opposition in a tizzy. Rahul Gandhi dismissed the polls as 'Modi polls'; another Opposition leader warned me that he would demand a public apology on air for the 'false numbers'. The Modi government, meanwhile, was already celebrating as if the match were over. News reports indicated that the government had already planned a grand swearing-in ceremony.

On Monday, 3 June, the day before the verdict, the stock markets were also cheering wildly. Through the month of May, the markets had been erratic, a crazy yo-yo suggesting growing uncertainty over the results and hefty profit booking, mainly by foreign institutional investors (FIIs). Now, the exit poll findings had erased all doubts about the verdict. The benchmark BSE Sensex leapt an astonishing 2,777 points to a record high in morning deals; some of the biggest market operators were known to be staunch BJP supporters. 'A big Modi win as predicted by the exit polls has made us bullish about India,' said a prominent market investor. Among the stocks leading the charge were companies linked to the Adani Group, known to be close to Prime Minister Modi.

Amidst this din of Modi cheerleaders, one soft-voiced political activist and academic sounded a note of dissent. Yogendra Yadav began his career as an insightful and professorial political analyst, often seen on TV, and is one of India's original psephologists. Now sixty-one he is a full-time political leader and founder of the Swaraj Abhiyan. Yadav was deeply involved in Rahul Gandhi's Bharat Jodo Yatra, had participated in the farmer agitation and has generally been a fierce critic of the Modi government. 'I really think all the pollsters have got it wrong,' he told me when I telephoned him the morning after the exit polls. For weeks, we had been exchanging notes from our travels. Spare, bearded and kurta-clad, often with a gamchha wrapped around his neck, Yadav had been travelling extensively across the Hindi heartland states. He was convinced that the mood on the ground was turning against the BJP, especially in Uttar Pradesh. We have worked closely together on election programming in the past, and while, like all pollsters, he has got some of his forecasts wrong—most famously in the 2004 general elections— Uttar Pradesh is the one state where Yadav has always scented the political winds correctly. But since he was now an Opposition politician, I wondered if he was a victim of wishful thinking. 'I know I have stuck my neck out, but I am certain the BJP is getting less than 272 [the halfway mark], probably ending up somewhere between 240 and 260,' he remarked.

Pradeep Gupta's 'char sau paar' forecast versus Yogendra Yadav's warning that the BJP would end up with fewer than the significant 272-seat tally: an election that was being considered a 'done deal' had suddenly triggered some excitement. Which is why 4 June saw the nation's eyes fixed on their TV sets and mobile phones. The electronic voting machines were opened at 8 a.m. sharp in more than a million (10 lakh) polling centres throughout India. The first ninety minutes on counting day are like net practice: voting numbers are splashed across screens by TV channels, but none of them have any relevance to the actual match play. The figures are either based on a handful of postal ballots or, in some instances, estimates that channel editors push to keep the TV screen buzzing (a rather unethical practice, one that can easily mislead audiences). Nevertheless, right through the first hour of coverage, the phrase 'char sau paar' was thrown about as if on loop. Hyperventilating anchors who had already declared victory for the BJP during the exit polls were now speculating on the scale of the impending triumph.

At 10 a.m. real trends became available. The early numbers suggested anything but one-way traffic. The BJP-led NDA was ahead, but the Opposition—INDIA—wasn't being cleaned out either. In fact, lo and behold, the Opposition was *leading* in key states, including Uttar Pradesh, West Bengal and Maharashtra. By noon, as the counting approached the halfway mark, one thing became abundantly clear: we were not witnessing a one-sided sweep but a fiercely competitive election. Even the more exuberant anchors were being forced to tone down their claims. Let alone 400, even getting to 272 was beginning to look like a stretch. Amidst the excitement over the unexpected results from several parts of the country, I whispered to my colleagues in the studio: 'Where is Gupta ji?'

In more recent elections, Gupta and I had celebrated getting exit polls right with an impromptu dance in the studio. We'd been criticized for our amateurish dance moves by those who think election shows shouldn't be reduced to tawdry infotainment. My children and a few well-wishers had warned me too: 'Please, no dancing today—sends out the wrong signal.' They needn't have worried. The exit poll findings were proving to be way off the mark. By 3 p.m., as the final results trickled in, the verdict was clear and astonishing. The NDA alliance would form the government but the BJP would not cross the halfway mark, unlike the two previous general elections. Forget 'char sau paar', even 300 paar was not happening, unlike in 2019. With most exit pollsters running for cover, a shell-shocked Gupta finally surfaced. This time his entry wasn't accompanied by the 'band, baaja, baarat' music that had marked his arrival during the exit poll. Instead, he tiptoed his way into the studio, aware that his track record and reputation as an ace pollster had taken their biggest hammering yet.

'So how did you get it so wrong in the big states?' was my direct question. Gupta, to his credit, acknowledged his errors. 'We were not able to capture the shifting caste alignments, especially the shifts in eastern Uttar Pradesh. We could not get the right responses from Bengal, where there is a "fear" factor, and in Maharashtra, the Dalit factor and new alliances made a big difference,' he admitted. Putting up a brave front, he stopped short of accepting complete defeat. 'Our assembly election results and seat share numbers in many states are right,' he remarked. As I pressed for an unqualified mea culpa, Gupta suddenly teared up. He had cried with joy in 2019 when his exit poll was remarkably accurate, but now a different range of emotions seemed to have hit him. He wept in mortification. The tears were not make-believe. Deeply and emotionally invested in his work, the stress of the past few days had finally caught up with him. 'Yes, I cried publicly because this for me is a passion project. I worked hard but got it wrong and let all of you down,' he later explained.

It wasn't just the news network that felt let down. Over the years, I had learnt to accept the ups and downs of exit polls: 'extrapolating vote shares into "exact" seats is injurious to health' ought to be a statutory poll warning. But while tough-skinned news anchors got to move on and call another election, retail investors in stock markets were left with little to cling to. With the exit polls proving way off the mark, the stock market panicked and crashed. The market lost an estimated Rs 30 lakh crore in value on counting day alone, the highest ever fall in a single day. The same exit polls that had pumped up the market just twenty-four hours earlier had now led to huge losses.

'It's the world's first stock market scam,' argued Praveen Chakravarty, a Congress leader and former investment banker. The Wharton School-educated Chakravarty is one of the Congress's data geeks and an expert markets watcher. He pointed to sudden frenetic activity in the stock market on Friday, 31 May, the day before the exit polls came out: more than double the previous day. Well over half the trading (around 58 per cent) was driven by FIIs. 'Why was there such intense trading, especially from foreign institutional investors on this single day? Surely it cannot be mere coincidence that an extremely rare event like the stock market trading doubling occurred exactly one day before multiple exit polls unanimously projected an enormous victory for Modi?' he asserted. He makes a valid point. Why did the trading volume double exactly one day before the exit poll results? Seasoned market watchers suggest that it isn't the FIIs who should be under the scanner, since they were net sellers of stock on 31 May, but domestic investors with deep pockets. Debashis Basu, who exposed the Harshad Mehta stock scam in the 1990s, wrote in the online magazine Moneylife: 'Some big investors hidden under the "retail" label are the real gainers. This is a wide category which includes NRIs but is far easier for the regulator to investigate.'

Adding to the conspiracy theories were intriguing remarks by Prime Minister Modi and Home Minister Amit Shah, who, in separate TV interviews during the election campaign, expressed confidence that the share market would touch new highs on counting day. 'I suggest you buy shares before 4 June; the market will shoot up,' was Shah's comment. 'Since when have our Prime Minister and home minister become share market advisors?' queried Supriya Shrinate, the tough-talking Congress spokesperson who was once an interrogative TV anchor with a business news channel.

The implication is obvious: Did the hectic stock market activities take place only because a group of investors had access to exit poll predictions before they were made public, and did these investors thereby profit from the alleged 'inside (mis)information'? Even more troublingly, were there links between the pollsters, stock market players and political party members who might also have had access to the poll findings? Whose money and on whose behalf were these investors investing? When I placed this question to Gupta, he retorted angrily, 'I have nothing to do with any stock market speculation, forget about a scam. The last time I did a significant trade in shares was in February 2024, well before the elections. During the elections, I invested around Rs 35,000 only.' When asked if he had shared his poll numbers with any political party or individual before the telecast, he became livid. 'I did not share the numbers even with you until the live studio show began. Where is the question of sharing them with someone else? I have clear ethics on this,' he insisted.

But Gupta, like many other pollsters in India, does have a potential conflict of interest that needs closer examination. He has been doing opinion polls for the BJP for several years. His consumer research arm has done 'impact assessment' surveys for Modi government schemes. His printing company has bid and won tenders for several lucrative government contracts, from printing LPG gas bills to railway reservation tickets with advertising rights. 'All these printing contracts are pre-2014, when Dr Manmohan Singh was Prime Minister,' claimed Gupta. He contributed to a book extolling Prime Minister Modi's election campaign expertise. He was also reportedly close to Mumbai BJP MP and Union Minister Piyush Goyal and Union Home Minister Amit Shah. 'Piyush and I were in the same class in Harvard Business School in 2013 for the Owner/President Management programme, but that doesn't mean I have a special relationship with him or Amit Shah or the BJP. It is not just the BJP; I have done polls and provided consultancy services to so many national and regional parties in between elections. But once the poll process starts, I do not engage with any party; then I am on my own,' he said. Have BJP members invested in his company? 'Of course not, the company is owned by me, my family and school friend—nothing to do with the BJP or any external party. I am open to any investigation,' he responded.

While a subsequent Securities and Exchange Board of India (SEBI) inquiry reportedly did not discover any evidence of market manipulation, the clouds of suspicion over exit pollsters have not entirely drifted away. At least Gupta openly admits to polling for the BJP and staying away from pre-election opinion polls on TV. But what of other pollsters who did not reveal their political party dealings? My inquiries indicate that many TV channel pollsters were also working closely with national and regional political parties. For example, Pradeep Bhandari, a much younger pollster, who often polled for the BJP under his Jan Ki Baat branding, never revealed it during his many TV appearances. In 2024, he conducted an exit poll that was telecast on NDTV, which showed the BJP-led NDA getting between 362 and 392 seats, again well off the final mark. 'I assure you that whenever I was polling for the BJP, I did not share my numbers on TV in any form,' he said. 'In 2024, I was not commissioned for any poll by the BJP.' But here is the nagging question: Can anyone who was contracted in the past or present by the BJP be free of political pressure to deliver favourable numbers? The sharp-talking Bhandari, who began polling in 2016, had done several news anchoring stints and was unapologetic about his pro-BJP leanings. In July 2024, he formally joined the BJP as a party spokesperson.

While an under-fire Gupta and others faced the exit poll heat, Yogendra Yadav relished the spotlight. He was, after all, the only pollster to have called it right amidst the 'char sau paar' cacophony. He was on air at 9 p.m. on results day, trying not to sound overly gleeful. 'To my mind, pollsters are just postmen; they should not be made the centrepiece of this. If they get it right, they are only doing their job; if they don't, they should aim to improve. And if they do get it right, I don't think dancing in the studio is a very good idea, and if they get it wrong, making someone cry in the studio is not a good idea,' was his sage advice. Yadav then delivered a punchline in his typically soft voice: 'I had given up psephology twelve years ago. I didn't want to, but I had to come into it as a political activist because I saw the tools of political survey were being misused to hoodwink the country, an attempt in which all the media channels, including yours, were a partner.'

As I listened to him, I could only break into a smile, partly to conceal my own sense of embarrassment and partly to accept our collective failure as media entities. After all, just three days ago, we had joined the drumbeat in predicting a massive victory for the Modi-led BJP. Now, we were all so deservedly being made to eat humble pie.

Meanwhile, the man whose star had suddenly dimmed was on a lonely flight back home to Mumbai. Pradeep Gupta was gradually absorbing the perils of getting an exit poll badly wrong in a high-stakes election. Just days earlier, a news anchor had described Gupta as 'the god of polling'. Now the 'god' was revealed to possess clay feet. The only consolation? He wasn't the only one. In 2024, other 'deities' too were knocked off their pedestals.

Ten years ago, the arrival of Narendra Modi on the national stage brought in its wake a new political animal: the professional 'election consultant-strategist'. Smart-talking, sharply dressed, reeling off numbers and wielding laptops, these 'consultants' soon became the rage. In the last decade every political party, national or regional, has used these data-crunching, event-management professionals at election time, often paying them hefty sums for their expertise. Traditionally in India, in the run-up to an election, low-profile, locally based 'karyakartas' (party workers) would go door to door or from mohalla to mohalla holding sabhas (meetings) and 'jan sampark' programmes. But once the consultants arrived on the scene, they created a sort of parallel universe inspired by an American presidential-style political playbook. Twenty- and thirty-something management nerds now took up positions in air-conditioned 'war rooms', tapping away at keyboards, poring over charts and diagrams and gathering micro-level data on constituencies. They began to organize campaigns for politicians, build political 'brands', reinvent politicians' social media profiles and even occasionally launch dirty wars online to pull down opponents through cleverly manipulated clips and memes. Even as the number of these 'consultants' proliferated, there was one 'OG' among them all, the guru and pathfinder of all political 'consultants': forty-seven-year-old Prashant Kishor, often referred to as 'PK' in the corridors of power.

Always dressed in a carefully casual style—perfectly matched trousers and shirts and trendy full-rim glasses—Kishor likes to describe himself as a salt-of-the-earth Gandhian; he often quotes the Mahatma to explain his fervour for politics at the grassroots. Yet Kishor's lifestyle is anything but. Often seen seated in a Mercedes or a BMW and flitting between five-star hotel lobbies across India's metros, Kishor is more Ralph Lauren than the Mahatma. Yet he has a striking CV. He was credited with playing a key role in crafting Modi's 2014 'Chai pe charcha' campaign and building the up-by-his-bootstraps chaiwallah persona: the earthy, dynamic outsider challenging a decadent Delhi elite peopled by the expensively educated and well-born. This gritty, 'authentic' persona was a runaway success. Modi was cast as the hardworking hero from the teashop who had got the better of Harvard-educated silver spooners. Post-election, though, the highly ambitious Kishor rapidly fell out with Team Modi when his demand to be appointed as the Prime Minister's 'chief of staff' was turned down by the BJP's old guard. Since then, Kishor has worked with a range of different politicians. Being ideologically amoral, he is expertly able to prise out a 'core brand' for his clients and project their USPs on multimedia platforms.

The list of Kishor's successes includes joining hands with the Janata Dal (United) (JD[U]) leader Nitish Kumar in Bihar in 2015, advising Captain Amarinder Singh of the Congress in Punjab in 2017, driving Jagan Mohan Reddy's comeback win in 2019 and piloting Trinamool Congress (TMC) supremo Mamata Banerjee's triumph in West Bengal in 2021. On the minus side, Kishor fashioned the 'UP ke ladke' campaign with Akhilesh Yadav and Rahul Gandhi in 2017, only to have it fall flat. The day before the results, he had sent me a WhatsApp message claiming the Samajwadi Party–Congress alliance would get more than 200 seats in the 405-strong Uttar Pradesh assembly: they ended up with just 47 as the BJP swept to a three-fourths majority. Lesser known is Kishor's central role in the TMC's Goa debacle in 2022. Parking himself in a five-star hotel in the seaside township of Dona Paula, Kishor tried to get a string of local leaders to switch sides, only to discover that Goa's politics is as treacherous as the ever-changing ocean tides and near impossible for flashy 'outsiders' to navigate. Kishor and team failed badly in Goa.

But the odd failure did not deter the ambitious Kishor from pushing ahead. In May 2021, after his successful Bengal adventure, he grandly announced that he was 'retiring' from political consultancy and transitioning into a new role. 'Every ten years one must be ready to make career shifts' is his mantra. A year later, he launched the Jan Suraaj movement, which he claimed would transform the politics of his home state of Bihar. Keen to shed his politics-by-laptop image and emerge as a grassroots activist-leader, he even embarked on a statewide 'padyatra' (walkathon) in October 2022. At the same time, Kishor never shut the door on his ambition to be part of mainstream political party set-up: in the summer of 2022, he almost joined the Congress, eventually opting out after a sharp disagreement on the nature of his involvement. A section of the Congress, especially those close to party leader Rahul Gandhi, were convinced Kishor was a BJP 'mole' and blocked his entry. 'Just see how deeply involved he was with Narendra Modi once, how many times he has shifted from one party to another—how does one trust a political mercenary like him?' said a Rahul Gandhi aide.

As the 2024 elections approached, Kishor found himself on the periphery of the political action: shunned by the Congress and seemingly ignored by Team Modi. In his cool, unflappable manner, he claimed his gaze was firmly fixed on the 2025 Bihar assembly elections. Curiously enough, he had kept a channel of communication open with one of his client-cum-friends, TMC leader Abhishek Banerjee, who still valued Kishor's inputs, even though, officially, another team from Kishor's original outfit, the Indian Political Action Committee (I-PAC), was working on the TMC campaign. In late 2023, Kishor was spotted taking a chartered flight to Vijayawada with Nara Lokesh, son and heir apparent to the (at the time) former Andhra Pradesh chief minister and Telugu Desam Party (TDP) leader, Chandrababu Naidu. With Andhra Pradesh heading into an assembly election battle at the same time as the 2024 Lok Sabha polls, Kishor had reportedly agreed to guide Naidu, who had just been granted bail after he was arrested in an old corruption case, in this no-holds-barred 'war' with the incumbent chief minister, Jagan Mohan Reddy. 'I met Chandrababu because we are old friends. We exchanged notes. But I was not his election consultant; that's a life I have given up completely,' insisted Kishor. Some of his erstwhile I-PAC colleagues have a different story to tell. 'He definitely played an advisory role in the Chandrababu Naidu campaign by basing himself in Hyderabad for weeks. It looked like he had fallen out and was trying to settle a score with Jagan Reddy, or maybe he was hoping Naidu will finance his 2025 Bihar election plans,' said a former aide. The high-stakes Andhra election, in fact, caused a split in Kishor's original start-up I-PAC consultancy team. One I-PAC group was working with Kishor's 2019 client Jagan Mohan Reddy; the other group, now rechristened ShowTime Consulting, was involved with Chandrababu Naidu's campaign. 'Look, Prashant is a guru to all of us; he started us off on this journey. I will always happily value his suggestions,' claimed Robbin Sharma, founder–director of ShowTime Consulting.

While the precise nature of Kishor's involvement in Naidu's campaign remains unclear, his not-so-infrequent TV appearances meant that he was never far away from the headlines. As a shrewd election strategist and skilled communicator, Kishor has a gift for predicting likely political scenarios and decoding and simplifying complex issues into short, sharp soundbites. His interviews with news channels and digital portals invariably go viral and get high viewership. He looks smart and talks smarter—a punch here and a broadside there. In an interview with Press Trust of India (PTI) editors ahead of the 2024 elections, Kishor predicted the BJP would get more than 300 seats while virtually writing off the Congress's chances of even coming close to 100 seats. He wasn't part of the 'char sau paar' club but still forecast a comfortable BJP victory. Even in Bengal, a state he had worked extensively in, he pointed to a big BJP win over TMC.

Mysteriously enough, despite his 'retirement', Kishor surfaced across several TV channels and web portals in what looked like a series of well-orchestrated appearances in the middle of May. The fourth round of polling had just finished, and he reiterated his view that the BJP would cross the triple century mark while the Congress would not even get into triple digits. This was around the same time that Yogendra Yadav was publicly stating that the BJP would fall under the 272 halfway mark. 'PK was brought in to talk up the BJP chances at the halfway point in the general election only to divert the narrative that was firmly shifting towards us,' insisted a Congress spokesperson. When an interview with the senior journalist Karan Thapar led to a fiery exchange between the two over a previous election assessment by Kishor for Himachal Pradesh that had gone wrong, the Congress social media cell went into overdrive. Memes and videos accusing a raging and blustering Kishor of being Modi- and BJP-friendly flooded social media.

Kishor, however, was unyielding. 'Look, I couldn't be bothered about what social media trolls have to say. If you see all my interviews, my assessment of the ground situation in 2024 has been consistent: "Brand Modi" is going down. Rural distress and unemployment are genuine concerns. Yes, my numbers may have been wrong, but you can't accuse me of doing interviews at the behest of any party, much less the BJP. Just look at the journalists I gave interviews to—on their long-pending requests. Can they be called pro-BJP journalists? This is such a ridiculous argument.'

The Congress, though, was unconvinced. The party was insistent that Kishor still had a backroom connect with the Modi government and the BJP. 'Everyone knows that the political consultancy business is a cash-driven enterprise. Please tell me why Kishor has never been questioned or raided by government agencies even though he is the country's most successful consultant?' contended a senior Congress leader. When I posed this question to Kishor in an interview, he countered angrily, 'Tomorrow I could ask why you haven't been raided, or why Congress leaders like Jairam Ramesh or K.C. Venugopal have not been touched. This is rubbish! Just pure frustration among some people.'

And yet, in the same interview, conducted just three days after the 4 June results, Kishor admitted to having erred by getting into the numbers game in the first place. 'I will never talk specific numbers again. That was my mistake,' he confessed. If pollster Gupta perhaps got carried away by the 'char sau paar' surround sound, strategist Kishor was guilty of mixing his armchair political assessments with definitive numerical predictions. Another high-profile individual, built up as the oracle of election prophecies, had been humbled. Kishor, the god of political consultants, was revealed to have been somewhat carried away by his own omniscience. He thought he was always right; voters proved that he was resoundingly wrong and out of touch this time. Kishor too was humbled in 2024.

=

Another 'god' failed in 2024.

It was a cool March evening in Delhi. The dates for the 2024 general elections had just been announced, causing political temperatures to spike across the country. At one of the capital's gleaming five-star hotels, a media house was holding its annual talk festival with a galaxy of heavy hitters from India and around the world. That evening, Home Minister Amit Shah had just finished his speech and settled down comfortably on a sofa in the speakers' lounge, a cup of tea at his elbow, to chat with the journalists crowding around him.

Shah looked gaunter than he usually does; his cheeks, covered in a salt-and-pepper beard, were noticeably narrower than before. After a health scare during the Covid pandemic his doctors had put him on a strict diet, and he had dropped over 20 kilograms. Once rotund and burly, he was now perceptibly slighter, and his spotless white kurta-pyjama hung a little loose on him. His eyes behind his glasses, however, were unchanged: they darted around, and he still had his trademark unblinking hard stare. His expression most of the time is impassive; nothing seems to faze him. When he talks his voice is low, a little menacing, with rough edges to his fluent Hindi.

A political heavyweight, Shah is the de facto No. 2 in the Modi government—and everyone in the room was acutely aware of his presence. All eyes were fixed on him and every word he uttered was mulled over and carefully examined. As he talked candidly it became clear that his appetite for a bruising electoral battle was as keen and sharp as ever. For such a fearsome figure, Shah's hands are rather uncharacteristically dainty. They are pale and heavily bejewelled; he wears a plethora of rings and charms to ward off bad luck. But so far luck had been on his side. Over the last decade the self-declared 'humble party karyakarta' from Ahmedabad had acquired a reputation for being a ruthless, some would say unscrupulous, election prizefighter. He was known to break parties, orchestrate defections, topple governments and use government agencies to intimidate and bully political rivals. A section of the media even dubbed him a modern Chanakya for his relentless emulation of the third-century philosopher's famous formula of 'saam-daam-dand-bhed' (by hook or by crook) as a template for a monarch to seize power. But Shah's not a philosopher. Far from it. What he is is an expert micromanager of electoral politics, using a mix of threats, allurements and shows of force. As the Prime Minister's point person and the political brains of the BJP, clearly it was Shah who was expected to deliver the promised 400 seats for Modi, his guru and mentor.

Ironically, the BJP's 'Abki baar char sau paar' slogan for 'Mission 400' was not coined by Shah; in fact, he was reportedly annoyed with it. A pragmatic politician, he was not keen on raising unrealistic expectations. "Char sau paar" means nothing unless we can offer a concrete promise along with it,' he warned an aide. The slogan was originally mooted at a meeting of senior BJP office-bearers and chief ministers in early January 2024 at which the home minister was absent. The meeting, called to review preparations for the big election year, was chaired by party chief J.P. Nadda, a genial middle-ranking leader who was suddenly catapulted into a frontal role. Suddenly, one of the senior leaders piped up with the 'Abki baar char sau paar' concept. 'This election should be about creating history under Modi ji's leadership. We scored a triple century last time; let's aim for 400 this time,' was the proposal. The idea received instant traction. Among those present at the meeting was Assam Chief Minister Himanta Biswa Sarma, once with the Congress but now one of Modi's most enthusiastic supporters and a very close associate of the home minister. Was Sarma among those who floated the 400 target? 'No, no, I don't get into any of these numbers. I just wanted to win maximum seats from Assam and the Northeast,' he claimed. Interestingly, post the general election result, no one from the BJP took responsibility for the misfiring 'char sau paar' campaign. At the time, though, it was considered a brainwave. As if on cue, toadying TV channels picked up the slogan: screaming primetime debates were held, virtually endorsing the '400-plus' plank.

Against the backdrop of this mounting pre-election excitement, I engaged the home minister in conversation. 'Amit bhai, is this 400-plus slogan a bit of a "jumla" (empty promise)?' I asked. It was probably the wrong question to begin an informal chat with, especially with a politician who has an aversion to 'secular' journalists. In 2015, Shah, then the BJP president, had first used the word in an interview to defend the Modi government's failure to act on its poll promise of putting Rs 15 lakh in every bank account once black money stashed abroad was brought back to the country. The promise, Shah claimed, was an election 'jumla'. The word haunted the government and gave the Opposition a stick to beat it with. Shah wasn't impressed with my question. 'Aapko hamare iss naare se itni takleef kyon ho rahi hai? Modi ji ke netritva mein hum kehte nahi, karte hain (Why are you so troubled by this slogan of ours? Under Mr Modi's leadership, we don't talk, we deliver),' he retorted.

But where will the additional numbers come from, I persisted. An unflustered Shah insisted that the BJP had done its homework. 'Iss baar chunaavi nateeje chaukane wale honge. Modi ji ki lehar hai (This time the election results will be surprising. There is a Modi wave),' he maintained. 'There is not one state where we will not increase our numbers. Even across the south we will win seats this time. Except for 2 seats in Manipur, which you can call tough, we are on the upswing in every part of the country.' The reference to Manipur was significant: the state has witnessed ethnic violence since May 2023, with the BJP-led Centre accused of doing precious little to stop the almost daily bloodletting.

I switched the conversation to specific states where the BJP might face a challenge while trying to repeat its 2019 performance. 'Amit bhai, in Maharashtra the opposition alliance against the BJP appears very strong. Would you concede that this is one state where you could lose seats?' I asked. 'Arre, you give Sharad Pawar too much importance. Has he ever won Maharashtra on his own strength? He is the "sargana" (kingpin) of corruption who ties up with local satraps to bargain for power. And let me tell you, even Uddhav Thackeray has sent feelers that he would like to rejoin us. We have made it clear that we won't take him back unless he apologizes for breaking ties with us in 2019,' said Shah, sounding supremely confident.

There has never been much love lost between the home minister and the Pawar–Thackeray duo, a power tussle that has disrupted Maharashtra's politics for nearly five years now. The Pawar family had already been split down the middle, with news reports indicating that Ajit Pawar's wife, Sunetra, could be contesting against Supriya Sule, Sharad Pawar's daughter, from the family bastion of Baramati. 'Yes, that is correct,' said Shah. 'When Ajit joined our alliance last year, we made it clear that he had to give us a commitment that he would be ready to challenge his uncle head-on, no half-measures this time.' This was a stunning assertion, one that revealed the Shah brand of brash politics. The home minister claimed that it was he who had actively encouraged a Pawar versus Pawar family 'war' in Baramati.

The conversation was getting more animated by the minute. I turned to Uttar Pradesh, the other key electoral battle. It is where Shah had built his reputation as a master election planner: in 2014, he was in charge of Uttar Pradesh when the BJP won 71 of the 80 seats, catapulting the party into a dominant position at the Centre. Shah's attempts at social engineering while bringing together a broad caste coalition under the BJP's umbrella are largely responsible for changing the political dynamics of the state for good. In 2022, however, it was Yogi Adityanath, or Ajay Singh Bisht, who led the party to an assembly triumph. Once a foot soldier in the Ram Mandir movement of the 1990s, the saffron-robed priest-turned-chief minister exemplified the BJP's politics in Uttar Pradesh: using Hindutva majoritarianism and appeals to religion to power its way to massive wins. There have been persistent reports of friction between Shah and Yogi, with speculation over a next-gen battle for supremacy. During our conversation, the home minister was riled by the theory of a possible war within the party. 'Lagta aap gossip zyada sunte hain. Ek baat jaan lijiye, iss baar hum UP mein assi mein se assi seat jeetenge (Looks like you listen to too much gossip. Be sure, this time we will win 80 out of 80 seats in UP)!' he exclaimed defiantly.

The conversation could have carried on. But Shah's aides signalled that he had to leave for another late-night meeting. I gently asked him one last time how confident he was of his poll numbers. His piercing gaze froze on me for just a moment. Facial intimidation is part of the Shah playbook, designed to bully opponents into submission. 'Ab 4 June ko baat karenge (We will speak now on 4 June),' he finally said with a shrug.

I did not meet Shah again on the campaign trail despite repeated attempts. But I managed to get a sense of the shifting mood in his camp from a senior BJP office-bearer who was regularly in touch with him. Apparently just before the seventh and final round of polling in late May, when my source called on the home minister, Shah betrayed a distinct sense of anxiety. At the best of times, Shah is known to sleep only for a few hours, working the phones till late into the night and then hitting the campaign trail at the crack of dawn. 'The morning I met him, he looked like he hadn't slept at all. Normally, he is energetic even at 7 a.m., but this time he seemed fatigued and lacking his usual confidence,' the office-bearer revealed. Conscious of the need to track every mood swing from a variety of fronts, Shah did not just rely on commissioned surveys: he had a mechanism to get daily ground-level feedback from party workers. The news wasn't as positive as he might have wished. 'Kuch local factors ki vajah se kuch jagah problem hai. Usse control mein la rahe hain (Because of local factors, there is a problem in a few areas. It is being controlled),' Shah admitted to the office-bearer.

And yet, just days earlier, Shah had publicly brushed off the possibility of the BJP failing to cross the 272-seat halfway mark. When asked by an interviewer if the BJP had a plan B in case it did not reach the majority mark, he replied confidently, 'Plan B is made only when there is less than a 60 per cent chance of plan A succeeding. I am certain that Prime Minister Modi will come to power with a thumping majority.' The bravado masked the growing disquiet within his core team.

On counting day, Shah remained at his home, a sprawling garden-enclosed bungalow—6-A, Krishna Menon Marg—in the national capital, watching the results. The previous occupant of the house had been the first BJP Prime Minister, Atal Bihari Vajpayee, who had suffered that famous shock defeat of 2004. Shah sat with his wife, Sonal, his lifelong companion, someone who has been his rock through good times and bad. When he was jailed in 2010 for an alleged involvement in an extra-judicial killing and not allowed to enter Gujarat for two years, Sonal alone stood firmly by his side. Since 2014, Shah's stars have been on the ascendant, his reputation growing with every electoral success. Could 4 June be any different? By noon, it was apparent that the 'local' factors were proving to be more than just an irritant, especially in Uttar Pradesh. Forget about getting 80 out of 80, the BJP, astoundingly, was trailing the Samajwadi Party–Congress alliance in the overall seat tally in the state. In Maharashtra too, the Pawar–Thackeray–Congress troika was proving to be a tough nut to crack, slowly pushing ahead of the BJP-led alliance. Sonal had prepared Shah's favourite dal-kadhi-chawal lunch, but the home minister waved it away, having lost his appetite. His only prophecy to have come true was that the BJP was losing in conflict-ridden Manipur. 'Char sau paar' proved to be a bit of a 'jumla' after all. The fantasy had imploded.

'I think the home minister was too overburdened this time,' explained a former BJP strategist. 'He was attempting to play too many roles, from plotting campaign strategy to handling party organization issues to choosing candidates to settling internal disputes to being a star campaigner. As a result, he took his eye off the ball for once.' The all-powerful Chanakya had been humbled by the voter. Shah's standing as the BJP's election grandmaster took a huge hit; 2024 turned out to be his biggest failure.

Narendra Modi was the Gujarat BJP state secretary in 1989, when, in an old-fashioned Rotary Club building in Palampur, a small town nestled in Himachal Pradesh's Kangra valley, the party passed a resolution demanding the construction of a Ram temple in Ayodhya. The 'Palampur declaration', as this came to be known, brought the BJP to the centre of the ongoing Ram Mandir agitation and established it as the political party of Lord Ram. In truth, a political party unable to grow its vote share under a dominant Congress seized upon a local agitation around a disputed shrine to haul itself towards power. In the process, it introduced Hindu majoritarianism into Indian politics and public discourse. A year later, in 1990, Modi played an important role in BJP leader and mentor L.K. Advani's Somnath to Ayodhya rath yatra, his first stab at national prominence.

Cut to 22 January 2024. Modi was no longer just a backroom figure or a nondescript Rashtriya Swayamsevak Sangh (RSS) worker slaving for his bosses. Today he was the lead performer, conductor and 'yajman' (chief patron) of the most defining event in the BJP's political history: the 'pran pratishtha' or consecration ceremony of the Ram idol at the brand-new Ram Mandir in Ayodhya. This ceremony was pitched as the ultimate symbol of Hindu revival and resurgence. It marked the culmination of decades of a bloody struggle and a cunningly crafted political movement to build a temple at the site widely believed to be the birthplace of one of the most revered deities in the Hindu pantheon. It was the BJP's moment in the religio-political sun. And no star shone more luminously than Prime Minister Modi himself.

But what role was Modi playing here? Politician? Priest? A leader using religion to boost his own cult? All of the above. The ceremony was meant to be sacred, a ritual before the inauguration of a Hindu temple.

The religious symbolism had been adroitly transformed into a made-for-TV spectacle, every little detail choreographed to perfection by the Prime Minister and his team. In the run-up to the ceremony, Modi had undertaken a rigorous eleven-day 'yama-niyama-anusthan' fast, including sleeping on the ground to perform his duties as the yajman. He had even embarked on a temple run across the country, visiting places of worship in Maharashtra, Kerala, Andhra Pradesh and Tamil Nadu before heading to Ayodhya. Every move Modi made was expertly captured on camera and the images shared far and wide, designed to stir a pan-India religious consciousness around Ram and the Prime Minister's persona. 'We wanted to showcase the grandeur of Hinduism not just to Indians but to the world; the images were being transmitted to billions of people. Naturally, the Prime Minister, as the leader of the country, would have a central role,' affirmed a senior BJP leader.

On the day itself, the Prime Minister was costumed like a god–king, in a gold kurta with a cream dhoti and turban—a typically standout figure in his sartorial choices. The cameras were once again transfixed on him as he performed the rituals along with the high priests of the temple before an audience of more than 7,000 people in Ayodhya and millions watching worldwide. The select gathering was made up of special invitees of the Shri Ram Janmbhoomi Teerth Kshetra. This body was formed after the Supreme Court, in a landmark judgment in November 2019, ruled that the disputed land on which the Babri Masjid was built would be handed over to a trust created by the Government of India to supervise the construction of the Ram Janmbhoomi temple. Not surprisingly, the trust is dominated by members linked to the Sangh Parivar, especially the Vishwa Hindu Parishad (VHP), which had spearheaded the temple movement. While personalized invitations were sent from the trust, the guest list had been thoroughly vetted by those in government. 'We wanted to make sure that not just the sant-sadhu samaj, which was involved in the temple drive, but celebrated Indians across every walk of life were invited to give it a truly diverse feeling,' claimed a trust official.

Business magnates like Mukesh Ambani, film stars like Amitabh Bachchan and cricket superstars like Sachin Tendulkar rubbed shoulders with saffron-robed mahants and sadhvis. Carefully allocated seats indicated the 'VVIP' status of the chosen few. Declining the invitation did not seem to be an option for the celebrities. A Mumbai-based business tycoon had an urgent board meeting in London. When he tried to find an excuse to wriggle out, he received a message from a well-wisher: 'Not attending is not a good idea, my friend. Your absence will be noticed.' Clearly, no one wanted to antagonize the all-powerful host. Fear and faith are but two sides of the same coin.

Political adversaries, however, had no such compunctions. The trust had made it a point to personally invite the heads of all the recognized political parties in the country. But most Opposition leaders were in no mood to oblige. The principal Opposition party, the Congress, was convinced that even the Ram temple construction calendar had been 'fixed' to give the Prime Minister maximum electoral mileage. 'The temple isn't even fully ready and yet the consecration ceremony is taking place only so that the Prime Minister gets his photo-op ahead of the general elections,' said senior Congress leader Digvijaya Singh. The temple construction committee chairperson, Nripendra Misra, rubbished the charge. The former principal secretary to the Prime Minister, Misra insisted that it was the temple trust members who were keen that the Ram Lalla idol be installed in the temple's sanctum sanctorum at the earliest. 'Our target from the moment I took over in 2020 was to inaugurate the temple by December 2023. That was always our deadline, which had nothing to do with the 2024 general elections timeline,' he asserted. What is true is that the temple wasn't ready: only the ground floor was complete; the first and second floors were still being constructed. Misra maintained that the Prime Minister's Office (PMO) had not interfered in the temple plans at any stage. 'Yes, the Prime Minister performed the "bhoomi pujan" in August 2020, and now he is part of the pran pratishtha ceremony. He is, after all, the Prime Minister of the country, isn't he?' argued Misra. To this day, the Ram temple at Ayodhya remains only partially constructed. In 2024, the politics of Ram remained similarly incomplete.

When the Prime Minister took on the role of yajman of the temple ceremony, the lines between the religious and temporal blurred, perhaps erased forever. In his address, though, Modi was careful not to step into the election terrain, choosing to focus instead on the cultural-civilizational roots of Hindutva nationalism. 'Our Ram Lalla will no longer live in a tent. He will now reside in a divine mandir. This is a temple of national consciousness. Ram is the faith, the foundation of India, the idea of India, the law of India, the consciousness of India and the glory of India,' he stated to thunderous applause. The grandiloquent prose was aimed at projecting Modi's PR image as a modern-day statesman–king, a practitioner of ruthless realpolitik at election time but now a wise Hindu philosopher. The others on stage with Modi—RSS Chief Mohan Bhagwat, Uttar Pradesh Chief Minister Yogi Adityanath, Uttar Pradesh Governor Anandiben Patel, the temple priests—were merely the supporting cast to the main show on display. No Union cabinet ministers were invited; all were politely told to take darshan at a suitable date later. Even the gathered audience—the rich and powerful citizens of India—were mostly Modi cheerleaders, watching the ceremonies awestruck on giant TV screens placed before them. Indian Air Force planes showered petals from above as Modi offered 'dandavat pranam' (lying prostrate on the ground) to the deity. The camera lens was reserved for one figure only; this was the supreme 'One nation, one leader' moment crafted to promote Brand Modi as the face of Ram Rajya. Religion was cynically used as a backdrop to boost a political cult.

Just days later, riding the emotional high generated by the Ram Mandir event among a large section of Hindus, the BJP's internal tracker poll showed the Prime Minister's popularity touching a new peak, his approval rating higher than 70 per cent. An *India Today* Mood of the Nation poll by CVoter showed that the BJP could win 304 seats on its own, one more than it won in 2019. When asked what Prime Minister Modi would be most remembered for, 42 per cent said the construction of the Ram temple and 19 per cent pointed to his raising India's global stature. 'In the end, it boils down to leadership, the trust people are reposing in the Prime Minister, not just because of the Ram Mandir but on a variety of issues,' said CVoter pollster Yashwant Deshmukh.

The extravagant mandir ceremony, in fact, marked the conclusion of a frenetic nine-month period in which Modi was literally everywhere, including, in the eyes of his loyal followers, on the moon. On 23 August 2023, the Chandrayaan-3 Mission successfully landed on the moon, making India only the fourth country in the world to master the technology of a soft landing on the lunar surface, after a forty-one-day voyage. The Prime Minister was attending the BRICS summit at the time in Johannesburg, but just as the lander completed its touchdown, Modi dramatically appeared on cue via video conference to join the celebrations, waving a tricolour. Even before the cameras could close in on the euphoric scientists at the Indian Space Research Organisation (ISRO) headquarters in Bengaluru, the Prime Minister quickly took centre stage yet again. 'We are witness to the new flight of new India; new history has been written. Though I was in South Africa for the BRICS summit, my heart and soul were here [in India],' enthused Modi. It was a perfectly choreographed event: a live telecast watched by millions of Indians with the supreme leader front and centre. Modi announced that the spot where the Vikram moon lander touched down would be called 'Shiva Shakti'. The messaging was complete. Union Science and Technology Minister Dr Jitendra Singh refuted any criticism that Modi had 'hijacked' a glorious moment for India's space scientists. 'Look, this was a special India moment and Modi ji, as the leader of the nation, naturally wanted to be there to share the joy,' gushed the minister. He credited the Prime Minister with creating an enabling milieu for the space research sector, which has seen more than 200 start-ups skyrocket into action.

A few weeks later, in early September 2023, Prime Minister Modi again captured eyeballs in his role as host of the G20 summit in New Delhi. As global leaders lined up for the annual event, Brand Modi's media-marketed moments were once again on display. Every photo-op was carefully curated, from the Prime Minister welcoming world leaders against the backdrop of a replica of the famous Konark Temple wheel to the grand stage at the newly unveiled Bharat Mandapam, the impressive venue for the event in Delhi's Pragati Maidan. The final act took place on a rain-soaked morning when the G20 leaders gathered at Mahatma Gandhi's samadhi at the iconic Rajghat; the photographs were international-standard marketing and communication moments. 'I think we were able to send out a powerful message of peace in the midst of global conflicts,' said Amitabh Kant, senior bureaucrat and G20 Sherpa.

There was another not-so-subtle message: Brand Modi equals Brand India. Across the country, thousands of G20 banners and hoardings bore only Modi's beaming face. A reporter from the online portal Newslaundry counted at least 963 G20 promotional installations on a 12 kilometre stretch of road from Indira Gandhi International Airport to the plush ITC Maurya and Taj Palace hotels in New Delhi, where most foreign dignitaries were housed. All hoardings had only Modi's photo. No other international head of state was visible. So was G20 basically 'Modi for 2024', a US presidential election–style pitch? 'Don't forget that as many as 220 G20 meetings were successfully held across India over nine months in every state, be it BJP- or Opposition-ruled. We were highlighting India's presidency above all else. As Prime Minister, naturally Mr Modi was also projected as a global leader,' countered Kant.

This obsession with being seen as a 'vishwaguru' had reached a stage where the Ministry of External Affairs (MEA) was only an extension of the inescapable Modi propaganda machine. 'We were asked by the MEA to ensure political leaders in the countries where we were posted tweeted and praised the Prime Minister as often as possible. Even the exact words to be used in the tweets were sent to us in advance,' admitted a former diplomat. These orchestrated Twitter (now X) campaigns didn't always go according to plan. For example, when the 2019 Chandrayaan Mission didn't succeed, the diplomats were in a spot. They had already recorded video messages and tweets from world capitals hailing India's achievement and praising Modi. When the lunar lander crashed due to a software error, the messages had to be hastily aborted at the last moment. 'We were scrambling through the night to erase the recordings,' an ex-diplomat said, laughing. From organizing diaspora events to arranging award ceremonies, diplomats had their work cut out to feed the Modi-centric foreign policy frenzy.

Unsurprisingly, *India Today* magazine's annual 2023 year-end issue chose Modi as its Newsmaker of the Year. Explaining the choice, editorial director and senior journalist Raj Chengappa wrote: 'Like the gods of Hindu mythology, he is a man of many avatars, some of which came to the fore in 2023 and enabled him to become, well, the man of the moment, for the moment and of the moment. He can look back at 2023 as his annus mirabilis even though for most world leaders this year was annus horribilis … in 2023, it was Cometh the Hour, Cometh Modi.'

The build-up was designed for an electoral avalanche: Modi was not just another mortal politician. He was an above-it-all supernatural being, an avatar of God himself. The template for the 2024 election battle had been set. Against an Opposition gaggle stood this one lofty, perfectly marketed demigod, perpetually shining in the media arc lights. A 'Modi shining' juggernaut, not unlike the BJP's failed 'India shining' blitz of 2004, was upon us.

=

'Pehle jab tak Maa zinda thi mujhe lagta tha shayad mujhe biologically janm diya gaya hai. Maa ke jaane ke baad, in saare anubhavon ko main jod kar dekhta hoon toh main convince ho chukka hoon ki Parmatma ne mujhe bheja hai (While my mother was alive, I believed that perhaps my birth was a biological one. Since her demise, when I view all my experiences, I am convinced that God has sent me).'

— Prime Minister Modi in an interview with News18,
14 May 2024

The 'non-biological' remarks likening himself to a messenger of God were made on the day the Prime Minister was filing his nomination from Varanasi, which was going to the polls in the final phase of an elongated seven-round general election. The setting was ideal: a boat ride along the Ganga, with the historic ghats in the backdrop. Exactly ten years ago, Modi had made a dramatic entry into national politics by deciding to contest from Hinduism's holiest of cities, a city of antiquity and pilgrimage. 'Maa Ganga ne bulaya hai (Mother Ganga has summoned me),' was Modi's catchy one-liner that reinforced his positioning as a devout Hindu above all else.

Like a fawning fangirl, the interviewer asked the Prime Minister to reveal the secret of his boundless 'urja' (energy), which she claimed has only grown with time. The response—'God has sent me'—was not a stray, off-the-cuff remark, as it turned out. On the same day, in another TV interview, the Prime Minister became emotional while likening his persona to that of Lord Krishna, both as a playful child in folklore and then as advisor to Arjun in the Mahabharata. A few days later, Modi was at it again. In an interview with News24, he said: 'Possibly God only has sent me for some work, for some purpose. And for the achievement of the purpose, he gives direction, education, ability, energy, inspiration … Call it "Daivya Shakti" (divine power) or "Ishwariya Shakti" (godly power). All this is not possible without it.'

Are these the irrational delusions of divinity of a putative autocrat or a shrewd politician's conscious attempt to influence the pious voter by crafting the self-image of a religious cult leader? 'A mix of both,' said Ashis Nandy. Dr Nandy is one of our wise men, among India's leading social scientists, who briefly encountered Modi when he was a rising young politician in the 1990s. He is of the opinion that Modi's repeated allusions to God are typical of a narcissistic mindset. 'This narcissism is a trait common to all authoritarian leaders who believe they are brought in to save the world. Modi is convinced that he is the "Chosen One", the leader who will provide deliverance to the teeming masses of India. Even the manner in which he changes his clothes constantly, flaunts new jackets and branded accessories, is all designed to show that he is a "Supreme Leader". It is just one grand, well-crafted performance aimed to set him apart from everyone else,' he said.

The aim is to project the idea that Modi rules by faith and magic and miracles; he is not just another politician who happens to win elections. In his seminal work, *The Revenge of Power*, author Moisés Naím writes about how autocrats are reinventing politics for the twenty-first century. One of the tricks for an autocrat to retain power is, 'More than leaders to their followers, they become stars to their fans.' Modi too is a beneficiary of this 'politics of fandom', omnipresent and omniscient.

Notably, this obsessive self-love is not a recent phenomenon. The repeated references to himself as God's messenger, routinely speaking about himself in the third person ('Modi ki guarantee') and the endless photo-ops are all part of a larger-than-life personality cult going back to his days as chief minister of Gujarat. Nilanjan Mukhopadhyay, author of a detailed biography on Modi, recalled asking him in 2012 where he got the idea for the Jyotigram Yojana, which successfully implemented power reforms in the state. 'You see, at times I feel I have God's gift for turning my ideas into action,' Modi had responded. When the biographer asked him about his teenage years reportedly spent wandering in the Himalayas, Modi rather enigmatically replied: 'Kabhi kabhi lagta hai main material duniya main aaya hi nahi hoon (Sometimes I think I have not entered the material world).' 'I think Modi has convinced himself that he is a divine child of destiny,' said Mukhopadhyay. When the Women's Reservation Bill was passed in Parliament in September 2023, Modi loftily pronounced, 'Perhaps God has chosen me for this sacred work to empower women.' Claiming to be 'divine' is a means of escaping day-to-day accountability, being above the law, above all public questioning. It is the standard tactic of the twenty-first-century autocrat.

This deification is boosted by the blind adoration of the followers of cult Modi. If Indira Gandhi was encircled by her 'chamchas' (loyalists), Modi too is surrounded by his 'bhakts' or obsequious sycophants. An official recalled the Prime Minister meeting a group of Non-Resident

Indians whose delegation head kept referring to Modi as an 'avatar of Lord Vishnu'. 'Instead of stopping him, the Prime Minister just smiled approvingly,' said the official. Even Champat Rai, general secretary of the Ram Janmbhoomi Trust, has referred to Modi in similar terms. 'In Hinduism, the king of the country is given the status of Vishnu. PM Modi is our unanimous leader, not a common person,' is his telling quote.

God's 'Chosen One' or simply an artful politician, the unending photographs in different locales suggest a manic craving to remain the centre of attention at all times. Be it releasing cheetahs into the wild, posing in front of a gigantic Sardar Patel statue or basking in the glory of Olympic medallists, Modi is unarguably the most photographed Indian politician. 'I don't know whether Modi discovered the selfie or the selfie discovered him, but he sure knows which camera angle will work,' a former aide remarked. Even global leaders are aware of Modi's photo obsession, and skilfully play on prime ministerial vanity. At an India–China summit in Mahabalipuram, Chinese President Xi Jinping gifted a porcelain plate with Modi's photo on it. It was, by all accounts, a treasured memento!

When Mumbai's Atal Setu trans-harbour bridge was inaugurated by the Prime Minister in January 2024, the official video footage released showed Modi walking imperiously on the bridge from different camera angles—alone. All the other dignitaries were edited out. 'It is the longest sea bridge in the country, in which the Maharashtra government and our Deputy Chief Minister Devendra Fadnavis have played a major role, but when it came to the key moment, the camera focussed only on one man,' said a Maharashtra government official.

Nor was this case a one-off. In May 2023, the new Parliament building was inaugurated. The building itself was not fully complete, looking more like a cross between a soulless airport departure lounge and a less-than-tasteful five-star hotel lobby. Opposition politicians disparagingly referred to it as 'the Modi Marriott'. The openness, elegance and historical depth of the old Parliament building were missing. As was the cross-party camaraderie of the famous Central Hall, where Nehru had delivered his defining 'Tryst with Destiny' speech. Maybe that's the way Modi wished the hastily constructed building to be designed. A fortress-like, unaesthetic monument built in silos, not an inclusive temple to democracy. Importantly, no invitation was sent to the President, as the Head of State, to inaugurate the new building or even attend the ceremony, leading to an Opposition boycott. When an Opposition member asked a Parliament secretariat official for an explanation, he was bluntly told, 'There is no rule being violated here; it is entirely the discretion of the government.' Apparently, the invitation cards with the Prime Minister's name had been designed well in advance. A rethink was ruled out.

When the official photo of the event was released, the only cabinet minister in the frame with the Prime Minister was Finance Minister Nirmala Sitharaman, but even she had been relegated to the margins. Instead of sharing the spotlight with his other ministerial colleagues, Modi was pictured with the saffron-robed priests who were the guests of honour inside Parliament: religious theatre with more than a dash of saffron had hijacked democratic norms and traditions. 'I had dressed up for the historic occasion only to find that the cameras were not meant to even look in our direction,' a minister said, chuckling. Ah, yes! The magical illusion of the moving camera, never far from the well-sculpted visage of the 'Chosen One'. Unsurprisingly, the PMO has a large in-house TV production crew that single-mindedly tracks the Supreme Leader at all times. The 'Modi-cam' is a 24/7 accompaniment, its ubiquity designed to hypnotize devout masses in a land of many devis and devatas.

Modi's headline-grabbing 'event-management' skill is a long proven one. Veteran journalist Sheela Bhatt recalls an election campaign in Gujarat in the 1980s when Modi was an emerging young BJP leader in the state. In a Congress-dominated political scene, the BJP would often complain of a lack of media coverage. 'I remember how Modi once suggested that the party gather 182 colourful raths in one big maidan in Ahmedabad to launch their poll campaign from each of the state's 182 assembly constituencies. Other party leaders were reluctant because of the costs involved, but Modi was insistent. Sure enough, the next day the gathering of raths was a front-page picture. Modi enjoys thinking big and out of the box. Everything for him has to be like a grand 70 mm presentation.'

Which might partly explain why Modi so readily bought into the 'Abki baar char sau paar' slogan. It was just the kind of eye-catching headline that would appeal to him. When the '400-plus' catchphrase was first suggested at the January 2024 BJP meeting, not everyone was on board. There was some scepticism that the slogan could backfire by creating a sense of complacency among party workers. But a buoyant Modi signalled approval and settled all doubts. The Prime Minister felt the 'char sau paar' slogan would serve multiple purposes. Not only would it enthuse the party machine to push for an even higher number of seats than in 2019 but it would also demoralize a weakened Opposition. There was also the unstated ambition of aspiring for a target that has only been achieved once before: in 1984, riding on the sympathy wave after the assassination of his mother, Indira Gandhi, Rajiv Gandhi won a record 415 Lok Sabha seats. 'The Prime Minister is constantly comparing himself to the Nehru–Gandhis; he wants to outdo them all the time,' admitted a BJP leader. Besting Rajiv Gandhi's record was a tantalizing prospect for the Nehru–Gandhi-obsessed Modi.

The Prime Minister chose the floor of Parliament in the first week of February to launch the party's election war cry. The moment he uttered the words 'Abki baar', the entire flock of BJP MPs thumped the tables and screamed, 'Char sau paar!' It was yet another well-choreographed exercise, aimed at enhancing the aura of invincibility around the Modi-led BJP. The Prime Minister, in fact, added his own twist to the 'char sau paar' narrative. 'Not only will the NDA get more than 400 seats, but I am also confident that the people of this country will definitely give the BJP 370 seats,' he declared. The 370 figure carried special significance: the 2019 decision to revoke Article 370 in Jammu and Kashmir had been a defining moment in the Modi government's ideological push. Modi even mocked the Congress, saying that its president, Mallikarjun Kharge, had also joined in the 'char sau paar' cry. Truth is, Kharge, in his Parliament speech, had only repeated the slogan to taunt the BJP's ambitious target.

But the party's hyperactive social media team cunningly edited the Opposition leader's remarks to suggest that he too was echoing the BJP's 400-plus declaration.

So did the BJP leadership succumb to their hubris in making 'char sau paar' the party's 2024 campaign calling card? Interestingly, a BJP pollster reveals that his tracker poll in mid-February showed the party hovering around the 300-seat mark, nowhere close to the 400-seat tally. 'I think the BJP leaders knew that 400 was not achievable but they just weren't willing to admit it publicly,' claimed the pollster. While an unctuous mainstream media totally bought into the 'char sau paar' hype, internal survey reports were much less convincing. In late February, the Prime Minister added another twist to the tale while addressing party workers in Madhya Pradesh. Modi now claimed that the 'Abki baar char sau paar' slogan had been coined by the public and not the party itself. 'Today there is one thing being heard everywhere: "Abki baar char sau paar." This has happened for the first time that the public itself has floated a slogan like this to bring back its beloved government. It has not been given by the BJP,' he proclaimed.

Somehow Team Modi had convinced itself that the 'char sau paar' slogan was resonating far and wide. Ground-level feedback showing a stronger Opposition in different states was disregarded as reflecting biased mindsets. Voices of local anti-incumbency were creeping through the noise. 'Rozgaar' (employment) and 'mehngai' were increasingly a growing refrain on street corners. Even more worryingly, the first round of polling saw a sharp dip in voter turnout, sparking fresh concerns of voter apathy. Even before the mismatch between fantasy and reality filtered through to the top leadership the campaign had already taken on a life of its own. The Opposition, the Congress in particular, began to strongly claim that the BJP's 400-plus goal was part of a devious plan to amend the Constitution and do away with reservations. By the time the BJP got ready with its counter, it was too late; the Congress had taken the lead on this narrative and run with it. 'I think the Prime Minister and his core team were carried away by the echo chamber effect. They were so absolutely certain of their own superhuman status that they didn't even think that "char sau paar" might come back to haunt them,' confessed a BJP insider.

It was only in the last week of the campaign that Modi almost conceded that 'char sau paar' might be unachievable. The Prime Minister was on a ceaseless whirl of media interactions, this time in conversation with TV news anchor Rajat Sharma, considered close to the BJP top brass. The audience was full of BJP supporters, raucously cheering every statement. Comforted by the non-stop applause, Modi admitted that the 'char sau paar' target was only meant for the BJP to try and improve its previous tally. 'If in your family a child achieves 90 marks and his competitor gets 30–40 marks, you will never tell your kid to settle for just 50 marks. You encourage your child to get 95 marks. In the same line, we set our 400 Lok Sabha seats target for our alliance,' he disclosed. In the same interview, Modi revived the 'messenger of God' theme. 'I believe God has ordained that I should work 24/7 till 2047 to achieve the aim of a Viksit Bharat (developed India) … God is showing me the path. God is giving me the energy.'

But days later the faceless voter delivered a message to the all-conquering, self-anointed messenger of God. The BJP lost in Faizabad–Ayodhya, the land of the Ram temple, by over 50,000 votes. In Varanasi, where Team Modi had hoped to break records, Modi's victory margin plummeted by over 3 lakh votes; he was even trailing in the early count. Forget 'char sau paar', the BJP was ending up with a much-reduced tally of 240 seats, and the NDA with less than 300. As the BJP marked a hat-trick of triumphs at the party headquarters, the celebrations lacked the usual fervour. When the Prime Minister drove in with his entourage, the chants of 'Modi, Modi!' were revived on cue, but the euphoria of past accomplishments was noticeably missing. Forced smiles. Awkward silences. No bombastic pronouncements. 'I think the feeling in the gathering was strange. We had won an election yet lost it!' admitted a BJP office-bearer.

For India, it was a parting of the clouds of authoritarianism. But for the BJP it was darkness at high noon. The self-styled gods of electioneering were brought well and truly down to earth. A decade of bruising, polarized majoritarian politics had seen a pushback. Hyper-confident pollsters, sharp-eyed strategists, rough-and-tumble politicians, even the most charismatic leader of our generation—they all became the gods that failed.

How did an election turn so dramatically? It is time to rewind to where it all began.

TWO

'Yeh Hindutva ki Sarkar Hai': The Amit Shah Factor

THE die was cast for the battle for 2024 on the day the Modi government was sworn in for a second term on 30 May 2019. Against the glittering backdrop of the imperious Rashtrapati Bhavan, its dome bathed in the luminous tricolour, fifty-seven ministers took oath along with Prime Minister Narendra Modi. But most eyes were transfixed on one round-faced, black-bearded man. As Amit Anil Chandra Shah stepped up to the podium, there was frenzied speculation about what portfolio the (then) BJP president would get. Shah had never been in the Union government, but in his five-year tenure as BJP president from 2014 onwards, he had earned a reputation for being a hard-nosed practitioner of realpolitik. Now, he was poised to make another great leap forward into ministerial authority.

TV channels flashed breaking news: Shah would be appointed as finance minister. The incumbent, the BJP's suave, urbane legal eagle, Arun Jaitley, was suffering from a prolonged illness and had already announced that he would not be joining the new cabinet. Shah was not just the BJP's chief strategist but also a crafty stock market investor, well-networked with the business and financial community. Amidst concerns about a faltering economy, the prospect of Shah being finance minister was attractive to the TV studio commentariat. However, Prime Minister Modi would prove the talking heads and opinion makers badly wrong—and not for the first time. Shah, it was officially announced only next morning, would be India's home minister, an acknowledgement of his newfound status as the second most powerful person in the country.

The home ministry is a labyrinth of dark corridors and interconnected rooms in the imposing North Block on Raisina Hill. Bureaucrats and their attendants can be seen scurrying around with files marked 'Top Secret' and whispering to each other in hushed tones, unlike the disorderly cacophony across most government offices. Climbing up the main staircase, a large portrait of a sombre-looking Sardar Patel, independent India's first home minister, comes into view. Patel's formidable legacy has shaped the power and authority of the home minister's office, and every successor has been dwarfed by his long shadow and towering achievements.

Shah's predecessor, Rajnath Singh, was a relatively amiable figure, an ardent follower of the Atal Bihari Vajpayee school of consensual politics. A two-time national BJP president and chief minister of Uttar Pradesh in 2000 at the age of just forty-nine, Singh could claim to be 'senior' to his ministerial colleagues, including the Prime Minister. During Modi 1.0, he was the de jure No. 2, presiding over cabinet meetings in the absence of the Prime Minister. But Singh was acutely aware of his limitations as a mass leader and was reluctant to rock the boat. Shah was different, dramatically so. 'When we walked into Rajnath ji's chamber, we never felt intimidated. He was a senior politician but not someone who threw his weight around. Mr Shah, on the other hand, exudes power and lets you know that,' recalled a retired home ministry bureaucrat.

Much of Shah's sense of power is derived from his proximity to Prime Minister Modi. Theirs is a relationship that was nurtured in Ahmedabad's highly competitive local politics in the 1980s, when Modi was the BJP's Gujarat state secretary and Shah was a young party activist. Shah was Modi's man Friday, his chief troubleshooter, his alter ego and, when needed, good cop to his bad cop and vice versa. Gujarat's jodi No. 1 was a pair of contrasting personalities with one common ambition: power. At all costs.

And yet, Shah was much more than his senior leader's factotum. Two anecdotes reveal the pugnacious style the younger partner in this long-standing equation has. The first came from an associate during Shah's days as a student politician in the RSS's Akhil Bharatiya Vidyarthi Parishad (ABVP) arm in Ahmedabad. In a college election, Shah was the ABVP candidate, pitted against a traditional rival, the Congress's National Students' Union of India (NSUI). The NSUI candidate for a key post was a woman, and the electoral college had a sizeable female student representation. 'We feared that the girls would all vote for the NSUI candidate and ensure their victory, so we needed a plan B,' recalled the associate. Shah, who was then joint secretary of the unit, hit upon an ingenious plan to get many of the girls to absent themselves on polling day. Phone numbers of the girls' homes were obtained from the telephone directory. This, remember, was a pre-mobile universe. Frantic calls were made to their parents, warning them of likely trouble on the campus on voting day. Sure enough the number of women voters dwindled on D-day as many girls stayed away from college, and Shah managed to squeak home. It was his first election victory. 'This is Amit bhai's mind; it's constantly coming up with new ideas,' the storyteller concluded with a laugh. Devious. Manipulative. Or just clever and resourceful. Either way, Amit Shah clearly learnt his lessons in election management rather early.

The second story was told to us by Shah himself. He claimed to have questioned the Vajpayee government's resolution to go ahead with the 1998 nuclear tests. Shah was then a first-time MLA, having just been elected to the Gujarat assembly in 1997. He had little access to the PMO, but that didn't stop him from writing to the Prime Minister, critiquing the decision to go nuclear. 'Now Pakistan will also test and we won't be able to use our superior army to recapture Pakistan-occupied Kashmir,' was the gist of Shah's argument. Vajpayee was curious to know who this defiant young legislator was and even gave Shah an appointment to meet him. At the meeting, Shah repeated his charge against the government on the nuclear issue, convinced that he was right. 'With Amit bhai, it is always nation and ideology first. He is a firm believer in the RSS's Akhand Bharat concept, and he will defend his position on it whatever the consequences,' claimed a party colleague.

The idea of Akhand Bharat was enunciated by the high priest of the Hindutva movement, Vinayak Damodar Savarkar, at the Hindu Mahasabha's nineteenth annual session in Ahmedabad in 1937. Savarkar defined it as: 'an India that must remain one and indivisible from Kashmir to Rameshwaram, from Sindh to Assam'. A portrait of Savarkar hangs prominently in Shah's home in Delhi. The country's new home minister was determined to take forward the Savarkarite legacy of a Hindu Rashtra built on the ideology of Hindutva. As Shah told a colleague, 'We haven't been voted to power by such a clear majority only to follow the Congress's style of ruling India. Yeh Hindutva ki sarkar hai (This is a Hindutva government). We must ensure that our ideological goals are achieved; there is no question of compromise.'

Home ministry officials and the rest of the country would soon find out just what this new political idiom of unapologetic Hindutva politics meant.

=

The removal of Article 370, which guarantees special status for Jammu and Kashmir, has always been inevitable for the Sangh Parivar. The saffron brotherhood has consistently held that Article 370, enacted by the Nehru cabinet in 1949, 'is a provision to break Kashmir from Bharat'. Almost every major political resolution of the RSS and the BJP (and its previous avatar, the Bharatiya Jan Sangh) and election manifesto(s) since the 1950s have reiterated the party's opposition to Article 370 and a promise to abrogate it if voted to power. The founder–president of the Jan Sangh, Dr Syama Prasad Mookerjee, who had spearheaded the agitation against special status for Jammu and Kashmir, died under mysterious circumstances in a Srinagar jail in June 1953. He had been arrested for entering the state without a government permit. The Jan Sangh slogan during the agitation was: 'Ek desh mein do vidhan, do pradhan, do nishan, nahi chalega, nahi chalega' (One country cannot have two Constitutions, two Prime Ministers and two flags). The long-serving RSS sarsanghchalak M.S. Golwalkar echoed this sentiment in 1967: 'There is only one way to keep Kashmir, and that is by complete integration. Article 370 must go; the separate flag and separate Constitution must go too.'

In 2009, during an interview with veteran BJP leader L.K. Advani, I had asked him if he had any regrets during his long political career. 'Well, not being able to scrap Article 370 is certainly a regret; removing it would have been a fitting tribute to our party's founder,' was his response. Mr Advani had been home minister in the Vajpayee governments between 1998 and 2004 but ruefully admitted that the BJP didn't have the majority to push forward with its core ideological agenda. 'We were a coalition government working to a common minimum programme. Had we been a majority, we would have certainly acted and removed Article 370. Even now, if we get a majority, we will do it,' Mr Advani had claimed. As it turned out, the BJP lost the 2009 general elections under Mr Advani's leadership. A decade later, however, the BJP had the kind of majority the Advani–Vajpayee era leaders could only have dreamt of.

Interestingly, when the BJP first won a Lok Sabha majority in the 2014 general elections, the party chose not to make any attempt to repeal Article 370. Nor did it touch another contentious provision, Article 35A, which confers special rights and privileges to the 'permanent residents' of Jammu and Kashmir, especially in matters of employment, education, property and settlement. Instead, in March 2015, after elections in the state threw up a hung assembly, the BJP formed an alliance with Mufti Mohammad Sayeed's Peoples Democratic Party (PDP). Prime Minister Modi described this partnership of ideological antagonists as a 'historic opportunity to fulfil the dreams of the people of Jammu and Kashmir'. It almost seemed too good to be true: an alliance that promised to bridge the divide between Hindu-dominated Jammu and the Muslim-dominated Kashmir Valley. Sadly, it proved to be a bridge too far. In June 2018, the

BJP withdrew support from the Mehbooba Mufti-led government (her father had passed away in January 2016), pushing a turbulent region back into the abyss of chaos and instability.

'The Modi government did actually consider repealing Article 35A in early 2019 itself but chose to defer any decision because there wasn't a consensus,' revealed a senior BJP leader. Article 35A, which stems from the special status granted by Article 370, had been introduced through a presidential order in 1954. A retired senior home ministry official confirms that repealing Article 35A was on the table as early as January 2019, in the run-up to the general elections. 'There was certainly a buzz that the Prime Minister might make a major announcement to set the political narrative ahead of a big election, but then Pulwama happened and all other Kashmir-related plans were pushed on the backburner,' disclosed the official. The terror attack in Pulwama on 14 February 2019—in which an explosives-laden vehicle rammed into a bus carrying Central Reserve Police Force (CRPF) personnel, killing 40 soldiers—transformed the election campaign, making national security and Pakistan-based terrorism a pivotal issue. Any major decision on revoking Kashmir's special status was postponed in the heat of an election battle dominated by Pulwama.

By June 2019, the Modi government no longer had any constraints. The election had been won with an even bigger majority than the last one, with the BJP alone securing a record 303 seats. Pakistan had been sent a firm message with the Balakot airstrikes. The Kashmir Valley appeared relatively tranquil. 'We must set the tone for the next five years in the first 100 days itself,' the Prime Minister said to the first cabinet of his new government. Each minister was asked to come up with a 100-day plan of action. Amit Shah, in his new role as home minister, was ready with his.

In early June, within days of the new government having been sworn in, a meeting was called at the PMO. Only three people were in attendance: Prime Minister Modi, Home Minister Amit Shah and National Security Advisor (NSA) Ajit Doval. It was a meeting of the 'P-3' or the most powerful troika in the government, as one official described them. A Prime Minister in complete command, a home minister itching to prove himself as a worthy No. 2, and a spook-turned-security-advisor who for decades had been obsessed with taming militancy in Kashmir. The agenda, reportedly, was to work out a timeline for revoking Article 370 and Article 35A. Doval did most of the talking, making it clear that any violent fallout from the decision would be handled by the security forces. 'We will pump in extra forces if required,' was his assurance.

Shah had only just taken charge in the home ministry, but he was clearly excited at the prospect of fulfilling a long-standing wish of the Sangh Parivar. 'We knew we were making history,' Shah would later boast to a group of journalists in his Parliament chamber. Prime Minister Modi, by contrast, did not say much at the P-3 meeting, listening carefully instead to what the NSA had outlined. When the presentation was over, he had only one 'demand': 'I want the entire process to be complete by 15 August,' he said. Shah and Doval nodded in unison. They had ten weeks to effect what hadn't been attempted in the previous seven decades: make Article 370 and Kashmir's special status obsolete.

Within hours of having got the green signal from the Prime Minister, Shah got to work with familiar zeal. The Kashmir division within the home ministry under then Home Secretary Rajiv Gauba was tasked with providing a road map for revoking Article 370. The top-secret operation was carried out on a 'need-to-know' basis. No official was given any additional details about the final plan. The security grid was worked out in co-ordination with the NSA's office and the army leadership in Delhi and Srinagar. Both Shah and Doval travelled separately to Srinagar to meet with the army commanders. The official reason given was to review the pre-Independence Day security arrangements. Meetings were held before dawn, one as early as 5 a.m., to avoid any media scrutiny. The message to the security forces was to ensure maximum boots on the ground in the lead-up to 15 August.

The legal dimensions of the revocation were handled by Shah's key legal advisor, Solicitor General Tushar Mehta, whom the home minister trusted implicitly. Mehta had been Shah's chief troubleshooter in Gujarat, appearing for him in several cases, including the controversial fake-encounter charges that had led to Shah being jailed in 2010. The Solicitor General chaired several rounds of confidential meetings to discuss each legal and constitutional step and its repercussions. One knotty question was whether the recommendation of the state's constituent assembly is required before the President can make any declaration regarding the modification or abrogation of Article 370. Since Jammu and Kashmir was under President's Rule and no assembly was in place, how could the Centre unilaterally change the provisions in Article 370? This could become an intractable issue, particularly because, in April 2018, the Supreme Court had ruled that Article 370 had attained permanency since the state constituent assembly had ceased to exist.

After rigorous scrutiny, Mehta suggested that to overcome any legal challenge, Article 370 could be rendered 'inoperative' while still remaining on the statute books. Moreover, the expression 'Constituent assembly of the State' under Article 370(3) could be amended to mean 'Legislative assembly of the State'. Since the legislative assembly of Jammu and Kashmir stood dissolved, the powers of the legislature were vested in Parliament under Article 356(1)(b) according to the Solicitor General. By this interpretation, a parliamentary resolution would be considered enough to bring about changes in Article 370 through a presidential order. While several top jurists questioned the constitutionality of the exercise as a subversion of basic federal principles, the Supreme Court in December 2023 unanimously upheld the power of the President to abrogate Article 370. The Court reasoned that Article 370 was only a 'temporary provision' and Jammu and Kashmir's special status could be removed.

Ironically, while the legal minutiae were being worked out in Delhi, the then Jammu and Kashmir governor, Satya Pal Malik, claimed that he was kept in the dark and not consulted in the lead-up to the revocation; he was only 'informed' about the decision at the very last stage. Malik was an unusual politician within the BJP's power arrangement. A Jat leader from western Uttar Pradesh, he had been mentored by the late Prime Minister Chaudhary Charan Singh in the Bharatiya Lok Dal. He then joined V.P. Singh's Janata Dal and only much later switched to a Vajpayee-led BJP in

2004, where he was eventually appointed party vice-president. Initially nominated as governor of Bihar in 2017, he was moved to Jammu and Kashmir in 2018 because the Modi government was reportedly looking for an experienced political hand to tackle the key state. 'I think I was sent to Jammu and Kashmir because the Prime Minister wanted someone who didn't have an RSS background and therefore was in a better position to have a dialogue with stakeholders in the Valley,' remarked Malik. Like many others in the political-administrative set-up, Malik was aware that the Centre was planning a 'big step' in Kashmir, but no specific details were shared with him till the evening before D-day. 'Suddenly, I get a call from the home minister asking me to call an urgent meeting of my advisors and recommend the removal of Article 370. There was no consultation—it was an order that had to be implemented at once,' he revealed.

By 3 August, Shah's 'Mission Kashmir' was in place, with security forces crawling all over the Valley. The budget session of Parliament was extended, the Amarnath Yatra was halted, citing security concerns, and schools and educational institutions were ordered to close. Internet services were suspended across the Valley. When some of us journalists met him in Parliament's Central Hall, Shah's calm demeanour didn't give anything away. 'Is it true, sir, that the government is planning to do away with Article 35A?' asked a senior journalist. 'What explains the heightened security in the Valley?' asked another. Shah, in his typically terse manner, refused to answer any questions. 'Please leave some things to the government; don't speculate too much, nothing is happening,' he said dismissively. Journalists looking for a sound bite were offered a plate of dhokla instead. When one of the journalists persisted with the Article 35A question, Shah interjected, 'Don't you think the people of Jammu and Kashmir should have equal rights as all other Indian citizens? Now, please have another dhokla!'

Shah spent the weekend of 3–4 August dividing his time between his Parliament office and the home ministry. While Home Secretary Gauba was liaising with Srinagar and the NSA's office, Shah was adding last-minute touches to the final act of his operation. In conversations with officials, the minister had revealed his impatience with what he called 'the family raj' politics of Jammu and Kashmir. 'Poori rajneeti badalni padegi (The entire politics will have to be changed),' was his conviction. Just setting aside Article 370 would not be enough unless the Centre had greater control over the turbulent Valley. The solution proposed was even more radical than just doing away with Kashmir's special status. The state would be downsized and divided into two separate Union territories: Jammu and Kashmir, and Ladakh. A state being downgraded to a Union territory was a first for the country. There is no clarity on who came up with the idea, but in a later media briefing Shah took full responsibility. 'Full statehood will be restored as soon as there is normalcy in the Valley' he emphasized. The definition of 'normalcy' was kept suitably ambiguous. Shah sounded like a snarling schoolyard bully, a headmaster out to punish an entire class for the sinful actions of a few. In the Centre's worldview, it seemed, the politicians and people of the Kashmir Valley could not be trusted. India's only Muslim-majority state had been split and downscaled. Shah had the Prime Minister's backing. And he wasn't going to be cowed down by any criticism of his actions. When I buttonholed him in Parliament's Central Hall for a response to the Union territory move, he snapped back: 'Aap secular liberal lobby chillate rahiye, decision lena hamara kaam hai (You secular liberal lobby keep screaming, our job is to take decisions)!'

Governor Malik maintained that he wasn't consulted on the decision to withdraw statehood from Jammu and Kashmir at any stage. 'While I fully supported the Article 370 move, I did not agree with the decision to downsize the state to a Union territory. Naturally, this would lead to hurt sentiments among people who felt they were being unfairly punished,' was Malik's take on the matter.

As Shah prepared to face Parliament on Monday, 5 August, and make the dramatic announcement, he went through all the legal formulations one last time with Solicitor General Mehta to make sure nothing had been left to chance. An eager Mehta would remain present in the Home

Minister's chamber in Parliament right through the Article 370 debate in case he was required to address any sudden legal complications. As someone who had built his political career in Gujarat's laboratory of Hindutva, this was Shah's chance to shine in the national saffron sun. His politics and religious biases coalesced in a moment of Hindutva conquest. As he would tell us later in self-satisfied tones, 'I have fulfilled the dreams of millions of Indians who have waited for this day!'

Gupkar Road in Srinagar is Kashmir's power address. It is home to the Valley's top politicians. At the best of times, the entrance to the chinar-lined street has a heavy security presence. The midnight hour of 4 August was the worst of times. Iron barricades went up and the police presence along the dimly lit road was dramatically increased. Dr Farooq Abdullah, three-time chief minister of Jammu and Kashmir, was fast asleep. He was getting an early night, having planned to leave for Delhi the next morning to attend Parliament. In the neighbouring bungalow, his son, Omar, was reading a book, having watched some TV. 'A little after 11 p.m., I started getting calls from my party colleagues that people were being rounded up and taken to the police station. And then suddenly, around midnight, the mobile phones went off. That's when I knew that something was amiss,' remembered Omar Abdullah.

The next morning, the landline phones too were not working. When he tried to step out of his house, Omar found that the gate had been padlocked from the outside. 'That's when I realized that my bodyguards were now my jailors. There was no official order, no documentation, no one came to share any information. It was only when the home minister spoke in Parliament that morning that we learnt what had happened,' he recalled indignantly. Hours later, after having been allowed to briefly meet his father for lunch, Omar was whisked away to Hari Niwas, once a sprawling estate overlooking the scenic Dal Lake, now a state government guest house. He had company. Another former chief minister, Mehbooba Mufti, had also been detained there. 'The one condition the magistrate imposed was that I must not meet Mehbooba at any stage. Now, we are not friends at the best of times, but I did send her a message that she should tell me when she decides to take a walk in the garden so that our paths wouldn't cross,' Omar admitted with a wry laugh.

While Mehbooba was moved to another guest house owned by the state tourism department a few days later, Omar would spend the next eight months in virtual solitary confinement in Hari Niwas. No newspapers or TV were allowed for the first five weeks. Omar spent his time reading, walking and cracking his favourite jigsaw puzzles. 'I guess my boarding school education helped me. I am someone who is comfortable in my own company,' he said. Omar was finally released in the last week of March, soon after the Supreme Court issued a notice on a habeas corpus petition filed by him. 'The day I was released was the day the Prime Minister announced the Covid lockdown. So I guess I just moved from one form of house arrest to another!'

For the Abdullahs, the dramatic turn of events smacked of political betrayal. 'There were rumours for weeks that the Centre was planning something, but none of us had a clue as to what was happening. One member of my party insisted that the Centre was going to remove Kashmir's special status and even split the state, but none of us believed him. We even laughed at his remarks. I guess he knew something we didn't,' Omar recalled. Just three days earlier, the Abdullah father–son duo had met with Prime Minister Modi at his Parliament office. The Centre's move to send in 100 additional companies of paramilitary forces and suspend the Amarnath Yatra had stoked speculation about an imminent major step in the Valley. 'We were getting mixed signals all the time. When we saw the governor, he assured us that there was no reason to be concerned, yet the ground reality was different. So we met the Prime Minister to convey our anxiety and seek reassurance that nothing would be done to rock the boat in the Valley,' said Omar. The Prime Minister reportedly assured the Abdullahs that they had nothing to worry about. 'Hamara koi aisa irada nahi hai (We have no such intention),' was his guarantee. Nothing was said in the meeting to suggest that the Centre was about to turn the Abdullahs' world upside-down. The PMO even put out an innocuous tweet with a photograph of the meeting. 'I can say this today, Mr Modi is not just a liar but a bloody good one,' remarked Dr Abdullah angrily.

Both Dr Abdullah and Omar had interacted with Prime Minister Modi during inter-state council meetings when each served as chief minister. They didn't have a special relationship, but there was no animosity either, especially between Dr Abdullah and the Prime Minister. Dr Abdullah said, 'He would always call me Farooq sa'ab, speak politely and in a soft tone. That day in August was no different. When we asked him about the rumours that the Centre was planning to do something drastic in the Valley, he looked at me with a smile, as if to suggest that I should trust him and not the rumour-mongers.'

Later, recalling Modi's honeyed—and, as it turned out, duplicitous—tones further added to the senior Abdullah's ire when he found out that he too was being detained, although no formal order was issued. The next day, when the home minister told Parliament that Dr Abdullah was not under house arrest, he was even more furious. With TV cameras gathered outside his Gupkar Road residence, Dr Abdullah went to the balcony and screamed: 'The home minister is lying to Parliament. Do you think I would stay in my house on my own will and not be in Parliament while my state is being burnt?'

The Abdullahs were not alone. More than 5,000 'preventive' arrests were made within a month of the Article 370 announcement, a majority of them under the Jammu and Kashmir Public Safety Act, which allows a detainee to be lodged in prison or under house arrest without a warrant, trial or court hearing for up to two years. Where the Abdullahs were arrested despite receiving assurances from the Prime Minister, PDP leader Mehbooba Mufti was treated even more peremptorily by the Centre. Till 2018, Mufti had been leading a coalition government with the BJP, enduring a rather tempestuous relationship with the Centre. She had unveiled an amnesty scheme for 'misguided' Kashmiri youth facing charges of stone pelting, a move that the BJP leadership frowned upon.

Shah seemed convinced that the PDP leader was partial to local militants and couldn't be trusted. 'I met him once in Delhi and he wouldn't even look me in the eye,' claimed Mehbooba, who inherited the chief minister's chair from her father, Mufti Mohammad Sayeed. Like the Abdullahs, Mehbooba too was angry about the manner of her arrest. 'They weren't even willing to give me time to pack my bags and were constantly searching my cupboards. It was almost as if I were a terrorist and not a former chief minister,' she said.

Governor Malik defended the arrest of politicians in the Valley. 'Look, you can't have leaders roaming the streets and screaming that rivers of blood will flow if Article 370 is removed. We had to arrest them to prevent any trouble,' he claimed. Malik argued that, increasingly, the Valley politicians were disconnected from ordinary citizens, and they, in turn, had lost faith in their leaders. 'I remember Mehbooba Mufti coming to see me the night before the Article 370 announcement and warning me that if the Centre touched Article 370, the Valley would explode. The next day, nothing happened. No one came out on the streets. We didn't have to fire a single bullet. Netas might have wanted violence but the people were fatigued with militancy,' was Malik's explanation.

At least the Abdullahs and the Muftis were kept in decent accommodations. A number of others who were detained were moved from one prison to another, some even transferred to the Tihar, Bareilly and Agra central jails under tight security. When the prisoners' families and journalists sought details under the Right to Information (RTI) Act on the number of people from Jammu and Kashmir who were detained in the Agra jail, the authorities refused to oblige, citing confidentiality and security concerns.

In May 2022, the news website Article 14 highlighted the case of Aasif Sultan, who was granted bail by a special court more than twenty months after he was first arrested, and then re-arrested by a counterintelligence Kashmir unit in what is described by lawyers as 'revolving-door detentions'. Aasif's father, Muhammed Sultan Sayeed, a former government official, was left totally distraught. 'I wanted to hug my son but there was no one to listen to me,' he narrated, anguished.

Sitting in Parliament, Home Minister Shah and Prime Minister Modi had no time for either sentimentality or dissent. The moment Shah moved the resolution seeking to revoke Article 370 and bifurcate the state, Opposition members erupted in protest. Two PDP members tore up a copy of the Constitution. The home minister remained unfazed. He spoke with zeal on what he described as a 'turning point'. He knew he had the numbers firmly on his side and, equally importantly, the unequivocal support of the Prime Minister. In a tweet that evening, Shah fulsomely praised Mr Modi: 'Today, Modi govt has corrected a long overdue historic wrong. I congratulate PM @narendramodi ji for his unwavering commitment towards ensuring unity & integrity of our motherland. This historic decision will usher in a new dawn of peace & development in J&K and Ladakh region.' The Prime Minister was quick to respond: 'Our Home Minister @AmitShah Ji has been continuously working towards ensuring a better life for the people of Jammu, Kashmir and Ladakh. His commitment and diligence is clearly visible in the passage of these Bills. I would like to specially congratulate Amit Bhai!' In their mutual admiration, Gujarat's jodi No. 1 was making it clear that this was a landmark decision for which they both took full responsibility, a decisive move that would shape the legacy of their second term.

Two days after Shah made his mark in Parliament, it was Modi's turn to take centre stage as he addressed the nation. Promising to usher in a 'new era' for Jammu and Kashmir, and Ladakh, he sought to explain the rationale for repealing Article 370: 'We as a nation, as a family, have taken a historic decision. A system due to which brothers and sisters of Jammu, Kashmir and Ladakh were deprived of many rights and which was a big obstacle to their development, that system has been done away with.' Right through his speech, the Prime Minister kept harping on the need for 'good governance', even invoking imagery from a previous era when Kashmir was the backdrop for many Hindi films. 'Article 370 and Article 35A did not give anything except separatism, corruption, terrorism and family rule,' he claimed, while raising a new slogan: 'Naya Bharat, naya Jammu Kashmir, naya Ladakh' (a new India, a new Jammu and Kashmir, a new Ladakh). The question of when statehood would be restored was left unanswered, beyond an assurance to the people of Jammu and Kashmir that 'slowly, slowly the situation will return to normal'. What was apparent, though, was that, howsoever contentious, there was no going back on the decision to revoke special status.

Modi 2.0 had drawn a line in the sand. Barely two months after being sworn in for a second time, the government had taken a 'historic' decision, one that had broken the status quo in the turbulent Kashmir Valley. In November 2016, more than two years after coming to power, the Prime Minister had dramatically announced the demonetization of Rs 500 and Rs 1,000 notes—a decision taken without any wider consultation and known only to Modi and a select few. The sudden disruption had caught those within and outside his government by surprise. In contrast, revoking Article 370 was not entirely unexpected. The build-up to it had begun during the 2019 election campaign and the idea was part of the BJP's enduring agenda. A senior Union cabinet minister said that when the demonetization plan was unveiled, there was complete silence in the cabinet meeting, with the ministers looking at each other in bewilderment. 'When we were told of the Article 370 plan on the morning of 5 August, the mood was very different. A few ministers even thumped the table and congratulated the Prime Minister and the home minister for their bold step,' claimed the minister.

The Modi government had got their timing spot on. The afterglow of another big win in the Lok Sabha election was still intact. The Prime Minister's 'neta No. 1' credentials had been reaffirmed by the victory. The Opposition, especially the Congress, in comparison, was in disarray, still recovering from another crushing electoral defeat. The government knew it had the numbers in Parliament to make an audacious move, even if the immediate fallout was chaotic. Unlike Modi 1.0, the 2.0 avatar didn't feel burdened by ally pressure or anxieties over pursuing its ideological goals. No one within the government or outside was in any position to raise a red flag of dissent. The February 2019 Pulwama terror attack meant that the public mood was firmly against any conciliatory gestures towards Pakistan or even a dialogue with stakeholders in Kashmir. An 'India first' nationalistic fervour was being tapped into. 'The Modi government has taken a decision that the country has been waiting for,' an emboldened home minister would tell us later in his Parliament chamber room.

A monthly tracker poll conducted by one of the BJP's in-house survey teams suggested overwhelming public support for the Article 370 move, with a spectacular 80 per cent public endorsement of the decision. An *India Today* Mood of the Nation poll in January 2020 revealed that 58 per cent of the respondents felt that the Modi government's abrogation of Article 370 would provide a permanent solution to the Kashmir issue. It was also listed by most people as a major achievement of the government. However, the decision to divide the state in two and convert both parts into Union territories did not attract equal favour. Around 50 per cent of those polled felt that the move violated the federal structure of the Constitution.

But the decision was not just about poll numbers. It was, as one BJP leader told me, about 'creating a "mahaul" (environment) where the Modi–Shah-led BJP would be seen as a party and a government with a difference'. This mahaul was reflected in the manner in which Shah responded to a question put by a journalist during a chamber briefing. 'Sir, don't you think such an important decision could have been taken after greater consultation with stakeholders to avoid any turmoil?' The home minister's response was typically blunt. In a blanket repudiation of the consensual mode of decision-making, Shah snapped: 'For seventy years, we have been consulting only, that is why no firm decisions were taken. Ab consultation nahi, action dikhega (Now no consultation, there will be action)!'

India's only Muslim-majority state had been downsized into a Union territory, a move tapping into deep undercurrents of Hindutva, invoking barely concealed sentiments of a 'Hindu' force subduing a 'Muslim' territory. A template for taking tough political decisions had been set within the first 100 days of the new government. A majority government was acting unhindered on its core ideological agenda. The Kashmir decree was only the first step. Soon the rest of the country would be drawn even deeper into the vortex of 'Hindutva first' politics.

In October 2019, just ahead of Diwali, Home Minister Shah had an important visitor. A senior RSS leader dropped in to have chai with the minister. The RSS leader congratulated Shah for the manner in which the Modi government had effectively abrogated Article 370. The RSS functionary had a request. There were a few Hindu families who had migrated from Pakistan and had been living in the national capital for years now, but their request for citizenship was stuck in endless paperwork. 'Can something please be done for them?' urged the RSS leader. Shah's response was immediate: 'Don't worry, we are going to fix this issue.'

While the move to invalidate Article 370 was core to the BJP's agenda, the proposed amendments to the Citizenship Act that would grant automatic citizenship to certain persecuted minorities across South Asia were no less important. Ahead of the 2014 elections, the BJP had promised to give shelter to Hindus persecuted in neighbouring countries as part of its election manifesto commitments. The Citizenship (Amendment) Bill (CAB) was introduced in the Lok Sabha in July 2016. It was referred to a parliamentary standing committee and was passed in the Lok Sabha in January 2019, but it lapsed when the term of the sixteenth Lok Sabha ended without the bill being passed in the Rajya Sabha. With many of its allies in the Northeast opposing the bill out of fear of citizenship being granted to massive numbers of illegal Bangladeshi migrants, the BJP didn't want to risk another flashpoint ahead of the 2019 general elections.

Shah himself had no such anxieties. In a press meeting in April 2019, he had explicitly stated: 'First the CAB will come. All refugees will get citizenship. Then NRC [National Register of Citizens] will come. This is why refugees should not worry but infiltrators should. Chronology samajhiye (Understand the chronology).' Even as BJP president, he made his intent clear on the election campaign trail. While addressing a meeting in Bongaon, Bengal, in May 2019, Shah reiterated: 'First we will pass the Citizenship Amendment Bill and ensure that all refugees from neighbouring nations get the Indian citizenship. After that a National Register of Citizens will be made and we will detect and deport every "ghuspaithiya" (infiltrator) from our motherland … We will ensure implementation of the NRC in the entire country. We will remove every single infiltrator except Buddha [sic], Hindus and Sikhs.' Shah's target audience, which cheered his announcement, included Bengal's populous Matua community, Hindu refugees who had crossed over from Bangladesh over time.

Until then, Shah had steered clear of expressly singling out Muslim migrants for discriminatory treatment, preferring instead to use the odious word 'ghuspaithiya', or infiltrator, in his election speeches. But the allusion to Bangladeshi Muslim immigrants was obvious. 'Infiltrators are like "deemak" (termites) in the soil of Bengal. A BJP government will pick up infiltrators one by one and throw them into the Bay of Bengal,' he warned at an election rally. It was the first time an open, plain and unequivocal religious slant was being brought into Indian citizenship laws. Shah's remarks were tweeted by the official BJP handle, only to be deleted much later. Nevertheless, it was a dead giveaway, a reflection of what many critics saw as an 'anti-Muslim' mindset, which formed the basis for the controversial bill.

The election triumph of 2019 convinced Shah that he was on the right track. As BJP president, he had revealed his party's commitment to amending citizenship laws to protect Hindu refugees. Now, as home minister, he was in a position to act. As he told a ministerial colleague, 'Jab janata ne majority di hai toh dabaav ki raajneeti nahi ho sakti (When the people have given us a mandate, we can't do politics under pressure).' But as a pragmatic politician with an ear to the ground, Shah was also aware that he was navigating a potential minefield. In August 2019, the Supreme Court-monitored final list of an NRC for BJP-ruled Assam had left out more than 1.9 million (19 lakh) applicants, many of them Hindus, who now faced the prospect of being rendered 'stateless'. Shah was under pressure from his own party in Assam to find a solution. Protecting 'Hindu interests' in Assam and beyond while singling out 'Muslim infiltrators' would have to be ensured through any new legal ploy. A nationwide NRC was a more complex exercise, but a law that prioritized citizenship for Hindu refugees was eminently doable.

As with Article 370, Shah's legal advisor, Solicitor General Tushar Mehta, was assigned the task of coming up with a lawful framework to amend the citizenship act. With typical vigour, Mehta got down to his assignment, carefully examining several judgments. His advice was clear: the conferment of citizenship was the sovereign function of any nation. 'As long as there is no arbitrariness in classification, there cannot be any legal impediment,' he observed. Since only persecuted minorities from select countries who had already entered India before 2014 were going to be conferred citizenship, he did not foresee any hurdles in implementing the law. Many constitutional experts saw it differently. Legal scholar Gautam Bhatia alleged that by dividing migrants into Muslims and non-Muslims, the law 'explicitly and blatantly seeks to enshrine religious discrimination into law, contrary to our long-standing, secular constitutional ethos.'

Once again, there appears to have been little consultation in the decision-making process. Attorney General K.K. Venugopal, the most senior legal officer in the government, was not involved in the initial drafting. The home ministry took the lead in this matter, while the law ministry was only 'informed' of the government's intent. 'We are all on the same page; there are no differences whatsoever,' then Law Minister Ravi Shankar Prasad would later claim. Any concerns over the constitutionality of the proposed law and political opposition were brushed aside. At another meeting with top officials, the home minister reportedly remarked irately: 'How will parties like the Congress object to this bill? Do you know that when Manmohan Singh was leader of the Rajya Sabha in 2003, he had asked the Vajpayee government to ensure minorities from Bangladesh were granted easy citizenship? Ab kis mooh se woh virodh karenge (With what face will they object)?' This bill, though, was different. It was specifically keeping out only Muslim refugees from the ambit of automatic citizenship. When doubts were raised over BJP allies like JD(U) not supporting the bill, Shah was equally dismissive. In his trademark browbeating style he said, 'This is a BJP government. We have 303 MPs. Unke kitne hain (How many do they have)?' (JD[U] had sixteen MPs.)

Shah knew he had the support of the only person who counted in the government: Prime Minister Modi. Pushing through the CAB was not on Modi's 2019 poll agenda, but the home minister convinced him that the bill could be passed in Parliament without much fuss. In the wake of the 'historic act' in Kashmir, this was seen as another big-ticket move that would further solidify the government's 'Hindu nationalist' credentials and push a dispirited Opposition further on the defensive. During Modi 1.0, consensus building was still seen as a possibility. In Modi 2.0, the SOP was 'act first, then discuss'. And no one epitomized this change in approach better than Shah. Unlike the abrogation of Article 370, during which the PMO was closely monitoring every move, this time the home minister was fully entrusted with the challenge of ensuring the smooth passage of the bill during the winter session of Parliament.

Shah was quietly confident but was taking no chances. He assigned his core team—Piyush Goyal, Dharmendra Pradhan and Bhupender Yadav—to speak to key allies and Opposition parties. The BJP had the numbers in the Lok Sabha but didn't have a majority in the Rajya Sabha. Shah's team was assured by the Biju Janata Dal and the Yuvajana Sramika Rythu Congress Party (YSRCP), both anti-BJP in their respective states but 'friendly' parties at the Centre, that they would back the bill. Shah personally spoke to Bihar Chief Minister Nitish Kumar, who was worried about his Muslim vote bank being further eroded. Kumar had initially opposed the bill in an internal meeting, but the call from the home minister did the trick. 'I think Nitish ji knew that state elections in Bihar were less than a year away and he was in no position to take on the BJP at the time,' said a senior JD(U) leader.

On 9 December 2019, Shah introduced the bill—which gave automatic citizenship to non-Muslims (Hindus, Christians, Parsis, Jains, Sikhs and Buddhists) who had come to India from Pakistan, Afghanistan or Bangladesh before 31 December 2014—in the Lok Sabha. It was passed a day later by a massive 311 to 80 votes. On 11 December, the bill was passed in the Rajya Sabha too, though by a narrower margin: 125 votes to 110. Attempts by the Opposition to make the legislation 'religion-neutral' were defeated. In both Houses, Shah was the centre of attention, dressed in an orange waistcoat. 'This bill is not even 0.001 per cent against Muslims—it is against infiltrators,' he insisted but then went on to catalogue the persecution, killings, rapes, murders and forcible conversion of non-Muslims and the destruction of places of worship in Islamic countries in the neighbourhood. 'Those who said religion should determine nationhood, they formed Pakistan … That was the idea of Pakistan,' Congress MP Shashi Tharoor remarked. To which the home minister retorted, 'The CAA would not have been needed if the Congress had not allowed Partition on the basis of religion. It was Congress that divided the country … Not us.'

This last riposte is typical of Shah, a pugilist politician eager for a verbal joust on religious nationalism. He has always worn his staunch Hindutva origins on his sleeve, only this time he had a national audience watching him on live TV. As a fervent right-winger, Shah unapologetically despises the secular consensus and takes pride in thumbing his nose at liberals and secularists. Having honed his skills in and risen to prominence from the communal cauldron of Gujarat, playing Hindu–Muslim politics is second nature to him. The CAB debate was another step towards ushering in a Hindutva worldview, one where Muslims would be regarded with suspicion, if not open hostility. When we met the home minister in his chamber after the bill had been passed, he appeared elated but was still combative as ever: 'Aap logon ko lagta hai ki yeh anti-minority law hai. Aap secularism aur tushtikaran ka chashma badaliye. Yeh samaj mein asli ekta banane ka kanoon hai (You think this law is anti-minority. You should change your views steeped in secularism and appeasement. This law will promote equality in society).'

I listened quietly, not keen to argue with a tough-talking, boastful minister clearly on a personal high. First, Article 370. Now, the CAA. The Modi government was on a roll and breaking new legislative ground. In Parliament, the Opposition had been silenced by the sheer force of the BJP's numbers. But outside the hallowed corridors, in the streets and by-lanes of the country, tempers were beginning to rise.

The Jamia Millia Islamia campus in south Delhi is an oasis of calm amidst a whirl of urban chaos. A verdant landscape provides sanctuary from the congested city areas that surround the university. A scenic cricket ground—the Nawab Mansur Ali Khan Pataudi Sports Complex—is a hub for sporting activity. A central mosque opposite the library is a space for quiet prayer and reflection. On most Sundays, the campus is fairly somnolent. Students stroll through its various centres of learning or read in the library. But Sunday, 15 December 2019, would prove to be very different. Even a distinct winter chill would not succeed in lowering the mounting political temperature.

For days, the students of Jamia had been feverishly debating the impact of the Citizenship Amendment laws passed by Parliament. While Jamia's faculty and student population mirror a growing diversity—superstar Shah Rukh Khan and cricketer Virender Sehwag are among its prominent alumni—its minority character is undeniable. For many young Indian Muslims from across the country, admission to Jamia is a passport to a better education. As the political commentary over the CAA laws became increasingly polarized, the campus began to feel the heat. Agitated students, convinced that the law was prima facie discriminatory against Muslims, felt the need to make their voices heard. A protest march was organized for the morning of Sunday, 15 December, with the students assembling outside the university campus. 'Our protest was meant to be symbolic and peaceful; we only wanted to send out a message that the youth were angry with the manner in which the Modi government had pushed through an unconstitutional law,' said Asghar Ahmed (name changed on request), one of the organizers.

By 2 p.m., the protest had gathered momentum. Shopkeepers in the neighbouring Jamia Nagar area had downed their shutters. The Okhla MLA Amanatullah Khan of the Aam Aadmi Party (AAP) held a 'peaceful' rally in the locality. As the numbers swelled, it was decided that the protestors would march towards India Gate via the city's main Ring Road. The local police, sensing trouble, began to put up barricades. But the crowd grew restive. Some protestors tried to climb the barricades. Around 4 p.m., two DTC buses and a motorcycle were set on fire by unknown arsonists. Stone throwing was reported in some areas. An outnumbered police force fired tear gas shells and charged the protestors with batons. By 6 p.m., as more incidents of arson were reported, it became apparent that this was no longer a peaceful students' protest but had become a violent situation that was spiralling out of control. 'Trust me, it was not the students who were behind the violence but outsiders who created trouble,' insisted Ahmed.

The authorities, though, were not prepared to make any such fine distinctions. Scores of policemen now barged into the Jamia campus in search of the leaders of the march. Tear gas shells were fired. Doors were slammed open. The main library was vandalized. 'Before we knew it, the police was smashing windows and beating anyone they could find in the library with batons. Many of us sustained head injuries and were bleeding profusely,' recalled a student. The next day when journalists asked the local police why they had entered a college library, their response was: 'When you burn buses and attack policemen, you aren't students in a library but goondas out to cause trouble.'

The conflicting versions of what happened in Jamia that Sunday couldn't hide the unmistakable reality. The CAA had triggered pent-up anger against the Indian state among anti-Modi government sections of society, mainly Muslims. Not just for students but also for many living in the areas surrounding Jamia, the CAA was symbolic of a political order in which Muslims were being reduced to second-class citizens. Coming on the back of Jammu and Kashmir losing statehood, the citizenship law amendments were seen as yet another step towards creating a Hindutva majoritarian state. In the eyes of the local population, the Modi–Shah duo was still identified with the Gujarat riots of 2002. Now the ghosts of the past had returned to haunt a new generation. Nothing that the Union home minister said in defence of the CAA would reduce that acute sense of mistrust and hostility. As one shopkeeper in the area remarked, 'For the men in khakhi, anyone who lives in Jamia and has a beard is a terrorist. Their actions are not about maintaining law and order but teaching us a lesson.'

By Monday morning, there was an uneasy calm around Jamia. A charred bus, broken library windows and bloodstained floors were grim reminders of the events that had unfolded the previous day. But the volcanic rage among the local population was far from extinguished. In the colony of Shaheen Bagh, a short distance from the epicentre of the Jamia violence, a group of elderly women had assembled on the street for a peaceful sit-in protest. Initially, there were just a few dozen of them, holding placards against the Jamia violence and the CAA laws. 'We thought it was just some group of parents of Jamia students who were staging a token protest; we never imagined that this would become a major flashpoint,' admitted a police officer.

Shaheen Bagh is a working-class neighbourhood adjacent to Jamia Nagar. Until the mid-1980s, it was an area that consisted of small vegetable farms, mainly owned by the Hindu Gujjar community. But as Gujjar families began to migrate to other parts, residents from the densely populated Jamia Nagar area moved here. The Babri Masjid demolition in 1992 accelerated the demographic shift. Muslims (and Hindus) were looking for security in communities populated by their own.

From being a mixed locality, Shaheen Bagh gradually transformed into a Muslim ghetto, overcrowded and poorly served by a crumbling civic infrastructure. With dirt roads, open sewers and erratic power supply, Shaheen Bagh epitomizes the sloth and decay of a middle-class colony from which the state has turned away. Shaheen Bagh has been left to its own devices by a government that couldn't care less. 'We have hundreds of daily complaints in Shaheen Bagh that no one attends to. Now, we had one more reason to complain, only this time, we were united in asserting our rights not just as citizens but also as proud Indian Muslims,' a local resident told me.

Within days, the 'small' protest by women that was blocking a main road leading to the industrial township of Noida began gathering eyeballs and momentum. Every evening, a few thousand women, young and old, were making their voices heard. It was a remarkable example of participatory citizens' action, a unique spontaneous mobilizing exercise of democracy-at-the-grassroots led by Muslim women in a traditionally male-dominated civic space. From octogenarian homemakers in hijabs or burqas to daily wage labourers in saris to young salwar-kameez-clad office-goers, Shaheen Bagh was representing a rare diversity of volunteer groups within the Muslim community. The lead taken by the women, often bringing their infants in arms to a voluntary and public-spirited sit-in, marked by energy and determination, set Shaheen Bagh apart from anti-CAA protests taking place in other parts of the country. With its ordinary women in makeshift tents, braving the Delhi winter, huddled together on mattresses and blankets, cradling their children, chatting, cooking, eating and sharing laughter, Shaheen Bagh was distinctive, a one-of-its-kind protest site in India. Shaheen Bagh fast became influential and inspiring. Art installations sprang up all around the protest site, skits and street plays were put on, graffiti and banners speaking out against the CAA and the Modi government appeared. The occasional Opposition neta would drop by to express solidarity, but it was obvious that the star figures were the women protestors.

What struck me while reporting from the area was the stoic spirit of the participants. This wasn't a gathering of rowdies but a disciplined congregation that had come together to celebrate their sense of personal and constitutional freedoms. It was their raw courage that was compelling at a time when dissent was being dangerously criminalized. I recall asking one woman whether she had a message for the home minister. 'Well, Amit Shah says that he will not budge an inch from his commitment to the CAA; then you go and tell him that we will also not budge an inch from this place. This land and this country are as much ours as they are his!' was the defiant response.

The home minister, though, was in no mood to listen or relent. 'Yeh sab sponsored hai; iske piche Opposition aur anti-national elements ka haath hai (This is all sponsored by the Opposition and anti-national elements),' was his terse and dismissive answer to reporters in Parliament. Shah was convinced that Shaheen Bagh was a political 'conspiracy', designed to force him to roll back the CAA laws: a climb-down that was out of the question. There was also the small matter of the Delhi assembly elections that were scheduled for February 2020. Five years earlier, AAP had swept to power in the assembly elections, a rare electoral debacle for the BJP. Shah was itching to avenge the defeat. If there is one politician the rough Shah intensely dislikes it is feisty AAP leader and Delhi Chief Minister Arvind Kejriwal. 'Jhootha aadmi hai (He is a liar),' was his rejoinder when we asked him about Kejriwal's political rise.

Shah plunged into the Delhi battle with characteristic aggression and typically crude and harsh campaign rhetoric. He personally supervised the nitty-gritty of the election strategy. The Shaheen Bagh anti-CAA protests became a backdrop to the heated election campaign, with the BJP accusing AAP and the Congress of 'minority appeasement'. While the Shaheen Bagh protests were remarkably peaceful, there was a deliberate attempt to whip up passions around the stir. Local BJP leaders would often refer to the Shaheen Bagh protestors in disparaging terms as part of the 'tukde tukde gang', a pejorative catchphrase used by the BJP and right-wing TV anchors to target anyone seen as anti-Modi government. First used to describe JNU students during the campus agitation in 2016, the phrase was now rudely and imperiously flung about to loosely refer to anyone who was part of the anti-CAA protests.

In an election rally on Republic Day, 2020, Shah gave voice to the BJP's anti-Shaheen Bagh sentiment when he urged the audience, 'Press the button with such anger that the current is felt in Shaheen Bagh and the protest ends. Your vote will make Delhi and the country safe and prevent thousands of incidents like Shaheen Bagh.' Here was a Union home minister and the second most powerful figure in the government openly telling his supporters to use the vote as a means to end Shaheen Bagh-like protests, potentially stirring a Hindu vote bank's anger against a 'Muslim protest'. It was once again an unashamedly vicious communal pitch aimed at consolidating the Hindu vote.

Shah's cue would be picked up by his vast army of enthralled supporters, each outdoing the other in venomous hate speech. Parvesh Verma, BJP MP from west Delhi, warned: 'Lakhs of people gather there [Shaheen Bagh]. People of Delhi will have to think and take a decision. They will enter your houses, rape your sisters and daughters, kill them … There is time today; Modi ji and Amit Shah won't come to save you tomorrow.' Though the ECI stepped in timidly and removed Verma's name from the BJP's star campaigner list, it was barely a rap on the knuckles for Verma's unlawful language. Verma was unrepentant. 'I heard protestors saying, "We want jihad" in Shaheen Bagh. We all know what jihad is … What happened in Kashmir can happen in Delhi too,' was his unapologetic defence of his incendiary remarks.

Verma wasn't alone. Just a day after the home minister's provocative speech, then Union Minister of State for Finance Anurag Thakur raised the pitch even further. At another election rally, Thakur was heard screeching in hysterical tones, 'Desh ke gaddaron ko (The country's traitors),' only for the audience to shout back, 'Goli maaro saalon ko (Shoot the traitors).' It was the most inflammatory, nasty, rabble-rousing hate speech imaginable, practically goading a large, unruly crowd to take up arms. It was clearly a violation of the Model Code of Conduct and a possible act of criminality, but the Delhi police, which just weeks earlier had charged into the Jamia campus and beaten up students for their anti-government sloganeering, now remained conspicuously inert and silent. The ECI was only a bit braver, asking for Thakur's removal from the BJP's star campaigner list.

I have known the smart-looking Thakur, now forty-nine, since his cricket administrator days. On one occasion, I even watched an India–

Australia test match with Thakur in Dharamshala, where he had built a stadium in his home state of Himachal Pradesh, with snow-capped mountains as the picturesque backdrop. Thakur's tenure as cricket administrator and Board of Control for Cricket in India (BCCI) president had ended in controversial circumstances when he was sacked by the Supreme Court for failing to implement the reforms drafted by a committee appointed by the apex court. Even more controversially, as the Himachal Pradesh Cricket Association chief, he declared himself captain of the state team in a Ranji Trophy game, only to be dismissed for a duck in his only first-class match. He seemed a genuine cricket enthusiast but, as with many politicians involved in the game, wanted to run the administration like a personal fiefdom. The son of Prem Kumar Dhumal, a former Himachal Pradesh chief minister, Thakur had been the president of the Bharatiya Janata Yuva Morcha. During Modi 1.0, he hadn't got much of a look-in. In 2019, he was made Union minister for the first time. Young and ambitious, he was keen to make up for lost time. How do you explain your rabid speech, I asked him. Initially, he denied making the speech. When confronted with the video, he responded testily. 'You are making too much out of it; it was an election rally, where some things will be said. I did not say "goli maaro"—it is the crowd that responded spontaneously to me!' was his lame excuse.

Yes, the minister didn't say 'goli maaro' himself, but he didn't stop the crowd from yelling out the incendiary chant. For an experienced political figure to lead a crowd to unleash violent war cries was an inexcusable disgrace. The young minister was being disingenuous too. A few weeks earlier, another hate-filled, rabble-rousing BJP politician from Delhi, Kapil Mishra, had led a pro-CAA rally, where he had explicitly said 'goli maaro (shoot them)' with specific reference to the Shaheen Bagh protests. Once again, the Delhi police chose not to act against Mishra, a former member of AAP who was now aligned with extremist Hindutva groups and frequently raised the most spiteful anti-Muslim slogans. 'Why are you linking me to someone else's comments?' Thakur argued. Why indeed. Because, quite simply, it was apparent that the minister was only echoing the BJP's election propaganda pitch. Violent language against Muslims was the tactic the BJP wanted to use to win elections.

Just days after Thakur's 'goli maaro' provocation, gunshots were heard near the Shaheen Bagh protests. Kapil Gujjar, a young man from Ghaziabad, fired three bullets into the air to spread panic in the area. While no one was injured and Gujjar was overpowered and arrested by the police, the message was loud and clear. The 'goli maaro' rhetoric was dangerously real.

Opposition leaders feared the Shaheen Bagh protests would stir a Hindu–Muslim divide and enable the BJP to reap electoral dividends in the Delhi elections. Delhi Chief Minister Arvind Kejriwal too was mindful of the possibility of the Shaheen Bagh 'factor' influencing voter choices. Kejriwal played tactical politics, consciously walking a tightrope. He determinedly refused to visit the protest site or speak out in support of the anti-CAA activists despite pressure from a section of his supporters. The Muslim vote was a key support base for AAP, but Kejriwal's election strategy revolved around not losing the urban middle-class Hindu vote. When I interviewed him on the campaign trail, his assistant made a strange request: 'You can ask Arvind ji any question you want but try and avoid focusing on Shaheen Bagh—it is very sensitive.' Kejriwal was somehow convinced that Shaheen Bagh was a well-laid BJP trap to change the election narrative. 'Why do you think the Centre is allowing the protests to continue unhindered in the heart of the city? The BJP wants this Shaheen Bagh movement to continue to divide people,' he argued.

On the night before the Delhi election results, Shah was attending the wedding of a veteran journalist's daughter at the India International Centre. When asked to predict the outcome, he expressed confidence in a BJP win. 'Main jaanta hoon, aap Kejriwal ki jeet chahte hain, par woh hoga nahi (I know you want Kejriwal to win, but it won't happen)!' he sniggered. As it turned out, the home minister's prediction went badly wrong. AAP swept the Delhi polls, winning 62 of the 70 seats in the Delhi assembly. The BJP won just 8. It marked a dramatic reversal from the Lok Sabha elections just months earlier, when the BJP won all 7 Delhi seats by a big margin. The voter, not for the first time, had made a distinction between a Lok Sabha and a Vidhan Sabha mandate.

Shaheen Bagh might not have influenced the electoral verdict, but it was apparent that Delhi was sitting on a tinderbox. A shrill poll campaign, rising anti-CAA sentiment in Muslim localities and a political leadership openly invoking Hindutva emotions—something had to give. Hindutva extremism requires the 'othering' of religious minorities, especially Muslims, to keep sustaining itself, and so it keeps provoking a cycle of reaction and counter-reaction. The deadly serpent of communal violence was about to be unleashed in the national capital with tragic consequences.

In February 2020, while the CAA issue continued to simmer, Prime Minister Modi was preoccupied with preparing to welcome a significant global visitor. The US presidential visit was a milestone for Prime Minister Modi. Unlike with Barack Obama, Modi had built a personal chemistry with Donald Trump. At a 'Howdy, Modi' event in Houston in September 2019, the Indian Prime Minister had openly endorsed the US President with a rousing cry of 'Abki baar, Trump sarkar' (This time, a Trump government). A senior diplomat involved in Indo-US negotiations says that Trump was totally 'charmed' by Prime Minister Modi. 'He is my kind of guy; he doesn't beat around the bush,' is what the US President reportedly told a key aide. Trump and Modi were both seen as uber-nationalist demagogues, expert actors in playing politics-as-reality TV who relished the media spotlight. If Modi had been feted by his American host in Houston, now the Indian Prime Minister would lay out the red carpet for the US President and the first family in Ahmedabad, the Prime Minister's home bastion.

The choice of Ahmedabad was unsurprising. Ever since he took over as Prime Minister in 2014, Modi has made it a habit to take his special guests to the city where his political career began. Gujarat offers a ready personal and emotional connection with the Prime Minister's past.

Here, Modi is monarch of all he surveys: it is where he is the ultimate folk hero, where the state apparatus is at his beck and call, and where adoring crowds may be summoned at the snap of a finger. The Motera Cricket Stadium on the outskirts of Ahmedabad was the chosen venue for a mega-event branded as 'Namaste, Trump', India's answer to 'Howdy, Modi', both events organized by Modi's dynamic Gujarati supporters. The stadium had been redesigned to accommodate more than 120,000 people, making it the largest cricket stadium in the world, part of an elaborate effort to put Gujarat on the world sporting map. Home Minister Shah's son, Jay, was now president of the Gujarat Cricket Association, a post previously held by both Modi and Shah. Motera was truly 'home' turf for the country's leadership. (In 2021, the stadium would be renamed Narendra Modi Stadium, a controversial rechristening aimed at giving a sense of permanence to Brand Modi.)

Ahmedabad was being given a facelift for the presidential visit. In Modi's typical style of putting on a show for international figures, the VVIP route avoided the grimier slum pockets. The national capital too was on high alert around this time. After spending a day in Ahmedabad, the Trumps would be flying into Delhi for the official engagements. Only, unlike a peaceful Ahmedabad, parts of Delhi were smouldering with CAA protests. On Sunday, 23 February, as Ahmedabad prepared to welcome the Trumps the next day, a group of anti-CAA protestors who were holding a protest near the Jaffrabad metro station in northeast Delhi, in solidarity with the Shaheen Bagh agitators, decided to block the main road just outside the station. The blockade proved to be the trigger that sparked a bloody cycle of events over the next seventy-two hours in Delhi. By the time the Trumps landed in India, parts of the national capital were engulfed in riots.

Within hours of the sit-in at Jaffrabad, local BJP politician Kapil Mishra arrived at the spot along with his cohorts and delivered a provocative speech warning the anti-CAA protestors to clear the street. The speech was delivered with the deputy commissioner of police (north-east Delhi) standing next to him, a sign of the BJP leader's political clout. Mishra then tweeted: 'Giving a three-day ultimatum to the Delhi police. Clear the roads in Jaffrabad and Chand Bagh of protestors. Don't try to reason with us after this because we won't pay heed.' Attaching a video with his tweet, he wrote: 'We will maintain peace until Donald Trump is in India. After that, we refuse to listen to even the police if the roads are not cleared … We will be forced to hit the streets.' It was a clear warning to the anti-CAA protestors, a menacing and sinister threat of bloodshed. Yet the police chose not to act right away even though the special branch and the intelligence wing sent multiple alerts to the northeast district police brass. Around 700 distress calls were made to the Delhi police on 23 February alone, but despite signs of an imminent flare-up, no preventive steps were taken. That evening, the first reports of stone throwing and clashes between pro- and anti-CAA supporters came in from the Maujpur area of northeast Delhi, and by the next morning, the violence had spread to nearby areas. By noon, parts of Delhi were caught in a full-blown riot-like crisis as Muslim and Hindu groups targeted each other. As the police fired tear gas shells and carried out a lathicharge, Head Constable Ratan Lal was shot at. He died of bullet injuries in Gokalpur. Intelligence Bureau employee Ankit Sharma's body was found stuffed in a drain near Delhi's Chand Bagh on 26 February, a day after he went missing. The police was convinced that anti-CAA protestors supported by 'Islamist gangs' were behind the targeted attacks on the police and Hindu homes. Tahir Hussain, an AAP councillor from the area, was later arrested and named a prime accused in the Sharma murder. The police recovered a significant cache of arms and ammunition from Hussain's premises. I managed to speak to Hussain on the phone while he was in hiding. He claimed he was being framed, but the evidence against him was damning. 'Tahir and his gang were prepared with weapons well in advance. This was not a riot but a pre-planned conspiracy that was hatched to incite violence,' a senior Delhi police officer insisted.

But the violence wasn't one-sided. Far from it. A viral video, for example, showed the Delhi police beating and kicking a group of young Muslims and forcing them to sing the national anthem and recite 'Vande

Mataram'. One of the men, twenty-three-year-old Faizan, succumbed to his injuries. I met his distraught mother, Kismatun, who was struggling to ensure a speedy and proper investigation. 'Hamari koi sunvai nahi (No one is listening to us),' she wailed. While Tahir Hussain was swiftly arrested, the policemen involved in beating up Faizan and in filming the video were not identified for a long time. It was only in July 2024, more than four years after the rioting, that the Delhi High Court ordered a Central Bureau of Investigation (CBI) probe into Faizan's death. In Hindu-dominated areas, Muslim homes and shops were targeted with equal ferocity by mobs armed with sticks and swords, waving saffron flags and chanting incendiary slogans. If the initial trouble had begun with clashes between Muslims and the police, by 25 February a retaliatory spiral of violence was unleashed, aimed at Muslim-owned shops and places of worship.

A graphic example of just how the copycat violence played out comes from two schools—one owned by a Hindu and the other a Muslim—in the Shiv Vihar area of northeast Delhi. The schools, DRP Convent and Rajdhani Public, which shared a common boundary wall, were targets of looting, arson and co-ordinated attacks by mobs. Officials in both schools blamed the 'other community' for the violence. In both instances, the police arrived at the spot after the worst was over. 'We kept making frantic calls to the police, but no one came,' a school official claimed.

As many as fifty-three people died in the Delhi riots, a final official toll revealed: thirty-eight Muslims and fifteen Hindus. While the violence drove a deep wedge between the two communities, the key question remains unanswered: Why was the Delhi police and the home ministry caught off guard by spiralling violence in the heart of the capital? This, after all, was a self-proclaimed 'muscular' government that claimed to be tough on law and order. Yet when put to the test, this 'strong' government was floundering for a clear-cut response. National Security Advisor Ajit Doval was pulled in to supervise the anti-riot operations as the home ministry struggled to handle the situation. With a number of senior police officers stuck in planning security for the Trump visit, the spread and scale of the violence had caught a depleted force by surprise.

Government sources insist that the violence was orchestrated by 'anti-national' forces, including the Islamist group the Popular Front of India, with the singular aim of discrediting the Modi government while a high-profile visitor was in the country. 'The anti-CAA protestors wanted global media attention for their cause. They chose the Trump visit to make their case by engineering the violence,' asserted a home ministry official. In their chargesheets, the Delhi police claimed that prominent anti-CAA voices, including former JNU student activists Umar Khalid and Sharjeel Imam—arrested under the stringent anti-terror law Unlawful Activities Prevention Act (UAPA)—played a key role in 'drawing sinister communal objectives at the cost of human lives'. The chargesheet refers to Khalid's 'rabid nature' and even cites a speech given by him in mid-February in Amravati in Maharashtra, where he had reportedly spoken about 'hitting the streets' during the US presidential visit. Khalid's lawyers argued that the speech had been edited with the deliberate intent of 'fixing' and persecuting a popular dissenting voice. 'A message of unity based on Gandhiji's teachings was given that day, but it was termed as terror. News channels that aired an edited video informed the investigating agency that their sole source was a tweet by a BJP leader,' they claimed.

I have met Umar Khalid on a couple of occasions, in the TV studio and during seminars in the national capital. Lanky and bespectacled, he struck me as a thoughtful, academically oriented young man who is a vocal critic of the Modi government's policies. He admitted to mobilizing support for the anti-CAA protests but insisted that he was against violence. 'It is you TV people who have labelled me an "urban Naxal". I speak for the human rights of the poor and the dispossessed; how does that make me anti-national?' he asked. In a polarized political climate, Khalid found himself being demonized in a cold-blooded media witch-hunt as part of the 'tukde tukde gang', an 'anti-national' who deserved to be locked up. The police case against Khalid was pathetically weak: based on WhatsApp messages and a political speech deemed illegal on vague grounds. However, being jailed under the UAPA laws meant he couldn't get bail. Khalid has been in prison for over four years now and is still incarcerated in 2024.

Khalid was not the only anti-CAA protestor in the crosshairs of the law. Two young, spirited and outspoken women student activists, Devangana Kalita and Natasha Narwal, were also arrested under the UAPA, on charges of fomenting the Delhi violence. Both admitted to being part of the street agitation but denied inciting or participating in violence. They spent more than a year in jail before being granted bail. When I interviewed them on the day they were released, they were amazingly defiant. 'The government can't scare us by throwing us in jail,' Narwal maintained. 'We have done no wrong.'

While the proof of these activists being involved in a riots 'conspiracy' is very sketchy, there may be a link between the Trump visit and the Delhi riots. The fact that anti-CAA protestors suddenly called for a blockade on the eve of a US presidential visit does suggest a well-considered strategy to intensify the protests at a crucial time. In fact, when Trump landed in Ahmedabad to a grand welcome, news channels were faced with a tough choice: focus on the bonhomie between the US President and Prime Minister Modi or spotlight the mounting violence in the national capital. The live images of burning cars and broken shops were colliding with the media-manufactured euphoria around the 'Namaste, Trump' rally in Ahmedabad. As we telecast the troubling pictures of the violence, an 'advisory' was received from the Ministry of Information and Broadcasting to be careful with any visuals that might incite trouble. Clearly, the Modi government didn't want the party in Ahmedabad to be disrupted by the grim reality on the ground in Delhi. If drawing attention to the rising anger over the CAA among people, particularly the Muslim community, was the primary purpose of the street protests, then the mission had been accomplished. The blood spilled on Delhi's streets was an unforgivable consequence.

But the root cause of the Delhi violence cannot be found in just the sequence of events of February 2020. The truth is that ever since the Modi government returned to power in May 2019, there had been no let-up in its belligerent Hindutva politics nor any concern for civil harmony. From the moment it decided to set aside Article 370 in Jammu and Kashmir and downsize India's only Muslim-majority state to a Union territory, the seeds of political and religious polarization were sown. The CAA was seen as yet another step in making India's large Muslim population feel vulnerable and exposed to the possible misuse of state power. The government's insistence that no Indian citizen would be affected by the amended law was never going to allay anxieties on the ground. In a surcharged atmosphere, people tend to be influenced by premonitions of potential catastrophe. Mistrust between a polarizing and aggressive Hindutva government in power and a restive, indignant citizenry, especially Muslims, on the street, was waiting to explode into an ugly confrontation. The Delhi riots were a tragic reminder for the government not to confuse parliamentary majority with religious majoritarianism. For Team Modi–Shah, the overwhelming 2019 mandate was seen as a licence to implement the Hindu Rashtra project with bruising, divisive single-mindedness. The fact that while the anti-CAA protestors were arrested, the pro-CAA groupings, with their 'goli maaro' incendiary rhetoric, remained untouched speaks volumes about the government's agenda. A partisan state that 'normalizes' hate speech and even rationalizes crimes against Muslims, including mob lynching, is never going to be trusted to act even-handedly.

I recall meeting Home Minister Shah in Parliament's Central Hall a few days after the Delhi violence. 'All you so-called secular people are responsible for this. You have brainwashed people into believing this government is anti-Muslim,' he remarked with cold rage. My response was to remind the minister that the contentious decisions on Article 370 and the CAA had not been taken by a 'secular intelligentsia' but by his home ministry and that the violence had erupted under his watch. 'Please be clear that the majority of voters are with us on these issues,' Shah retorted with supreme self-confidence.

The first nine months of Modi 2.0 had revealed the strengths and limitations of unchecked authoritarian and confrontational Hindutva politics. Team Modi–Shah had taken hard decisions on potentially contentious issues that previous governments had chosen to avoid in an attempt to keep the peace. The politics of consensus evolved by past governments was now ceding space to the unbridled politics of constant confrontation. Hubris acquired from a series of electoral triumphs had built a sense of near invincibility. Extreme arrogance combined with the politics of religious hatred made for a combustible mix. In the process, new fault lines were being exposed. Hate was in the air; demons of communal conflict had been let loose once again. The 'Sabka saath, sabka vikas' (Together with all, progress for all) slogan of 2014 had been buried within the first year of Modi 2.0, and though the government kept insisting that its welfare benefits were meant for all Indians, not just Hindus, on the ground it had lost the trust of India's Muslims. The Hindu–Muslim divide was complete, creating a large group of disaffected people who would wait till 2024 to respond through the ballot. Home Minister Shah's antagonistic brand of politics had revealed an unremorseful Hindutva coarseness. The mask of reasonableness epitomized by the previous home minister, Rajnath Singh, was well and truly off. Within the Sangh Parivar, Shah's ideological zealotry was endorsed. But for the wider public, he was a more feared than admired political figure. Meanwhile, what would it take to unify a scarred and conflict-ridden nation? A once-in-a-lifetime pandemic was about to achieve what our political leadership could not: a virus would unite where religion had divided.

THREE

'Taali Bajao, Thali Bajao': The Covid-19 Challenge

THE month of March in the national capital is peak wedding season. The last flush of spring before the summer sets in is an ideal period for nuptial celebrations. In early March 2020, J.P. Nadda, BJP president, hosted a glittering reception for his son's wedding in Lutyens' Delhi. A cavalcade of cars lined up outside his Motilal Nehru Marg residence. Prime Minister Modi was the star guest. But while the cameras clicked away on the lawns, the real action was taking place in a VVIP room designated only for special invitees. A group of senior BJP politicians had gathered around a table where Home Minister Amit Shah was holding court. An eager participant in the conversation was Shivraj Singh Chouhan, former Madhya Pradesh chief minister. 'Amit bhai, Scindia ji ka kya karna hai? Aap jo kahenge woh hoga (Amit bhai, what do we do about Scindia? We will follow whatever you say),' was Chouhan's cryptic question. Shah smiled and nodded. And with that, the BJP's 'Operation Lotus', the code name for toppling governments, was set in motion in Madhya Pradesh.

Less than a week later, as the country was celebrating Holi, Congress leader Jyotiraditya Scindia called on the Prime Minister at his residence, with Home Minister Shah also present. Just twenty-four hours earlier, on 10 March, his late father Madhavrao's seventy-fifth birth anniversary, Scindia had quit the Congress, his party for almost two decades, walking out along with twenty-two MLAs in Madhya Pradesh. In a resignation addressed to the interim Congress president Sonia Gandhi, he wrote: 'While my aim and purpose remains the same as it has always been from the very beginning, to serve the people of my state and country, I believe I am unable to do this anymore within the party.' The resignation of the Gwalior royal family scion along with his supporting MLAs pushed the fifteen-month-old Kamal Nath-led Congress government to the brink.

Scindia's defection was not surprising. He had been chafing at the bit ever since the Madhya Pradesh verdict of December 2018, which saw the Congress edge out the BJP in a cliffhanger. While he had reluctantly accepted the veteran leader Kamal Nath as chief minister, he wanted assurances about his role in the state Congress. As a star campaigner and key member of the Rahul Gandhi 'youth' brigade, Scindia was promised an 'important' say in the new government in Bhopal. 'Forget about any position, all I wanted was respect within the party for me and my supporters. Promises were made but never kept,' he would claim later. When Scindia surprisingly lost the 2019 Lok Sabha elections from the family bastion of Guna, he was rapidly sidelined and denied a shot at becoming the state Congress chief. Even a promised government house in Bhopal did not materialize. Efforts by a prominent media baron to broker peace between Scindia, (then) Chief Minister Kamal Nath, and former chief minister and the Congress stalwart Digvijaya Singh also failed. The two senior Congressmen were determined to cut their junior colleague down to size. When Scindia protested against the non-fulfilment of promises in the Congress manifesto, Kamal Nath dared him to carry out his threat of a street protest against the state government. The chief minister was certain that Scindia's bark was worse than his bite. When Scindia's name was not announced in the initial Rajya Sabha list from the Congress, he felt his time was up. 'I tried to raise my concerns with the Gandhis, even met with Sonia ji and Rahul ji, but no one was listening,' he alleged. Pushed to a corner, Scindia opened a channel of communication with the BJP.

The BJP shares an unusual relationship with the Scindia family. Jyotiraditya's grandmother Vijaya Raje Scindia was one of the original benefactors of the Jan Sangh, his aunt Vasundhara Raje had been the BJP's Rajasthan chief minister, and his other aunt Yashodhara Raje a minister in a previous Madhya Pradesh government. Yet Jyotiraditya's father, Madhavrao, broke with the rest of the family in 1980 to join hands with the Congress, and the son followed suit, aggressively opposing the BJP and denouncing its Hindutva ideology. During the 2018 elections, the BJP had even mocked Jyotiraditya's 'royal' tag, contrasting him with 'common man' Shivraj Singh Chouhan. 'He doesn't understand the ground realities of Madhya Pradesh because he sits in a palace,' Chouhan had remarked dismissively.

Yet, in a peculiar twist, Chouhan was now relying on Scindia's 'revolt' to bring down the Kamal Nath government and become chief minister once again. A key player in getting Scindia to switch was BJP leader and spokesperson Syed Zafar Islam. The suave Islam is like Scindia, an investment banker-turned-politician. As one of the few Muslim faces in the BJP, he was keen to make a mark and would enthusiastically defend the Modi government in TV debates. The task of ensuring that the Scindia rebellion went off smoothly was assigned to Islam. He worked with the young Congress leader in contacting all the rebel MLAs and giving them specific assurances on ministerships and other benefits. As a first step, seventeen MLAs were flown—for 'safe-keeping'—to a resort in Bengaluru. Karnataka was ruled by the BJP at the time, which meant the state machinery was completely in the party's control. 'We had originally taken a few dissident MLAs to Gurugram, but the Congress leadership managed to contact them and get them back. This time, we ensured that the whole operation was kept top secret and no one could reach the MLAs in Bengaluru,' revealed Islam. The 'party with a difference' was now adept at luring MLAs with its 'no-rules-apply' politics and toppling Opposition governments, another sign of the 'new' BJP under Team Modi–Shah.

With the numbers clearly against him, the wily and experienced Kamal Nath, a veteran of many political battles, decided on one final roll of the dice. There had been a steady stream of reports from global news agencies, warning of a rapidly spreading virus that needed immediate attention. Covid-19 was the name given by the World Health Organization (WHO) in February 2020 to the disease caused by the novel coronavirus, SARS-CoV-2, first detected in the Wuhan province in China in late 2019. By mid-March, several offices, schools and colleges were following a government advisory on wearing masks outdoors and practising social distancing as a preventive response to the virus. With the BJP pushing for a no-confidence vote, Nath suggested that the House be adjourned as a precautionary measure. The Madhya Pradesh Speaker N.P. Prajapati, a Congressman, swung into action and announced an adjournment of the House on 16 March for ten days because of the mounting fear around coronavirus. Nath hoped the ensuing ten days would give his government some breathing space to woo back the rebel MLAs.

Meanwhile, there was also pressure for Parliament to be adjourned as a safety measure. But the presiding officers in both Houses of Parliament did not relent. On 18 March, when four TMC MPs entered the Rajya Sabha wearing black masks, then Vice President Venkaiah Naidu in the chair asked them to remove them, claiming that it was against the rules of Parliament. When several Opposition MPs called for a curtailment of the Parliament session, Union Minister of Minority Affairs Mukhtar Abbas Naqvi objected. 'Showing any panic will not be in the national interest,' he insisted. The irony was stark. On the one hand, the Modi government was advising citizens to mask up and limit large gatherings, and on the other, MPs in Parliament who were trying to follow the advisory were being accused of a 'panic' reaction. Congress MP Rajeev Gowda sarcastically remarked in Parliament, 'Coronavirus doesn't know we are MPs!'

Kamal Nath was convinced that the decision not to curtail Parliament was taken under pressure from the Prime Minister and home minister's office. 'The Centre refused to adjourn Parliament even though Covid cases were rising only because they wanted to ensure that the Madhya Pradesh government was first toppled. Had Parliament adjourned, the MP assembly too would have adjourned, and the BJP's plans would have got derailed,' he insisted. Not even a looming pandemic would be allowed to stand in the way of the Modi-led BJP's all-out quest for power.

The BJP leadership realized it needed to act quickly. Chouhan moved the Supreme Court, which ordered that a video-recorded floor test be held on 20 March. Knowing his game was up, Kamal Nath resigned hours ahead of the floor test. On 23 March, Chouhan was sworn in as chief minister of Madhya Pradesh for the fourth time in a closed-door ceremony at the Raj Bhavan in Bhopal. No party leaders and not even the media were invited; a Covid-induced lockdown had just been announced in Bhopal. The next morning, on 24 March, the Congress boycotted the trust vote and Chouhan proved his majority on the floor of the assembly. That very evening at 8 p.m., giving just four hours' notice, Prime Minister Modi announced a complete lockdown of a nation of a billion people for twenty-one days, beginning at midnight. With a Congress state government toppled and a BJP government installed in its place, the Modi government was finally ready to focus on the challenge that lay ahead. A once-in-a-century pandemic.

Whether the Modi government delayed in announcing the lockdown only to ensure Operation Lotus in Bhopal was completed successfully is a question I posed to then Health Minister Dr Harsh Vardhan. A soft-spoken, genial figure and an ENT surgeon by training, who had entered the party in the Vajpayee–Advani era, Dr Harsh Vardhan brushed aside the question. 'My entire focus was on Covid management. I had nothing to do with what was happening in Madhya Pradesh; that was purely a political issue being handled by the party and the Prime Minister,' he replied. Whether or not the lockdown was delayed in March 2020 to bring down an Opposition-led government will remain just one of the many unanswered questions swirling around the Covid story. But the sequence of events had yet again given a glimpse into the darker, Machiavellian side of Modi's politics.

The Prime Minister's televised addresses to the nation are much-awaited news 'events'. In November 2016, Modi had dramatically announced the demonetization of Rs 500 and Rs 1,000 notes, a move that had sent the entire country into a spin. Since then, every prime-time broadcast by Modi has been watched with a mix of fear and eagerness. The one on 24 March, however, was a little different. The cryptic tweet from the Prime Minister read: 'Will address the nation at 8 p.m. today … on vital aspects relating to the menace of Covid-19.' There was an audible sigh of relief in the newsroom. For once there would be no last-minute surprises: this was going to be an address on the virus and not a dramatic economic or political policy decision. At the time, the country had officially reported 515 Covid cases and 10 deaths.

Modi had already addressed the nation once on 19 March on his government's efforts to combat the rapid spread of the Covid virus. In that speech, he had called for a one-day-long self-imposed 'Janata curfew', during which no one would step out of their homes. Terming the situation 'grave' and worse than any world war, he stressed on the need to avoid panic buying and assured citizens that the government was taking all steps to ensure there were no disruptions in the supply of essential commodities. There was also a final piece of advice for the citizenry: 'From doctors to nurses, hospital staff, sanitation workers, airline employees, government staff, police personnel, media people, people associated with train-bus-auto rickshaw services, and home delivery agents; all have been selflessly serving others, without caring about themselves … The nation is grateful to them all, and citizens should express their gratitude to these people on Sunday.' So, on 22 March at 5 p.m., for five minutes, as state administrations blared a siren, people were asked to stand on their balconies and terraces and doorsteps and clap, ring bells or bang thalis (steel plates). 'Taali bajao, thali bajao,' was the Prime Minister's message to an anxious country, which had just been put on high alert. The messaging was bizarre. In the midst of a pandemic, millions of Indians were being asked to create a lot of noise—to scare away the virus, perhaps? Modi's brand of secretive superstition (he's known to be obsessed with the number eight) and gormless magical thinking (in 2014 he had expounded on the wonders of ancient plastic surgery practised 2,000 years ago, as exemplified in Lord Ganesh's elephantine head) were being played out, ahead of scientific solutions to a lethal disease. Or was there a method to the madness?

Months later, a senior government official told me that the 'taali-thali' idea—and the subsequent 'Diya jalao' (light a lamp) campaign—was entirely the Prime Minister's idea. 'Modi ji saw it as a morale booster, a unique way to create a sense of unity and common purpose in a difficult period,' he argued. When I suggested that the 'taali-thali' concept was rooted in a delusional 'all is well' anti-science fantasy, and particularly ill-timed given the looming medical crisis, the official caustically remarked, 'But didn't people come out in their millions and follow the Prime Minister's advice? That is the hypnotic power of Modi that none of you liberal elite will appreciate.' The 'hypnotic power' of Prime Minister Modi had pushed the masses towards an irrational act of collective obedience. A rational mind would be scornful of the 'taali-thali' messaging, but the vast majority of the country were clearly happy to follow the leader. Prime Minister Modi was not just another politician but a feel-good guru, a lucky-charm-dispensing shaman or even a sort of psychedelic witch doctor, a cult figure for his followers, using his massive communication armoury to prepare the nation for a 'war' of a very different kind.

On 24 March, the Modi government finally officially declared 'war' on the virus. In his nationwide address, a grim-faced Prime Minister, his voice sounding suitably grave, announced an unprecedented national lockdown, starting midnight, for the next twenty-one days. 'From midnight tonight onwards, the entire country—please listen carefully— the entire country shall go under a complete lockdown. In order to protect the country, and each of its citizens, a full ban is being imposed on people from stepping outside their homes. There is a "lakshman rekha" on your doorstep. Even one step outside your house will bring coronavirus inside your house. If the situation is not controlled in twenty-one days, India could go twenty-one years behind,' he warned.

From feel-good guru to prophet of doom and gloom, Modi's transformation was sudden and dramatic. Just two days ago, the country had been urged to clap and bang steel plates, and now 1.3 billion (130 crore) people were being asked to stay at home, that too at four hours' notice. From 'celebration' one moment to 'sacrifice' the next, Modi had dragged the entire country through an emotional roller coaster. Television ratings suggest that Modi's lockdown address was the most watched TV event in the history of the country, viewed live by a record 197 million (19.7 crore) people across 201 channels. This was disaster television at its peak.

It took a while for the enormity of what had just been broadcast to sink in. My first thought was whether I should cancel my dentist appointment scheduled for the next morning. Millions of other Indians obviously had far more urgent concerns. Daily grocery supplies disrupted, transport services halted, schools shut down, offices closed. How would the millions living in slums, chawls and single-room tenements, often as many as six to eight people in a 10-by-10 square-foot room, actually observe the latest buzzword: 'social distancing', defined not just as avoiding mass gatherings but also as reducing close contact between individuals to slow the spread of the virus? Social distancing was a privilege for the middle class, but for the vast majority who lived in tiny shanties it was next to impossible. Would these multitudes of anonymous Indians be able to endure an extended twenty-one-day lockdown? And what if the virus kept spreading and the timelines were further extended? How would the poor, especially those who survived on daily wages, be able to bear the brunt of this stay-at-home 'farmaan' (order) put in place overnight?

Most Indians were given virtually no time to even think about these crucial questions. The midnight lockdown was announced in a prime ministerial address that began at 8 p.m. and ended just before 9 p.m.: effectively, the nation was given less than four hours to shut down their lives. 'We had no choice. Had we delayed the lockdown period, there would have been total chaos,' countered Dr Harsh Vardhan, who, as health minister, was expected to monitor the spread of Covid-19. But surely essential services, shelter and transport could have been arranged for those who were stuck and far away from home? 'All these big decisions were taken by the Prime Minister's office and the home ministry; we were only acting under their guidance,' he confessed.

The mild-mannered Dr Harsh Vardhan's admission only confirms what many suspected. The all-powerful, authoritarian PMO and the home ministry were the driving force behind all major lockdown decisions. All others, including cabinet ministers and state governments, were only meant to execute the instructions. An RTI report filed by the BBC in March 2021 revealed that most government departments, both at the Centre and in the states, were not consulted prior to the lockdown being implemented. 'How can they say that no one was consulted?' claimed a home ministry official. 'Most state governments were in touch with us and had already initiated their localized lockdowns.'

The truth is, the decision-making apparatus to tackle the Covid-19 virus was highly centralized. On 11 March 2020, the Ministry of Home Affairs passed an order invoking the Disaster Management Act, 2005, under which the home ministry has absolute powers, through bodies like the National Disaster Management Authority, to take any necessary steps to manage a disaster situation. On the same day, the Modi government also ordered states to implement the Epidemic Diseases Act, 1897 to enforce its advisory. First enacted as a response to the Bombay plague that had led to the deaths of thousands, this archaic nineteenth-century law was now being used to contain a virus in the twenty-first century. The state exercised limitless authority over citizens' lives, massively restricting their liberties and freedoms. 'There was perfect co-ordination between the Centre and the states when it came to implementing the measures, be it quarantining, mandatory screening, sealing borders or lockdown controls. We were constantly talking to each other,' claimed a home ministry official.

And yet, as the strict lockdown began to take effect, it soon became apparent that the 'war' the Modi government was waging against the virus was proving to be most devastating for the poor, costing them jobs and, in some cases, their lives. The twenty-one-day 'sacrifice' would end up being a much longer, far more tortuous ordeal. No 'taali' or 'thali' noise would stop the virus from spreading.

'Urban India didn't care about migrant workers till now. The pandemic has given a face to those who were "invisibilised" and are being cared about now only because elite and middle-class Indians have lost their services.'
—Award-winning journalist P. Sainath in an interview with
India Today, 10 April 2020

On 28 March 2020, four days after Prime Minister Modi announced a national lockdown, an unprecedented migration began. This was the massive migrant exodus of 2020—an epic movement of millions. Panic-stricken, desperate people poured out of India's cities, infants and aged in tow, ready to walk, cycle or travel in makeshift carts all the way home to distant villages. From New Delhi to eastern Uttar Pradesh. From Mumbai to Assam. From Hyderabad to Chhattisgarh. With most bus and train services brought to an abrupt halt by Modi's brutal diktat, people took to the only transport they had—their legs.

From the moment the lockdown was enforced, reports began trickling in of desperate people across the country scrambling to find a way to get to their homes. Stray images of migrant families walking or cycling on the highway with their meagre belongings appeared on TV screens. As rumours spread of buses that would take migrants home, large crowds, comprising mainly migrant labourers, gathered at major transport hubs across cities. At the Anand Vihar bus station on the Delhi–Uttar Pradesh border, hundreds of people clambered over each other to locate the last few buses that remained in the hope that these would take them back to their villages. With most national news channels headquartered in Noida, just across the border from Delhi, the looming migrant exodus crisis finally entered the breaking-news cycle of newsrooms.

That evening, I took a detour from the office to reach Anand Vihar. The scenes on ground zero were heart-wrenching. 'We have been thrown out of our rooms by the landlord who wants us to pay him rent in advance. How do we pay him when we don't have any work?' a young man from Bihar's Siwan district told us tearfully. Many of the despairing voices were of daily wagers, several of whom worked on construction sites in the city. With food supplies running out, they were frantically looking to get away to the security of their villages. Distraught Delhi government officials struggled to handle the crowds, pleading with the migrants to go back. Four days earlier, the Prime Minister had warned people against large gatherings. The milling crowds were a reality check; in a country of 1.3 billion people, enforcing a sudden lockdown was never going to be easy. The trauma of despairing people left to fend for themselves would become a recurring theme; the chaos at Anand Vihar was only a teaser of what was to unfold in the coming weeks.

The initial reaction of the Modi government to reports of the migrant exodus was one of denial. On the day the Anand Vihar rush was reported, a senior government official rang up news channels asking them 'not to spread panic'. 'You are making it out to be as if the whole country is on the road,' was the complaint. State governments too were reluctant to admit to the scale of the problem. Rather than face up to the crisis, the Centre and state governments were busily passing the buck, failing to come up with a co-ordinated response. 'We are ready to send people home, but it is for the Uttar Pradesh and Bihar governments to have the transport ready,' contended a Delhi government official.

Typically, it needed an unspeakable tragedy for the 'system' to fully wake up. On 9 May, sixteen people were run over by a freight train near Aurangabad in Maharashtra while they were sleeping on railway tracks after a long journey on foot. The victims had left Jalna town, where they were working in a steel factory, after their employer refused to pay their wages. Without a daily wage and struggling for food, these labourers were desperate to get back home to their village in Madhya Pradesh at any cost. Their mutilated bodies were found on the blood-spattered railway tracks.

The anguish of the relatives of the victim was palpable. 'Gareeb ki koi sunvai nahi hai desh mein (There is no one to listen to the poor),' they said when interviewed. That conversation went viral across social media.

'Managing' the media narrative has been an intrinsic part of the Modi power playbook, perpetually and obsessively focused on ensuring that the mainstream media, in particular, doesn't raise inconvenient issues and social media is 'influenced' by their supporters. However, the unfolding humanitarian crisis threw the government's media managers off guard; they couldn't 'manage' the narrative any longer. The government had no choice but to act, provide some real relief to the poor, hungry, faceless migrant who was at the heart of the crisis. Where initially the Centre was reluctant to even acknowledge the mass public suffering, it was now compelled to ramp up public transport services. Here too there was chaos in the early stages as the government rolled out Shramik Special trains. When we reported that migrants leaving Mumbai were complaining that they were being forced to pay for their train tickets, the irate railway minister, Piyush Goyal, insisted that this was 'false information'. 'Only Opposition-ruled states are charging migrants to board trains,' claimed a BJP spokesperson. A day later, we ran another story exposing how migrant workers in BJP-ruled Gujarat were being asked to shell out Rs 600 to board a train to Uttar Pradesh—the government's lie had been caught on camera.

The fact is that with no clear-cut policy in place, the unplanned deployment of bus and train services led to frenzy, turmoil and untold miseries on the ground. A railway circular claimed 'the local state government shall hand over tickets to passengers cleared by them and collect the ticket fare and hand over the total amount to the railways'. While the Congress accused the government of exploiting the stranded workers by charging them money, the BJP claimed that the railways were already bearing 85 per cent of the travel cost and charging the remaining 15 per cent to the states. Caught in the midst of another political tussle were countless poor, suffering Indians. Denial. Deflection. Distraction. Government accountability was at a premium. An unfeeling

Modi government was busy scoring political points while the loss of life continued unabated.

A classic example was provided by a war of words on Facebook and Twitter between Shiv Sena leader and then Maharashtra Chief Minister Uddhav Thackeray and Piyush Goyal in the third week of May. Thackeray claimed in a Facebook address that against the state government's demand for an average of eighty trains daily, only thirty-five or forty trains had been made available, even though Mumbai had the highest demand for carrying stranded migrants and students. Goyal responded with a series of twelve tweets till 2 a.m., repeatedly asking the Maharashtra government to submit the list of passengers to be ferried to their home states as per procedure. 'Where is the list of 125 trains from Maharashtra? As of 2 a.m., received list of only 46 trains' was the final late-night tweet. A 'war' on social media was hardly what the country needed in an emergency. Couldn't the minister have just picked up the phone and sorted it out, our reporter asked Goyal, himself a Mumbaikar. 'I'm sorry but the chief minister was lying in public and needed to be called out,' was the combative answer. The BJP and Shiv Sena had been allies in Maharashtra till their bitter falling out in 2019. Seemingly, the wounds of that wrangle were still raw. At a time when mass welfare and relief were the need of the hour, bitter competitive politics was not just jarring but cruel.

Could the Prime Minister, who was holding regular meetings with chief ministers and senior officials from state governments, have stepped in and ensured a smoother process to transport the migrants? 'Please appreciate that India is a vast country and to expect everything to work smoothly from day one is a bit unfair,' a senior railway official contended. Could the co-ordination have been better, I asked. 'This was a sudden and unimaginable crisis. There was a national lockdown, the fear of the Covid-19 pandemic was spreading and yet our officers were working night and day to help people. You journalists only look at the negatives. Why don't you ever appreciate the great work the Indian railways did in ferrying so many people safely to their homes?' was the official's argument.

The railways eventually ran as many as 3,740 Shramik Special trains in May alone, ferrying more than 6 million (60 lakh) stranded migrants to reach their home states by mid-June. A defiant railway minister refused to accept that the train movement could have happened sooner. 'It was only when we saw that the migrants were unwilling to stay in the designated camps that we started the trains. After all, containment and lockdown are about staying where you are,' argued Goyal. He also blamed the states for the delayed response. 'Migrants would come to the station and could not be transported because several states were unprepared for one reason or the other,' was his charge.

The truth is the scale of the migrant crisis created by the lockdown overwhelmed not just the railways but the entire government machinery. The result was policy ad-hocism: new government orders were issued almost on a daily basis, leading to more confusion. The controversy over whether to charge migrants for rail tickets was a prime example. The Modi government could claim that they tried their best, even turning adversity into opportunity at times. The manufacture of personal protective equipment (PPE), masks and sanitizers on a massive scale is cited as an example of effective, result-oriented action, or what the Modi government likes to call a 'mission mode' 'atmanirbhar' (self-reliant) approach. 'When the pandemic hit, we weren't equipped to manufacture PPE kits and relied on imported protective equipment. A year later, we were manufacturing 2 lakh kits and 2 lakh N95 masks every day. Isn't that a remarkable achievement?' asked a health ministry official. But the self-glorification rang hollow against the death toll that inched ever upwards.

It was only by the end of May 2020, almost two months after the original twenty-one-day lockdown was announced, that the government seemed to slowly be coming to grips with the situation and began taking the first tentative steps towards 'unlocking' the country. By then, India had officially recorded more than 250,000 Covid-19 cases and 7,200 deaths. On 30 June 2020, the Prime Minister was on air once again—the sixth time since the coronavirus outbreak. This time to announce 'Unlock 2.0', a plan to discharge services in a phased manner and extend the Centre's free food for the poor scheme—Pradhan Mantri Gareeb Kalyan Anna Yojana—at a cost of over Rs 90,000 crore to over 800 million (80 crore) Indians. This was Prime Minister Modi playing 'annadata' (a giver of food) in a crisis, with his sharp focus on the 'gareeb kisan' (poor farmer) as his calling card. 'We may not have got everything right, but you must realize that Prime Minister Modi never switched his gaze from minimizing the suffering of the poor during Covid. That's why the poor trust and vote for him,' remarked a former PMO official. The free ration for 800 million Indians would eventually save the Modi government from voter anger in the post-Covid-19 era.

But here is the burning question: Could the misery of millions of poor Indians have been reduced with a less severe lockdown? Most medical experts believe that a lockdown was needed to break the chain of infection and, crucially, give the government machinery more time to prepare in dealing with an unprecedented pandemic. 'It was the right thing to do. Without the lockdown, the infections would have spread at a rate that would have made it impossible for our hospitals to handle,' insisted Dr Randeep Guleria, the former All India Institute of Medical Sciences (AIIMS) director, a member of the Centre's Covid task force.

But there were a few who believed that the same goal could have been achieved with better planning and execution. Among those to raise an early red flag was the erudite Rajiv Bajaj, the managing director of Bajaj Auto. In a series of interviews, Bajaj described the lockdown as 'arbitrary' and 'misguided'. In June 2020, he went a step further during a recorded conversation with Congress leader Rahul Gandhi. 'The lockdown definitely decimated the economy. You flattened the wrong curve: it is not the infection curve, it is the GDP [Gross Domestic Product] curve. This is what we have ended up with, the worst of both worlds,' was his assertion. The plain-spoken corporate leader wasn't far off the mark. Official figures show that the GDP in April–June (Q1) of 2020-21 collapsed by more than 23 per cent—a record in itself and the worst among the big economies. By the government's own calculations nearly 25,000 micro and small enterprises closed down between 2020 and 2023, while millions of jobs, mainly in the unorganized sector, were lost.

The BJP, incensed that the industrialist was in a dialogue with an Opposition leader, was quick to hit back. Its spokesperson Syed Zafar Islam told me on a TV debate, 'Everybody has the right to have an opinion, but please understand, Rajiv Bajaj is not an expert on Covid-19 and how to deal with it.' The response was typical of the manner in which the Modi government dealt with any public criticism of its handling of the pandemic: arrogantly dismissive and full of contempt for any alternative view, with party spokespersons spitting personal invectives on TV and elsewhere. In an unimaginable crisis, when pushed for answers, the mood was always one of denial. For example, Minister of State for Home Affairs Nityanand Rai, in a written reply to Parliament in September 2020, claimed that reports of large-scale migration of labourers had been triggered by 'fake news'. 'The migration of large number of migrant workers was triggered by panic created by fake news regarding duration of lockdown and people, especially migrant labourers, who were worried about adequate supply of basic necessities like food, drinking water, health services and shelter,' he stated.

To blame 'fake news' for a humanitarian crisis that stretched over several weeks was to shrug off any accountability for administrative lapses. It was almost as if the Modi government was bent on shooting the messenger for reporting the reality of thousands of anguished citizens who had struggled during a hard, agonizing lockdown that had completely disrupted economic activity for months.

Santosh Gangwar, the minister of labour and employment at the time, told Parliament that an estimated 10.4 million (1.04 crore) migrant workers returned to their home states during the 2020 lockdown, while maintaining that the ministry did not have any data on migrant workers who lost their jobs and lives during Covid-19. That evening, I debated the issue on prime-time TV with the strapline: 'Modi government in denial mode: Did no labourers lose jobs or lives during the lockdown?' The next day I bumped into a senior BJP politician at Delhi's India International Centre, the tree-shaded, low-slung, high-profile building where seminars and conferences are known to set national policy agendas. 'When will you stop spreading negativity? Can't you see the great work the Modi government is doing in providing relief to so many people?' was his accusatory remark. I was a bit taken aback by the shrill tone adopted but quickly gathered myself to remind the politician that taking welfare measures in an emergency-like situation is the government's duty. 'Fact is, people have suffered immensely; some have died, including those who were run over by a train while sleeping on the tracks due to sheer exhaustion,' was my response. 'So you will now blame us for migrant deaths? Did we tell people to sleep on railway tracks?' he countered. I walked away from the heated exchange but was left wondering why there was such a peculiar lack of sympathy, why greater compassion wasn't being shown. True, managing the lockdown wasn't easy, and government resources had been stretched to the limit, but living in denial wasn't ideal either. In a regimented top-down decision-making system, empathy was the missing link.

The unwillingness to face public criticism or scrutiny was marked by opacity in functioning. On 27 March 2020, within days of the lockdown being announced, the PM CARES Fund was formed by the Prime Minister to extend assistance to Indian citizens in the midst of the Covid-19 public health emergency. Modi made a public appeal to donate generously to the fund, whose proceeds would be used for a variety of Covid relief measures. Yet there already existed a Prime Minister's National Relief Fund since 1948 as a primary focal point for mobilizing public donations in the event of natural disasters like floods and earthquakes. 'We wanted to control and streamline the process to ensure well-targeted action with a fund that would be specifically used to fight the Covid crisis rather than a generic disaster management fund,' explained a government official. 'Control' being the operative word.

Mumbai-based advocate Manoj Harit detailed a telling 'chronology' for the fund rollout. The initial tweet announcing the fund was published at 4.51 p.m. on 28 March. At 5.09 p.m., through another tweet, the Indian Administrative Services Association committed Rs 21 lakh, and less than ten minutes later, at 5.18 p.m., actor Akshay Kumar, a professed admirer of the Prime Minister, committed to donating Rs 25 crore. By 5.34 p.m., PhonePe had shared a link through which people could contribute to PM CARES. Clearly, this was a well-planned exercise designed to sound a drumbeat of approval around the Prime Minister's initiative. 'The synchronization of the rollout cannot be a coincidence, especially given the well-known obsessive media management and expertise of the regime,' argued Harit.

A journalist colleague dashed off several RTI queries on the fund's status and its key donors. Each time, he was stonewalled with a negative response. In a detailed affidavit to the Delhi High Court in January 2023, the PMO asserted that PM CARES is a public charitable fund that is not controlled by the Union government or any other government organization and, therefore, is not obliged to disclose third-party information.

Prima facie, this explanation seems totally absurd. The PM CARES Fund website, hosted on a government URL, says that the Prime Minister of India is its chairperson (ex-officio) and the ministers of defence, home and finance are its ex-officio trustees. The fund is administered on an honorary basis by an additional secretary/joint secretary in charge of it in the PMO. Donations to the fund had been given exemption under the Foreign Contribution (Regulation) Amendment Act (FCRA). The Union government had reached out to corporates and public-sector undertakings, asking them to contribute to the fund; a total amount of Rs 3,076.62 crore was collected in 2020 as per the website. Thousands of crores raised in the name of the fund were spent on purchasing ventilators, oxygen cylinders and vaccines using government machinery and resources.

It required a determined RTI activist, Commodore Lokesh Batra (retd), to expose the lack of transparency and doublespeak on the fund's status. Since all contributions towards the PM CARES Fund were 100 per cent exempt from income tax, the RTI activist sought to know the basis for the exemption. In its reply, the office of the Commissioner of Income Tax (Exemption) said, 'PM Cares fund has been registered under the Registration Act, 1908 and being a body owned by, controlled by and established by the Government of India,' but it does not meet the definition of a 'public authority' under the RTI Act. However, the trust deed of the fund released in December 2020 states: 'There is no control of either the central government or any state governments, either direct or indirect, in the functioning of the trust in any manner whatsoever.' As Commodore Batra put it, 'If there is no government control, then how is the entire fund being run and supervised by government officials, and why is the Prime Minister's photo there on every Covid-related government initiative, be it vaccines or ventilators, that has used fund resources?' The fact is, the PM CARES Fund was a key weapon in the Modi government's armoury to control the financing and distribution of Covid relief. It ensured the rapid deployment of resources in the fight against Covid while also boosting the Prime Minister's image. Only, no questions could be asked on its internal functioning or sources of funding.

Slipping into silent mode when posed difficult questions by public-spirited citizens is standard operating procedure for the Modi government. But during the Covid period, the refusal to address discomfiting issues only aggravated the crisis. The Modi government's muteness was nowhere more shocking than when egregious conspiracy theories targeting Muslims as Covid carriers were being floated. The trouble began in March 2020. Within days of the lockdown being announced, a gathering of the Tablighi Jama'at, an Islamic missionary organization, in the south Delhi neighbourhood of Nizamuddin was singled out by the authorities and held responsible for the spread of coronavirus across India. The convention, which had been cleared by the Delhi civic authorities, was attended by several thousand people, including many foreign delegates. A number of those who attended the convention unknowingly contracted Covid and took it back to the towns and villages where they lived.

When the reports first trickled in, social media went berserk. The hashtag #CoronaJihad, actively promoted by prominent members of the BJP's IT cell, encouraged the idea that this was an 'Islamic' conspiracy to target Indians. Kapil Mishra, the Delhi BJP leader, was among the first to put out an incendiary tweet: 'Tablighi Jama'at people have begun spitting on doctors and other health workers. It's clear their aim is to infect as many people as possible with coronavirus and kill them.' No one from the BJP hierarchy in the Delhi state unit or at the Centre repudiated what was clearly a hateful, absurd and communally provocative remark. Soon rumours began circulating of Tablighi Jama'at members refusing to go into quarantine, assaulting hospital staff and throwing bottles of urine at Hindus. More deadly hashtags labelling the Tablighis as #CoronaTerrorists followed. News channels too blamed the Tablighis for being coronavirus 'superspreaders'.

Instead of acting swiftly to quell the rumours, the police in several BJP-ruled states began rounding up members of the Tablighi Jama'at and placing them and their contacts in quarantine. The Uttar Pradesh police even went to the extent of offering Rs 10,000 for information on anyone who had attended the gathering. While a number of Tablighis did test positive, to accuse them of being primarily responsible for the spread of the virus was a malicious act characteristic of a divisive political agenda. After the initial denials over the impact of the lockdown on migrant labour, the state machinery was now guilty of demonizing an entire community: Muslim men in beards were suddenly targeted as virus spreaders and socially boycotted. In Karnataka, former BJP MP Anantkumar Hegde denounced the Tablighi Jama'at as terrorists. An audio clip was shared in WhatsApp groups urging people not to let Muslim fruit and vegetable vendors into their areas, saying they were spreading the virus through their produce. Posters appeared in cities like Mangalore and Meerut saying Muslims would no longer be permitted to enter certain neighbourhoods. Dividing citizens on the basis of religion and spreading the virus of hate and bigotry in the midst of a public health crisis was perverse.

The fact that the Centre and several state governments did nothing to challenge these allegations nor took any action against the hatemongers was an abdication of their constitutional duty, negligent and unconscionable. It marked a moral collapse in the country's fight against Covid. A case in point in early April 2020 was that of Mehboob Ali, who had returned to his village in Bawana in northwest Delhi after attending a Tablighi Jama'at conference in Bhopal. He was immediately accused by neighbours of being a 'corona terrorist', dragged into a field and beaten with sticks and stones until he bled from his nose and ears. He barely survived the gruesome attack. Nor was he the only one. Across the country, there were reports of attacks on Muslim vegetable vendors in particular. Northeast Delhi had seen bloody communal riots in the weeks prior to the Covid emergency. The violence had stopped but not the spiralling narrative of religious hatred. Not for the first time, innocent citizens were the worst sufferers of this appalling religious prejudice. The Covid threat would pass sooner or later, but the virus of communal strife would remain a festering sore.

India woke up to a new year in 2021 after a traumatic twelve-month period. The Modi government was now ready to celebrate a fresh start. There were distinct signs of the virus slowing down. While masks were still mandatory in public places, strict lockdown rules had been eased in most parts of the country, temporary Covid centres were being shut down, shops, offices and restaurants had begun to open, markets were filling up, airlines were increasing flights, even board examinations for schools were being scheduled. The Reserve Bank of India (RBI) announced that India was 'bending the Covid infection curve' and rather poetically declared that the economy was 'breaking out amidst winter's lengthening shadows towards a place in sunlight'. While much of the Western world, especially the United States, was experiencing another surge of the infection, India was being projected as a standout country in the fight against Covid.

In January 2021, addressing the World Economic Forum via video conference, the Prime Minister claimed that India had defeated the doomsday predictions. 'It was predicted that India would be the most affected country from corona all over the world. It was said that there would be a tsunami of corona infections in India … but the number of people infected with corona today is rapidly decreasing,' Modi boasted. On 21 February, senior leaders of the BJP and all state unit chiefs met to adopt a resolution thanking Prime Minister Modi for his 'visionary leadership' in effectively handling the pandemic and getting the country back on the path to growth. In the first week of March, addressing a Delhi Medical Association meet, then Health Minister Dr Harsh Vardhan went a step further, declaring that the country was 'in the end game' of the Covid-19 pandemic. The minister didn't forget to praise Prime Minister Modi's leadership during a time of global crisis, claiming that 'India has emerged as an example to the world in international co-operation.' Details were triumphantly shared of India's role as 'the world's pharmacy', supplying 55.1 million (5.51 crore) doses of the vaccine to sixty-two countries. The self-congratulatory messaging, typical of a sycophantic and obsequious political culture, proclaimed Modi-led India to be a 'vishwaguru', and the Prime Minister a 'vaccine guru'.

The government's optimism was based on a sharp drop in reported infections. From a peak of more than 90,000 cases per day on average in mid-September 2020, infections had steadily declined. By mid-February, India's case count had officially reduced to 11,000 cases a day. The seven-day rolling average of daily Covid deaths had slid to below 100. The Union health ministry's daily press briefings had stopped. Even the Covid task force meetings were shorter and less frequent. 'There was a feeling among officials that the worst was over. Maybe it was Covid fatigue, but we just took our eye off the ball,' admitted a retired government officer.

In the last week of February, the ECI announced a schedule for five state elections in which 186 million (18.6 crore) people were eligible to vote for 824 assembly seats. Polling in West Bengal would be held over as many as eight phases, an elongated election schedule that reflected the intense, at times bloody, political competition in that state. A few days later, in mid-March, the cricket board allowed more than 130,000 fans, mostly unmasked, to watch two international games between India and England at the Narendra Modi Stadium in Ahmedabad. The poll bugle and the cricket matches were clear signs that India was looking at life beyond Covid-19.

And if elections and cricket—two of India's national obsessions—were on track, could religious gatherings be far behind? In early March, having got the nod from the Centre, the Uttarakhand government announced plans for the Kumbh Mela by the banks of the Ganga in Haridwar, even though the Covid case count had begun to rise once again. The festival attracts lakhs of pilgrims and was projected as the first major public celebration in the country since the onset of the pandemic in 2020. A health expert who was being consulted by the Centre's Covid-19 task force revealed that he had attended a meeting in Delhi where specific concerns were voiced over the Kumbh becoming a superspreader event. 'At the meeting, most officials agreed with my assessment that it might be best to postpone the Kumbh or, at the very least, downsize the month-long celebration. All agreed. So the next day, I was rather shocked to see a full-page advertisement featuring the Prime Minister, inviting devotees to the festival and assuring them that it was "clean" and "safe" to take a holy dip.'

So why did the Centre allow the Uttarakhand government to go ahead with the Kumbh Mela despite warnings? Typically, there is the usual Centre versus states blame game. 'We wrote to the state government on more than one occasion warning them about "inadequate" preparations at the Kumbh, but they kept assuring us that the situation was under control,' claimed a former Union health ministry official. But this explanation was a feeble attempt to shirk responsibility. The Centre, specifically the home ministry, had arrogated to itself vast powers under the Disaster Management Act during the pandemic, and could have easily monitored and controlled the state government's handling of the situation. Uttarakhand was BJP-ruled, so there was little possibility of the administration defying any central diktat.

Allowing the Kumbh Mela in Haridwar to proceed as planned was actually a gigantic mistake—a result of the triumphalist smugness that had overwhelmed the Modi government ever since the Covid numbers had begun to decline at the start of the year. It was the RSS–BJP Sangh Parivar's way of announcing to the country that India had little to fear from Covid. On a news show during this period, when I asked a BJP spokesperson about the need to postpone the Kumbh Mela, I was accused of being a 'Hindu-phobic' liberal who was unaware of ground realities. Faith had taken over from reason, as had local politics. The Uttarakhand elections were just a year away, and the BJP was already gearing up for the fight. In early March, the BJP had effected a change in guard in Dehradun, replacing then Chief Minister Trivendra Singh Rawat with a relative political lightweight in Tirath Singh Rawat, who enjoyed RSS backing. While Trivendra Rawat had insisted on strict Covid protocols for the Haridwar Kumbh, his successor was more than happy to indulge the priests and local traders who had opposed the protocols, which included a compulsory RT-PCR test for the attendees. He argued that the test would dissuade devotees from visiting the holy city for the customary dip.

On 12 April, as India registered another 169,000 Covid cases, overtaking Brazil as the second-worst-hit country, 3 million (30 lakh) people gathered by the banks of the Ganga to take the ritual dip. Religious fervour took over as Covid protocols were washed away in the river. Scores of the jostling faithful jumped into the water, without regard for social distancing. Among those participating in the rituals was Tirath Singh Rawat, who had publicly proclaimed that 'faith in God will overcome the fear of the virus'. He too wasn't wearing a face mask. As a senior Uttarakhand police official remarked, 'It was total madness and we were in no position to enforce any rules when the chief minister himself was violating Covid protocols.' The Haridwar Kumbh Mela was a peak point of the religious hysteria constantly encouraged by the Modi-led regime.

By 15 April, more than 2,000 devotees had tested positive for Covid-19. Just two days later, the Modi government backtracked and called for the Kumbh Mela to be seen as a 'symbolic' occasion without involving further elaborate and crowded rituals. However, it was too late. By the time the festival ended on 28 April, more than 9 million (90 lakh) people had taken the holy dip. Thousands of them returned to their homes across the country without being tested or quarantined, all of them potential carriers of the virus. No records are available of just how many Kumbh pilgrims tested positive, but it is obvious that the religious festival was a potential superspreader. There was an 1,800 per cent increase in Covid cases in Uttarakhand alone during the Kumbh Mela. But unlike in 2020, when the Tablighis were called out by the state and civil society and vilified for organizing a much smaller gathering, no one dared challenge the Kumbh organizers for having wilfully violated Covid protocols. On 2 July, less than four months into his tenure, Tirath Singh Rawat resigned. The ostensible reason: Rawat was not a member of the Uttarakhand state assembly and needed to get elected within a six-month period, but as there was uncertainty over when by-elections would be held, he thought it best to step down. The more plausible explanation is that the Centre was looking for a scapegoat for the disastrous mismanagement of Covid protocols during the Haridwar Kumbh Mela.

But what of the Modi government and the Centre, which had green-lighted the Kumbh, cricket matches and a frenetic five-state election campaign? Who would be accountable for the renewed surge in Covid cases? In February, the Prime Minister was hailed by his colleagues as a Covid 'conqueror' who spearheaded India's emergence as a 'vishwaguru'. Now, barely sixty days later, the Modi government was about to enter its darkest period in power. A calamity of its own making unfolded. The lethal second wave caught Modi and his government totally unprepared.

=

Narendra Modi fights elections like a general going to war. Right through the month of March and early April 2021, the Prime Minister was in his battle fatigues, criss-crossing the election-bound states. His particular focus was on West Bengal, where the BJP had sensed an opportunity to take down the Mamata Banerjee government. In the Lok Sabha elections of 2019, the BJP had won 18 of the 42 seats in Bengal, the first time the party had crossed double digits in the state. Home Minister Amit Shah, in particular, was convinced that the BJP would breach the Bengal fortress in 2021. At a closed-door interaction in Kolkata with journalists, Shah insisted that Mamata Banerjee's time was up. 'Just you wait and see—we will create history in Bengal,' he declared confidently.

Shah's buoyancy was based on what he called the 'Modi factor'. Modi is the BJP's mascot in every election, and Bengal was no different. By the first week of April, the Prime Minister had addressed nine rallies in the state; he was scheduled to attend over twenty rallies by the time the eight-phase election campaign concluded. Not just the Prime Minister but almost every senior BJP leader and Union minister was assigned a Bengal district to track. By the middle of April, all of the BJP's heavy artillery had been deployed to carpet-bomb the state. The party's Bengal in-charge Kailash Vijayvargiya crowed, 'There will not be a single one of Bengal's 294 constituencies that we will not have covered by the end of this campaign. Yeh kamal ka toofan hai (This is a storm of the lotus).'

On 17 April, the Prime Minister addressed a large rally in Bengal's Asansol. Typically, his prime target was the Bengal chief minister, whom he routinely taunted with a guttural and mocking 'Didi, O Didi' jibe, which was dubbed singularly offensive by political opponents and activists. Dressed in a long-sleeved saffron kurta and sporting a flowing white beard, designed perhaps to bring to mind the great Bengali national icon Rabindranath Tagore, Modi thanked the audience for coming for the meeting in such large numbers. 'Everywhere I look, I only see people. Aap logon ne toh aaj kamaal kar diya (You have performed a miracle today).' There was no mention in the speech of the urgent need to observe social distancing or crowd control as per Covid protocols.

On the day of the Asansol rally, the country had just registered the second consecutive day of more than 200,000 cases. There had been more than 1,000 deaths over a twenty-four-hour period. And yet here was the Prime Minister, encouraging the cheering crowds to gather in even larger numbers. It was the lowest point in India's fight against Covid, a moment when basic safety norms were compromised by the country's top leadership in an attempt to win an election. 'Why are you only blaming the Prime Minister? Has Mamata Banerjee stopped her rallies?' a combative Vijayvargiya argued when criticized for organizing the PM's rallies even as Covid cases were rising. But surely the Prime Minister, as the foremost leader in the country, was expected to set an example for the rest to follow? Had the campaign blitzkrieg extinguished all common sense?

Just five days later, reality hit home: the country was well and truly in the midst of a second Covid wave. On 22 April, hit by an unprecedented surge, India recorded over 300,000 new confirmed cases, the highest single-day tally recorded anywhere in the world since the onset of the pandemic. Faced with rising public outcry over large political gatherings, the Prime Minister was forced to cancel his next round of election rallies in Bengal. Instead, his office said, he would be parked in the national capital to chair a series of meetings on Covid management, including a virtual interaction with chief ministers of states reeling under a heavy Covid caseload. Home Minister Amit Shah too was pushed to cut down his physical rallies. The Calcutta High Court stepped in and faulted the ECI for not doing enough to ensure appropriate Covid protocols were followed. The Madras High Court went a step further, saying murder charges should be imposed on the constitutional body for being 'the only institution responsible for the situation that we are in today'. The scathing observations could not mask the terrifyingly grim reality. The entire Indian state, not just the ECI, had completely failed in its duties.

How did the Prime Minister, who is otherwise so conscious about his public image and messaging, get it so horribly wrong in the summer of 2021? A senior government official talked of pressure from the party to get Modi to 'aggressively' lead the poll campaign. 'You see, the Prime

Minister at election time is a karyakarta first. The party draws up the campaign schedule and the Prime Minister makes sure that he puts party above all else in this period,' he explained. But surely a global pandemic demanded a more reliable, socially conscious approach from a leadership that had been constantly lecturing citizens to be more careful in combating the virus. 'Yes, we got the optics badly wrong,' admitted the official but then contended, 'It's easy to blame the Prime Minister in hindsight, but which state government covered itself in glory during this critical period?' As always, passing the buck is the last refuge of a government unwilling to be held accountable for its abject failure. Meanwhile, the delusions of a self-obsessed ruler took a massive toll as the deadly second wave rampaged through India.

Over the next ten weeks, between April and June 2021, the mighty Indian state was brought to its knees. The Delta strain of Covid 2.0 was a fast-spreading, far deadlier virus that left the country numbed and shattered. India's medical infrastructure was strained and on the verge of collapsing. The images in this period were dire. Covid patients literally gasping for breath amidst a critical shortage in oxygen supply. Desperate relatives searching for an ICU bed or a gas cylinder. Cremation grounds running out of space. Makeshift funeral pyres sending the stench of death into the air and, perhaps the most striking visual of all, corpses floating down the Ganga, including in the Prime Minister's home constituency of Varanasi. The horrifying images of bloated bodies being dumped across several villages into the holy river illustrated an inescapable truth: the grip of Covid had extended way beyond just the major cities and into every corner of the country.

The Modi government's initial reaction to the Covid 2.0 crisis was, yet again, denial. When the visuals of funeral pyres in Varanasi were first shown on TV, a senior government officer rang up with a complaint. 'Where are you getting these visuals from? Many of them are dated; the situation is not as bad as you are making it out to be,' he claimed. This was followed by another phone call from an Uttar Pradesh information department officer who was similarly aggrieved at visuals of scores of bodies seen buried in the sands along the riverbank. 'This is not a new practice. People have been coming here for years to carry out the last rites, and many of them opt for sand burial because of a caste or community tradition. Even dumping the body in the Ganga is not new; it has nothing to do with Covid,' I was told by the officer. When I questioned him about the sheer number of bodies buried in the sand, the officer sounded annoyed. 'You just want to show negative stories about Covid; why can't you do some positive news instead?' he argued.

The unwillingness to face bare facts or provide hard data typified the government's approach to the devastating second wave. In February 2022, the then Minister of State for Jal Shakti Bishweswar Tudu, in response to a specific question in the Rajya Sabha, blandly told the Upper House that 'the information regarding number of Covid-19-related dead bodies estimated to have been dumped in the River Ganga is not available'.

The Modi-led NDA was rechristened the 'No Data Available' government by critics. The under-counting of Covid deaths in particular was a troublingly recurrent theme. A WHO report in May 2022 claimed that more than 4.7 million (47 lakh) people in India, nearly ten times the official figure of 481,000, died in the first two Covid waves in 2020–21. The government was quick to rubbish the report, alleging that the methodologies and sample sizes were flawed. But the actual death numbers in the Covid years—far greater than what was officially reported—is a reality the government cannot mask forever, not even in the Prime Minister's home state of Gujarat. For example, when Covid-19 infections peaked in April–May 2021, Ahmedabad officially recorded at least three times as many total deaths as in the same period in the previous two years: 30,247 deaths as compared to an average of 8,337 in the previous years. This is as per data provided by the Ahmedabad local administration to an information activist. And yet the Gujarat government's health ministry data shows fewer than 1,000 Covid deaths in April–May 2021. In July 2024, researchers from several universities, including Oxford University, using mortality data from the National Family Health Survey (NHFS) 2019–21 estimated that there were almost

1.2 million (12 lakh) excess deaths in 2020 alone, eight times the official number of Covid-19 deaths in India that year.

Did the Modi government lie to the Indian people about the number of Covid deaths as part of a gigantic cover-up? In a tweet on the WHO data, Congress leader Rahul Gandhi remarked: '47 lakh Indians died due to Covid pandemic. NOT 4.8 lakh as claimed by the Govt. Science doesn't LIE, Modi does.' The BJP hit back, its spokesperson Sambit Patra accusing Rahul and the Congress of 'defaming' the Prime Minister and 'lowering India's image'. But the response begs the question: How does falsifying the death count of its own citizens redeem a country's image? This is post-truth politics, where facts and truth don't matter. Instead, the country is transformed into a republic of lies, where authoritarian governments escape scrutiny by shouting down dissenters, treating them with indifference or levelling threats. But in a democratic society, political leaderships are accountable to the people. In normal times, a government might have got away with the lies, but in the pandemic, there was no place to hide. That the Modi government still seems to have got away with it was only because a mostly spineless media allowed it to.

When not in denial, the Modi government's other Covid strategy was to deflect attention to the states. After all, it wasn't just the Centre that had been caught napping with the dramatic spike in Covid cases— the states too were on the back foot. In Delhi—the city where the oxygen crisis was the most acute—the Centre put the Kejriwal-led state government in the dock. The Modi government claimed that proposed oxygen plants in four hospitals were delayed as the Delhi government had not submitted 'site readiness certificates'. When I posed this question to Chief Minister Kejriwal, his response was testy: 'The Centre controls the purse strings. They are only trying to hide from their abject failure in setting up oxygen plants.' The crossfire only reflected the gaping trust deficit between key stakeholders in an emergency.

Amidst conflicting claims, it was clear that governments, both at the Centre and the state, could have been far better prepared to deal with the disaster. For example, an investigation by news website Scroll reveals that it took eight months after the pandemic struck in March 2020 for the Modi government to invite bids for new oxygen plants. In October 2020, the Central Medical Services Society, an autonomous institution under the Union health ministry, floated an online tender calling for bidders to establish pressure swing adsorption (PSA) oxygen plants in 150 districts of the country. The total outlay for these 162 plants (twelve were reportedly added later) was Rs 201.58 crore, money allotted from the PM CARES Fund specifically set up for Covid relief. In April 2021, as the second wave ravaged the healthcare systems in the country, the health ministry confirmed in a tweet that only thirty-three plants had been installed.

'No one could have anticipated the scale and intensity of the second Covid wave. It is easy to criticize the government, but the astronomical numbers in India are such that no country's health infrastructure could have handled it. The government has moved heaven and earth to get oxygen to hospitals; what more can they do?' Dr Devi Shetty, renowned cardiac surgeon, told me in an interview at the peak of the crisis in May 2021.

The numbers in a populous country like India were indeed overwhelming. But the question remains: Could the government have foreseen the crisis and been better prepared to mitigate its impact? For example, crucial genome sequencing to detect the most dominant variants was not prioritized, and there was no co-ordinated national effort to track the variants early. The Indian SARS-CoV-2 Genomics Consortium (INSACOG) was set up only in December 2020, again several months after the pandemic had begun, with the specific mandate of tracking Covid variants in the country. An *India Today* report in May 2021 reveals how INSACOG faced hurdles from the very beginning. It was initially allocated Rs 115 crore for a six-month period, funds that were to come through the Department of Biotechnology. But the first tranche, a reduced amount of Rs 80 crore, only came at the end of March. The body also did not receive samples from several states, many of which didn't even have nodal officers to ensure the collection and transport of samples to the labs or cold storage plants where they could be preserved before or during transport. As a result, INSACOG fell far short of its objective of sequencing 80,000 samples by February 2021. It could manage only 3,500. It was only in March 2021 that INSACOG could determine that the deadly B.1.617 variant—the driver of the second Covid wave—had been found in 20 per cent of the samples from Maharashtra, more than any other state.

'That the variant was spreading and contagious didn't ring alarm bells till it was far too late,' Dr Rakesh Mishra, former director at the Hyderabad-based Centre for Cellular and Molecular Biology (CCMB), told *India Today* magazine in an interview. To make matters worse, there were territorial battles for control within the medical bodies. For example, the Indian Council for Medical Research (ICMR) was managing the pandemic when it didn't really have the domain expertise. 'The ICMR was getting Covid samples from labs across the country but for some inexplicable reason just wouldn't share the results with others,' revealed noted virologist Dr Shahid Jameel, who resigned as the chairman of the scientific advisory board of INSACOG in May 2021.

This also raises questions over the functioning of the national task force for Covid set up by the Prime Minister. Headed by noted paediatrician and public health expert Dr V.K. Paul, its members included Dr Balram Bhargava (then director-general of the ICMR), Dr Randeep Guleria (then director of AIIMS) and Dr Sujeet Kumar Singh (then director of the National Centre for Disease Control). 'The members are all accomplished professionals in their fields, but they just didn't have the power or authority to challenge the political executive and tell them where things were going wrong,' pointed out a health expert.

The political leadership was, in fact, missing in action at this critical time. A report in *Business Standard* in May 2021 that analysed the Prime Minister's public engagements during the Covid period is telling. 'Mr Modi made 82 public appearances—physical as well as virtual—in the seven-month period from March to September 2020. In the next four months, he made 111 such appearances. From February to April 25, 2021, he clocked 92 public appearances (including election campaign speeches). This was followed by 20 days of public absence, the longest since Covid-19 began.' In effect, during the deadliest Covid period, the Prime Minister was invisible. Where Modi had constantly communicated with citizens during the first Covid wave and the ensuing lockdown, in the frightful second phase the 'Supreme Leader' had gone missing, perhaps unwilling to face up to a grim news story. 'The PM was monitoring the situation and holding daily briefings. When he is on TV, you call him a "prime-time Prime Minister"; when he is not on TV, you don't think he is working. What do you really expect him to do?' queried a government official.

An *Outlook* magazine cover in May 2021 was a blank white page with the word 'Missing' on it in large font. Below, it said that the 'Government of India', age '7 years', had gone missing during the ruinous second Covid wave, and that if the government is found, 'citizens of India' should be 'informed'. An *India Today* cover the same month was just as damning: titled 'The Failed State', it had harrowing images of dead bodies lined up on a street for the last rites. After seven years in power, the Modi government was facing intense media scrutiny for the first time. Its credibility to govern was being called into question. In August 2021, *India Today*'s biannual Mood of the Nation survey reflected the shifting mood. The percentage of people who found Mr Modi to be most suitable as India's next Prime Minister fell from 38 per cent in January 2021 to 24 per cent in August. This was the Prime Minister's lowest popularity rating in the seven years he had been in office. The horrendous second wave of Covid had left its stamp on the Prime Minister. The gung-ho 'vishwaguru' branding now appeared like a terrible nightmare. Modi desperately needed a political resurrection. Fine words were no longer enough to restore public trust. This time, he needed to walk the talk.

=

Dr Harsh Vardhan is an early riser, a habit he developed during his teenage years when he attended the local RSS 'shakha' (branch). On 7 July 2021, after finishing his pre-dawn walk, the then Union health minister was preparing for another long day in the office. The amiable doctor-politician was literally thrown into the deep end as health minister in Covid times. At the time, Dr Harsh Vardhan had been a politician for more than three decades, won several elections and almost become the chief minister of Delhi in 2013, but nothing had prepared him for the particular onslaught of the virus. As the head of the group of ministers that had been set up to combat Covid-19, Dr Harsh Vardhan was a key ministerial figure in the Modi government's crisis management team. 'I think for about eighteen months in 2020 and 2021, I used to only get home after midnight and sleep for only a few hours. I was like a doctor on round-the-clock duty,' he recalls.

Like an alert doctor, he never missed a phone call. While the second wave of Covid raged, the minister would get calls at all odd hours as despairing friends and acquaintances sought his help for an ICU bed or an oxygen cylinder. By early July, it seemed that the worst was over in Delhi at least. The emergency calls became fewer in number. Still, when his mobile rang that morning, he instantly picked it up. Only this time it wasn't a desperate patient but BJP President J.P. Nadda on the line. 'Harsh Vardhan ji, I have been asked to inform you to hand in your resignation as minister. Would you please communicate the same to Rashtrapati Bhavan? The Prime Minister will speak to you later,' was the brief message.

Politics is as ruthless as it can be rewarding. For months, Dr Harsh Vardhan had been a key figure in the Modi government's Covid management plans. Now, with a snappish call from the BJP president, he was being asked to put in his papers in a sudden cabinet reshuffle. In the capital's power corridors, word had already filtered through that the Prime Minister was 'not happy' with the minister's performance, especially during the second wave, when the government machinery was accused of having gone 'missing'. Amidst growing criticism, Home Minister Shah had taken a frontal role in supervising the Covid arrangements in oxygen-deficient Delhi, while the Covid task force chief, Dr V.K. Paul, was handling the media; the health minister was suddenly consigned to the sidelines. 'You can ask any official in my ministry—I put my heart and soul into the Covid effort. Just because I wasn't in front of your TV camera all the time, doesn't mean I was missing,' retorted Dr Harsh Vardhan. The soft-spoken minister wasn't quite TV savvy. When I had asked him for an interview during the second wave, he was persuaded with much difficulty and only after I sent him a list of questions in advance. 'I will record my answers instead of coming live,' he had told me then. The media heat was getting to him. As was the political pressure of a government pushed on the back foot.

Earlier in the year, in April, Dr Harsh Vardhan had found himself in the middle of an unseemly row with former Prime Minister Dr Manmohan Singh. As the number of Covid cases was rising, Dr Singh had written to Prime Minister Modi suggesting ways to fight the pandemic, while raising doubts over the Centre's vaccine policy. 'The key to our fight against Covid-19 must be ramping up the vaccination effort,' wrote Dr Singh while sharing a five-point prescription. Although the letter was addressed to the Prime Minister, Modi did not respond. Instead, a day later, it was Dr Harsh Vardhan who waded into the debate. While a public display of petulance was uncharacteristic for the good-natured minister, in a written rebuttal to Dr Singh, he accused the Congress party of 'spreading negativity'. 'It seems that those who drafted your letter or advised you have done a great disservice to your standing by misleading you regarding material already in the public domain,' he wrote. The buzz was that the letter had been drafted in the PMO and the minister was only the messenger. 'A cabinet is a collective responsibility; it doesn't matter really who drafts the letter, but as health minister I felt duty-bound to respond to a former Prime Minister and clear the air,' Dr Harsh Vardhan later told me.

In essence, Dr Harsh Vardhan became the fall guy for what was seen as the miserable failure of the health infrastructure system during the peak Covid period. Facing flak for inertia and incompetence, the Modi government needed to hold someone accountable. A relatively low-profile health minister became the soft target. Just days before being removed, the minister had been allegedly upbraided by the Prime Minister at a cabinet meeting. 'I see that some of you only send out birthday wishes on social media instead of communicating what work is being done by the government in the fight against Covid,' Modi reportedly harangued the gathering, his eyes moving in the health minister's direction.

Dr Harsh Vardhan was an old-style politician, not exactly well versed in social media outreach, a key aspect of the Modi government's strategy. 'Why didn't the government act against members of the Covid task force who were appointed by the PMO and who were involved in all major decision-making? Harsh Vardhan ji is an honest, decent man, the kind who has less space in the cut-throat politics of today,' an assistant to the former minister pointed out.

Mansukh Mandaviya, a relatively unknown Rajya Sabha MP from Gujarat, succeeded Dr Harsh Vardhan as health minister. Having won an MLA seat once in 2002, Mandaviya was seen as part of the next generation of BJP Gujarat politicians who were handpicked by Prime Minister Modi. Brought into the Rajya Sabha in 2015, he had no mass appeal but became the youngest general secretary of the BJP in Gujarat. Then, at forty-nine, he was entrusted with a key portfolio. 'Mansukh bhai is quietly efficient but also a total "yes man" who will never go against what Modi says, just the kind of person the Prime Minister wants in his core team,' said a Gujarat BJP member.

The country had a new health minister, but the PMO was now even more hands-on in dealing with the crucial ministry. The Modi government may have hit out at Manmohan Singh, but it also quickly took on the suggestions Dr Singh had outlined in his missive: get the vaccine programme on track to counter the Covid surge. It was the silver bullet that the country desperately needed to prevent the pandemic from becoming a total catastrophe.

═

'Not one, not two, as many as three coronavirus vaccines are being tested in India … along with mass production, the roadmap for distribution of vaccine to every single Indian in the least possible

time is also ready. As soon as the scientists give the green signal, the country will begin large-scale production of those vaccines.'
—Prime Minister Narendra Modi during his Independence Day speech at Red Fort on 15 August 2020

'As the world's largest vaccine-producing country, I want to give one more assurance to the global community today … India's vaccine production and delivery capacity will be used to help all humanity in fighting the crisis.'
—Prime Minister Narendra Modi during a prerecorded speech to the United Nations in September 2020

Despite the Modi government's ambitious vaccine-production plan, in April–May 2021, as the second wave of Covid led to an explosion of cases, India struggled to play catch-up in the vaccine race. While the Centre boasted that it had vaccinated 143 million (14.3 crore) people since the drive began on 16 January 2021, the fact was that barely 7.9 per cent of the adult population had received their first vaccine dose compared to 57 per cent in the US and 60 per cent in the UK. Many states like Maharashtra complained of a shortage of vaccines even as the Centre blamed them for poor planning and distribution. All of a sudden, ramping up vaccine production from 3–4 million (30–40 lakh) a day to at least 8–10 million (80–90 lakh) a day became urgent.

Ironically, in the months leading up to the second wave, India had exported 65 million (6.5 crore) doses of the vaccines free of cost across the world as part of the Vaccine Maitri mission. Indian embassies across the world were being urged to project India's 'vaccine diplomacy' as evidence of the Modi government's 'soft power' and commitment to the global Covid challenge. 'We were told to bring out glossy pamphlets to showcase our vaccine exports with images of Prime Minister Modi prominently displayed. It was seen as a really big deal,' recalled a former diplomat. When Brazil received 2 million (20 lakh) doses of vaccines in January, then Brazilian President Jair Bolsonaro invoked a Lord Hanuman image while thanking Prime Minister Modi on Twitter: 'Dhanyawaad Bharat' was the message. The Prime Minister was quick to reply: 'The honour is ours.' Modi's international image was being assiduously cultivated even as India fell short of vaccinations.

By April 2021, the Vaccine Maitri drumbeat fell silent as the export policy had to be dramatically reversed. Complacency gave way to chaos as the Covid death toll began to rise sharply. When the vaccine rollout began earlier that year, in January, the government had placed orders for less than 17 million (1.7 crore) vaccine doses. A further 110 million (11 crore) doses were ordered only in March as cases began to rise. In a country of 1.4 billion people, these were minuscule amounts. 'Without finger-pointing, the fact is that we were taken by surprise by the intensity of the second wave. We had planned to vaccinate step by step with the initial focus on the vulnerable groups, especially frontline workers and those above sixty-five. The second wave, though, spared no one and left us struggling to reset the entire vaccine programme,' admitted a member of the Prime Minister's Covid task force.

Unfortunately, that wasn't the only botch-up.

On 1 May 2021, at the peak of the second wave, the Modi government, under pressure from states, declared a shift to a Liberalized Pricing and Accelerated Covid-19 Vaccine Strategy, by which domestic vaccine makers would be free to sell 50 per cent of their production to state governments and private players. The other half would go to the Centre, which had made a commitment to vaccinate all those above forty-five free of cost. This meant the states were now free to source vaccines from domestic and global suppliers. But barely a month later, in the first week of June, the Prime Minister announced that the country would revert to a centralized vaccine procurement system and provide free vaccines to all adults, not just those above forty-five years. The announcement came within a week of the Supreme Court asking for an affidavit from the Centre explaining how the sum of Rs 35,000 crore allocated in the Union budget for vaccines had been spent so far, why there was differential pricing and why free vaccines were not being made available to all.

Under intense criticism for the vaccine shortage and predatory pricing, the Prime Minister tried again to shift the blame onto the states and even the media for the vaccine policy confusion. 'Some people questioned the lack of choice for states and why the Centre was deciding everything. Flexibility in lockdown and "one size does not fit all" arguments were made. Many types of pressures were exerted and certain sections of the media houses ran a campaign to this effect as well,' he claimed in his June address.

Listening to the Prime Minister's speech with rising anger was then Telangana Chief Minister K. Chandrashekar Rao. At an earlier virtual meeting of chief ministers with the Prime Minister, he had complained of his views being ignored by the Centre. 'I don't understand this. When the central government was exporting vaccines instead of ramping up domestic production, Modi was taking all the credit. Now, after the second wave of Covid, when things have gone bad, he is blaming us for the vaccine shortage. This is not done,' complained Rao. The mercurial Rao attempted to create a coalition of non-NDA chief ministers, dialling many of them for support. Kerala Chief Minister Pinarayi Vijayan had already written to eleven non-NDA state chief ministers to take a united stand in demanding free vaccines from the Centre. Facing the heat from all sides, the PMO turned to the two companies who were at the heart of the 'Made in India' vaccine programme: the Pune-based Serum Institute of India and the Hyderabad-based Bharat Biotech.

The two companies are chalk and cheese in their lineage. A chance conversation with a veterinarian led Serum Institute's chairperson and managing director, Dr Cyrus S. Poonawalla, inheritor of a 70-acre stud farm, to venture into investing in the vaccine business in 1966 and then steadily expand it. His son and company CEO, Adar Poonawalla, was born with the proverbial silver spoon, which he was looking to shine further. In April 2020, when the world was reeling under the lockdown blues, the impeccably turned out, UK-educated Poonawalla, just forty at the time, announced a partnership with Oxford University's renowned Jenner Institute to start human clinical trials on a single vaccine candidate. Given the urgent need for a vaccine that could be rapidly scaled up, Poonawalla declared that he would take the financial risk and manufacture millions of doses of the planned Oxford vaccine ahead of the approval. 'It was a risk but a well-calculated one,' Poonawalla told me later. The Covishield vaccine project had got a head start.

If Adar Poonawalla is the flashy, smart-suited, next-gen business leader, occasionally seen in the company of Bollywood A-listers, Dr Krishna Ella, the founder–chairman and managing director of Bharat Biotech, is the complete opposite: a bespectacled first-generation entrepreneur who hails from a farming family in Vellore. A molecular biologist by training, he went to the US for higher education on a scholarship and built his vaccine business from scratch with his wife, Suchitra Ella. Their decision to invest in the Covid-19 vaccine suddenly pitchforked the low-profile couple into the limelight. While Poonawalla was part of a global consortium led by multinational pharma giant AstraZeneca, the Ellas chose to tie up with the ICMR. The Covaxin vaccine project was a 'Made in India' initiative, leading to speculation over the links between the company and the Modi government. Had Bharat Biotech funded the BJP in return for preferential treatment, we asked Krishna Ella on a programme. He responded in a defiant tone: 'I haven't got any Gates Foundation money; I have not got any money from the Government of India. We have conducted the clinical trials at our own cost and manufactured 20 million (2 crore) doses at our risk. I never said the government should be the sole buyer of my vaccine. I am doing this not as a business venture but because I think it's my moral responsibility as a scientist to do this for my country.'

Moral responsibility or a sharp business opportunity, it was to the Poonawallas and the Ellas that the Modi government turned to as the vaccine programme battled a supply shortage amidst mounting Covid cases. From being miserly with funds in 2020, in May 2021 the government sanctioned grants totalling a little over Rs 4,500 core to expand capacities. The Serum Institute was now expected to raise its production of Covishield doses from 70 million to 100 million (7 crore to 10 crore) by July, while Bharat Biotech would push its doses of Covaxin from 30 million to 58 million (3 crore to 5.8 crore) by August. In January 2021, Adar Poonawalla stirred a controversy by claiming that only three vaccines passed the test of scientific evaluations—Pfizer-BioNTech, Moderna and Oxford-AstraZeneca—and that the others were 'safe like water' and their effectiveness had not been tested. An angry Dr Ella snapped back, 'We do 200 per cent honest clinical trials and yet we receive a backlash; some companies have wrongly branded me like water.'

With the spat playing out in public, the PMO intervened as peacemaker. Prime Minister Modi personally spoke to both parties and promised full support. With a new health minister who reported on a daily basis into the PMO, a dashboard with specific vaccination targets was established, supervised directly from South Block. By August 2021—by which time the worst of the second wave was over—vaccine availability had crossed over 150 million (15 crore) doses a month. When, in October 2021, India achieved the one billion (100 crore) vaccine doses milestone, the Prime Minister invited the Poonawallas and the Ellas for high tea and showered them with fulsome praise. The vaccine manufacturers too couldn't stop gushing over the Prime Minister. 'Without Mr Modi's vision, none of this would have been possible,' said Adar Poonawalla admiringly.

The BJP went a step further, kickstarting a 'Thank you, Modi ji' pan-India campaign. BJP state governments were asked to advertise in newspapers, while local units put up banners and posters of the Prime Minister hailing India's billion vaccine doses achievement. The party's social media unit plastered the campaign across digital platforms. Earlier, the University Grants Commission had asked central universities to put up posters on campuses thanking the Prime Minister for the free vaccination drive. Even students of the Kendriya Vidyalaya-run central schools were asked to record scripted videos thanking the Prime Minister for cancelling the final exams amidst the second wave. The videos were posted on social media accounts and tagged with #ThankYouModiji. Within a short time, Modi's crack PR team had turned the pandemic into an 'event' and aligned it perfectly with his branding as a 'Supreme Leader'. 'Didn't Indira Gandhi align her image to the Twenty Point Programme?

Then why should anyone crib if Modi ji was identified with the vaccine initiative?' asked a BJP leader.

This Modi-style 'event management' was seen again on 17 September, when official estimates claimed that more than 25 million (2.5 crore) Covid-19 vaccine doses had been administered in a single day—the highest since the vaccine drive had begun—on the Prime Minister's birthday. A major chunk was administered in the large BJP-ruled states, with Karnataka, Bihar, Uttar Pradesh, Madhya Pradesh and Gujarat accounting for more than 2 million (20 lakh) doses each. The Prime Minister was quick to use the media—from Twitter to Facebook—to thank medical officials and beneficiaries: 'Yesterday was a very emotional day for me. With the efforts of all of you it became a very special day for me,' he gushed in a video address to healthcare workers in Goa. Then Health Minister Mandaviya described the record as 'India's gift to the Prime Minister'. Political flattery was alive and well even in a pandemic.

There was a twist in the tale, though. In Madhya Pradesh, for example, a number of people who had not received their vaccine shots were issued vaccine certificates, including, in at least one instance, in the name of someone who had died of Covid months earlier. As the government's own CoWIN portal showed, the surge in vaccinations on the Prime Minister's birthday was not a consistent trend. On either side of the birthday, there was a significant dip in daily vaccine numbers. 'Since all efforts were geared towards making a splash on the PM's birthday, supplies were stockpiled to ensure we made 17 September a record-breaking day,' a former health ministry official admitted.

The 2021 'birthday vaccine bash' was, in fact, a prelude to a twenty-day Seva and Samarpan campaign launched by the BJP to mark Modi's twenty consecutive years in office (he had become Gujarat chief minister for the first time in October 2001). The extended birthday celebrations included BJP leaders arranging for 50 million (5 crore) people to send postcards to the Prime Minister, thanking him for his efforts in public service. Under the existing 5-kilo-free ration scheme, the government distributed around

140 million (14 crore) ration bags with the Prime Minister's picture stamped on each one—and a 'Thank you, Modi ji' message.

It was almost as if the government was urging citizens to shake off the haunting images of death and despair by projecting a glossy, feel-good aura, a make-believe, media-manufactured universe in which the Prime Minister was Superman, the sole saviour. Just months ago, the country had gone through the trauma of a second Covid wave in which the official death toll crossed 400,000 (the unofficial figure as pointed out earlier was, according to some estimates, several times higher). On just one day, 10 June 2021, India had reported 6,148 deaths, the highest single-day toll from Covid-19 in the world. And yet, instead of grieving over the monumental loss of lives, by the end of 2021, the country, or at least the Modi government, was in a celebratory mood. The worst was over; it was time to get the propaganda machine back on track.

In May 2021, then Information and Broadcasting Minister Prakash Javadekar had rather boldly announced that India's adult population would be 'fully vaccinated' by December 2021. By the end of the year, 64 per cent of India's 940 million (94 crore) adult population was fully vaccinated and around 90 per cent had received the first dose—an undeniably impressive achievement after the catastrophe that had befallen the country in the summer of 2021. Each vaccine certificate carried a picture of Prime Minister Modi, a credit-taking exercise designed to convince the Indian voter that the larger-than-life leader had been their benefactor in the Covid emergency. The same photograph was a red rag to his political opponents, though. West Bengal Chief Minister Mamata Banerjee was especially incensed and even threatened to stay away from any Covid meeting called by the Prime Minister. 'How can you carry only one person's photo when the fight against Covid is a collective effort? Will you also show the Prime Minister's photo on a death certificate tomorrow?' she raged.

Perhaps, the final word here must go to BJP President J.P. Nadda (Union health minister in Modi 3.0 and Modi 1.0), who, during a political rally in poll-bound Himachal Pradesh in November 2023, told voters: 'PM

Modi ne vaccine banakar aapki raksha ki; ab BJP ki raksha karne ki baari aapki (PM Modi protected you by making the vaccine; now it is your turn to protect the BJP).'

From 'taali-thali' performer-in-chief to 'vishwaguru' to now being credited as 'vaccine maker–protector', Modi had not only survived political ruin but also emerged stronger after the Covid pandemic. Where any other national leader might have struggled to counter criticism over an economically devastating lockdown and the muddled handling of the harrowing second wave, the Prime Minister's cheerleaders tom-tommed the Covid response as a major achievement of the Modi government. An *India Today* Mood of the Nation poll in January 2022 found that 82 per cent of respondents held a positive view of the Central government's Covid-19 vaccination rollout efforts. Was public memory actually short? Had the government's astute event management made a difference? Had the Opposition failed to raise its voice? Had the media forgotten to hold the government accountable? Or was Prime Minister Modi simply a teflon-like figure who had weathered the storm and continued to enjoy the trust of a majority of Indians?

As a senior Opposition leader later told me: 'If a leader can derive political benefit from a messed-up response to a pandemic, then what is left to say?'

Except in India there is always a fresh challenge lurking around the corner. Only this time, it wasn't an unknown virus in the air but a human adversary on the ground that the Modi government would have to deal with.

FOUR

'Jai Jawan, Jai Kisan':
The Farmers' 'Revolt'

NARENDRA Modi's cabinet meetings are often designed to surprise. 'With Modi ji, it's a case of expect the unexpected. Forget about us, I don't think even the Prime Minister's shadow knows what is going on in the top leader's mind,' a cabinet colleague told me, laughing. On 5 June 2020, there was palpable anxiety over the future among the ministers assembled in South Block. With the lockdown still in place in different parts of the country, they were keen to voice their troubles in dealing with migrant labourers and the economic distress brought on by the pandemic. But Covid relief wasn't on the cabinet agenda; rather, surprisingly, agriculture was. 'We are bringing in three long-pending agricultural reforms as ordinances that will transform agriculture and raise farm incomes,' declared the Prime Minister. Then Minister of Agriculture and Farmers' Welfare Narendra Singh Tomar was asked to circulate the proposed changes to bewildered cabinet ministers caught totally off guard. Trying to push through pivotal laws with a possible thunderclap impact on farmers' livelihoods when the country was battling a crisis smacked of misplaced priorities and dictatorial tendencies. At a time when a calming hand was needed, the Modi government had yet again turned to disruption.

The three ordinances (which have since become laws) were the Farmers' Produce Trade and Commerce (Promotion and Facilitation) Ordinance, 2020; the Farmers (Empowerment and Protection) Agreement on Price Assurance and Farm Services Ordinance, 2020; and the Essential Commodities (Amendment) Act, 2020. The intention, said the Prime Minister, was to create barrier-free trade of farmers' produce outside the state-controlled markets and introduce a more liberalized agriculture marketing system. 'We have liberalized trade and industry, but we have left agriculture highly regulated. Now is the right time to give our farmers a chance to get the best prices for their produce by making farming more competitive,' asserted Modi.

Listening to the Prime Minister's plan with mounting concern was Harsimrat Kaur Badal, a three-time Shiromani Akali Dal MP and then Union minister for food-processing industries. A lively and articulate politician whose husband, Sukhbir Singh Badal, was also an MP, she was known to speak her mind on a variety of issues. Ministers are not known to voice their dissent in Modi's cabinet meetings but Badal, the lone Akali Dal representative in the Central government, raised a red flag. 'I kept arguing that these ordinances should not be pushed through like this and that it will lead to unrest. It is only when I was assured by the Prime Minister that no bill would be passed without consultation with the farmer stakeholders that I backed off,' she revealed. The Prime Minister deputed Tomar and Home Minister Amit Shah to resolve the issue with her.

For the next three months the Akali Dal leader kept pushing Narendra Singh Tomar and Amit Shah to set up a meeting with the farmer unions. Tomar was reportedly busy with the Madhya Pradesh assembly by-elections, and Shah had been taken seriously ill and was hospitalized over a Covid-related infection. 'I kept banging on every possible door but there was no one there to listen,' claimed Badal. It was a familiar story in the Modi government. No minister wanted to tangle with a contentious issue without the Prime Minister's express approval. Even the agriculture minister appeared clueless and disinterested. Home Minister

Shah was the only one who had the political heft, but he was bedridden at the time.

Three months later, in September 2020, as Parliament began a discussion on the three farm bills, Sukhbir Badal suddenly announced in the Lok Sabha that his wife would be quitting the Modi government in protest. Within moments, Badal had walked out and dropped off her resignation letter in the Prime Minister's chamber in the Lok Sabha. She tweeted: 'Proud to stand with farmers as their daughter and sister.' What many do not know is that Badal had, in fact, offered her resignation a day before the formal handover. Meeting with Tomar, Defence Minister Rajnath Singh and BJP President J.P. Nadda, she had informed them that it would not be possible to stay in government if the farm bills were passed in Parliament. 'Aag lagegi (There will be fire),' she had warned, adding, 'I cannot compromise on this.' The three leaders tried to play down the possibility of a widespread farmers' agitation, seemingly unaware of the anger building on the ground. 'Kuch dino mein sab kuch theek ho jayega (All will be well in a few days),' Rajnath Singh reportedly told the Akali Dal leader.

A week after Badal's resignation, the Akalis took their protest a step further by announcing their decision to quit the BJP-led NDA. The Akalis were the BJP's oldest ally, having first joined hands with the Bharatiya Jana Sangh (the BJP's predecessor) in 1967. Forging a pre-poll alliance for the 1997 Punjab assembly elections under the leadership of Akali Dal patriarch Parkash Singh Badal, the two parties had shared power in Punjab and Delhi. Parkash Singh had enjoyed an excellent relationship with the BJP leadership, especially former Prime Minister Atal Bihari Vajpayee. 'Whenever Badal sa'ab was in Delhi, he would always meet with Atal ji and Advani ji; it was a bond forged when they were all jailed together in the Emergency years,' recalled an Akali leader.

The Akali–BJP bonhomie diminished once Modi became Prime Minister in 2014. Having been a party secretary in charge of Punjab in the late 1990s, Modi had immense respect for senior Badal but little time for the ambitious but more controversial next generation. In his campaign against corruption and 'pariwaarwaad' (family raj), the Badals, facing a slew of charges, were an obvious target within the NDA camp. Modi's No. 2, Union Home Minister Amit Shah was even less enthused about the long-standing tie-up with the Akalis. As BJP president, while on a tour of Punjab, he reportedly told his colleagues that the alliance needed a rethink. 'How will we grow in Punjab if we only remain a junior partner? Anti-incumbency Badal family ke khilaaf hai par nuksan hamara ho raha hai (Anti-incumbency is against the Badal family but we are the ones losing out),' he asserted.

That the two sides had stuck on for a while was only because the Akalis had a friend in Delhi in Arun Jaitley, a key member of the first Modi government. Jaitley, himself a gregarious Delhi-based Punjabi, had cultivated his relationship with the Badals for years. In 2014, Parkash Singh Badal insisted that Jaitley contest a Lok Sabha election for the first time from Amritsar. 'We will ensure your victory,' he promised. As it turned out, Jaitley lost to Captain Amarinder Singh, the formidable Congress leader from the Patiala royal family. Jaitley, though, remained grateful to the Badals for their support and kept the alliance going till the 2019 general elections. But when Jaitley passed away soon after, in August 2019, the Akalis knew that the countdown to a split had begun. 'Fact is, Amit Shah didn't want this alliance from the moment he took over as BJP president. He was looking for any excuse to end it,' said Naresh Gujral, a former Akali Dal MP.

With the Punjab elections scheduled for early 2022, the Akalis knew that they had to make their move first. The growing public anger over the farm laws left them with few options. 'These agri-marketing bills are lethal and disastrous for farmers. They will destroy all that Punjab has built over the last fifty years. The Centre's stand only shows its insensitivity to Punjabis and issues of the Sikh community,' proclaimed Sukhbir Badal while announcing the break from the BJP.

Having been ousted from power in Punjab by the Congress in 2017 and in danger of being reduced to a marginal third player by the rising clout of AAP in the region, the Akalis were playing an emotive card in a desperate attempt to shore up their agrarian Sikh vote base. Only it was too late for them to restore credibility among voters who were still seething over their excesses when the party had formed the government. Unbeknown to the Centre, the farm bills were already a hugely contentious issue across rural Punjab. The fury that was smouldering in the countryside would soon reach the borders of Delhi.

The Prime Minister's aura as a leader no one dared to challenge was about to face its first major hit, not from a political rival but from a weatherbeaten yet valiant figure ready to brave the elements and roar out his protest against perceived injustice: the kisan. Kisan (farmer) power would now bring an imperious Modi to his knees.

On 14 September 2020, Parliament met for the first time in six months. With the pandemic-induced lockdown in place, there had been a long gap between sessions. Since the infection was still in the air, MPs were asked to be extra cautious. Parliament hours were truncated: while the Lok Sabha would sit in the morning, the Rajya Sabha would have an evening sitting. Masks were mandatory even though the MPs sat in seats enclosed by glass partitions that were designed to prevent the spread of the virus. Covid-related health concerns were expected to dominate a relatively low-key Parliament session. 'We hadn't met our fellow MPs for months; many had suffered personal tragedies during Covid. We thought the gathering would be a moment to reflect on and review the government's Covid responses,' said senior Congress MP Digvijaya Singh.

It wasn't just the fallout of the Covid pandemic that should have worried MPs. Prime Minister Modi claimed to enjoy a 'special' relationship with Chinese President Xi Jinping: images of the two leaders sitting on a swing together near the Sabarmati riverfront in Ahmedabad in 2014 had gone viral. However, in June 2020, India and China had engaged in the worst border skirmish between the two countries in sixty years. The Indian Army and China's People's Liberation Army fought each other in the Galwan valley in Ladakh in the western sector of the Line of Actual

Control, the de facto boundary between the two neighbours. Soldiers were seen attacking each other not with guns but with iron rods and clubs on a dangerous ridge. The incident had resulted in the deaths of twenty Indian and at least four Chinese soldiers. The bloody confrontation, the latest in a series of border intrusions by the Chinese army, had caught the Modi government unawares. Yet, at an all-party meeting called days after the Galwan clashes, Modi was seen downplaying the conflict. 'Neither have they [China] entered our border nor has any post been taken over by them,' he said emphatically. Rather than acknowledge the gravity of the situation, the Modi government had slipped into denial mode—again.

When Congress MP Manish Tewari demanded a discussion in Parliament on the Chinese transgressions in Ladakh, the government refused to engage. The official reason given was 'national security'. 'I put up sixty-five questions in Parliament on China's border violations and not one was answered, not one,' an irate Tewari told me. 'It was as if the government just didn't want to talk about China since the debate would only embarrass the Modi government and affect the Prime Minister's "muscular" leader image.' Strict instructions were given to BJP spokespersons not to participate in any television debate with the Opposition on Chinese aggression. The focus, instead, was on a rabble-rousing call for a 'boycott' of Chinese products. The Chinese-owned social media app TikTok was banned with much glee as if that would force a troop pullback. The orchestrated hysteria was meant to temporarily deflect from the vexed border situation without addressing core issues. By 2023–24, India's trade deficit with China had risen to 85 billion dollars, only highlighting strategic geo-economic vulnerabilities in the relationship. The stand-off in Ladakh was not fully resolved despite numerous meetings between military officers on both sides.

Denial and distraction are part of the Modi power playbook. Rather than face up in Parliament to the external threat, an internal conflict was ignited. On the opening day of the 2020 monsoon session of Parliament, then Agriculture Minister Narendra Singh Tomar introduced the three contentious farm bills in the Lok Sabha to replace the ordinances cleared by the cabinet in June. With the BJP's clear majority in the Lok Sabha, the bills were quickly passed through a voice vote. When two of the three farm bills were introduced in the Upper House on a Sunday morning, Opposition MPs were instantly on their feet, demanding the bills be sent to a select committee of Parliament for a review. In the chair was Deputy Chairman Harivansh Narayan Singh of the JD(U)—a BJP ally then too—who promptly rejected the Opposition's demand and instead moved to pass the bills by a voice vote. 'How can you move such a major legislation by a voice vote? Let there be physical voting,' demanded the TMC's Derek O'Brien. When the chair refused, a group of Opposition MPs rushed to the well of the House, attempted to tear up the rule book and tried to snatch the deputy chairman's microphone. Leading the protests was an incensed O'Brien, who strongly denies that he ripped the rule book. 'Can anyone show any video of us trying to tear any rule book? I will resign from Parliament if they can. Do you know that they cut off the Rajya Sabha TV feed only so that the nation could not see how they were murdering democracy by pushing a bill through? If even one member asks for a division and physical voting, how can the chair deny me that right and force a voice vote like this?' he raged.

I have known Singh since his days as the learned editor of the successful Ranchi-based Hindi newspaper *Prabhat Khabar*. Singh is a soft-spoken man of letters who was close to the JD(U) leadership and to Bihar Chief Minister Nitish Kumar in particular. As Rajya Sabha MP, he had reportedly built a good equation with Prime Minister Modi, who liked his low-key approach. When I asked Singh about the farm bill controversy, he was reluctant to speak out. 'Everyone has seen the behaviour of the MPs. I went strictly by the rules. What more can I say other than my conscience is clear?' he claimed. In a letter to then President Ram Nath Kovind, Singh wrote, 'The members of the Upper House indulged in violent activities in the name of democracy. They attempted to threaten the chair. Every rule, system of the Upper House was flouted.'

A day after the chaos, then Rajya Sabha Chairman and Vice President Venkaiah Naidu announced that eight MPs were being suspended for their 'unruly behaviour'. 'What happened during the farm bill passage is unfortunate, unacceptable and condemnable. It was a very bad day for the Rajya Sabha,' he said. Among the suspended MPs was O'Brien, the leader of his party in the Upper House. 'Instead of suspending us, Mr Naidu should have told the country why he wasn't sitting in the chair when such a major bill was being passed. Truth is, even the Vice President, as a farmer's son, didn't want to be associated with this black day and so stayed away!' argued the TMC leader. The buzz among the Opposition MPs was that Singh had stepped in at the last minute to supervise the voice vote because Naidu didn't want to get tangled up in the controversial issue.

It wasn't just O'Brien who was incensed. The well-spoken and polished Naresh Gujral was the Akali Dal representative in the Rajya Sabha. Since the farm laws were top priority for his party, he requested he be given a little extra time to speak. His original allotted time was twelve minutes but at the last moment, it was cut down to just two and a half minutes by Venkaiah Naidu's office. 'Even the treasury benches were ready to hear me out, but Venkaiah ji was not. It was like he was working under someone's instructions that day,' says Gujral.

Meanwhile, Modi remained haughtily unruffled by the bedlam in Parliament. Over the years, both as Gujarat chief minister and now as Prime Minister, he has often disregarded legislative niceties. He speaks of Parliament being a 'temple of democracy' but in reality expects both Houses to fall in line before an all-powerful chief executive. Modi has always regarded a majority mandate as license to adopt monarchic disdain for the very democracy that has given him his post. Debates on contentious issues are avoided, budgets are passed without discussion, Opposition members who protest are routinely suspended and fewer bills are sent to committees for scrutiny (only 16 per cent of the bills in the Modi government's second term were sent to parliamentary standing committees for an in-depth review, unlike, say, in Manmohan Singh's final term, when the number was as high as 75 per cent). 'The Prime Minister believes that unruly legislatures constrain the executive from taking tough decisions,' a former PMO official disclosed. In the Modi style of decision-making, Parliament is a rubber stamp for executive fiat. A bulldozing, heavy-handed approach is interpreted by the Modi government as 'decisive' governance, when, in fact, in a democracy, it achieves the opposite and only leads to chaos.

This time too the Prime Minister wasn't in any mood to oblige the Opposition. Without referring even once to the ruckus and protests, Modi euphorically described the passage of the farm laws as 'a watershed moment in the history of Indian agriculture'. 'For decades, the Indian farmer was bound by various constraints and bullied by middlemen. The bills passed by Parliament liberate the farmers from such adversities. These bills will add impetus to the efforts to double income of farmers and ensure greater prosperity for them,' he tweeted.

For Modi, 'gareeb' and 'kisan' are key players in his election playbook. He habitually invokes his commitment to the poor and the farmer in every election speech. In February 2019, just ahead of the Lok Sabha elections, he had launched the Pradhan Mantri Kisan Samman Nidhi, which would provide financial support of Rs 6,000 per annum to all farmer families, payable in three equal instalments. The scheme, designed to shore up the farmer vote bank, delivered spectacular results electorally, as seen in the BJP's performance in the 2019 elections.

But income support to farmers wasn't all Modi promised. In February 2016, he pledged to double farmer incomes in six years, by 2022–23; it was to be his 'gift' to the country in the seventy-fifth year of Independence. It was an attractive promise but typically fanciful. The Doubling Farmers' Income Committee (DFIC) set up by the Modi government had estimated the annual income of a farming family in 2015–16 to be Rs 96,703 or about Rs 8,000 per month. Doubling farmer income by 2022 meant an annual income of Rs 1,72,694 at 2015–16 prices or around Rs 2.5 lakh at 2022 prices, which would have required farmer incomes to grow at an annual rate of 10.4 per cent. In reality, the growth was barely around 4 per cent and farmer incomes were nowhere close to the promised target. Then Agriculture Minister Narendra Singh Tomar admitted as much in a written reply to Parliament in December 2022, in which he said that the average monthly income of a farmer is Rs 10,218, some way away from being doubled. The figures were just not adding up.

But in the Modi political playbook, hard figures matter less than clever, flamboyant optics. The focus is often on a 'big bang' effect, intended to grab headlines and set the narrative. Which is why the farm laws were being 'marketed' as the government's 'grand plan' to enrich Indian farmers. The *Do Bigha Zamin*-style sepia-tinted images of farmers in penury, toiling in loincloths in bucolic countrysides, were replaced by colourful promotional videos of farmers equipped with modern tools and poised for prosperity. 'It is wrong to suggest that the farm laws were unplanned or that there was no consultation while drafting them. We consulted several top economists and policy makers before going ahead,' insisted a NITI Aayog official. The NITI Aayog, which had replaced the Planning Commission soon after Modi took over in 2014, was a key nodal agency in driving the farm laws initiative. But while many leading economists supported the farm laws, a key stakeholder was missing from the consultative process: the farmer organizations. 'Such is the goodwill the Prime Minister has among the people that we thought the farmer bodies would be convinced by his personal commitment to the kisan,' remarked a government official.

He couldn't have been more wrong. Parliament could be bulldozed into submission by the sheer weight of numbers, but bullying India's doughty farmers into accepting a legal architecture without a sustained dialogue was never going to work.

＝

Agriculture is to rural Punjab what trade is to urban Gujarat. The kisan and his 'kheti' (farm) are central to the Punjabi Sikh identity. Their fierce attachment to land was described to me by a Sikh farmer leader as a fight for 'zameen' (land) and 'zameer' (self-respect). It was in Punjab that the 'Green Revolution' first took off in the 1960s, and by the mid-1980s Punjab's annual rate of increase in the production of foodgrains was more than double that of the country as a whole. While Punjab had

17,459 tractors per 100,000 holdings, the all-India figure was only 714. The enterprising, hard-working Jat Sikh farmer was at the heart of this social and economic transformation.

However, post-1980s Punjab was no longer the picture-perfect agricultural state. Fragmented landholdings, declining productivity and market pressures had pushed wheat–paddy agriculture into crisis mode. Agrarian distress had even led to suicides among small and marginal farmers. A 2022 report based on field research claimed that just six districts of Punjab saw 16,594 suicides between 2000 and 2018. Where once Punjab was defined by agrarian prosperity, it was now being captured on celluloid through tragic stories of drug abuse and youth crime. The film *Udta Punjab* revealed a state in decline.

Even Punjab's politics was in flux. The Akali Dal, which had been the dominant regional party of the state and in power for a decade between 2007 and 2017, had become the target of growing public anger over charges of rampant corruption and 'family raj'. The Congress, which had benefitted from the anti-incumbency sentiment, was beset with infighting. Then Chief Minister Amarinder Singh, scion of the Patiala royal family, was accused by his own party leaders of being aloof and disconnected. Younger voters who had tired of the old elites were gravitating towards AAP, seen as a rising anti-establishment force. 'The farm laws couldn't have come at a worse time for Punjab; we were a troubled state sitting on a volcano,' remarked Dr Pramod Kumar, a Chandigarh-based academic.

The Centre may have pitched the farm laws as 'reforming' and 'transforming' agriculture, but in the villages of Punjab, they were seen as an attempt to unsettle traditional agricultural practices. 'Agriculture may flourish with reforms but farmers will perish,' contended Dr Kumar. For the Punjab farmer, the laws were viewed as an imposition, a high-handed attempt by the Centre to disrupt their way of life. Key figures in Punjab's rural way of life were the 'arhtiyas' or commission agents, who facilitated trade between the farmer–cultivators and the actual buyers, be they private traders or a government agency like the Food Corporation of India (FCI). While justifying the need for the farm laws, the Modi government had insisted that these would free the farmer from the clutches of the arhtiyas. But the arhtiyas were more than just monopolistic 'brokers' cutting a deal. Each district-level Agricultural Produce Marketing Committee (APMC) mandi has scores of licensed arhtiyas who not only manage the entire crop purchase and sale but also provide financial support to farmers in crisis. In Punjab, most arhtiyas are Jat Sikhs, fully integrated with the local farmer community. 'The lawmakers sitting in their Delhi bungalows may think of the arhtiyas as middlemen who are exploiting us, but for many farmers, they are a lifeline who will be with us through good times and bad. Will any corporate lend us cash for a marriage or medical emergency in the village like the arhtiya does?' asserted Gurmeet Singh, a Sangrur-based farmer and protestor.

When the farm ordinance decision was first announced, the Congress immediately accused the Modi government of 'selling out' farmer interests to billionaire corporates, more specifically Mukesh Ambani and Gautam Adani, the country's two richest men who were in the cross hairs of routine Opposition attacks. 'The "Adani–Ambani Farm Laws" have to be revoked. Nothing less is acceptable,' tweeted Congress leader Rahul Gandhi. Fearing a backlash, the Ambani-led Reliance Group promptly issued a statement saying it had never undertaken any contract farming and had no intention of entering the agriculture sector. Adani was more vulnerable since the company's agri-logistics business was already running grain storage facilities in Punjab and Haryana. A WhatsApp campaign among farmer groups spread the rumour that the Adani Group was planning to 'take over' the agri-marketing business in Punjab. 'In our minds, there is a connection between Adani and Prime Minister Modi. All these reforms are only meant to benefit big corporates,' claimed Dr Darshan Pal, a leader of the Krantikari Kisan Union (KKU). Truth or propaganda, the battle lines had been drawn.

On 24 September 2020, barely four days after the Rajya Sabha had 'passed' the farm laws, Punjab's farmers began a three-day 'rail roko' agitation. The initial response of the Modi government was to downplay the protests as being 'limited' to a few pockets in Punjab. Then Chief

Minister Captain Amarinder Singh was not as sanguine. He had previously backed private investment in agriculture, but with the Akalis breaking their alliance with the BJP, Singh couldn't afford to be seen soft-pedalling on farmer concerns. 'I want to caution the Modi government: Punjab is a border state; don't play with the sentiments of the people. This issue will explode if the farm laws are not rolled back,' he warned.

Captain Singh was prescient in his warning. Within weeks of the initial rail roko agitation, the farmer unions in Punjab and Haryana called for a nationwide road blockade and, raising a 'Delhi chalo' slogan, marched towards the national capital to protest the farm laws. The Delhi police denied them permission to enter the city, citing Covid-19 protocols that were still in place. When the farmers pushed ahead undeterred, they had to face water cannons and baton attacks from the police at various places. 'I saw the visuals of the violence on television and knew that this was big trouble. The Sikhs are a fiercely proud and patriotic people, but if you dare them with use of force, they will not sit back,' remarked Captain Singh. He recalled speaking to the home minister and requesting him to quickly find a compromise solution. Under orders from the home ministry, the Delhi police backed off. But the farmers dug in for a long-term agitation and set up encampments along Delhi's borders. 'It was almost winter, temperatures were falling … We were sure the farmers would go back instead of camping out in the cold,' said a home ministry official.

The home ministry's assessment was yet another ill-informed miscalculation. When I visited the Singhu border, the epicentre of the protests in mid-December, it was apparent that the agitating farmers had prepared for the long haul. Outside the tents, traditional Sikh langars (community kitchens) were set up, serving food night and day to the scores of people who had assembled. Sacks of ration were piled up. Large handis (cooking vessels) were being filled with fresh milk to make delicious kheer. Fresh produce lined the road. 'We have enough food to last us a year; no farmer will ever go hungry. We are here to stay until the government withdraws the farm laws,' one of the volunteers told me. With food, music and even a fitness centre, the atmosphere in the Singhu area was festive but also politically charged. Every evening, the farmer leaders would make fierce anti-Modi speeches from a makeshift podium. It was apparent that the angry Sikh farmers had declared 'war' against the Modi government; it were as if a rumbling had begun from deep within the earth itself. Farmers stood against Modi, immovable and determined.

The farm laws issue was stirring not just the Punjab farmer. Unrest was slowly spreading to neighbouring areas too. Across western Uttar Pradesh and Haryana, the Jats have been the traditionally dominant agrarian caste. For decades, the politics of the region had revolved around the powerful 'khap' panchayats of the community. In the 1980s, Mahendra Singh Tikait had emerged as an influential farmer leader in the region when he formed the Bharatiya Kisan Union and organized a campaign in Muzaffarnagar demanding that farmers' electricity bills be waived. Most famously, Tikait's rally on Delhi's Boat Club lawns in 1988 had drawn nearly 5 lakh farmers to the venue. But gradually his control over the farmers appeared to wane and with his death in 2011, the union was in the wilderness.

Enter Mahendra Singh Tikait's son, Rakesh. A Delhi police constable in the 1980s, he shed his uniform to join his father's movement, but while Tikait senior was disdainful of electoral politics, Rakesh was keen to get involved. Stout, bearded and sharp-eyed, sometimes with the kisan's turban or sometimes a topi on his head, the younger Tikait had contested elections unsuccessfully in western Uttar Pradesh twice. The Punjab farmers' agitation was just the opportunity he was looking for to make a name for himself. Within days of the Punjab farmers announcing their march to Delhi, Tikait decided to align his farmers body with the anti-farm-laws movement. 'We did not ask him to join—he volunteered,' recalled farmers' union leader Dr Darshan Pal.

When I first interviewed Tikait in December 2020 at Delhi's Ghazipur border, one of the protest sites, where he had assembled with his supporters, it was obvious that he was relishing the sudden media attention. Tikait had the perfect rustic look, dressed in a white kurta-dhoti with the green kisan 'andolan' (protest) cap on his head and green-white gamchha around his neck, beard unkempt and greying. 'Jat aur Sikh bhai-bhai hain; hum sub kisan putra hain. Modi sarkar ko yeh kala kanoon wapas lena hoga (Jats and Sikhs are brothers; we are all farmers' children. The Modi government will have to take back these black laws)!' he warned to loud cheers. When I asked for his specific objections to the farm laws, he brushed my question aside: 'Yeh sab baad mein … mujhe aaj bahut logon se milna hai (All that is irrelevant … I have to meet many people later today). He then showed me his mobile phone and boasted: 'Abhi meri Sharad Pawar se baat hui (I have just spoken to Sharad Pawar).' From constable to serial agitator to full-fledged political leader, Tikait now clearly saw himself in the big league.

Farmers, politicians and activists—the Samyukt Kisan Morcha (SKM), an umbrella body set up by the protestors—were posing an unexpected challenge to the Modi government. Through the 2020 December chill, the protesting farmers stayed put at the various sites on Delhi's borders, their spirits undaunted. As the new year dawned, the Modi government realized that the optics of angry kisans huddled in tents in winter weren't helping its battered image, damaged as it was by the muddled Covid-19 response. But could a government that prided itself on its political machismo bend before street protestors?

The farmer protests suddenly catapulted Narendra Singh Tomar, then Union agriculture minister, into the national limelight. Thickset, balding and in his mid-sixties, Tomar was a three-time MP from Madhya Pradesh. As a long-time BJP organizational man, he had hoped to become state chief minister when the Kamal Nath government was brought down in 2020. However, though Prime Minister Modi liked him—he is from an influential OBC community and was projected as a 'kisan putra' (farmer's son)—the party chose continuity over change and stuck with Shivraj Singh Chouhan as chief minister. Tomar might have continued to function below the radar as agriculture minister, but now he became the 'face' of the Modi government's outreach to the protesting farmers.

In mid-December 2020, Tomar wrote an emotional letter to the 'farmers of the country':

As agriculture minister, it is my responsibility to break the conspiracy that is being spread in the name of farm laws between the government and the farmers sitting on protest near Delhi's borders. I belong to a farmer's family and since childhood, I have experienced the tough life of farmers. And I also know what it takes to grow or sell crops. A lie is being spread in the name of MSP and mandis. The fact is that nothing is going to change.

The letter was a follow-up to a series of meetings that Tomar and Union Commerce Minister Piyush Goyal had held with the agitating farmer representatives. The meetings, by all accounts, were a 'non-starter'. 'Yeh mantri hamein hamari jagah dikhana chahte thhe. Humse aise baat ki jaise hum unke kabil nahi (These ministers wanted to show us our place. They spoke to us like we were not their equal),' was how Tikait described the dialogue. Tomar remembered it differently. 'We were very open. We kept telling them that we would make amendments to address all their concerns. But they didn't want any compromise and insisted on a legal guarantee on MSP [Minimum Support Price], which was not possible,' he said. The mistrust even extended to food choices. During the lunch break, the farmers chose to have their own langar food and not that offered by the government delegation.

A legally guaranteed MSP was a specific bone of contention. Under the MSP regime, the Centre recommends a price at which twenty-three crops, including wheat and paddy, can be procured from farmers. Farmers wanted a fixed MSP based on a cost-plus pricing formula devised by the National Commission on Farmers, headed by celebrated agricultural scientist Dr M.S. Swaminathan, to be 'guaranteed' by law, irrespective of prevailing market conditions. 'Not only is it financially unviable, a legally guaranteed MSP goes against basic market demand–supply principles and will lead to endless litigation over compensation, and there will be little crop diversification,' explained leading agrarian economist Prof. Ashok Gulati, a proponent of the urgent need for wide-ranging agriculture reform. He was one of the experts consulted by the agriculture ministry. Interestingly, even Congress leader Rahul Gandhi spent an hour with him. 'I pointed out to Rahul that Modi's farm laws were more or less identical to what the Congress had proposed in its manifesto, so why not support them and take credit.' said Prof. Gulati. 'But I guess competitive politics is a different ballgame.' Curiously, Modi, as Gujarat chief minister, had recommended an MSP guarantee by law in 2011. In Indian politics, where you stand depends on where you sit: one rule when in Opposition, another in power!

While Tomar and Goyal were attempting to resolve the issue, the one minister who might have been able to take the negotiations forward was kept out of them. Rajnath Singh had been agriculture minister in a previous Vajpayee government and had built good connections with farmer bodies, especially in his native Uttar Pradesh. Tomar did consult with Rajnath Singh privately and was told to find a 'middle path'. But when it came to the actual negotiations, Singh was not directly involved. 'Rajnath ji as a senior minister and with his consensual nature could have handled the farmers issue better,' admitted a BJP leader.

With the dialogue making no headway, the government attempted to 'divide' the farmers, or so Tikait claimed. 'Kai baar mujhe phone aaye ki "Aap Dilli chaliye, hum aapki one-to-one baat sabse bade neta se karate hain, ek baar mil lo, aap ke liye sab fit ho jayega, kitne din sangharsh karoge?" (I got many phone calls saying, "Come to Delhi, we will organize a one-to-one meeting with the biggest leader, just meet once, we will 'fit' everything for you, how long will you agitate?")' Tikait said that this was a 'conspiracy' to break the agitation, which he refused to be part of. 'I made it clear: no one-to-one meeting; either you meet all farmer leaders or none at all,' he asserted. Tikait was reportedly in touch with a few BJP leaders from western Uttar Pradesh who were trying to convince him to withdraw from the protests, especially after the Supreme Court passed an order on 12 January 2021 staying the implementation of the farm laws and appointing an 'expert committee' to listen to the farmers' grievances.

Ironically, the court order only seemed to embolden the farmer bodies to intensify their protests. The farmer unions had already announced a plan of action that would include a first-of-its-kind tractor rally on 26 January 2021. 'After the court verdict, we wanted to make it a peaceful victory parade for farmers. After all, many of the soldiers who march on Republic Day are the sons of farmers. "Jai jawan, jai kisan" was our slogan,' said Prabhjot Singh, one of the organizers of the rally. After some persuasion, the Delhi police gave permission for the rally while charting out a fixed route from the protest site through the national capital. The rally would be a turning point for the farmer agitation in more ways than one. With dialogue having failed and attempts at dividing the farmers proving unsuccessful, the government threw one last gambit: its media and social media outriders began demonizing the protesting farmers as anti-national 'Khalistanis'.

It was then Union Law Minister Ravi Shankar Prasad who initially claimed in December 2020 that the farmer protests had been 'overtaken' by the 'tukde tukde gang', a shrilly damning phrase that entered the BJP's lexicon after the student protests at Jawaharlal Nehru University (JNU) in 2016 against the execution of 2001 Indian Parliament attack convict Afzal Guru. Since then, the term has been used routinely by party leaders to stigmatize political opponents as 'nation breakers'. Another Union minister, Raosaheb Danve, claimed that China and Pakistan were behind the farmer protests. With unnamed 'intelligence sources' pointing to an 'ultra-left Naxal' hand, even Narendra Singh Tomar and Piyush Goyal called for the media to 'investigate' who was behind the farmer protests. Since the agitation was being spearheaded by Punjab's Jat Sikh farmers, it didn't take long for these allegations to draw in the Khalistani factor.

Khalistan is a sensitive issue in Punjab, a grim reminder of the separatist violence that tore the state apart in the 1980s. Invoking the spectre of a Khalistani hand in the farmer agitation was seen as a ploy by the Modi government to discredit and delegitimize the entire protest movement. The insinuation incensed the farmers; they refused to be cowed down by a propaganda campaign. 'All you media people who are calling us Khalistanis should get out from here. Hum kisan hain, aatankwadi nahi (We are farmers, not terrorists),' they shouted. When tempers are running high, it often takes only one incident to set off an inferno. The Republic Day tractor parade was that spark.

On 25 January, the day before the planned tractor march, Punjabi actor Deep Sidhu rather dramatically announced that the farmers would march towards Red Fort the next day. None of the other farmer unions who were part of the SKM had endorsed this announcement. Sidhu's credentials to participate in the farmer protests were suspect. Accused of having extremist links, he was spotted in a viral video, wearing black attire and a white turban, arguing with police officers at the farm protest site, demanding the opening of road blockades. I had first met Sidhu during the 2019 election campaign in Gurdaspur. At that time, he was part of actor-turned-politician Sunny Deol's entourage. Keeping up with Deol on the campaign trail wasn't easy since he wasn't punctual with his schedules, but Sidhu helped organize an interview for us with the star candidate. Afterwards, he often telephoned me to boast about his appeal among the youth. 'I can easily win the next elections in Punjab. I have an entire army of supporters with me,' he bragged.

This Deep Sidhu-led private 'army' was widely held to be responsible for the violence that erupted on Republic Day during the farmers' parade when some individuals—later identified as Sidhu's supporters—deviated from the approved route, clashed with the police, forcibly entered the Red Fort and hoisted a Sikh religious flag on an empty flagpole. 'We had given a fixed route and clear dos and don'ts to our members; we had even told them to fly the national flag on each tractor and maintain discipline. It wasn't our farmers who were behind this violence but an unruly mob who had their own agenda,' insisted an SMK leader.

As tear gas shells were fired and barricades breached, the 'peaceful' farmer movement became tainted with violence. Communal and separatist undertones threatened to hijack the agitation. The Modi government was quick to hit back. That night, Ravi Shankar Prasad was back on news channels, reasserting his claim that a 'sinister' design was behind the farmer protests. His 'tukde tukde gang' contention had been vindicated, he argued.

Within hours of the violence erupting, the administrative machinery swung into action. The district magistrate gave orders for the Ghazipur protest site to be vacated; electricity was disconnected; the farmers' makeshift tents were removed; and barricades were placed along the road. On the afternoon of 28 January, paramilitary forces surrounded the main podium. On the stage, the farmers' leader Tikait held forth, addressing his followers and declaring that he was ready to court arrest. Reports began to come in that a group of BJP supporters had also arrived on the site and were demanding that the farmers be removed. It was at this time that Tikait had his moment of high emotion. In a passionate speech, he accused the BJP of 'betraying' the Jats of western Uttar Pradesh who had supported the party in recent elections. 'Itna bada dhoka, itni badi gaddari (Such cheating, such betrayal),' he cried, his voice breaking and his eyes welling up for the cameras. TV channels immediately aired the pictures and protestors got energized. Tikait's teary-eyed pleas to his followers to fight on went viral. If the Republic Day violence had been a big setback to farmer unity, Tikait's impassioned speech lifted drooping spirits. Almost overnight, a farmer–leader was born.

At the Singhu border, where the Punjab farmers had assembled, there was similar frenetic activity. The day after the Republic Day fiasco, a group of around 100 people entered the protest site and began shouting slogans and throwing stones. No one is quite sure who was behind this slogan shouting and stone pelting, but the agitating farmers were convinced that 'outsiders' linked to the BJP were involved. 'They wanted to drive us out from the site while the police just watched,' claimed Harmeet Singh, a farmer leader. That the police was keen to force the farmers out became clear when the protest site was suddenly surrounded by multiple barricades. Concrete cement blocks and concertina wires were put in place as if in a war zone; even sharp nails were driven into the roads. These measures were designed to isolate the protestors. In more than two dozen districts of Haryana, internet services were suspended. Ironically, the state's heavy-handedness only made the farmers more determined to stay put. 'We had food stocks with us that could last for a year; I had promised my father that I wouldn't come back till we won this war,' a young farmer remarked.

And 'war' indeed it was, one that the government wasn't winning in the public arena. So far, the Modi government's success had stemmed from its control over the popular narrative. Now, terrifying images of iron nails and barricades put up on main arterial roads revealed what the Centre was doing to citizens: using the violent power of the state to intimidate farmers into submission. On one side were the brave farmers shivering in the north Indian winter, while on the other side were Modi and his elite coterie ensconced in their heated Lutyens' bungalows. In the war of narratives, it was a no-contest. This time, it was Modi's opponents who sped away with the narrative and with the sympathy. 'PM as "tanashah" (dictator)' became a catchline that began to gain traction, especially across north India's farmer belt.

Modi responded with characteristic vindictiveness and lack of feeling. Instead of reaching out to the aggrieved farmers, on 8 February 2020, while replying to the Motion of Thanks on the President's address in Parliament, he launched a stinging attack on the protestors, accusing them of being 'andolan jeevis' (professional protestors). 'These parasites feast on every agitation. When they are not in front, they operate from behind the curtains; they cannot survive without agitation,' Modi ranted. He even accused the protestors of being supported by a new Foreign Direct Investment, which he described as 'foreign destructive ideology'. 'We need to save the country from such an ideology,' he warned. The speech was delivered by a furious, rabble-rousing politician, not a statesman-like Prime Minister. Modi was floundering in the face of the farm agitation. He had, quite simply, lost the plot. Those who fed the entire country, the farmers, were now being shrilly targeted by none other than the Prime Minister. Any hope for a dialogue was now at an end. The farmers were determinedly carrying on with their protests; an obstinate Prime Minister was refusing to engage with them—how long could the impasse continue?

=

Located in the Rohilkhand region on the Indo-Nepal border, Lakhimpur Kheri is not just Uttar Pradesh's largest district but also its 'sugar bowl'; much of the local economy depends on the sugar cane that is grown and processed here. The fertile soil of the district, which is nourished by the many rivers that criss-cross the Terai belt, attracted enterprising farmers from Punjab to migrate here in the early 1950s after Partition. The Sikh agriculturalists of Lakhimpur Kheri, many of whom own sugar cane farms, have much in common with the Punjab farmers, and identified strongly with the farm protests on Delhi's borders. The agitation echoed powerfully here. Unpaid sugar dues owed to farmers by the privately owned sugar mills had added to a sense of restiveness. The local farmers were looking for an opportunity to express their grievances. Uttar Pradesh Deputy Chief Minister Keshav Prasad Maurya's visit to the area on 3 October 2021 was a sign for the farmers to escalate their protests against the farm laws. Several of them gathered with their tractors at the helipad in Lakhimpur with black flags. Maurya's host was then Union Minister of State for Home and local BJP MP Ajay Mishra 'Teni'. The minister had organized an annual wrestling tournament in his home village in Tikunia, at which Maurya would give away the prizes. Only this time, the 'dangal' celebrations took a tragic turn.

Around 2 p.m., as the farmers were returning from their protests, a convoy of SUVs allegedly led by Ashish Mishra, the Union minister's son, came rushing in from behind. One of them ploughed into the crowd and knocked some of the farmers down. When the farmers tried to block the way, the other two SUVs accelerated forward and ran over the injured, crushing them to death. Four farmers, all Sikhs, were mowed down by the speeding SUVs. Clashes broke out between the farmers and those in the convoy; four more people—three local BJP workers and a journalist—

were killed. As the grisly video of the violence went viral, even the most partisan of news channels were screaming 'cold-blooded murder'. A Union minister's son allegedly leading a VIP convoy that caused the deaths of unarmed agitating farmers: the optics could not have been worse for the Modi government. Worse still, Ajay Mishra had been caught on camera just days earlier warning the protesting farmers: 'sudhar jao' (mend your ways) or else he would 'mend them himself' within minutes. 'If I decide to show them my true power, then they will have to leave not only their villages but also the district,' he boasted. It was an open threat that exposed the minister's thuggish inclinations and further embarrassed the Modi government.

'We realized that what had happened in Lakhimpur was indefensible; we just didn't know what to say initially,' admitted a senior BJP leader. As part of the damage control, party spokespersons were informed that no one was to go on TV and defend the minister or his son. The Prime Minister and other top government ministers were also conspicuously silent. When I tried to speak to Mishra, I was curtly told by his assistant, 'Aap jaise TV patrakar se hum kyon sawaal le (Why should we take questions from a TV journalist like you)?' The only BJP politician who spoke out was Varun Gandhi, MP from the neighbouring Pilibhit constituency. 'The video is crystal clear. Protestors cannot be silenced through murder. There has to be accountability for the innocent blood of farmers that has been spilled,' he tweeted. The BJP did not respond to Gandhi's remarks. Instead, he and his mother, Maneka Gandhi, were dropped from the BJP's new list of national executive members. In 2024, Varun Gandhi would be denied a ticket.

Interestingly, while the Centre was silent and prevaricating in acting against Mishra and his son, Uttar Pradesh Chief Minister Yogi Adityanath swung into action and promised 'no one will be spared'. Within a week of the incident, the minister's son, who had been absconding, was arrested. A special investigation team (SIT) of the Uttar Pradesh police was set up to handle the case. The SIT report described the farmer deaths as a 'pre-planned conspiracy', not just a case of negligent driving, and filed charges of murder, criminal conspiracy and rioting. The minister's son would have to stay in jail a while longer.

And yet, despite the growing clamour for the minister to step down, the Modi government did not touch Mishra, who was previously charged in a murder case where the complainant claimed that Mishra 'shot [his] son in his head at a main road in broad daylight' in Tikunia during a panchayat election battle in 2000. The case dragged on for years—Mishra was finally acquitted by the Supreme Court in 2024—but that did not stop him from being inducted into the Modi government in a cabinet reshuffle in July 2021 as part of a delicate caste-balancing act. The political buzz was that since Mishra was a Brahmin leader from Uttar Pradesh, the BJP did not want to disrupt caste equations in the state. Mishra, a two-time MP, had just undertaken an 'ashirwad' yatra across the Rohilkhand region in an attempt to shore up support for the BJP in the Brahmin community.

But it wasn't just the caste factor that was protecting Mishra. The minister had a patron in Home Minister Amit Shah, who was closely monitoring politics in Uttar Pradesh. Within weeks of the Lakhimpur Kheri horror, Shah was sharing the stage with his junior minister at a police event in Lucknow, where, ironically, law and order was the focus. 'Zameen se juda, dynamic leader hai, chunaav jitna jaanta hai (He is a grassroots leader, knows how to win elections),' Shah reportedly told a ministerial colleague. When journalists queried the home minister on the Opposition's demand for Mishra's removal, his answer was typically combative: 'Just because someone's son may have committed a criminal act, why should the father resign? Show me how Mishra is personally involved.' The ghastly criminal acts attributed to Mishra obviously counted for nothing when measured against his political weight. Just another example of the chilling electoral calculations of the 'new' Modi-led BJP. In fact, setting aside the controversy, Mishra was given a BJP ticket from Lakhimpur Kheri in the 2024 Lok Sabha elections. Campaigning for him, Shah promised voters to make the sitting MP a 'bada aadmi' (big man) if re-elected. Mishra lost by 34,000 votes.

The home minister's handling of the Lakhimpur Kheri violence reveals the mindset of the Modi–Shah leadership style—both in Gujarat and now at the Centre. A controversial minister might be quietly dropped in a reshuffle but not in response to a demand for their resignation from the Opposition. A Gujarat Congress leader once asked Modi during a customary all-party meeting in Gandhinagar why a particular minister who was accused of corruption had not been removed from his cabinet. 'Sarkar hamein chalani hain, aap aur vipaksh ko nahi (We have to run the government, not you and the Opposition),' was Modi's dismissive response. Modi rules by striking fear in others. When you keep demonstrating you are capable of the unthinkable, opponents are stunned into silence.

Days after the Lakhimpur Kheri killings, Prime Minister Modi had an important visitor. Senior politician and former Jammu and Kashmir governor and then Governor of Meghalaya Satya Pal Malik had sought an urgent meeting. Malik, whose self-image was that of a 'kisan putra' from his days as a young leader in the Lok Dal in the 1970s, was incensed by the farmer deaths. 'So many farmers have died; you need to put a stop to it by taking back the farm laws, else it will cost you in the next election,' was his appeal to the Prime Minister. Modi apparently stared at him balefully and then shot back: 'Satya Pal ji, you don't have to worry so much. These farmers will soon give up their protests and go home.' The tea being served remained untouched as the Prime Minister got up mid-conversation and the governor made a hasty exit. 'He looked at me as if I had committed some sin by raising the issue of farmer deaths,' claimed Malik. 'That day, as I left the Prime Minister's residence, I made up my mind that I didn't want to meet Modi again. Until that moment, I always thought of him as a leader whose heart beat for farmers, but I realized that all he cared for was his personal image and his chair. He could tweet and comment on a death anywhere in the world but not a word of sympathy for our farmers who had died.' Not one to shy away from a political joust, Malik launched a no-holds-barred tirade against the Modi government on the farm laws issue. A governor speaking out against the Centre was highly unusual. 'I am a farmer first, then a public figure. If the Prime Minister wants me to resign, I will do so right away. I have no love for this chair,' he told me in an interview at the time.

The rebellious Malik was not asked to quit, and he continued to make his displeasure clear until his gubernatorial term ended in October 2022. In April 2023, he hit the headlines once again, this time in an outspoken interview for the news portal The Wire with Karan Thapar. In the interview, Malik accused the Prime Minister of silencing him as the Jammu and Kashmir governor. He also detailed alleged security lapses leading to the Pulwama terror attack ahead of the 2019 elections. Was he trying to settle scores with Modi by speaking out now? 'Badla nahi, badlaav hona chahiye (Not revenge but change is needed),' was Malik's sharp one-line reply. The Prime Minister, characteristically, did not respond to Malik's unproven charges. In the Modi power playbook, replying to any criticism is a mark of defensiveness: he doesn't deign to respond to anyone who challenges him.

=

The anti-farm-laws agitation had stretched on for almost a year by now and was showing no sign of ending anytime soon. The Prime Minister's confrontational attitude towards the protestors and silence on the Lakhimpur Kheri episode had not aided matters either. The viral images of the farmers being brutally mowed down had not just incensed the protesting farmers but also sharpened public opinion in their favour. An October 2021 monthly tracker poll commissioned by the BJP showed that the farmer disquiet could affect poll outcomes, especially in the crucial state of Uttar Pradesh. To a pointed question in the survey, an overwhelming majority of farmers said that the government must withdraw the farm laws. In early November, Union Minister of Road Transport and Highways Nitin Gadkari met the Prime Minister, referred to the discontent over the farm laws and suggested a tactical retreat. It was a throwback to 2015, when the government had pulled back from contentious land acquisition laws after protests from the Opposition and farmer organizations. However, this time, Modi was not keen to budge and apparently told Gadkari that he would not succumb to 'pressure tactics'. 'Agar hum dabaav mein aate toh aapko lagta hain ki hum yahan tak pahunchte (Do you think I would have reached here if I was susceptible to pressure)?' was Modi's pointed rejoinder to his senior colleague.

A few days after Modi's meeting with Gadkari, RSS Chief Mohan Bhagwat telephoned the Prime Minister. The Modi–Bhagwat relationship is one of convenience, based on well-defined responsibilities and a mutual commitment to the larger Hindu Rashtra ideal: the RSS leader does not intrude into the Prime Minister's daily governance space, while Modi mostly stays away from the RSS's cultural programmes. In the Vajpayee years, the RSS leadership was at times openly critical of the Prime Minister. Not any longer. The balance of power is heavily weighted in favour of the political executive, and Bhagwat knows his limitations. Even during the strict Covid lockdown, when a few voices within the RSS hierarchy had reportedly expressed a sense of disquiet over the distress of migrants, Bhagwat had chosen not to escalate the issue further. This time, the RSS sarsanghchalak was being pushed to resolve the standoff by the Sangh affiliate, the Bharatiya Kisan Sangh, which insisted: 'We need a minimum support price as a legal guarantee during the sale and purchase of agriculture produce.' This remained one of the prime demands across farm unions.

When Bhagwat mentioned the need for a rethink on the farm laws to the Prime Minister, the initial response was reportedly dismissive and pugnacious. 'It is just a few andolan jeevis who are keeping this protest going; the majority want them,' maintained Modi. But within days of the conversation with the RSS chief, Modi's office set off alarm bells. The BJP's on-ground feedback machine, based on inputs from local leaders, confirmed what the internal poll tracker surveys were pointing out: an overwhelming majority of farmers in Uttar Pradesh wanted a withdrawal of the farm laws. 'We were not surprised that Punjab farmers were against the new laws, but to find similar results from Uttar Pradesh was worrying,' said a senior BJP leader.

Prime Minister Modi is a domineering, high-handed figure who thrives on conflict and is reluctant to be seen bowing to pressure. In his calculus, Uttar Pradesh was not just another battleground state. It was his 'karmabhoomi' too now, the state with which he had built a deep personal and political attachment. Confronted with the inevitable, he could not bear to lose face, but he could not give the Opposition a whiff of an opportunity in the battle for Uttar Pradesh either. Finally, at a meeting with Narendra Singh Tomar, Amit Shah and Rajnath Singh, Modi told them of his decision to withdraw the farm laws. The key was to do it in such a way that the Prime Minister could seize the moral high ground. An aide suggested Guru Nanak Jayanti, which was just a few days away, on 19 November 2021, as the right time to make the announcement. 'It will strike the right chord with the protestors, a majority of whom are Sikhs,' was the rationale. Always conscious of getting the optics right, Modi jumped at the idea. Few politicians can best him at seizing the moment. Politics for Modi is performative, a drama that he enacts with detailed attention to scripts and costumes. It is also about rotating to a strategic flexibility when needed.

'Whatever I did, I did for farmers. What I am doing, I am doing it for the country.' With these words, the Prime Minister announced that he was withdrawing the laws that had sparked off a year-long agitation. The announcement, the biggest, clearest and most embarrassing climb-down for Modi since he took office in May 2014, was made without the usual fanfare, not at prime time but at 9 a.m., just as people were getting ready to celebrate Guru Nanak Jayanti. Modi's prime-time appearances are usually about creating dramatic and disruptive moments where he is fully in control. This time, he had to appear humble in defeat and even apologize, an extremely rare occurrence. 'I apologize to the people of the country. Despite several attempts we were not able to convince farmers.'

But Modi's apology was not accompanied by any regret over the deaths in Lakhimpur Kheri or reports that scores of farmers had died during the protest (SKM later claimed that 702 farmers had died during the agitation). Instead, Modi insisted that his government had done 'everything possible' to help farmers. 'In the over five decades of my life, I have witnessed the struggle of farmers closely. That is why after becoming Prime Minister, my government gave farmers' issues primacy,' he claimed. This was typical Modi-speak. Even in defeat, thoroughly rebuffed by a genuine people's agitation, Modi tried to recapture the 'gareeb kisan' after having tear-gassed and lathicharged them.

In taking back the farm laws, Modi had exposed a chink in his seemingly indestructible armour. His bellicose politics could corner his political opponents, but he couldn't combat restive farmers and their evocative 'Jai jawan, jai kisan' slogans. Certainly not before a major election cycle that had to be won at all costs. While the decision bought him a temporary truce, Modi's carefully nurtured pro-farmer image was never quite the same again. Seven years into power, the all-powerful Prime Minister was looking vulnerable for the first time. While Modi was still a dominant figure in Delhi, in state elections the BJP was finding it increasingly difficult to replicate its Lok Sabha success, as we saw in two crucial battles that shattered Team Modi–Shah's claim to political invincibility.

FIVE

'Khela Hobe': Pawar Saheb and Mamata Didi

A TELEVISION journalist working at a round-the-clock news channel is like a doctor in an emergency ward: always on call. But even journalists, like doctors, are entitled to switch off occasionally. On 23 November 2019 my plan was to go for a long walk with my dog, have a hearty breakfast and then catch up on some sleep in the afternoon. Which is why when my mobile phone began to furiously ring at 7.30 a.m., I was half tempted to switch it off. The number flashing on the screen was from the India Today assignment desk. When I answered, the voice on the other end was hyperventilating: 'Breaking news! We need your live phone interview urgently. The swearing-in ceremony in Mumbai is about to begin at Raj Bhavan. Devendra Fadnavis and Ajit Pawar are already there.' My colleague was sounding incoherent, but the last bit of information shook me out of my stupor. Wait a minute. Swearing-in? Who? Fadnavis and Ajit Pawar taking oath at dawn? Was I dreaming of a parallel political universe?

The night before, I had anchored a live news show that stretched on till midnight on the unfolding political drama in Maharashtra. 'NCP–Shiv Sena–Congress Maha Vikas Aghadi alliance firmed up; Uddhav Thackeray set to be new Maharashtra chief minister' was the late-night news flash. On my way back from the office, I had even sent the Shiv Sena leader a good luck message. Thackeray had replied with a thank you emoji, followed by a 'Jai Maharashtra' greeting. Now, less than eight hours later, I was live on air once again, only to announce that Devendra Fadnavis was being sworn in as the chief minister of Maharashtra with Ajit Pawar as his deputy. The British Prime Minister Harold Wilson had famously said that a week is a long time in politics; apparently in Maharashtra, even a few hours can be long enough.

Then Nationalist Congress Party (NCP) chief Sharad Pawar too had slept in late that morning after a difficult meeting with the Congress and Shiv Sena leaders to sort out last-minute hitches in the alliance formation. The meeting at Mumbai's Nehru Centre had seen an acrimonious exchange between Pawar and the Congress leader in charge of Maharashtra at the time, Mallikarjun Kharge, over the speaker's post: the Congress was insisting on the post for the party, but the NCP wasn't ready to concede. An infuriated Pawar had unexpectedly walked out of the meeting, hastily followed out by his nephew and senior NCP leader Ajit Pawar. On reaching home, Sharad Pawar frantically worked the phones till late evening to sort out matters. The one NCP leader he wasn't able to connect with was his nephew, whose mobile was switched off. 'Ajit dada has gone to meet his lawyers for some urgent work,' he was told. Pawar retired for the night, hopeful that despite the initial hiccups the alliance government was on track. At around 7 a.m., he was woken up by a party MLA informing him that Ajit Pawar was at Raj Bhavan with BJP leader Devendra Fadnavis. 'The swearing-in is about to start, Saheb,' he was told. As a seasoned political campaigner, the seventy-nine-year-old Pawar 'Saheb' wasn't easily flustered. In a political career spanning nearly five decades, he had seen many ups and downs. He had been Maharashtra's youngest chief minister at thirty-eight, although he had missed out on the Prime Minister's post on more than one occasion. A cancer survivor, his sheer resilience is arguably his biggest asset. Seemingly unruffled, Pawar rang up his daughter, Supriya Sule, an MP who lives in the same leafy

Silver Oak Estate complex in South Mumbai. Sule was already up and about, and was alerted to the news by her husband, who was switching channels when he caught the news break. 'I assure you we didn't know what was going on. Ajit dada being sworn in with Fadnavis ji—it all seemed a bit unreal, to be honest,' Sule said.

The Pawars are a tightly knit family, held together by shared emotional, political and business ties. Ajit, affectionately referred to as 'Ajit dada' by family and friends, is the son of Sharad Pawar's elder brother Anantrao. After his brother passed away, Sharad Pawar had taken Ajit under his wing, encouraging him to nurture the family stronghold of Baramati near Pune. At just twenty-three, with Sharad Pawar's support, Ajit was elected to the local sugar co-operative factory board, a stepping stone to a political career in Maratha-dominated western Maharashtra. 'For Saheb, Ajit is like the son he never had, someone whom he has been very protective of,' claimed a family friend. Temperamentally, though, uncle and nephew are very dissimilar. While Pawar Saheb is a patient and calculating politician, Ajit is an impetuous and hot-headed leader. 'Saheb has a wide circle of friends and contacts and can build bridges with anyone. Ajit dada is not as sophisticated; he can be a real fightercock when he doesn't get his way,' revealed the family associate. 'He is a good administrator who takes quick decisions but can lose his temper easily,' said a bureaucrat who has worked closely with Ajit. Allegations of corruption too have swirled around him. In 2012, Ajit resigned from the Maharashtra cabinet after he was accused of being involved in a major irrigation scam when he was the water resources minister.

While the senior Pawar had national ambitions that had taken him to Delhi, Ajit has always focused on state politics. He became deputy chief minister for the first time in 2004 in a Congress–NCP alliance government. 'Ajit dada is a very efficient organizer and resourceful politician. When Saheb was in Delhi, it was he who managed all the key party tasks in Mumbai and Pune. From men to money, he handled everything. Saheb was very dependent on him,' disclosed an NCP leader.

Which is also why when the news first broke that morning of Ajit Pawar's 'rebellion', the buzz was that such a major step couldn't have been taken without the uncle's knowledge, if not consent. 'Why would I agree to Ajit joining hands with the BJP when I was the one who stitched together an agreement with the Congress and the Shiv Sena to form a government? What Ajit did in being sworn in with Fadnavis that morning did not have my approval,' countered Sharad Pawar when we asked him about the sudden swearing-in. And yet, second-guessing the political moves of a canny senior leader like him isn't easy. Pawar is a man of few words and an inscrutable mind; the running joke in Maharashtra's political circles is that when he says no it probably means a yes, and when he says yes it means a maybe. If a government being sworn in at the crack of dawn wasn't dramatic enough, the backstory of how the Maharashtra power game was playing out is even more striking and gives an insight into the grimy and complicated behind-the-scenes deal-making in twenty-first-century Indian politics.

═

In October 2019, the Maharashtra assembly elections had given a clear majority to the BJP–Shiv Sena pre-poll alliance, but the BJP fell short of a majority on its own, winning only 105 seats in the 288-member assembly, well below the majority mark of 145. By contrast, the NCP won 54 seats, a surprisingly strong performance for a party that had been written off by many pollsters. An image of the octogenarian Pawar addressing a public meeting in the pouring rain in Satara had gone viral—a symbol of his indefatigable spirit. In normal course, the BJP–Sena government should have been sworn in almost right away since they had a clear majority: with the Shiv Sena's 56, they had 161 seats out of 288. But leadership battles in India are far from 'normal'. The Shiv Sena claims they had been promised a 50-50 power-sharing 'deal', including a stab at the chief ministership. The BJP insists that no such arrangement had been agreed upon. The so-called 'deal' had reportedly been worked out between Amit Shah and Uddhav Thackeray during a private meeting in February

2019 at the latter's residence in Mumbai. When I asked Shah about it, his answer was typically aggressive. 'Uddhav ji jhooth bol rahe hain (Uddhav Thackeray is lying). Please show me one statement or piece of paper where I have said that the Shiv Sena will get the chief ministership of Maharashtra. Our stand was clear: whoever got more seats would get the chief minister's post. That was non-negotiable.' With the BJP getting more seats than the Shiv Sena, then incumbent Chief Minister Fadnavis was seen as the natural contender for the top job. In fact, just ahead of the elections, when at a public event I had asked the even-tempered Fadnavis about a possible tussle over the chief ministership, he had dismissed it as a non-issue. 'I am confident that I will be sworn in once again as chief minister; there is no debate on this between us and the Shiv Sena,' he claimed. Listening to him intently in the audience was the Sena's youthful leader Aaditya Thackeray, who responded with a smile: 'I think you journalists should leave this to us to work out.'

So what suddenly went so wrong for the original 'saffron' allies to part ways in bitterness in just over a month? The BJP claims that it was the Sena that 'betrayed' them by starting secret negotiations with the NCP–Congress alliance. 'Uddhav ji wanted the chief minister's post. They kept telling us that there was no question of parting ways and yet they were looking for a way out,' remarked Fadnavis. Sanjay Raut, Shiv Sena MP and a close confidante of the Sena leadership, had a very different story to tell. 'Do you know that Uddhav ji and I must have telephoned all the top BJP leaders dozens of times to decide on government formation, but they had all switched off their phones? We were even ready for the deputy chief minister's post, but the BJP didn't even want to talk to us,' he said.

The pugnacious Raut is a noteworthy character in Maharashtra's game of thrones. A former journalist, Raut first met then Shiv Sena chief Bal Thackeray in the 1980s, when he did a two-part interview with him for a Marathi newsmagazine. The senior Thackeray was impressed and offered the young, ambitious journalist an opportunity to edit the party's mouthpiece, *Saamna*. Raut's sharp, at times acerbic writing style and aggressive espousal of Hindutva politics made him a perfect fit for the magazine, which is the voice of the party's first family. In 2000, he was sent to the Rajya Sabha, where he quickly made a mark as a street-smart political operator, befriending a number of senior politicians, including Sharad Pawar. 'I would sit with Pawar Saheb in Parliament's Central Hall and sometimes go to visit him at home. We had ideological differences, but he was always gracious enough to give me time,' recalled Raut. It was at one such meeting, ahead of the 2019 Maharashtra elections, that Pawar reportedly mentioned the possibility of forging a grand alliance against the BJP. 'The BJP will finish the Sena as it is finishing all its regional allies one by one. If we want to prevent Maharashtra's politics from being dictated by Delhi, then we must look at options,' the wily Pawar reportedly told Raut. It was an idea that appealed to Uddhav Thackeray too. The soft-spoken Thackeray had been feeling uneasy for a while, chafing under Amit Shah's bossy approach towards the alliance. 'I had a good equation with Prime Minister Modi, but with Shah it was different; he was always taking us for granted,' claimed Uddhav. In one heated exchange, the home minister reportedly told Uddhav that the Sena needed the BJP and not vice-versa. 'Yeh Bal Thackeray ka zamana nahi hai (This is not the age of Bal Thackeray),' was a stinging remark by Shah, which Uddhav took to heart. Raut too confided to a journalist once that the cause of the uneasiness between the BJP and the Shiv Sena was not Modi but Amit Shah.

On results day, as the final Maharashtra numbers flashed on screen, Thackeray realized that he finally had some options. While the Shiv Sena may have won just 56 seats, the BJP could not form the government without the Sena's support. The NCP too would need the Sena if it wanted to stitch together Pawar's 'grand alliance against the BJP' idea. Egged on by Raut, Thackeray picked up the phone and spoke to Pawar a few days after the results. For years, the Pawars and the Thackerays have dominated Maharashtra politics. Despite their political fights, Sharad Pawar and Bal Thackeray were unfailingly courteous to each other in person. Now, Pawar dangled bait in front of Uddhav Thackeray: 'If the BJP won't treat you with respect and you actually decide to quit the alliance, why don't we work out an alliance?' The phone conversation ended with no commitment but with an agreement to remain engaged with Raut as the designated interlocutor.

Within days of Pawar's first phone conversation with Uddhav Thackeray, there were signs of a breakthrough. Uddhav was 'persuaded' by Raut to meet Pawar and discuss the terms of the alliance. A key figure in influencing the Sena leader was his wife, Rashmi, who had shown a keen interest in the political goings-on in the state. 'If there is one person Uddhav totally trusts, it is his wife. Rashmi tai convinced him to ditch the BJP and hitch up with the NCP–Congress alliance,' claimed a Thackeray family confidante. A face-to-face meeting was set up at a five-star hotel in Mumbai for the principal stakeholders. Uddhav indicated that he was ready to accept Pawar's power-sharing offer. 'I want a public guarantee that the chief minister's chair will first be given to the Shiv Sena,' was his primary condition. A beaming Pawar replied in the affirmative but asked for time to get a nod to his 'grand' alliance idea from the Congress leadership. But even before the NCP leader had initiated a dialogue with the Congress, Uddhav did something unusual. He asked Raut to instantly connect him on the phone to Sonia Gandhi. Raut didn't have her mobile number but somehow managed to touch base with 10, Janpath. Uddhav had never met or spoken to the Congress president before. The Sena and the Congress had been ideological adversaries for years. Now, suddenly, the Sena leader was keen to directly hear her response to a potential alliance. Sonia Gandhi was reportedly taking aback by an entirely unanticipated call but politely agreed to discuss the issue first with Pawar and her own party leaders.

A veteran of many power battles, Pawar has had a tumultuous relationship with the Gandhi family over the years. In 1978, when Pawar first broke away from the Congress, it was in the immediate aftermath of Indira Gandhi's post-Emergency defeat. Instead of standing by Sonia Gandhi or even his original mentor, Y.B. Chavan, an ambitious Pawar charted his own path and tied up with the rival Janata Party. When Indira Gandhi came back to power in 1980, she dismissed the Pawar-led government in Maharashtra. Pawar returned to the Congress in 1987, when Rajiv Gandhi was the Prime Minister, but he never quite achieved complete reconciliation with the Gandhis. When Sonia Gandhi took over in 1998, Pawar felt he was being undermined as the party's leader in the Lok Sabha. In 1999, he initiated an open revolt against Sonia Gandhi's leadership, insisting that the Congress could not propose the 'foreign-born' Sonia as the party's prime ministerial candidate. Expelled from the party, he formed the Nationalist Congress Party (NCP), only to enter into a power-sharing arrangement with the Congress in Maharashtra soon after. 'How does one trust someone who keeps making these U-turns?' Sonia Gandhi reportedly said to an aide about Pawar's political somersaults. 'Loyalty' is most valued to be a member of the Congress president's coterie: Sonia Gandhi's world is firmly divided between her 'loyalists' and those she remains wary of. The NCP leader, for his part, insisted he was a Congressman at heart. 'I joined this party in the early 1960s, when Jawaharlal Nehru was Prime Minister. The Congress is my first home,' he once told me in a rare emotional moment.

Sonia Gandhi had taken over as the interim Congress president following Rahul Gandhi's resignation after the 2019 Lok Sabha defeat. When Pawar raised the issue of a 'grand' Maharashtra alliance—that would include the Shiv Sena—with her, she was non-committal. Sonia is not known to rush into decisions; she treads cautiously. She called a meeting of her trusted aides, including Ahmed Patel and A.K. Antony, at her 10, Janpath residence. While Ahmed Patel, ever pragmatic, suggested that the party should be open to forming a government with whoever could keep the BJP out of power in a key state like Maharashtra, A.K. Antony and a few other senior Congress leaders warned that an alliance with a 'communal' party like the Shiv Sena would be the 'kiss of death' for the Congress. Sonia too appeared inclined to accept the Antony line. 'Let me also get a few more views,' she said. The crucial 'view' was that of her son, Rahul Gandhi, no longer Congress president but still the main decision-maker within the party. Rahul's verdict was even more clear-cut: there was no question of aligning with a Hindutva party like the Shiv Sena.

The Congress's reluctance to ally with the Sena created a predicament for Pawar. But just as his strategy was falling apart, there was a dramatic twist in the tale. A proposal was floated—no one is quite certain first by whom—for a BJP–NCP alliance. Pawar's nephew Ajit Pawar and NCP Rajya Sabha MP Praful Patel jumped at the idea of a tie-up with the BJP. 'It will be a game-changer in Maharashtra politics and a win-win for all,' the duo insisted. Patel is a bit of an oddity in Maharashtra's Maratha-centric rural politics. The tall, sharply dressed, Mumbai-based Gujarati industrialist-turned-neta's family owns a flourishing tobacco trading business with beedi-making fields across the Vidarbha region. His father, Manoharbhai Patel, had been a Congress MLA and a friend of the Pawars. When Pawar returned to the Congress in 1988, he took a young Praful under his wing and sent him to the Lok Sabha in 1991. The suave, private-school-educated Praful 'bhai' became his mentor's eyes and ears in Delhi. 'Saheb likes those who can combine sharp politics with strong entrepreneurship. Praful bhai was the perfect choice for him when he moved to Delhi in the early 1990s,' observed an NCP leader. Pawar's 'man in Delhi' was well connected across the political spectrum. As the NCP's leader in charge of Gujarat and civil aviation minister in the United Progressive Alliance (UPA) government between 2004 and 2014, Patel had built good equations with both Modi and Shah, who were then spearheading the BJP government in Gandhinagar. 'I have always believed in maintaining friendships across the political aisle. It was no different with Modi ji and Amit bhai,' said Patel. Shah was also a former chairman and director of the Ahmedabad District Co-operative Bank, so there were common business contacts too. Though both Gujaratis, Shah and Patel were contrasting characters. The BJP leader was a 24/7 politician with little time for social gatherings, while the anglicized Patel enjoyed the high life and the company of Delhi's elite circles. Despite being in opposing parties, the duo maintained a regular line of communication.

Interestingly, this was not the first time the idea of a BJP–NCP alliance had been mooted. The NCP had initially backed the Fadnavis-led BJP government in Maharashtra in 2014, but plans for a formal alliance never took off. A second attempt in 2017 also did not fructify. A key behind-the-scenes player on both previous occasions was Gautam Adani, the Ahmedabad-based business magnate who had excellent relations with both Pawar and Prime Minister Modi. The idea of an alliance with Pawar appealed to Modi. 'This government can do with someone of Sharadrao's experience; an alliance will be a good step,' was Modi's positive response. Coincidentally, P.K. Mishra, one of Modi's most trusted bureaucrats in the PMO, had served as agriculture secretary when Pawar was Union agriculture minister in a UPA government. Among the 'informal' proposals on the table was for Pawar's daughter, Supriya, to become a Union minister and for Pawar to head a national statutory body on agriculture with a senior cabinet rank.

While Modi asked Home Minister Shah and the BJP's Maharashtra chief ministerial face Fadnavis to lead the top-secret negotiations, Pawar deputed Ajit Pawar and senior NCP leader Praful Patel to represent him. That Fadnavis was willing to work towards forming a government with the NCP shows how quickly power politics can flip. Right through the 2019 Maharashtra election campaign, he had targeted the Pawar family, promising to prosecute Ajit Pawar for his alleged role in the irrigation scam and to reinvestigate other cases as well. Fadnavis had even boldly claimed that 'time was up' for the ageing Pawar when the BJP successfully wooed several local NCP leaders into switching sides. The ultimate act of 'war', however, was an ED inquiry against Pawar on the eve of the election. 'The BJP wants to finish me politically, but I am ready to face any inquiry,' had been Pawar's uncharacteristically aggressive response while threatening to march to the ED office. But now, after a fortnight of waiting for the Shiv Sena to act, and growing restless to be sworn in as chief minister—a position he believed was rightfully his—Fadnavis agreed to play ball. Meetings were set up in Mumbai and Delhi to work towards a BJP–NCP alliance, away from the media glare. A leading corporate guest house in Delhi was one of the meeting venues.

Meanwhile, with Maharashtra's politics in a state of suspended animation, then Governor Bhagat Singh Koshyari, a former BJP chief minister in Uttarakhand and a staunch RSS man, swung into action. He imposed President's Rule in Maharashtra on 12 November. No party or alliance, he claimed, had been able to prove majority. The governor was accused of working to a script prepared by the Centre to pave the way for a BJP-led government. Governors in the Modi years have been charged with being openly partisan, and the Mumbai seaside Raj Bhavan occupant was no different. 'His only motive behind declaring President's Rule was to give the BJP enough time to cobble up numbers by hook or crook,' claimed Shiv Sena's Raut. The BJP counters this by claiming that President's Rule was actually pushed by the Pawar camp. 'The NCP leaders said that they needed some more time so that Pawar Saheb could travel across Maharashtra and prepare his cadres for a tie-up with us,' claimed a BJP leader.

The announcement of President's Rule put pressure on all parties to break the impasse. The first to blink was the Congress. A delegation of Maharashtra Congress legislators met Sonia Gandhi and told her that the party might break up if the proposal to become part of the government was rejected. 'The BJP has already sent feelers and are promising money and ministerships—we need to decide fast,' warned Ashok Chavan, a former Maharashtra chief minister himself. Sonia consulted her team again. Ahmed Patel suggested that a common minimum programme be worked out between the potential allies. 'The Shiv Sena of Uddhav Thackeray is not the Sena of Bal Thackeray. They will be more accommodative,' he argued. A call was set up between Sonia Gandhi and Uddhav Thackeray, followed by another one between Rahul Gandhi and Aaditya Thackeray—and an in-principle agreement was sealed. After its debacle in the 2019 Lok Sabha polls, the Congress desperately needed to be part of any power-sharing deal in Maharashtra.

When Pawar called on Sonia Gandhi at her 10, Janpath residence, what he heard left him surprised and elated. 'Our party is ready for a tie-up with the Shiv Sena. Ahmed bhai [Ahmed Patel] will discuss the modalities with you,' she informed Pawar. His team of Ajit Pawar and Praful Patel had been closeted with the BJP leadership, discussing possible government formation. But now, Sonia Gandhi had green-signalled an alliance with the Shiv Sena. Pawar instinctively knew what he needed to do. In a BJP-led government, he would never be able to call the shots. In an NCP–Shiv Sena–Congress alliance, he would be kingmaker and the main power centre. 'When you are playing a card game and you suddenly have all the aces in the pack, why will you bet on an uncertain hand?' said a long-time Pawar watcher. This was power politics as high-stakes poker, where every player was gunning for the big prize. Thus was the Maha Vikas Aghadi (MVA) alliance formed between the Congress, Shiv Sena and NCP.

There was one final twist in the tale. With an alliance agreed upon, the chief ministerial choice needed to be settled. This time, Pawar met Uddhav Thackeray again for a one-on-one meeting at another five-star hotel in Mumbai, where Pawar told Thackeray, 'Only you can lead this alliance now. You will have to be the chief minister. No one else will be accepted by all sides.' It took Thackeray a few moments to realize the import of the remark. After all, his father and role model, Bal Thackeray had consciously rejected the lure of office when the Sena–BJP alliance first came to power in Maharashtra in 1995. 'Whoever becomes the chief minister, the remote control will always be with me,' was the Sena supremo's famous one-liner. Bal Thackeray was a tough-talking demagogue whose politics revolved around a combative style, but Uddhav Thackeray, a passionate photographer-turned-politician, was shy and ever-smiling, less inclined to pick up a fight. Now, Pawar was making him an offer his father would have probably rejected outright. 'My hands were shivering when I shook hands with Pawar that day, I had never wanted or expected to be CM,' confessed Thackeray to a friend. BJP leaders in Maharashtra had a different take. 'This is what Uddhav wanted all the time, don't be fooled by his "I am not interested in power" innocent talk,' they maintained.

Much later, when I asked Pawar about the negotiations with the BJP, he admitted that it was only a plan B in case all else failed. Plan A had always been the 'grand alliance' in partnership with the Shiv Sena and the Congress. 'There was no government in place and Maharashtra was heading for President's Rule. So I allowed Ajit and Praful [Patel] to talk to the BJP to see if something came out of it. But I never agreed to the tie-up,' he insisted. It was a masterful—if unethical—double game played by a hardened power politician.

On 20 November, eight days after President's Rule was declared in Maharashtra, Pawar sought a meeting with Prime Minister Modi. The winter session of Parliament had just begun, and the buzz was that Pawar wanted to consult the Prime Minister on issues related to agriculture and the co-operative sector. A memorandum to help 'distressed farmers' in Maharashtra was handed over to the Prime Minister. But this was merely a ruse. The real reason for the meeting was to communicate to the Prime Minister that a BJP–NCP alliance in Maharashtra would not be possible. 'The Prime Minister did feel let down but didn't show it,' claimed a BJP leader. By contrast, Amit Shah was fuming. 'Didn't I tell you that Pawar cannot be trusted? He used us to get the Congress to support the Sena,' Shah told his team. Fadnavis was just as incensed, having been 'robbed' of the chief minister's chair. 'We shook hands and reached a complete agreement with the NCP on all issues, including ministerial portfolios and even who would be the guardian minister for which district. It was all very smooth until we were suddenly ditched by Pawar at the last minute,' he claimed.

'Revenge' was thus in the air when Shah agreed to Fadnavis's last-ditch plan to break the NCP by aligning with Ajit Pawar. 'He doesn't want to go with the Congress,' was Fadnavis's contention. 'Okay, do it, but do it soon,' instructed Shah, eager to teach Pawar a lesson in powerplay. Bhupendra Yadav, then the BJP's national general secretary in charge of Maharashtra and Shah's trusted troubleshooter, was assigned to fly down to Mumbai and open a dialogue with Ajit Pawar. 'A majority of the MLAs will come with me,' promised Ajit, driven by reckless ambition and the expectation that in siding with the BJP, the cases against him would be dropped or watered down. When, on 22 November, Shah was informed that Ajit Pawar had agreed to a deal, the home minister decided to move quickly. Prime Minister Modi was 'apprised' and assured that the BJP had the numbers to stake claim. 'Do it tonight itself, no waiting for the morning. If Pawar comes to know of this plan, he will stop it,' were Shah's clear-cut instructions to Fadnavis. At 12.30 a.m., Governor Koshyari obligingly sent a petition to the Centre to lift President's Rule in Maharashtra. Without any delay, the petition was forwarded to then President Ram Nath Kovind, who gave his assent at 1.30 a.m. No constitutional authority had bothered to check the veracity of Fadnavis's claim to form a majority government or ascertain Ajit Pawar's professed numbers. It was an overnight coup where political skullduggery had triumphed over any letter of the law or constitutional morality.

What Shah, Fadnavis and Ajit had not anticipated was Pawar's ability to control the political chessboard in Mumbai. Having come to terms with his nephew's 'revolt', Pawar quickly connected with all the turncoat NCP MLAs, one by one. Ajit Pawar had an excellent rapport with many MLAs, but he couldn't match his uncle's stature and emotional appeal. One NCP MLA said that Saheb had reminded him of how he had helped his father when his business was collapsing. 'Pawar Saheb has a personal equation with so many MLAs; they are like his family,' insisted Jitendra Awhad, NCP leader and a Saheb loyalist. As the 'rebel' MLAs slowly returned to Saheb, Ajit Pawar found himself isolated. When the Supreme Court intervened, questioning the governor's midnight call and ordering a floor test in the assembly, Fadnavis and Ajit Pawar knew the game was up. Fadnavis resigned on 26 November, barely three days after being sworn in. Ajit Pawar returned to the NCP fold, chastened and defeated. On 28 November 2019, Uddhav Thackeray was sworn in as the chief minister of Maharashtra at the iconic Shivaji Park. He claimed that he had fulfilled his father's ambition of flying a saffron flag over Maharashtra. What went unremarked was that he had achieved the goal by aligning with the very parties his father had steadfastly opposed for much of his career.

Watching this power shift play out on television was an enraged Amit Shah. Ever since he had risen to prominence on the national political stage in 2014, the home minister was eulogized for his 'Chanakyaniti' by media cheerleaders. Maharashtra 2019 was a rare instance of his political strategy stumbling, and it had left him eager for revenge. Over the next few years, vendetta politics would continue to rumble in the state and have a big impact on political equations in 2024. Once considered an oasis of stability, Maharashtra was now entering a period of unimagined chaos driven by bitter politics and conflicting ambitions. The constantly shifting alliances and nifty deal-making only reflected an unscrupulousness that has coarsened politics across the country. Repeated hung assemblies have meant that there are no ideological 'parties with a difference' any longer— only leaders with permanent interests. Even Machiavelli would have found it tough to keep up with Maharashtra's manipulative politicians. In fact, in the past fifty years, Fadnavis is the only Maharashtra chief minister to have completed a full five-year term, when he first took office in 2014. The prize of controlling Mumbai, India's commercial capital, means that the stakes are even higher here.

While a victorious Pawar sat back to revel in his success, Shah turned his attention to another state, one that many in the BJP, including the home minister himself, had been obsessed with for years. The power game swiftly shifted from western India to the east coast. The Bay of Bengal's waters may seem calm on the surface, but its depths are mysterious.

=

West Bengal has special political and emotional resonance for the BJP. Not only does it send the third-largest group of MPs to the Lok Sabha after Maharashtra and Gujarat, which makes it highly significant politically, but it is also the home of the Jana Sangh founder Syama Prasad Mookerjee, a central figure in the Sangh Parivar pantheon. President of the Hindu Mahasabha between 1943 and 1946, Mookerjee was a staunch opponent of the plan to turn a 'united Bengal' into an independent province. Instead, in 1947, he pushed for the partition of Bengal to create a state for Bengali Hindus within the Indian union—a move in which thousands died. Establishing the party's presence in West Bengal was seen by the BJP as a crucial mission to revive and reinvigorate Mookerjee's scarred legacy. Not surprisingly, when Shah first took over as BJP president, 'Mission Bengal' became one of his priorities. Over the next five years, West Bengal was the state he travelled to most often apart from his home base of Gujarat. 'When Amit bhai talks of winning Bengal, there is always a glint in his eye,' a BJP leader from Bengal remarked.

The 2019 Lok Sabha elections provided some hope to the BJP that a 'conquest' of Bengal was not such a far-fetched dream: the BJP won an impressive 18 of the 42 seats, with a 40 per cent vote share. In a state where the BJP's seat tally and vote share had never crossed double digits, this was projected as a breakthrough moment. 'Today we have conquered India, tomorrow it will be Bengal,' Shah promised a group of Bengal BJP leaders who had come to greet him on the general election success.

For TMC leader and West Bengal Chief Minister Mamata Banerjee, however, the 2019 results were a wake-up call. Ever since she had first breached the red citadel in 2011, Banerjee had established herself as Bengal's unquestioned supremo. 'I am not just Bengal's "Didi" but also the "Dada"—everyone is with me,' she joked. Slight yet formidable, the white-sari-clad Mamata Banerjee is one of India's last genuine mass leaders, with an unerring political instinct and sharp foresight. She had swept every election in the state over an eight-year period, between 2011 and 2019, from assemblies to panchayat. Her critics accused her of resorting to strong-arm tactics, misusing the state machinery and empowering local party militias to browbeat any potential rivals. The once-mighty left parties were battered into submission. The BJP, though, was a very different proposition. It had the hunger and resources to challenge Didi's dominance. In 2017, the BJP delivered its first blow when it got Banerjee's right-hand man, Mukul Roy, to switch sides. A strong organizational leader, Roy had played a crucial role in building up the TMC in the state. His departure exposed a chink in Banerjee's armour: in power, and busy with managing the administration, she was slowly becoming disconnected from her second-level leadership. The BJP's 'Jai Shri Ram' war cry was beginning to resonate in parts of Bengal. Taking advantage of the state's sizeable Muslim population, the BJP began to make inroads in areas where it was possible to ignite Hindu–Muslim passions by accusing the chief minister of pandering to minorities. When a poll survey in 2019 showed the BJP gaining ground, a livid Banerjee accused the poll agency and the television channel broadcasting it of having been 'bought' by the BJP. 'They are all being paid by the BJP; they are all agents of Modi–Shah,' she cried. The final results, though, confirmed what the pollsters had warned. The lotus was beginning to bloom in Bengal. For weeks after the 2019 results, Banerjee did not speak to anyone, not even to party colleagues. She locked herself in her Kalighat home-cum-office, struggling to digest the emergence of the BJP as a serious contender for power in Kolkata; her insecurity bordered on paranoia. A former TMC MP recalls how Banerjee sent him an angry WhatsApp text accusing him of being hand-in-glove with the BJP. 'I tried to explain to Didi that she still had won more Lok Sabha seats than the BJP so she did not need to despair. Instead of listening to my viewpoint, she accused me of having a secret "deal" with Amit Shah and blocked my number from her phone.'

Convinced that she was surrounded by 'enemies', Banerjee needed someone she could trust implicitly. Among the few people who had unfettered access to her was her young nephew, her elder brother's son Abhishek Banerjee, a shy-looking, bespectacled youth with an unassuming air. Unlike his aunt, who had fought her way up from the dingy streets of Kalighat, clashing head-on with left cadres in pitched battles, to the highest seat of power in the state, Abhishek had had a relatively cushy landing in politics. An MBA by training, Abhishek had launched a company, Leaps and Bounds Infra Consultants, just ahead of his aunt's 2011 assembly win, which catapulted her to power in the state. Later that year, Abhishek tiptoed into politics, making a low-profile entry while launching a new youth wing of the TMC called 'Yuva'. He was given a ticket to contest from the Diamond Harbour constituency for the 2014 Lok Sabha elections. Riding the Mamata wave, he became one of the youngest ever MPs at twenty-seven. By 2019, he had become much more than just an MP. He was the TMC's organizational point-person, his aunt's eyes and ears and her 'go-to' crisis manager, whom she had come to increasingly rely upon. Mamata Banerjee's growing dependence on her nephew alienated many of the TMC's old guard. It also gave the Opposition a handle to beat the chief minister with. 'This is a pishi–bhaipo (aunt–nephew) government now,' sniggered BJP leader Dilip Ghosh. Shah was even more scathing. 'This is a government of tolabaji, tushtikaran and bhatijakaran (extortion, appeasement and nephewization),' he alleged. Reports of local businessmen being called to meet Abhishek at his swanky apartment complex on Kolkata's Harish Mukherjee Road had been doing the rounds for a while. 'He has amassed immense wealth with properties in Singapore, Bangkok and Dubai,' claimed Ghosh. Abhishek strongly denied all these accusations. 'The BJP only knows how to make allegations; let them prove their absurd charges,' he told me later in a rare interview.

The slew of corruption charges against her nephew disturbed Banerjee initially. While Abhishek, by all accounts, has expensive tastes, the chief minister has made simplicity the cornerstone of her public image, of which she is extremely conscious. 'I am a "simple man"!' is her constant refrain. Even after taking office, she has continued to live in her original home in Kalighat, instead of moving into the official bungalow. The Banerjees are a tightly knit family and fiercely protective of each other. When Abhishek was targeted, Banerjee defended him within the party and outside. Now, when his aunt was being challenged by an ascendant BJP, it was the nephew's turn to stand protectively by her side.

Abhishek suggested that the TMC rope in well-known election strategist Prashant Kishor to combat the BJP as part of its 2021 Mission Bengal. Banerjee had been introduced to Kishor in 2015 by her Rajya Sabha MP Derek O'Brien at the swearing-in of the Nitish Kumar-led government in Bihar. An old-style politician who relied on her connection with the masses, Banerjee wasn't too swayed by the smooth-talking Kishor or his formidable election-management record. 'All these people want too much money for their work. We are not a rich party like the BJP,' she confided in a colleague. The younger, more tech-savvy Abhishek, though, was impressed with what Kishor had achieved with the Modi-led BJP's campaign in 2014 and then with the Nitish Kumar–Lalu

Yadav pitch in Bihar in 2015. 'He is the kind of person we may need one day in Bengal,' he admitted to O'Brien.

The go-getting Kishor was on a high at the time, moving from one electoral success to another. Having built his reputation as an integral member of Team Modi in 2014, he had since worked on many winning campaigns across parties. His career took another turn when, in 2018, Nitish Kumar appointed him the national vice-president of the JD(U) within weeks of his being inducted into the party. Kishor had worked on Nitish's 2015 Bihar re-election campaign and built a personal equation with the Bihar chief minister. 'Because Kishor was not a traditional politician, an otherwise insecure Nitish did not feel threatened by his rise,' said a senior Patna-based journalist.

By the following year, however, the picture was not quite as rosy. Kishor was finding that life as a politician was very different from that of a professional strategist. For many within the party, he was an overambitious upstart who was positioning himself as a potential successor to an ageing chief minister. At one party meeting, a senior JD(U) leader reportedly questioned Kishor's proximity to Kumar. 'Some of us can't meet Nitish ji for weeks, but this man who has never won an election is walking in and out of the chief minister's residence as if he is the de facto chief minister. Who is he to tell us what to do?' Caught in a political tug of war in Bihar, in the lead-up to the 2019 elections, Kishor turned his attention to Andhra Pradesh, where his political consultancy, I-PAC, worked on Jagan Mohan Reddy's successful campaign. Election over, Kishor's organization was on the lookout for a new client to boost their bottom line. This is where the enthusiastic Abhishek Banerjee stepped in. The duo hit it off instantly. 'I was really impressed with Abhishek's willingness to go the extra mile in professionalizing the TMC,' claimed Kishor. Feeling the BJP's heat, Mamata Banerjee gave her approval to her nephew's suggestion to bring the strategist on board. It was a costly multi-crore contract, but Abhishek was able to convince his aunt that the party needed expert advice ahead of the 2021 West Bengal assembly polls.

The TMC was founded in 1998 as a breakaway faction of the Congress. While claiming to espouse the cause of 'regional nationalism', the party essentially revolved around the combative grassroots-leader persona of Mamata Banerjee and her fierce antipathy towards the left government in the state. Banerjee is gutsy, armed with dollops of courage. 'Do you know how many times the police have beaten me with lathis? These veteran Congress leaders only sit in AC rooms in Delhi bungalows. I am the one who is fighting on the streets,' she cribbed. This street-fighter image is what made her the direct beneficiary of the growing disaffection with left rule. Her 'poriborton' (change) war cry became a rallying point for Opposition voices in the state. But having emphatically captured power in a tsunami election in 2011 and then having retained it five years later, Banerjee was accused of failing to rein in her local 'dadas' or strongmen who controlled district politics. Charges of extortion—party 'syndicates' demanding 'cut money' on every deal—were frequent. 'There was no real "poriborton" on the ground in Bengal, only a growing lumpenization and change in the party affiliations of the gang leaders who called the shots,' said Shikha Mukherjee, a veteran Kolkata-based journalist.

'Our first challenge in Bengal was to improve the TMC's image by reconnecting its top leadership in Kolkata with the voters who were unable to air their grievances freely,' revealed Kishor. The strategist had shifted base to Kolkata in 2020, operating either from Abhishek's residence or from a plush suite in a five-star hotel in the city. His I-PAC team of over 100 recruits—many of them young graduates in their twenties—set up office in Salt Lake City. They were tasked with fanning out across the state to get responses from ordinary voters on how they perceived the local Trinamool leadership. The idea would eventually culminate in a statewide Didi ke Bolo (Tell Didi) campaign, where citizens were invited to share their complaints on an online portal or to a specified WhatsApp number that would be directed to the chief minister's secretariat. 'I think the biggest help we got from Prashant's team is that they created an effective feedback mechanism that enabled us to get the party organization back on track,' claimed O'Brien, who was the party's media in-charge. The image reshaping didn't end there. Under Abhishek Banerjee's supervision, local TMC leaders and MLAs were urged to spend a few days every month visiting their constituents and even staying in people's houses to build a rapport with the voters. 'Some of the MLAs didn't like being told what to do by us "outsiders" and even complained to Mamata Banerjee, but the best thing about her was that she gave us a free hand,' recalled Kishor. An ambitious Duare Sarkar (Government at Your Door) programme was launched by the West Bengal government to ensure that benefits of various social welfare schemes were directly delivered to potential beneficiaries. Camps were set up in districts where government officials would explain the benefits of various schemes. 'Mamata Banerjee's government had a number of welfare schemes involving direct cash benefits, especially for women. Duare Sarkar enabled us to ensure that the "cut money" middlemen couldn't deny people their due. It was a game-changer,' claimed a government official.

In January 2021, ahead of the all-important assembly polls scheduled for March, I interviewed Mamata Banerjee for the first time since the 2019 Lok Sabha setback. 'I am giving the BJP an open challenge,' she asserted confidently. 'They can bring whoever they want—Modi ji, Amit Shah ji, Nadda ji—no one can defeat us in Bengal because the people are with us.' The anxiety of 2019 seemed to have given way to renewed self-belief. Interview over, Banerjee asked me to watch a promotional video on her phone: colourful visuals of the chief minister and her rallies were set to a catchy tune. 'It is our election theme song. Do you like it?' she asked. My Bengali isn't very good, but the song's slogan, 'Khela hobe' (The game is on), was unmissable. A young TMC leader, Debangshu Bhattacharya, had composed and uploaded the tune on social media first. 'I wrote it in just twenty minutes before a TMC rally. Didi liked it very much and told me that she was going to make it the party's election anthem,' said Bhattacharya. As I was leaving, Banerjee gave me a thumbs up. 'Khela hobe, Rajdeep ji, khela hobe,' she exclaimed. A few weeks later, Prime Minister Modi would hit back with a counter: 'Khela shesh, Didi (The game is over)!' The battle for Bengal, arguably one of the most fiercely contested and politically charged state elections, was ready for the final countdown.

===

For Amit Shah, the news that Prashant Kishor was handling Mamata Banerjee's campaign was a red rag. Shah and Kishor had fallen out in the aftermath of the BJP's 2014 victory. After all, there was space for only one self-styled election Chanakya in the Prime Minister's core group. The home minister knew he had a challenge on hand but remained optimistic about scripting history in Bengal. His major task was to find a homegrown 'face' to take on the Bengal chief minister's mass appeal. The name at the top of his list of potential contenders was that of former India cricket captain and contemporary Bengali folk hero Sourav Ganguly, or 'Dada', as he is affectionately called. Unlike many of his cricketing peers, Ganguly is a genuinely keen tracker of politics. As a symbol of Bengali pride, he is a much sought-after public figure. Both the left and the TMC had offered to send him to the Rajya Sabha, offers that he had politely declined. 'You know I am happy contributing to cricket in whatever way possible. Plus I have too many other assignments to be tied down in Parliament,' was his explanation. Born into a wealthy family that runs a flourishing printing business, Ganguly lives in a sprawling multi-storey bungalow in Kolkata's Behala area. After retiring from cricket as one of India's most feted captains, Ganguly has had fingers in many lucrative pies. His face continues to be splashed across Kolkata's billboards advertising a range of products. He was the host of a successful Bengali TV quiz show, and he has invested in several companies, including a local football team. As a local Bengali sports journalist told me, 'There are two things that Ganguly has perfected: a cover drive and sensing a business opportunity.'

In 2015, Ganguly became president of the Cricket Association of Bengal with support from the TMC leadership. As a flagbearer of a staunch and confident Bengali identity, Mamata Banerjee was keen to have the state's sporting and film heroes firmly in her tent. Getting Ganguly to switch allegiance publicly wasn't going to be easy, but Amit

Shah had an ace up his sleeve. As a cricketer, Ganguly had had his fair share of run-ins with cricket board officials. Now, Shah was about to offer him the big prize: presidentship of the BCCI. This move, he hoped, would bring Ganguly squarely within the BJP's sphere of influence. 'Is it true that you are angling for the BCCI presidentship and maybe even becoming chief minister of Bengal one day?' I had asked Ganguly during a book release event in Kolkata in 2017. 'This is the problem with you journalists, all mindless speculation. I am happy where I am,' was his testy rejoinder. The 'I-am-not-interested-in-politics' stance was a façade; Ganguly was certainly ambitious and, more crucially, did not appear averse to being part of the BCCI's power axis.

The BCCI elections are marked with intrigue and backroom deals. As part of the deal-making during the October 2019 elections, Ganguly was offered the post of vice president or chairmanship of the Indian Premier League's (IPL) governing council, which he declined. It was widely believed in cricket circles that Brijesh Patel, a former test player from Karnataka, was the preferred choice for president for an influential section of the BCCI, including former board president N. Srinivasan. Congratulatory messages were already pouring in and a press release announcing Patel as the president was being drafted, when there was a sudden, dramatic change in plan. After the board meeting in Mumbai, Ganguly was in his suite at Trident Hotel when his phone began to ring. On the line was Anurag Thakur, Union minister of state for finance and corporate affairs and a former BCCI president himself. 'Dada, I am pleased to inform you that we feel you will be the right person to head the BCCI,' was Thakur's brief message. Ganguly wasn't sure initially if this was a prank or a genuine offer. However, as soon as he accepted, the earlier press release announcing Patel as BCCI president was hastily withdrawn and he was made head of the IPL governing council instead. Ganguly, the captain who had restored Indian cricket's reputation in its darkest hour post the match-fixing controversy, would now helm Indian cricket administration, the first test cricketer to head the sport's most powerful and cash-rich body. His support act as board secretary was the home minister's young son, Jay Shah. The BJP's imprimatur on the cricket board was apparent. So why the last-minute change? The one-word answer: politics. Amit Shah had decided to play the 2021 Bengal election card. Working the phone lines furiously, the home minister used the weight of his office to get key board members like Srinivasan to reluctantly change their minds. Shah's gameplan was simple: first, make Ganguly the BCCI president, then bring him on board as a potential BJP chief minister candidate in the next state elections. 'Just ensure that he is gently reminded that we got him the post,' Shah reportedly told Thakur, who was his point of contact with the members of the BCCI.

On record, all the key stakeholders, including Shah, have denied there was any 'deal' in making Ganguly the board president and insist the BCCI's 'independent' election process had not been compromised. 'Trust me, there was never a quid pro quo; no one ever told me that I would have to give the BJP my support in return for being made the board president,' insisted Ganguly. Whether any 'deal' was spelt out or left unsaid, the BJP leadership was convinced that Ganguly would, at the very least, campaign for them in the 2021 Bengal elections. 'Not everything has to be spoken out loud, but the message within our fold was that Ganguly would be with us at the crucial time,' claimed a Bengal BJP leader. By December 2020, with just a few months left for the Bengal elections, the BJP leadership decided to make its move. Thakur reportedly tried to convince Ganguly to join the BJP. Ganguly felt he was in a bind. The offer was tempting, but he also realized that formally joining a party would mean his reputation as a universally loved Bengali icon would become embroiled in hyper-partisan politics. Besides, his own feedback from speaking to journalist friends was that the battle for Bengal was far from a cakewalk for the BJP. If anything, Mamata Banerjee, with whom he still had a warm personal equation, was in the lead. 'I don't think I am ready for this,' he told Thakur. In January 2021, Home Minister Shah visited Kolkata with the ostensible purpose of overseeing the poll preparations. His real agenda was to try again and get Ganguly to swing in the BJP's direction. But even as Shah was landing in Kolkata, there was a news flash of Ganguly being suddenly admitted to hospital after complaining of chest pain. An angioplasty was performed and a stent was inserted. With blockages being reported in his heart, Ganguly was advised bed rest. Instead of discussing weighty matters around elections, Shah rang up to inquire about the star cricketer's health. When I asked Ganguly if his hospital visit had been an attempt to avoid meeting the home minister, he retorted: 'How can I feign a heart condition? You are again engaging in baseless speculation.'

And yet, despite Ganguly's repeated denials, there were persistent rumours that the cricketer might make a last-minute appearance on a BJP stage. On 7 March 2021, the BJP was set to launch its Bengal campaign with a rally at the Brigade Parade Ground in Kolkata. The Prime Minister himself was slated to address the crowd. 'Don't be surprised if Ganguly lands up there,' a Bengal BJP leader told us on the morning of the rally. News channels were furiously speculating and cameras had lined up outside Ganguly's home. Ganguly was neither picking up my calls nor answering my messages. At 2 p.m., he finally responded: 'How many times do I have to say it: I am not joining politics!' Instead of Ganguly, it was 1980s celluloid superstar Mithun Chakraborty who was introduced to the enthusiastic crowd in the ground. With Mission Ganguly failing, Amit Shah had settled for second best. Chakraborty had met the RSS chief, Mohan Bhagwat, a few days earlier and apparently pledged support to the BJP. In the 1970s, the actor was associated with the Naxalite movement, the armed, ultra-left struggle that had influenced many Bengali youth at the time. In 2014, he had become a TMC Rajya Sabha MP but barely attended Parliament, never asked a single question in the House and resigned in 2016. Now, he was back in the political arc lights, this time claiming to have a 'spiritual connection' with the RSS.

In October 2022, during the election for a new BCCI president, Sourav Ganguly's hopes of being renominated were dashed. In 2019, Shah had needed the star cricketer for his political agenda. Unfortunately, Ganguly hadn't delivered. Now, he was expendable. Ahead of the elections, at a meeting of the BCCI's top brass in the home minister's Delhi residence, former board president Srinivasan declared that he would not support Ganguly again. 'No one has been a two-term board president. Besides, even as board president, he has been advertising products and consulting for IPL teams; there is a clear conflict of interest,' he argued. Nobody contradicted him. Instead it was decided that another former test player and a World Cup winner, Roger Binny, would replace Ganguly as board president. As a sop, Ganguly was offered the IPL chairmanship, a post he politely declined, choosing instead to be a director of cricket with the Delhi Capitals franchise. While Ganguly was out, Jay Shah, still in his early thirties, would continue as the all-powerful board secretary. He was, after all, the home minister's son and the administrator who enjoyed undiluted power and patronage. In the cricket board, like in national politics, there are no permanent friends or enemies, only permanent interests.

=

'Didi, O Didi.'

A three-word taunt that Prime Minister Modi aimed at Mamata Banerjee through the last stretch of his high-decibel 2021 Bengal campaign, but which eventually returned to haunt him. Many political observers saw it as a misogynistic catcall, a leering, mocking slur against a veteran woman leader, unbefitting the Prime Minister of the country. But it was part of a conscious BJP strategy to get under Mamata Banerjee's skin, make her respond angrily and turn the state-level election into a battle between the Prime Minister of the country and a chief minister. 'Once Sourav Ganguly refused to join the election battle, we had very few options left; it had to be PM versus CM,' confessed a BJP strategist. The volatile Banerjee has a reputation for flying into a rage when provoked. In the 2019 election campaign, BJP workers were urged to disrupt her rallies and roadshows with chants of 'Jai Shri Ram'. A video of her getting out of a car and confronting sloganeers chanting 'Jai Shri Ram' had gone viral in 2019 and given the BJP an opportunity to portray Banerjee as being 'anti-Hindu'. This time, her team was much more careful. As Kishor would tell me later, 'Our biggest challenge in Bengal was to ensure we didn't make any major mistakes. Keeping Didi calm in the face of the constant attacks on her was crucial.' Instead of getting riled up, the TMC strategists cleverly framed the Prime Minister's heckling of their leader as gender injustice as well as the victimization of Bengalis. Regional pride was invoked: 'Bangla nijer meye kei chaye' (Bengal wants its daughter) was the response. Modi and Shah were branded as 'outsiders' from Gujarat, while the TMC was projected as a party upholding Bengali pride, a torchbearer of Bengali culture, fighting for Bengali sub-nationalism against an arrogant New Delhi, a party that would protect the state's interests. Bengal versus Delhi is a narrative that has gained political currency over the years; the left had used it repeatedly when it ruled the state. 'It isn't as if the Prime Minister had something against Mamata Banerjee; it is just that when you are in the heat of an election campaign, a few harsh things will be said about your opponent,' claimed Kailash Vijayvargiya, the BJP leader in charge of the Bengal campaign.

The Modi–Shah duo, though, is not the kind to give up easily. Despite Covid warnings, Modi continued to campaign aggressively and relentlessly in Bengal till ECI protocols forced him to back off in the final leg of an elongated eight-phase campaign. He was driven by more than a desire to win the election: there were festering wounds from the past that dogged the Modi-versus-Didi confrontation. In 2002, when Banerjee was an ally in the BJP-led Vajpayee government, she had joined the chorus for Modi to be sacked as Gujarat chief minister in the aftermath of the communal violence. 'The Prime Minister doesn't forget or forgive easily. He wasn't going to let Didi defeat him easily,' admitted a senior BJP leader. Shah, who despite being the country's home minister was now spending more time in Bengal than anywhere else, hadn't given up the fight either. In December 2020, he succeeded in getting Suvendu Adhikari, a trusted aide of Banerjee, to switch sides. Adhikari was the TMC's strongman from East Medinipur and had played an important role during the 2007 Nandigram land agitation, which catapulted Banerjee to power in the state. But as the TMC's youth-wing chief, he came into conflict with Abhishek Banerjee, who had set up his own parallel youth outfit within the organization. The chief minister's patronage of her nephew meant that Adhikari found himself on the wrong side of a power struggle within the party's next-gen leadership. A senior journalist narrated witnessing how, during one of her rare visits to Delhi, while greeting the TMC MPs, including her nephew, in Parliament's Central Hall, Banerjee made it a point to tell Adhikari, who was accompanying her, to organize tea for everyone. 'When Didi wants to send a message, she doesn't make eye contact and asks you to make tea instead,' laughed a TMC MP. While the grim-faced Adhikari didn't have Ganguly's star appeal, he was still considered a prize catch by the BJP. Shah proposed that he fight from Nandigram, the Adhikari family citadel, in an attempt to send a tough message to the Banerjee camp. Adhikari had won the seat in the 2016 assembly elections by a whopping 80,000 votes. 'When we heard that the BJP was putting up Adhikari as their candidate, we felt that Mamata must take up the challenge and also contest from there. A true leader has to be seen as unafraid,' remarked Kishor. Banerjee would lose the Nandigram battle, but she won the war.

Apart from individual battles, what Amit Shah had really counted on was religious polarization in a state where the Muslim population is more than 30 per cent. In the 2019 general elections, the BJP's rise was driven by charges of 'Muslim appeasement' against the chief minister. The campaign was especially effective in Dalit- and Adivasi-dominated areas, where the BJP's vote share had shown sharp growth. Branding her as a pro-Islamist 'Jihadi Didi', the BJP IT cell shared images across WhatsApp groups of Banerjee offering namaz against the backdrop of Islamic motifs. At the time, Mamata Banerjee had responded irately to the 'pro-Muslim' tag, but now she kickstarted her campaign in Nandigram by flawlessly reciting shlokas from the Hindu Chandipath. 'I am a Hindu woman too. Don't play the Hindu card with me. Tell me, do you know how to be a good Hindu?' she retorted. The BJP's rabble-rousing attacks on Banerjee's politics had already consolidated the Muslim vote firmly behind her. Now she was reaching out to Hindu voters too, especially women, the main beneficiaries of her targeted welfare programmes. 'When you are assured of a majority vote of a large minority, you only need to make sure that the majority community isn't alienated and a sizeable enough section will still vote for you,' contended Kishor. With an overwhelming vote among Muslims, increased vote share among poorer Dalit and Adivasi groups and the staunch support of women voters, Didi was firmly on track to beat back the BJP juggernaut.

On 10 March 2021, in the middle of Banerjee's campaign in Nandigram, there was a sudden news flash: 'Mamata Banerjee injured, rushed to hospital'. Her foot was hurt as the car door slammed on it while she was waving to the gathered crowds. 'This is a conspiracy to kill her; a few unknown people pushed her into the car,' TMC MP Sukhendu Sekhar Roy, who was accompanying her, was caught shouting. The video footage seemed to suggest that the incident was perhaps an accident, the result of the car door striking a pole along an overcrowded lane. Hours later, images of Banerjee in hospital, looking visibly distressed, with her foot in plaster, were splashed across the internet. The X-ray report showed a fracture in her left ankle. Three days later, Banerjee emerged from the hospital in a wheelchair. 'I will campaign across Bengal with my broken leg and in a wheelchair,' she promised. Then she added for good effect, 'Khela hobe!' Months later, when I asked her if the wheelchair was aimed to garner voter sympathy, she looked genuinely offended. 'Please see my left ankle—it is still swollen,' she replied. She emphasized that she would have preferred walking and meeting people to addressing gatherings from her wheelchair. 'Do you know I walk 30,000 steps at top speed every day and keep a count on my smartwatch? Why would someone like me use a wheelchair unless I had no option?' she argued. Whether by accident or design, a lone determined woman in her trademark white sari and rubber chappals in a wheelchair became the defining image of the 2021 Bengal election campaign.

Though the tide appeared to be turning in the TMC leader's favour, Amit Shah remained convinced that the BJP's formidable machine would win in the end. In early April, I met the home minister at a Kolkata hotel soon after a press conference where he had boldly claimed that the party would win more than 200 seats in the 294-member assembly. 'What makes you so sure? The women and minorities votes still seem to be with Mamata,' I pointed out. The home minister replied in his typically combative manner: 'You spend too much time with pollsters in the studio. Zameen par aaiye, asal parivartan ho raha hai (Come on the ground, real change is taking place)!' I promised to exchange notes with the home minister after the results.

When the West Bengal results were declared on 5 May, one party did get over 200 seats, but it wasn't the BJP. The TMC won a standout 215 seats, completing a hat-trick of wins in the state. The BJP won 77 seats, its best-ever performance by some distance but nowhere close to what a super confident Shah had claimed just weeks earlier. Didi had won her do-or-die 'khela', perhaps even more convincingly than she herself might have expected. Interestingly, this was the biggest blow the Modi–Shah duo had suffered in a major state election since Bihar 2015. 'The aura of media-created invincibility is over. Now you decide who is the real Chanakya!' a buoyant Kishor, who had played a vital role in the TMC's campaign strategy, declared.

First, checkmated by 'Saheb' in Maharashtra, and now, trounced by 'Didi' in West Bengal. It was apparent that state-level contests in India were a completely different ballgame compared to a national election. Veteran, rooted local chieftains like Sharad Pawar and Mamata Banerjee had demonstrated that they could tap into powerful regional sentiments and their own wide, well-established networks to beat back a rampaging force like the BJP machine. When confronted with an existential threat, regional parties could marshal their energies in do-or-die battles, harnessing to themselves the incredibly powerful plank of local identity, local dignity and local culture. The roots of a federalized multi-party system run deep in Indian soil, and humiliating or mocking popular local leaders only results in the voters' disapproval. It was a trend that would continue into the 2024 electoral battle, making single-party dominance an unrealized goal. The Maharashtra and Bengal setbacks meant that the Modi–Shah duo desperately needed to get the BJP election machine back on track. The ultimate battleground was now more critical than ever in this volatile game of thrones: Uttar Pradesh.

SIX

'UPYOGI' in Saffron:
The Bulldozer Mandate

NO Prime Minister in India has been quite as paranoid about having a negative image in the media as Narendra Modi. He is a dedicated follower of TV news and an obsessive tracker of social media trends. A critic once called the Modi government 'of Twitter, by Twitter and for Twitter'. In mid-May 2021, during the deadly second wave of Covid, Modi was aghast to see live images of three bodies being pulled out of the Ganga in his home constituency of Varanasi on a leading Hindi news channel. The headline screamed: 'Bihar se lekar Uttar Pradesh tak, Ganga mein laashein hi laashein (From Bihar to Uttar Pradesh, there are only corpses in the Ganga)'. The people who were being interviewed blamed both the state government and the Centre. 'Yahan koi vyavastha nahi hai, na Yogi ji ki na Modi ji ki. Hum shav bahane ke liye majboor hai (There is no arrangement here by either the Yogi government or the Modi government. We are forced to throw the bodies in the river),' wailed a young man who had just dumped his elderly father's body in the flowing river.

The explicit images of the Covid calamity on screen reportedly incensed the Prime Minister. 'You had told me the situation is under control. What is this happening in Varanasi?' he demanded. 'When Modi ji is angry, he doesn't say much. His tone and a few words are enough for us to know that Pradhan Mantri ji gusse mein hain,' remarked an official. The Prime Minister's ever-alert media team and information and broadcasting officials were already connecting with several news channel editors and asking them to avoid telecasting pictures of dead bodies. 'This is a very sensitive issue that is against the broadcasting code. You cannot just show dead bodies like this. Do you want your licence to be suspended?' an editor was warned by a ministry official.

Sitting in his Lucknow residence, Chief Minister Yogi Adityanath too was watching the grisly pictures of bodies floating down the river. Like the Prime Minister, Adityanath is also intensely conscious of his media image. Ever since his unanticipated ascent to power in 2017, he has allowed very little bad news about his government to filter out. Strict rules are in place for 'managing' the media narrative. Anyone who questions the official version of news events risks inviting the wrath of the state machinery. District administration officials are issued specific instructions to keep track of and investigate 'negative' news stories and seek explanations for 'false' narratives that 'tarnish' the image of the Yogi government. Several journalists have had FIRs filed against them by the state government for critical reporting.

In 2019, a journalist who recorded a video of schoolchildren being served salt and roti as a midday meal in a government-run school in Mirzapur was accused of 'conspiring' to malign the state government. A case was instantly registered. In 2020, a reporter for a Kanpur-based newspaper who had exposed the sand mafia and land grabbers was shot dead while he was returning home with a friend on a motorcycle. The same year, an FIR was registered against independent digital news portal Scroll's executive editor, Supriya Sharma, for a report that said people in the Prime Minister's adopted village in Varanasi were facing hunger during the Covid-19 lockdown. A report published by the Committee against Assault on Journalists claims that 138 cases were registered against journalists in 'Yogi raj' between 2017 and February 2022, 48 journalists were physically assaulted and 66 were booked or arrested; 78 per cent of these cases were recorded during the pandemic in 2020 and 2021.

Controlling the information and propaganda machine on behalf of the Yogi government during the crucial pandemic period was Navneet Sehgal, a 1988-batch IAS officer. Like any successful babu in the Uttar Pradesh administration, the imposing suit-clad Sehgal had mastered the craft of dexterously moving from serving one government to the next. He had worked closely with Mayawati when the Bahujan Samaj Party (BSP) leader was chief minister, then became a key member of Akhilesh Yadav's office and was now in charge of the information department in the Yogi government. 'Yeh kya ho raha hai, Sehgal ji? Isse band karvaiye (What is happening, Sehgal? Put a stop to it)!' was the chief minister's clear-cut instruction to his principal troubleshooter even as the images of dead bodies floating in the Ganga went viral.

For Sehgal, this was yet another challenge. The chief minister wanted him to make sure, in a blatant act of censorship, that stories of Covid miseries didn't get out to the wider world. Typically, Sehgal contacted newspaper and channel editors and owners in Lucknow and Delhi with a direct missive: 'Stop showing dead bodies. You are needlessly sensationalizing the story. If you go on like this, we will have to act.' Sehgal, now Prasar Bharati chairman, denies pressurizing anyone. 'I was only pointing out that these water burials are an age-old tradition in parts of UP; why link it to Covid?' he said, bland and disingenuous. A news editor in Lucknow recalled being warned by an official that 'negative' reporting would mean no government advertising support in the run-up to the state assembly elections.

Elections indeed were on top of everyone's mind. Uttar Pradesh was going to the polls in early 2022 and, from a political viewpoint, the deadly second wave of Covid couldn't have been more ill-timed. For the BJP, Uttar Pradesh was a fortress that they could not afford to surrender, even if battered by a virus. No chief minister in the state had been re-elected since N.D. Tiwari in 1985 and none after serving a full five-year term since Independence. While Yogi and the BJP were taking on history, Prime Minister Modi had a more immediate objective: to ensure that his relentlessly cultivated image as a governance guru was not affected by the negative publicity over Covid 2.0. Varanasi, Modi's 'karmabhoomi', was now the epicentre of the floating dead bodies and the subject of concentrated media coverage, which for once wasn't quite the treacle-laden, gushing, rah-rah propaganda the government was used to. Nevertheless, the media narrative would be managed with a few phone calls, but bringing the ground situation under control would require greater focus.

In this moment of crisis, the Prime Minister turned to his trusted aide Arvind Kumar Sharma, a bureaucrat-turned-politician. A 1988-batch Gujarat cadre officer, Sharma had worked closely with Modi in both Gandhinagar and Delhi. He was part of the Prime Minister's core team, an unassuming, hard-working officer, very good at project implementation, just the kind of quietly efficient, unquestioning bureaucratic figure Modi likes having around him. In January 2021, Sharma took voluntary retirement from the civil services, but just three days later he joined the BJP, exchanging his government attire for a saffron topi. Within a week, he was the party's nominated candidate for the Uttar Pradesh legislative council election and then appointed the BJP's state vice president, sparking speculation over his future role in the Yogi government. Was he going to Uttar Pradesh as the Prime Minister's eyes and ears or was he there to impose checks on the Yogi government? When he was initially asked the question, Sharma had seemed a trifle embarrassed. 'I am here to work for the people as desired by the Prime Minister; please do not speculate,' was his uncomfortable response. Now, in June 2021, as Covid numbers began to mount—the official death toll in Uttar Pradesh had crossed 20,000 by the end of May—Sharma was summoned by the Prime Minister and given a well-defined role: to ensure that the alarming situation in Varanasi was brought under control.

The decision to make Sharma the man in charge of Covid management in Varanasi and its neighbouring districts was taken by the PMO without consulting the Yogi government; it was simply 'informed'. 'It wasn't as if the Centre and state were working at cross-purposes; we just wanted to ensure that the best person was given responsibility for what was clearly a distressing state of affairs that needed urgent attention. Yogi ji was in charge in Lucknow, but Varanasi is, after all, the Prime Minister's home constituency,' was how a senior government official explained the decision. The domineering Modi never likes to cede control of decision-making. When he sets his mind on something, he wants it done at once and at any cost.

On taking charge in Varanasi, Sharma immediately got cracking. The area was facing a familiar problem: an acute shortage of ventilators and oxygen cylinders. Having a prime ministerial mandate made a big difference. When an Aurangabad-based agency pleaded helplessness upon being informed of the pressing need for an oxygen-generating plant and cited backed-up orders from across the country, it was sternly told: 'This is not just another order; this is for the Prime Minister's constituency.' The next day, the oxygen plant machine was on its way, bringing significant relief to the main government hospital in Varanasi. Ventilators and oxygen cylinders too were sourced from different parts of the country, with Gujarat pitching in with 400 cylinders. With a round-the-clock Covid response centre in place, Sharma and his team were able to quickly fill the gaps in the system and bring a measure of control to the spiralling crisis in the city.

For Yogi Adityanath, though, the prime ministerial intervention in Varanasi seemed like a vote of no confidence in his government's management of the pandemic. In a sprawling state, Covid had exposed the government's limited hospital and primary health infrastructure. A fiercely contested panchayat election in March–April 2021 had only ended up facilitating the spread of the virus—teachers on poll duty were among the early casualties. The Haridwar Kumbh Mela, unwisely allowed to proceed in neighbouring Uttarakhand in April, had also become a superspreader. Still the government kept insisting that there was nothing to worry about. In fact, the chief minister himself tested positive for Covid, and then the next day, on 15 April, he tweeted from his official handle: 'There is no need to worry about Covid, the Uttar

Pradesh government is with you.' It was a statement divorced from the grim ground reality. Most of Uttar Pradesh's hospitals were overrun with patients and, with a growing shortage of beds and oxygen, struggling to ensure basic Covid treatment. The situation in rural Uttar Pradesh was worse. Families were not provided basic Covid-testing facilities in many districts. Many of the deaths were not even registered as being related to Covid-19. And yet, right through these calamitous weeks, the chief minister kept up his buoyant 'all is well' messaging, almost as if he were living in an alternate universe. Denying truths, avoiding reality and, instead, disseminating feel-good propaganda on an industrial scale was par for the course for a government in denial.

But the images of the bodies floating in the Ganga were the ultimate wake-up call. Did the Modi government think at any stage about replacing the chief minister during the second Covid wave? It's a direct question I posed to a senior BJP leader from Uttar Pradesh. 'I know that Modi ji was not happy initially with the response of the Uttar Pradesh government, but I don't think there was any plan to change the chief minister. It wasn't as if this was the only state that was suffering because of Covid. You replace one chief minister, you will have to hold others accountable too,' was the defensive answer I got. And yet, because of its overwhelming political relevance, Uttar Pradesh was like no other state on the national map: its prized 80 Lok Sabha seats are key for the BJP's position in New Delhi. Nor was Yogi Adityanath just another BJP chief minister. In the few years that he had been in power, the rabble-rousing, diminutive prelate in saffron robes with his ear jewels and shaven head had already established himself as a recognizable Hindutva figure for the BJP rank and file. In election campaigns across the country, Yogi Adityanath, with his aura of saffron zealotry, was the biggest crowd puller for the BJP apart from the Prime Minister himself. 'When we prepared any campaign schedule anywhere in the country, candidates would demand at least one Yogi rally,' a BJP election strategist revealed.

The question 'After Modi, who?' was periodically blowing in the wind, with speculative reports suggesting that Home Minister Shah saw the

1972-born Yogi, over a decade younger than him, as a future competitor for the top post. Was Gujarat's jodi No. 1 looking to cut Yogi down to size ahead of the crucial 2022 Uttar Pradesh election? It was an unanswered question that would return to haunt the BJP in its 2024 general election campaign too.

On 21 November 2021, with Covid fatalities finally under control and the delayed vaccination drive having taken off, a photograph of the Prime Minister and the Uttar Pradesh chief minister walking side by side, with Modi's arm on Yogi Adityanath's shoulder, was tweeted by the latter. 'Hum nikal pade hai pran karke / Apna tan-man arpan karke / Zid hai ek surya ugana hai / Ambar se ooncha jana hai / Ek Bharat naya banana hai (We have set out with a vow, pledging our body and mind. We are determined to create a new sun and go further than the skies to build a new India).' More than these words, it was the picture-perfect photo that spoke volumes. The Prime Minister and the chief minister were on the same page for Mission Uttar Pradesh: one, the national emblem of the BJP's rise, and the other, its Uttar Pradesh mascot. It was, as the BJP propaganda machine would repeatedly emphasize, a 'double engine', a dig at states not led by a BJP chief minister and that, presumably, were only single engine.

Just weeks later, in December 2021, while addressing a rally after laying the foundation stone of a 594-kilometre-long Ganga Expressway in Uttar Pradesh's Shahjahanpur, Prime Minister Modi coined a new phrase: 'Uttar Pradesh plus Yogi bahut hai UPYOGI' (Uttar Pradesh plus Yogi is very useful). It seemed almost as if the chaos and deaths caused by Covid had become a fading memory. Political optics were being artfully constructed around the chief minister's being a 'man of action', someone who was 'eliminating mafias' and transforming Uttar Pradesh into an idyllic state of Hindutva machismo and cleverly photographed infrastructure development. The Uttar Pradesh 2022 election template had been set.

⚌

Barely a week into his chief ministership in March 2017, Yogi Adityanath had called a meeting of the state's senior police officers. Most of them were meeting the new chief minister for the first time, and as the agenda had not been spelt out, they were visibly nervous, unsure of what to expect. A stern-looking Adityanath looked around the room impassively and firmly demanded, 'Mujhe agle hafte mein Uttar Pradesh ke sabhi gang aur unke gang leaders ki list chahiye (Within the next week, I want a list of Uttar Pradesh's gangs and gang leaders).' For a few moments, there was silence, until the chief minister thumped the table with his fist: 'Sabhi gangsters ko message clear hona chahiye: Yogi ki sarkar mein koi baksha nahi jayega. Zero tolerance (The message must be clear to all gangsters: no one will be spared in the Yogi government)!'

An officer present at the meeting recalled how the chief minister's harsh tone had alarmed many of his colleagues. 'One of us did raise concerns over possible police excesses, but he was promptly shut down with a warning not to go against orders. We knew that very day that we were dealing with a very different chief minister, someone who wasn't going to play by conventional rules.' Nor was Adityanath afraid of airing his contentious views in public. In an interview on *Aap Ki Adalat* in June 2017, the chief minister uttered a bellicose warning usually heard from streetside toughs rather than constitutional authorities: 'Agar apradh karenge, toh thok diye jayenge (If they commit crimes, we will knock them down).' This 'thok denge' attitude of the chief minister was seen as giving the Uttar Pradesh constabulary a virtual 'licence to kill'. In the first year itself, a poster released by the chief minister's office claimed that 1,038 encounters had taken place in which thirty-two people were killed and 238 injured. An investigative report in *The Indian Express* pointed out that between 2017 and 2023, Uttar Pradesh witnessed 186 'encounter killings' (killings by security agencies outside the judicial process, which should be abhorrent in a democracy), which worked out to more than one alleged criminal being killed by the police every fifteen days. When it came to police firing to injure, the number went up to as high as 5,046—more than thirty alleged criminals being shot at and injured every fifteen days. Most of these 'encounter deaths' went unquestioned and unchallenged. Routine magisterial inquiries were completed and disposed of, without any objections being raised. 'Encounters have been "normalized" in Uttar Pradesh under the Yogi government; the entire criminal justice system is being short-circuited,' senior lawyer Sanjay Hegde pointed out.

The numbers don't tell the full story. A significant number of 'encounters' occurred in western Uttar Pradesh, in districts like Meerut, Muzaffarnagar, Saharanpur and Baghpat—areas with a large Muslim population. Unsurprisingly many of the 'gangsters' killed in these parts were Muslim. Uttar Pradesh's gangs are often organized along sharp caste and community lines. Blood-soaked rivalries reflect the social fault lines and political affiliations of the gang leaders. The best example is in Adityanath's own constituency of Gorakhpur, where clashes between two rival groups led by gangster-turned-politicians Hari Shankar Tiwari and Virendra Pratap Shahi—one a Brahmin, the other a Thakur—killed dozens of people and scarred eastern Uttar Pradesh's politics through the 1980s and '90s. 'In Uttar Pradesh, you often have to see gang wars through the prism of caste and community because many gang leaders see themselves as protectors of their caste and community interests first,' a veteran police officer revealed. Two of eastern Uttar Pradesh's prominent gangster–politicians, Atiq Ahmed and Mukhtar Ansari, were routinely branded 'Muslim' dons even though their support base extended beyond the community. Ahmed was shot dead by three assailants outside a government hospital in Prayagraj in April 2023 when he was being taken for a medical examination by the police. The killing was captured on live television. An unfazed Yogi called it 'the end of mafia raj'.

Yogi Adityanath was born Ajay Mohan Singh Bisht in a remote village in Uttarakhand in 1972. His life changed in 1993, at the peak of the Ram Janmbhoomi movement, when he went to Gorakhpur to visit the Gorakhnath temple and got the chance to meet Mahant Avaidyanath, the head priest and one of the most vociferous supporters of a Ram temple in Ayodhya. Avaidyanath convinced the young Ram bhakt that he was a 'born Yogi' and declared him his heir apparent in 1998. That year Yogi Adityanath was also named the BJP's Lok Sabha candidate from Gorakhpur in place of his mentor. Sharat Pradhan, senior journalist and author of a biography on Yogi Adityanath, points out that while the Gorakhdham peeth claims to stand for an egalitarian order in which all communities, including local Muslims, are accommodated, political Hindutva in the 1990s spurred the young Adityanath to carve out a distinct identity for himself as an anti-Muslim, rabble-rousing leader. 'As a religious mobilizer, Yogi Adityanath can claim to do social and spiritual work across communities, but as a politician, he is an unapologetic, hardline Hindu zealot who wears his religion on his sleeve,' analyses Pradhan.

In his formative years as a politician, Adityanath created a Gau Raksha Manch, or a cow protection group, that soon transformed into the Hindu Yuva Vahini (HYV), a militant Hindu vigilante outfit that consciously stoked anti-Muslim communal discord. In 1999, activists of HYV entered a Muslim-dominated village in Maharajganj in a fleet of cars, where they were accused of inciting Hindus and digging up graves. When Adityanath's fleet was obstructed by a group of Samajwadi Party workers who were protesting against the BJP government in the state, the protestors were allegedly beaten up and fired upon, and one person died. A case was registered against Adityanath for murder, trespassing a Muslim graveyard, defiling a place of worship, rioting and promoting enmity between communities. The murder charge was eventually dismissed by an Allahabad High Court's special court for MPs and MLAs in 2019. Pradhan says, 'From that moment in Maharajganj, a militant Hindu demagogue was born.'

Over the next decade, the HYV was frequently involved in communal flare-ups in and around Gorakhpur. Adityanath's role in inciting mob violence often came under the scanner. In one particularly inflammatory speech in 2005, Adityanath can be heard threatening: 'Agar ek Hindu ka khoon bahega, kam se kam dus aise logon ki hatya karvayenge (If even one Hindu is killed, we will kill at least ten of them).' While declaring that he wouldn't allow any 'tazia' procession in the Gorakhpur district, he exhorted his followers to 'use them to burn Holi in celebration'. Adityanath's militia, a private saffron army, was on the march, often storming into Hindu–Muslim marriages, claiming that they were acts of 'love jihad', a term that Adityanath would routinely use in his speeches to target interfaith marriages. His malevolent supporters would threaten anyone who transported or stored meat, accusing them of cow slaughter.

Once installed as chief minister, Adityanath was keen to live down his past as an HYV militia chief and be seen as uniformly tough on law and order. 'We were given instructions to arrest any leader, Hindu or Muslim, who took the law into their hands. In that sense, the chief minister wasn't playing favourites or asking us to discriminate between communities,' insisted an Uttar Pradesh police officer. And yet, the perception was growing that the 'war' against criminal mafias was a euphemism for a war against Muslims. 'Look, you can't spend decades spewing venom against Muslims and attacking them and then suddenly claim to be enforcing rule of law equally. Like it or not, Muslims felt hounded,' said Rashid Ahmed (name changed on request), a Meerut-based social worker. Ahmed points to one of the first decisions taken by the Yogi government: ordering the closure of 'illegal' slaughterhouses. This was a clear example of discriminatory politics. 'Yogi will never touch any unlawful businesses of his Thakur caste, but the moment it is a Muslim who is involved in supposed illegality, the police will act with total impunity. Even butchers who had run their meat businesses for years were targeted and rendered unemployed overnight,' he said.

A fervid Yogi Adityanath was unfazed by the criticism. In 2018, a civil society group working mainly in the Muslim neighbourhoods of western Uttar Pradesh put together a detailed report of alleged excesses by the police against local Muslims and sought an appointment with the chief minister through a senior government officer. After much persuasion, the officer agreed to take their case to the chief minister's office. For weeks there was no response. When the officer broached the issue with a bureaucrat close to the chief minister, he was told not to pursue the issue any further.

This unashamedly divisive, 'political Hindu' worldview, where Muslims were either demonized or rendered invisible, was projected by

Adityanath in the run-up to the 2022 elections. When asked at a media conclave how he would counter the Opposition's charge that the chief minister was promoting 'Thakur raj' even at the cost of antagonizing the BJP's Brahmin leadership, the response was immediate: 'Yeh ladai usse bahut aage ja chuki hai. Yeh ladai assi banam bees ki ho chuki hai (This fight has already moved ahead from there. It has become a fight of eighty versus twenty).' The reference was hardly subtle: Muslims accounted for 19–20 per cent of Uttar Pradesh's population. The chief minister, who had sworn an oath on the Constitution, was pointing out that the 'real' battle was not between Brahmins and Thakurs; he was vowing a religious war between majority Hindus and minority Muslims.

Barely twenty-four hours after making the controversial remark, and amidst loud protests from Opposition leaders who accused Adityanath of playing blatant communal vote-bank politics, the chief minister was at it again. Asked to explain his 'eighty versus twenty' comment, Adityanath refused to back down. 'Eighty versus twenty is a reality. The 20 per cent are those people who oppose Ram Janmbhoomi, Kashi Vishwanath Dham, the development of Mathura–Vrindavan ... those who sympathize with mafias and terrorists.' It was an atrocious attempt at stirring the communal pot and consolidating the Hindu vote bank. A month later, just ahead of the second phase of polling in Uttar Pradesh, Adityanath claimed that his remarks were not made in the context of religion or caste. 'I said 80 per cent are with the BJP and 20 per cent always oppose us and will do so this time too. This 20 per cent includes those who oppose vaccines, women's security, welfare schemes for the poor, highways, medical colleges and so on. I didn't mention religion or caste anywhere,' he clarified. It was cunning dog-whistle politics. First underscore your fanatical 'political Hindu' credentials unapologetically to set the narrative and then expressionlessly deflect any criticism by claiming you were speaking in generic terms.

Unlike the BJP politicians of a previous era, Adityanath clearly appeared unbothered with any constitutional norms whatsoever, nor did he seem to fear that the ECI might crack down on his viciously incendiary rhetoric. His politics was rooted in the post-Babri demolition era, a period when Muslim-bashing was gradually being normalized and when the idea of a saffron-robed Hindu agitator–monk leading India's most populous state was no longer seen as undermining a secular republic. The sant-sadhu samaj had joined the Ram Janmbhoomi chorus in the 1980s and '90s. Then, the 'trishul' (trident) became a familiar religious symbol of a new-found Hindutva aggression. Now, having made the transition to the chief minister's office, Adityanath found his own defining weapon to represent his style of governance: the bulldozer.

The first time Adityanath used the word 'bulldozer' in the public domain was in September 2017, when he warned that he would bulldoze the properties of those involved in crime. It was, however, in early 2020 that the bulldozer was 'weaponized', not to target criminal gangs but to spread fear among anti-CAA protestors, most of whom were Muslims. The protestors had clashed with the police in many places, leading to arson and rioting. The Yogi government responded by putting up banners in Lucknow with photographs, names and addresses of those accused of vandalism during the protests, part of a 'name and shame' policy. Notices were issued to them seeking compensation for damages with a warning that their property would be confiscated if the fine was not paid. The threat of a bulldozer razing the homes of the accused was the final step. 'It was crazy,' raged Sadaf Jafar, a Lucknow-based politician–activist who would later contest the 2022 elections on a Congress ticket. 'We were being treated as criminals in a trial not being conducted in a court of law but in Yogi raj, where only one man's diktat mattered.'

When the Supreme Court stepped in and directed the state to refund the money recovered from the anti-CAA protestors, the Uttar Pradesh government went ahead and passed a law that would allow them to legally confiscate properties as damages. In this rough-and-ready system of 'bulldozer justice', the Yogi government defended its actions by claiming it was only enforcing law and order. 'The chief minister has given strict instructions that we are only to use bulldozers against criminal elements and the mafia,' claimed Prashant Kumar, then assistant director general of police (law and order) and the key officer in charge of the bulldozer drive. In 2020, the property of criminals like Vikas Dubey, whose gang had killed eight policemen in a shoot-out, was razed.

However, the line between hardened criminals and protestors was blurred. In stone-pelting incidents across Uttar Pradesh in June 2022 over a BJP leader's inflammatory remarks on the Prophet, the properties of the alleged 'masterminds' behind the protests were swiftly demolished. The chief minister's media advisor, Mrityunjay Kumar, tweeted a picture of a bulldozer with a shockingly prejudiced post: 'Remember, every Friday is followed by a Saturday.' Haryana BJP IT–in-charge Arun Yadav tweeted: 'Friday being stone day, Saturday should be declared as bulldozer day!' The bulldozer demolitions led the Opposition to lampoon Adityanath with the moniker 'Bulldozer Baba'. Once again, the Supreme Court intervened, not to stop the bulldozer from rolling on but to diffidently caution that 'demolitions have to be in accordance with law and they cannot be retaliatory'.

But travelling through the mohallas and by-lanes of a sprawling state during the 2022 campaign, it was apparent that the demolition drive had struck a chord with voters. In a state where the previous Akhilesh Yadav-led Samajwadi Party government had been accused of going 'soft' on criminals and 'appeasing' Muslims, Adityanath had pitched himself as a muscular leader of a 'strong' law-and-order state, a Hindutva avenger–hero who had zero tolerance for anyone with a 'Talibani' mindset, a communal jibe squarely aimed at the Muslim community. As a consequence, the bulldozer, hitherto associated with construction projects and demolition work, had now entered the political lexicon as a symbol not only of unhindered state power but also of a majoritarian offensive on the vulnerable.

When I asked a Jat family I met in a village on the outskirts of Muzaffarnagar about whom they would vote for, they enthusiastically responded, 'Hum bulldozer ko vote denge!' Ironically, the family had participated in the farmer protests against the Modi government in 2020. All around us, the bulldozer and the lotus, the BJP's official symbol, were being used interchangeably. In fact, the image of a bulldozer was even spotted at a few Adityanath rallies. I asked the male member of the family why he would vote for the BJP when just months earlier he had been railing against the Centre on the farm laws. 'Woh alag baat hai. Yahan Yogi ji ne kanoon theek kiya hai. Ab hamari beti shaam ko bagair darr ke bahar ja sakti hai aur hamare gaon mein ab poori shanti hai (That is a different story. Here, Yogi ji has fixed the law-and-order situation. Our daughter can go out unafraid in the evening and there is complete peace in the village).' The angry Jat farmer in Delhi was a 'political Hindu' in his village first, then a kisan. Challenging this sharpened Hindu identity politics was never going to be easy for a weak and divided Opposition.

Akhilesh Yadav, leader of the Samajwadi Party, likes the good things in life. He enjoys family holidays—his favourite destination is London, where he spends several weeks every summer—and he loves sport, especially cricket and tennis. When he was the chief minister of Uttar Pradesh, Yadav had built a sprawling football field and gymnasium within the premises of the official residence. His easy-going lifestyle is in marked contrast to the rustic upbringing of his late father and Samajwadi Party Founder, Mulayam Singh Yadav, who was born into a farming family and would travel 20 kilometres from his western Uttar Pradesh village of Saifai to reach his college. A trained wrestler, Mulayam Singh had to cross a lake that would flood during the monsoon. It meant lifting his bicycle on his shoulders and tying it up to a banyan tree (the cycle would later become the party symbol). Senior journalist Rahul Shrivastava, who tracked Mulayam Singh's career for years, relates a story that reveals the humble origins of 'Netaji', as the leader was fondly called. Mulayam Singh had got a job as a teacher in the same college where he used to study. One day, he was at the home of Lallaji, the owner of the college, when the telephone rang. Lallaji asked him to answer the phone, but Mulayam Singh had never seen or handled a phone. When he picked up the phone, he was terrified, not knowing how to use it. The caller on the line kept shouting 'Hello-hello,' but Mulayam Singh thought he was saying 'hilo-hilo' (move-move). He shot back angrily, 'Tum hilo! Hum kyon hilein (You move! Why should I move)?' and banged the phone down.

Akhilesh Yadav, by contrast, was born into VIP privilege, Mulayam Singh having become an MLA at the age of twenty-eight. 'It has all come too easily for him. Mulayam fought all the tough political battles and virtually handed power to Akhilesh on a platter,' a former party functionary said. Akhilesh 'Bhaiya', as his party workers call him, was one year short of his fortieth birthday when he became Uttar Pradesh's youngest chief minister in 2012. Five years later, when he was voted out, he seemed unable to comprehend the reasons for his defeat. 'We did so much work and yet people have rejected us. Hamara kaam nahi, yeh Modi ji ka jadoo chala hai (It's not our work but Modi's magic that has worked)!' he claimed.

Yet Yadav possesses sharp instincts and, though outwardly easy-going, has inherited from his father a keen sense of political possibilities in Uttar Pradesh. In the run-up to the 2022 elections, as the Yogi government battled Covid and the death toll mounted, the Samajwadi Party leader was convinced that the wheel was turning in his favour. An industrialist friend recalled meeting a cheery-looking Yadav amidst the second Covid wave in the summer of 2021. 'When I asked him about the election campaign, he sounded super confident. "Covid ne Yogi raj ko bhee khatm kar diya hai (Covid has finished Yogi raj)," were his words to me.' Apparently, Yadav had commissioned a poll that suggested growing anti-incumbency. When the *India Today* Mood of the Nation poll in August 2021 also indicated voters' anger, he was even more convinced that the tide was turning. 'Uttar Pradesh ko chalana Yogi ji ke bas ki baat nahi (Running Uttar Pradesh is beyond Yogi),' he remarked, adding that a few BJP MLAs had even been in touch with him and wanted to switch sides. He crafted alliances with smaller OBC-led parties, hoping to become a catalyst for change.

However, buoyed by his poll numbers, a complacent Yadav made a cardinal mistake for any politician: he took the 2022 election result for granted. When he should have been out and about raising public awareness against the Yogi government on Covid mismanagement, he chose to stay indoors. While the chief minister galvanized the administrative machinery into action and the tireless BJP cadres fanned out across the state, the Samajwadi Party was in stasis, directionless, almost as if it was waiting for its leader to take the initiative. While the Covid storm raged, Yadav spent several weeks in London, staying at a plush hotel in the city. 'It is wrong to say that I was missing in action during Covid. I had gone to London to drop off my daughter, who had got college admission there,' he insisted. 'It is you media persons who built this perception because that is what the BJP wanted you to do.'

Yadav cannot blame the media for his own failings. When the vaccines were being rolled out in early 2021, he created a stir at a press conference in Lucknow by saying he would not take 'the BJP's vaccine'. 'I will not get the vaccine now. I am telling you about myself. Am I going to trust a vaccine given by the BJP?' he raged. Yet, just months later, when the government intensified its vaccine drive at the peak of the second wave, he did a U-turn. 'Seeing the public outrage, the Centre has given up politicizing the corona vaccine. I was against the BJP's vaccine but welcome the vaccine of the Government of India. I will also now get vaccinated. I appeal to those who could not get vaccinated for lack of vaccines to do so now,' he tweeted. When I asked him about the change in stance, he appeared unruffled: 'Rajneeti mein paristhiti badalti rehti hai (Circumstances keep changing in politics).' Truthfully, Yadav had made a blunder by allowing the BJP to mock his anti-vaccine position. In this unforgiving social media age, it was a gaffe that allowed the Centre to deflect from its own shortcomings and push the Opposition on the defensive.

While Yadav was living in his own bubble, Uttar Pradesh's other big regional player, Mayawati, had almost entirely fallen off the political map. The Samajwadi Party and the BSP had tied up just ahead of the 2019 general elections, ending decades of a bitter feud between Uttar Pradesh's two principal regional parties. Yadav's reaching out to Mayawati, respectfully addressing her as 'bua' (father's sister), was seen as a potential political game-changer. As it turned out, both 'bua' and 'bhatija' (nephew) were swept away by the Modi wave. Within days of the defeat, Mayawati unilaterally announced that the alliance was over and that the BSP would fight future elections on their own. 'Bua' was back to being 'Behenji' (sister), the name by which she was more popularly known. The official reason for the break-up was 'the Samajwadi Party's behaviour', which she indicated was no longer acceptable.

The real reason for the split was reportedly Mayawati's fear of being targeted by the BJP government at the Centre. 'If there are two things Mayawati is afraid of, they are the prospect of going to jail and losing her security cover,' said Danish Ali, who was one of the ten MPs elected on a BSP ticket from Uttar Pradesh in 2019 and was appointed the BSP's parliamentary party leader in the Lok Sabha. According to him, Mayawati was convinced that the BJP would send the ED after her if she challenged them politically. The BSP leader had a slew of corruption charges pending against her and members of her family, including her brother. When the ED called her brother in for questioning, Mayawati was terrified that she would be next in line. 'By breaking with the Samajwadi Party and lying low, Mayawati bought herself immunity from any coercive action,' claimed Ali. He shared a personal anecdote to support his argument of a tacit BSP–BJP 'arrangement'. During the course of the contentious CAA debate in Parliament in December 2019, Ali had interrupted the home minister's speech, insisting that Shah was spreading communal discord with his remarks. Amidst the din, a colleague passed a slip to Ali saying 'Behenji' wanted to speak to him urgently. The MP rushed out to the party office in Parliament and rang up his leader. 'What kind of behaviour is this? How can you interrupt the speech of the home minister?' she had yelled. When Ali tried to explain himself, Mayawati screamed back: 'I don't want to hear anything you say. You will not ever argue with the home minister. Jaante nahi ho yeh kitne khatarnak log hain (Don't you know how dangerous these people are)?' In December 2023, Danish Ali was suspended by the BSP for going against the party line. 'On every contentious issue, be it Article 370, triple talaq or CAA, Mayawati wanted us not to challenge the BJP. When I warned her that we were being seen as a B team of the BJP, she shouted and asked me to leave the room,' he alleged.

Not surprisingly, in the run-up to the 2022 Uttar Pradesh polls, Mayawati was mostly invisible, hidden away in her palatial mansions in Delhi and Lucknow, rarely interacting with her legislators. Though she still kept a tight grip on party affairs, she was grooming her nephew Akash Anand to handle the nitty-gritty issues concerning the organization. A party that had been nurtured by its founder, Kanshi Ram, with the promise of social and political empowerment for Dalits was now the fiefdom of the family of the 'Dalit ki beti'. Meeting Mayawati was now very difficult, getting an interview even more so. Her chief interlocutor remained Satish Mishra, a senior lawyer–politician who handled all her cases. When I requested a meeting with Mayawati ahead of the 2022 Uttar Pradesh elections, his terse response was: 'Let me see; she is very busy.'

Mayawati's relatively low-key 2022 campaign suggests that she wasn't busy as much as disinterested. Rather than energetically criss-crossing the state, she focused on a handful of major rallies in key large towns. I attended one such rally in Agra, once a BSP bastion but now slowly becoming a BJP stronghold. The crowds were still there, especially among her core Jatav vote base, but the enthusiasm for their leader was conspicuously absent. I recall speaking to a senior journalist at the rally who explained the momentum shift rather well. 'In Uttar Pradesh, Dalits have tasted power. There was a time when they felt that Mayawati was their sole ticket to power. Now it is Modi,' he remarked. Interestingly, in her Agra speech, Mayawati spent more time targeting the Congress than the BJP. 'The Congress never recognized the great contribution of Dr Babasaheb Ambedkar for Dalit upliftment, which is why they did not give him the Bharat Ratna during their rule,' she declared. Ironically, an identical charge was made earlier by the BJP too. The 'B team' (of the BJP) dig would haunt Mayawati, a once-heavyweight, tall leader whose rapid decline eventually led to fresh caste alignments in the 2024 general elections.

For the Congress party, Uttar Pradesh is like a black-and-white-era film, often considered through the lens of the past. The fulcrum of the party's dominance in Indian politics for the first four decades after Independence, the state is seemingly now a BJP stronghold for the most part. Repeated attempts to revive the Congress in Uttar Pradesh have met with little success. In the 2012 assembly elections, Rahul Gandhi led the Congress campaign by taking on both the Samajwadi Party and the BSP, only to be wiped out. Five years later, in 2017, the Congress leader joined hands with Akhilesh Yadav—the duo was branded as 'UP ke Ladke' by ace political strategist Prashant Kishor—but that campaign didn't take off either as the BJP swept to power. Just two months ahead of the 2019 general elections, the Congress delivered another googly by appointing Priyanka Gandhi Vadra as the party's general secretary for Uttar Pradesh (East), while Jyotiraditya Scindia was put in charge of Uttar Pradesh (West). The sudden appointments threw the party into further disarray. 'It was frankly ad hoc and bizarre beyond belief,' recalled a senior Congress leader from the state. 'Neither Priyanka nor Scindia had built any connection with ground workers across Uttar Pradesh. If you had to give them a responsibility, at least give them some time to build a network in the state.'

The last-minute choice of Priyanka was especially curious. For years, the party had positioned the charismatic Gandhi daughter as their 'Brahmastra' (ultimate weapon) to take on the BJP, convinced that she had a magnetic appeal reminiscent of her grandmother Indira Gandhi. Ahead of the 2017 elections, poll strategist Kishor even pushed for Priyanka to be announced as the Congress's chief ministerial face, only to be rebuffed by the party leadership. Until now, her campaigning had been confined primarily to the family bastion of Amethi–Rae Bareli, but now she was expected to make an instant impact and take on an ascendant BJP and a numerically strong Samajwadi Party–BSP combine. 'It was crazy to throw Priyanka into the deep end without even giving her a chance to learn how to swim,' said a Congress watcher. Predictably, the 2019 Lok Sabha campaign was a disaster, and the Congress won just one seat: Sonia Gandhi's Rae Bareli citadel. In a clear sign of a 'wave' election, even Amethi was lost.

By the time the 2022 election cycle began, Priyanka had begun learning to navigate Uttar Pradesh's choppy waters on her own. A miffed Scindia had left to join the BJP; Rahul Gandhi had quit as party president and become an MP from Wayanad in Kerala. The responsibility for reviving the Congress rested almost entirely on Priyanka. In the three years since the Lok Sabha debacle, she had tried to transform a moth-eaten state party unit into a battle-ready outfit. One of her first decisions was to replace actor–politician Raj Babbar with Ajay Kumar Lallu, a two-time MLA from an OBC community, a belated attempt by the Congress to recognize the changing caste equations in the state and the OBC-ization of Uttar Pradesh politics. Next, she began the arduous process of revamping party units at the block level, drafting in younger, newer faces. When she first took over, she was astonished to find more than 500 members in an ageing Uttar Pradesh Congress executive committee. These leaders had held the same position for thirty years and were refusing to yield any space to the next generation. Some of these old-timers had even appointed their drivers and personal bodyguards as district committee members. 'We seem to have more leaders than workers in the party,' Priyanka confided to an aide. A leaner seventy-five-member committee with specific responsibilities and a more representative caste balance was set up.

The organizational revamp, however, only widened the fault lines within the party. In June 2021, Jitin Prasada, considered a Rahul Gandhi loyalist, quit the party to join the BJP. When asked by a colleague if the reason for his departure was ministerial ambition, he snapped back angrily, 'You expect me to stay in a party where decisions are taken without any consultation?' Prasada was reportedly peeved with a few appointments Priyanka had made in his home district of Shahjahanpur without his knowledge. Six months later, R.P.N. Singh, another Uttar

Pradesh leader from the Rahul brigade, quit the party in a huff and joined the BJP, saying, 'This isn't the Congress I have been part of for thirty years.' Singh, now a BJP Rajya Sabha MP, had reportedly tried to air his grievances to Rahul Gandhi, only to be told that he should speak on Uttar Pradesh affairs to his mother and sister instead.

Neither Prasada nor Singh is a mass leader, but both are political inheritors born into influential families from Uttar Pradesh long associated with the Congress. Both were made ministers in Manmohan Singh's cabinet in 2009 on Rahul Gandhi's intervention, but neither was confident any longer of winning an election on a Congress ticket. Personal ambition may have been a driving factor in switching sides, but so was the sense that the Congress was now operating on a different wavelength. Neither blamed Priyanka by name, but it was obvious they couldn't fully reconcile to their political 'junior' calling the shots. Party insiders cited Singh's regular absence from office-bearer meetings called by Priyanka as a glaring example of how the internal dynamics were playing out. Matters reached a stage where Singh, then a party general secretary in charge of Jharkhand, reportedly harangued and shouted at Priyanka for a full hour on the phone. He later apologized for his outburst, saying his mother had admonished him for using harsh language.

For Priyanka's critics within the party, a major grouse was her personal assistant, Sandeep Singh, who was accused of throwing his weight around. Sandeep, who hails from eastern Uttar Pradesh, was a JNU student leader once associated with an extreme left student outfit that had shown black flags to then Prime Minister Manmohan Singh. Later he had become part of Rahul Gandhi's core 2019 election team, even writing some of his speeches. The controversial 'Chowkidar chor hai' slogan in the 2019 campaign was reportedly coined by him. Now a member of Priyanka's inner circle, the live wire and politically alert Sandeep was virtually a gatekeeper to the Congress leader. When I was to interview Priyanka during the 2024 campaign, Sandeep suggested a midnight meeting at a dhaba on the Lucknow–Rae Bareli highway for a pre-interview debrief. 'The good thing about Priyanka is that unlike her brother, you can reach out and communicate with her often; the not-so-good thing is that she expects you to deal with Sandeep and his team on local constituency issues. Who is a greenhorn like him to give instructions to those of us who have spent years toiling for the party?' remarked a former Congressman.

Yet, despite these internal challenges, Priyanka, at least, was showing some fighting spirit at a time when most other Uttar Pradesh Opposition leaders seemed reluctant to hit the streets. An illustration of this was provided in September 2020, when she led a Congress march to Boolgarhi village in Hathras district, where four upper-caste men had allegedly gang-raped a young Dalit woman on 14 September. The victim succumbed to her injuries two weeks later, and in an eerie and macabre move, the police hurriedly cremated her body in the early hours of the morning of 29 September without either the knowledge or consent of her family. The death and sinister pre-dawn cremation sparked a furore in the media, with news channels taking up the story aggressively and questioning the Uttar Pradesh administration's role in a possible cover-up and the injustice being done to a poor Dalit family in an area where caste discrimination is still an everyday reality.

This was the moment when Priyanka Gandhi Vadra stepped out into the heat of the Uttar Pradesh battlefield. 'What has happened in Hathras is proof that the Yogi government has failed to protect a Dalit ki beti despite their brave talk of law and order,' she claimed in a TV interaction. With Mayawati not speaking out strongly and Akhilesh Yadav in London, Priyanka suddenly became the face of the protest. 'She may not admit it, but Priyanka is keen to have a bigger political profile beyond just being Rahul Gandhi's sister, or Rajiv and Sonia's daughter, or the granddaughter who looks like Indira Gandhi. She relishes the arc lights and wants a piece of the action,' contended a family friend. Seizing the chance, Priyanka, accompanied by her brother, Rahul, decided to lead a march by a Congress team to Boolgarhi. When the Uttar Pradesh police stopped them for violating a public order prohibiting the assembly of four or more people, the defiant Gandhis decided to return two days later. This time, the Gandhis' convoy ran into heavy police deployment, but they refused to turn back. As clashes broke out between the Congress workers and the police, Priyanka alighted from the vehicle and attempted to shield the workers. A policeman held the Congress general secretary by her kurta and pushed her away. The incident was captured on camera and replayed incessantly across news channels. A chastened Uttar Pradesh police was forced to apologize and order an inquiry. The Gandhis were eventually allowed to meet the grieving family in Hathras. This wasn't quite Priyanka's Belchi moment—in 1977, Indira Gandhi had famously ridden on an elephant to reach the remote Bihar village of Belchi, where thirteen people, including eight Dalits, were burnt alive—but it was the closest she had come so far to acquiring a political profile beyond the 'entitled dynast' stereotype.

A year later, in October 2021, Priyanka hit the road again. This time she journeyed to another Uttar Pradesh flashpoint: Lakhimpur Kheri, where eight people were killed in clashes after a convoy allegedly led by Union Minister Ajay Mishra Teni's son ran over a group of protesting farmers. Section 144 was imposed and there was a large police presence in the area. Keen to reach the spot, Priyanka, along with Congress MP Deepender Singh Hooda, tried to give the slip to her security cover and sneak into the area at nightfall. A fifty-member Uttar Pradesh police team chased and finally caught up with her at 4 a.m. at the district border. A fracas ensued, with the police trying to shove her into their jeep and even punching her assistant, Sandeep. When Priyanka refused to budge unless shown an arrest warrant, the police hastily produced an order on WhatsApp. She was detained in a police guest house in Sitapur district for three nights.

Priyanka Gandhi's 'arrest' became prime-time news. Sitting in the guest house, she managed to connect with a few news channels on Zoom and accused the police of manhandling her. Her assistant even released a video showing Priyanka sweeping the floor in the room where she was lodged. 'I actually do clean the places I stay in if they are dirty in any way. It's a practice I follow from my Vipassana Meditation courses, so it wasn't theatrics. I was cleaning on my own and a colleague took the video and released it without informing me,' she claimed. Unintended or not, the visual was a made-for-TV moment. The BJP called it 'photo-op' politics, but it was apparent that the Congress leader was capturing eyeballs.

The growing publicity meant that Priyanka became the de facto face of the Congress in the 2022 Uttar Pradesh battle. Just a few days after the Lakhimpur Kheri incident, she played the woman card, announcing that 40 per cent of the tickets in Uttar Pradesh would be reserved for women. From Hathras to Lakhimpur Kheri via Unnao, where she spoke for a rape victim who died after being set on fire by her alleged rapists, Priyanka was being recast as a street-fighter politician taking on the Yogi government. A catchy new slogan and well-packaged video were unveiled: 'Ladki hoon, lad sakti hoon' (I am a woman and I can fight). Her team was confident. 'Our videos are going viral; this time we will make a mark in Uttar Pradesh.'

But while her supporters were busy pumping up the volume, behind the scenes Priyanka knew that it was a losing battle for the Congress. Away from the media glare, Priyanka quietly reached out to Mayawati to explore the possibility of a poll tie-up with the BSP. She phoned Mayawati at least four times seeking a meeting in either Lucknow or Delhi, but on each occasion an excuse was made to put off any interaction. 'I guess Behenji has her compulsions,' she told her party colleagues.

As a gruelling seven-phase Uttar Pradesh election campaign drew to a close in the first week of March 2022, Union Home Minister Amit Shah was holding court with journalists and poll watchers on the lawns of the Taj Ganges in Varanasi. Shah prides himself on his expertise in election analysis. Uttar Pradesh, in particular, had been his stomping ground ever since he was appointed in charge of the state ahead of the 2014 general elections. 'We are definitely winning the election,' affirmed Shah, 'but I don't want to give you a number.' This was a little unusual: Shah would often challenge his own party by throwing out a seat number to aspire to. Was he being cautious? 'Dekho, number dena aap ka kaam hai; mera lakshya party ko chunaav jitana hai (Giving a number is your task; my aim is to make the party win the election),' was his sharp rejoinder to media queries.

The home minister's low-key response reflected a certain anxiety within the BJP camp. The party's internal surveys had shown that a chunk of the sizeable anti-BJP vote was being cornered by Akhilesh Yadav. A multi-cornered contest had become a bipolar battle with the Muslims, Yadavs and even a section of the non-Yadav OBCs consolidating around the Samajwadi Party, which had tied up with the Jat-dominated Rashtriya Lok Dal. The Yogi government was also facing backlash from farmer groups over 'aawara pashu' or stray cattle that were devouring standing crops across the state, a direct consequence of the ban on slaughtering cattle. Varanasi and much of eastern Uttar Pradesh were in the final phase of polling, and Shah was now banking on Modi's popularity to ensure a last-minute surge. True to his playbook, the Prime Minister held a final mega roadshow in his home constituency, travelling through the city in an open-top vehicle as well-organized crowds showered petals on him and chanted 'Jai Shree Ram' on cue. The Prime Minister, zealous about his camera appearances, wore a saffron cap and a gamchha around his neck. 'In Uttar Pradesh, there is a visible "Modi effect". In every constituency that the PM goes to, we have seen a 2–3 per cent bump for the party candidate,' remarked a BJP pollster. As expected, a day after Modi's visit to the city, the BJP's daily mood tracker reported a sharp upturn for the BJP. When Shah saw the poll numbers, he seemed to relax a bit. But he issued a warning to his team: 'Make sure no booth is missed out on polling day—every vote counts!'

In Uttar Pradesh, the home minister relied mainly on one person to supervise the BJP's formidable poll machine: Sunil Bansal. Prior to being handpicked by Shah ahead of the 2014 Lok Sabha elections, Bansal was a low-key RSS pracharak (worker), previously associated with the ABVP, with his roots in Rajasthan. He was the ideal backroom organizer, meticulous with his planning and ready to put in long hours. The BJP's electoral successes in Uttar Pradesh pitched him as a rising star and a firm

Shah loyalist. While the bureaucrats reported into the chief minister, the party's sanghatan (organization), including its vast booth-level network, would report into Bansal, making him a key figure in the power apparatus in the state. 'Every senior ministerial appointment in Uttar Pradesh is done only after Bansal's approval. Yogi ji may be the chief minister, but the real power centre in the party is Sunil ji,' claimed an Uttar Pradesh BJP leader.

When Yogi's council of ministers was to be sworn in, a majority of the ministers first reached Bansal's office at the BJP's Lucknow headquarters to take his 'blessings', including Danish Ansari, the lone Muslim face in the cabinet. Ansari was reportedly strolling in a local market, when he suddenly got a call from Bansal asking him to reach his office immediately. Ansari was taken aback when he was informed that he was being made a minister. 'I had to hurriedly buy a new outfit for the occasion,' he said with a laugh. While an all-powerful Bansal was moved out of Uttar Pradesh to become a BJP national general secretary in August 2022, the seeds of division between the 'Yogi camp' and the 'Shah–Bansal' combine had been sown. When the 2024 elections came around, these dual power centres would end up working at cross-purposes, affecting the BJP's performance in the state.

The final numbers in the 2022 Uttar Pradesh assembly polls were above the BJP's expectations. In the 403-member Uttar Pradesh assembly, the BJP won 255 seats, a clear majority. A thirty-seven-year jinx had been broken with Yogi Adityanath becoming the first sitting chief minister to return to power since 1985. Though the BJP had won fewer seats compared to the 312 in the previous 2017 assembly poll, its vote share had actually climbed from 39.6 per cent to 41.2 per cent. As Shah had feared, the Opposition vote had mainly gone to the Samajwadi Party, whose vote share was up by a substantial 10.2 per cent and who had won 111 seats this time, as opposed to 47 previously. The once redoubtable Mayawati won just 1 seat in a state where in 2007 she and the BSP had won a clear majority. The Congress too was similarly wiped out, winning just 2 seats and only 2.33 per cent of the vote. In as many as 387 of the 399 seats the party contested, it lost its deposit, a sure sign of a total debacle.

So what explains the BJP's success in Uttar Pradesh despite the anti-incumbency factor, the staggering number of Covid deaths and the massive exodus of migrants in 2020, thousands of whom had toiled home on foot back to Uttar Pradesh's villages? What explains the win amidst Uttar Pradesh's complex caste arithmetic? 'The presence of Modi ji and Yogi ji at the top and Bansal and team's micro-management at the bottom—no one can match us in Uttar Pradesh,' was how a BJP leader described the 2022 triumph. While the core Hindutva voter was firmly with the BJP, the incremental vote had come through the party's sizeable labharthi constituency, especially the free ration kits, which targeted more than 150 million (15 crore) people. Yogi's bulldozer imagery was constitutionally untenable but politically effective. The 'UPYOGI' model had come to symbolize Hindutva power. The chief minister was no longer a 'fringe element' but a popular leader, his 'tough on law and order' image a key factor in drawing in votes, his foul, polarizing rhetoric resonating with deep-seated anti-Muslim prejudices.

No Opposition party or leader could match the BJP's organizational strength and mass connect: Akhilesh Yadav had successfully pitched himself as the prime face of the Opposition but hadn't been able to grow exponentially beyond the party's core Muslim–Yadav vote; Mayawati, a pale shadow of her former self, had completely surrendered her political equity by not even putting up a fight; and Priyanka Gandhi Vadra was unable to translate her telegenic presence into a more tangible party revival on the ground.

A day after the 2022 Uttar Pradesh results, an upbeat Shah called a meeting of BJP office-bearers to discuss Gujarat, his home state as well as the next big election battleground that year. 'This time, it is Mission 150. We have to set a new record for maximum seats in Gujarat.' The mood in the Congress headquarters, in contrast, was sullen and dispirited. Not only had the party been wiped out in Uttar Pradesh, but it had also lost its government in Punjab to the start-up challenger AAP, which swept the polls there. Even in tiny Goa, where the party had been hopeful of wresting the state on the back of anti-incumbency, the BJP returned to power. 'It really felt like we were a sinking ship without a captain to steer it,' admitted a Congress office-bearer. The captain they had hoped would lead from the front was still recovering from the 2019 election setback. But with Priyanka's struggles in Uttar Pradesh and Sonia in semi-retirement, Rahul Gandhi was squarely back in focus.

Could the Congress's eternal heir apparent attempt another re-invention despite past missteps? It was time to script an unlikely, potentially game-changing, political comeback.

SEVEN

Rahul Gandhi's 'Mohabbat ki Dukaan'

LIKE so much else in the grand old party, the Congress Working Committee (CWC) too is a pale shadow of its former self. For over two decades, since Sonia Gandhi first took over as Congress president in 1998, elections to the party's apex executive body were not held. Instead, the committee was packed with 'nominated' members who were all Gandhi-family loyalists. Meetings were held infrequently, and the vigorous debates that had once characterized CWC deliberations were now replaced by one-line resolutions authorizing the party 'high command' to take decisions on behalf of the party. Which is why when Rahul Gandhi called an emergency CWC meeting on 25 May 2019, just two days after the Congress had suffered another embarrassing general election defeat, party workers were surprised. 'With Sonia ji, the approach was to stay patient and not break from the status quo unless it was a crisis. With Rahul Gandhi, it's just the opposite; he always wants to shake things up by attempting something dramatic,' affirmed a senior CWC leader.

Rahul Gandhi had taken over as Congress president in December 2017, elected unopposed as was now the norm. The 'coronation' of the fifth-generation Nehru–Gandhi family member had been in the pipeline for a few years, but the Congress leader had shown a marked reluctance to take over from his mother. Now, at forty-seven, he had finally picked up the baton just eighteen months ahead of the general elections. His ascent was greeted with much enthusiasm, in the hope that he would bring some much-needed youthful energy and direction to a comatose organization floundering in the face of Narendra Modi's meteoric rise. 'I remember in the first meeting chaired by Rahul, we felt he would take us back to the Rajiv Gandhi days, when there was so much excitement about a generational change,' recalled a Congress MP. When the Congress formed a coalition government in Karnataka in the summer of 2018 and then swept that year's winter elections in the Hindi heartland by winning Rajasthan, Madhya Pradesh and Chhattisgarh, the sense of anticipation was even greater. Even sceptics, who were unsure of Rahul Gandhi's vote-gathering abilities, were silenced. In the euphoria of the assembly election triumphs, a 'Rahul versus Modi' contest was no longer considered a daunting challenge. 'There were actually Congress leaders who, in January 2019, were beginning to talk about who would get which portfolio *when*, not *if*, the Congress returned to power,' a CWC member admitted, laughing. The May 2019 general election results burst the Congress bubble. A party accustomed to being in power was now confronted with the discomfiting reality of being in the Opposition for *another* five years, if not longer. A Lok Sabha tally of just 52 seats, up only 8 from the 44 in 2014, was a body blow. In 2014, the party had deflected the blame onto Manmohan Singh's increasingly effete coalition; this time the Gandhi family leadership could no longer escape scrutiny.

The 25 May CWC meeting was pitched as a postmortem, an opportunity for quiet introspection. Only Rahul Gandhi had a slightly different plan. With all the Congress grandees having assembled at the party's 24, Akbar Road headquarters, he stared at the forlorn-looking faces and then broke the stillness with a sharp opening remark: 'I have failed, you have failed, we have all failed.' Minutes later, he was more scathing and pointed in his observations. 'How many of you in this room supported me in the campaign against corruption in the Rafale aircraft deal? How many of you spoke of corruption in the Modi government? Why was I left alone to take up the fight against the BJP?' he asked. When a few Congress members tried to interject, he brushed them off dismissively; the then president wasn't finished with his plain speaking. 'There are those of you in this room who were more interested in campaigning for your children than in assisting the party,' he alleged, glaring in the general direction of Ashok Gehlot, the then Rajasthan chief minister who had spent days campaigning for his son, Vaibhav, from the Jodhpur seat. The BJP and its allies had swept all 25 seats in the state. Then Madhya Pradesh Chief Minister Kamal Nath was not at the meeting, but that did not stop Rahul from accusing him of pushing for his son Nakul's candidature from his Chhindwara bastion. 'Kamal Nath informed us himself that as CM he had the right to field his son,' claimed Rahul. (Nakul Nath was the only Congress candidate to win from MP, a state where the BJP won the remaining 28 seats.) As Rahul's tirade continued, a hush fell. Finger-pointing is not unusual among Congress factions, but personal attacks in a CWC meeting are uncommon. 'We had expected the meeting to lift our morale; instead Rahul's stinging remarks left us feeling even more demoralized,' lamented a CWC attendee. Rahul himself had lost from Amethi. He had managed to win only from a second 'safe' constituency, Wayanad. 'If you can't win your own Lok Sabha seat, how can you blame the rest of us? Why not just accept that there was a Modi wave?' argued a Congressman who has since left the party.

But it wasn't just Rahul Gandhi who spoke out angrily. In a three-hour meeting that was getting increasingly heated, Priyanka Gandhi Vadra sprang to her brother's support. The Congress general secretary who had taken an organizational role only months ahead of the polls was just as livid. She claimed that her brother had fought the election virtually on his own, and while everyone else had desisted from attacking Modi, he had done so at great cost to himself. 'Many of those who are lecturing us for weaknesses in the organization are the very ones who have destroyed it,' snapped Priyanka, according to a CWC member.

Barely had the meeting attendees recovered from the criticism of their failures when Rahul dropped a bombshell. 'As leader of the party, I take moral responsibility for this defeat. I wish to resign as party president. I would urge you to accept my resignation and appoint someone else in my place. Let that person not be from our family so no one can say that the Congress is family-controlled,' he emphasized. Rahul's decision to resign was just as unexpected as the condemnation that had preceded it. It appeared to shake those present out of their somnolence. 'There is no question of you resigning. You need to lead the party into the future and strengthen it,' they protested. Even those who had been at the receiving end of a tongue-lashing from the Congress president joined in the chorus rejecting the resignation.

But Rahul refused to change his mind. Amidst the clamour, he walked out of the room abruptly, leaving a perplexed gathering wondering what was to come next. In a sense, Rahul Gandhi's strident tone at the CWC meeting should not have come as a surprise. In closed-door meetings with his aides, Rahul Gandhi had often spoken out against the party's 'old guard', the ageing group of leaders who had assembled around his mother, many of whom had been inducted into politics when his father, Rajiv, was Prime Minister. Rahul Gandhi's childhood was scarred by tragedy and bloodshed, and early in life he witnessed unimaginable violence and betrayal. He had seen his father criticized and his mother taunted mercilessly. All of this had left him hurt and angry with those who he felt had 'exploited' his parents' goodwill for their personal benefit. 'How many of these leaders defended my father when he was attacked by V.P. Singh on Bofors? How many of them stood by my mother when she was being slandered for her foreign origins?' he once complained to a friend. This inner rage and unresolved hurt sometimes expressed itself in contempt for the political class in general.

Watching the CWC drama unfold was Ahmed Patel, an archetypal representative of the 'old guard', an older generation of Congressmen with whom Rahul was not quite comfortable. While Sonia Gandhi was Congress president, Patel, or 'Ahmed bhai', as he was popularly known, was arguably the most powerful politician in the Congress. As political secretary to the Congress president, he was not only the eyes and ears of the leader but also the party's chief troubleshooter and go-to person on all key issues. But ever since Rahul Gandhi had taken over the presidentship in 2017, Patel had been slowly marginalized and ousted from the core decision-making circle. Nevertheless, he was still fiercely committed to the Gandhis, having got his first big break under Rajiv Gandhi's leadership in the 1980s. 'Somebody in Rahul's team told him that I am a wheeler-dealer, but what they don't realize is that I deal on behalf of the Gandhis, and always in their best interest,' he had told me once.

Now with Rahul Gandhi insisting on stepping down as Congress president, Patel was worried. The entire old guard of the party might be forced to step aside to make way for Team Rahul to take over and restructure the party. An anxious Patel turned to Sonia Gandhi to intervene. 'What purpose will resigning serve? If Rahul doesn't take back his resignation the party will be in danger of splitting. This is what the BJP wants; this is their gameplan,' he cautioned. Sonia Gandhi heard her trusted aide out but pleaded helplessness. 'I have already tried to reason with him but you know how it is with Rahul: once he has made up his mind it is difficult to get him to change it.' For a month after the volatile CWC meeting, Rahul Gandhi almost 'disappeared' from the public gaze, staying mostly indoors at his 12, Tughlaq Lane residence and refusing to meet any Congress office-bearer in his capacity as party president.

On 6 July 2019, barely six weeks after having announced his intention to step down, Rahul Gandhi ended all speculation by formally announcing his decision to resign in an emotional and combative four-page open letter. 'As president of the Congress Party, I am responsible for the loss of the 2019 election. Accountability is critical for the future growth of our party. It is for that reason that I have resigned as Congress president,' he wrote in the letter. Charging the RSS–BJP with having compromised every institution in the country, he urged Congress workers to be ready for an ideological fight. 'It is a habit in India that the powerful cling to power, no one sacrifices power. But we will not defeat our opponents without sacrificing the desire for power and fighting a deeper ideological battle. I was born a Congressman, this party has always been with me and is my lifeblood and forever that way it shall remain,' he concluded.

The letter, in a way, was typical of Rahul Gandhi's political beliefs. He was firmly caught in the middle of cut-throat power politics and yet desired to rise above the muck. In 2013, at a Congress session in Jaipur, he had piously referred to 'power' as 'a poison', even as the party faithful loyally exhorted him to become the prime ministerial face. Ironically, while his letter urged Congress cadres to fight the Sangh Parivar ideologically, Rahul was choosing to resign at the very moment when the party needed him to lead the fight from the front. He was in power politics and yet out of it, a party mascot but also a self-proclaimed political ascetic: a puzzling dichotomy that had left the Congress looking increasingly rudderless and thoroughly confused.

While Rahul Gandhi had taken the high moral ground by resigning, the more urgent task of finding a replacement as Congress president was left to Ahmed bhai. An apprehensive Sonia Gandhi turned to her long-standing confidante to resolve the crisis. For Patel, this was a chance not just to settle the upheaval in the Congress but to restore his own relevance within the party. Rahul Gandhi had made it clear that he would stay out of the consultative process of choosing a successor. Patel and a small group of senior Congress leaders initiated the process but couldn't find a widely acceptable name. Patel's own preferred choice was Mukul Wasnik, the soft-spoken, low-profile but well-networked leader from Maharashtra who was a staunch organization man. Wasnik was reluctant; 'Mujhe isme padna nahi hai (I don't want to get into this),' he pleaded.

On 10 August 2019, seventy-seven days after the CWC resignation drama had first played out, when the party's executive body met again, there was still no consensus on a name to replace Rahul Gandhi as party president. Wasnik had quietly dropped out. A group of Rahul's supporters continued to insist the Gandhi legatee take back his resignation. But Rahul simply would not budge. As the meeting dragged on, Patel cautioned Sonia that a non-Gandhi party president was not a workable idea. 'You will have to take over, madam,' he insisted. It was a possibility he had already broached with her a day earlier. When Sonia had consulted them, Rahul had reportedly been firmly against her taking up the post, but Priyanka was less so. 'I will do it but only for a year, till you find someone else,' was Sonia's compromise offer to Patel. The veteran Congressman jumped at her suggestion. It was late at night when it was announced that the party's longest-serving president, Sonia Gandhi, would once again return as interim Congress president. The Congress, it seemed, was umbilically tied to its first family. The BJP's time-tested jibe of 'pariwarwaad' (family rule) would resonate even more intensely, pushing the Congress on the back foot yet again.

In a party wedded to the status quo, rebellion is frowned upon. Faction fighting may be intense in the Congress, but under the gaze of its ubiquitous high command, rebellious leaders usually fall in line. Which is why, on 23 August 2020, a minor explosion in the party sent out shockwaves when a group of twenty-three Congressmen wrote a letter to Sonia Gandhi, seeking organizational elections and a complete overhaul of the party. When the letter was made public, a sense of near disbelief spread among Congress watchers. More so because the letter 'bomb' was released while Sonia Gandhi was in hospital. The twenty-three senior leaders who had signed the letter included MPs and several former Union ministers and chief ministers. They would be christened the 'G-23', an informal grouping of change-seekers, if not rebels. 'Even after fourteen months of the 2019 electoral verdict, the Congress party has not undertaken any honest introspection to analyse the reasons for its continued decline. The uncertainty over the leadership has demoralized the Congress workers and further weakened the party. There has been an erosion of the support base with leaders and functionaries leaving the party in a number of states. In view of the gravity of challenges facing the party, it is now an imperative to urgently establish an "institutional leadership mechanism" to collectively guide the party's revival.'

The signatories wouldn't admit to it, but the five-page letter was the first serious challenge to Sonia Gandhi's leadership since veteran Maharashtra leader Sharad Pawar had walked out of the party over Sonia's 'foreign origins' issue in 1999.

'We were reformers and not rebels,' insisted Kapil Sibal, lawyer–politician and a key member of the G-23. 'We respected and valued Sonia Gandhi's contribution to the Congress, but we also realized the urgent need for a change in style of functioning.' As one of the country's top lawyers, Sibal was a bit of an oddity in the group. Driven by a personal commitment to constitutional values, he is known to fight many pro bono cases for those at the receiving end of state tyranny. There was little personal ambition driving Sibal but a burning desire to revive a party in decline. Many of the others in the G-23, though, were professional politicians struggling to deal with an extended period out of power.

The most high-profile of these 'rebels' was Ghulam Nabi Azad, the party's leader in the Rajya Sabha and a veteran politician who had started his career under Indira Gandhi's tutelage in the 1970s. Possessing dollops of old-world charm, the tall, smiling Kashmiri was a 'family loyalist', a euphemism for those whose political journey revolved around their proximity to the Gandhi family. So why did this faithful party leader raise a banner of revolt? 'I had no problem with Sonia ji; my issue was with Rahul Gandhi and his style of functioning. Every time I reached out to her, she would tell me to speak to Rahul. Every time I tried to speak to Rahul, his aides would tell me to speak to his mother. How can a party run with two power centres, one of whom is inaccessible even to those who had worked with his grandmother and father?' complained Azad. Rahul's inaccessibility to party leaders had long been the subject of frustrated whispers in the Congress power circles. Many of these leaders, including senior MPs, did not have his mobile number and had to go through the rigmarole of contacting his team of relative political amateurs to seek an appointment. 'The problem with Rahul is that he says he is not interested in power, yet he is the most powerful person in the Congress,' grumbled another G-23 member. While Rahul stayed away from the daily grind of party politics, he still had veto power over crucial decisions taken by the Congress, including key appointments. Azad's supporters claimed that their leader was assured a Rajya Sabha seat from Tamil Nadu with the support of the ruling Dravida Munnetra Kazhagam (DMK), a party with which he had a long-standing relationship. 'Rahul struck off Azad sa'ab's name only because he was convinced that there was some special friendship between Prime Minister Modi and Azad sa'ab. How can you do party politics when you are suspicious of your own leaders?' asked an Azad follower. In August 2022, when the former Jammu and Kashmir chief minister finally quit the party, I asked him if being denied a Rajya Sabha seat was a factor in his decision. 'Rubbish,' he replied angrily. 'Do you think that after being in a party for fifty years, I will leave over a Rajya Sabha membership? I left because there is no place in Rahul Gandhi's Congress for anyone with self-respect.'

It wasn't just Azad. A majority of the G-23 leaders were increasingly upset with the 'Rahul way' of playing politics: a certain impatient ad-hocism in decision-making coupled with a know-it-all insouciance. Bhupinder Singh Hooda, former chief minister of Haryana, for example, was miffed because he wasn't given full charge of the Haryana unit ahead of the 2019 assembly elections. Instead, a Rahul Gandhi loyalist, Ashok Tanwar, who would later quit the party, was pitched as the state Congress chief. 'Had I been allowed a free hand, I would have won Haryana for sure,' insisted Hooda. The canny septuagenarian was a close ally of Ahmed Patel, placing him on the wrong side of shifting power equations. Another former chief minister in the G-23 mix was Maharashtra's Prithviraj Chavan, a measured and dignified party elder who was upset with being marginalized in the state after the party's defeat in the 2014 assembly polls. Chavan had reportedly been seeking an appointment with Rahul Gandhi for months to air his grievances but with little success. 'How do you function when there is no communication?' he lamented to a colleague.

Two relatively younger and articulate MPs, the dashing, telegenic Shashi Tharoor and the smart and well-spoken Manish Tewari, were also annoyed at being passed over for party leadership in the Lok Sabha. Instead, Adhir Ranjan Chowdhury, a five-time MP from West Bengal, was appointed the leader of the Congress in the Lok Sabha. Chowdhury had built a reputation as a tough guy, having taken on both the Communist Party of India (Marxist) (CPI[M]) and the Mamata Banerjee government, but was obviously lacking the high oratorical skills required for parliamentary debate. 'In the Congress party, we have a knack for choosing the wrong person for the right task,' said a G-23 member, laughing. The decision was reportedly taken by Sonia Gandhi as Congress parliamentary party chairperson without any consultation with the MPs. When an agitated Tharoor approached the Congress leadership seeking clarification for why he wasn't considered for the post, his concerns were brushed aside. 'Adhir is a five-time MP; he is senior to you,' he was told. Another theory was that Adhir was chosen because he didn't have any appeal outside his constituency of Berhampore, while a Tharoor or a Tewari leading the Opposition charge in Parliament might attract national attention. 'In the Congress, talented people make those around them deeply insecure,' opined a senior leader.

Interestingly, the embryonic idea of a 'reformist' grouping within the Congress was first mooted at a dinner meeting at Shashi Tharoor's well-appointed, book-lined Delhi residence. 'This wasn't some kind of conspiracy against the party or the Gandhis, just a free and frank exchange of views between concerned Congress leaders. I am a reformist, not a revolutionary,' insisted Tharoor. That initial meeting was also attended by P. Chidambaram, the former finance and home minister, who would later distance himself from the signatories. 'I was very clear that nothing could be done without the concurrence of the Gandhis, so I think it was rather graceless that a letter should be shot off and made public when Sonia Gandhi was in hospital,' said Chidambaram.

As it turned out, the G-23 'rebellion' soon fizzled out. Individually and collectively, the group didn't have the political heft or support from the Congress rank and file to demand change. An informal tea in December 2020 at Sonia Gandhi's 10, Janpath residence, with the usual fare of mint-chutney sandwiches and cookies, was enough to break the ice. In characteristic style, she tried to play down any crisis, insisting that she bore 'no ill-will to any dissenters'. 'My doors are always open for you, and I assure you your concerns will be addressed,' she told the gathering, which included key members of the G-23. While Sonia Gandhi and Priyanka played peacemaker, Rahul Gandhi was more defiant. 'By attacking the party leadership, you are only playing into the BJP's hands,' he reportedly told one of the dissenters. The divergent approaches towards the G-23 members from within the Gandhi family is revealing. In her two decades as Congress president, Sonia Gandhi's working style was largely consensual. She was always conscious of the need to take along even those with whom she didn't always see eye to eye. For example, Pranab Mukherjee was the party's choice for President of India in 2012 even though Sonia Gandhi couldn't fully trust a leader who had fallen out with her husband. Showing political maturity, she even made peace with Sharad Pawar despite his attack over the prickly 'foreign origins' question. 'Sonia ji knows her strengths and limitations, when to throw a carrot and when to wield a stick. She is, in that sense, a consummate power politician,' remarked a senior CWC member.

By contrast, Rahul Gandhi's attitude towards party members who were not ideologically aligned with him seemed impetuous and unyielding. For Rahul, the RSS–BJP 'Hindu Rashtra' agenda is enemy No. 1, anathema to his own pluralist views. Conscious of how valiantly his progressive forbears had struggled against Hindu extremism for the cause of constitutional values, Rahul believes fighting Hindutva is his supreme ideological mission, and anyone who deviates even slightly is regarded with suspicion. 'He wants to be an ideologue in a political party whose only ideology is power,' pointed out a former Congressman who left the party because a group close to Rahul accused him of hobnobbing with the BJP. 'I went to a dinner party being hosted by a BJP MP who happens to be an old friend. The next thing I know is I get a WhatsApp message accusing me of being a "turncoat". It was crazy,' revealed the leader, who did join the BJP eventually. Rahul Gandhi's supporters, though, denied the accusation that their leader was responsible for any friction within the party. 'Rahul ji is a genuine democrat who is looking to effect a structural and generational change within the Congress. When he says he doesn't want power for himself but to make a difference to society, he genuinely means it,' argued a long-standing Rahul aide.

***

Few doubted Rahul Gandhi's sincerity, but many questioned his political acumen. While Sonia Gandhi had carefully chosen Ahmed Patel, the mild-mannered, genial, seasoned politician with connections across the aisle, as her political secretary, Rahul's 'go-to' political aide was the party's general secretary (organization), K.C. Venugopal, a Kerala Congressman who had entered the Lok Sabha for the first time in 2009. 'When the UPA was in power and if an Opposition leader or an industrialist needed help, Ahmed bhai would not hesitate to pick up the phone and oblige,' said a former Congress MP. By contrast, the grim-faced Venugopal, once a fiery student activist who had cut his teeth in Kerala's bitterly contested Congress-versus-left politics, was an 'outsider' to Delhi's power elite; he didn't have Patel's wide network of contacts and was not well-versed in Hindi. For a party whose precipitous decline in the Hindi heartland was at the core of its crisis, a Kerala leader unfamiliar with north Indian politics being placed in a central organizational role was seen as a strange appointment. Brijlal Khabri, a Dalit leader from Uttar Pradesh who was briefly appointed the state Congress president in October 2022, disclosed how he found it very difficult to build any kind of rapport with Venugopal. The rustic, village-born Khabri can only speak in Hindi. 'I met Venugopal ji only a couple of times, but it was difficult to have any kind of conversation because he didn't know Hindi and I didn't know English. Every time I tried to make a political point he would just nod and say okay, okay.' When Khabri was removed from his post less than a year later, he learnt of his removal from a WhatsApp message sent by a journalist friend. 'No one even bothered to call me or inform me that I was being removed,' he said. India's most populous and politically influential state was apparently not on the priority list of the Congress leadership. 'What we needed was an astute Hindi-speaking politician from north India; instead we got a non-Hindi-speaking leader, who doesn't even know the names of Uttar Pradesh's districts, being put in charge of rebuilding the party,' lamented a state Congress leader. It was Venugopal who reportedly persuaded Rahul to contest from Wayanad in Kerala as an additional seat to Amethi in 2019, a move that seemed to signal the Congress's retreat from north India's crucial battleground state.

The Congress leadership's lack of judgement in dealing with the intricate and at times tortuous power politics of north India was in evidence elsewhere as well.

When the Congress won the Rajasthan assembly polls in 2018, Ashok Gehlot, the battle-hardened, street-smart, seasoned neta who had been chief minister of the state twice before, was chosen to lead the government over his younger, more flamboyant rival, Sachin Pilot. A trifle inarticulate on occasion, the kurta-pyjama-clad Gehlot always puts everyone at ease with his laidback air. He had entered the political ring in the Indira–Sanjay Gandhi era in the 1970s, a pre-TV age when politicians didn't care much for sartorial choices. Sachin Pilot, by contrast, cuts a striking figure, almost an advertisement for twenty-first-century Indian politics. A dynast like Rahul Gandhi, he is young, tall, handsome, always smartly attired, as well as telegenic and tech savvy. Approachable and very communicative, he has never hidden his ambition to become chief minister. However, unlike Gehlot, Pilot didn't have too many allies in the well-entrenched Congress cliques of the national capital. As part of the compromise formula that was worked out with Gehlot and Pilot, Rahul Gandhi had reportedly 'promised' the latter that he would be made chief minister 'some time soon'.

By July 2020, however, it was clear that the astute Gehlot wasn't going anywhere in a hurry. Though Pilot was deputy chief minister, all key files and appointments were controlled by Gehlot's office. 'Our leader could not transfer even a constable if he wanted to,' claimed a Pilot aide. Matters reached a head when FIRs were filed under sedition laws of the Indian Penal Code (IPC) after a mobile intercept reportedly revealed conversations about the purchase of MLAs to topple the Gehlot government in which Pilot's name was mentioned. Pilot was issued a notice asking him to appear before the police to record his statement. 'Yes, that was the trigger point for me to revolt. Just imagine, I am the deputy chief minister and state Congress president and the police arrives at my door and involves me in a sedition case,' expostulated Pilot.

Angered by what he believed was a 'conspiracy' by the chief minister to throw him out of the party, Pilot rebelled and left Jaipur with at least a dozen of his loyal MLAs, vowing not to return until Gehlot was removed. With some of the MLAs parking themselves in a hotel in Manesar in BJP-ruled Haryana, there was growing suspicion that the 'revolt' was a bid by the BJP to unseat another Congress-ruled government. 'We have phone conversations between these rebel MLAs and BJP leaders in Delhi and money transactions being discussed,' Gehlot insisted. As the crisis dragged on, to avoid 'poaching', that unique Indian sport of MLA hunting, Gehlot shifted the bulk of his loyal MLAs to a resort in Jaisalmer. BJP Union Minister Gajendra Singh Shekhawat, who had defeated Gehlot's son in the Jodhpur seat in 2019, was allegedly the key point of contact for the rebels. Pilot, on the other hand, was just as adamant that he never made contact with any BJP leader. 'I have invoices of all hotel bills, legal fees and every single payment we made. My MLAs and I paid for everything from our own pockets,' he asserted.

Internal rebellion or another possible 'Operation Lotus' (the codename for the BJP's attempts to topple Congress governments), these events alarmed the Congress party leadership significantly. Already, the Madhya Pradesh government had collapsed in March 2020; the party couldn't afford to lose another government. In August, a month after Pilot's 'rebellion', peace was brokered between the two warring sides, with Ahmed Patel and Priyanka Gandhi Vadra playing interlocutors. Patel was very close to Gehlot, while Priyanka was seen as her mother's voice. Rahul Gandhi refused to get involved in the negotiations. Under the pact that was reportedly agreed upon, Gehlot would stay on as chief minister but Pilot's men would be accommodated as ministers, and the younger leader was promised once again that he would be made chief minister before the next election cycle in 2023. Pilot waited it out with increasing restiveness until September 2022, when Gehlot was asked by Sonia Gandhi to become the party president in her place in Delhi and Pilot was told to prepare to take over in Jaipur. Gehlot initially agreed but, when informed that it was his archrival who would be replacing him as chief minister, did the unthinkable: this time he engineered a revolt against the high command's decision.

A two-member committee comprising Mallikarjun Kharge and Ajay Maken was deputed to travel to Jaipur as party observers. Their task was to call a meeting of the state legislature party and obtain a one-line resolution authorizing the party high command to choose the new chief minister. But while the two observers waited for the MLAs to gather at the chief minister's residence, a parallel meeting was being conducted by state minister and Gehlot loyalist Shanti Dhariwal, where new conditions were put forward: they would not accept a chief minister from the Pilot camp and the decision on the chief ministership could only be taken after the presidential elections were over. 'MLAs blackmailing the Congress high command by putting conditions—I have never seen anything like it,' admitted a distraught Kharge, who, in a twist of fate, would become Congress president just a month later. And yet, instead of confronting the Gehlot challenge head on and forcing him to step down and accept the post of party president, the Congress's central leadership backed off. Gehlot was allowed to stay on as the chief minister.

An increasingly tired Sonia Gandhi, now in her seventies and battling ill-health, with no Ahmed Patel by her side (he had passed away in November 2020), was struggling to impose her writ on even the old guard. The organization in-charge, K.C. Venugopal, did not have the experience or political heft to force a senior leader to fall in line. A reticent Rahul Gandhi continued to distance himself from the nitty-gritty of political management. A leadership vacuum stared the once-mighty Congress in the face. 'Nothing shows just how weak the Congress high command had become better than Gehlot's act of defiance. It was a clear message to all that even the Gandhis could be challenged,' admitted a senior Congress leader. Gehlot would later apologize to Sonia Gandhi for his non-cooperation but also, reportedly, managed to get an assurance that no disciplinary action would be taken against him. The shrewd Gehlot had outmanoeuvred Pilot yet again. A week before the 2023 winter Rajasthan assembly polls, Gehlot and Pilot were finally seen on stage together at a Rahul Gandhi rally, but it was too little, too late. A hopelessly fractured Congress lost Rajasthan. A majority of the 'loyal' ministers whom Gehlot had backed were defeated.

If Rajasthan was a case of the Congress failing to deal swiftly with a fractious battle of bickering rivals, Punjab became an example of the party's uncanny ability to self-destruct. The Congress had won Punjab under Captain Amarinder Singh's leadership in 2017. The erstwhile raja of Patiala, with his resplendent turban, spotless kurtas and superbly styled beard and moustache, has a commanding presence and lives life king-size, his luxurious farmhouse residence near Chandigarh reflecting his fine tastes in whisky, art and books (many authored by him) on military history. Captain Singh's regal lifestyle made him a bit of a loner in Punjab's faction-ridden politics. He was accused by his MLAs of being inaccessible and of outsourcing the daily tasks of governance to a small team of bureaucrats. 'What do you mean by inaccessible? Just because I don't hold a daily durbar of the usual political sycophants doesn't make me unapproachable,' he retorted.

While the 'Captain' was confident of handling the brewing discontent among legislators, there was one leader who was turning publicly mutinous. Cricketer-turned-TV-comic-showman-turned-politician Navjot Singh Sidhu had earned a reputation as an unguided missile that might explode at any time. He had switched from the BJP to the Congress just ahead of the 2017 elections after triggering an open war of words with the ruling Akali Dal leadership, then allies of the BJP. He had even flirted with joining AAP, which was leading the anti-corruption charge against the Badals, the first family of the Akalis, but the negotiations gave way at the last moment when Sidhu insisted on being projected as chief minister. Weaning Sidhu away to the Congress was achieved by political strategist Prashant Kishor, who at the time was handling Amarinder Singh's campaign. Kishor convinced the Congress high command that Sidhu would be an asset. Desperate to win the election, Singh reportedly agreed to even make Sidhu deputy chief minister, a promise he would later go back on. 'The 2017 battle against AAP was easily the toughest election I have fought. We brought in Sidhu because he was a crowd-puller with star appeal,' recalled Kishor.

Sidhu was undoubtedly a star. His TV persona was as a quick-witted punster, earning him a niche in the sports and entertainment space. But Singh was never convinced that Sidhu could make the transition from celebrity to politician. 'When you are a minister in the government, you have to abide by rules and be disciplined; you can't be a showman in a TV studio,' was Singh's complaint. Their first clash came over Sidhu's insistence on continuing with his TV appearances while being a minister. The chief minister saw it as a conflict of interest, but Sidhu insisted otherwise. 'I do my government duties between 9 a.m. and 6 p.m. What I do after that is nobody's business,' was his defiant response. He was allowed to appear on shows after the Punjab advocate-general gave him legal clearance. A more acrimonious exchange occurred soon after, in 2018, when Sidhu defied the chief minister's explicit instructions and attended Pakistan Prime Minister Imran Khan's swearing-in ceremony in Islamabad. 'Imran is an old friend from my cricket days; how can I not go if invited?' was Sidhu's defence. Yet when photos of Sidhu being embraced by then Pakistan army chief General Javed Bajwa at the function went viral, the visit became an acute embarrassment for Singh. An alleged relationship with a Pakistani woman journalist notwithstanding, Singh, a former military man and fierce nationalist, had consistently taken a hard line on Pakistan. Speaking in the Punjab assembly, a furious Singh had once invoked Punjabi sentiments to protest against Pakistani support to cross-border terror: 'I want to tell this to General Bajwa: if you are a Punjabi, we too are Punjabis, and you dare try to enter our territory, we will set you right.'

As the 'war' between the two Sardars rapidly deteriorated into frequent bouts of public recrimination, Sidhu resigned from the cabinet in July 2019 after his portfolio was changed. He released his resignation letter addressed to Rahul Gandhi on Twitter and informed the chief minister only much later. Singh was fuming at what he considered a breach of protocol. 'Does this unstable man have any idea of how the cabinet system runs?' he raged. Sidhu appeared unbothered. By addressing the letter directly to Rahul, he had made his point. He had a direct line to the Gandhis and was accountable only to them, not the chief minister. Priyanka Gandhi Vadra, in particular, was Sidhu's 'go-to' person in Delhi and was reportedly asked by the party to play peacemaker since she was the one person he trusted. On more than one occasion, Sidhu suddenly drove down unannounced from Chandigarh to pour out his angst to the Congress leader. 'Handling Sidhu's mood changes isn't easy, but Priyanka was very patient and accessible, and that gave us a temporary respite,' said a Congress office-bearer.

By mid-2021, matters had reached a point of no return. Sidhu hit the road ahead of the 2022 Punjab assembly elections, addressing public meetings where he spoke critically of the chief minister for not acting against the previous Akali government on charges of drug trafficking, corruption and sacrilege. When photographs of a beaming Sidhu with Priyanka and Rahul Gandhi appeared on social media, speculation mounted of a possible change of guard in Punjab. An incensed Amarinder Singh sought Sonia Gandhi's intervention to clear the air. 'I told her that if she wanted me to resign, I would do so right away. But I wasn't going to tolerate the humiliation of being attacked by a political novice who instead of being served a disciplinary notice was happily being indulged by her kids,' claimed Singh. The chief minister had known Rajiv Gandhi from his schooldays in the Doon School and was a family friend who organized chopper rides for the Gandhi family when they travelled for holiday getaways to Himachal. In fact, when a Congress leader once suggested that Singh should refer to Rahul Gandhi as 'Rahul ji' like other Congressmen, he laughed it off, saying, 'Bloody hell, maybe Rahul should refer to me as "Uncle ji"!'

In an attempt to manage the escalating crisis, Sonia Gandhi reportedly assured Amarinder Singh that he was still the high command's preferred choice. She even constituted a three-member committee to resolve the infighting by talking to both sides. It was a typical Sonia Gandhi move: try to douse the flames by deferring an immediate decision. But unknown to the Patiala royal scion, his kingdom was about to be snatched away. A section of the Congress alleged that Singh was in touch with Home Minister Amit Shah and had struck a deal. Separately, a survey conducted by the party showed that the chief minister was hugely unpopular among the local population and MLAs. 'I don't think we can win Punjab under Captain's leadership—that's very clear from the findings,' Rahul Gandhi reportedly told Harish Rawat, the then party general secretary. While the mother was calling for truce, the son was seeking to shake things up. Not for the first time, the Congress was in an utterly confusing crisis of its own making.

In July 2021, when Sidhu was finally appointed president of the Punjab Pradesh Congress Committee, Amarinder Singh was allegedly kept in the dark. 'Do you know the first time I heard about it was when you interviewed Harish Rawat on TV, who said a compromise formula has been worked out under which Sidhu would be party chief and I would stay on as chief minister?' Singh told me angrily. 'Is this how a party functions?' he raged. Nor was he allegedly kept in the loop when a sudden meeting of the Congress legislature party was convened in September 2021. With a majority of the MLAs against him, a decision was finally taken by the Congress high command to replace the chief minister. 'I was having breakfast at home, when my media advisor told me that the news channels were flashing breaking news about a meeting of MLAs where I would be asked to step down. Can anything be more humiliating after all the years I gave to this party?' he complained. Without waiting for the meeting, Singh informed Sonia Gandhi that he was resigning but not before lashing out at the man he held chiefly responsible for his ouster. 'There is no question of ever supporting Sidhu, who is clearly mixed up with Pakistan and is a danger and disaster for Punjab and the country,' he thundered.

Bewilderingly enough, the Congress didn't even have a ready replacement for their long-serving chief minister. A mercurial Sidhu was never going to be acceptable to a majority of the MLAs. Finding a consensus was proving difficult. Finally, the high command broke the deadlock with a surprise pick: Charanjit Singh Channi, a three-time MLA but relatively junior in the party hierarchy. 'He is the first Dalit Sikh chief minister of Punjab; his appointment will be a game-changer,' enthused Rawat. Channi's appointment was endorsed by Rahul Gandhi, who was pushing for greater Dalit representation at leadership levels in the party. When Sidhu heard of Channi's nomination, he went ballistic and threatened to quit the party. Priyanka, who was holidaying in Shimla, was drafted in yet again to pacify the raging Sardar, but he went ahead and announced his resignation as Punjab Congress chief on Twitter without informing anyone. This time, even Priyanka refused to indulge his rebellious act.

A change in leadership just five months ahead of the assembly polls would prove to be an unmitigated disaster. The Congress's Punjab soap opera had played out for months in the public domain, and an unforgiving voter was in no mood to be swayed by the party's Dalit card. In the Punjab assembly polls of 2022, AAP, barely a decade old, swept to a massive win, bagging 92 out of 117 seats, riding a wave for change. Charanjit Singh Channi, the new chief minister, contested from 2 seats, lost both and then mysteriously departed from the country after corruption charges were filed against him during his short term in office. Sidhu too lost from Amritsar and was then jailed for a year after a 1988 road rage case came back to haunt him. After leaving the Congress, Amarinder Singh initially formed his own party, lost from his bastion in Patiala and then joined the BJP.

What, though, of the idealistic fifth-generation dynast who was still the de facto leader of the Congress? As the party lurched from one electoral debacle to another, the rank and file grappled with an uncomfortable question that it had refused to confront for years: Was Rahul Gandhi really a serious politician with the drive and ambition to revive a depleted

Congress? Did he have the right political instincts, or was he a liability who derived his position purely based on his family surname? Helming the party to two massive general election defeats, losing major states, opting to resign as party chief, failing to lift the morale of demoralized workers, making poor judgement calls, yet remaining seemingly untouchable within the Congress ecosystem—Rahul Gandhi was like a solitary oarsman on a broken raft that was about to sink into swirling waters. After two decades in public life, Rahul Gandhi was at a crossroads. He may not have won the hearts of the public, which was still entranced by the Modi cult, but could he at least earn the goodwill and respect of his own flock? He would find out on a yatra of self-discovery that silenced all his critics.

If politics awarded marks for physical fitness, Rahul Gandhi might easily compete for the top spot. He's a natural sportsman, extremely fit and athletic. He is a black belt in aikido, a Japanese martial art, has trained in the close-combat martial art jujitsu, is a skilled sword-fighter and expert cyclist, and has even completed a professional scuba-diving course. 'When Rahul is in the gym doing his daily workout, it's like he enters another world. He is always focused and incredibly strong,' said a friend.

Rahul's fitness levels were about to be put to the test. In May 2022, at a Congress 'Chintan Shivir' or 'brainstorm' session in Udaipur, it was announced that Rahul Gandhi would be embarking on a nationwide Bharat Jodo 'padyatra'. A mass-contact yatra had been in the offing since 2020, but it kept getting postponed due to Covid-19. The electoral debacle in Uttar Pradesh was arguably the final wake-up call. A beleaguered Congress was desperately searching for a revival potion. A Congress party concept note that I accessed ahead of the yatra reads: 'Bharat Jodo Yatra is not a one-off event in the run-up to the 2024 elections. It is a sacred mission, a national pilgrimage through which India rediscovers itself and like-minded Indians turn into fellow travellers. For the Congress, it is a journey to reconnect with the people and to its own founding principles.'

The objectives spelt out reflected this core idea of the yatra.

- Shift the national mood from negativity, hatred and defeatism to positivity, unity and hope.
- Strengthen the national resolve to challenge the divisive politics of the BJP and the RSS.
- Bond with forces, organizations, individuals who are struggling to save the idea of India.
- Rejuvenate the Congress by reclaiming the nationalist legacy and heritage of the Congress.
- Cultural and ideological expansion by incorporating new icons.
- Radical shift in the public image of the Congress party and its leadership.

This agenda note had reportedly been prepared by Yogendra Yadav. 'I may have prepared a concept note for Rahul, but the idea of a padyatra was entirely his. It was his insistence on the rigour of a padyatra when the original suggestion was more for a phased campaign of political activities,' said Yadav. The soft-voiced, cerebral Yadav, an expert analyst of politics and a committed civic activist, was now a core member of the Bharat Jodo Yatra team. One of the founding members of AAP, he had since set up his own political organization, Swaraj Abhiyan, which had associated itself with a range of citizens' campaigns, including the 2020 farmer agitation. Interestingly, in a TV show in May 2019, in the aftermath of the Lok Sabha elections, Yadav had told me that the 'Congress party should die'. Now, just three years later, he was part of the brains behind making the Congress live again and reinvigorating both the party and its leadership. 'My commitment is not to any party but to principles. Rahul Gandhi is standing up for the principles embedded in our Constitution that I unflinchingly believe in,' he claimed.

Yadav may have provided the intellectual veneer to the yatra, but there were other experienced Congress hands who were handling the nuts and bolts. Digvijaya Singh, the two-time former Madhya Pradesh chief minister, was entrusted with leading the planning for the yatra along with K.B. Byju, a former Special Protection Group officer, and Alankar Sawai, Rahul Gandhi's chief assistant who was seen in party circles as his eyes and ears. Canny, forceful and a long-time RSS baiter, Singh is one of the few 'old guard' Congress leaders to have built an equation with Rahul Gandhi. The veteran politician has many connections with left-leaning civil society groups who were seen as useful allies in this mammoth exercise. 'We wanted to involve all those people whose voices were being shut by the BJP's "dadagiri",' said Singh. This readiness to take on the RSS–BJP frontally was Singh's trademark, and a long career fighting the Sangh Parivar was a quality that appealed to Rahul. Singh is a hardline secularist and never ashamed to admit it. 'Too many of our senior leaders are scared of Modi, but not Digvijaya ji,' Rahul told an aide.

Tasked with managing the headlines during the yatra was Jairam Ramesh, another Congressman whose trenchant criticism of the Modi government made him a Rahul favourite. An English-speaking intellectual, Ramesh had worn several hats in public life, effectively making the transition from an IIT-trained policy nerd to a minister in the UPA government to now driving the Congress's media and communication engine. An unapologetic Nehruvian, it was Ramesh who guided Rahul Gandhi in his early years in politics. When Rahul journeyed to Amethi in 2004, a first-time candidate from the family seat, Ramesh was constantly by his side, managing his publicity. He had also played a role in shaping Rahul's left-of-centre political ideology, including his scathing attacks on corporate groups like the Adanis. 'If Rahul Gandhi has this intense dislike for the Adanis, it is because Jairam has convinced him that these business groups are cronies of Prime Minister Modi,' claimed a long-time Congress watcher.

Yet the academically inclined, cerebral Ramesh had also shown disdain for the traditional rent-seeking Congress netas, and this had sparked some internal conflict. Once, when a Congress chief minister was reportedly close to signing a contract with the Adanis, Ramesh had raised a red flag, Rahul Gandhi had intervened and the deal had been scuttled. As a party ideologue, Ramesh was handpicking young professionals aligned to Rahul Gandhi's left-leaning worldview to supervise the Congress's 'war room' efforts. Ramesh was known to be an excellent draftsman who could set the party line on important issues, but some perceived his approach to be too meddlesome, at times resulting in ruffled feathers within the old guard. Ghulam Nabi Azad, for example, blamed Ramesh for pushing him towards the exit. 'He was the one who carried tales against me to Rahul Gandhi. He may speak and write English well, but how does that qualify him to become a leader? He is a drawing room neta,' fumed Azad.

As communications chief, Ramesh's challenge was to handle a hostile media. 'Why do you direct all your questions only to the Opposition? Rahul is holding press conferences in every state along the yatra route. Has Modi held even one during his tenure as Prime Minister?' was his sarcastic response to journalists complaining of lack of access to the Congress leader. During the yatra, Rahul gave interviews to popular young YouTubers but steadfastly refused to give any to the mainstream media outlets. 'He is convinced that you've sold yourselves to the BJP,' said an aide. When I asked Ramesh for a possible interview with Rahul Gandhi, he pleaded helplessness. 'I can help organize anything for you during the yatra, but this, I am afraid, you will have to negotiate directly with Rahul,' he said with a laugh.

While entry into Rahul Gandhi's inner circle may have been restricted, a 4,000-kilometre-long Kanyakumari-to-Kashmir padyatra meant that the Congress leader was now finally breaking the inaccessibility barrier with his party's restive rank and file. In a meeting with the 'Bharat yatris'—a name given to the hundred-odd Congress supporters who would be his co-travellers on the arduous journey—Rahul Gandhi spoke of the yatra as a form of 'pashchatap' (atonement) and 'tapasya' (penance). 'We have lost touch with people so we need to atone. We are not asking for votes in the yatra but this is a tapasya to reconnect with the masses,' he emphasized. During a closed-door interaction with civil society activists, when he was greeted with a promise of 'total support'—'We trust you, Rahul ji'—he shot back with a disarming smile, 'Please don't trust politicians.' It was apparent that Rahul Gandhi was all fired up and determined to walk the talk.

The yatra schedule was gruelling. Every morning for over 140 days, between 7 September 2022 and 30 January 2023, the yatris would wake up to an alarm set for 4 a.m., sometimes even earlier. The daily walk of around 25 kilometres would kick off at 6 a.m., often in pitch darkness, especially in the chilly north Indian winter. A yatri recalled requesting Rahul if the yatra timings could be changed because of the dipping temperatures. 'Jab kisan char baje subah uth sakta hai khet mein paani daalne ke liye, toh hum kyon nahi uth sakte (If the farmer can wake up at 4 a.m. to water his fields, why can't we)!' was the rejoinder. Often criticized for shying away from a political challenge, Rahul Gandhi was now leading by example—a young captain charging at the head of his army. The critics who were convinced that Rahul would quit the yatra and go abroad for a holiday were being proven wrong. Clad in his preferred attire of a white T-shirt, jeans and sneakers, Rahul was among the first to arrive at the yatra's starting point every day. He stayed in an air-conditioned container with a bed, a couch and an attached bathroom. It was comfortable but without the frills of a Lutyens' bungalow. Many of the other yatris lived in more spartan mobile vans, often four to six of them rooming together and using a common toilet. Rahul also chose not to shave during the yatra, and he soon developed a bushy, unkempt greying beard. Gone was the mincing brat from Lutyensland; in his place stood a Parashuram-meets-Che Guevara-style figure, the dishevelled anti-establishment yogic look becoming his signature appearance on the yatra. His insistence on wearing only the white T-shirt, at times even in the biting north Indian winter, was reportedly the outcome of his meeting a group of young girls in torn clothes. 'They were shivering in the cold. That day, I vowed that I would also only wear a T-shirt,' he claimed. When a young man struggled to break the security cordon to greet him, Rahul reached out and hugged him. Apparently, the tearful man whispered: 'Nafrat ke bazaar mein aapne mohabbat ki dukaan kholi hai (In the market of hate, you have opened a shop of love).' With that,

Rahul Gandhi found the catchy one-liner that would become the yatra's theme and his own calling card: Mohabbat ki dukaan.

The 'Mohabbat ki dukaan' slogan symbolized a political message of compassion, an alternative to the 'Modi hai toh mumkin hai' (Anything is possible as long as Modi is around) triumphal mantra of the BJP cheerleaders. Where Rahul Gandhi was pitched as a gentle soul talking of love and affection, the Prime Minister was contrasted as a '56-inch' bombastic nationalist trapped in his own imperious personality cult. Humility versus hubris. Inclusion versus exclusion. Softness versus braggadocio. And yes, love versus hate. A template for a fight against the Modi worshippers had been set. A yatra that had started slowly and with limited expectations was now picking up momentum. Video clips of Rahul Gandhi hugging the elderly, lifting and kissing children and chatting with farmers were shared widely. Professionally produced drone shots of the milling crowds with background music went viral on YouTube. Team Rahul had hired the Mumbai-based brand and advertising company Teen Bandar to film the entire yatra and create a buzz on social media. Prashant Chari, co-founder of Teen Bandar, says he was impressed by Rahul Gandhi's focus and discipline. 'We were entering Nanded in Maharashtra from Telangana and it was getting late. Rahul had walked all morning but still had the energy to do a late-night border crossing on foot to address a rally. He just never seemed to tire,' recalls Chari.

Rahul's boundless energy was visible to all, and enabled the yatra to gather traction and much-needed impetus. Be it participating in a boat race in Kochi or getting drenched in the rain in Mysore, he was unflinching in his goal of connecting with common people on the ground. 'All the public interactions we've filmed with Rahul have been natural and instinctive. Even a spontaneous bike ride in Ladakh was his idea to connect with Indians from every corner,' remarks Chari. 'It all worked because there is an authenticity to his personality that people hadn't seen before.' Striding, running, swimming, rowing, gunning his bike, cradling children, hugging the elderly, being perpetually surrounded by people— this was a brand new Rahul, at least in public perception. The Congress's ideological mascot and conscience keeper was now revealing his hitherto reserved, closed-off inner self to a wider world.

So were the photo-ops and sound bites part of a conscious image makeover? In 2020, Rahul Gandhi had rejigged his personal communications team. Srivatsa Y.B., a forty-year-old Youth Congress activist from Karnataka, who had worked on the state unit's social media campaigns, was brought in and given a clear brief by Rahul: 'Align my communication to show the world who I really am. Show, not tell.' Srivatsa set about putting together a small team to recast Rahul Gandhi's image among the masses. Rather than engage with mainstream media, which Rahul was convinced could never be neutral towards him as long as Modi was in power, Srivatsa and team created alternate platforms around social and digital media. This included a volunteer system of young Congress supporters on Instagram and Twitter who were enlisted to amplify the messaging. 'The man you see in his personal videos is the real Rahul Gandhi, totally committed to common people's concerns and wanting to learn more,' said Srivatsa. For example, when Rahul Gandhi met a group of bike mechanics, he apparently spent three hours with them learning how to fix a bike—and four hours acquiring brick-laying skills while chatting with construction workers. Yogendra Yadav insists Rahul Gandhi wasn't performing for the camera at any stage. 'Let me assure you that none of these videos are scripted theatre. Rahul is not a political strategist but more of a spiritual being, someone with strong convictions, a progressive outlook and genuine empathy for the poor.'

But Rahul's spiritual inclinations, seemingly inspired by Gandhian values, could not mask the stark reality confronting the Congress. Demoralized by successive electoral defeats, could the party afford the luxury of being led by a dreamy idealist who didn't want to get trapped in the murky world of political powerplay?

The fact that the yatra spent nineteen days traversing through Kerala—now Rahul's adopted home as Wayanad MP—but didn't touch the crucial battleground state of Uttar Pradesh or the two states—Gujarat and Himachal Pradesh—going to assembly elections in November 2022 didn't go unnoticed. 'Our yatra map wasn't decided keeping elections in mind but was simply taking the most feasible route between Kanyakumari and Kashmir,' claimed Digvijaya Singh. A Gujarat Congress leader recalled the frantic exchange of WhatsApp messages between Congress party functionaries about whether Rahul Gandhi should campaign in Gujarat at all. 'One leader told me that if Rahul campaigns here and we are badly defeated, he will be blamed, so why take the risk. How can you ever win elections with such a defeatist mindset?' argued the Gujarat Congressman. Eventually, Rahul campaigned for just one day in Gujarat, a sign perhaps that the Congress leadership had almost given up the fight in Prime Minister Modi's home state.

So what really did Rahul Gandhi and the Congress achieve by undertaking this strenuous expedition in 2022? Purely as a test of physical endurance, the yatra had undoubtedly boosted Rahul's image. Once repeatedly lampooned by the BJP as a 'pappu' (a dumb kid), and accused by his critics of flitting in and out of politics, and of taking a 'break' in the middle of a Parliament session, Rahul was now seen as a tenacious leader willing to stay the course. Importantly, it earned him the respect of his own party at a time when the Nehru–Gandhi family aura, seemingly lacklustre, was clearly not delivering votes. 'Name one Opposition leader who has consistently taken up the issues that Rahul has—Covid, China, jobs, farmers, cronyism. It is only Rahul who has kept taking the Modi government head-on and being proven right every time,' argued the party's combative media head Pawan Khera. The yatra also instilled a sense of self-belief in the Congress workers when morale was low. 'Every time Rahul Gandhi says "daro mat" (don't be scared), we feel a sense of pride and confidence. If our leader can do it, we can too,' said Youth Congress chief B.V. Srinivas, part of the next-gen team within the party. Rahul was finally earning his inheritance.

But did the yatra really change the national mood or indeed transform the Congress's political fortunes? The BJP won a record number of seats in the 2022 Gujarat assembly elections and triumphed with its allies in three northeastern states where elections were held within weeks of the yatra concluding in February 2023. The Congress did manage to recapture power in Himachal and crucially regain Karnataka in May 2023, but there was no evidence that the yatra itself had downsized Prime Minister Modi's influence or reduced the gap between the two main national parties. 'I don't think you can see the yatra purely through a cost-benefit analysis in a TV studio debate. It is my belief that the yatra brought hope to millions who felt left out and disillusioned by a divisive and authoritarian regime. To use words like "mohabbat" and attempt to bridge the gap between communities is an act of courage in today's India. Rahul Gandhi showed that courage,' affirmed Yogendra Yadav.

Courageous. Strong-willed. Truthful. People-centric. Rahul Gandhi's reinvention—at least in the hearts and minds of Congress supporters—was complete. Still, the nagging question remained unanswered: How was the Congress going to plot a political comeback against a formidable BJP machine?

In the summer of 2020, even as the country was grappling with the Covid lockdown, Sonia Gandhi was despairing about the state of the Congress and her family's hold over the party. With Rahul having given up the party presidentship in the aftermath of the 2019 debacle, Sonia Gandhi was expected to find a revival tonic. Over her long career helming the Congress, Sonia had been a status quo-ist, never keen to rock the boat. But desperate times call for desperate measures. In her hour of need, she turned to Prashant Kishor, the ace election strategist. Kishor was working on the TMC's 2021 Bengal assembly campaign at the time but had parallelly built an equation with Sonia Gandhi, with Priyanka playing interlocutor. He had worked on the Congress's 2017 Uttar Pradesh election fight, even pushing for Priyanka to be made the party's chief ministerial face. While Sonia Gandhi had vetoed that idea, she seemed more open to considering Kishor's suggestions this time around. So in a twelve-hour Zoom conversation spread over three days, Kishor presented a long-term Congress recovery plan to her, which included 100 slides just on the vexed leadership question. 'I was very impressed with her focus. She genuinely wanted to see change,' he claimed. The conversation, however, didn't move forward as concerns over Sonia Gandhi's health and the G-23 'rebellion' took priority. Kishor too was caught up in preparing and strategizing for the fierce battle for Bengal.

Nearly a year later, in May 2021, Sonia Gandhi engaged with Kishor again. Mamata Banerjee had just been triumphant in the Bengal election, and Kishor's stock was high. The Congress president indicated that she wanted the election wunderkind to come on board but also that she needed to consult with her son first. 'We need to get things moving soon. I need a time-bound decision,' insisted Kishor. A month later, Kishor met Rahul with his blueprint for the Congress. 'Rahul was in broad agreement with my proposals but didn't seem as enthused as Sonia Gandhi,' recalled Kishor. Among the various ideas thrown up was the suggestion for a non-Nehru–Gandhi to be made party president, with Rahul Gandhi taking over as Congress parliamentary party leader and Priyanka Gandhi Vadra being given a key organizational role. 'This wasn't the only leadership solution. I offered different combinations and a complete package on how to reconstitute the party,' said Kishor.

Rather than bite the bullet, Sonia Gandhi appointed a committee of senior leaders, including A.K. Antony and Ambika Soni, to evolve a consensus on Kishor's induction into the party. After all, Kishor's initial success had been with Prime Minister Modi, and in many Congress eyes he was still a 'Modi man'. The committee came back with a suggestion that Kishor prove himself in the next round of assembly elections in early 2022, which included Uttar Pradesh, Punjab, Uttarakhand and Goa. 'I made it clear to them that I wasn't a day trader who could bring instant results. I was looking at a long-term ten-year plan that could at the earliest begin with Gujarat 2022 [towards the end of the year],' revealed Kishor. The Congress baulked at the idea. The proposal to draft Kishor was put on hold.

A miffed Kishor went ahead and planned Mamata Banerjee's sudden bid to expand into Goa. 'One day Kishor is talking to us, the next day he is working with Trinamool to defeat us in Goa; how can we trust such a person?' alleged a Congress leader who was involved in the negotiations. Kishor denies he encouraged the Bengal chief minister to contest the Goa elections only to spite the Congress. 'The aim was to defeat the BJP. If the Congress wasn't willing to do it, Mamata, after her great victory in Bengal, was the next best bet,' he maintained. As it turned out, politics in the small, scenic west coast state is very different from what it is on the eastern seaboard; the TMC drew a blank in Goa.

Now, an impatient Kishor dialled the Congress leadership for another round of meetings. The party had lost badly in all the assembly elections in March 2022, and time was running out for the much-talked-about revival plan. This time, Sonia Gandhi showed greater urgency and summoned a high-level meeting of senior CWC members and Congress chief ministers at her 10, Janpath residence. Kishor was asked to make his 350-slide presentation to this group. Nor was this meeting kept a secret. Over three days, with TV cameras parked outside the venue, Kishor shared his plans for restructuring the Congress with the party's top leaders. 'Most members agreed to my suggestions. P. Chidambaram was even tasked to action the plan. But when it came to the crunch, they didn't want to create the model of an empowered action group that would have full authority to reorganize the party. They offered me a general secretary (elections) post, but I didn't want to be just another glorified Congress member,' said Kishor. A senior Congress leader shared his own version of events: 'Prashant Kishor is overambitious. He wanted to be the second most important person in the Congress after Sonia ji. No one can just come and take over the party like this overnight.' The deal fell through. Kishor and the Congress parted ways.

So what does the botched 'Mission PK' tell us about the state of the Congress? That India's oldest party was prompted to actively engage with an 'outsider' like Kishor clearly shows the profound depth of its internal crisis. Sonia Gandhi is highly risk-averse and generally unwilling to disrupt party hierarchies, which makes her taking the lead in this matter surprising, to say the least. Perhaps, her political instincts had convinced her that the Congress needed a major shake-up. Yet even she could not persuade her son to greenlight Kishor's entry into the party. In fact, Rahul Gandhi left on a foreign trip mid-way through Kishor's presentation at 10, Janpath. 'I don't know whether it is out of insecurity or plain overconfidence, but maybe Rahul Gandhi thinks he has better ideas than me for the Congress's future growth. Good luck to him,' remarked Kishor. A member of Team Rahul said the Congress leader was uncertain about Kishor's affiliations: 'We think he is a gun for hire, a mercenary who will go with anyone who gives him the best deal. Please don't forget he made his name by promoting Modi as PM.' Quite simply, the trust deficit between Rahul and Kishor was too deep to be bridged.

With Kishor no longer in the picture, the Congress would need to fix its house without external help. Appointing a new party president was a long-pending issue. Sonia Gandhi had taken over in August 2019 as interim president with the assurance that a replacement would be found through the much-delayed organizational elections. Typically, the Congress had dilly-dallied over the leadership question, with many workers still hoping that Rahul Gandhi would return. But with an adamant Rahul refusing to accept any official post and preferring to embark on his yatra instead, Sonia Gandhi turned to old Gandhi-family loyalists to find a way out. Her first choice was Ashok Gehlot, someone who had wide experience in handling the party's convoluted, byzantine power networks, but when he refused to quit as Rajasthan chief minister, the Congress leadership was stuck.

This was when Shashi Tharoor decided to throw his hat into the ring. A man of many parts—MP, author, diplomat, public speaker—Tharoor is a bit of an iconoclast in an archaic Congress system that prefers its leaders to remain mostly submissive and stay out of the headlines, and certainly not a run-of-the-mill Congressman. Good-looking, with stylish sartorial choices, his signature hair flip and sharp intellect, the articulate Congress MP made an instant mark soon after first becoming an MP in 2009. He has legions of fans, and is a rockstar among a younger, urban, English-speaking demographic. At a literary festival in New Delhi once, as Tharoor held forth on his latest book, a young woman stood up in the crowd to ask, 'Are you open to offers of marriage?' Such is the boundless appeal of Shashi Tharoor. Yet somehow the Congress has been unwilling to give him the space and attention that his popular appeal warrants. In 2017, Tharoor had become the founder–chairman of the All India Professionals' Congress, a group of working professionals who support the Congress, but he wasn't really able to break into any of the Congress's key decision-making bodies. 'Because he is a lateral entrant into politics with a mind of his own on most issues, his detractors in the party have always accused him of not being a team player,' asserted a Tharoor supporter.

For Tharoor, the decision to contest the presidential election was a chance to not only raise his profile within the party but also impress upon the Congress leadership the need for an open contest instead of a 'fixed' match. 'I think my contesting will strengthen the Congress's democratic ethos and show that we do have genuine internal democracy,' he claimed. Rahul Gandhi had insisted on a free and fair election, but not everyone in the party was as willing to play by the rules. 'We got phone calls from a senior Congress leader close to 10, Janpath warning us not to attend any presidential election campaign meeting called by Dr Tharoor,' revealed a party delegate from Kerala, the three-time Thiruvananthapuram MP's home state. When Tharoor went to the Delhi Congress headquarters, only three delegates turned up to meet him. 'We were told by our Congress leaders that if we were seen at Tharoor's meeting, our careers would be finished,' divulged a Delhi Congress delegate. Clearly, not all Congress leaders were comfortable with the virtues of inner-party democracy. Tharoor remained undaunted in his cross-country effort to garner support, even though he knew it was a losing battle.

With Gehlot ruling himself out and Tharoor unwilling to withdraw from the contest, it was left to K.C. Venugopal to find a more 'suitable' choice. While Digvijaya Singh was asked to keep his nomination papers ready, Venugopal worked on the party's Rajya Sabha leader, Mallikarjun Kharge, to accept the role. A veteran leader from Karnataka, a well-known

Dalit face who had risen through the ranks, a staunch Gandhi-family loyalist—whose children are named Priyadarshini and Priyank after Indira Gandhi and Priyanka—Kharge ticked all the boxes. He was never going to challenge the supremacy of the Gandhi family, so his reassuring presence would ensure continuity with change. The ageing Kharge was initially unsure. 'You are asking me to wear a crown of thorns at this age in life,' he warned Venugopal in their late-night meeting. Finally, just a day before the nomination process concluded, Kharge agreed to contest as party president. When several prominent CWC members accompanied him to file his nomination, it was apparent that there would be only one winner. 'He is our unofficial "official" choice,' quipped one CWC member.

When the results came in, as expected, Kharge had won—with 7,897 votes to Tharoor's 1,072. It was a mismatch but not quite the overwhelmingly one-sided contest many had anticipated. When Sonia Gandhi became Congress president in 2000, her opponent, Jitendra Prasada, received just 94 votes. In comparison, Tharoor had managed a respectable showing. 'You can say what you want as mediapersons, but our poll was free and fair unlike the BJP's, where the RSS decides who leads their party,' insisted Madhusudan Mistry, head of the Congress's election authority. Interestingly, while Kharge's campaign managers had had the backing of the party's hierarchy, Rahul Gandhi had steadfastly refused to take sides. He had even brought forward his yatra by a month to avoid being in Delhi when elections were held. 'When anyone asked Rahul ji whom he preferred as president, his firm reply was, "I am focused on my yatra. I have nothing to do with this election,"' claimed Venugopal, now firmly entrenched as a key power centre within the party, a bridge between the old order and the new, and involved in every major decision.

Interestingly, though, even as Kharge began building his own team of trusted aides with the intention of establishing his political authority, Team Rahul continued to loom large. In December 2022, though the Congress was swept aside in Gujarat, it won in Himachal Pradesh. Party leaders were uncertain how to mark the occasion. 'We thought of putting up solo posters congratulating Kharge ji for the Himachal success since this was the first win as party president, but then were told not to forget to congratulate Rahul and Priyanka. In the end, we were a little confused, so we played it safe by showing all three faces,' admitted a party official. The truth is, while Kharge was party president, the Gandhi family was still the de facto final port of call on key issues. 'Kharge suggests, Rahul approves, Venugopal executes. It is a system of power-sharing that ensures a division of responsibility,' remarked a Congress old-timer.

After a prolonged period of uncertainty and turmoil, when its leadership slip-ups and even its very existence as a viable political force had been called into question, the grand old party seemed to be finding its feet again. The Congress had an experienced president at the helm, but the party's talisman now was undoubtedly Rahul Gandhi. Be it flying off to London to deliver lectures at Cambridge University, or sharing touchy-feely YouTube videos of meeting farmers one day and truckers the next, or even interacting with chocolate makers in Ooty, Rahul Gandhi was determinedly recasting his image as a neta with a difference. He was now a fierce party ideologue and not a backroom strategist, a leader with the common touch, disinterested in any deal-making and taking on the storm clouds of politics in his stride. It was almost as if the Congress's mascot was staying in public life on his own terms, unchained by convention or rules of power politics. An endearing figure for his admirers, entitled dynast to his opponents—public opinion remained sharply divided on Rahul Gandhi's latest avatar. Years of being savagely tormented and taunted by the BJP and still standing defiant and undeterred had paradoxically awakened in Rahul Gandhi a certain indomitable spirit. He had been verbally abused, but he never retaliated, choosing instead to comfort the suffering and the neglected. He was a staunch anti-Modi critic in public forums but also fiercely guarded in his private space. One aspect hadn't changed, though: when he did take off on a quiet holiday, his party was as clueless as the prying media.

In August 2023, when he undertook a private visit to Goa, the local Congress unit and the media in the state were understandably excited. 'He will be meeting with a range of people on the visit, including business persons and karyakartas,' a local Congress leader informed the Goan media. Imagine the surprise when a photo was received by Pramod Acharya, editor of Prudent, a leading Goan cable channel, of Rahul Gandhi not with karyakartas or businesspeople but cuddling Jack Russell terrier puppies in north Goa's Mapusa. 'We were not sure initially whether the pictures were fake or not, but we later got the video of Rahul playing with the puppies at the home of Stanley Braganca, whose wife, Sharvani, runs a dog kennel. We thought he had come to revive the Goa Congress, but I guess he had other things in mind!' Acharya said, laughing. Weeks later, Rahul Gandhi would share a video on his YouTube channel of him 'gifting' a cute puppy—Noorie—to his mother. 'I'd like you all to meet the newest and cutest member of our family. Unconditional love and uncompromising loyalty, there is so much this beautiful animal can teach us,' was his message while sharing the video. Cynical political watchers may snigger, but the images became widely popular among Instagram-addicted youth. Clearly, the 'Mohabbat ki dukaan' pitch was alive and well and gaining Rahul Gandhi a fan following.

But what of the enfeebled party that was still struggling to find its route back to power? Rahul Gandhi may have been marching to his own beat with a puppy at his heels, but the Congress, indeed the entire Opposition, was facing a more ferocious bloodhound unleashed by Modi: a legally 'weaponized' ED, a terrifying, all-powerful government agency out to change the rules of the political game.

EIGHT

'Hamare Saath ED Hai': Washing Machine Politics

IT was a mid-summer evening in May 2023. Despite the air-conditioning in the Nashik hotel room, NCP leader Chhagan Bhujbal was sweating profusely. As he sipped a glass of his favourite whisky, he looked and sounded anxious. He had a greying beard, tired eyes and a gaunt look on his face; the spring in his step that had characterized his adventurous political career was missing. Just a few days earlier, he had received yet another notice from the ED in an alleged money laundering case. The original case had been filed in 2016, and the matter had been dragging on ever since. Accused, along with his son and nephew, of irregularities in awarding contracts worth over Rs 100 crore to a Mumbai developer, Bhujbal had already spent two and a half years in jail before he was granted bail. The lengthy period in jail had adversely affected his health, and he was constantly popping pills. 'I can't sleep at night just thinking of my days in prison. I am seventy-five now, but they [the ED] are still gunning for me,' he moaned.

'But you are such a senior leader. I am sure Sharad Pawar will help you,' I responded. 'When you are in trouble, you are alone in life. Who was there to assist me when I was in jail? Matlabi hai saari duniya

(The world is selfish),' Bhujbal lamented, asking his aide to prepare another round of drinks. He recalled how Anil Deshmukh, former home minister and another senior NCP leader, was released after spending thirteen months in jail on money-laundering charges. Upon his release, Deshmukh had alleged he was made an 'offer' in jail to join the BJP if he wanted 'protection' from the law. 'Ab woh mujhe bhi Deshmukh ji ki tarah phasana chahate hain (Now they want to trap me like Deshmukh),' alleged Bhujbal.

Bhujbal, who is a former Maharashtra deputy chief minister, joined Pawar when the latter broke away to form the NCP in 1999. He started his career in the Shiv Sena as one of Bal Thackeray's key lieutenants. Bhujbal grew up in extreme poverty, living in a tiny one-room tenement near Mumbai's Byculla market. His family sold flowers and vegetables on the roadside to make ends meet. Now, like so many Maharashtra politicians, he spearheads a vast business empire that stretches across several sectors, from educational institutes to real estate to agriculture. 'I am a self-made man who has come up the hard way because of my own efforts. The only reason that the agencies are after me is because I come from a humble OBC community. Do you think they will treat any upper-caste politician like this?' he fulminated. The OBC factor was Bhujbal's calling card: in a Maratha-dominated political milieu, he used it frequently to emphasize his relevance.

Bhujbal's life story is compelling; the reasons for his imprisonment less so. The charges of corruption are well-documented, but I was trying to be as empathetic as possible and listened patiently to his woes. 'There is only one solution now. We have to join hands with Modiji and the BJP. Even Pawar Saheb knows this, only he can't seem to make up his mind,' he said as large plates of chicken tikka and seekh kebab were placed on the table. Bhujbal is a generous host. The whisky bottle was almost empty by now. But how will joining hands with the BJP help your case, I asked. 'Come on, why are you acting innocent? Everyone knows what is happening,' he retorted.

Just weeks after this conversation, in July 2023, I was woken up from a Sunday snooze by a colleague on the news desk. 'We need you live on air right away. The NCP has split. Ajit Pawar is being sworn in along with a few more NCP leaders, all of whom are joining the Eknath Shinde-led BJP–Shiv Sena government,' he informed me. As I scanned the names of the new cabinet ministers, one name stood out. Chhagan Bhujbal was back in government. A few days later, I met Bhujbal at his official bungalow in Mumbai's plush Malabar Hill area. He had lived in ministerial comfort for much of the previous three decades and seemed completely at ease here—a sharp contrast to the nervous Opposition politician I had met in that dark Nashik hotel room. 'I assume you are sleeping well now?' I quipped. 'Yes, yes, I am so relaxed now, I can't tell you—it is like a rebirth,' was Bhujbal's cheery response. His broad smile was back.

As it turned out, the sense of relief in the Bhujbal household was not unfounded. In December 2023, the ED withdrew its petition in the Bombay High Court seeking the quashing of a 2018 order that had granted Bhujbal and his nephew Sameer bail and allowed them to renew their passports and travel abroad. The case was for all practical purposes put in cold storage. Bhujbal was no longer a marked man.

Bhujbal was not alone in feeling comforted by the change in political affiliations. The leader of the breakaway NCP group, Ajit Pawar, had a slew of corruption charges against him. A state Anti-Corruption Bureau inquiry into an alleged Rs 70,000 crore irrigation scam when he was water resources minister was still being monitored by the Bombay High Court. Meanwhile, the ED was investigating apparent irregularities in loans given by the Maharashtra State Co-operative Bank. While the ED chargesheet didn't mention Ajit Pawar specifically, properties belonging to companies allegedly owned by him and his family members were attached. In particular, the ED investigation was reportedly focusing on Ajit Pawar's wife, Sunetra, who was a majority shareholder in one of the companies under the scanner. 'When Ajit dada was told that his wife could be summoned and even arrested by the ED, he panicked,' claimed an NCP leader.

A desperate Ajit met with his uncle Sharad Pawar, along with two senior NCP MPs, Praful Patel and Sunil Tatkare, to find a solution. In July 2022, the ED seized four floors of a commercial building owned by Patel in connection with a money-laundering case involving gangster Iqbal Mirchi, a member of underworld don Dawood Ibrahim's gang. Tatkare too was facing an ED probe into corruption and land-grabbing charges. The trio pleaded with the NCP founder–president to tie up with the BJP. 'They told me that the BJP was a better bet for the future, but all they actually wanted was protection from the ED. I made it clear that they were free to leave but I would not join them,' claimed Sharad Pawar.

With the senior Pawar refusing to take the bait, Ajit Pawar and Patel revived their earlier conversation with the BJP. The deal was rather simple. At least half a dozen senior NCP leaders had ED cases against them, which would be withdrawn or put on the backburner in return for political support. Patel denies the charge of a deal or a quid pro quo. 'This wasn't about any of us but about saving the party. Our choice was between a divided Opposition and a Narendra Modi-led strong Centre. We chose stability,' he argued.

Notably, just days before the breakaway group allied with the BJP, Prime Minister Modi had referred to allegations of scams against NCP leaders, including the irrigation scam in which vast amounts were ostensibly spent on irrigation projects, but the state's irrigation potential barely registered any increase, thus leading to allegations of massive graft. Addressing a BJP booth-workers meeting in Bhopal, Modi warned of zero tolerance against the 'corrupt' NCP. 'We should have a "ghotala" (scam) metre for them,' he declared. Maharashtra's BJP Deputy Chief Minister Devendra Fadnavis too had promised to send Ajit Pawar to jail in the alleged irrigation scam. Now, he was set to share the post of deputy chief minister with him. 'We are partners in developing Maharashtra,' was his pithy response to the brazen, cynical shift in the party's stand.

Ironically, it was Mumbai BJP leader and former MP Kirit Somaiya who had played a key role in pushing the enforcement agencies to act against the NCP leaders, including Hasan Mushrif. Somaiya revealed documents that he claimed proved Mushrif's involvement in fraud and money laundering. Later, when Mushrif was sworn in as a minister in a power-sharing arrangement with the BJP, Somaiya admitted to feeling embarrassed but not disheartened. 'Sometimes in politics you have to sacrifice your personal goals for the party. Yes, my crusade didn't reach its logical conclusion, but at least we formed a government in Maharashtra,' he said. In February 2024, the Mumbai police's Economic Offences Wing filed a closure report against Ajit Pawar in the co-operative bank case, claiming that a criminal case was filed 'due to mistake of facts'. The irrigation scam inquiry too petered out. The ED no longer showed any urgency in pursuing the cases against Mushrif, Patel or Tatkare. The CBI too filed a closure report in an Air India merger case against Patel just months after he joined the NDA. Like Bhujbal, all the NCP leaders who switched over could sleep peacefully.

***

The template for political immunity from prosecution was set a year earlier, in June 2022, when the Uddhav Thackeray-led MVA government in Maharashtra was toppled after a dramatic coup staged by Eknath Shinde, a close aide of the Shiv Sena chieftain. An energetic political go-getter, seen sporting a flaming red tilak on his forehead and a well-trimmed beard, the short-statured Shinde, a senior minister in the MVA government, was eyeing the chief minister's chair while Uddhav Thackeray was convalescing in hospital after spinal surgery in December 2021. 'I am doing all the hard work for the party and the government, but the credit is going entirely to Uddhav ji and now to his son Aaditya. Why should I work under a kid like Aaditya?' a frustrated Shinde complained to a party colleague. Matters came to a head when the party's Thane strongman was reportedly kept waiting in an anteroom for more than an hour at Varsha, the chief minister's official residence, only to be told that

Uddhav ji was unwell but he could meet Aaditya or Thackeray's wife, Rashmi, instead. 'That was the day I decided enough is enough, I will not compromise my self-respect any further,' claimed Shinde.

'What absolute rubbish!' countered Sanjay Raut, MP and Shiv Sena (UBT) spokesperson. 'Uddhav ji gave Shinde ji a free hand in running his ministry and the party in Thane; he trusted him completely. There was no interference.' According to Raut, Shinde's rebellion was triggered by a discreet ED inquiry into two of his associates, including a prominent builder. 'He was worried that the inquiry would soon reach his doorstep, and he feared he would be sent to jail,' asserted Raut. If the Uddhav camp is to be believed, a month before he quit the party, a tearful Shinde had pleaded with the Sena leadership to ally with the BJP, else he would be arrested. 'I am a grandfather now; I don't want to be jailed,' he had cried.

Sensing an ambitious Shinde's restiveness was Union Home Minister Amit Shah, who had a score to settle, having been checkmated by the Uddhav Thackeray–Sharad Pawar duo in 2019. Shah claimed that he had rung up Shinde in November 2019 itself, minutes after the Thackeray-led government was sworn in. 'I told him that whenever he felt suffocated by the Thackerays, he should call me,' he revealed. The only other politician kept in the loop was Fadnavis, still seething at the manner in which the Sena had ditched him in 2019. When the Shah–Shinde–Fadnavis troika met in Delhi, Shah warmed up to the feisty Sena leader and assured him full support if he could break the party and form a government. 'It will not be easy, but I will try,' promised Shinde, who was keenly aware of the clout of the Thackerays within the Sena rank and file.

Formed as a nativist sons-of-the-soil party in Mumbai in the 1960s, the Shiv Sena is a network of local 'shakha pramukhs' (branch heads) and their dedicated cadres, bound together by a regionally assertive 'Maharashtrian first' sentiment, a shared militant Hindutva identity and the personality cult of party founder Bal Thackeray. While the charismatic Balasaheb was alive, he was the unquestioned supremo, feared and admired in equal measure. After his death in 2012, the leadership baton passed to his son

Uddhav, whose low-key appearance, soft voice and unassuming style were in marked contrast to his father's imposing, larger-than-life image. By 2019, Uddhav's son Aaditya had entered the political fray as well and became the first Thackeray family member to contest an election. Educated in English-language schools, the slightly built, jeans-clad, well-spoken Aaditya is a millennial-generation politician, more comfortable speaking at a conclave on climate change than leading street protests. Many Shiv Sainik workers, with their combative politics of 'thokshahi' (rule by force; the Sena's original trademark), could not relate to Aaditya's more urbane style of functioning. 'We have an emotional connection with the party because of Balasaheb, but you can't expect us to automatically transfer loyalty to the grandson,' explained a senior Sena leader.

Shinde, in his white long-sleeved shirt and matching trousers, was a dominant figure in Thane, a sprawling district near Mumbai. Where he once plied an autorickshaw on crowded streets, he now moved around in a fleet of cars and owned a large farmhouse with a private helipad, proof of how the Sena had transitioned from a 'Marathi manoos' regionally chauvinist force into a wealth-creating political enterprise. But could the loyal Thane satrap, however resourceful, take on an enduring family legacy and actually split a party in power? A man of few words, Shinde had two weapons in his armoury as he set about his mission to take down his leader. The first was the unstinted backing of the Union home minister. The second was the looming presence of the ED.

Like with the NCP, there were a number of Shiv Sena leaders too on the ED's radar. Among them was Pratap Sarnaik, another ambitious autorickshaw driver-turned-three-term MLA from Thane. Profiting from his political contacts, Sarnaik had built a lucrative real estate and hospitality business in and around Mumbai and Thane. A vociferous supporter of the Thackerays, Sarnaik's home was splashed with pictures of him with the party's first family. 'I would be nothing without their blessings and support,' he declared. Yet, despite Uddhav Thackeray being Maharashtra chief minister, Sarnaik was a troubled man. In 2021–22, the ED raided Sarnaik and his business associates and took possession of more than 100 plots belonging to a firm owned by the Sena MLA. A Thane-based builder who was close to Sarnaik was also arrested by the ED in a National Spot Exchange Limited money-laundering case. With the net tightening around him, a despairing Sarnaik dashed off an open letter in June 2021 to Uddhav Thackeray: 'In my personal opinion, it is imperative that we patch up with Honourable Prime Minister Narendra Modi. A lot of our supporters feel that by doing so the harassment that Pratap Sarnaik, Anil Parab and Ravindra Waikar and their families are facing will stop. I have been fighting a legal battle over the last seven months with no support from the state government or any other leader.' (Parab and Waikar were also Sena MLAs under the ED lens. Waikar left the Shiv Sena (UBT) in March 2024 to join the Shinde-led group as the ED closed in on him. He contested and won the 2024 elections from Mumbai North-West by just 48 votes. Subsequently, the Mumbai police closed a case against him for the illegal construction of a hotel on municipal land.)

Sarnaik's letter raised eyebrows. A Sena MLA close to the chief minister was publicly claiming that the ED was harassing him and advocating an alliance with the BJP to save him from the law. 'I kept telling Uddhav ji that we should go back to the BJP. Big netas have connections in Delhi and can always be protected, but what happens to karyakartas and MLAs like us who have to suffer,' said Sarnaik. Thackeray pleaded helplessness to stop the ED investigation. 'They are after me and my family too; we all have to fight,' was the Sena chief's defiant response.

A despondent Sarnaik began considering his options—and when Shinde offered the opportunity to switch sides, he decided to grab it. The duo was engaged in a turf war in Thane, but that didn't seem to matter, given the looming threat of intense harassment and possible imprisonment. A meeting with Home Minister Shah was the clincher. Uddhav supporters claimed that Sarnaik wept before the home minister, terrified that he would be sent to jail if he didn't join the defecting MLAs. 'Yes, I did meet Mr Shah in Delhi before joining the breakaway group, but please don't believe the stories being planted against me. My only request to Amit bhai was to give me an assurance that I would not be hounded by the enforcement agencies. Once he promised that, there was no turning back,' claimed Sarnaik, who pointed out that the cases against him were still being heard in courts.

Like Sarnaik, another Thackeray loyalist, Yashwant Jadhav, was also in a tizzy. In May 2022, he was summoned by the ED on allegations that he had purchased properties in Mumbai by paying through an illegal 'hawala' route. Months earlier, the Income Tax department had cracked down on Jadhav and attached forty-one properties allegedly owned by him and his aides. As a former standing-committee chairman of the Brihanmumbai Municipal Corporation, Jadhav had controlled some enormously lucrative money-spinning civic contracts. The Income Tax department even found a diary at Jadhav's residence that detailed suspicious entries worth crores. One of these included a Rs 50 lakh watch and another a Rs 2 crore 'gift', both presented to Matoshree, the Thackeray residence in Bandra. When asked about it, Jadhav nonchalantly claimed that he was referring to his mother as 'Matoshree'!

Jadhav's wife, Yamini, was a Sena MLA from Byculla in central Mumbai. With the couple being repeatedly summoned by the ED and the Income Tax department, panic set in. Shinde's call to them was a boon; they almost instantly agreed to join him. 'We tried to convince Uddhav ji to return to the path of Hindutva and ally with the BJP, but he was adamant. We are Hindutva-waadis first,' was Yashwant Jadhav's public defence. In an attempt to give an emotional edge to her defection, Yamini released a video claiming that she had been suffering from cancer for several months but that the top Sena leadership hadn't bothered to visit her. 'I was left alone,' she cried. The rhetoric and tears couldn't hide the truth: the Jadhavs didn't want an ED or an Income Tax department sword hanging over their future.

A similar case was that of Bhavana Gawali, a five-time Sena MP. In August 2021, the ED carried out multiple raids on properties linked to the parliamentarian after an FIR lodged by the police accused her of misusing government grants and embezzling funds worth Rs 14 crore. Pursuing the case against her was none other than Kirit Somaiya, claiming he had irrefutable evidence of her involvement. Like the others, Gawali too was looking for a way out. When she was contacted by the young MP Shrikant Shinde, son of the aspiring chief minister, she unhesitatingly declared her support for the Shinde camp. 'Just no ED harassment, please,' she reportedly implored. On record, though, she insisted that she had switched allegiance because she was a supporter of Prime Minister Modi.

Not surprisingly, when Shinde finally made his big move and broke away from the Shiv Sena in June 2022, the numbers were overwhelmingly in his favour. As many as forty of the Shiv Sena's fifty-six MLAs and twelve of the party's nineteen MPs chose to join hands with him. The MLAs were first driven to a Surat resort, then flown to a hotel in Guwahati, before finally arriving in Mumbai via Goa ten days later. As they travelled from one BJP-ruled state to another, the MLAs were provided state 'protection': local police officers accompanied them at all times. While Shinde was the face of the rebellion, the operation was personally supervised by Home Minister Shah from Delhi. 'Amit Shah ji ne humko bahut madad di (Amit Shah helped us a lot),' a Shinde-supporting MLA admitted. During their stay in a Guwahati hotel, the MLAs were looked after by Assam Chief Minister Himanta Biswa Sarma. 'He assured us that we were in safe hands,' revealed one of the defectors.

The destabilization and eventual downfall of the Opposition-led Maharashtra government in the summer of 2022 was a glaring instance of the ED being 'weaponized'. The Modi government stood accused of abusing the ED's coercive powers and drawing a supposedly independent agency meant to act against criminality into a battle for supremacy between two warring factions of a rival political party. 'Why do you keep saying "ED, ED"? Many of us who left had no ED cases. We broke away because we wanted to revive the original Hindutva alliance,' said Deepak Kesarkar, a senior Shiv Sena minister. 'All those charged continue to be probed; no one is being let off,' maintained Amit Shah. And yet, all the evidence suggests that the cases built up by the ED against those who switched sides were either slowed down or rendered redundant. No one who joined the Eknath Shinde camp has been convicted or jailed for any of the alleged crimes they were once being investigated for.

In contrast, the voluble Uddhav loyalist Sanjay Raut, who had become a one-man army defending the Thackerays, was arrested by the ED in August 2022, weeks after the new Shinde-led government was sworn in. Raut was accused of money laundering in a slum redevelopment case in Mumbai and imprisoned for three months. When he was granted bail, the Bombay High Court, in a stinging order, described his arrest as 'ab initio illegal'. 'He was arrested for no reason. This truth is glaring … It is only then due to the court intervention that he could get a room with some ventilation in ED custody. All this prima facie indicates that his arrest is nothing but a witch-hunt and annihilation of his valuable rights,' stated the court order.

A Rajya Sabha MP, Raut claimed that at least three BJP leaders in Delhi had contacted him before his arrest and offered to bail him out provided he ditch the Thackerays and help topple the MVA government. Accusing the ED of being part of a 'criminal syndicate of the BJP,' Raut wrote to then Vice President Venkaiah Naidu in February 2022, seeking 'protection from the abuse of power to perpetuate intimidation and harassment of MPs'. He even warned at a press conference just days ahead of his arrest that he had obtained video evidence to expose ED officials who were extorting money by blackmailing local businessmen. The alleged video was never released, but Raut was spoiling for a fight with the ED. 'Do you know that on the day the ED officials raided my house and eventually arrested me, they kept telling me, "Sir, uparwalon se boliye, woh sambhal lenge (Why don't you speak to those on top; they will sort this out),"' he disclosed.

Raut's version is contested by ED officials who claim that they act on evidence and not political inclinations. But the whispers in the power corridors repeatedly echo two words to describe the ED's actions against political figures: 'washing machine'. 'Sarkar mein jao, sab paap dhul jaate hain (Join the government, all your sins are washed). ED is like Lalita ji in the famous Surf ad,' chuckled Raut. It is an efficient washing machine indeed: go in stained and dirty if in the Opposition, come out on the other side as a member of the BJP, squeaky clean.

While few would admit to ED 'protection' on camera, Harshvardhan Patil, a former Congress minister who switched to the BJP before the 2019 Maharashtra assembly polls, admitted at a public gathering, 'Why did I join the BJP? Everything is easy-going and peaceful now. I get sound sleep as there are no inquiries.' An embarrassed Patil later clarified that his remarks were 'misinterpreted'.

Jitendra Awhad, a former MVA government minister in Maharashtra and one of the few senior NCP leaders to have remained in the Sharad Pawar camp, shared an interesting anecdote. Apparently, when the toppling machinations were on, Awhad met one of the Sena leaders involved in the coup and asked him to consider his personal equation with the Thackeray family before taking a final call. 'They made you what you are and now you are betraying them. The Sainiks and the public won't forgive you,' Awhad cautioned. The Sena leader retorted confidently: 'Let the elections decide who is with whom. For now, I know only one thing: hamare saath ED hai (the ED is with us).'

Touché.

The Enforcement Directorate headquarters are located on the leafy Dr Abdul Kalam Road in the heart of Lutyens' Delhi. A three-storey complex spread over several wings, the large premises are a marked change from the small, dingy rooms of the previous headquarters in Lok Nayak Bhawan near Khan Market, which the ED shared with other government departments. The shift in address reflects the rising clout of an organization that was set up in 1956 as a small enforcement unit to investigate cases of violation of the Foreign Exchange Regulation Act, 1947 within the Department of Economic Affairs. It was named the Enforcement Directorate a year later, in 1957, but did not take a frontal role in major financial crime investigations. It was the high noon of a socialistic outlook, and the ED often ended up focusing on small transactions in foreign currency instead. During the Indira Gandhi years in the 1970s, Income Tax was the more feared government department. Ridiculously high tax rates meant that any raids to seize stashes of 'black money' from politicians and businessmen instantly grabbed headlines. The ED had preventive detention powers under punitive laws like the Foreign Exchange Regulation Act (FERA) and the Conservation of Foreign Exchange and Prevention of Smuggling Activities Act, 1974 (COFEPOSA), but the targets were usually gold smugglers and import–export companies, not politicians.

The first time the ED acquired a political profile was during Rajiv Gandhi's tenure in the mid-1980s, when he appointed the pensive-looking Vishwanath Pratap Singh as his finance minister with a mandate to weed out corruption. V.P. Singh brought on board his trusted officer Bhure Lal as enforcement director. A 1970-batch IAS officer, Lal, with his impressive moustache, soon became a dreaded figure, using his departmental powers to investigate and raid several leading businessmen, from the Ambanis to the Thapars. Each raid was accompanied by a rush of publicity. V.P. Singh was using the ED to build his image as 'Mr Clean', an artful positioning that would lead him to challenge and undermine Rajiv Gandhi over the Bofors scandal and eventually become Prime Minister himself in 1989. And so the ED took its first steps into a rather murky political realm.

But with economic liberalization in the 1990s, there was a gradual recognition that harsh anti-business laws needed to be reviewed and foreign exchange treated as an asset rather than a scarce resource. FERA was replaced by the less draconian Foreign Exchange Management Act (FEMA) in 1999, and a violation of FEMA laws was ruled a civil offence with no direct imprisonment. But FEMA wasn't the only new legislation that was put in place. Amidst a growing global clamour to clamp down on drug trafficking and its links to money laundering, the PMLA, 2002 was enacted, a criminal law with stringent bail conditions, including reversing the burden of proof onto the accused to prove their innocence. According to Section 45 of the PMLA, bail can be granted to an accused in a money-laundering case only if twin conditions are satisfied: there should be prima facie satisfaction that the accused has not committed the offence and is not likely to commit any offence while on bail. Drafted and passed by the Vajpayee-led NDA government, it was notified by the Congress-led UPA government in 2005, a rare instance in which both major parties were in broad agreement. 'It wasn't our baby; it was only handed over to us under commitments we had made as a member of the international Financial Action Task Force,' insisted lawyer–politician P. Chidambaram, who was the UPA's finance minister. But did he not foresee the potential for misuse of an excessively harsh legislation? 'How was I to know the next government would weaponize the law?' he responded.

The Act may have passed from one government to the next, but it was tightened further in the NDA years through a series of amendments that expanded the scope of what constituted a 'scheduled offence' under it. Many of the amendments between 2015 and 2019 were brought in as money bills to avoid any rigorous parliamentary scrutiny in the Rajya Sabha. Widening the ambit of money laundering, a 2019 amendment clarified that 'proceeds of crime' under section 3 of the PMLA include 'any property that may directly or indirectly be derived or obtained as a result of any criminal activity relatable to the scheduled offence'. As a result, the Act doesn't differentiate between a terrorist and a mere car dealer, and anyone suspected of dealing with laundered money, even unknowingly, can be arrested or have their assets frozen or seized. 'It's crazily draconian,' said Abhimanyu Bhandari, a leading specialist in PMLA law. 'An FIR may be filed against a property dealer in Gurugram for cheating, but if you have bought a flat from him, the ED can draw you in by linking you to the proceeds of his crime. It just makes it so easy to fix anyone you want.'

Rather than strike down some of the harsh provisions of the PMLA, in July 2022, a three-judge bench of the Supreme Court, which was presided over by Justice A.M. Khanwilkar, upheld the constitutionality of the Act, effectively ratifying the wide investigative powers of the ED and stringent bail provisions. While deeming ED officers to be distinct from the police, the apex court also upheld section 50 of the PMLA, which empowers ED officials to record statements on oath from any person, which are admissible in court unlike those made to the police. The judgment was delivered just two days before Justice Khanwilkar's retirement. Khanwilkar was also part of the bench that dismissed the plea of Zakia Jafri, widow of slain MP Ehsan Jafri, who was killed in the 2002 Gujarat riots. Zakia Jafri had challenged the clean chit given to sixty-four people, including Narendra Modi, in the riot cases. On the basis of the court ruling, the Gujarat police on the very next day arrested activist Teesta Setalvad and former Indian Police Service (IPS) officer R.B. Sreekumar on charges of fabricating evidence. In February 2024, Justice Khanwilkar would be appointed as chairperson of the Lokpal of India, a weighty post-retirement sinecure. His PMLA ruling is under review by a larger Constitution bench after an appeal was filed, but no final judgment has been passed. With the review process delayed, the Supreme Court in August 2024 was constrained to emphasize that bail is the rule and jail is the exception even in PMLA cases.

'The PMLA judgment is a black spot on the Supreme Court. The ED has been weaponized to serve its political masters,' warned Dushyant Dave, senior advocate and a trenchant critic of an alleged executive–judiciary nexus. Dave's warning, which came just days after the Khanwilkar judgement, would prove prescient. The ED is now easily the most powerful—and dreaded—agency in the country. It has become a hulking behemoth, basically supervising investigations into almost every suspected major financial offence. It's been called the 'new god who controls everything'. All that the government needs is a pliant but effective departmental leadership that is willing to exercise untrammelled powers and, as alleged by the Opposition, use those coercive powers to prosecute political adversaries on behalf of the government. Finding an officer who will be his master's voice isn't difficult in India's vast bureaucratic set-up; the Modi government would find its ideal recruit soon enough.

Few knew who the chief election commissioner of the country was until T.N. Seshan gave the post dramatic visibility in the 1990s. Even fewer perhaps knew who the chief of the ED was until the balding, moustachioed, sleepy-eyed Sanjay Mishra, with his unblinking stare, stepped into the post in November 2018. Seshan relished his media prominence; Mishra, by contrast, was the shadowy all-powerful figure who transformed the image of the central agency without hogging the headlines for himself. An Indian Revenue Service officer from the 1984 batch, the Lucknow-born biochemistry graduate began his career as an assistant director in the Income Tax department. Batchmates recall him being a quiet performer, very meticulous in his work. 'He is a no-nonsense stickler for rules who can't be bullied by anyone easily but someone who also has strong likes and dislikes,' was how a colleague described him.

A profile of him in *The Indian Express* recounts how Mishra, an assistant director in the ED in charge of the Agra–Jaipur division at the time, carried out a raid on receiving information about a Rs 20 lakh hawala transaction. During the raids, it was revealed that the suspect was a businessman from Pakistan's Sindh province and had fled to India because of religious persecution. Apparently, Mishra filed the case but made some 'adjustments' to ensure the suspect wasn't judged harshly. A journalist who tracks the ED says that Mishra's reputation for being 'non-corrupt' meant that it wasn't easy for the usual well-networked 'fixers' in the national capital to access him. 'A middleman once sent an expensive watch as a Diwali gift to the director. It was promptly returned with a stern warning not to attempt to bribe him,' said the journalist.

A publicity-shy hard taskmaster who couldn't be bought, but with razor-sharp political antennae, Mishra was just the kind of quietly efficient officer the Modi government was looking for to handle a crucial investigative agency. Interestingly, Mishra did a nine-year stint, beginning in 1994, in Ahmedabad in the Income Tax investigating department, where he reportedly caught the eye of both the BJP and Congress leaderships. An early benefactor was Congress leader Ahmed Patel, who was impressed by Mishra's readiness to go the extra mile when taking up politically sensitive cases. It was the Congress which gave Mishra his big break: he was appointed as joint secretary in the Ministry of Finance when Pranab Mukherjee was finance minister.

By 2013, as the winds of change drifted through the corridors of power, Mishra quickly built an equation with the emerging Team Modi with a Gujarat-based business house allegedly playing an important mediatory role. 'Sanjay is low profile but very sharp and ambitious; he surely knows how to politically manipulate the system to rise up the ladder,' asserted a batchmate. When he was first made ED director in 2018, a few eyebrows were raised among those who still saw him as 'Ahmed bhai's man' in the system. But within a few months all doubts were erased. Cases involving Opposition leaders were now in fast-forward mode. In June 2020, an ED team landed up at Ahmed Patel's house to record his statement in a money-laundering case involving a biotech company promoted by the Sandesara brothers, who had fled the country. 'That was a key moment. If there is one politician whom Team Modi–Shah intensely disliked, it was Ahmed bhai. They were convinced that it was Patel who had hounded them in Gujarat on Sonia Gandhi's instructions. With the ED reaching his [Patel's] doorstep, Mishra had passed the crucial loyalty test,' said an ED watcher. Clearly, Mishra knew which side of his bread was buttered and worked accordingly to ruthlessly and single-mindedly pursue his bosses' interests.

Despite being appointed for a two-year term, Mishra got an unprecedented three extensions, eventually completing nearly five years in office. Initially, when the Supreme Court ordered him to step down after the first extension, the Modi government went so far as to promulgate an ordinance in November 2021, which was later ratified by Parliament, giving it the power to extend the ED director's tenure to five years. In July 2023, though the Supreme Court deemed the Centre's repeated extension orders illegal, it allowed Mishra to continue till September 2023 because the government claimed his inputs were necessary for an ongoing global review by the Financial Action Task Force, the global money-laundering watchdog. Even after Mishra's retirement, the Modi government did not appoint a full-time director to replace him. 'It is obvious that with every extension, the Modi government was only rewarding and incentivizing the ED director to go after Opposition politicians. Even the courts seemed powerless to stop this abuse of their own orders,' said lawyer–activist Prashant Bhushan.

I sent many text messages to Mishra seeking an appointment to listen to his side of the story, but he wasn't willing to meet. ED officers who worked under him insist that his tenure should be seen as a 'golden period' in the agency's history. 'His instructions to us were very clear: don't spare anyone. The PMLA law is tough, so show that you mean business—that was his message to us,' claimed one officer.

However, the bare facts of the ED's operations in the last decade raise disturbing questions over its 'political' role. In September 2022, an *Indian Express* investigation revealed that of the 121 politicians who had come under the ED's lens since the Modi government came to power in 2014, as many as 115, or 95 per cent, were Opposition leaders whom the agency booked, raided, questioned or arrested. In sharp contrast, in the UPA decade (2004 to 2014) only 26 leaders were probed by the ED, which included 14 from the Opposition, or 54 per cent. The ED's defence is that their cases are registered after proper scrutiny. 'In most of the money-laundering cases that have gone to trial, we have succeeded in getting a conviction. And the court has taken cognizance of all our chargesheets. If this was a political witch-hunt, then why didn't the court throw out the case instead of denying bail repeatedly to the accused?' argued a senior ED official.

In data released in 2023, the ED claimed that it had registered 5,906 cases for economic offences since 2005 and got convictions in 24 of the 25 cases where the trial was concluded. But the conviction statistic is misleading. In a seventeen-year period, the agency could conclude only 25 cases, or a mere 0.42 per cent of the total cases; the rest are caught in endless litigation and delays, making the elongated process itself the punishment. The agency argued that only 176 of the total cases registered, or 3 per cent, involved present and former politicians. 'The cases against politicians are highlighted by the media, but what of the hundreds of others we are acting against?' contended an ED official. As per a government reply in Parliament, the number of raids conducted by the ED during an eight-year period, between 2014 and 2022, saw a twenty-seven-fold increase to 3,010 searches as compared to 112 raids in the UPA period from 2004 to 2014. Attachment of the proceeds of crime also saw a quantum leap from Rs 5,436 crore in the UPA years to over Rs 1,00,000 crore in the Modi period. 'Just because we are far more proactive in PMLA cases now, we are being singled out,' claimed an ED official.

However, the ED's argument falls flat when invoked in the political realm. In case after case, a distinct pattern of selective action is noticeable wherein Opposition politicians and governments are dragged under the PMLA scanner, while BJP-led governments, or BJP politicians, or the accused who switch sides to the BJP are rarely, if ever, prosecuted. It almost seems as if the ED works to a well-calculated action plan aimed at muddying the political waters, no more than a sword arm of the state, ever ready to fling the noose around the Opposition. 'If politics was an eleven versus eleven sport, we could play it, but what happens when one side has a twelfth man [the ED] with total powers to disqualify any of your players whenever it chooses?' asked Dr Abhishek Manu Singhvi, Congress leader and senior lawyer. What happens when the umpire is biased?

Take the case of Karnataka Congress strongman and Deputy Chief Minister D.K. Shivakumar. Over the years, DK, as he is popularly known, had built a reputation for being a 'resourceful' politician, one of the few Congress leaders who still had access to financial muscle power. However, in 2017, searches were conducted by the Income Tax department at DK's homes in Bengaluru and Delhi, and a sum of Rs 8.59 crore was allegedly seized. Significantly, the raids were conducted at a time when DK played a pivotal role in whisking away forty-four Congress MLAs from Gujarat to a resort near Bengaluru ahead of a crucial Rajya Sabha poll in which Congress leader Ahmed Patel was pitted against Home Minister Shah. The moment Patel squeaked home to a narrow win, DK became a marked man. An ED case for money laundering was filed against him based on the Income Tax raids. 'A BJP leader from Karnataka warned me at the time that I would be finished politically,' claimed DK.

Barely a year later, DK was in the line of fire once again. The 2018 assembly elections in Karnataka threw up a hung verdict. The BJP was the single largest party but was still nine MLAs short of a majority. The BJP's B.S. Yediyurappa was ready to stake a claim to form the government, but he needed a section of the Congress or the Janata Dal (Secular) (JD[S]) MLAs to support him. 'I was approached by a senior BJP leader and told that if I switched over with my MLAs to the BJP, I would get the deputy chief ministership, plum portfolios and my cases would be closed. If I didn't join, I would be thrown into jail,' alleged DK. The Congress leader rejected the offer, Yediyurappa's government lasted barely three days and a JD(S)–Congress government was sworn in instead. But by 2019, once the BJP had swept the Lok Sabha polls, the tide turned again. This time, even DK could not stop defections from the Congress. Within weeks of a new BJP government taking over in Karnataka, DK was arrested by the ED in September 2019. A month later, he was granted bail, but he and his family members continued to receive summons from the agencies almost every week. 'One day it was the CBI, the next day Income Tax, then ED … Even my daughter was not spared,' he said.

DK recalled a chance meeting with a top Union minister at an airport lounge in which he was reminded of his refusal to join hands with the BJP in 2018. 'I was told clearly that I was paying the price for my unwillingness to break with the Congress and for defying the BJP leadership,' he claimed. In March 2023, the Supreme Court dismissed the money-laundering case against DK, pointing out that the ED had not been able to establish money laundering as the source of all the recovered cash.

Contrast DK's case with that of Assam Chief Minister Himanta Biswa Sarma, another 'resourceful' Congressman who switched to the BJP just ahead of the 2016 assembly elections after a well-publicized falling out with the Gandhis. An ambitious Sarma was hoping to be anointed as successor to the then Congress chief minister, the long-serving Tarun Gogoi, but the party leadership wasn't giving any assurances. Like DK,

Sarma too is a well-networked politician with a wide range of business interests. While he was a minister in the Gogoi government, Sarma was implicated by the BJP in a chit-fund case and in a Guwahati water-supply project scam in which politicians were allegedly bribed by the American multinational company Louis Berger International. Sarma faced CBI questioning and raids in the chit-fund case in 2014, but the moment he joined the BJP, the probe stalled. In the Louis Berger case too, he wasn't questioned by any central agency. Once he switched sides, neither the CBI nor the ED seemed interested in pursuing the alleged scam. 'My name has never been there as an accused in any file record in this case; this is only an attempt to tarnish my image,' maintained Sarma. For his Congress friends-turned-foes, this was a prime example of 'washing machine' politics. 'Imagine, the BJP brings out a booklet in 2015 naming Sarma as a key suspect in the scam, and when he joins the party, the case is forgotten. If this is not a washing machine, then what is?' queried Gaurav Gogoi, Congress MP from Assam.

While enforcement agencies claim that inquiries in these cases haven't been closed, the perception that the ED's powers are being misused to influence the course of state and national politics is unmistakable. The reality is that in cases that target Opposition politicians, the ED has been hyperactive, while staying silent in matters involving a politician from the ruling party or someone who has switched over to it. The destabilizing impact of this on Opposition-ruled governments exposes a nefarious agenda of the Modi government. Even the timing of notices, raids and arrests seems to match a political calendar.

Sample the ED casebook:

- In March 2024, within days of the general elections being announced, Chief Minister Arvind Kejriwal was arrested by the ED in the Delhi liquor policy probe. The ED had been probing the case of alleged payoffs since August 2022 and had already arrested several key AAP leaders, including Delhi's deputy chief minister, Manish Sisodia, in February 2023. Kejriwal had just tied up with the Congress to fight the seven Delhi Lok Sabha seats. 'My team was very clearly told by a senior government officer that I would not be arrested if I broke the alliance with the Congress,' claimed Kejriwal. The ED countered by saying that nine summons were issued to Kejriwal for questioning but that the chief minister skipped them all. No cash recoveries were made in the case, nor a money trail established, but the ED insisted their inquiries would nail Kejriwal's alleged role.

- Also arrested in March 2024 was K. Kavitha, daughter of former Telangana chief minister and Bharat Rashtra Samithi (BRS) chief K. Chandrashekar Rao, in the same liquor case. Ahead of the 2023 Telangana elections, with whispers of a BJP–BRS post-poll tie-up, the ED did not arrest Kavitha despite multiple interrogations. Once the BRS lost the polls, the ED moved in. While she described her arrest as 'illegal' and denied all charges, the ED claimed she had 'confessed' to paying a Rs 100 crore bribe to Kejriwal and his deputy Manish Sisodia.

- In July 2020, when the Ashok Gehlot government faced a revolt from his deputy Sachin Pilot, the ED raided Gehlot's brother, Agrasen, in connection with a probe into the alleged diversion of fertilizers in 2007–09. The Congress claimed that the 'raid raj' was timed by the Centre to try and topple Gehlot's government. In October 2023, weeks before the Rajasthan assembly elections, Vaibhav Gehlot, the chief minister's son, was summoned by the ED in an alleged foreign exchange transaction case.

- In February 2021, weeks before the West Bengal elections, first the CBI and later an ED team served summons to TMC leader and MP Abhishek Banerjee's wife, Rujira Banerjee, in connection with an alleged coal pilferage case. The case has dragged on since, despite the Banerjees having been interrogated on several occasions.

- In August 2023, ED raids were conducted on close aides of then Chhattisgarh Congress Chief Minister Bhupesh Baghel just ahead of the state elections. Those raided included key financiers of the Baghel campaign—an attempt to squeeze Congress funding at a crucial time. Just days before the actual polling, the ED issued a statement that it was probing kickbacks amounting to Rs 508 crore allegedly received by Baghel in connection with an investigation into a Dubai-based online betting site. The ED claimed the site was being used to launder money through 'benami' bank accounts. Baghel stoutly defended himself, pointing out that his government had filed seventy-two FIRs in the case and asked the Centre to act against the accused. But his protestations came too late. The BJP's media team had already flooded WhatsApp groups and local news channels with reports of Baghel's 'Dubai connection'. 'There are several pictures of Mahadev App promoters with senior BJP leaders in Chhattisgarh, including a sitting governor, yet we were put in the dock while elections were on,' lamented a Baghel aide.

- In February 2024, just ahead of the general elections, the ED arrested Jharkhand Mukti Morcha leader and then Chief Minister Hemant Soren in connection with an alleged land scam. Soren is a Congress ally who claimed that he had rejected several offers to switch sides. The BJP had unsuccessfully tried to topple his government in 2023. While granting him bail, the Jharkhand High Court observed that 'there exist reasons to believe' that Soren was not guilty of the PMLA offence he was accused of.

In sharp contrast, those Opposition leaders who crossed over to join the BJP or allied with it appear to have got 'protection' from the law. An *Indian Express* report in April 2024 detailed how, out of twenty-five Opposition leaders who were facing a corruption probe and who subsequently crossed over to the BJP, as many as twenty-three got a reprieve. The cases against them either slowed down or were closed.

- In September 2021, the ED filed money-laundering charges against several TMC leaders in Bengal for their alleged role in cash transactions in the 2016 Narada sting case. A prominent name missing was that of Suvendu Adhikari, who defected from the TMC in December 2020 and became the BJP's face in the 2021 West Bengal assembly elections. While his name was mentioned in a CBI chargesheet, sanction for his prosecution was kept pending with the Lok Sabha speaker.

- In 2018, Income Tax raids were conducted on the properties of TDP leader C.M. Ramesh soon after the TDP split from the BJP. The charge was that a firm linked to Ramesh had siphoned off Rs 100 crore. In June 2019, Ramesh, then a Rajya Sabha MP, quit the TDP and joined the BJP. With no further action in the case, Ramesh contested the 2024 Andhra Pradesh elections on a BJP ticket and won.

- In March 2024, the CBI closed a corruption probe against senior NCP leader Praful Patel regarding alleged irregularities in the leasing of aircraft when Patel was Union aviation minister in the UPA-I government. Patel had played a key role in the Ajit Pawar-led NCP faction switching over to the BJP in July 2023.

- In November 2020, Raninder Singh, son of Captain Amarinder Singh, former Punjab chief minister, was questioned by the ED in an alleged money-laundering case. A year later, Amarinder Singh quit the Congress and eventually joined the BJP. The case against his son has made no headway since.

'To understand the functioning of the central agencies, especially the ED, you just have to go into the chronology of each case. This is a lawless force of the ruling party, which knows no rules or boundaries while it fixes opponents and spares its own. How is it that hundreds of BJP MLAs and MPs aren't touched but Opposition leaders are hounded?' asked lawyer–politician Kapil Sibal.

Interestingly, it was only after 2019 that the ED truly bared its fangs. This coincided with a change in guard in the North Block, with political lightweight Nirmala Sitharaman taking over as finance minister from Arun Jaitley and Amit Shah replacing Rajnath Singh as the home minister.

In the Jaitley–Singh regime, the ED had been relatively subdued, but with Shah playing enforcer-in-chief, there was no holding it back. Officially, the ED reports to the revenue department in the finance ministry, but now it was reportedly taking direct orders from the home minister.

An instructive case study is the arrest of senior Congress leader P. Chidambaram in August 2019, just months after the Modi government was sworn in again. The sword of punitive action had been hanging over the former finance and home minister since 2014, but a less hostile Jaitley was reportedly reluctant to give a go-ahead to the agencies. While being political adversaries, as senior advocates, Jaitley and Chidambaram were part of a common legal fraternity and had even socialized with each other on occasion: the latter was a prominent invitee to Jaitley's daughter's wedding. The CBI first raided Chidambaram's residence in 2017 but did not make an arrest. Shah, however, was convinced that the former UPA home minister had a hand in his being arrested by the CBI in July 2010 in a fake-encounter case in which he spent just over three months in jail. 'Both Modi ji and Amit bhai have long memories; they don't forget or forgive easily,' said a Gujarat BJP leader. Chidambaram was arrested by the CBI on 21 August 2019. Just five days later, Jaitley, who was critically ill, passed away. After fifty-five days in custody, the Congress leader was re-arrested for custodial interrogation by the ED. He would eventually spend 105 days in jail, twelve days more than Shah's confinement in 2010. Shah appeared to have had the last laugh even if it meant waiting almost nine years.

The case against Chidambaram goes back to 2007, when the CBI and ED were probing alleged irregularities in the Foreign Investment Promotion Board (FIPB) clearance to INX Media, a company owned by Peter Mukerjea and Indrani Mukerjea. In 2015, the Mukerjeas became the prime accused in the murder of Sheena Bora, Indrani's daughter. While still in jail facing trial, in July 2019, Indrani suddenly turned approver in the INX case, claiming that she had bribed Chidambaram's son, Karti, to 'fix' the FIPB clearance. While Chidambaram refused to go into the case details, an associate tellingly remarked, 'Imagine arresting a former home minister on the dubious claims of a murder accused when the FIPB file clearance was signed by top finance ministry bureaucrats.' An ED official maintains that the case against the father–son duo is based on evidence, and investigations are ongoing. 'Nothing is closed,' was the official mantra. Interestingly Indrani Mukerjea, who accused Chidambaram, was granted bail in 2022, and she was recently even the subject of a Netflix documentary.

Another politically surcharged ED investigation is the much-publicized probe into the Gandhi family. In June 2022, Sonia and Rahul Gandhi were sent notices to appear before the agency over money-laundering allegations in the *National Herald* case. The origins of this case stretch back to 2013, when BJP leader Dr Subramanian Swamy filed a complaint before a trial court alleging cheating and misappropriation of funds in the Gandhis' acquisition of the *National Herald* newspaper and its properties. Swamy stated that the Gandhis had bought into the newspaper's erstwhile publishers, Associated Journals Limited, through a 'not for profit' organization called Young India, in which they had a majority stake. The mercurial Swamy has had a roller-coaster relationship with the Gandhi family: though he claimed to be close to Rajiv Gandhi, he has over the years launched a series of vituperative attacks on Sonia Gandhi. In 1999, he organized a tea-party meeting between Sonia Gandhi and J. Jayalalithaa, the All India Anna Dravida Munnetra Kazhagam (AIADMK) leader and five-time Tamil Nadu chief minister, a coming together that eventually led to the fall of the Vajpayee government. But the bonhomie didn't last long, and Swamy went back to being on the warpath against the Gandhis.

A 'dangerous enemy' to have, Dr Swamy kept urging for action in the *National Herald* case. The ED, probing money-laundering charges, closed the case in early 2015, only to reopen it a few months later. In December 2015, Sonia and Rahul Gandhi were granted bail, but the PMLA case dragged on. 'It's quite crazy. There is no transfer of any property, no complainant who claims to have been cheated, not one, and yet the ED refuses to close the case,' argued Singhvi, lawyer for the Gandhis.

ED officials claimed that their investigation was ongoing and that closing the case was not possible till 'all angles' had been explored.

Matters reached a head when the mother–son Gandhi duo was summoned for questioning to the ED headquarters in June 2022. Until now, despite the rising animosity between the Modi government and the Congress, the Gandhis hadn't been touched by the agencies. 'Summoning them was an act of pure vendetta by the Prime Minister only because he had been summoned by investigators in the 2002 riots case,' claimed Congress leader Shaktisinh Gohil, referring to the day-long interrogation Modi was subjected to by the Special Investigation Team looking into the 2002 Gujarat riot conspiracy charges. If Modi spent around eight hours in the interrogation room, Rahul Gandhi's questioning took more than thirty-six hours over four days. 'The fact is the ED only had a two-page questionnaire, yet they dragged it on for four days by repeating the same questions again and again. It was only meant to harass and intimidate,' maintained a member of the Gandhis' legal team. Apparently, the ED's standard modus operandi is to prolong the interrogation with long gaps in between the questioning only to keep an accused on edge. According to a journalist who tracks the ED, in one instance an accused was made to stand on a bench for six hours in an interrogation room only as a show of power by ED officers. The ED denies any such harassment.

A month later, it was Sonia Gandhi's turn to be questioned over three days, only this time the ED team was a little more accommodating as her health was fragile, and she had been in and out of hospital. 'We warned the ED officers that if anything happened to Sonia ji, they would be accountable,' said an aide of Priyanka Gandhi Vadra, who was allowed to accompany her mother to the ED headquarters. While the Gandhis seemed unruffled by the long hours of questioning, a weakened Congress was suddenly roused from its stupor. Party workers and leaders hit the streets, organizing high-decibel demonstrations and protests, courting arrest. An excitable media, meanwhile, furiously speculated about the fate of the Gandhis. 'Let's get one thing clear: this case is not about arrests or conviction because there is nothing in it. It is only meant to keep the political pot boiling. Surkhiyon mein rakhna hai (To be kept in the headlines),' asserted Singhvi. When asked why no arrests have been made in the case, ED officials simply clam up: 'Let's wait and see; the legal process is still on.'

The cryptic response is typical of the opaque functioning of an all-powerful agency that is seemingly accountable to no one. Whether the Gandhis or indeed any of the Opposition politicians who are in the ED's line of fire are actually convicted or set free, in the criminal justice system, especially under the PMLA, with its stringent bail provisions and expanded scope of offences, the 'process is the punishment'. In March 2023, fourteen Opposition parties approached the Supreme Court, arguing that the Centre was arbitrarily using the ED to arrest and institute criminal proceedings against Opposition leaders who had dared to raise their voice against the Modi government. The plea called for setting specific pre- and post-arrest guidelines in PMLA cases. Rejecting the plea, Chief Justice D.Y. Chandrachud observed, 'A political leader is basically a citizen. As citizens, we are all amenable to the same law. Political leaders do not enjoy a higher immunity.' In a country where lakhs of citizens remain under trial for years, the Chief Justice's stand is unexceptionable. However, the order has meant no let-up in an enforcement regime where ruling party members remain protected and Opposition leaders face the heat. 'The ED's discriminatory actions have ensured that the basic concept of a level playing field no longer exists in our democracy. Hopefully, one day, the courts will also realize this,' said Singhvi.

'A level playing field': a concept at the very heart of electoral democracy, a constitutional principle of equality before the law that has been dismantled bit by bit in the Modi decade. The ED's selective actions have meant that no Opposition-led government has breathed easy, suffocated as they are by the constant threat of arrest. There are damaging accusations also of the ED being used to extort money from businesses, small and big, in return for political 'protection' from the Modi government. In February 2024, a joint investigation carried out by news websites The News Minute and Newslaundry revealed:

- At least thirty companies that donated nearly Rs 335 crore to the BJP between the financial years 2018–19 and 2022–23 had also faced action by central agencies during this period.

- At least twenty-three of these companies had never made any donations to the BJP between 2014 and the year they were raided.

- At least four of these companies donated a total of Rs 9.05 crore within four months of the central agency visit.

- At least six of these companies, which were already donors to the party, handed out a heftier amount in the months following the searches.

- Six other firms, which had donated to the BJP previously, faced central action after they skipped donations in one financial year.

- Only three of these companies donated to the Congress during this same period.

In March 2024, the Supreme Court literally forced the State Bank of India to disclose the details of the electoral bonds received by it to fund political parties. More than 50 per cent of the bond monies went to the BJP, another sign of how electoral politics was not a level playing field by any stretch of the imagination. Once again, a distinct pattern of possible quid pro quo deals linked to ED action was detected. At least fourteen of the top thirty companies that had purchased electoral bonds between 2019 and 2024 faced action from central or state probe agencies in this period.

- Future Gaming and Hotels Pvt. Ltd, a Tamil Nadu-based lottery company that purchased bonds worth Rs 1,368 crore, was being investigated by the ED, which had attached its properties worth Rs 409 crore in a money-laundering case. A substantial chunk of Future Gaming's bond money went to the ruling DMK government in Chennai and the TMC in Bengal, proof that compromised businessmen are on the right side of power—in states and at the Centre.

- Eleven infrastructure firms bought bonds worth Rs 506 crore close on the heels of investigative action by the ED or the CBI.

- Telangana-based Megha Engineering and Infrastructures Ltd, which purchased bonds worth Rs 584 crore, was the BJP's largest donor. The company was probed by the Income Tax department and the ED in 2019 and is now handling several major infrastructure projects across the country.

- Hyderabad-based businessman Sarath Reddy's family firm, Aurobindo Pharma, donated Rs 25 crore through bonds to the BJP. Interestingly, in May 2023, the ED had not opposed his bail in the high-stakes Delhi liquor case, and a few months later, when Reddy turned approver, his testimony was used to arrest Delhi Chief Minister Kejriwal.

'I think you are making huge assumptions that the money is given by these companies after ED raids or in return for any special favours. For all you know, they gave money and the ED still went knocking at their door,' argued Finance Minister Nirmala Sitharaman when quizzed on the issue at a media event. 'This is nothing but the legalization of bribery through bonds,' countered P. Chidambaram. 'The BJP's "hafta vasooli" (extortion) strategy is simple. Raid a target through the ED, CBI or IT and then seek hafta (protection money) for the company's protection,' alleged the Congress's Jairam Ramesh. 'Chanda do, dhandha lo (Give donations, get business),' was the party's one-line attack. 'The Congress is the Gangotri (fountainhead) of corruption,' Ravi Shankar Prasad of the BJP hit back.

Washing machine. Extortion department. Election department. Or a tough investigative agency exposing the grimy underbelly of a corrupted political system? As the charges flew thick and fast, the cacophony couldn't obscure the obvious. The ED was right in the middle of a fiery political contest, one in which the ruling dispensation held all the aces. The 'weaponization' of the ED by the Modi government had completely changed the rules of the political game. The constitutional commitment to a level playing field in Indian politics had been buried. A dominant ruling party now had an extra player on its side with unrestrained powers to disrupt, disadvantage and demolish any opponent at a time and place of its choosing. The Congress too had misused agencies when in power, most notably during the Emergency years under Indira Gandhi. But surely the failings of the past cannot be justification for brazenly egregious intent and action in the present.

'The essence of tyranny is the ability to use a harsh law selectively against your enemies,' said senior Supreme Court lawyer Sanjay Hegde. In such a milieu, what chance did the Opposition have, much less one that was scarcely united or credible?

NINE

'Yeh Adani ki Sarkar Hai': The Making of the INDIA Alliance

BILLIONAIRE tycoon Gautam Adani is a soft-spoken, seemingly bashful man of few words. When he celebrated his fiftieth birthday in 2012, a few close friends and family members wanted to make a big splash. The Ahmedabad-based business magnate politely refused. 'My best is yet to come—there is no need to celebrate just yet,' he responded in typical low-key style. But in December 2022, the media-shy Adani, or Gautam bhai, as he prefers to be addressed, had little choice but to step out of the shadows. *Forbes* magazine had just headlined Gautam bhai's ascent as India's richest person and, briefly, the second-richest person in the world, according to its Real-Time Billionaires list. The market capitalization of his ports-to-power conglomerate had grown ninefold in just three years. His personal net worth at the end of 2022 had climbed to a staggering $125.8 billion (as per the *Forbes* figures). For the first time since 2008, there was a change in the mega-rich pecking order: Gautam bhai had pipped Reliance Industries' Mukesh Ambani to the top spot.

From being anointed *India Today* magazine's 'Newsmaker of the Year' to appearing on the popular prime-time show *Aap Ki Adalat* on India TV, Adani was the undoubted flavour of the season. Every media outlet wanted a slice of the Adani life story. A tenth-standard dropout becoming the richest Indian in the world was the ultimate fairy tale come true. 'We were getting thousands of congratulatory messages from across the globe. Gautam bhai was excited but tried not to show it. He even spoke privately to many editors and politicians to thank them for their support over the years,' revealed an Adani aide.

The euphoria lasted all of four weeks. On 24 January 2023, US-based investment research firm Hindenburg Research published a scathing report accusing Adani of engaging in 'brazen stock manipulation' and 'fraud' through a maze of offshore shell companies. Adani stocks tanked, and his personal fortune tumbled by $80 billion in just a month. One politician, in particular, was jubilant, convinced that he had found the smoking gun for a controversy he had been waiting to expose for years. 'I remember meeting Rahul Gandhi a week after the Adani story broke, and his first reaction was to exclaim, "Wasn't I bloody right!"' said a Congress office-bearer.

From the time he was pitchforked into a leadership role in the Congress ahead of the 2014 Lok Sabha elections, Rahul Gandhi had targeted the Adani Group and its alleged connections with Modi. 'If you want to expose Modi, the route is through his business friends. Adani's money is Modi's bounty and vice versa. This is oligarchic capitalism, Modi-style,' he told a colleague. Rahul's focus on Adani's wealth and political links was almost obsessive, to the point where he was unwilling to listen to any alternative views. A former Congressman recalls suggesting to a family friend of the Gandhis that maybe the party should 'go slow' on Adani since the well-networked industrialist was a Congress funder too. 'The next thing I know is that I am in the doghouse, accused of being soft on Adani,' recollected the leader.

Why is Adani such a red rag to Rahul Gandhi? Apparently, when the UPA was in power, the first-generation entrepreneur had tried to reach out to Rahul Gandhi through a range of contacts, starting with Robert Vadra, whom he invited to his Mundra port facility in Gujarat, a visit described by the business magnate as a 'routine' one. 'I call so many people to see what we have built; Robert was only one of them,' he claimed. Subsequently, a few attempts at fixing a meeting in Delhi were made, first through Ahmed Patel and later through Kamal Nath, who had never hidden his closeness to Adani and, as commerce minister, was a keen votary of big business. But neither was able to make any headway when it came to persuading Rahul Gandhi to even meet the businessman. Sharad Pawar, another leader with whom Adani enjoyed a strong personal rapport, was also consulted to explore the possibility of sorting out matters. A cautious Pawar chose to stay away from playing peacemaker.

The Adani–Gandhi tangle dates back to the pre-2014 period, when Rahul Gandhi was given a comprehensive briefing by a party colleague on how Modi and Adani were benefitting each other through their close proximity. Though Adani got his initial business boost in the 1990s, when a Chimanbhai Patel-led Congress government was in power in Gujarat, his spectacularly exponential growth coincided with Modi's rising political clout after 2002. This was the period when Adani founded the Resurgent Group of Gujarat (RGG), an organization of local businessmen, to counter the Confederation of Indian Industry (CII) which had criticized Modi's handling of the 2002 riots. With Adani as chairperson, the RGG became a driving force behind Modi's Gujarat growth story. The report presented to Rahul contained information about the mega infrastructure projects that Adani was handling in Gujarat and detailed the many instances in which land was given for these projects by the Modi government at allegedly throwaway prices. When Modi was anointed the BJP's prime ministerial candidate in 2013 and flew around in one of Adani's private planes while campaigning, Rahul took that as evidence of cronyism. In 2024, an investigative report in Scroll pointed to how most Adani projects outside India were announced within months of Prime Minister Modi visiting that country or meeting its head of state. While the Adani Group insists that it won all projects fairly, the Congress leader was unrelenting. 'Rahul feels very strongly that India is being overrun by crony capitalists, whose riches are primarily because of the political favours they have received to corner scarce public resources,' said a Gandhi family friend. One of the first public campaigns Rahul Gandhi spearheaded was in Odisha in 2008, when he supported protests by tribal groups against a Vedanta bauxite mining project in the eco-sensitive Niyamgiri Hills. The Congress-led UPA was in power then, and the environment ministry rejected the Vedanta bid.

Adani, for his part, was convinced that Rahul Gandhi was surrounded by a group of 'leftist' advisors who had 'poisoned' the Congress leader's mind against him and were using him as a pawn in the larger political battle with Modi. When I asked him about his Modi connection, he shot back: 'I have set up infrastructure projects—all of which I have won after due bidding—in twenty-four states across the country, some of which are Congress-ruled. How can I be accused of only working with the BJP?' Adani's ire was especially directed at Jairam Ramesh, the Congress MP who, like Rahul Gandhi, was unequivocal in his criticism of the Adani Group business model. Ramesh, as Union environment minister, had sparred with many leading business houses over clearances for projects that were allegedly in violation of the Forest Rights Act. The Adanis, with interests in big-ticket mining in states like Chhattisgarh, were often in the minister's crosshairs. Later, as chief spokesperson and party ideologue, Ramesh had become even more combative in his trenchant attacks on the group. 'Rahul is criticizing us all the time, but it is actually Jairam who is shaping the agenda against us,' Adani told a business associate.

Both Jairam Ramesh and Rahul Gandhi belong to what may be loosely described as the 'barefoot development' stream within the Congress. While not exactly against entrepreneurship, this stream of thought prides itself on its grassroots-oriented approach and publicly prefers to stand on the side of renowned left-leaning economists rather than with corporate industry bodies. Rahul holds tenaciously to this line even though it has often been derided as 'champagne socialism' or an elite left-y faddishness. The Hindenburg report, then, was just the opening he had been waiting for to embarrass the Modi government. With just days remaining for the 2023 budget session of Parliament and the highly visible nationwide

Bharat Jodo Yatra drawing to a close, the timing of the report could not have been better. Using the platform of the President's address debate in Parliament, Rahul Gandhi, his unkempt salt-and-pepper beard making him look like a cross between a dishevelled Karl Marx and a fresh-off-the-padyatra crusader, held forth on the alleged Modi–Adani equation for most of a forty-minute-long speech. 'People want to know about the Modi–Adani relationship. Rules were overlooked to favour Adani. From Tamil Nadu, Kerala to Himachal Pradesh, we have been hearing one name everywhere: "Adani". People used to ask me how it is that Adani enters any business and never fails. There should be a case study on Adani by business schools such as Harvard on how the relationship between business and politics works ... Narendra Modi should get a gold medal in this. The real magic started when the PM came to Delhi. In 2014, Adani was in the 609th spot on the list of richest Indians [in the world] and now has climbed to top spot,' he announced. For months, Rahul had publicly attacked the Modi government as 'Yeh Adani ki sarkar hai (This is Adani's government).' Now, he had brought his battle cry to Parliament.

Rahul Gandhi held up pictures of Adani and the Prime Minister lounging in the five-star comfort of a private aircraft and mentioned specific projects, including airport tenders, in which favours were allegedly doled out. The Congress leader specifically mentioned the Mumbai international airport, alleging that India's busiest airport was taken away from the Hyderabad-based GVK Group—'hijacked' by using central agencies like the ED and the CBI—and given to the Adanis. Speculation over just why a leading infrastructure corporate had sold the profitable airport in India's commercial hub had swirled around for months. GVK issued a denial, but Rahul's charges made front-page headlines. 'The moment Rahul took on Adani inside Parliament, you knew the gloves were off. It showed to our party rank and file that our leader was not going to back off in this fight with Modi,' said a Congress MP.

The treasury benches became incensed. A concerted counteroffensive was launched. Union Minister Kiren Rijiju challenged Rahul Gandhi to furnish proof of his allegations against the Prime Minister, while Lok

Sabha Speaker Om Birla disapproved of photos being waved in the House. The speaker, already facing Opposition charges of open partisanship, ruled that all references to Adani be expunged from Rahul Gandhi's speech. News channels were warned by the speaker's office not to quote any expunged words in their prime-time debates. 'There were a lot of angry exchanges that evening in Parliament. The sense you got was that the government was unhappy that the speaker had not intervened earlier to stop Rahul Gandhi's constant jibes about an alleged Modi–Adani quid pro quo deal inside Parliament,' said a senior journalist who was witness to the heated exchange in Parliament.

The next day, Modi hit back. No reference was made to the contentious 'A' word nor was there any response to the specific charges made by the Congress leader. Instead, in an angry speech laced with familiar populist rhetoric, the Prime Minister chose to invoke his special equation with the people of the country. 'Modi is a member of 25 crore families of the country. The faith of 140 crore citizens is my biggest protection, which your lies cannot breach. The 80 crore citizens who get free rations can hardly trust these people who make false allegations,' he countered. There was even a reference to Rahul Gandhi's dig about the need for a Harvard University study on Adani's rise. 'Many people here have a craze for "studies" from Harvard University. One study revolves around the fall of the Congress. I believe every big university will study the downfall of the Congress and even those responsible for it.'

Generally, most Modi–Gandhi political bouts are hopelessly one-sided: a demagogic, loud communicator with a 'jatra'-style melodramatic delivery versus an inexpert public speaker whose articulation skills have never been his strong suit. And yet, this was one round where Rahul Gandhi had undoubtedly landed a few stinging punches. It wasn't as if the Modi–Adani nexus charges were new. The astronomical increase in Adani's wealth coinciding with Modi's meteoric ascent had been the subject of political commentary for a while. Only this time the Hindenburg report had given crucial third-party ammunition to back what was considered Rahul Gandhi's personal campaign against the

Prime Minister until then. Even media houses that were reluctant to discuss the Modi–Adani question were forced to debate the ticklish issue. 'I think Rahul Gandhi has hit Narendra Modi where it hurts. Let the Prime Minister respond with facts to our charges and not mere bombast,' argued Supriya Shrinate, the Congress's social media head. The BJP, though, was unwilling to send its official spokespersons on TV programmes to debate the Adani question. Instead, the party's media machine reportedly rang up pliant channels and urged them to look for 'other' issues to take up. In Parliament, BJP MPs repeatedly disrupted the House, calling on Rahul Gandhi to 'apologize' for the allegedly 'anti-India' remarks he had made at a gathering in London on the state of democracy in the country. The Modi government, it seemed, had much to hide on the Adani connection. But the diversionary ploys weren't quite working. For once, the war of public perception was being won decisively by the Congress.

Typically, the government's response was to urgently look for a more effective 'weapon of mass distraction,' one that would take the gaze firmly away from the fallout of the Hindenburg report. In the third week of March, shortly after the Adani controversy, the ideal issue was 'found'. On 23 March 2023, Rahul Gandhi was convicted and sentenced to two years' imprisonment and fined Rs 15,000 by a Surat court in a criminal defamation case filed by Purnesh Modi, a Gujarat BJP MLA. The case revolved around certain remarks made by Rahul Gandhi at an election rally in Karnataka in 2019: 'I have a question. Why do all of them—all these thieves—have Modi, Modi, Modi in their names? Nirav Modi, Lalit Modi, Narendra Modi. And if we search a bit more, many more such Modis will come out.' It was an over-the-top taunt made in the heat of an electoral campaign. Prima facie, a two-year sentence for criminal defamation seemed ridiculously excessive punishment. No one had been similarly punished for over a century under the law.

The facts of the case made it even more suspicious. After the lawsuit was filed in April 2019, Rahul Gandhi had appeared in person before the chief judicial magistrate of Surat, A.N. Dave, in June 2021 and recorded his statement. Then, mysteriously, the complainant, Purnesh Modi, approached the Gujarat High Court, seeking a stay on the trial, a plea that was accepted in March 2022. Strangely, the complainant and not the accused was seeking a stay on the trial. Even more inexplicably, in February 2023, just days after Rahul's headline-grabbing Lok Sabha speech, Purnesh Modi moved the court to have the stay vacated. A.N. Dave had just been replaced by Harish Verma, who, within weeks of the stay being vacated, convicted Rahul Gandhi. Verma would soon be promoted to the cadre of district judges. 'The chronology of the case says it all. Even the most ardent critic of Rahul Gandhi will recognize that what happened was grossly unjust,' said Dr Abhishek Manu Singhvi, Rahul's lawyer.

Within twenty-four hours of the conviction order, the Lok Sabha secretariat issued a notification disqualifying Rahul from his Parliament membership. As per Section 8(3) of the Representation of the People Act, 1951, 'A person convicted of offence and sentenced to imprisonment for not less than two years shall be disqualified from the date of such conviction and shall continue to be disqualified for a further period of six years from his release.' The speaker's office, under pressure to act swiftly, had wielded the rule book to disqualify the Congress leader less than two months after expunging his Adani remarks. The speaker, Om Birla, an oleaginous, smarmy BJP MP from Kota, had been plucked out of relative obscurity to occupy a high-profile post. 'He is the kind who will stand to attention if the Prime Minister even glances his way,' sniggered an Opposition MP.

Criticized for missing umpteen opportunities in the past, this time Rahul Gandhi emerged in fighting form, retorting that he was being victimized for speaking the truth on the Modi–Adani issue. The Opposition too rallied around him, accusing the Modi government of political vendetta. On 22 April, Rahul vacated his official residence in Lutyens' Delhi. Images of his luggage being loaded in trucks as he bid farewell to his house staff went viral. Significantly, the BJP's internal tracker poll in April showed that the majority opinion, even among the party's supporters, was that the eviction was unfair and smacked of vindictive harassment. 'We misread the mood on this issue. Rahul got all the sympathy because of his disqualification as an MP,' admitted a BJP spokesperson.

The BJP had got its strategy badly wrong. In a desperate bid to deflect attention from the Adani storm, they inadvertently conferred a halo of victimhood on Rahul Gandhi. Even worse, events had firmly positioned Rahul as the prime challenger to Modi, a stout-hearted leader unafraid to raise inconvenient questions, even at great personal cost. While Rahul's disqualification was eventually set aside in August 2023, when the Supreme Court stayed the lower court conviction order, the months in parliamentary 'exile' made him a rallying point for the anti-Modi forces. The all-important question now was, could Rahul Gandhi and his party translate sympathy into votes in the build-up to the battle for 2024?

Few states are as electorally complex as Karnataka. For almost four decades, voters here have made starkly divergent choices in state and general elections. It is this magically scenic land, with its forest-lined rivers and misty hillsides decorated with gushing waterfalls, that was the first big test for the Congress in the aftermath of Rahul Gandhi's dramatic disqualification from the Lok Sabha. With just a year left for the next general elections, Karnataka's 2023 assembly elections were, in the words of Congress General Secretary Randeep Surjewala, a 'do or die' battle for the party. While the Congress had won Himachal Pradesh in December 2022, they had not defeated the BJP in a direct fight in a major state since the winter of 2018. 'I remember telling our state leaders that they were not just fighting to win power in Bengaluru but they were leading the charge to keep the Congress alive in India,' said Surjewala.

In hindsight, he need not have worried. Karnataka is one of the few states where the Congress seemed well-stocked with the crucial weapons required to take on the formidable BJP election machine. In the veteran Kuruba warhorse Siddaramaiah and the tough-talking, flamboyant D.K. Shivakumar, the party had two strong regional bosses, the former a wily politician with a genuine mass connection, the latter a highly resourceful organizer. The differences between them were sharp, but they appeared willing not to let the conflict play out on the electoral battlefield. Almost a year before the election, Rahul Gandhi had brought the two leaders together and worked on a truce. 'I think once these heavyweights came on the same page, half our battle was won,' asserted Surjewala.

The Congress also had a lesser-known 'weapon' on their side: the party's newly minted election strategist, Sunil Kanugolu. The Bengaluru-based Kanugolu joined the Congress as head of their election strategy committee in mid-2022, soon after the party's negotiations with Prashant Kishor came unstuck. Kanugolu had first imbibed his poll-planning skills as part of Prashant Kishor's original start-up team that worked on Prime Minister Modi's 2014 Lok Sabha campaign. Unlike the high-profile Kishor, the thick-set, bespectacled Kanugolu prefers staying out of the headlines. He is reserved and low-profile, the quintessential backroom operator, unwilling to give even a sound bite on camera. While Kishor moved on, Kanugolu stuck on with the BJP, working closely with Amit Shah on the 2017 Uttar Pradesh Vidhan Sabha victory. His career then took another turn when he worked with both Dravida parties in Tamil Nadu at different points, before bagging an assignment with the Congress, a party he claimed to ideologically identify with. Karnataka was a chance for him to prove his mettle in a set-up that was different from the BJP's unyielding, take-no-prisoners and to-hell-with-everything-else approach.

The quick-thinking Kanugolu's chief contribution was to introduce some of the BJP's successful attributes into the Congress's sluggish election-planning structure. A more professional ticket-distribution system was set up based on extensive ground surveys, and media campaigns that would gather traction were charted out in detail. One such campaign was the popular 'Pay CM' poster blitz, a sly dig at the corruption charges against then BJP Chief Minister Basavaraj Bommai. Banners sprang up overnight across Bengaluru city, including near the chief minister's residence and the BJP headquarters, inviting the public to scan a QR code on the poster and file complaints against bribery. The 'Pay CM' slogan resonated at a time when the Karnataka contractors' body alleged that they had to pay 40 per cent commission to get public work contracts. 'It was Sunil's idea to hit the BJP early in the battle. Before they could respond, "Pay CM" quickly became part of common parlance. It gave us a head start,' acknowledged Shivakumar.

Corruption was the Congress's primary offensive weapon against the BJP in Karnataka. The party also came up with 'guarantees' of their own—five, in fact—to offer the voter. The word 'guarantee' was first used electorally by the Congress in Assam in 2021 and later in Himachal Pradesh in 2022 in an attempt to convince voters that the grand old party would actually act on promises. Now, however, it tried to scale up the promises. Free electricity, monthly cash assistance of Rs 2,000 for women, 10 kilograms free rice for the poor, free bus travel for women and cash handouts for unemployed youth—the Congress's five 'guarantees' were further backed by the assurance that LPG cylinders would be priced at Rs 500. 'Do give us some credit. Long before the Prime Minister copied our idea and came up with "Modi ki guarantee", there was "Congress ki guarantee",' said Surjewala.

While the Congress was getting its act together, the BJP, for once—but not entirely unexpectedly—was floundering. Karnataka is not a 'natural' BJP state. The party has never won a majority on its own in the assembly elections here. The BJP's core vote bank is the politically influential Lingayat community, but an entrenched caste bloc can also limit a party's appeal among other competing caste groups. Not surprisingly, the BJP's tallest leader in Karnataka, B.S. Yediyurappa, was widely seen as its Lingayat face. A clever and astute politician, Yediyurappa had shepherded the party for more than two decades. The idea of a regional strongman having complete control of a state is antithetical to the Modi–Shah model, where alternate power centres are looked upon with suspicion. In July 2021, when complaints about Yediyurappa's family being involved in an uncontrolled 'commission raj' were received by the PMO, the BJP leadership finally decided to act. The seventy-eight-year-old chief minister was told to step down as part of a generational change, but he was unwilling to give up, going so far as to seek the help of a local seer to 'manage' the situation. But the Centre was adamant. If Yediyurappa did not cede power, there was always a lurking fear amongst his supporters that the case files against him could be reopened. In the 'new' BJP, it's not just the Opposition that is threatened with ED action—even party colleagues can be intimidated. A tearful Yediyurappa halfheartedly gave up his chair to Basavaraj Bommai, a relative political lightweight—a sign that the BJP unit in Karnataka was caught in a bitter power tussle between Yediyurappa loyalists and the Centre.

A key figure in the Karnataka BJP's game of thrones was B.L. Santhosh, the party's powerful national general secretary (organization), responsible for co-ordination between the RSS and BJP at all levels. An RSS pracharak, his career rise mirrored that of Prime Minister Modi. Round-faced and with a thin moustache and the fixed gaze of the ideologue, Santhosh is always attired in a spotless white shirt and dhoti, and invariably sports a red tilak. Having worked closely with the BJP organization in Karnataka, he now wanted a greater say in the politics of his home state, much like what Modi once had in Gujarat. 'Santhosh is very ambitious. Like Modi ji, he doesn't want to be just an invisible pracharak but hopes to be the chief minister of Karnataka one day,' claimed a Bengaluru-based BJP watcher. While Team Modi–Shah was focused on the national picture, it was left to Santhosh to handle the nitty-gritty of the Karnataka campaign.

Santhosh's influence extended not just to the choice of candidates but also to the revival of the Sangh's Hindutva ideological agenda in the state. In the build–up to the 2023 Karnataka elections, the BJP raked up a series of religious issues and encouraged Sangh affiliates to ratchet up the communal temperature in an attempt to polarize the electorate and distract from the corruption taint against the Bommai government. This was a leaf out of the Modi–Shah campaign book. Critics have often accused the BJP's leadership of stepping on the accelerator of religious hatred and communal antipathy to storm through an election. From disallowing Muslim girls to wear hijabs in schools to calling for a boycott of halal meat to preventing Muslim vendors from participating in traditional temple festivals, there was an all-out attempt to stoke the Hindu–Muslim divide. As the Hindutva hotheads and extremists took centre stage, the affable Bommai silently looked the other way. 'It is you people who are constantly making these hijab-halal references. I am focusing on governance,' was his standard response to journalists. Off the record, he admitted to his aides that the Hindutva appeal would not work in 'secular' Karnataka.

In the final stretch of the Karnataka election, the BJP campaign was marked by growing nervousness that bordered on desperation. The state Congress, in its manifesto, promised to ban the Bajrang Dal, equating the right-wing Hindutva group with the Islamic PFI, claiming that both groups were promoting enmity and hatred. The BJP seized upon the reference to the Bajrang Dal, which was reportedly slipped in without the concurrence of the central Congress leadership. On a whistle-stop tour across Karnataka, Prime Minister Modi began his speeches with a rousing cry of 'Bajrang Bali ki jai!' Modi appealed to voters to chant 'Jai Bajrang Bali' while exercising their franchise. When it comes to campaigning, Modi has repeatedly shown his willingness to plumb the depths of religious divisiveness if it means winning an election.

With the Prime Minister attracting large crowds, the Congress was initially worried. Could the Bajrang Bali war cry shift the poll narrative and divert attention from the more basic 'guarantees', including cheap gas cylinders? Could Lord Hanuman be a poll weapon? 'It was only when we did a spot poll after a PM rally that we felt somewhat reassured. Bajrang Bali was only an issue for the BJP's core voters,' said a member of the Congress strategy team.

The results of the 2023 Karnataka elections confirmed these surveys: the Congress won a clear majority with 135 seats, while the BJP came trailing in with 66. The humble LPG cylinder had trumped the strident, hate-filled Hindutva plank. Even the Prime Minister's call for a 'double engine' government, where a vote for the BJP in Karnataka was being pushed as a vote for the Centre, hadn't worked. 'If you want development in Karnataka, vote for "double engine". If Congress comes to power, the Siddaramaiah government will put a stop to all central schemes,' BJP President J.P. Nadda announced in a campaign speech, a highly unconstitutional veiled threat that amounted to 'vote BJP or lose central government funding'. But the BJP's 'double engine' had been derailed by the voter. No to Hindutva. Yes to 'guarantees'. The Karnataka voter had chosen Bengaluru over Delhi. Local over national. The Congress had defeated the BJP in a direct fight—on the back of an earlier victory in Himachal Pradesh. Could the tide be turning? Had the Congress firmly established itself as challenger No. 1 in the battle for 2024? Or were other Opposition leaders also eyeing the big prize? Most crucially, if the need arose, could all these Opposition leaders with conflicting ambitions and shifting ideologies fight the BJP as a united front?

=

Patna in midsummer is a steaming hot cauldron. In the third week of June 2023, the political temperature was rising in a city that relishes the sights and sounds of politicians at play. Nitish Kumar, Bihar's long-serving chief minister, was hosting an array of netas across the political spectrum. The road from Patna airport was festooned with cut-outs of leaders from different parts of the country, representing twenty-six small and large parties. The invitee list read like a who's who of India's Opposition politicians. While Mamata Banerjee was holding court at one table, her left adversaries Sitaram Yechury and D. Raja were engaged in animated conversation at the next. Fresh off the Karnataka win, Rahul Gandhi was relishing the extra attention, while AAP leader Arvind Kejriwal scribbled away on a piece of paper in another corner. Hindutva flagbearer Uddhav Thackeray shuffled around nervously, whereas Kashmir's stormy petrel Mehbooba Mufti was all smiles. Akhilesh Yadav was tucking into lunch, and Tejashwi Yadav was showing off his fancy watch. The elders at the gathering—Sharad Pawar, Mallikarjun Kharge, Lalu Yadav and Farooq Abdullah—were more subdued, each having witnessed too many twists and turns in their long stints in electoral politics. If there was one thing that held this diverse gathering of Opposition leaders together, it was the prospect of joining hands to defeat Prime Minister Modi. 'Didn't left and right come together to bring down Indira Gandhi in 1977?' reminded Nitish Kumar when journalists questioned the intent of the meeting.

But the summer of 2023 was not quite the high noon of 1977, when a rag-tag Janata Party army had defeated the mighty Indira Gandhi. Nor was there a towering Jayaprakash Narayan or JP-like figure, someone whose moral stature and lifelong public service could make them a unifying mascot. The Opposition had commanding state leaders, but none could match Narendra Modi's pan-India appeal, and the parties themselves did not have the wherewithal to compete with the BJP's organizational machinery or access to resources.

West Bengal Chief Minister Mamata Banerjee, for example, had been in power for more than a decade in Kolkata, but her attempts to expand her footprint nationally had come a cropper. In 2021, soon after she won the state poll for a third time, she was goaded by election strategist Prashant Kishor and her nephew Abhishek Banerjee to bring Goa into the TMC's fold. 'Goa is a small state with a large minority population—Christians and Muslims—you will have a big edge over your opponents,' was Kishor's advice. Buoyed by a hat-trick of wins in Bengal, an ambitious Banerjee bit the bullet. A campaign blitzkrieg was launched in the state, hoardings with Banerjee's face were erected across the Goan countryside, while Kishor parked himself in a five-star luxury hotel in Dona Paula, near the state capital, Panaji, in a bid to lure local strongmen over to the TMC. Among Kishor's targets was the fifty-one-year-old ambitious South Goa leader Vijai Sardesai, a former deputy chief minister and the head of Goa Forward, a small regional outfit. But the 'deal' fell through. 'Kishor offered to project me as chief minister and promised to bankroll the entire campaign. But he wanted us to merge our party with Trinamool, which we were reluctant to do. Why should Kolkata dictate to Goa?' argued Sardesai. Even an exchange of Bengali and Konkan-style saris when Banerjee visited Goa during the festive period could not resolve this thorny problem.

The Goa leader's argument lies at the heart of the Catch-22 situation that confronts regional parties attempting to grow nationally. Mamata Banerjee's TMC is steeped in Bengali ethos, and while Goa may share Bengal's love for fish and football, its political ethos—built around village panchayat cliques and deep-rooted ties to villages and Comunidades—is tough to penetrate for outsiders. 'Kishor thought he could buy an election with money power, but in Goa, our local connections matter more than anything else,' said Sardesai. The TMC–Kishor camp had a different story to share, claiming that the Goa Forward leader used his negotiations with the TMC to strike a better deal for himself with the Congress. 'He was never serious about coming with us. He just used Mamata di's name to bring Rahul Gandhi to the bargaining table,' asserted a TMC leader. When the results were declared, the TMC had got out for a duck, without winning a single seat, and the BJP had managed a relatively comfortable win in the 40-member assembly, the division in the anti-BJP votes only making their task easier. 'The TMC was the BJP "B team" in Goa, out to cut the "secular" votes,' insisted Sardesai.

The 'B team' charge is one which another overtly ambitious politician, Arvind Kejriwal, has routinely faced from his critics. While Banerjee has been unable to break out of her Bengal-centred image, a politically smart Kejriwal acquired a national saliency within a decade of forming AAP, a party packed with young, educated change-makers, free of the baggage of dynasty, religion, caste or region. No other political start-up in recent times has stamped its presence on the national scene so dramatically. Not only did Kejriwal win three consecutive elections—two of them by massive margins in Delhi—but he also swept the important border state of Punjab in March 2022. The Punjab triumph convinced Kejriwal that he was the most appropriate future challenger to the BJP and Prime Minister Modi. 'Arvind has always seen himself as an equal to Modi when it comes to political mettle, a David who has the self-belief that he can defeat Goliath. That's why he took on Modi way back in 2014 in Varanasi, even though we knew victory was highly unlikely,' said Ashutosh, former AAP leader.

Kejriwal had now set his sights on Modi's home state, Gujarat, which was going to assembly elections in November 2022. At a meeting at the chief minister's residence, his partymen were surprised with detailed presentations made on AAP's Gujarat strategy, right down to booth-level operations. 'I don't think we have seen Arvind as excited in a long while as he was talking about Gujarat that day,' said an aide. At the meeting, one of his colleagues asked him how he would answer criticism about AAP's presence in Gujarat damaging the Congress's chances by dividing the anti-BJP vote. 'For twenty-five years, the Congress has not been able to fight the BJP in Gujarat; now we should get a shot at it,' was Kejriwal's clear-cut response.

What many do not know is that while publicly seeking to occupy the challenger No. 1 space in Gujarat, Kejriwal was trying to work out a seat-sharing pact with the Congress behind the scenes. He tried to connect with Rahul Gandhi initially, but was rebuffed by a wary Rahul. 'I am not the Congress president and I don't decide on alliances. Why should I be meeting Kejriwal at this juncture?' Rahul reportedly told his aides. His route to Rahul blocked, Kejriwal reached out to Sonia Gandhi. The two had a telephone conversation, at the end of which Sonia Gandhi 'promised' to get back after speaking to senior leaders. But there was no revert. A cautious Sonia Gandhi, as is her style, wasn't willing to make any pre-poll commitments. The deal fell through, making it even easier for the BJP to romp home in their bastion, with a record 156 seats in the 182-member assembly. AAP too managed to make a mark, winning 5 seats with nearly 13 per cent vote share. In Gujarat's tribal belt, Kejriwal even outscored the Congress in several seats. 'How can we trust someone who is targeting our vote bank across the country?' argued a Gujarat Congress leader. The trust deficit would always haunt Kejriwal as he jostled for more space in the political sun.

The 'trust factor', or lack of it, had dogged another potential prime ministerial challenger in the Opposition ranks. The ultimate political survivor, Sharad Pawar was by far the most senior leader at the Patna luncheon, the only one in the group whose political career had begun in the 1960s. But when he split from the Congress to become Maharashtra's youngest chief minister at thirty-eight, Pawar acquired the reputation of being a leader who could switch sides whenever convenient. Now eighty-two, Pawar was less inclined to further any immediate political ambition.

In July 2022, he almost signed up to be the Opposition's joint nominee for the post of President, only to back out at the last moment. 'He gave us a go-ahead initially, but suddenly, when we were about to propose his name, he declined,' recalled an Opposition leader. Kingmaker, not king, was his chosen role. 'How can I be Prime Minister with only a handful of MPs? I only want to ensure that the Opposition sticks together at this time,' he told a close friend. What was unsaid was his desire to ensure a secure future for his daughter and MP, the young and articulate Supriya Sule, within a wider coalition.

Pawar may have become a reluctant challenger, but the host of the Patna gathering certainly wasn't. Nitish Kumar is from the storied batch of Indian politicians who cut their teeth in the Emergency years of the mid-1970s, inspired by the clarion call for 'Sampoorna Kranti' or 'Total Revolution' given by veteran socialist leader Jayaprakash Narayan. Idealistic student activist then, hard-nosed leader with a sharp instinct for political survival now, Nitish Kumar has been sworn in as chief minister of Bihar a record nine times. His political acrobatics in shifting from one side to the other have earned him the rather unflattering nickname 'Paltu Kumar' (loosely, flip-flopping leader). But through all the dexterous power shifts, Nitish Kumar has retained one fierce ambition: to be Prime Minister one day. Which is partly why the inexorable rise of Modi had left him, like many other politicians of his generation, a little flummoxed. Modi, after all, came from a relatively politically lightweight state like Gujarat, not the Hindi heartland states—say, a Bihar or an Uttar Pradesh (which between them accounted for a little less than a fourth of the Lok Sabha seats). Unlike Modi, Nitish Kumar had been both a chief minister and a Union minister in the Vajpayee government. 'Yeh Modi ji aap mediawalon ka creation hai (Modi is a creation of you media fellows),' he once said dismissively of the Prime Minister.

Nitish Kumar does not like Modi and has made no secret of it. In 2013, when Modi was made the BJP's prime ministerial candidate, Nitish Kumar was the first to break away from the BJP-led NDA while claiming to be the torchbearer of 'secular' politics. BJP leader Arun Jaitley had telephoned

Kumar from London asking him not to take any precipitate decision. Jaitley and Kumar shared a warm personal equation, and the former's intervention was designed to hold the alliance together. 'Arun ji, main aapka sammaan karta hoon, par main inke [Modi] saath kaam nahi kar sakta. Woh communal hain; democratic nahi, tanashah hain (I respect you, Mr Jaitley, but I can't work with Modi. He is communal; he is not a democrat but a dictator),' was Kumar's defiant response.

The break-up with the BJP pushed Nitish Kumar into the arms of Lalu Yadav, his long-time political rival in Bihar. While their alliance swept the state assembly elections in 2015, it was a fraught relationship. Competitive Mandal movement warriors, each seeking to widen his own sphere of influence and make a bid for Bihar's top job, were never going to be able to forge a lasting partnership. In 2017, Nitish Kumar claimed he was 'suffocated' by Yadav family corruption and returned to the NDA's fold, effectively accepting Modi's dominant position at the Centre. And yet, he kept a line to the Congress, and Rahul Gandhi in particular, open, hopeful of leading an anti-Modi grouping in the future. In 2018, Nitish Kumar spent a week in Delhi, along with Prashant Kishor (then in the JD[U]), pushing for a 2019 general election tie-up with the Congress. But when a wary Rahul Gandhi didn't meet him, Nitish Kumar was distraught and felt isolated. 'I think after Nitish's return to the NDA, Rahul couldn't bring himself to fully trust Nitish again. Rahul has always been more comfortable with Lalu than Nitish,' said a Bihar Congress leader.

But nothing is permanent in politics. Especially in volatile Bihar. In July 2022, Nitish Kumar switched loyalties again. This time he broke with the BJP and joined hands with the Yadavs and Congress once again. The split in the Shiv Sena and the toppling of the Maharashtra government just weeks earlier had convinced Nitish Kumar that the BJP was planning an Eknath Shinde-like coup against him: in the 2020 Bihar assembly elections, the JD(U) was reduced to just 43 seats, the party's lowest tally since allying with the BJP. Reports that the BJP had used a youthful Chirag Paswan to target Nitish Kumar sent the latter into a seething rage. 'As he gets older,

Nitish trusts no one, and he sees conspiracies around him all the time,' claimed a former JD(U) leader.

Back in an anti-Modi group, Nitish Kumar sensed his opportunity to play a pivotal role in national politics, possibly as an Opposition alliance convenor. Within days of the Congress's victory in Karnataka, he hit the road, meeting a cross-section of Opposition leaders and inviting them to be part of a 'secular' 'democratic' coalition. One Delhi-based leader recalled Nitish Kumar getting emotional during their meeting. 'Yeh hamara aakhri mauka hai iss tanashah ko hatane ka (This is our last chance to remove the dictator),' was the Bihar leader's passionate pitch. Now, as he sat at the high table in Patna, surrounded by leaders from across the country, Nitish Kumar was a step closer to his ultimate goal: the Opposition's national 'face' who would take on Modi.

The Patna meeting was not the final act of making some spectacular announcement about a potential challenger to Prime Minister Modi for the 2024 general elections. Rather, it was an icebreaker, a useful starting point, one that many of its stakeholders hoped would create some momentum with less than a year left for the general elections. 'Har kranti Patna se shuru hoti hai (Every revolution starts in Patna),' enthused Lalu Yadav. Recovering from a kidney transplant operation, the visibly weakened former chief minister seemed to be relishing the prospect of another no-holds-barred electoral combat. The Opposition alliance had been forged. A fellowship of the electoral ring was formed.

A month later, the alliance partners met again, this time in the more luxurious environs of the Taj West End in Bengaluru. Their successful political conquest of Karnataka meant that the Congress could now afford to host a more lavish get-together. The plush five-star hotel in the heart of Bengaluru was cordoned off for the VVIP gathering. But neither the salubrious surroundings nor the sumptuous buffet could resolve the nitty-gritty of alliance-building. Seat-sharing and the choice of a convenor were not on the menu. Only two major announcements were made: a decision to meet in a month in Mumbai and, more interestingly, the name of the alliance. 'The Indian National Developmental Inclusive Alliance,' declared Congress President Mallikarjun Kharge. A tongue-twister in its expanded form was quickly shortened into a catchy single word: INDIA.

The name 'INDIA' was reportedly floated by Mamata Banerjee and endorsed by the Congress. Not everyone was on board, especially Nitish Kumar. Already peeved at not being formally anointed convenor, he was even more put out when his suggested name—'IMF', or India Main Front—found few takers (given its echoes with Washington-based international monetary bodies perceived to be bullying India). He protested at the 'unilateral' decision-making, but was eventually cajoled by Sitaram Yechury into not walking out of the meeting. 'This alliance is being taken over by the Congress,' Nitish grumbled irritably.

But the minor rumblings did not affect the big picture. This was an enormously significant moment for the Opposition. A twenty-six party 'big tent' alliance, including parties led by seven state chief ministers and accounting for 142 members of the Lok Sabha, had taken shape. Not only did it now have a high-recall name, but by the next day it also had a well-spun tagline: 'Judega Bharat, jeetega India' (Bharat will unite, India will win). 'It's going to be INDIA versus Modi in 2024,' cheered the TMC's Derek O'Brien. Misplaced optimism or the hint of a mood swing? India awaited an answer.

TEN

'Kaun Banega Challenger': The Battle for the States

WHEN asked for his mantra for success, Amit Shah once told a junior BJP colleague, 'Life or politics, never take anything for granted.' As he watched the political situation unfold through the first half of 2023, the home minister's razor-sharp antennae had picked up worrying signals. It wasn't just the assembly election defeat in Karnataka that troubled him. In Delhi, a street agitation by several women wrestlers, including Olympic medallists, accusing BJP MP and Wrestling Federation of India (WFI) chief Brij Bhushan Sharan Singh of sexual harassment had spiralled out of control. Viral videos and images of some of India's top sportswomen protesting on the streets had horrified public opinion—and greatly embarrassed the Modi government. Most of the champion wrestlers were from BJP-ruled Haryana, and it didn't take long for the links between politics and sports to play out. 'The Congress and the Hoodas in Haryana are backing the wrestler protests; it is politically motivated,' claimed Anurag Thakur, then sports minister, who was tasked with defusing the situation.

The real story is murkier. The man in the eye of the storm, Brij Bhushan, was a six-time MP from Uttar Pradesh, a political 'bahubali' (strongman) with a criminal record. I had first met him in the 1990s when he was charged under the Terrorist and Disruptive Activities (Prevention) Act for sheltering members of the Mumbai underworld in his official Delhi residence. 'The entire case is cooked up. So many people from my constituency come to stay in my home. How can I monitor each one?' he had argued. Bhushan was eventually let off in the terrorism case but remained under the scanner on multiple other charges, from murder to kidnapping. Significantly, he was seen in BJP circles as part of Home Minister Shah's 'group of influence', a Thakur from Uttar Pradesh who could act as a check on Yogi Adityanath's rising clout. When the sexual harassment charges were initially made against him, Brij Bhushan had instantly turned to Shah for help. 'I have done no wrong,' he insisted. The home minister reportedly asked Brij Bhushan to 'stay silent' and remain 'under the radar'. When I tried to buttonhole the MP at his Delhi residence, a security guard warned me: 'If we see you here again, we will break your camera!'

For Deepender Hooda, the clean-cut, bespectacled young Congress MP, the wrestlers' protest was an opportunity to stake his claim to be a defender of his community. The protesting women wrestlers were all Jats, a few of them from the Hooda family bastion of Rohtak in Haryana. An ambitious and go-getting Hooda had been chief of the Haryana wrestling federation till 2020, before he was forced out by Brij Bhushan, who ran the national wrestling federation like a personal fiefdom. 'This isn't about politics. Our women wrestlers are the pride of our community and the state,' stated Hooda. When the wrestlers began their protest in January 2020, they had insisted on keeping politicians away from their agitation. But in April, when no action was taken against Brij Bhushan despite assurances from the sports ministry, the protest took a political turn. Backed by Hooda and, allegedly, by a leading industrial house involved in sports, the wrestlers upped the ante. In a dramatic move, the wrestlers threatened to immerse their Olympic and World Championship medals in the Ganga. 'We got calls from Mamata Banerjee and Arvind Kejriwal pleading with us not to take any extreme step. Priyanka Gandhi met us. They all promised to support us but nobody from the BJP bothered about us,' said Vinesh Phogat, a multiple gold medallist at the Commonwealth Games.

'Instead of listening to us and acting against the MP, the government is engaging in a character assassination campaign,' said Sakshi Malik, an Olympic bronze medallist. Apparently, Haryana government officials had been sent to the homes of the wrestlers to pressurize the families into withdrawing the protest. Many of the Olympians were employed by the state government and were warned that they would lose their jobs if they didn't end their protests. In one instance, a story investigated by Al Jazeera's website revealed how a young complainant was reportedly threatened with a warning: 'Aapko dope ke case mein phansa denge (We will frame you in a doping case).' Soon after, officials from the National Anti-Doping Agency (NADA) arrived at the residential wrestling academy where the complainant was training and forced her to take a dope test. A few days later, she received a notice claiming that traces of a banned substance had been found in her samples. A delegation of Haryana's wrestling coaches met then Sports Minister Anurag Thakur to raise the issue of alleged fake doping charges, but the notice was not withdrawn. She remained suspended. It was only seven months later that NADA issued her a clean chit. It was too late. The young wrestler's three-year sponsorship deal had been cancelled and her career pushed to the brink. 'Saam, daam, dand—they tried everything,' said Bajrang Punia, an Olympic medallist who, according to the sports ministry, was the 'ringleader' of the protests. Ironically, Punia claimed to be a supporter of Modi. But when he dialled in to seek the PMO's intervention, he received no answer.

With no solution in sight, the wrestlers, who had been living in makeshift tents in Jantar Mantar in the heart of the capital, decided to march towards the new Parliament building on inauguration day. The Delhi police swooped in and detained the wrestlers. The orders to break up the protest had come directly from the home ministry. The images of female Olympic wrestlers being brutally dragged on the streets and into police vehicles went viral. The same Olympians who had been feted by the Prime Minister at his residence when they won medals for the country were now being treated like street thugs. Their protest made the wrestlers symbols of an anti-Modi government sentiment. While Punia was offered a Congress ticket from Rajasthan in the 2023 assembly elections, Malik was proposed as a Congress Lok Sabha candidate from Mathura in 2024. Both eventually turned down the offers. Vinesh chose to step into the political ring and contest on a Congress ticket from Jhulana in the 2024 Haryana assembly elections. She had just been controversially disqualified from a gold medal round at the Paris Olympics and felt she had little to lose. 'I would have never joined politics if the Prime Minister had stood by us when we needed him,' she insisted.

Modi's Beti Bachao, Beti Padhao programme was undermined in full public view by his own pusillanimous and conspicuous silence on the wrestlers' demands. Public sympathy was almost totally with the wrestlers. 'We lost the perception war,' admitted a BJP leader. 'Olympians versus netas is no contest.' The wrestlers' protests, on the back of the earlier farm agitation, were mishandled by an instinctively autocratic, ill-advised government, unsure and incompetent in the face of dissent. The government's prevarication would have an electoral impact too. In the 2024 general elections, the Congress dominated the Jat belt across Haryana and Rajasthan.

Unfortunately for the home minister, there was more bad news in store. He was campaigning in Karnataka when he learnt that ethnic violence had erupted in Manipur between the Meitei and Kuki-Zo groups. Scores of people were killed and thousands had become homeless. Manipur, like Haryana, was BJP-ruled. State Chief Minister N. Biren Singh, a former Congressman, was also a part of Shah's growing 'circle of influence' within the party. When a group of BJP MLAs from Manipur had mooted the possibility of a chief ministerial change, Shah shot it down. 'Chief minister badalne se kuch nahi hoga (Nothing will happen by changing the chief minister). This is a very sensitive issue,' the home minister bluntly told the MLAs. The sixty-three-year-old Biren Singh is an interesting character, a rugged politician who was once a star national footballer. At his Imphal residence, pride of place is given to a picture of him clasping the prestigious Durand Cup, awarded at India's oldest annual domestic football competition, with the 1981 Border Security Force team. 'Football is my first love, politics only came later,' he said with a smile. After spending years in the Congress, he switched to the BJP just ahead of the 2017 Manipur elections. His son-in-law, R.K. Imo Singh, from a well-known Congress family, also defected to the BJP. He is president of the Manipur Cricket Association and reportedly part of BCCI secretary Jay Shah's clique. 'Every Manipur politician has some connection with Delhi; there are wheels within wheels,' said Pradip Phanjoubam, a senior Imphal-based journalist.

While Shah made a three-day visit to Manipur in May 2023 to review the on-ground situation, Prime Minister Modi resolutely stayed away from Imphal, refusing to even tweet about the bloody violence that had engulfed the state. It was only in July, when a horrific video of two women being paraded naked by a large mob in Manipur's Kangpokpi district went viral, that Modi finally broke his silence. The Prime Minister prides himself on his Northeast outreach; no other Prime Minister has visited the region more often. But when put to the test in Manipur, the Modi-led government was seen floundering and in denial. 'The ultimate measure of a man is not where he stands in moments of comfort and convenience, but where he stands in times of challenge and controversy,' said Martin Luther King, Jr. When faced with challenge and controversy, events like the farm protests, or wrestlers' agitation, or the violence those in Manipur, inevitably, a darker aspect of Modi's character reveals itself: escapist, irresponsible, unfeeling. In sharp contrast to Modi, Rahul Gandhi leapt into action once again, visiting relief camps in Manipur and meeting displaced people across communities. 'We don't believe in photo-op politics,' argued Nalin Kohli, the BJP's national spokesperson, in vain self-defence. But sometimes a photo does resonate. Images of Rahul embracing tearful Manipuri women made a compelling statement. A silent Modi versus an empathetic Rahul Gandhi—Manipur underscored the contrasting approaches to a crisis of the two principals. The tide of perception was slowly turning.

I got first-hand experience of an absentee state in Manipur under rather unusual circumstances. In late June 2023, a human rights activist friend called in with a request. 'Can you report the story of Vungzagin Valte?' she pleaded. I had no clue who Valte was, but when she recounted the horror story, I was shaken out of my stupor. Wending my way through a congested south Delhi colony, I reached the tiny ground-floor flat where Valte, a three-time BJP MLA from Manipur, was staying, convalescing from a near-death experience after being assaulted on the street in the heart of Imphal. A close associate of the chief minister, Valte is a Kuki. He was targeted by a Meitei-led, well-armed mob at a short distance from Biren Singh's official residence. Nothing could have prepared me for the sight of Valte, painfully crippled, his body twisted, battered and bruised, his speech badly affected by the attack and alleged electric shocks. He had been airlifted out of Imphal and taken to a hospital in the national capital. Staying at a relative's home, the Valte family was beside themselves with worry and grief. 'My husband was almost killed, and yet no one has been arrested, no one comes to even see us,' cried his wife. It was hard not to tear up. If this was the condition of an MLA's family, imagine the ordeal of ordinary Manipuris in relief camps. Manipur is a tiny state in a corner of India, but in the run-up to the 2024 battle it became symbolic of the political leadership's failure to provide a healing touch. In the general elections of 2024, the BJP was wiped out of Manipur, losing both seats in the state.

=

The BJP election war room takes its internal poll surveys seriously. The feedback comes from several private polling agencies and from an extensive RSS–BJP network on the ground. In June 2023, the party's monthly opinion-tracker poll showed it was trailing in Madhya Pradesh and Chhattisgarh, where assembly polls were due in November, along with Rajasthan and Telangana. While losing a southern state like Karnataka— where governments changed every five years due to an inefficient local unit that had messed up its strategy—was still understandable, how could the BJP be losing to the Congress in the Hindi heartland? With the 2024 general elections just a year away, this was a major alarm bell.

The poll findings were the subject of intense discussion at a high-level meeting called at the Prime Minister's residence in early June, around the same time that the INDIA partnership was taking shape. Modi, Shah, BJP President J.P. Nadda and organization secretary B.L. Santhosh stayed closeted in a room. The quartet comprised the BJP's Big Four, each assigned specific roles within a tightly controlled party system. Modi was the charioteer of the election machine, the Supreme Leader and final decision-maker; Shah was the strategist and chief organizer with ears firmly to the ground; Nadda was the dutiful follower, expected to implement orders; Santhosh, a bit chastened by the Karnataka defeat, remained a co-ordinator between the party and the RSS. When Shah referred to the disquieting Madhya Pradesh and Chhattisgarh data, the Prime Minister was unimpressed. 'Bas hamein mehnat aur karni padegi (We will have to work harder),' he emphasized. 'With Modi ji and Amit bhai, you must understand, every election is like going into a new battle. If you lose one, don't give up, just make sure you get the next one right—that is their firm message to us,' said a BJP functionary.

Madhya Pradesh, the sprawling state that was the Sangh Parivar's citadel, was of particular concern. Not only was the BJP trailing in the opinion poll, but also then Chief Minister Shivraj Singh Chouhan's ratings were plummeting. A few months earlier too, Chouhan's poll numbers had been unimpressive, leading to speculation that after seventeen years in power (with a short interregnum in 2018–19), the party leadership might replace the long-serving chief minister. In fact, high-level BJP sources confirmed that the decision to effect a leadership change had been taken in February 2023 itself but was held back at the last moment after top RSS leaders interceded on Chouhan's behalf. Now, the latest poll numbers led to a renewed conversation over Chouhan's future; the feedback was that there was 'thakavat' (fatigue) more than anger over 'Mamaji', as he was popularly referred to. But there was a glaring lack of available options. The decision to replace the chief minister was put on hold till Amit Shah had submitted a final report of the ground situation. In June 2023, the Prime Minister flew to Washington for an all-important India–US bilateral visit. Shah was now asked to take full charge of election planning. 'Amit bhai ke nirdeshon ke anusaar plan banaiye (Make your plan as per Amit Shah's instructions),' the Prime Minister directed before he boarded the plane to the US. The other members of the Big Four could only nod quietly.

The home minister has, by all accounts, an insatiable appetite for electoral jousting. From the first college election he fought in Ahmedabad in the early 1980s, his winner-takes-all, mercilessly competitive, cold-blooded mentality has set him apart. Boosted by the Prime Minister's vote of confidence, Shah set about his task. As a first step, he commissioned another detailed survey of the voter mood in all the election-bound states, including an assessment from local karyakartas and booth workers. Trusted aide Bhupender Yadav was put in charge of Madhya Pradesh. Veteran leader Om Mathur was asked to handle Chhattisgarh. Union Minister Pralhad Joshi was given the responsibility of Rajasthan. Prominent BJP leaders were identified from across the country and asked to park themselves in specific districts for the three months leading up to the elections. For example, Vishwajit Rane, a senior Goa minister, was given responsibility for a cohort of six Indore district seats. He would not only have to report to the state in-charge but also hold booth-level meetings, submit weekly reports and attend frequent video conferences presided over by the home minister. 'With Amit bhai, there is no concept of night and day. He can even ask you to do something at midnight and you just have to ensure it gets done. I have never seen such micromanagement,' said Rane, who was earlier in the Congress.

From selecting candidates two months in advance to focusing on the competitive seats that needed extra attention, Shah was keen to create an upbeat mahaul that would suggest the BJP had overcome the setback in Karnataka and was firmly back in the election game. As part of the strategy to lift worker morale, Shah recommended sending Union ministers to fight state elections. One of the ministers recalled being rung up by Shah at midnight and being informed of his decision.

'I remember asking Amit bhai whether my being asked to fight a state election was a demotion since I was an MP and a minister. His reply was straightforward: "Politics mein koi demotion-promotion nahi hota; aap pehle BJP ke karyakarta hain, phir leader. Ab jaake chunaav jeeto (There is no concept of promotion-demotion in politics; you are a BJP worker first, then a leader. Now, go and win the election)." It was another lesson for me in the Amit Shah school of election management,' said the one-time minister who is now an MLA.

The internal survey for the poll-bound states had another interesting finding. While the popularity of state-level BJP leaders was uneven, Prime Minister Modi's own ratings were rock solid. The conclusion drawn was that the 2023 state elections would have to be fought solely on the name of the Prime Minister. 'Koi double engine nahi—iss baar har rajya mein ek hi engine chalega, Modi ji ka engine (No double engine—this time in each state only one engine will run, Modi ji's engine),' was Shah's unambiguous message to his team. To combat the Congress's 'guarantees' that had worked so effectively in Karnataka, the BJP came up with a counter slogan based on the various schemes launched by the Central government: 'Modi ki guarantee'. 'People trust Modi ji; his guarantee will always carry more weight than anything the Opposition has to offer,' was Shah's reasoning. Simple. Focused. Effective. 'Modi ki guarantee' would become the BJP's core election message for both the assembly elections and the 2024 general elections. Only the results would turn out to be very different in both.

On 3 November, just days ahead of the assembly polls in Madhya Pradesh, at an election rally in Ratlam, the Prime Minister announced that his government would extend the free-ration scheme under the Pradhan Mantri Garib Kalyan Anna Yojana for another five years. The scheme was put in place during the Covid period and had targeted 800 million (80 crore) 'poor people'. 'For the next five years, the stoves of 80 crore people in my country will keep burning. This is Modi's guarantee,' he stated. Elections are full of 'promises' made by parties, not all of which are kept. Modi, however, claimed that this was not just a poll 'promise' or a point on the BJP's agenda; this was the Prime Minister's personal commitment. Like all autocrats, Modi speaks about himself in the third person, bypassing the party and connecting directly with the voter.

The Modi-centric campaign meant that no local leader, not even a four-time sitting chief minister, would be projected in publicity material as the sole 'face' of the party. In a clear sign of the changing times, a Jan Ashirwaad Yatra was launched in the state almost simultaneously from five different locations. But unlike in previous elections, it was led by different state leaders and not just Chouhan. When the Chouhan cabinet suggested renaming a subsidized meal scheme Mama ki Thali, the proposal was shot down. Where the Centre did relent is in allowing the chief minister to push ahead with his Ladli Behna scheme for women. Launched in March 2023, it promised a monthly cash handout of Rs 1,000 to all eligible women beneficiaries (women from families below a certain income level). By June 2023, 13 million (1.3 crore) women in the age group of twenty-one to sixty had enrolled. The Ladli Behna beneficiary women would turn out to be a decisive vote bank for the BJP in Madhya Pradesh.

While an embattled Chouhan had fallen timidly in line and, in a demonstration of hand-rubbing obsequious humility, eventually accepted the concept of 'collective leadership' in Madhya Pradesh, in neighbouring Rajasthan, the BJP's only north Indian woman satrap, the stylish, outspoken and on occasion rather haughty Vasundhara Raje wasn't willing to give up without a fight. A two-term former chief minister, she was by far the most popular BJP leader in the state. Unwilling to be seen as just another state leader, Raje insisted that her future role be clarified before she plunged into the campaign. Shah, though, was unbending. He had never seen eye to eye with the Rajasthan leader, critiquing her in the party's inner circles for not being a 'team player'. 'What is this fuss over "collective leadership"? This has always been our stand before an election,' was his unambiguous message. When a despairing Raje parked herself in Delhi for a week to try to address her grievances with the party leadership, she did not get an appointment with either the home minister or the Prime Minister. 'I think the message to Vasundhara ji was eventually communicated through Santhosh ji. She would have to be part of the team and all leadership choices would be made after the polls,' said a Rajasthan BJP leader. Raje did eventually join the BJP's Parivartan Yatra campaign in Rajasthan, but her trademark zest was missing.

Perhaps the trickiest assignment for Shah was Chhattisgarh, a state where the Congress had swept to power in 2018 with a massive majority. 'I must confess, most of us within the party had given up on Chhattisgarh. Even our internal surveys were putting the Congress comfortably ahead about three months before the elections,' admitted a BJP official. Shah, though, was unwilling to concede defeat without putting up a fight. 'Chhota rajya hai; teen-char per cent ke swing se mahaul badal jayega (It is a small state; a 3–4 per cent swing can make a difference),' was his reasoning. The state's politics was sharply divided between the tribal districts and the plains. In 2018, the Congress had swept the tribal belt, winning a record 11 out of 12 seats in Bastar and all 14 in Surguja. 'In our very first strategy meeting on Chhattisgarh, Om Mathur ji told us to focus on the tribal seats and do whatever it took to win back the Adivasi vote,' recalled Vishnu Deo Sai, who would later become the first tribal chief minister of the state.

The sustained outreach campaign in the tribal districts included a familiar ploy: prey on religious fears and work people up into a communal fever pitch. The BJP built up a propaganda campaign over growing religious conversion among the tribal population. The RSS, through its tribal-focused Vanvasi Kalyan Ashram, had already raised the issue of tribals being converted to Christianity. In the run-up to the elections, the entire Sangh Parivar machinery pumped up the volume on conversions, using booth-level WhatsApp groups to spread their hate-laced hype regarding 'church activities'. 'They will take away your land and your gods,' cried one such incendiary video, clearly aimed at dividing the tribal population along religious lines. The BJP also reminded voters that President Droupadi Murmu was the Modi government's pick. The Prime Minister also announced big-ticket schemes for tribal welfare as proof of the Modi government's commitment to Adivasis. In the final stretch of the campaign, Amit Shah instructed the local unit to prop up and even fund candidates from smaller tribal parties, like the Gondwana Gantantra Party and a then newly formed tribal group called the Hamar Raj Party, in an attempt to further divide the anti-BJP vote. It was a tactic the Modi–Shah duo had successfully experimented with in local municipal and panchayat elections in Gujarat in their formative years in politics. Divide rivals' votes by propping up competitors in the anti-BJP space. 'BJP ko main pole banao, baaki ke vote katao' (Make BJP the main pole, and divide the others' votes) was their time-tested strategy. The BJP's announcement of the Mahatari Vandana Yojana, a Ladli Behna-like initiative targeted at married women in the state, was a key moment for the mass outreach in Chhattisgarh and would prove crucial here on voting day. The scheme aimed to provide financial assistance of Rs 1,000 per month to eligible women and ensure their economic empowerment; camps were organized across the state to fill out forms for women voters. To reach out to the state's paddy farmers, the BJP promised a special bonus above the minimum support price (MSP). In Delhi, the Centre was unwilling to concede to the farmers' higher MSP demands; in Chhattisgarh, an election had to be won. 'If you want to understand how the RSS–BJP election machine works, just do a case study of their 2023 Chhattisgarh campaign. Tribal versus non-tribal, Hindus versus Christians, bankrolling small parties and independents, promising cash handouts to women and farmers—I don't think there is anything the BJP didn't do to reclaim the state,' said a BJP pollster. The party's governance deficit may be glaringly obvious at times in daily administration, but during an election campaign, the Modi-led BJP springs into all-systems-go mode.

In sharp contrast, the Congress failed to build on the Karnataka momentum. Fresh from aiding the party's win in Karnataka, an eager Sunil Kanugolu and team landed in Bhopal to work on the Congress campaign in Madhya Pradesh—only to run into an obstinate brick wall in seventy-seven-year-old party veteran Kamal Nath, the party's chief ministerial face and campaign driver. 'You will have to report to her,' Nath told

Kanugolu, indicating twenty-nine-year-old Nikita Khanna. She was the US-returned daughter of a friend of the Congress leader who had worked with a United Nations agency but had zero election experience. 'I was involved in the election war room but so were many others; we were a team,' claimed Nikita. When Kanugolu flatly refused to do Nath's bidding, the Congress leader was incensed. Nath had insisted upon a free hand to run the Congress campaign and was unwilling to take any guidance from an 'outsider' who was not part of his coterie of long-standing loyalists.

Like many contemporary election strategists, Kanugolu relied on data and on-ground surveys. When the data showed that Chouhan and the BJP were catching up, especially on the back of the successful implementation of the Ladli Behna scheme, he suggested a shift in focus: the woman voter, he advised, was key. 'I don't need advice from all you backroom guys. Do you know how many elections I have fought and won? I have been winning elections since before you were even born,' was the nine-time MP Nath's enraged response. When I asked Nath about his run-in with Kanugolu, he brushed it aside: 'I only wanted to know what he was bringing to the table with his team, but he couldn't provide me with any concrete details.'

In a last-ditch attempt to broker peace, the Congress leadership asked Randeep Surjewala, part of the party's Karnataka success, to move to Bhopal as general secretary in charge. It was too late, however. One morning, Nath's men arrived at the location where Kanugolu and his fifty-member team of young data geeks and strategy wonks were working and asked them to vacate the premises within twenty-four hours. 'If you don't leave, we will throw out your computers,' they warned. A visibly shaken Kanugolu hurriedly left Bhopal after having worked on the campaign for barely a month. 'If the Congress continues to lose to the BJP, it is because of leaders like Kamal Nath who just won't change with the times and think they know it all,' he muttered to a friend.

The Congress campaign in Madhya Pradesh was centred entirely on Kamal Nath. No other leader was given a look-in. One of Sanjay Gandhi's storm troopers in the 1970s, an ever-smiling charmer in his youth, Nath is known for his big business links and has always been a dedicated Gandhi family loyalist. Despite being touched by controversy over the 1984 anti-Sikh riots, he has proved his cred as an effective politician, winning successive victories from his constituency, Chhindwara, since 1998. A resourceful poll manager, Nath undoubtedly had the experience needed to win again. But he wasn't quite the 'team' leader the Congress needed in a tough fight. When the INDIA alliance proposed a joint rally in Bhopal to kick off the campaign, Nath reportedly vetoed it, saying it would be a 'distraction'. He even refused to accept a proposed seat-sharing pact with the Samajwadi Party. Instead, he chose to play his own version of competitive Hindutva politics, never missing an opportunity to project himself as a Hanuman bhakt and even 'sponsoring' a section of the local sant-sadhu samaj to flaunt his Hindu identity. 'Get this straight, the BJP does not have a monopoly on Hinduism. Do you know that I have built the largest Hanuman temple in Chhindwara? Do you know that it was Rajiv Gandhi who opened the Babri Masjid locks in Ayodhya?' he argued. A 'soft Hindu' projection has never really worked for the Congress in the Hindi heartland, and Nath's strategy was badly misplaced. There were even conspiratorial whispers in Bhopal's power corridors that Nath might have done a backroom 'deal' with the BJP to avoid being tangled in the ED's crosshairs. An ongoing ED–CBI investigation into alleged fraud and money laundering by the Congress leader's relative had only added to the speculation. 'What utter rot!' expostulated Nath. 'Do you really think I didn't want to defeat a force that brought down my government by unholy means?'

In the final analysis, blaming Nath alone for the Congress's Madhya Pradesh debacle would be unfair. If the party was unable to capitalize on the creeping anti-incumbency against the BJP, it is because the Congress organization in the state, and elsewhere, had become feeble and ragged after two decades of being out of power. The 2018 election, when the Congress edged ahead of the BJP and formed a government for fifteen months, was an aberration. The truth is, the party structure in Madhya Pradesh had been monopolized by followers of Nath and Digvijaya Singh, two leaders who were hardly representative of the change the voters were looking for. Unlike the BJP, which had demonstrated its strength and flexibility by successfully evolving the idea of a 'collective leadership' while playing the Modi card aggressively, the Congress remained constrained by past thinking and lacked a credible leadership to manage its factionalized state unit. In sharp contrast, the BJP in Madhya Pradesh, like in Gujarat, benefitted from a deep-rooted Sangh Parivar network across the state. Unsurprisingly, the party was wiped out in the state assembly polls of 2023—and would be wiped out in Madhya Pradesh in the 2024 general elections as well.

If Madhya Pradesh was a missed opportunity, neighbouring Chhattisgarh turned out to be an appalling self-goal. In August 2023, three months ahead of the assembly election, every poll pointed to a clear win for the Bhupesh Baghel-led Congress government, which had swept to power in 2018. 'You can go through a dozen internal surveys, be it of the BJP or Congress—each and every one put us on top. When everyone tells you that you are winning, I guess it can breed overconfidence at times,' admitted Vinod Verma, a close aide of Baghel.

In 2013, almost the entire Congress leadership in Chhattisgarh had been wiped out in a Naxal attack in the horrific massacre at Jhiram Ghati. Taking the reins in 2018 in Chhattisgarh, Baghel had proved to be a popular and rooted leader, symbolizing a robust rebound of the Chhattisgarh Congress from the horror of the Jhiram Ghati killings. This time too his team was certain that the forceful Baghel would pull off another Congress win. But under the surface of optimism, discontent was brewing at the local level. Baghel's rough-edged aggression was unsuited to a Congress culture not known for encouraging strong regional satraps. The chief minister exerted total control through the state bureaucracy, alienating many district-level Congress workers who were looking for a share in the spoils of power. 'He was way too dictatorial in his functioning; even his own ministers were petrified of incurring his wrath,' remarked a Raipur-based journalist. When tribal groups organized themselves under the banner of the Sarva Adivasi Samaj in the Bastar belt, the chief minister was accused of ignoring their demands, including ensuring greater autonomy for gram panchayats. In 2018, the Congress had swept Chhattisgarh's tribal belt, winning 25 out of 26 seats; in 2023, the party would win just 4.

Baghel's main rival for the top post was Tribhuvaneshwar Saran Singh Deo, a genteel politician of royal lineage. With his neatly combed iron-grey hair and aquiline features, the Delhi University-educated Deo, now a titular maharaja, looks every inch the local aristocrat. His family once ruled the tribal-dominated Surguja district. Deo conceded the chief minister's seat to Baghel in the battle for the post in 2018 amidst reports that Rahul Gandhi had brokered a truce by which both leaders would share the top job for two and a half years each. But in 2021, when it was time for a handover, Baghel refused, claiming he had the support of the majority of MLAs. Initially, the Congress leadership was inclined to effect a change—Baghel even reportedly handed in his resignation—only to backtrack at the last minute. Deo met all the top Congress leaders and was assured that he would be made chief minister soon. 'Our leader was even told to fix a swearing-in date, but suddenly the high command did a complete U-turn,' cribbed a Deo supporter. While the official reason given was Baghel's credentials as a prominent OBC leader, word has it that as an important fundraiser for the Congress, he had earned considerable goodwill among the party leadership. In particular, Baghel had built a strong equation with Priyanka Gandhi Vadra, fully supporting her campaigns in Uttar Pradesh and Himachal Pradesh. 'I hate to say this but Baghel ji was like our trusted ATM; he contributed wholeheartedly to every election we fought,' admitted a Congress official.

The soft-spoken and ever-courteous Deo lost out and was eventually offered an olive branch: deputy chief ministership in June 2023. But by then the Congress camp was split into different factions, each looking to weaken the other. To contain the internal wrangling, the previously planned campaign slogan, 'Bhupesh hai toh bharosa hai' (In Bhupesh we trust), was tweaked to 'Congress hai toh bharosa hai' (In Congress we trust) under instructions from the party's central leadership. Posters too would now display other state leaders, not just the chief minister. 'Our own poll survey showed that if you removed the face of Baghel ji from the campaign, we would lose around 20 seats. And yet our Delhi leaders in their wisdom decided that we must fight the elections with a collective leadership in Chhattisgarh,' lamented a Baghel loyalist. As the assembly elections drew closer, Baghel himself was cornered by a slew of corruption charges and ED investigations, all of which pushed the Congress on the back foot in a crucial phase. The party was trounced in Chhattisgarh, losing badly even in Deo's bastion of Surguja, which they had swept five years earlier. The BJP won an absolute majority with 54 out of 90 seats.

If the Congress squandered a likely victory in Chhattisgarh, in Rajasthan the party almost miraculously pulled off a triumph when most pundits had totally written off their chances. Internal polls in early 2023 showed the Congress trailing well behind the BJP. This wasn't surprising; Rajasthan had seen governments alternating every five years for almost three decades. The public spat between then Chief Minister Ashok Gehlot and his young rival Sachin Pilot hadn't helped matters either. In a desperate attempt to salvage his position, Gehlot reached out to Naresh Arora, a sharp-suited, savvy election specialist who had worked on Congress campaigns since 2016 and was part of D.K. Shivakumar's Mission Karnataka team. 'When I met Gehlot ji for the first time in January 2023, I asked him straight away: Are we fighting to win or only to avoid an embarrassing defeat? When he made it clear that he wanted a winning strategy, I dived in,' said the smooth-talking Arora, who allegedly set up a team of 2,000 employees of his company, DesignBoxed, to fan out across the state to collect poll data and work on strategy.

Over nine months in 2023, Gehlot went through a complete image makeover. A low-key, unassuming politician was transformed into a Modi-esque, larger-than-life chief ministerial figure. If Modi had made the Ayushman Bharat health insurance scheme his calling card nationally, Gehlot's Chiranjeevi health insurance scheme, with enhanced benefits, became a key selling point in the state. 'Every welfare scheme in the country, even at the state level, was identified with Modi ji. We needed to change that,' pointed out Arora. A major outreach initiative was designed. This entailed setting up Mehngai Rahat (price-rise relief) camps across Rajasthan, which would help eligible beneficiaries get relief under various government schemes, including access to LPG cylinders at Rs 500 as an anti-inflationary measure. The attempt to project Gehlot, wise, senior, moderate and welfarist, as a pro-poor, benevolent chief minister who would deliver reassuring stable governance did have an impact. In the run-up to the elections, every opinion poll showed the Congress leader as being more popular than his rivals on either side of the political divide. The template of 'guarantees' or welfare-benefit promises that had succeeded in Karnataka seemed to be working here too. The BJP was forced to respond with a 'Modi ki guarantee' counter to offset the Gehlot factor.

And yet, as is often the case with the Congress, an individual-centric campaign was frowned upon by a section of the party. 'This Arora fellow only wants to spend huge monies in showcasing the chief minister. He doesn't care about anyone else, not even the Congress party organization,' was the complaint made by the state party chief, Govind Singh Dotasra, who was reportedly involved in a slanging match with Arora. 'I tried to explain to them that you can't have two captains in a ship. If Gehlot wins, the Congress wins. But the Congress organization let Gehlot down,' was Arora's counter.

Gehlot is the party's tallest leader in Rajasthan, but he is also a practised hand in dealing with factional politics. As the chief minister's stature rose, several of his MLAs came to be accused of corruption and neglect. But instead of acting against the tainted MLAs, the chief minister's office was seen to be 'protecting', even indulging, them. When a survey report recommended that thirty-nine out of the 113 sitting MLAs be dropped, Gehlot hesitated to act. Nor was the Congress central leadership willing to bite the bullet. 'It is very easy to say "drop a sitting MLA", but don't forget that these are the very MLAs who stood by me when the BJP was inducing them to defect with all kinds of allurements,' was Gehlot's defence. In the end, only eight MLAs were struck off the candidates' list. This would prove to be a crucial error. Many of the sitting MLAs lost. The party leadership's inability to resolve the grievances of a sulking Pilot, who still commanded considerable support among the caste-conscious Gujjar community, was another critical failure on the part of the Congress. Pilot complained to a party colleague: 'I was only given a chopper and asked to campaign across the state in the last few days. Until then, I was entirely shut out from decision-making.' However, the Gehlot camp insisted that Pilot was disinterested because he wanted the chief minister to lose. The fact is that in the last fortnight of the campaign, when Arora planned a 'guarantee yatra' across the state, many of the party's leaders from its 'star campaigner' list were simply not available. 'Make no mistake, it is not the BJP that defeated the Congress in Rajasthan, it is the Congress, especially those who sit in Delhi and know nothing of the ground situation,' asserted the election planner. Notably, in the 2024 general elections, a more focused and nimble Congress organization would win 11 out of 25 seats in Rajasthan when most pundits predicted a total rout. This begs the question: Did the infighting within the Congress scuttle its chances in 2023?

Although the Congress couldn't achieve a turnaround in Rajasthan, it managed one in Telangana. Here too, the surveys in the first half of 2023 had written off the party's chances. The fledgling state, which was formed at the initiative of the Congress central leadership in 2014, was now the fortress of K. Chandrashekar Rao, or KCR, the crafty politician and leader of the Telangana movement who had been running things with total command for a decade. When KCR renamed the Telangana Rashtra Samithi party as Bharat Rashtra Samithi (BRS) in October 2022, the aim was to project himself as a national leader. 'I am going to take my Telangana model across the country. We will be the real challengers to the BJP in the future,' he boasted.

The eager, ambitious KCR was not short of funds. One of his associates revealed that the Telangana chief minister was ready to fund the entire 2024 Opposition INDIA alliance campaign provided he was made convenor of the grouping. 'KCR is convinced that he is a better administrator than anyone else, including Modi,' said a former BRS leader. Projecting himself as a genuine farmers' leader, he even planned a 'Mission Maharashtra', hoping to kickstart his national ambitions from the neighbouring state. In early 2023, BRS posters were splashed across Maharashtra towns like Nanded, the skyline punctuated by the party's distinctive pink banners. 'Abki baar, kisan sarkar' (This time, a farmers' government) was the slogan KCR was taking to the voters.

But while KCR, functioning in solitary splendour from a farmhouse on the outskirts of Hyderabad, was setting his sights on Maharashtra and beyond, he seemed oblivious to the ground slipping away from him on his home turf. The Congress, once a dominant party in the Telangana region, was suddenly back in contention. Having been eased out of Madhya Pradesh by the Congress's old guard, election strategist Kanugolu had shifted base to Hyderabad, where he found himself in the warm embrace of a youthful leadership hungry for power. Until 2023, Revanth Reddy was scarcely known outside Telangana. The ebullient and charismatic Reddy had started off his political journey as an ABVP activist before joining the TDP and then finally switching to the Congress in 2018. In 2015, he was arrested by the KCR government in an alleged cash-for-votes case just ahead of his daughter's engagement ceremony. While he managed to get bail for a few hours to attend the engagement, he vowed revenge. 'From that day, I had only one mission: defeat KCR and teach him a lesson for what he made my family go through,' said Reddy.

With Kanugolu and team providing the micro-level backroom support, Reddy took the battle into the KCR camp, accusing the chief minister of promoting 'family raj' in Telangana. In a public meeting in June 2023, he threw an open challenge to KCR. 'You have 104 MLAs [in a 119-member assembly], and if you are a real man, give tickets to all your sitting MLAs. If you are so sure of winning, just do it.' Normally a canny operator, an overconfident KCR fell into the trap. Weeks later he announced that he was renominating all his sitting MLAs (only two were eventually denied a ticket). 'The day he made the announcement, we knew we had a chance to capitalize on the anti-incumbency against sitting MLAs. KCR scored the biggest self-goal,' said a buoyant Reddy, grinning. He was bang-on in his assessment. The Congress-led alliance won 64 seats in a 119-member assembly, the BRS just 39. For the first time since Telangana was carved out as a separate state in 2014, the Congress was tasting power.

The results of the four main state assembly elections were announced on Sunday, 3 December 2023, billed as the 'semifinal counting day' before the big 2024 finals. Confident of a strong showing, a Congress office-bearer in Delhi had placed an order for laddoos to be distributed among the media and party supporters at noon. 'Even if we win two states, it will be positive for us. If we win three, it will be a bonus, and if we win all four, then it's the end of Modi,' exclaimed the Congressman. In contrast, the BJP office—normally a hive of activity on counting day—was more subdued. 'Let's wait for a few hours, then we will know who should be celebrating,' observed BJP spokesperson Syed Zafar Islam.

By noon, the direction of the poll winds was clear. The BJP was inching ahead in a tough battle in Rajasthan. Surprisingly, despite the tight contest predicted by many exit polls, the party was sweeping Madhya Pradesh. Even more unexpectedly, the lotus was even blooming in Chhattisgarh. Only Telangana was providing the Congress some southern comfort. A 3–1 result in favour of the BJP was a decisive victory in an election cycle where five years earlier the party had lost in all the three Hindi-speaking states. The promised laddoo order at the Congress headquarters never materialized. Instead, it was the BJP office that erupted in celebration with laddoos and jalebis. The party was convinced that the winter polls of 2023 had set the stage for the summer storm of 2024. For the long-suffering Congress, a year that had started with rare optimism was ending in a familiar slough of despair.

＝

The Bihar chief minister's sprawling, heavily fortified bungalow on Patna's 1, Anne Marg has been Nitish Kumar's official residence for almost two decades now. Across the road, at 7, Circular Road, is another house that was allotted to him when he briefly lost his chief ministership in

2013. Where once Kumar would regularly hold 'janata durbars', access is now tightly controlled. Only a few close aides have easy entry. On 3 December, as the assembly election results were declared, three of his key JD(U) partymen came to converse with him behind closed doors. Ministers Sanjay Jha, Ashok Choudhary and Vijay Chaudhary were an inner-circle troika who had, over time, become the eyes and ears of the chief minister. 'The chief minister does nothing without consulting them; they almost control Nitish ji and he is fully dependent on them,' admitted a former JD(U) colleague.

Nitish Kumar's health concerns had been the subject of much speculation for months in Patna's power corridors. 'The chief minister is not himself anymore. He easily forgets things and tends to ramble,' a senior IAS officer said, describing an interaction with Kumar. At an Opposition INDIA alliance meeting in Mumbai, Kumar had met a DMK delegation led by Chief Minister M.K. Stalin. A few minutes after Stalin left the room, Kumar turned around to his partymen and asked, 'Yeh kaun thhe? Inka naam main bhool gaya (Who was he? I have forgotten his name)!' While no one would spell out exactly what was wrong, Kumar's bouts of forgetfulness and distinct short-term memory loss were worrying. Compromised cognition and forgetfulness are tragic impairments in the lives of many senior citizens and can seriously affect daily activities.

The more immediate cause for anxiety was Kumar's own position within the INDIA group. Kumar had played a critical role in bringing the disparate forces together, but even six months after the Patna soiree, there was little sign of any progress. His claim to be made alliance convenor had not been publicly endorsed either. The announcement was to have been made in September in Mumbai, but the press release was held up at the last moment because of a 'lack of consensus'. Just who had prevented the announcement from being made is unclear, but fingers are pointed at a small group of leaders within the alliance who were wary of Kumar's ambitions, including long-time 'frenemy' Lalu Yadav. 'Had Nitish been made convenor that day, he would have never left us, and the 2024 elections would have been ours,' lamented an INDIA alliance member.

Part of the alliance's problem was the Congress's laser focus on the 2023 assembly polls. 'Whenever we tried to raise the need for urgent talks on seat-sharing for the general elections and a common minimum programme for the alliance, the Congress leadership said they were busy with electioneering for the assembly polls. It was very frustrating,' remarked a senior ally member. The Congress was clearly hoping for a strong showing in the assembly polls, which would have strengthened their claims to a leadership role in any seat-sharing talks. But now, their resounding defeat in the important Hindi heartland states had shattered that hope. 'We knew then that we would now be under great pressure from every party in the INDIA alliance to accede to their demands,' conceded a Congress leader.

What the Congress perhaps wasn't aware of is that even before the December 2023 results, Nitish Kumar's team had already begun negotiating with the BJP for a return to the NDA fold. Kumar's close aide Sanjay Jha was the main interlocutor. A former BJP Yuva Morcha leader close to the late Arun Jaitley, Jha had switched sides and joined Kumar in 2013, when the initial JD(U)–BJP break occurred, reportedly with the consent of his mentor, Jaitley. 'Jha has always been a go-between for the BJP and the JD(U); he has friends on both sides of the divide,' claimed a senior Bihar journalist. In November 2023, weeks ahead of the election results, Jha, along with Ashok Choudhary and Vijay Chaudhary, had met BJP leaders, including BJP President J.P. Nadda. The troika had more or less convinced Kumar that the INDIA alliance was a losing proposition. 'They will never make you convenor as long as the Congress and leaders like Mamata Banerjee are around,' was their stand.

While Nitish Kumar weighed his options, a despondent and defeated Congress, reeling from its assembly poll losses, was running out of time and options. A day after the December results, when party president Mallikarjun Kharge's office dialled the INDIA allies seeking an urgent meeting, many of them didn't respond or cited their inability to attend at short notice. Even the relatively mild-mannered and good-natured Akhilesh Yadav, still smarting from the Congress's refusal to give him a single seat in Madhya Pradesh, said he was occupied. Mamata Banerjee too claimed she was 'unavailable'. The raft of Opposition leaders RSVPing 'no' to a meeting was embarrassing. 'We will now hold a meeting "at a date convenient to all",' was the Congress's response.

When the INDIA alliance meeting finally took place in mid-December, it was a hastily organized affair by the Congress in Delhi at the Ashoka Hotel. 'They haven't even ensured a proper lunch or tea,' grumbled one of the allies. The contrast with the elaborate spread when the alliance had met at the Taj West End in Bengaluru in July could not have been starker. 'We had just come to power in Karnataka then, so the mood was celebratory, but now that we had lost in the assembly polls, naturally the mood was downbeat,' confessed a Congress spokesperson. In power politics, the à la carte menu for gatherings can sometimes be an indicator of the well-being of a party. But the limited food options were the least of the INDIA alliance's worries. Suddenly in the meeting, the unpredictable Mamata Banerjee hurled a bouncer. She suggested that the alliance choose a leadership 'face' right away and proposed Mallikarjun Kharge as her prime ministerial choice. Her suggestion was instantly seconded by AAP leader Arvind Kejriwal. Only a day earlier, when she met the media over tea, Banerjee had ruled out any individual being projected as an INDIA alliance prime ministerial nominee. In less than twenty-four hours, she had changed her mind. 'We were totally blindsided by what Mamata di did. We didn't know what to say,' admitted a Kharge aide.

While the Congress president and most of the other leaders stayed silent, Nitish Kumar began to fume. He was infuriated. Having initiated the efforts to stitch together an Opposition alliance, he now found himself being sidelined at a key moment. 'Yahan hamare liye ab koi jagah nahi hai; aapka kehna sahi tha (There is no place for us here; you were right),' he grumbled to his aides.

No one has a clear answer as to why Mamata Banerjee made the unexpected pitch for Kharge, but it is evident that she was unwilling to concede a leadership role to Nitish Kumar, whom she considered a direct competitor. Perhaps the octogenarian Kharge seemed like a safer bet. 'Mamata di felt that announcing a veteran Dalit figure like Kharge as prime ministerial contender was just the kind of smart strategy that would disrupt the BJP's plans and create a real impact,' insisted a TMC MP. 'Remember, India has never had a Dalit Prime Minister.'

Political cunning or smart strategy, Mamata Banerjee had set the cat among the INDIA pigeons. For Nitish Kumar, in particular, it was endgame. His switch over to the BJP was now inevitable. That very night, the Jha-led power troika called up Vinod Tawde, the BJP's general secretary in charge of Bihar, to express their willingness to return to the NDA fold. Senior JD(U) leader Rajiv Ranjan Singh, better known as Lalan Singh, who wasn't in favour of the move, found himself speedily removed as national party president. 'He is negotiating with Lalu Yadav to break the party,' was the troika's whisper campaign against Lalan Singh. An insecure, mentally fragile Kumar swallowed this narrative.

Meanwhile, talks between the BJP and JD(U) escalated from Tawde to Nadda and all the way up to Amit Shah. The Union home minister was no admirer of Kumar's brand of political gymnastics and didn't trust him an inch. 'If he wants to ally, let him give us the chief ministership this time,' he proposed initially, but Kumar, who only months earlier had been eyeing prime ministerial glory, was not agreeable. Keenly aware that he needed to deliver a body blow to the INDIA alliance on the eve of the Lok Sabha elections, Shah, pragmatic as ever, backed down. The demoralization that Kumar's departure would bring to the INDIA alliance (given that he had been one of its primary architects) was the clincher. In early January 2024, a final call between the two principals, Kumar and Prime Minister Modi, sealed the deal. While Modi reportedly didn't say much in the conversation, Kumar was effusive in his praise for the Prime Minister. He sought only one sweetener: a Bharat Ratna for former Bihar chief minister and Mandal movement icon Karpoori Thakur. 'Imagine, a leader who wants to challenge Modi is pleading with him for a Bharat Ratna as a sop. This is what Nitish ji has been reduced to,' said a former colleague.

Ironically, just days after the Modi–Kumar phone call, an INDIA alliance meeting was held via video conference. At the meeting, from which Mamata Banerjee notably stayed away, Kumar was finally offered the post of convenor by the Congress. 'No, no, let someone else do it. I can only take up a post if my name is acceptable to all,' was the Bihar chief minister's noncommittal response. His mind made up, he was only playing for time. On 23 January, a Rashtrapati Bhavan communiqué announced a Bharat Ratna for Karpoori Thakur. Just five days later, Nitish Kumar was sworn in as Bihar chief minister for a record ninth term—after switching sides for the fifth time in ten years.

'The day Nitish ji left the Opposition alliance, we were certain it was game, set and match for us in 2024,' said a BJP leader involved in the negotiations. It wasn't an empty boast. Nothing is ever a done deal, especially in Indian politics, but coming on the back of a demoralizing assembly election result, Nitish Kumar's departure was seen as a mortal blow for the Opposition. The vexing question—'Kaun Banega Challenger'—had been answered. Frankly, there was no challenger to Modi in sight.

Or so it seemed.

ELEVEN

'Modi ki Guarantee' vs 'Samvidhan Khatre Mein Hai': A War of Narratives

THE BJP's election machine in the Modi–Shah era is like a high-speed treadmill without an off button. Unrelenting. Unyielding. Unlimited. On the morning after the December 2023 assembly election results, the BJP Lok Sabha MPs' WhatsApp group received a brief message: 'Please be in Parliament by 11 a.m. sharp to celebrate and honour Prime Minister Modi ji for leading us to this great victory.' Previous governments had customarily marked assembly election victories as party events held outside Parliament, which did not interfere with parliamentary functioning. But for the Modi government, every poll triumph was a self-congratulatory occasion to be cheered both inside and outside Parliament. The act was well-rehearsed. The Prime Minister entered the Lok Sabha like a returning monarch and, as if on cue, party members rose in unison, thumped the tables and exultantly called out the Prime Minister's name in ringing repetition, like back-up singers preparing the stage for the lead performer.

This day was no different. With then Parliamentary Affairs Minister Pralhad Joshi leading the chorus, the MPs began furiously chanting,

'Teesri baar Modi sarkar', 'Baar baar Modi sarkar', 'Modi! Modi! Hat-trick! Hat-trick!' In his front-row seat, the Prime Minister sat impassively, pretending not to hear the chants even as the Parliament cameras kept an unwavering focus on him. Lok Sabha Speaker Om Birla smiled benignly without saying a word, allowing the chanting to reach a crescendo. The intent was clear. The BJP wanted to send a message to the beleaguered Opposition and the all-important voter: buoyed by its successes in three key states, a Modi-led BJP was poised for a rare hat-trick of wins in the 2024 Lok Sabha elections.

'The BJP has converted even the sacred precincts of Parliament from a temple of democracy into a court of a king. It is absurd,' remarked Congress MP Gaurav Gogoi. The BJP leadership, though, appeared unflustered with the criticism. A BJP MP disclosed that even the 'Modi, Modi' chants were closely monitored by the Prime Minister's hawk-eyed team. 'It's like you are in a Bigg Boss studio and someone is watching over you all the time,' said the backbencher MP.

The Bigg Boss analogy is apt. Modi as the undisputed supremo, Shah as the trusted election-in-charge are jodi No. 1, unchallenged and seemingly unstoppable. They are like a tag team of heavyweight professional political wrestlers, competing together since Gujarat's municipal elections in the 1980s. And they are in no mood to stop or step aside. All major decisions, including the choice of chief ministers, are taken by the all-powerful duo with limited consultation and in total secrecy. A case in point is the appointment of the Gujarat chief minister in 2022. Party observers, led by then Agriculture Minister Narendra Tomar, were sent from Delhi to Gandhinagar to meet the newly elected BJP MLAs. When the legislature meeting began, Tomar was still clueless about the leadership's preferred choice for the post. 'We will inform you in due course,' was the cryptic message from the Prime Minister's office to the minister. For forty-five minutes Tomar tried to buy time by addressing the MLAs on a range of issues while anxiously waiting to hear from Delhi. He was running out of things to say when suddenly a chit with a name was thrust into his hand. When he announced the name—Bhupendra Patel, a first-time

MLA, seated in the last row—the room was stunned into silence. The big bosses in Delhi had plucked a relatively unknown MLA for the top post. In the 1980s, Indira Gandhi was accused of bypassing state units while choosing chief ministers. Team Modi–Shah had embraced the Indira-style 'high command' culture with even greater authority.

The choice of chief ministers for the three Hindi heartland states in the winter of 2023 was made just as secretively. Dr Raman Singh, a three-time chief minister of Chhattisgarh, was passed over for the much younger Vishnu Deo Sai, the first Adivasi from the state to hold the post. Singh's removal was not entirely unexpected. He had been in the running for the governor's seat earlier. More surprising was the manner in which Shivraj Singh Chouhan, long-serving Madhya Pradesh chief minister, was overlooked. The BJP had just won an impressive two-thirds victory after a tough battle, and man-of-the-match Chouhan was hopeful of retaining the top job. After all, the Ladli Behna scheme of cash handouts to women that had struck a winning chord with voters was his brainchild. After the results, Chouhan was eagerly receiving garlands from jubilant supporters, posing for photos with women voters, holding review meetings with bureaucrats and even planning on an auspicious swearing-in date, until he was informed that the party had chosen someone else. Ujjain strongman Mohan Yadav, not a recognizable figure outside Madhya Pradesh, was his unlikely replacement. 'Chouhan ji lobbied furiously with the RSS and his contacts in Delhi, but the Big Two had already sealed his fate,' remarked a supporter. The choice of Yadav was electorally strategic. The BJP wanted to reach out to the influential Yadav community in Uttar Pradesh and Bihar. On the day he was sworn in, LED screens were put up across the Yadav-dominated areas of Bihar to leverage the occasion for the crucial Yadav vote. An unswerving party karyakarta, the amiable Chouhan fell in line, contested the Lok Sabha elections, won by a huge margin and eventually became Union agriculture minister. Getting the combative Vasundhara Raje to similarly accept that her time in neighbouring Rajasthan was up, however, proved to be more problematic. Soon after the BJP crossed the halfway mark, Raje began rounding up her loyal

MLAs, hoping to put pressure on the high command. But to no avail. Defence Minister Rajnath Singh, one of the few central leaders with whom Raje enjoyed a good rapport, was sent as a party observer to Rajasthan. 'So whom are you making chief minister?' an agitated Raje reportedly asked him soon after his arrival in Jaipur. An embarrassed Singh mumbled something about the choice being left to the MLAs, but the truth is that the decision had already been taken in Delhi. Bhajan Lal Sharma, another first-time MLA but staunch organizational man, would be the new chief minister. At the legislature party meet, a visibly irritated Raje was handed a chit at the last minute and coerced into proposing his name. 'Vasundhara was seething at being ignored but didn't dare speak out,' said one of her loyalist MLAs. Retreating into the shadows, Raje chose not to campaign in the Lok Sabha elections except in her son Dushyant Singh's Jhalawar–Baran constituency and even tacitly backed a few Congress candidates. Raje's silent 'rebellion' would prove costly. The BJP, which had swept Rajasthan's 25 seats in 2019, would win just 14 in 2024.

An Adivasi, an OBC and a Brahmin—the chief ministerial changes in the Hindi heartland states were one aspect of Team Modi–Shah's caste-based 'social engineering' calculations aimed at effecting a generational shift in leadership ahead of 'Mission 2024'. Their larger game plan had been initiated in the summer of 2022, almost two years before the general election calendar began. The BJP had just won the crucial Uttar Pradesh assembly elections and had seized the poll momentum, but there was also genuine concern that ten years of anti-incumbency might slowly begin to bite at some stage. The challenge was to recharge the organization before complacency set in. 'If we have to win the 2024 elections by a big margin, then we have to get the organization back in top shape again,' Shah told an office-bearers' meeting in May 2022.

At that time, there was no specific 'char sau paar' target set, but the home minister was already plotting a strategy to ensure the BJP crossed its 2019 figure of 303 seats. In a detailed presentation to party functionaries, he listed the 224 seats that the BJP had won in 2019 with more than

50 per cent vote share. 'Now we need to target another 100 seats that we lost last time to be sure of victory,' claimed Shah. Most of the BJP's big wins in 2019 had come from north and west India, where the party won more than 80 per cent of the seats, blanking out the Opposition in half a dozen states. There was little headroom to expand in these regions. But the east and south of the country still held potential opportunities for growth.

Consequently, the BJP kicked off the Lok Sabha Pravas Yojana, an ambitious outreach programme aimed at strengthening the party's presence in constituencies where they had finished second or third in 2019 or won by a small margin. They identified 144 'difficult' but winnable electorates (the number would later increase to 160) and made them focus areas. These target seats were further divided into clusters of three or four constituencies, and each cluster was entrusted to a senior minister or MP. The leader in charge would have to travel every month to these constituencies, interact with party workers right down to the booth level, assess the delivery of government programmes on the ground and then provide detailed feedback to the central leadership. In the 'new' BJP, the lines between party and government functioning were increasingly blurred. Ministers involved in the Pravas Yojana were given a 144-point programme sheet to work on. And even high-ranking ministers were drafted into the project. External Affairs Minister Dr S. Jaishankar was deputed to visit Thiruvananthapuram, while Finance Minister Nirmala Sitharaman was given a Telangana cluster to supervise. As one minister remarked, 'We were expected to perform ministerial duties on weekdays and party work on weekends—no holidays, no breaks!'

Another key aspect of Shah's Mission 2024 was what a party insider jokingly called the 'M&A' approach: mergers and acquisitions. Shah had identified three large states where a double-digit loss in seats couldn't be ruled out: Maharashtra, Bihar and Karnataka. In Maharashtra, where the BJP-led NDA had won 42 of the 48 seats in 2019, the stakes were especially high. Despite splitting the Shiv Sena and forming a government in 2022, the BJP was worried that the wide Opposition alliance ranged against it was a formidable force. To further shore up its ranks, the BJP prodded a break-up in the NCP in July 2023 by using the ED as a weapon of fear and 'protection'. It meant a tie-up with Ajit Pawar, whom the BJP had once vociferously denounced as 'highly corrupt'. A BJP–Shiv Sena–NCP alliance was fortified by engineering splits and defections.

In Bihar, the BJP decided to reach out to Chirag Paswan, the young Lok Janshakti Party leader, who had built a decent following among Dalit youth in particular. Ahead of the 2020 Bihar assembly elections, Paswan was encouraged by the BJP leadership to go solo to downsize Chief Minister Nitish Kumar. 'Chirag was told by Amit Shah ji to fight hard against JD(U) candidates but not target the BJP,' admitted a BJP Bihar leader. The aim was to ensure that the BJP became the single largest party and that Nitish Kumar's post-poll bargaining power was reduced. A high-risk strategy but a gamble Team Modi–Shah was willing to take. Their style, right from the Gujarat days, has been to constantly keep their rivals, within and outside the party fold, on the edge. Once the elections were over, just a year later, Paswan found himself out on the road, literally. The dapper-looking politician who had tried to make a career in Bollywood with no success now found himself in the midst of a real-life drama. Government officials landed up at his 12, Janpath bungalow, where his father, the late Ram Vilas Paswan, had lived for years, and asked him to immediately vacate the house. A desperate Chirag Paswan, who happily referred to himself as Modi's 'Hanuman', contacted several senior BJP leaders, including Shah's office, but no help was forthcoming. Many leaders didn't even take his call. Truckloads of household items had to be shifted out overnight. The Modi government had chosen Chirag Paswan's uncle Pashupati Kumar Paras as Union minister. The nephew was left out in the cold. His mother was in tears at being suddenly evicted from a house that carried many family memories. 'It was humiliating, but in life all of this strengthens you,' Chirag Paswan confessed later. Team Modi–Shah's dealings with Paswan exemplify their 'use and throw' politics of convenience.

By July 2023, with Nitish Kumar having switched over to the Opposition, Team Modi–Shah needed Paswan again. Party chief J.P.

Nadda, who enjoyed a warm relationship with the Paswan family, was assigned the task of courting him. Keen to end his political isolation, Paswan jumped at the opportunity to return to the national mainstream. On his return, at an NDA meeting, Modi made it a point to clasp Paswan's hands and embrace him. 'He is like a father figure to me,' claimed the Bihar leader. Use. Throw. Use again. Amidst shifting allegiances, the NDA alliance was strengthened. When Nitish Kumar returned in January 2024, the circle was complete. 'This is the flexibility of the Modi–Shah leadership; no one is a permanent enemy for them,' said a BJP watcher.

In Karnataka too, ideological elasticity was at play. During the 2023 assembly elections, former Karnataka chief minister and JD(S) leader H.D. Kumaraswamy was repeatedly targeted by the BJP and accused of corruption and dynastic politics, but the Congress win in Karnataka had scuppered the party's plans. Now, as they prepared for the 2024 polls, the BJP couldn't afford another jolt in a state where they had won 25 out of 28 Lok Sabha seats in 2019. The easygoing Kumaraswamy was a consummate dealmaker. He had been chief minister in alliance with both the BJP and the Congress at different times. But sitting in his ranch-style farmhouse on the outskirts of Bengaluru, Kumaraswamy wore a troubled look. The Congress was eyeing his JD(S) MLAs and he was staring at political irrelevance. 'Yes, I opened a conversation with Amit Shah ji, and he was most willing to engage,' he later revealed. The home minister proposed a merger of the JD(S) with the BJP. A down-and-out Kumaraswamy was willing, but his father, H.D. Deve Gowda, preferred an alliance. The partnership was announced in January 2024, although the negotiations had begun months earlier. While Prime Minister Modi was targeting 'pariwarwaad' in Delhi, a political family was being conveniently co-opted in Bengaluru. 'In politics, you have to think of the future, not be tied to the past,' was Karnataka BJP chief B.Y. Vijayendra's defence. He too, as the son of a former chief minister of Karnataka, B.S. Yediyurappa, was a beneficiary of family politics. For Team Modi—Shah, election wins matter above all else. Election victories are the be-all and end-all of their politics. Governance, slogans, mottos, policies and vicious polarization—

all of it is geared towards winning elections at any cost, a single-minded, hyper-competitive manic craze for power rarely seen in Indian politics. And indeed, in the 2024 elections, the BJP–JD(S) alliance would prove a winner, securing important seats in southern Karnataka that the BJP might otherwise have lost.

Not all alliance 'dealmaking' worked out, though. In Punjab, for example, Shah agreed, after initial reservations, to resume talks with old BJP ally the Akali Dal. In the past, the Akali Dal had been the senior partner and contested 10 seats in Punjab, and the BJP the remaining 3 seats. This time, Shah was adamant about a '50-50' arrangement. Punjab BJP President Sunil Jakhar was deputed to work out the modalities. The final offer was 7 seats for the Akali Dal and 6 seats for the BJP—'Take it, or leave it!' The Akalis baulked at the idea, claiming that seat-sharing was an issue of 'self-respect'. Shah was unyielding. The negotiations broke down. For the first time in decades, the two parties contested a Lok Sabha poll separately. The BJP drew a blank, and the Akalis won 1 seat.

While Shah supervised the alliance-making, a high-level 'joining committee' was set up to handpick individuals from other parties and decide on inductions. The committee included Union Minister Bhupender Yadav, Assam Chief Minister Himanta Biswa Sarma, National General Secretary Vinod Tawde and General Secretary (Organization) B.L. Santhosh. State units could send recommendations, which would be screened by the committee. The main criteria was 'vote-gathering skills'. 'Even if a person could get one vote, they would be useful,' said a committee member. Another quipped, 'We were no longer the Bharatiya Janata Party but the "Bharti" (recruitment) Janata Party.' Congress leaders were prized defectors. By now, at least ten former Congress chief ministers had joined the BJP fold.

Not every proposed high-profile entry went through smoothly, though. For example, Kamal Nath, the former Madhya Pradesh chief minister and nine-time Congress MP, was preparing to join the BJP in early March 2024, having just been trounced in the assembly polls. Getting Kamal Nath, someone considered close to the Gandhi family, to cross over was ideal pre-election optics to propagate the impression that the Congress was a sinking ship. Nath had reportedly contacted the Prime Minister through a common business magnate friend. The plan was to induct Nath and his son Nakul, the sitting Chhindwara MP, at a grand event in Delhi. The date and timing were being worked out when Nath flew into Delhi from Bhopal on his private aircraft. But at the last minute, Team Modi–Shah received feedback that Nath's induction would anger party cadres, especially the Sikh community, given his alleged involvement in the 1984 anti-Sikh riots. 'Despite a lot of pressure to take him in, we decided not to take the risk,' disclosed a senior BJP leader. Officially, the party denies they were close to stitching a deal with the Madhya Pradesh Congress leader. The veteran Congressman also refutes any plan to defect, insisting he remains a 'loyal' partyman. Nath may have stayed back, but across Madhya Pradesh, hundreds of Congress workers did change sides, further depleting party ranks. Nath himself was scarcely visible in the 2024 campaign outside of his Chhindwara pocket borough. The BJP won all 29 seats in Madhya Pradesh.

Team Modi–Shah's 'mergers and acquisitions' strategy was proving to be a mixed bag. Where it worked, like in Karnataka, it brought the party crucial extra seats. But where it didn't, like in Maharashtra, it only spread discontent in the ranks. No one from the BJP will speak out publicly, but there is a distinct sense of unease amongst RSS and BJP leaders at different levels regarding the manner in which an ideologically driven, zealous party has now increasingly become hostage to entirely short-term election calculations. As one party leader explained, 'Just think of our workers who have dedicated their lives to this party now being asked to campaign for Congress leaders who are given BJP tickets the moment they switch sides. Isn't it demoralizing?' In 2024, as many as 116 of the BJP's 441 candidates—over 25 per cent—were 'imports', a majority of them from the Congress. 'Instead of a Congress-"mukt" (Congress-free) Bharat, we are becoming a Congress-"yukt" (Congress-filled) BJP,' lamented a BJP office-bearer. But Team Modi–Shah was unperturbed by the criticism, because they always had one ace left to play with: the enduring popularity of Prime Minister Modi.

=

Narendra Modi is an obsessive political campaigner, driven by frenzied energy and intense self-belief. An old Modi associate from his Gujarat days claimed that even as a young pracharak, he hated losing at anything. 'I remember once having a bet with him as to who could walk faster to reach a public meeting in Ahmedabad. When I reached slightly ahead of him, he was angry and refused to speak to me for a day or two,' recalled his contemporary. This 'win-at-all-costs' attitude might partly explain why Modi never switches off from election mode, why he's always rousing his troops to seek more votes.

Barely had the Pravas Yojana of ministers and MPs ended, when another outreach initiative was launched by the Modi government in November 2023. The Viksit Bharat Sankalp Yatra, flagged off by the Prime Minister himself, aimed to raise awareness and monitor the implementation of his government's flagship beneficiary schemes, like Ujjwala Yojana, Awas Yojana and Ayushman Bharat. 'We wanted to ensure that the promised benefits were reaching the intended beneficiaries and there were no leakages in between,' said a BJP office-bearer. Camps were organized across districts where citizens could raise their concerns with government officials and expect instant redressal. The BJP was armed with lists of lakhs of labharthis of government programmes, all of whom were seen as a captive vote bank. 'From creating WhatsApp groups to setting up call centres, we were in touch with lakhs of beneficiaries across India,' revealed a BJP leader involved in the micro-level planning. Over 150 call centres were set up across the country, each handling a cohort of three Lok Sabha constituencies with teams of around seventy-five young recruits, hired on short-term contracts and paid around Rs 7,000–10,000 a month, all working the phones to push the BJP's messaging. Jarvis Technology and Strategy Consulting—a private political consultancy firm, one of the many working with the BJP—was handling the call centre project of connecting with labharthis from across the country. It was a gigantic, resource-rich exercise, typical of Team Modi–Shah's scaled-up election management style over the past decade. So much meticulous planning and energy has gone into creating this vast election-winning machine that governance, day-to-day administration and policy-making have inevitably been put on the backburner in the build-up to any election.

And yet, in 2024 something was missing. In 2019, the labharthi outreach was seen as key to the BJP's success, the party claiming that the over 200 million (20 crore-plus) beneficiaries of government schemes had given it a cutting edge among voters. Five years on, the labharthi machine was beginning to sputter. For example, call centres were encouraging labharthis to click selfies along the Viksit Yatra route and upload them on their Facebook or Instagram pages. Only this time the labharthi engagement was much less enthusiastic. 'I think the growing "technocratization" and outsourcing of event-based politics has run its course for the BJP in the past decade. Technology brought efficiency in systems, but the human connection lost out,' said Rajat Sethi, a political strategist who has worked with BJP campaigns. MLAs and MPs were accused of being inaccessible to workers, while complaints of mid-level party leaders taking a commission to speed up the delivery of benefits were now more frequent. Although new schemes were announced, like PM Vishwakarma Yojana, to provide support to traditional artisans and craftspeople (mainly from OBC communities), and Lakhpati Didi, to aid rural women through self-help groups, there were reports of uneven implementation on the ground. For example, mandatory registration on websites was proving to be cumbersome for many potential applicants. A senior BJP office-bearer admitted, 'Be it our karyakarta or a labharthi, everyone wants to feel wanted, not just on some impersonal mobile app but also through real-life interaction. Maybe we are paying the price for trying to scale up and become too big, too soon.' While the welfare scheme beneficiaries remained an asset for the party, their votes could no longer be taken for granted.

The much-hyped Viksit Bharat Sankalp Yatra itself was not without controversy. It was being promoted as both a government and a party event. On stage, bureaucrats were seen rubbing shoulders with local BJP members, and off stage, officers of joint secretary or deputy secretary rank were deputed as district 'rath prabharis' to showcase the government's achievements. The Opposition alleged that state funds were being used to promote a political yatra in the run-up to the general elections, with the clear intent to further the interests of the ruling party. When the yatra completed fifty days in January 2024, the Press Information Bureau issued a statement claiming that as many as 100 million (10 crore) people had already participated in the yatra. Promptly, party leaders and ministers put out identically worded effusive messages congratulating the Prime Minister. Separately, the Ministry of Defence (MOD) was tasked with setting up 822 'selfie points' in prominent places like railway stations and airports, where citizens could take pictures with a cut-out of Prime Minister Modi. Another MOD order directed soldiers on annual leave 'to spend time on promoting government schemes'. The politicization of the bureaucracy and even the military was disturbingly apparent. 'If this is not a brazen attempt to misuse state machinery and subvert service rules, what is?' asked Pawan Khera, the Congress's media head. BJP President J.P. Nadda shot back in a tweet, 'It baffles me to see the Congress party having an issue with public servants reaching the grassroots to ensure saturation of schemes. If this is not the basic tenet of governance, what is?' The fact is, back when Indira Gandhi engaged the services of her then assistant Yashpal Kapoor (still a government officer) for electioneering purposes during the 1971 polls, it was dubbed 'electoral malpractice' and she was dismissed as Prime Minister by the Allahabad High Court in its famous judgement of 12 June 1975. Modi's wholesale use of the government apparatus for election purposes makes Indira Gandhi's action look like a mere traffic violation in comparison.

However, the political slugfest could scarcely mask the impracticalities of what was the central plank of the BJP's 2024 re-election bid: a 'Viksit Bharat' by 2047, when the country would celebrate 100 years of independence. This would be preceded by an 'Amrit Kaal' (golden period)—a 'Modi ki guarantee', his personalized promise of transforming lives. Previously, Modi had sold the vision of a 'New India' by 2022; now, he was being even more ambitious and asking his supporters to dream even bigger and higher by setting 2047 as a target date. BlueKraft Digital Foundation, another Modi government-affiliated research and advocacy group, initiated a 'Viksit Bharat ambassadors' programme, aimed at attracting college students and young professionals to spread the Prime Minister's vision. Around fifty initiatives, from public meetings to marathon runs, were organized across the country in the run-up to the elections to drive community engagement. Celebrities like spiritual leader Sri Sri Ravi Shankar, badminton champion Saina Nehwal, and film actors Rajkummar Rao and Vikrant Massey were roped in to interact with audiences. 'We wanted young India to know what a "Viksit Bharat" means. Our endeavour went beyond just seeking their votes; we were asking the young to visualize a truly developed India,' said Hitesh Jain, a Mumbai-based BJP lawyer–politician who is a director at BlueKraft. But dream-spinning has its limits even if the dream merchant enjoys the trust of his people. The country had just gone through five tough years, especially during the Covid pandemic. The Viksit Bharat plank was colliding with the harsh realities on the ground of unemployment and inflation. 'We were talking of how India will look in 2047 when most voters want to know how their lives will change in the next six to twelve months,' admitted a BJP poll strategist. 'This is where we got the 2024 narrative badly wrong.'

In February 2024, at a closed-door meeting with a group of party MPs, the Prime Minister unveiled his Viksit Bharat vision. The Ram Mandir consecration ceremony had just taken place and was being hailed as a grand 'Hindu civilizational moment'. Amidst the excitement of the momentous occasion, the expectation was that Modi would pitch fulfilling the Ram Mandir promise as his trump card. But the Prime Minister adopted a different approach, counselling the MPs to focus their poll campaign on the government's achievements in lifting millions of

Indians out of poverty and on highlighting India's position as the fifth-largest economy in the world instead. 'Jo pichle saath saal mein nahi hua, humne dus saal mein karke dikhaya hai. Voter ko Viksit Bharat chahiye (What could not be done in sixty years, we have achieved in ten. The voter wants a developed India).' On the eve of elections, Modi's Ram Mandir-propelled Hindutva religiosity was gradually taking a backseat to his familiar nationalist-populist tactic as the Supreme Leader who alone could restore the power and glory of a 'Viksit Bharat'.

This was an interesting narrative switch. For weeks before the Ram Mandir inaugural ceremony, the entire Sangh Parivar had been galvanized to take the mandir issue to the masses. The VHP had led the way, urging people to visit temples and light a 'Shree Ram Jyoti' in their neighbourhoods. The Ram temple trust handed 'akshata' (sacred rice) to VHP volunteers to further distribute in 5 lakh villages. A mass 'teerthyatra' (pilgrimage) was planned to enable 5 million (50 lakh) people to visit Ayodhya between January and April. As the yajman, of the rituals at Ayodhya, the Prime Minister had been a focal point, visiting other temples across the country prior to the Ram Mandir's consecration. And yet, just days later, Modi wasn't asking his MPs to highlight the mandir construction but to emphasize his government's pro-poor welfare schemes and infrastructure projects: be it free ration for the poor, highways across the country or his latest ambitious initiative—Har Ghar Nal, which promised tap water to every rural household. 'There are only four castes in the country, poor, youth, farmers and women. They will remain our priority,' he told a labharthi audience via a video-conference. Typically, Modi had coined an acronym for this too: GYAN (knowledge), which stood for 'gareeb', 'yuva' (youth), 'annadata' and 'naari' (women). After the Mandir triumphalism, this marked a back-to-basics welfarism, one that aimed to touch a wider electorate, especially the poor. Simply put, Ram was important but not without rations in the kitchen. 'I think the Prime Minister instinctively realized the limits of mandir politics: it could secure the core voter but not the crucial incremental vote,' remarked a BJP poll strategist. The Hindutva project's cultural-ideological agenda, so electrifying thirty years ago, in the mid-1990s, was running out of steam now. You cannot shoot the same arrow twice. Hindutva needed to be balanced with the ground realities of how to woo voters with more tangible benefits.

Unsurprisingly, when the BJP released its 'sankalp patra' or manifesto in the run-up to the 2024 elections, 'Modi ki guarantee' was its dominant theme. The party was now totally subsumed under a one-man cult figure. The sixty-seven-page manifesto listed out specific 'guarantees', with the Prime Minister's photographs splashed all over. In all the party's outdoor hoardings, booked months in advance and placed at key vantage points across towns and cities, the 'Modi ki guarantee' slogan, with life-size images of the Prime Minister, was a constant. 'I think we printed twice as many Modi posters compared to 2019; the number runs into several lakhs,' a BJP publicity team member disclosed. The main idea was to carpet-bomb the skyline in a manner that would 'invisibilize' and demoralize the Opposition even before the election campaign took off. Modi's face was everywhere: from billboards to newspapers to airport kiosks to railway station banners. Only the guarantee changed across geographies depending on the demographics of the area. In upwardly mobile Bengaluru, 'world-class infrastructure' was the guarantee; in Jammu, it was the decision to abolish Article 370; in rural Bihar, it was the promise of drinking water and a pucca house. Modi was the BJP's pied piper, Prime Minister, 'pradhan sewak', feel-good guru and dream merchant—all rolled into one larger-than-life persona. In the party's successful 2019 campaign, hyper-nationalism had been the overarching message; in 2024, it was the range of welfare benefits and infrastructure projects being promised under the Viksit Bharat umbrella. 'Every survey we did showed that the Prime Minister was way above his rivals in popularity. Why would we not make him our mascot?' said a BJP leader. To amplify the noise around 'Modi ki guarantee' and 'Viksit Bharat', a war room was set up, supervised by Union Minister Ashwini Vaishnaw, a former IAS officer and IITian, described by one BJP leader as 'Modi ji's latest blue-eyed boy'. Armed with years of business and administrative experience, the grey-haired, soft-spoken but sharp-eyed Vaishnaw is the quintessential backroom figure, adept at financial and big-tech media management, two key elements of any election campaign.

Several other notable BJP election backroom figures were also urged by the Prime Minister to contest the Lok Sabha elections for the first time. Union Minister Piyush Goyal was given the relatively safe seat of Mumbai North, Bhupender Yadav contested from Alwar, while Dharmendra Pradhan was sent to Sambalpur. 'The idea was to get as many ministers as possible to prove their election credentials and create a buzz in those states at the same time,' explained a BJP strategist. Rajeev Chandrasekhar, an entrepreneur–politician who had joined the BJP only in 2018 after having been an independent Rajya Sabha MP from Karnataka for more than a decade, was inducted into the Modi government in 2021 during a cabinet reshuffle, an elevation that indicated increasing political heft. The tech-savvy Chandrasekhar was keen to get a ticket from Bengaluru, his home city and a BJP Lok Sabha fortress. The party's Karnataka unit was less enthused. They saw the anglicized Chandrasekhar as an 'outsider'. Instead, Chandrasekhar was pushed into a high-stakes battle in Thiruvananthapuram against the Congress's Shashi Tharoor. The BJP was determined to show it meant business in Kerala, a state where it had never won a Lok Sabha seat previously. Chandrasekhar's family roots were in Kerala, but he had never lived there. 'A first-time candidate taking on a three-time high-profile MP—we had nothing to lose,' insisted the BJP leader's aide. A combative, tough-talking Chandrasekhar plunged into the battle, matching Tharoor word for word. It was a 'war' of the English-speaking elites, Nehruvian poster boy versus a 'new' India businessman, pedigree against financial muscle. In a neck-and-neck fight, Tharoor squeaked home by just over 16,000 votes. 'It was a bloody tough contest; they threw everything at me,' he remarked. The voluble Chandrasekhar would be one of seventeen Modi ministers to lose. With another dozen ministers being denied a ticket, it meant that as many as 29 of the 72-member Council of Ministers either lost or were replaced, a clear sign of a change in the air.

The ministers were all banking on the unshaken belief that the Modi persona would overwhelm local issues and intimidate the Opposition. The 'char sau paar' slogan was an intrinsic part of this 'One nation, one leader' strategy. Kicking off his election campaign in the Adivasi-dominated pocket of Jhabua in Madhya Pradesh in early February, Modi had asked voters to ensure polling of an additional 370 votes in each booth compared to the previous elections for the BJP to win 370 seats and cross 400 with its allies. Leading from the front, Modi addressed as many as 206 rallies and roadshows during an arduous three-month-long campaign, criss-crossing the country with boundless energy, addicted as he is to fighting and winning elections. Said an awestruck ministerial colleague, 'As a campaigner, he is in a league of his own. I have seen him looking tired in the plane, but the moment he touches down and sees the crowd, he is totally recharged.'

Against a skilled campaigner with the entire arsenal of the BJP election machine behind him, could a bedraggled-looking Opposition stop the seemingly inevitable Modi march to another big victory?

=

Congress MP Ajay Maken is a bit of an all-rounder, performing a variety of roles in the grand old party. A three-time MP and MLA from Delhi, he was the youngest speaker of the Delhi assembly, head of the party's communications team and a Union minister in the Manmohan Singh government. But ahead of the 2024 elections, the sixty-year-old Maken faced the biggest challenge of his political career. As party treasurer, he was expected to ensure the Congress had sufficient funds to fight the general elections. By no means an easy task. After the Congress lost power in 2014, donations from industrial houses had begun drying up. Business groups that had supported the Congress in the past were reluctant to finance the party and risk the wrath of the Modi government. Significantly, the two biggest corporate barons, Gautam Adani and Mukesh Ambani, did not donate to the Congress at all. Rahul Gandhi's trenchant critique of 'crony capitalists' had only made things tougher for the party's finances.

Desperate to shore up its funds and create a much-needed buzz around the party, the Congress launched a first-of-its-kind crowd-funding exercise in December 2023. Maken and his team spearheaded an online Donate for Desh campaign, inviting people to contribute in multiples of Rs 138 to mark 138 years since the party's formation. Trying to cash in on Rahul Gandhi's popularity among Congress supporters, the Congress leader's trademark white T-shirts, signed by him, were promised as a gift to anyone donating Rs 670 or more. For a party that had traditionally relied on hefty funding from big business houses to now be selling T-shirts as merchandise in return for small donations was another sign of testing times. In the space of fifty days, the party earned around Rs 25 crore from the campaign. 'It's not so much the money we got—the crowd-funding was primarily a political exercise to motivate our workers and connect them with the party,' said Maken.

But the party's financial worries were about to intensify. In February, with the countdown to the 2024 general elections having begun, Maken sent an urgent message to journalists on the Congress beat: 'Major breaking news, press conference in an hour. Please cover live.' At the press conference, he dramatically announced that eleven Congress bank accounts had been frozen by the Income Tax department after a penalty was imposed for the late filing of its 2018–19 tax returns. Maken had spent much of the previous day on the phone with the party's chartered accountants, who were haggling with bank officials. 'They are saying that you can't touch the money unless we get a court order,' relayed one of the accountants. 'Don't leave the bank premises. We are trying our best to sort it out,' replied Maken. A month later, with no solution in sight, the Congress leadership escalated the issue. Sonia Gandhi made a rare appearance at the party headquarters, accompanied by Congress President Mallikarjun Kharge and Rahul Gandhi, accusing the BJP of 'crippling' the principal Opposition party. 'The Income Tax department forcibly took away Rs 135 crore from our accounts, but still we were not allowed to operate them. Not only that, but the Income Tax department also sent us fresh notices for the recovery of Rs 3,500 crore, including financial year

1993–94, *thirty-one* years after assessment. This was pure tax terrorism,' raged Maken.

The Congress-versus-Income-Tax-department tangle and its timing only exemplifies how the battle for 2024 wasn't anywhere close to being a level playing field. A majority of the Congress candidates received anywhere between Rs 2 crore and Rs 3 crore as election funding from the party, unlike the BJP, which had a generous double-digit multi-crore budget for its nominees (no one will share the exact election spend but at least one BJP MP admitted to getting more than Rs 10 crore from just the central party kitty). A newly elected Congress MP said he was reluctant to organize a big rally in his constituency because of the massive costs involved. 'In desperation, I asked a local private contractor who is a friend to pick up half the tab. When he backed out at the eleventh hour, I just decided to stick to a more basic door-to-door campaign, which actually worked far better,' he said, relieved.

The financial crunch was only the latest in a series of crises facing the Congress ahead of the general elections. Losing in the three Hindi heartland states in December 2023 had dealt a crushing blow to the party's morale, worsened further by Bihar Chief Minister Nitish Kumar's decision to break away from the Opposition INDIA alliance and join hands with the BJP in early 2024. Then, in a fit of pique, Mamata Banerjee announced that she would not partner with the Congress in Bengal, expressing doubts about the party's ability to cross even 40 seats nationally. Apparently, during a seat-sharing discussion between TMC and Congress leaders at the INDIA alliance meeting in December, Rahul Gandhi was reportedly lounging nonchalantly in his seat opposite Banerjee, conveying, according to an observer, an air of casual disrespect towards the senior three-time chief minister and the country's only woman chief minister. 'I can give you 2 seats; the rest we will fight,' Banerjee told him. Rahul wasn't impressed. 'Don't forget, we can damage you in Bengal,' he warned. The Congress leader's words stung the Bengal chief minister, and she reacted with a flash of her characteristic quick temper. 'You try and "damage", we will "manage",' she shot back and walked out. Banerjee's ire was also directed at Adhir Ranjan Chowdhury, the Congress's Lok Sabha leader and West Bengal chief, who routinely targeted her. 'If you want an alliance, remove Adhir first,' she reportedly told Kharge on the phone. The party president promised to resolve prickly issues but seat-sharing talks between the two sides remained deadlocked. The last straw was when Rahul Gandhi decided to make Bengal part of the route of his Bharat Jodo Nyay Yatra, his final mass contact programme ahead of the elections. 'What is the need for him to come to Bengal like this? He should have at least consulted us before taking any decision. We are the main party here,' Banerjee complained to an aide. A section of the Congress was convinced that Banerjee had struck a backdoor 'deal' with the BJP to dent the INDIA alliance further and was looking for an excuse to opt out. 'How do you expect any alliance when there is such a huge trust deficit on both sides?' asked a TMC leader.

The TMC would eventually fight the Bengal elections on its own while the Congress partnered the left, a decision that would cost the INDIA alliance an additional four to five seats in the final analysis.

Amidst confusing signals, the Congress appeared unsure of the way forward: whether to strengthen the INDIA alliance or fortify its own ranks first. The party's decision to stay away from the Ram temple pran pratishtha ceremony in January had exposed ideological fault lines within. During a closed-door meeting, several Congress leaders had been in favour of attending, fearing that a 'boycott' would be seen as 'anti-Hindu'. Amongst those in support of attending the Ram Mandir ceremony was Congress MP Rajeev Shukla, the journalist-turned-politician with a reputation for cultivating friends across parties. 'Our fight is against the BJP and not Ram,' remarked Shukla.

The Congress's ambivalence on religious identity politics was all too familiar. At a Raipur plenary session in 2023 to finalize an election roadmap, the party's posters and advertisements had included images of many well-known freedom fighters, but Maulana Azad's was strikingly excluded. The local Chhattisgarh Congress leadership apparently saw Azad as a 'Muslim leader' and wanted to 'play it safe'. 'We had to intervene at the last minute to ensure that a portrait of Azad was prominently displayed on the stage backdrop,' disclosed a Congress leader. Some sections of the party were infected by the BJP's narrative-setting on uber-Hindutva and unsure about how to challenge it, if at all. However, neither Kharge nor Rahul Gandhi had any such doubts. While viewpoints differed, the party president, backed by Rahul Gandhi, was firm in his belief that the Ram Mandir ceremony was primarily a political platform for the Sangh Parivar ahead of the elections. 'Prime Minister Modi wants to mix religion with politics; why should we attend and endorse it in any manner?' asserted Kharge, who was deeply influenced in his formative years by Ambedkar's teachings. It wasn't an easy call to make but one which suggested that the Congress was finally willing to take a stand and distance itself from Hindutva politics. For Rahul Gandhi, in particular, the decision was seen as a moment of truth. In the 2017 Gujarat elections, Rahul had embarked on a temple-hopping campaign, his party emphasizing his 'janeu-dhari' (Brahminical) Hindu credentials. At the time it had seemed like a desperate attempt to compete with the BJP for Hindu votes, one that yielded limited benefit. Now, the party leadership was keen to make a distinction between Hinduism and Hindutva, even if it meant taking a gamble and 'boycotting' the Ram Mandir ceremony. Hinduism was the true spiritual calling that the party deeply respected; Hindutva was only the BJP's weapon to seek political rewards. 'The decision to stay away from the Ram Mandir inauguration was a defining moment for us. We now had clarity on the secularism versus soft Hindutva debate, unlike in the past,' said Gurdeep Singh Sappal, a working committee member and key functionary in Kharge's office.

Not everyone was in agreement with the party chief's assessment, though. Among the first to jump ship was Milind Deora, considered close to the Gandhi family. Deora, who had just been appointed the party's joint treasurer, had been restless for a while, having been passed over twice for a Rajya Sabha nomination from Maharashtra. More comfortable in the company of corporate leaders like Mukesh Ambani, the US-educated Deora was unable to handle Rahul Gandhi's anti-big-business political vocabulary. He used the Ram Mandir decision as an excuse to switch to the ruling Shiv Sena under Eknath Shinde, which had promised him a Rajya Sabha seat. 'It really wasn't about any post. I just felt that the Congress had lost its connection with the people. Be it the Ram Mandir or the economy, the Congress was on the wrong side of history,' he claimed. The timing of Deora's resignation was significant. It came on the day Rahul Gandhi was about to launch his Bharat Jodo Nyay Yatra from Imphal. In fact, all the senior Congress leaders were flying into Imphal on a cold, foggy January morning by private charter from Delhi. Deora's name was on the passenger list. Waiting for the flight to take off, the Congress leaders switched on the TV in the VIP lounge to catch the latest news. Imagine their surprise when the headlines weren't about the yatra but Deora's resignation! A few weeks later, another Congress leader from Maharashtra, former chief minister Ashok Chavan, joined the defectors' queue. 'I was just unhappy with the direction the party was going in. I tried to explain my viewpoint to the party leadership, but no one was ready to listen. The BJP was very welcoming, so I thought, why not try it out,' he said. Curiously, just days before resigning, Chavan had been actively involved in seat-sharing talks with the party's allies in Maharashtra. 'He never gave us an inkling that he was set to leave; it was all very sudden,' said a Maharashtra Congress leader. A well-networked, skilful organizer, Chavan was instantly rewarded with a Rajya Sabha seat by the BJP. Ironically, the BJP had gunned for Chavan in 2010 for his alleged role in the Adarsh Co-operative Housing Society scam, forcing him to quit as chief minister, but now the Adarsh case was pushed to the backburner as the party wanted a grip over Chavan's home district of Nanded. The 'washing machine' was at work again.

These high-profile exits only added to the palpable sense of doom and gloom within the Congress ranks. An internal party assessment based on feedback from state units suggested that the party might struggle to cross its 2019 tally of 52 seats. At a working committee meeting in February, a senior Congress MP expressed concern that the Congress might end up with 'just twenty-five or twenty-seven seats'. Even Sunil Kanugolu, the party's ace election strategist who had played an important role in the Karnataka and Telangana victories, was cautious in his assessment. While his team was involved in constituency-wise surveys and poll management, he opted out of planning the entire Lok Sabha exercise, maintaining that 'too little time' was left to execute a national strategy. When Kharge urged senior leaders to contest the Lok Sabha elections, many of them politely refused. One former chief minister bluntly told the Congress president that contesting the elections in a one-sided atmosphere 'was a waste of time and money'.

One Congress leader, though, was undeterred. Amidst the pessimistic outlook, Rahul Gandhi decided to go ahead with his Manipur to Mumbai Bharat Jodo Nyay Yatra in January 2024. The decision to embark on a yatra so close to the general elections was another contentious call. A few Congress leaders wanted Gandhi to focus instead on planning the party's election strategy, including the tricky issue of ticket distribution. 'How can Rahul ji be away when crucial decisions have to be taken?' they contended. But Gandhi was adamant, insistent on marching once again to his own beat, now more confident in his own ideas after the relative success of the Bharat Jodo Yatra. 'A yatra is the only way to connect with the masses, and a mass-connect programme is the only way for us to revive the party,' he maintained. This was a new Rahul Gandhi, on his feet, constantly engaging with common people, perhaps sublimating his own childhood anger and hurt as a victim of violence into a larger cause of justice for the weakest and most helpless. When the party began its screening committee meetings in March to decide on candidate selection, Gandhi was on the road, and it was left to Congress President Kharge to take the final call. 'Except for a few seats, like insisting on a ticket from Delhi for Kanhaiya Kumar [the former student leader], Rahul mostly stayed away from the messy process of candidate selection. On one occasion, we literally had to force him to join us via video-conference,' claimed a senior Congress leader.

Where the previous Bharat Jodo Yatra had been an ambitious walkathon from Kanyakumari to Kashmir, the Nyay Yatra was a modified version because of time constraints. Dressed in his now easily identifiable white T-shirt, Gandhi and party leaders walked every day but also travelled by bus to cover longer distances. The choice of Imphal as a starting point for the yatra was also noteworthy. Manipur had been caught in a terrifying cycle of ethnic violence since May 2023. While Prime Minister Modi hadn't visited the state even once, Gandhi had made it a point to visit the relief camps where thousands of people driven out of their homes were living in misery and hardship. By kicking off this Nyay Yatra from Manipur, Rahul was once again putting the state in the national consciousness, his way of showing empathy for its displaced people. Empathy for the weak, poor and dispossessed was becoming Rahul Gandhi's badge of identity.

Repurposing 'Nyay', or justice, as an electoral calling card was a risky option. For sceptics, including some within the Congress, the concept was seen as too abstract. In the 2019 Lok Sabha elections, the Congress had used the term as a core political slogan, but it found no resonance. The party even developed the idea into a manifesto promise of a basic income-support scheme for India's poorest, roping in Nobel laureate and economist Abhijit Banerjee to give it shape, but the post-Pulwama-Balakot strident nationalism meant that 'Nyay' never registered among voters. Now, the Congress dusted off 'Nyay' again—but with one important difference: it was linking the concept to specific 'guarantees' for key voter blocs, including a) women who were promised Rs 1 lakh a year; b) a right to apprenticeship for youth who would be given a 'guaranteed' placement with a stipend of Rs 1 lakh for a year; c) a promise of a loan waiver for farmers; d) a Rs 400 'guarantee' for labour under the National Rural Employment (MNREGA) programme; and e) a caste census aimed at providing social and economic justice to OBCs, Dalits and Adivasis in particular. Critics wondered how a Congress government would fund its populist promises, but the manifesto committee members insisted they had done the math. 'The Congress manifesto was drafted after taking into account the financial implications of each promise. The promises were to be rolled out and fulfilled over a five-year period, so we were confident of achieving targets,' claimed P. Chidambaram, chairperson of the manifesto committee.

Of these promises, the most controversial was the caste census, seen by many as a divisive and potentially counterproductive idea. In 2009, Congress leader and then Union Minister Veerappa Moily had pushed for a caste count in the 2011 Census. But the caste-wise data was never released, after many Congress leaders opposed it. Now, Rahul Gandhi had not only revived it but made it a principal talking point of the Nyay Yatra. It was a noticeable shift in direction, initiated at the Congress Chintan Shivir in Udaipur in May 2022, where Rahul spoke passionately of the need to 'transform' the Congress party and break the rich–poor divide. Less than a year later, in February 2023, at its Raipur meet, the Congress made a landmark organizational change, amending its Constitution to provide 50 per cent reservation to Dalits, Adivasis, OBCs, minorities and women in the working committee and all key party positions. OBCs, in particular, made up a sizeable caste group that had gravitated towards the BJP in the Modi era. To challenge OBC-led Hindutva politics, the Congress needed to build a new caste coalition centred on greater representation for non-upper-caste groups. Interestingly, the idea had been seeded by a group of left-leaning academics, including French political scientist and South Asia specialist Christophe Jaffrelot. When Rahul Gandhi visited Paris in September 2023, he had a long meeting with Prof. Jaffrelot. 'I have been writing for a while that the best way to combat Hindutva is to build a counter-narrative around caste, but I don't think it's accurate to say that I prompted Rahul's thoughts. He was already on that path,' said Jaffrelot. Congress leaders maintained that Rahul's caste census formulation was his own agenda. 'Make no mistake, this change was driven by Rahul ji out of conviction, not convenience,' insisted Gurdeep Singh.

For years, the BJP had mocked Rahul Gandhi, calling him 'Pappu', a nickname intended to dismiss him as a non-serious politician. If the Bharat Jodo Yatra had forced a rethink in people's perception of Rahul Gandhi, the Nyay Yatra was being seen as a complete reinvention. Positioning himself as an on-the-ground warrior for social justice and economic equality, Rahul was entering unfamiliar terrain for a traditional mainstream party like the Congress. OBC reservations, particularly, have been the trademark of the Mandalite parties of north India, whose rise in the 1990s coincided with the decline of the Congress. Now Rahul was endorsing reservations as a crucial step towards wealth redistribution: 'Jitni abaadi utna hak' (Rights proportionate to population) was his belligerent slogan, one that even some Congress leaders were worried might backfire. 'The Congress has always been a very conservative party when it comes to caste, so naturally there will be some resistance. But Rahul Gandhi was very clear from the beginning: The Congress must become a force of social engineering and change,' said Pushparaj Deshpande, director of the Samruddha Bharat Foundation. Founded as a trust to promote constitutional values, the foundation was working closely with the Congress and Rahul Gandhi, and organized at least three town-hall meetings during the 2024 election campaign, where the Congress leader interacted with Dalit, Adivasi and OBC community influencers. The BJP's social media influencers ran a noisy campaign to discredit the foundation, claiming it was being funded by 'anti-India' forces like billionaire businessman George Soros. 'All our funding is local and we have nothing to do with any foreign business entity,' insisted Deshpande.

The image of being a political 'revolutionary' transformed Rahul Gandhi's communication style too. He now became much more direct and spontaneous. Informal, unfussy, now on a motorbike, now in a dhaba, he was ever ready to mingle with the people, revealing a politician far more at ease in his common public interactions than in formal settings delivering set speeches. For example, Rahul made a sudden decision to meet vegetable vendors and loaders at 5 a.m. at Delhi's Azadpur market after a video on Lallantop, a Hindi news portal, showed a vendor breaking down because he didn't have money to buy tomatoes. When Rahul arrived at the mandi, people gathered around him instantly. 'Hum khush hain ki aap aa gaye; koi hamein yaad nahi karta (We are happy you have come; no one remembers us),' remarked a loader, a Dalit from Bihar, clasping the Congress leader's hand. The contrast with visuals of Modi, an expensively dressed Caesar, and his security posse arriving at neatly choreographed events and his one-way, top-down, imperious manner of engagement could not have been more striking.

During the Nyay Yatra, clambering atop a jeep, Rahul would suddenly pick up the mic, call out to someone in the crowd, hop over to their side, place an arm around their shoulders and strike an impromptu conversation, often on caste politics. If the Bharat Jodo Yatra revolved around the softer 'Mohabbat ki dukan' theme of harmony, the Nyay Yatra's caste references were provocative, at times overly confrontational. On one occasion in Raebareli, Rahul triggered a needless controversy when he asked a journalist to reveal the caste of the owner of the TV channel he worked for. 'Kya woh OBC hain? Nahin. Kya woh Dalit hain? Nahin (Is he OBC? No. Is he Dalit? No),' he asked. Even before the reporter could reply, Congress workers in the audience roughed him up. It was an unsettling episode, one that highlighted the dangers of disruptive and, at times, divisive political messaging. 'What happened at Raebareli was unfortunate, but please don't ever forget what Rahul ji has had to endure from a hostile media for so long,' said a Congress leader.

For Team Rahul and the Congress, the Nyay Yatra, despite initial misgivings over its timing, was having the desired impact. A template was set. If in 2014 and 2019 the BJP had successfully pigeonholed Rahul as an entitled 'naamdar' (dynast), the elite power 'insider' going up against Modi, the quintessential 'son-of-a-chaiwallah' 'outsider', he was now recast as a new-age dishevelled radical, an angry rebel fighting for the have-nots by challenging the status quo. Take, for instance, Rahul Gandhi advocating for young military recruits during the Nyay Yatra. The Agnipath scheme had been initiated by the Modi government in June 2022 to recruit soldiers for a four-year-long short-term service. These soldiers would be known as 'Agniveers' (fire warriors). The scheme could not have been more ill-timed. For two and a half years before that, planned military recruitment had remained suspended because of the Covid pandemic. Now, the Agnipath scheme added to the uncertain climate. 'For many youth, this came as a total shock. Many had cleared their exams and were waiting to be recruited by the armed forces and now suddenly found themselves over-age, helpless, with nowhere to go because in one stroke the entire pending recruitment process was cancelled,' said Major General Yash Mor. Typical of major decisions taken by the Modi government, even the armed forces leadership was kept in the dark about this one. A hasty announcement made stealthily and without adequate consultation or preparation was bound to recoil. There were violent protests among the youth in several parts of north India, who feared that their hopes of a permanent career as army jawans had been dashed. In states like Haryana and Rajasthan, where, traditionally, young men join the armed forces in large numbers, driven in part by the high rate of unemployment, Agnipath was a potent issue. 'Joining the army is part of our social ethos. Every year, more than five thousand youth from Haryana join the forces. How can you suddenly disrupt their lives!' argued Congress MP Deepender Hooda. Interestingly, Hooda's team co-ordinated with army exam coaching centres across Haryana to highlight the issue, a sign that the Congress was now far nimbler in its responses.

Rahul Gandhi, who met with some of the protestors on his travels, agreed to take up their cause. Team Rahul prepared lists of youth across the country who had lost out because of the new recruitment process and created numerous WhatsApp groups to connect with them on a regular basis. Some of the youth protestors were invited to an interaction with Rahul at 10, Janpath. When one of them broke down in tears, Rahul assured him that he would force the Modi government to scrap the scheme. The Congress leader's sustained campaign had an impact, with the defence ministry undertaking a post-election review of the Agniveer programme and recommending suitable changes. If Modi had positioned himself as a staunch nationalist, Rahul was identifying himself as an anti-establishment people's crusader. 'Modi ji only spoke about deshbhakti; Rahul ji was walking the talk,' said a member of the team.

With Rahul taking the lead, 'Nyay' became part of the political lexicon even before the actual election campaign took off, a counter to the BJP's

'Modi ki guarantee' and 'Viksit Bharat' pitch. 'In 2019, Mr Modi and the BJP set the agenda; now we had the narrative clarity that enabled us to compete for mindspace,' claimed media head Pawan Khera. A key element here was the Congress's decision-making process, which, unlike in 2019, was far more focused and better co-ordinated. While communications chief Jairam Ramesh was the visible face, with his hard-hitting tweets and snappy sound bites, the publicity engine was driven by a strong collective comprising Ajay Maken, Gurdeep Singh Sappal, Pawan Khera and Supriya Shrinate, the social media chairperson. 'We were unafraid this time, so we didn't hesitate to punch back when attacked,' said the tough-talking Shrinate, whose aggressive demeanour on TV debates characterized the 'new' Congress approach.

In 2019, the Congress's social media campaign had revolved around the 'Chowkidar chor hai' slogan, an abusive attack on Modi that backfired spectacularly. A section of the Opposition erred in raising the issue of Modi's marital status, a private matter, which didn't go down well with voters. When Supriya Shrinate took over the social media department in 2022, her brief was clear: be forceful but keep the campaign political, not personal. One of the first things she did was hire young animators. The idea of caricaturing the Prime Minister in Instagram reels and memes was a risky one but added an edginess to the Congress communication campaign. The animated video showing Modi as an inflated balloon—a reference to the Prime Minister's 'jhoot ka gubbara' (balloon of lies), as Rahul Gandhi called it—that was pricked by a child went instantly viral and gathered millions of views. 'We quickly realized that the one thing Modi didn't like was his ego being punctured, so that's exactly what we set out to do,' said Shrinate.

The aim was to stay away from personal jibes that would allow the Prime Minister to play the victim card, but be unsparing in targeting him politically. When Modi spoke of 'parivarwaad', the Congress posted a list of all the dynasts who were now members of the BJP. On corruption too, the Congress was no longer defensive. Old tweets and sound bites of the BJP on newfound allies like Ajit Pawar were circulated along with the image of a washing machine. When a BJP ad campaign banged on about how an INDIA alliance government would mean a new Prime Minister every year, the Congress responded promptly: 'Chalo, maan liya sarkar to hamari hi banegi (At least they are accepting the government will be ours).' Video bites of common people complaining of price rise and unemployment were spread on social media through a network of volunteers. 'I think we had a freshness to our videos that appealed to the young, while the BJP was stuck in the past, still viciously attacking Rahul Gandhi as a "pappu" and "shehzada". Both Rahul and India had moved on, the BJP hadn't,' remarked Shrinate. The data supported her claim. The average likes for the Congress's Instagram videos at the peak campaign period were 122,000, while the BJP's were much lower, at 26,945. On YouTube too, between March and May 2024, the Congress garnered 613 million views, and the BJP around 150 million. It was a dramatic transformation for a party that until now had lagged well behind the BJP in the social media communication game.

But old habits die hard. Not everything went to plan. Initially, the advertising campaign was relatively low-key, the party not spending any of the allotted funds on outdoor publicity in the first three election phases. 'There were still people in the system who did not believe we could put up a fight, so they were reluctant to spend money. In hindsight, it may have cost us fifteen or twenty seats,' admitted a Congress office-bearer. By the last stretch, though, the notoriously fractious party was actually battle-ready. 'In 2019, there were many gaps in our system, expenses that were not accounted for. This time we made sure that the entire campaign was streamlined with proper auditing and no leakages,' said Maken.

Equally significant, but perhaps less acknowledged, is the role played by the party war room led by Sasikanth Senthil, a former Karnataka cadre IAS officer who joined the Congress in 2021 after quitting the bureaucracy over his opposition to the revocation of Article 370 and the passage of the CAA. 'The fundamental building blocks of a diverse democracy are being destroyed,' he argued. An energetic organization man, idealistic and fiercely anti-BJP, Senthil played a key role in mass outreach. A man of few words, he didn't carry any of the trappings of power, preferring to walk around Delhi's streets in sturdy sandals. A team of over 700 persons across thirty-eight state-level war rooms headquartered in the Lutyens' Delhi bungalow of the Telangana Congress's Uttam Kumar Reddy was tasked with co-ordinating the ground campaign. A key aspect of the drive was sending out as many as 8 crore cards outlining the Congress's 'Nyay' promises in twelve languages. Each card, printed in an A4 format, was delivered to candidates and taken to the doorstep of voters at least ten days before every phase of the election. The Congress didn't have the booth-level management to match the BJP, but it was attempting last-mile connectivity for once. 'If the BJP machine is focused on tech-driven solutions, we kept our focus on the human element, constantly interacting with our workers to give them a sense of involvement. We were a connect centre, not a war room,' said the forty-five-year-old Senthil, now an MP from Tamil Nadu.

Senthil represents the new generation of Congress leaders gathered around Rahul Gandhi. They are not privileged dynasts, but committed political activists keen to identify with public-spirited campaigns. Other war room members like Vaibhav Walia and Varun Santhosh, in their kurta-jeans-jhola look, are also part of this generational shift—polar opposites of the spiffily attired family legacy 'baba log' politicians whom Rahul Gandhi once hung around with. Senior leaders in the party were wary of them, concerned that they were driving the party towards taking radical left positions on critical issues. 'The "new" Congress is being hijacked by those with an NGO mindset who can't see beyond their own narrow ideology,' said an ex-Congressman who left the party ahead of the 2024 elections. Senthil laughs off the criticism. 'I actually think the BJP is a command-and-control party; it is the Congress that is a genuine mass organization of which I am a small part,' he declared.

A rebooted Congress led by a reinvigorated leader on a mission versus a tried-and-tested BJP election machine led by a charismatic political strongman: the stage was set for the battle of 2024.

=

India is probably the only country where the electoral process has been elongated rather than curtailed over time. On 16 March 2024, the ECI announced a forty-four-day seven-phase voting period, the second longest since the first parliamentary elections were held in the country in 1951–52, lasting four months. Nearly 970 million (97 crore) registered voters spread across 10.5 lakh polling stations in 543 constituencies would decide the fate of more than 8,000 candidates in the fray. An Indian general election is a mammoth exercise, but did it really need such a stretched-out schedule, especially in peak summer, when the heat would affect voter turnout? Surprisingly, even Maharashtra, a state with no history of political violence, was set to have a five-phase election. The Opposition was certain the poll timetable was designed to give the BJP the advantage, allowing Prime Minister Modi to campaign across the country while exhausting some of his cash-starved rivals. 'You want us to start campaigning in March for an election that will end in June. The Prime Minister will travel everywhere in his official aircraft and we will have to make do with limited resources. How is it free and fair?' asked Sanjay Raut of the Shiv Sena.

'Not a level playing field' was an argument the ECI brushed aside, preferring to hide behind a bureaucratic wall. After its initial press conference to unveil the election calendar, the ECI resolutely stayed away from further media interactions. Just days before the poll schedule was announced, the Centre appointed two of the three election commissioners under an amended law by which the Supreme Court Chief Justice was removed from the selection committee and replaced by a Union cabinet minister. The Opposition had repeatedly written to the ECI seeking time to raise its demand for 100 per cent counting of the VVPAT, but the poll body refused to meet them. 'We are not against electronic voting machines, but we want a complete VVPAT count for a free and fair election. Why is the EC not even willing to meet us?' demanded Congress leader Jairam Ramesh. One Opposition leader branded the ECI as a 'chai-biscuit' body. 'Every time we meet them, they politely offer us chai and biscuits and then do nothing to address our concerns,' they said.

Paradoxically, the long-drawn-out election schedule would eventually work in the Opposition's favour, giving them more time to get their act together. The sense of urgency in the Opposition ranks intensified when, just five days after the elections were announced, in an unprecedented move in a parliamentary democracy, Delhi Chief Minister Arvind Kejriwal was arrested by the ED on money-laundering charges in the Delhi liquor policy case. The ED had been gunning for Kejriwal for months, sending him several summonses to appear before the agency for questioning, so when he was arrested, it wasn't entirely a surprise. Kejriwal, in fact, had been preparing for it while steadfastly maintaining that there was no money trail to implicate him in an investigation that began eighteen months earlier. 'They just want to prevent me from campaigning in the 2024 elections. My team members have been told by the BJP that if I break with the INDIA alliance, I will be saved, else I will be jailed,' he claimed.

Arresting a high-profile Opposition leader within a week of the elections being announced was a calculated risk that the Modi government was willing to take. To arrest a sitting chief minister days before an election campaign smacked of shameful political calculation and once again revealed a manic and vindictive drive to crush the Opposition with state power. At the heart of it was Prime Minister Modi's personal grudge against the AAP leader. From the moment Kejriwal tangled with Modi and contested against him in the 2014 Varanasi Lok Sabha election, he had become a marked man. 'Modi ji can engage with other Opposition leaders, but when it comes to Kejriwal, he sees red,' admitted a Delhi BJP leader. A TV news channel editor recalled being rung up by a government official when a Kejriwal interview was telecast during prime time. 'You seem to be promoting a zero MP party like AAP all the time. Be careful,' the official warned.

For the INDIA alliance leaders, Kejriwal's arrest was an ominous sign. Clearly, the sounding of the election bugle didn't imply that enforcement agencies would dial down the pressure. In January, Jharkhand Chief Minister Hemant Soren, another INDIA alliance partner, had also been arrested by the ED in an alleged land scam case. The fractious allies now had no option but to band together. When AAP decided to hold a 'Save

Democracy' rally in the capital, a majority of the INDIA alliance partners arrived in a big show of strength. Until then, there was still uncertainty whether the Congress would actually tie up with AAP in Delhi, given past animosities on the ground. 'I guess it required an arrest for the Congress to wake up to the reality that this time we had to swim or sink together,' remarked an AAP leader.

Another trigger was the Chandigarh mayoral election in January 2024, where a combined AAP–Congress candidate was defeated by the BJP nominee after the presiding officer, Anil Masih, a BJP minority cell member, declared eight votes invalid. The backstory here is revealing. While the AAP–Congress combine had a majority of the councillors with them, the BJP didn't want to give up without a fight. National General Secretary Vinod Tawde was deputed to Chandigarh to oversee the election. The hyperactive Tawde managed to convince two AAP councillors to switch, but the BJP still needed a few more people to defect. 'Don't worry, I will do the needful,' an eager Masih reportedly told the BJP leader. The original plan was to declare two votes invalid, but the overenthusiastic Masih declared eight invalid. The illegal act of the presiding officer invalidating ballots was caught on camera. The Supreme Court had to step in to overturn the verdict. 'Imagine, if a Chandigarh mayoral poll can be rigged, what will happen in a national election?' remarked AAP MP Sanjay Singh.

Interestingly, a Chandigarh-like scenario was almost replicated in the Surat Lok Sabha seat. The Congress candidate's nomination was rejected by the returning officer after his three proposers submitted identical affidavits claiming they had not signed the document and that their signatures had been forged. When the Gujarat Congress wanted to cross-examine the proposers, they were told that the men were 'missing', as was their candidate. By the time they surfaced, it was too late. All other candidates also withdrew from the contest and the BJP nominee was declared unopposed, a rare occurrence in a Lok Sabha poll. 'The men who claimed their signatures were forged were moving around under police protection, but we were given no access to them,' complained Gujarat

Congress chief Shaktisinh Gohil. In BJP-dominated Gujarat, no one could challenge the state machinery: unsurprisingly, the BJP would win 25 of the 26 seats in the state.

The 'Save Democracy' rally at the Ramlila Maidan in late March thus became a platform for the Opposition to find common ground. At the meeting, every speaker raised their voice against what was described as the Modi-led BJP's 'dictatorship'. The 'Democracy versus dictatorship' battle cry would serve as a template for the INDIA alliance campaign, an attempt to revive what one Opposition leader called 'a 1977 moment'. Though Modi is no Emergency-tainted Indira Gandhi, his populist demagoguery still commanded support. 'Things will change now; this election will be people versus Modi,' insisted D. Raja, the veteran Communist leader. 'Wait and see, Modi ki guarantee equals zero warranty,' chided Derek O'Brien of the TMC.

In the first week of April, ten days before the first phase of polling, Jyoti Mirdha, the BJP candidate from Rajasthan's Nagaur (and formerly with the Congress), called for voters to help realize the BJP's 'char sau paar' target. 'Several tough decisions need to be taken in the country's interest, and for that we have to make constitutional amendments,' she proclaimed. Nor was she the first BJP leader to say so. In early March, Anantkumar Hegde, a BJP MP from Karnataka, had voiced a similar sentiment. Hegde was a loudmouth, known to court controversy, and was denied a party ticket after his frequent ill-tempered remarks. But Mirdha was a contestant whose comments instantly went viral. Another BJP leader, Lallu Singh, the sitting MP from Faizabad–Ayodhya, joined the chorus. 'A government can be formed with 272 MPs, but to amend the Constitution, we need a two-thirds majority,' he was seen saying in another viral video. The Congress latched onto the remarks. 'It is clear from these statements that BJP and PM Modi hate the Constitution and democracy. By abolishing the Constitution given by Babasaheb, BJP wants to snatch away the rights of the people,' the party tweeted from its official handle.

Just twenty-four hours later, at a rally in Chittorgarh in Rajasthan, Congress President Kharge raised the 'Samvidhan' issue. 'The

Constitution is in danger; even "aarakshan" (reservations) are not safe under this government. That is why they want "char sau paar",' warned Kharge. Accompanying him at the rally was Rajasthan Congress chief Govind Singh Dotasra, who claimed that the speech was a turning point in the campaign. 'Suddenly, everyone was talking about Samvidhan and not about Modi ki guarantee,' he asserted. Kharge was not just Congress president but also a Dalit. The symbolism of his raking up 'reservations under threat' was not lost in the din. The BJP responded angrily, its party spokespersons accusing the Congress of deliberately spreading falsehoods. 'I want to make it clear that till the BJP is in politics, we will not let anything happen to reservations. We will not let the Congress end it either,' stressed Home Minister Shah at a rally in Chhattisgarh.

The home minister was right. No political party could afford to end reservations in a charged political environment. The Opposition was stoking an imaginary fear. But in the clamour of an election campaign, emotional narratives can gather momentum of their own. Which is exactly what happened with the 'Samvidhan khatre mein hai' slogan. While the Prime Minister green-lit the 'char sau paar' slogan in January 2024 as he looked to break new records, what Team Modi–Shah failed to do was explain exactly what a 400-plus parliamentary majority for the BJP would mean for the voter and the country. 'The mistake we made is that we said "char sau paar" but beyond the magical number we didn't really offer any clear promise to the voter,' admitted a BJP leader. 'Maybe we should have said, "Abki baar char sau paar toh PoK pe vaar" or something like that!' After ten years in power the BJP was struggling to find a compelling narrative and slowly creating a marked disconnect between the political leadership and the voter.

An open-ended 'char sau paar' slogan provided the Opposition the ammunition they were desperately looking for. Almost out of nowhere, a talking point had been found, one that would reach a crescendo when the election entered its final stretch with Rahul Gandhi flashing a copy of the Constitution at all his rallies. The leather-bound pocket edition of the Constitution, measuring roughly 20 centimetres in length and 9 centimetres in breadth, became a persuasive election weapon. Having aggressively pushed for a caste census and more reservations, the 'Samvidhan khatre mein hai' refrain was seen as the logical next step in the party's messaging. 'Rahul was presented a pocket Constitution copy by Jairam Ramesh and he thought holding it up at rallies was a good way to connect his wider social justice plank with people,' said a Congress office-bearer.

While the Congress and the Opposition drew political mileage from the 'Samvidhan' debate, especially in the Hindi heartland, the real drivers of the campaign were under-the-radar NGO activists, YouTube journalists and influencers from Dalit groups. Away from the cacophony of traditional mainstream media, a silent revolution was underway in alternative fora, especially on widely watched digital and social media platforms. Thirty-five-year-old Sumit Chauhan, a well-spoken young man who can be seen on YouTube wearing T-shirts with images of Ambedkar, likes to describe himself as an anti-caste Dalit 'community journalist'. With his punchy videos, he has built a subscriber base of over 1 million followers on YouTube and more than double that number across platforms for his Hindi language portal, The News Beak. After working at mainstream news channels, or what he dismissively calls 'Manu-stream media', for seven years, he broke away in 2019 to create a unique space for himself as a content creator of stories that affected marginalized communities, especially Dalits. 'We have been raising concerns about atrocities against Dalits for years. For us, the BJP represents Hindu Rashtra and caste supremacy, which we are resisting,' he said. The threat of a domineering BJP government changing the Constitution was already being discussed on several Dalit-led YouTube channels when the election controversy broke. 'The anti-Hindutva sentiment was already there on the ground; the Opposition parties just cashed in on it,' claimed Chauhan.

It is difficult to estimate the precise impact of the 'Samvidhan khatre mein hai' campaign, but the final results suggest that the Opposition had a distinct edge in the first phase of polling. In Rajasthan, where the issue was triggered, the Congress won an astonishing 8 out of the 12 seats that went to the polls in the first round. In Uttar Pradesh's round one, the results were just as surprising: 6 of the 8 seats in the western part of the state, where there are large Dalit and Muslim neighbourhoods, were won by the Samajwadi Party–Congress alliance. In Maharashtra too, the Opposition would win 4 of the 5 seats that initially went to the polls in the Vidarbha region. The INDIA alliance, in fact, won 64 of the 102 seats that polled in the first phase, and the BJP just 35. Something entirely unforeseen was happening on the election battlefield. An Opposition written off by most pollsters and analysts was clawing its way back into the race, even edging ahead in crucial states. The saffron party urgently needed a counter, a change in style and strategy. 'Modi ki guarantee' wasn't working. It was time to go back to the basics.

Banswara, a tribal-dominated Rajasthan district bordering Gujarat and Maharashtra, is famous for its ancient bamboo forests and traditional handicrafts. Its tryst with national headlines came just once in the 1960s, when the stylish batsman Hanumant Singh, from the royal family of Banswara, scored a century in his test debut. But on 21 April 2024, the small town sprang onto front pages again. Addressing a rally in the district, Narendra Modi claimed that if the Congress came to power, it would seize and redistribute wealth to Muslims, labelling them 'infiltrators' and 'those who have more children'. 'When they [the Congress] were in power, they said Muslims had the first right to the properties of the state. This means that they would collect the properties and give them to the ones who have more kids. They will give it to the ghuspaithi. Do you want to give away your hard-earned money to intruders? This is what the Congress manifesto says: the amount of gold owned by our mothers and daughters will be measured, collected and distributed. They will disseminate your wealth among those people. These urban Naxals will not even spare your mothers and sisters their mangalsutras. They will go that far …'

The Prime Minister of India had just delivered a textbook example of horrendous, toxic hate speech, laced with communal dog-whistles and disgraceful and shameful lies. Forget the well-spun dream of 'Viksit Bharat', the self-styled 'pradhan sewak' of the country had gone back to the unapologetic anti-Muslim rhetoric that first earned him national notoriety in the aftermath of the 2002 Gujarat violence. It was a rabid, bigoted speech, villainizing India's 200 million (20 crore) Muslims as 'infiltrators' and looters of Hindus' wealth, and mocking them for allegedly having more children. The fearmongering was unashamedly blatant.

Why did the Prime Minister choose to change tack so suddenly from a campaign revolving around his welfare 'guarantees' and the aspirational vision of a 'Viksit Bharat' to one tugging at the baser instincts of the voter? Why was Modi suddenly whipping up hatred? Part of the answer must lie in the timing of the speech. Just two days had elapsed since the first round of polling, a round marked by low voter turnout. The BJP's internal tracker surveys had revealed worrying signs. While Muslims had come out in large numbers to vote, the BJP's core voter was missing, perhaps complacent in the belief that the party was sure to cross 'char sau paar'. The intense north Indian heat may have been another explanation for low turnout numbers, but clearly there was little enthusiasm amongst voters. Moreover, the Congress campaign and manifesto centred on cash 'guarantees' and the 'Constitution is in danger' was gathering traction. An aggressive Rahul Gandhi was pushing a pro-poor agenda with 'mehngai', 'rozgaar', an 'X-ray' of wealth distribution and a 'khatakhat' (speedy) promise of cash guarantees becoming his constant refrain. The word 'khatakhat', in particular, was drawing an enthusiastic response from an increasingly transactional voter. Every time Rahul Gandhi would utter the word, part of popular street lingo, a wild cheer would erupt from audiences. 'Our feedback system amongst our volunteers on Instagram and other social media channels showed that "khatakhat" was gathering traction; every video mentioning it was going viral,' recalled Y.B. Srivatsa, Rahul's communications head. Elated by the response, the Congress went into a 'khatakhat' overdrive, pushing the idea in every possible forum.

'The "khatakhat" campaign's spread was purely organic; no one planned it as such,' said Srivatsa.

The BJP needed a counter to the politics of competitive economic populism. Simply dismissing the Congress promises as 'revadi' (freebies) wasn't working any longer. 'The feedback from the ground surveys after round one did indicate that this was not the "done deal" we presumed it would be. The anti-BJP vote was consolidating, while our voter had not come to the booth in many areas,' disclosed a BJP strategist. Ergo, it was time to return to a familiar trope. For the BJP and the wider Sangh Parivar, that meant Muslim-bashing. The Muslim as an 'enemy figure' has been the saffron brotherhood's ideological glue for decades. The rise of the BJP is linked to its successfully branding the Congress, its principal adversary for power, a party of 'Muslim appeasers'. The appeasement tag has stuck to the Congress since the Shah Bano case in the 1980s, when Rajiv Gandhi's government overturned a Supreme Court judgment on the maintenance rights of a divorced Muslim woman. Now, Modi was reviving the 'appeasement' charge, only this time through crudity, indecencies and open falsehoods. His reference to the Congress ensuring Muslims had the 'first right to resources' was in the context of a speech made by his predecessor, Dr Manmohan Singh, in 2006 during an address to the National Development Council. But the remarks were taken out of context. Dr Singh had not just referred to Muslim minorities but also to SC/ST, OBC, other minorities and women as the government's 'collective priorities'. The charge that the Congress manifesto promised to 'survey' and 'redistribute' gold and property to Muslims was also prima facie absurd. It was outlandish, insane and fantastical. The forty-six page 'Nyay Patra' did speak of 'growing inequality of wealth and income', which it promised to address 'through suitable changes in policies', but there was no mention of private property being confiscated, let alone seizing the mangalsutras of Hindu women. Nor, for that matter, any reference to transferring benefits to Muslims anywhere. Even the familiar charge of Muslims producing more children had been debunked by the government's own most recent National Family Health Survey, which showed a decline in fertility rates across communities. So why was Prime Minister Modi consciously spreading lies? 'Look, on a campaign trail many things are said in the heat of the moment. When the Congress was falsely stating that the Constitution will be changed and reservations will be scrapped by a BJP government, wasn't that a bald lie that needed to be called out first?' argued a senior BJP leader.

But Banswara wasn't just a typical heat-of-the moment speech. It was a deliberate move to energize the BJP's rank and file after a disappointing first-round outcome. Part strategy, part rabble-rousing instinct, and marked by a touch of desperation, the lowest-common-denominator speech was designed to recapture the war of narratives that was edging towards the Opposition, especially the Congress. Shockingly, the ECI chose not to admonish Modi, even though the Banswara speech was a barefaced violation of the code of conduct. Initially refusing to comment, the commission then sent a notice to BJP President Nadda instead of much-needed admonishment, censure and punishment for the speechmaker. Trying to play it safe, they also sent a notice to Congress President Kharge on Rahul Gandhi's poll speeches. The commission was drawing a false equivalence. The Banswara remarks were the most egregious instance of a communally poisonous speech, one which should have attracted instant action from a professedly neutral body. Instead, four weeks after Banswara, the commission issued a feeble statement urging restraint from all sides in making speeches on caste and religious lines. It marked another new low for the top election body that was clearly unwilling to take on a political supremo.

Nor was Banswara a one-off. The news portal Scroll produced a detailed review of Modi's speeches in the week after Banswara. In almost every speech, not only did the Prime Minister repeat his charge of the Congress serving only Muslim interests, but he also made claims that were based on lies or half-truths. In a speech in Sagar in Madhya Pradesh, Modi alleged that the Congress in Karnataka had instituted reservations based on religion through illegal means. A fact check reveals that while a Congress government in Karnataka in 1962 had included certain Muslim castes in an OBC list based on the recommendation of an official panel, it was in 1994 that the H.D. Deve Gowda-led JD(S) government brought all Muslim communities in Karnataka under the OBC list, and carved out a 4 per cent sub-quota for them. The JD(S) was now a BJP ally. In Surguja, Modi warned that the Congress was planning to introduce an 'inheritance tax' if it came to power. 'Your children will not get the wealth that you accumulate. The Congress will snatch it away from you,' he declared. In Gujarat's Banaskantha, Modi sounded even more hysterical. 'Beware, the Congress will snatch away your "bhains" (buffalo). If you have two buffaloes, the Congress will take away one,' he warned. The remarks came just hours after the Congress's overseas wing chairman, Sam Pitroda, said in an interview to news agency ANI that an inheritance tax was an 'interesting idea'. An enraged Pitroda claimed that his remarks were deliberately distorted. 'It was a complete set-up by a section of the media that was acting like agents of the Modi government. I was discussing the US position on inheritance tax, and the news outlets made it seem like I was referring to India,' he said. Caught in a bind, the Congress quickly distanced itself from Pitroda's comments.

The Congress had initially decided not to react to Modi's charges at all. 'We knew that if we responded to the Hindu–Muslim politics being unleashed by the BJP, we would be moving away from our own welfare plank; we just didn't want to play on their pitch,' pointed out a Congress media cell member. Interestingly, when the Congress did hit back on the Banswara diatribe, it was Priyanka Gandhi Vadra who led the charge. While the tall, striking and articulate Priyanka is a crowd-pulling campaigner, the party leadership had appeared reluctant in the past to fully unleash her on the election trail, perhaps concerned that her light might outshine her brother's. This time, the gloves were off. In a rally in Bengaluru, Priyanka lashed out at Modi's 'mangalsutra' comment. 'When there was war, Indira Gandhi donated her gold. Meri ma ka mangalsutra iss desh pe kurban hai (My mother's mangalsutra was sacrificed for this country),' she said, referring to the assassination of her father, Rajiv Gandhi. It was an emotional response but just the kind to strike a chord amongst the wider public. The 'mangalsutra' pushback would define Priyanka's role in the Congress campaign. If Rahul was the social justice crusader and Kharge was projected as the down-to-earth political veteran, Priyanka was the charismatic presence who could take on sensitive issues with a more personal touch. 'We now had our own trishul to take on the BJP's "double engine",' said a Congress leader gleefully.

By pushing the politically edgy vocabulary of 'Samvidhan', 'khatakhat' and 'mangalsutra', the Congress had seized the poll narrative. On each occasion, it was the BJP that was pushed on the back foot. Modi insisted that his government had no plan to change the Constitution, but the on-ground whisper campaign was tough to counter. He mocked Rahul's 'khatakhat' jibe, but the word was stuck in people's minds. And Priyanka's emotive invocation of her mother's mangalsutra had settled that debate too. In 2019, the Pulwama terror strike had given Modi and the BJP the decisive edge in narrative-building. Modi's one-liners like 'Ghar mein ghuskar maara' were echoing across the country, consolidating his image as an uber-nationalist. In 2024, it was Rahul Gandhi's speeches that were gathering more eyeballs, especially on YouTube and other social media. The narrative war was no longer one-sided. Nor was the leadership contest.

The clearest sign that even a consummate campaigner like Modi was rattled came during a rally in Hyderabad in the first week of May, when the Prime Minister invoked the Adani–Ambani duo to attack the Congress. 'For five years, these people [the Congress] abused Adani–Ambani, but once the elections were announced, they stopped. Kitna maal uthaya hai? Kaale dhan ke kitne bore bharkar ke rupaye maare hain (How much loot have you collected? How many sacks of black money have you taken)? How many tempo-loads of money have arrived for the Congress? You have to answer the nation,' he screeched. It was a sudden, inexplicable charge. For a decade, Modi had never uttered the contentious A–A words despite being constantly provoked by Rahul Gandhi. Now, he was referring to them in a language that was rough and unfathomable. Rahul Gandhi was quick to hit back: 'You also know that they give money in a tempo. Is it your personal experience? The country knows who is the driver and helper of the BJP's tempo of corruption!' Every BJP leader and strategist I spoke to is clueless as to why Modi dragged Adani–Ambani into the poll war of words. 'Why would we even think of playing on a Congress pitch and expose ourselves to needless controversy?' admitted a BJP strategist. 'I think the "Samvidhan khatre mein hai" slogan had got under the Prime Minister's skin and he was looking to somehow shift the headlines.'

And yet, despite struggling to match the Opposition's 'Samvidhan' rhetoric, the BJP maintains that its Banswara ploy worked in energizing voters. In the three election rounds that followed Modi's incendiary speech, the voting percentage in the Hindi heartland states did increase, and the party won more than 60 per cent of the seats, sweeping states like Madhya Pradesh and Gujarat, traditional BJP bastions, and it gradually regained some of the momentum it had lost in the first round in Uttar Pradesh and Rajasthan. At the halfway mark of this election marathon, the BJP was certain a third consecutive majority victory was very much in sight for Team Modi–Shah. What could change? The crucial last stretch was about to see a dramatic reverse swing in the tale.

TWELVE

'Hawa Badal Rahi Hai': The States That Turned

POLITICAL gossip is more pervasive in Lucknow than the intoxicating perfumes of its famed 'attar' bazaars. From bun maska and tunde kebabs at street corners to governmental manoeuvres and 'pher-badal' (reshuffle) at the Vidhan Bhavan, the city is as thrilling for a gastronome as it is for a political watcher. In early May 2024, as the temperature soared, so did the election chatter. Had Yogi Adityanath been excluded during the campaign, or had the Uttar Pradesh chief minister voluntarily distanced himself from it? Yogi's alleged turf battle with the BJP's central leadership, especially Home Minister Amit Shah, was being whispered about in hushed tones in Uttar Pradesh's power circles, as was the possibility of a change in guard in Lucknow after the elections if the party won big.

No one is quite sure who started the 'Yogi is on the way out' rumour or how or why. Government sources in Lucknow claimed that the buzz first began after the 2023 winter elections, when Shivraj Singh Chouhan was replaced in Madhya Pradesh and Vasundhara Raje was sidelined in Rajasthan. The BJP pointed a finger at the AAP leader, the canny Arvind Kejriwal, who, a day after being granted bail by the Supreme Court so he could join the election campaign, claimed that the Centre was preparing to leave the saffron-robed monk out in the cold after the 2024 Lok Sabha elections. 'If a BJP government is formed, they will first dispose of Yogi Adityanath and then make Amit Shah the Prime Minister of the country. Prime Minister Modi is asking for votes for Amit Shah. Will Amit Shah fulfil Modi's guarantee?' asked the Delhi chief minister. It was a politically shrewd yet mischievous remark, designed to foment trouble in the BJP ranks—and it was enough to excite the gossip bazaar. The next day, the Samajwadi Party leader and Uttar Pradesh's other principal political player, Akhilesh Yadav, latched onto it. 'Tell me, why don't we see Yogi's picture on the BJP hoardings? Why has Uttar Pradesh's double engine suddenly become a single engine? Will BJP do to Yogi what they have done to Shivraj Chouhan in Madhya Pradesh?' he asked with an impish smile.

Gossip is at its juiciest when there is a kernel of truth to it. The Shah–Yogi story fits into this category. A next-gen battle over who might succeed Narendra Modi in the future was the subject of much political speculation. Shah was Modi's de facto No. 2, the BJP's crisis manager and chief poll strategist, while Yogi Adityanath was a highly popular leader from the country's numerically decisive state. Now, in the heat of another big election, the internal tug of war was getting traction once again. After speaking to multiple sources, I learnt that Yogi was deeply unhappy with the BJP's choice of Lok Sabha candidates. He had reportedly proposed a list of names, but hardly any of his suggestions were accepted. One of the sitting MPs Yogi strongly batted for was former army chief and then Union Minister General V.K. Singh, who had won the 2019 elections from Ghaziabad by a massive 5.6 lakh votes. When he saw that General Singh's name was missing from the 2024 list, Yogi became incensed. 'How can you drop someone of his stature? This will send out the wrong message,' Yogi cautioned at an internal party meeting. The warning went unheeded. General Singh had reportedly fallen out of favour with the central leadership.

Thoroughly put off that the chief minister's nominees were being ignored, the Yogi camp blamed the charmed circle around the home minister, especially Sunil Bansal, the influential BJP general secretary referred to by Adityanath's supporters as 'Chhota Chanakya'. Another 'suspect' was the director of a national news TV network who had easy access to Shah and was accused by his critics of 'deal-making'. 'These guys sitting in their air-conditioned rooms in Delhi seem to know more than us on the ground in Uttar Pradesh,' argued a Yogi supporter.

Amit Shah undoubtedly had a special interest in Uttar Pradesh. It was here, after all, as general secretary in charge of India's most politically crucial state, that he had acquired a national profile by spearheading the BJP's spectacular 2014 win. Shah had his own loyalists in the Uttar Pradesh BJP unit, not all of whom saw eye to eye with Yogi Adityanath. The hands-on organizational man Bansal was one of them, deriving his power from his proximity to the central leadership, but in August 2022, he was moved out of his post as Uttar Pradesh BJP organizational secretary and given charge of West Bengal, Odisha and Telangana instead. His departure established Yogi, the face of the BJP's impressive 2022 assembly victory, as the only power centre in the state. 'Yogi takes decisions without consulting any BJP leader; no minister, no MP, no MLA has any role in governance. Only a handful of bureaucrats matter,' lamented an MLA. 'At least when Bansal ji was around, we could complain to him— now there is no one.'

Accusations that the chief minister was promoting members from his Thakur community at the cost of the BJP's Brahmin and OBC leaders added to the murmurs of discontent. Keshav Prasad Maurya, Yogi's deputy chief minister and the party's OBC face, was the leader of the dissident group. Maurya was convinced that Yogi's loyalists had conspired to defeat him in the 2022 assembly polls. Even though the chief minister and his deputy lived just 75 metres away from each other on Lucknow's Kalidas Marg, the city's VVIP hub, they hadn't visited each other's residences in almost five years. The only time Yogi came calling was once in 2021, to bless Maurya's newly wed son and daughter-in law. He had skipped the marriage ceremony and reception, which was attended by the top brass of the Sangh Parivar. 'A few senior RSS leaders had to persuade Yogi to at least maintain cordial relations with his deputy in public, but the truth is, there was a complete breakdown in ties,' confessed a senior Uttar Pradesh leader.

The BJP's predicament in Yogi-led Uttar Pradesh was not unlike that faced by the party during the Modi years in Gujarat. Then, as chief minister, Modi was blamed for sidelining all potential challengers to his chair. Now, Yogi, a saffron-clad self-proclaimed 'monk' endorsed by the party's rank and file for his extremist Hindutva stance but accused by his peers of running a one-man show, was facing similar charges. As decision-making became excessively centralized in both Delhi and Lucknow, the fault lines within the BJP widened. District-level BJP leaders and karyakartas complained that if there was a power struggle brewing at the top, there was no one to listen to their grievances on the ground. 'In 2024, Uttar Pradesh was a state with a million political mutinies,' said Rahul Shrivastava, a journalist who has tracked Uttar Pradesh's politics for more than three decades.

Jaunpur, a scenic but rough town in eastern Uttar Pradesh, is an example of just how the not-so-picturesque power games were playing out. The BJP central leadership had allotted the party ticket to Kripashankar Singh, a long-serving Congressman in Mumbai who switched to the BJP only in 2021. Singh was among the 100-plus BJP candidates who had defected from the Congress in the last decade and been rewarded with a ticket, a source of much disquiet within the party and concern for the RSS, which prized loyalty above all else. Originally from Jaunpur, Singh arrived in Mumbai in the early 1970s. He reportedly sold vegetables to make ends meet and eventually became the Congress's north Indian face in the city. Ironically, the BJP had led the charge against Singh in a disproportionate assets case, from which he was ultimately discharged. Now, he was part of the saffron army, and had shifted base from his swanky apartment in Pali Hill to the dusty dirt-tracks of Jaunpur to try his luck. Within party circles, there was speculation that Singh, a surprise choice, had used a Mumbai 'big money' connection to get the ticket, an allegation he strongly denied. 'I am now Modi ji's soldier; yeh meri dharti hai (this is my home),' he told me on the campaign trail.

Though Singh was elated at getting the ticket, it wasn't going to be smooth sailing in a traditionally tough constituency. The BSP, which won the Jaunpur seat in 2019, had announced Srikala Reddy Singh, wife of the jailed gangster–politician Dhananjay Singh, as their candidate. Just days later, when Dhananjay, the unchallenged 'bahubali' of Jaunpur, was released from jail on bail, the Union home minister sternly told him: 'You must get your wife to withdraw.' After much persuasion, she reluctantly stepped aside and Dhananjay declared his support for the BJP. Dhananjay was seen as a 'prized asset', a leader who had some influence across at least three constituencies of eastern Uttar Pradesh (Purvanchal).

But Chief Minister Yogi Adityanath wasn't pleased at the turn of events. Having made the drive against mafia leaders his calling card, he now found that a fellow Thakur and history-sheeter from his home turf of Purvanchal was being wooed by the BJP leadership in Delhi. While Adityanath did attend a rally in Jaunpur, he was reportedly not keen to strengthen Dhananjay's hand and refused to share a platform with him. Inter-Thakur rivalry in Uttar Pradesh can be nasty at times. Caught in the middle of it was Kripashankar Singh, already facing the 'outsider' tag. He would lose the 2024 Jaunpur election to the Samajwadi Party's Babu Singh Kushwaha by 99,335 votes. Amidst the BJP's internal wrangling, the large OBC vote and even a sizeable section of the BSP's Dalit vote consolidated behind Kushwaha.

Another example of power politics in Uttar Pradesh involved an even more recognizable BJP 'bahubali'. Brij Bhushan Sharan Singh was a six-time MP who was in the eye of a major controversy after serious and damning charges of sexual harassment were made against him by several medal-winning Indian women wrestlers. While Brij Bhushan reluctantly stepped down as chief of the wrestling federation, he wasn't willing to give up his Kaiserganj seat in central Uttar Pradesh. The central BJP leadership was placed in an awkward predicament: obliging Brij Bhushan would leave the party open to the charge of siding with an alleged sexual predator, but alienating him could affect the party's chances in at least two or three constituencies where the leader held sway. Caught in a bind, the BJP leadership attempted a compromise. 'We will give the ticket to your son Karan instead,' was BJP President J.P. Nadda's offer. Even though Shah took the final decisions, the formal task of informing leaders on ticket selection was usually left to the more affable BJP president. Brij Bhushan, who insisted the harassment charges against him were false, wasn't impressed with Nadda's offer. 'If you don't give me the ticket, I will contest as an independent and win. Jo karna hai karo. Main aapki baat nahi manoonga (Do what you want. I won't listen to you)!' A despairing Nadda rang up the home minister and requested him to intervene. One phone call from Shah did the trick at the last moment. 'I only agreed to step aside when Neta ji called me; after all, who doesn't want to see their son rise?' Brij Bhushan, who was considered close to Shah, later told me.

But the story doesn't end there. While campaigning for his son, Brij Bhushan spoke out against Adityanath's 'bulldozer policy'. The Kaiserganj strongman had a long-running feud with Yogi Adityanath, whom he considered his 'junior', Brij Bhushan having entered politics in the late 1980s as part of the Ram Janmbhoomi movement. 'It is very difficult to build a home. I understand your pain and sorrow, which is why I am against bulldozers,' he told a gathering in Gonda. When I interviewed him at his sprawling farmhouse, Brij Bhushan claimed that he was one of the few BJP leaders whose supporters included local Muslims too. 'The people are with me even if some powerful people are conspiring to finish me,' he said. I asked him if he was referring to Adityanath. 'Ab kuch baatein camera par nahi keh sakte (There are a few things that cannot be said on camera),' was his telling response. Unhappy at being pushed into a corner by the party leadership, Brij Bhushan restricted his campaign to ensuring his son's victory. And while Karan Bhushan Singh won the Kaiserganj seat by 1.48 lakh votes, across central Uttar Pradesh, the BJP faced surprise defeats.

It wasn't just the leadership that was caught in tussles. Even the RSS–BJP karyakartas—the foot soldiers who are the party's organizational fulcrum—were feeling alienated. In Meerut, where the BJP replaced its sitting MP with Arun Govil, renowned for his portrayal of Lord Ram in the iconic 1980s TV serial *Ramayana*, the mood was more sullen than celebratory. For local BJP workers, the glum-faced Govil was an 'outsider', someone who had little connection with the area. 'He may be a star, but will he stay amongst us?' wondered a Meerut-based BJP functionary. Govil was TV's Ram to the wider world, but to the BJP's own cadres, he was a celebrity being imposed from the top. He even reportedly wore gloves while shaking hands and was reluctant to let people put garlands on him. When a TV channel wanted to interview the actor, his entourage was keen to negotiate a guest appearance fee. On-screen Ram was yet to adjust to the demands of off-screen politics. Govil eventually scraped home by just over 10,000 votes.

Another glaring instance of an 'outsider' being parachuted into the election race was when the BJP dropped its sitting MP and gave a ticket from Shravasti in central Uttar Pradesh to Saket Misra, son of Nripendra Misra, chairperson of the Ram Mandir construction committee and a former bureaucrat in the Prime Minister's office. An IIM Calcutta graduate and global investment banker, Misra had worked abroad for several years before returning home to 'contribute to nation-building'. He had joined the BJP in 2018 and worked as an advisor to the Purvanchal Development Board. But the local BJP unit in Shravasti saw him as a lateral entrant who had benefitted from his 'VVIP connections'. 'We talk of the Congress being a party of the "baba log", but in 2024 we also had our own privileged elite,' says an Uttar Pradesh BJP office-bearer. Misra lost the Shravasti seat by nearly 77,000 votes.

The brewing resentment over the choice of several BJP candidates meant that dispirited cadres and divided leaders were not pulling together. Overconfidence and the certainty that the Modi factor would overwhelm all else allowed a degree of complacency to creep into the BJP's planning. Added to that was the unshaken belief that, despite the petty wrangling over tickets, Shah, the consummate strategist, and his election management skills would triumph in the end. The exuberance and conviction turned out to be badly misplaced. But the reason for a poll defeat is not always a party's own flaws. Sometimes the opponent is able to capitalize on those flaws in unforeseen ways. And in Uttar Pradesh in 2024, fifty-one-year-old Akhilesh Yadav was in his prime and ready to prove his mettle.

'Hawa badal rahi hai; apna time aa raha hai (The wind is changing; our time is coming),' said Akhilesh Yadav with a confident smile. We were on a roadshow in the heart of Lucknow, wending our way through the quaint cobbled streets of Hazratganj towards the bright lights of Gomti Nagar. All along the route, Samajwadi Party workers were clamouring to get a glimpse of their Akhilesh 'bhaiya'. Every now and then, Yadav would stop the bus and step out to wave to the crowds milling around him. 'Kya aisa josh aapne pehle dekha hai (Have you seen such frenzy before)?' he asked, beaming. I was struck by the enthusiasm of his supporters but wasn't sure if it would translate into an electoral triumph. In the last decade, Yadav had been dealt four consecutive defeats at the hands of an ascendant BJP (two assembly and two Lok Sabha elections), and there was a sense that the Samajwadi Party leader's youthful buoyancy never matched ground realities. 'This time, our PDA will be too strong for them, just you wait and see,' he assured me.

'PDA' was the acronym Yadav had coined for his social engineering project that aimed to bring together 'pichhda' (backward), Dalit, and 'alpsankhyak' (minorities) and 'aadhi abadi' (women) on one platform. On paper it was a potent alliance, one that was designed to move the party away from the narrow Muslim–Yadav confines of his father the late Mulayam Singh Yadav's political base. And yet, it wasn't a new experiment. In the 2022 assembly elections, Yadav had attempted to broaden his appeal by reaching out to non-Yadav OBC leaders. But he still wasn't able to stop the BJP juggernaut. In fact, the effort to recraft the Samajwadi Party into a more inclusive force had begun in 2013, when Yadav, as chief minister, celebrated Karpoori Jayanti to mark the birth anniversary of Karpoori Thakur, who became Bihar's chief minister in 1970–71. Thakur was popularly known as 'Jan Nayak' and is regarded as the leading light of the EBC community from neighbouring Bihar. As a *Caravan* magazine cover story of July 2024 detailed, the Samajwadi Party made hectic attempts to embrace and co-opt EBC, OBC and Dalit figures in the eighteen months leading up to the 2024 elections. The rapidly changing social dynamics reflected in Yadav's intelligent ticket selection too. 'I have only given five Yadavs [all his family members] and four Muslims tickets this time. There are fifteen Dalits and twenty-seven non-Yadav OBCs in my list,' he emphasized. In a state where caste alignments are key, he was getting his arithmetic right. The twelve tickets he gave the Kurmi community, for example, revived the party's base amongst a widely spread social group.

The Samajwadi Party leader was also playing the alliance game judiciously. In the 2019 general elections, Yadav had tied up with Mayawati, but the bua–bhatija combine was an uneasy alliance because the BSP leader was reluctant to give equal space to her political competitor. This time, Yadav had chosen to ally with the Congress and Rahul Gandhi. In 2017, the duo, branded 'UP ke ladke', had stumbled before the might of the BJP. Bitter recriminations followed, with Yadav cribbing that the Congress leadership didn't even take his calls or answer messages, and the Congress claiming that Yadav wanted to 'finish off' their party in the state. Circumstances brought them together again under the INDIA alliance umbrella. The Congress was a declining force in Uttar Pradesh, with limited ground presence, but Yadav was willing to accommodate them with 17 of the 80 seats. Rahul Gandhi's yatras had made him a popular figure among minorities in particular, and only an alliance could consolidate a key vote bank. 'After some initial hard bargaining, Akhilesh was one of our easiest allies to negotiate with. No airs, no arrogance, even though he was the much bigger party in Uttar Pradesh,' said Avinash Pandey, Congress general secretary in charge of Uttar Pradesh. The negotiations had the odd funny moment too. For example, the Congress list mistakenly included the late Mahaveer Prasad.

Someone in the party had forgotten that he had passed away a decade ago! (The Congress denied the story, saying it was a canard spread by a 'mischief-monger'.)

And yet, no caste calculations or alliance management can work if the ground is not restless for change. The seven-phase polling in the vast state began in western Uttar Pradesh, and it was here that the first signs of the 'badalti hawa' (shifting winds) were noticed. There was an uneasy uncertainty in the air. The 'Samvidhan khatre mein hai' narrative spread like wildfire, especially in Dalit pockets. India Today's correspondent Preeti Choudhry recalled meeting sixty-two-year-old Somvati and her grandson Rajbir in a village in Saharanpur. Both said they would vote for the 'gathbandhan' (Samajwadi Party–Congress alliance). Somvati had always voted for Behenji (Mayawati) and the 'hathi' symbol of the BSP, while her grandson, a first-time voter, was impressed by Modi's oratory. So why were they shifting their vote this time? 'We have heard in a nukkad sabha that if the BJP comes to power, they will do away with aarakshan and even do away with the SC/ST Act,' said Somvati. The unlettered elderly lady had no clue about the 'Samvidhan' but was worried she might lose reservation benefits. 'For most villagers, the only thing that matters is reservations in education and government jobs; it's their lifeline,' said Choudhry. With Mayawati typecast as the 'B' team of the BJP, the Samajwadi Party–Congress got a large chunk of the Dalit vote across Uttar Pradesh. The Congress's Imran Masood won the Saharanpur seat by more than 60,000 votes. A Dalit–Muslim tactical alliance on the ground was proving decisive.

If Dalits were anxious about reservations, the country's youth were angry and restive about jobs. Outside an IAS exam coaching centre in Barabanki, I met a group of young men in their mid-twenties. They had all voted for the BJP in the 2022 Uttar Pradesh assembly elections, but at least half of them were now planning to vote for the Congress. 'I twice voted for the BJP in 2019 and 2022 because I thought they would ensure jobs. But all we have got are paper leaks and more paper leaks. If a government can't conduct an exam properly, how can they ask for our vote!' fumed one of the young men. While question papers of government recruitment exams getting leaked was a national crisis, in Uttar Pradesh it seemed to have reached epidemic proportions. Just weeks before the elections, the Uttar Pradesh constable examination paper had leaked, affecting more than 4.8 million (48 lakh) aspirants. For an entire generation, paper leaks had come to symbolize corruption and incompetence. Moreover, with many public sector undertakings downsizing or preferring short-term contractual employment, government job opportunities had reduced significantly. 'At least Rahul Gandhi and Akhilesh are talking about "janata ki baat", Modiji only gives us his "mann ki baat",' quipped another youth. Travelling through Uttar Pradesh since 2014, one would hear the occasional expression of discontent but rarely such sharp criticism of the Prime Minister. Now, Modi too was being mocked by disillusioned young voters. The Congress's Tanuj Punia, a thirty-nine-year-old IIT graduate with a big Instagram following, won the Barabanki seat by more than 2 lakh votes.

Among the images that stood out during the Uttar Pradesh campaign was one of a joint Rahul–Akhilesh gathbandhan rally in Phulpur. The duo was running late and the crowd was getting impatient in the sweltering heat. Yet they stuck around, waiting for the leaders to arrive. When the choppers landed, the crowd, mainly youth from the surrounding areas, became uncontrollable, breaking the barricades and rushing to the stage. The meeting had to be cut short due to security concerns. It was a frenzied crowd, not seen in Uttar Pradesh in a long time, certainly not at a Congress event. As we struggled to make our way out from the gathering, a young man in a bright yellow shirt with the words 'Rock On' emblazoned on it spotted our camera and turned excitedly to us. 'Sir, aapne Rahul ji aur Akhilesh ji ko dekha? Poora khatakhat maza aa gaya (Did you see Rahul and Akhilesh? It was great fun)!' If 'khatakhat'— the word Rahul Gandhi had linked to the speedy delivery of cash guarantees—had become a part of common parlance, then clearly change was in the air. The once-derided 'UP ke ladke' had well and truly arrived. Rahul Gandhi and Akhilesh Yadav, lively, youthful figures with a mass appeal, were scoring over pompously ceremonial BJP leaders armed with the same old empty promises in their multiple-vehicle convoys.

The second standout moment for me in Uttar Pradesh was in Varanasi, Modi's home turf. We were drinking chai by Assi Ghat, when a few locals joined us for an impromptu 'chai pe charcha'. Opinion was divided on how a decade of 'Modi raj' had changed Varanasi. Modi's supporters pointed to the increased tourist traffic as a direct consequence of the Prime Minister's focus on Varanasi as a centre of faith and tourism. The critics were just as emphatic in claiming that all that had happened was the 'Gujaratification' of the historic city. 'All the new hotels and restaurants are being set up by "outsiders"; all contracts are going to Gujarati businessmen,' they lamented. The heated debate was only settled when someone offered meetha paan as a sweetener. The chai shop has been a mandatory stop for me since 2014, but this was the first time I was hearing angry voices of dissent among the faithful customers who swear by Hindutva politics. 'You have to make a distinction between Modi and the BJP; people still admire Modi, but they do not like the local BJP leadership, which is seen as corrupt and non-performing,' pointed out Utpal Pathak, a Varanasi-based journalist.

When the results were announced on 4 June, the turnaround was official. The Samajwadi Party had won 37 seats and the Congress 6. The BJP was pushed to second place with 33 seats, with the party's vote share down by over 8 per cent. The BJP lost even in the Ram Mandir homeland of Ayodhya–Faizabad. In Varanasi too, where Modi's election managers had promised a record-breaking 'Abki baar 10 lakh paar' (10 lakh-plus this time) victory, the margin collapsed to just over 1.5 lakh votes, a big loss of face for a sitting Prime Minister. 'I couldn't believe it,' said a senior Uttar Pradesh BJP leader. 'I thought we might lose some vote share, but to lose so many seats was unthinkable.' Akhilesh Yadav was predictably jubilant: 'Didn't I tell you: hawa badal rahi hai!'

The BJP election results' post-mortem placed the blame for the Uttar Pradesh debacle on a variety of issues: overconfidence; listless cadres; the impact of the Samvidhan–reservation controversy on Dalits; Muslim consolidation; unfilled government job placements; non-Yadav OBCs like Kurmis shifting away; anti-incumbency against sitting MPs. It was a lengthy list, but no one wanted to confront the elephant in the room: the looming presence of Team Modi–Shah, who had centralized all core decision-making and ended up isolating Chief Minister Adityanath. A senior RSS leader claimed that when Chaudhary Bhupendra Singh was appointed the Uttar Pradesh BJP president in 2022, the local unit was not even consulted. 'There is a gradual Congressification of the BJP that we have to be careful about,' he warned. In the Indira Gandhi era, all power in the Congress was concentrated around the Prime Minister's office, which eventually led to state leaders being diminished and becoming disconnected from party workers. The RSS has always harped on 'collective leadership' and shunned 'vyaktipuja' or worship of an individual, but it was now having to cope with an overwhelming personality cult from within its own ranks.

Significantly, in an interview with *The Indian Express* just after the fourth phase of polling, BJP President J.P. Nadda claimed that the party had grown beyond the RSS. 'In the beginning, we were less capable, smaller and needed the RSS. Today, we have grown and we are capable. The BJP runs itself,' he declared. Nadda's remarks only added to the sense of unease within the Sangh Parivar, the general impression being that the party chief was echoing a Modi–Shah line. 'Look, if they don't need us, its fine, we will carry on with our social work,' said the RSS leader. He pointed out that in states like Madhya Pradesh and Gujarat, where the RSS network was strong and fully involved in the campaign, the BJP had swept the polls. But in places like Uttar Pradesh and Haryana, where the organization felt sidelined, the cadres just didn't get involved. 'Think of where the BJP would be if they didn't sweep Gujarat and MP,' the RSS leader said pointedly.

The truth is, for Home Minister Shah in particular, the Uttar Pradesh results were a wake-up call, a major dent to his reputation as a political Chanakya. His supporters insisted that he tried everything, including a last-minute tie-up with the Jat-dominated Rashtriya Lok Dal (RLD) in western Uttar Pradesh, to shore up the BJP's fortunes. The BJP–RLD 'deal' revealed the rough-and-ready nature of the Shah school of 'saam-daam-dand-bhed' politics. In the third week of January, the Samajwadi Party and the RLD announced a seat-sharing pact. Forty-five-year-old Jayant Chaudhary, a Texas-born graduate of the London School of Economics and an RLD leader, was part of the INDIA alliance at the time. But the final seat negotiations were taking too long, and Chaudhary was running out of patience. When Shah learnt this, he asked one of his key men to start a private conversation with the RLD leader. Chaudhary had been receiving feelers from local BJP leaders for a while, only this time the home minister himself came on the phone line to take the dialogue forward. On the table was an offer of 2 Lok Sabha seats. The RLD leader pushed for a few more, but Shah is a tough negotiator. Faced with a 'take it or leave it' situation, Chaudhary asked for additional inducement: a posthumous Bharat Ratna for his grandfather and Jat kisan leader Chaudhary Charan Singh. The home minister readily agreed, and shortly afterwards the deal was clinched. The carrot of a Bharat Ratna had secured the BJP another INDIA ally. 'Who doesn't want to be on the winning side in an election? The BJP looked a certain winner, so why wouldn't I choose to be with them?' Chaudhary told an aide. In the INDIA alliance, the RLD leader was likely to spend five more years in the Opposition; with the BJP, he was in line for a Union ministership. The lure of power had trumped all else.

Unfortunately for the BJP, this time Chaudhary's own Jat vote bank wasn't fully convinced by the switch. After all, just five years earlier, in 2019, his father, Ajit Singh, had been defeated by the BJP's Jat strongman Sanjeev Balyan, by a slender margin of 6,000 votes, in a prestige battle in Muzaffarnagar, where counting had gone on till late into the night. Now Chaudhary was expected to campaign not only for the man who had vanquished his father but also for the party that had evicted Ajit Singh from an official bungalow in 2014. Jat pride was at stake. 'I was covering the election in the campaign bus with Balyan and Jayant, and throughout the journey they didn't say a word to each other,' recalled journalist

Preeti Choudhry. Balyan lost the Muzaffarnagar seat this time. While the RLD won its 2 seats, the party's Jat vote did not get transferred to the BJP candidates who were battling local anti-incumbency. The rugged Jats of western Uttar Pradesh remained suspicious of the BJP in the wake of the farm protests of 2020–21. In politics, chemistry matters as much as arithmetic.

The shock defeats across Uttar Pradesh were a major factor in the BJP's dwindling tally in 2024. At the onset of the campaign, a survey done by a consultancy firm that worked for Team Modi–Shah had predicted a 'minimum' of 70-plus seats. Now, having secured less than half the projected number, the bubble had burst. The seemingly impregnable machine had been seriously challenged, its limitations dramatically exposed. As it turned out, Uttar Pradesh wasn't the only headache for Shah. The BJP's celebrated tactician was about to get another reality check.

⸻

Baramati in western Maharashtra is the pocket borough of the Pawars, the most enduring family in the state's politics. Just over 100 kilometres from Pune, Baramati is an upwardly mobile small town. Shopping malls, multiplex theatres and even a biotechnology institute have been set up here. The Pawars are robust political entrepreneurs. From colleges to hospitals, milk dairies to vineyards, there is scarcely any productive activity in the town that doesn't bear their stamp, and their obvious efforts to turn a sleepy mofussil town into a hub of activity have been amply rewarded by the voters. Since 1967, when the family patriarch Sharad Pawar first contested from here, the Pawar writ has run unchallenged in Baramati. Pawar's daughter, Supriya Sule, is a three-time MP from Baramati; his nephew Ajit Pawar has been the local MLA since 1991. 'Nothing moves in Baramati without the consent of the Pawars. They are the modern-day rulers of this area,' said a local journalist.

But in 2024, the Pawars faced an unprecedented war within. Ajit Pawar's decision to break away from his uncle in 2023 had pitted 'Dada' (Ajit) against 'Saheb' (Sharad). The Pawars' party, the NCP, was split down the middle, the two factions battling each other over the party's name and symbol. As mentioned earlier, Home Minister Shah had placed a stern condition while accommodating Ajit Pawar as a BJP ally: Ajit would have to nominate his wife, Sunetra, as his NCP faction's candidate against his cousin Supriya. Still smarting from past antagonisms, Shah wanted to defeat Sharad Pawar on his home turf at all costs. So did Devendra Fadnavis, the BJP's deputy chief minister in the Maharashtra government. 'No compromise this time on Baramati,' was the home minister's firm message when a prominent industrialist reportedly tried to intercede to avoid a battle within the Pawar family.

Supriya 'tai' (sister) versus Sunetra 'vahini' (sister-in-law)—this was easily the most high-stakes family battle in Maharashtra politics in 2024. 'They meet at all festive functions, be it Ganesh Chaturthi or Diwali, like one big happy family, but when it comes to elections, they are now fighting tooth and nail to defeat each other—it's crazy,' remarked a family friend. At risk was a political legacy built over half a century across western Maharashtra.

Eighty-three years old and ravaged by oral cancer, the senior Pawar had taken his daughter's election as a personal challenge, a fight to restore his wounded pride. For the sixty-four-year-old Ajit, breaking away from the NCP was a chance to step out of his uncle's shadow and establish a claim for leadership in Maharashtra. Ajit is very much the hands-on local toughie who knows how to 'manage' elections with his vast network of contacts. When he agreed to a rare interview at 6 a.m. at his sprawling bungalow, supporters were already queuing up for an audience. I asked him to confirm what Shah had told me earlier. Had the Union home minister, itching to take revenge against the senior Pawar, pushed him to nominate his wife as the candidate against his cousin? 'No one can push me. I am doing what is best for our party; family comes later,' he claimed. But Sunetra Pawar, demure and retiring, a political novice, was distinctly uncomfortable in her new role as a vote-seeking politician. A woman of very few words, she seemed to find the media attention distinctly unsettling. 'Please don't ask me too many questions,' she pleaded.

The outgoing and vivacious Supriya Sule, by contrast, is easily the most camera-friendly member of the Pawar family. Educated in an English-medium school in Mumbai, she's an effective speaker in Parliament, regularly raising her voice on a variety of issues. But having lived mostly in Mumbai and Delhi, she was dependent on Ajit Pawar's contacts for electioneering in Baramati. Ajit had reportedly issued strict instructions to his supporters to stay away from Supriya's meetings. 'Dada is a grassroots leader but also a bit of a bully; many people in Baramati are scared of him,' admitted a local NCP leader.

While Ajit Pawar was playing on people's 'fear' factor, Sharad Pawar was counting on sympathy for the manner in which the party he had founded had been split apart by an ambitious nephew who had publicly asked him to 'retire' from politics. The senior Pawar was not just seen as a political family head but in Baramati's bazaars he was also acknowledged as the leader who had put a nondescript township on the national map. Despite being hurt by her cousin's betrayal, Sule herself refused to say a word against her opponent. 'I am not going to run a negative campaign and wash any dirty linen in public. Let people vote for me on my track record as an MP,' she insisted. She confessed that taking on a family member wasn't easy. Moreover, she had an additional impediment. The NCP's familiar clock symbol had gone to the Ajit Pawar faction. In every speech, she had to remind the voter that she was contesting on a new symbol, a 'tutari' (a musical instrument).

If NCP voters were confused over a symbol, BJP voters were even more puzzled by the shifting political alignments. After all, the BJP leadership, including Prime Minister Modi, had previously accused Ajit Pawar of large-scale corruption. In a 2014 campaign rally, a belligerent Fadnavis had promised to send Ajit to jail. When one BJP state leader reportedly raised the issue with the party high command, he was shouted down by the home minister. 'If you don't work for Ajit Pawar, we won't give you a ticket for the assembly elections,' he was warned by Shah. The terrified politician reluctantly fell in line.

A similar story was playing out across western Maharashtra. BJP workers were being asked to campaign for the same NCP leaders whom they had steadfastly opposed for decades. 'In Delhi, the Prime Minister talks about taking about corruption, on fighting against dynasty politics, and here we are being asked to line up behind Ajit Pawar, whom our own leaders have often targeted as a symbol of corruption and dynasty politics,' fumed a BJP leader from western Maharashtra.

While the Pawar family power game continued to make headlines, voters in this part of Maharashtra were battling a serious livelihood crisis. An extended period of low rainfall had led to brutal water shortages and aggravated rural distress. Villagers were lining up in long queues for water, often paying Rs 200 a week for a mid-size drum from a private tanker. A few villagers we met professed disinterest in the election; they had more immediate concerns. 'I don't care which Pawar wins, I want water,' a middle-aged woman raged. But they were a minority. Most others said they would vote for Sule. 'It is about our "asmita" (pride); we don't like gaddars (traitors) who deceive their own family,' said an elderly farmer.

'Gaddar'. A potent word that had come to symbolize the underlying chaos and acrimony in Maharashtra politics, a reminder of coarsened deal-making that would haunt the ruling alliance. Two regional parties in the state were split under the express instructions of Team Modi–Shah, with Fadnavis as chief executor. Their plan to divide and rule may have been disguised as calculated political strategy, but the voter, anonymous and silent, had still seen through the charade. An undercurrent of anger and anti-incumbency was coursing through the state's politics. On counting day, Sule and her sister-in-law Sunetra Pawar were briefly engaged in an electoral battle, but slowly Sule pulled away, eventually winning by over 1.5 lakh votes. The battle of the Pawars in Baramati had been settled, at least for now. Across Maharashtra, the BJP-led alliance won just 17 of the 48 seats, down from a massive 41 seats in 2019. The BJP itself won just 9. From Dalit voters shifting allegiance to the Congress in Vidarbha to Maratha reservations creating a caste schism in Marathwada, Maharashtra's politics was in a state of intense churn.

Like in Uttar Pradesh, here too internal power fights were hurting the BJP. High-performing Union Minister Nitin Gadkari was convinced that there was a conscious attempt being made by 'forces in Mumbai and

Delhi' to defeat him in his Nagpur citadel. In the capital's corridors of power, the plain-speaking Gadkari was believed to be the only minister who didn't blindly toe Team Modi–Shah's line. Dropped from the BJP's all-powerful Central Parliamentary Board in 2022, Gadkari had let a senior RSS leader know that he would not to take any further 'humiliation' lying down. When his name was not included in the BJP's first list of Lok Sabha candidates, there was more speculation over his future. Sensing an opportunity to stir trouble in the rival camp, Shiv Sena (UBT) leader Uddhav Thackeray made a public offer to Gadkari to join the Opposition alliance. 'We can even considering making you our prime ministerial nominee,' was a behind-the-scenes 'informal' proposal. Gadkari, a committed BJP–RSS man, politely refused. Although the senior leader did eventually get the ticket, all was not well. In Nagpur, to his outrage, he found a massive number of names 'missing' from the voters list in his stronghold areas. While he still won by over 1.3 lakh votes, he wasn't his usual ebullient self during the campaign. At one of his rallies, the severely diabetic Gadkari even fainted in the searing heat. 'I am a loyal party soldier, but don't expect me to get involved across Maharashtra beyond a point,' he told a BJP leader.

The Maharashtra debacle was an unexpected setback for Team Modi–Shah and for the BJP's state unit. A defeated Fadnavis offered his resignation, which was turned down. His critics within the party accused him of sidelining other leaders and of taking decisions without consulting anyone. A shell-shocked Shah stayed silent. His plan to checkmate Pawar had failed miserably.

The hawa had shifted dramatically in India's two biggest election states. Would the third largest provide any solace?

In the first week of February 2024, barely a fortnight after the Ram Mandir inauguration, the BJP's election strategists were in for a pleasant surprise. The party's weekly tracker survey showed the BJP surging ahead in West Bengal, with high recall for the mandir issue and Prime Minister Modi's popularity at a peak. It predicted 'at least 25-plus seats in Bengal'. The BJP doesn't have just one survey team. A political consultancy firm, Nation with NaMo (earlier called Association of Billion Minds), works almost entirely as Team Modi–Shah's in-house ground-feedback agency. There are others too, including Axis My India, which does much larger opinion polls, and Varahe Analytics, which does specific data crunching, especially in the southern states. All the surveys were pointing in one direction. The BJP was well ahead of Bengal's ruling TMC. 'In a large state like Bengal, we will make up what we may lose elsewhere,' was the party leadership's overall assessment. In 2019, the BJP had won 18 of the 42 seats in Bengal, a major turnaround for a party that had previously struggled in the state. Now, it was aiming even higher.

Interestingly, even the TMC's internal polls were showing a rising graph for the BJP. Until then, certain that she could beat back the BJP charge, Chief Minister Mamata Banerjee had initially trained her guns on attacking the Congress–left combine. Part of her strategy was to allow the anti-Mamata vote to be divided between her rivals. The ascent of the BJP amidst the Ram Mandir excitement, however, changed the dynamics. Just days ahead of the Lok Sabha polls being announced, the Centre decided to finally frame the CAA rules, after nine extensions and exactly 1,521 days after the Act was notified in January 2020. 'We have delivered on yet another commitment,' proclaimed Shah. The delivery was timed to woo Bengal's large Hindu Matua community, which had migrated from Bangladesh.

Nor did the party limit itself to playing only the Hindu card. In mid-February, women in a village in Sandeshkhali, a riverine island in the Sundarbans, levelled land-grabbing and sexual exploitation charges against local TMC strongman Sheikh Shahjahan and his henchmen. For the next month, Sandeshkhali dominated national media headlines. 'Mahila' (women) voters were Banerjee's secure vote bank; the allegations in Sandeshkhali struck at the core of her support base. If women voters drifted away from her, Banerjee would be in serious trouble. When I sought a reaction to the goings-on in Sandeshkhali, she angrily retorted,

'You people in Delhi are buying into the BJP's propaganda; this is all a conspiracy to "badnaam" (defame) Bengal.'

Like in the 2021 West Bengal assembly elections, Banerjee was back to playing on a familiar pitch, positioning the Modi government as 'Bengal Virodhi'. Only this time the contest was for power in Delhi, not Kolkata. 'Our tracker polls did show that a number of people who wanted Didi as CM also wanted Modi as PM; that was our biggest hurdle to overcome,' admitted Pratik Jain, a member of the I-PAC team working on the TMC campaign. As a first step to retain her mahila vote, Banerjee doubled the monthly income support for women under the flagship Lakshmir Bhandar scheme to Rs 1,000 in the state budget. 'The Modi government denies us funds, but I will always stand by you,' she repeatedly told Bengal's women.

While a veteran politician, by now a three-time chief minister, four-time Union minister and seven-time MP, was getting her act together and planning astutely, the BJP surprisingly pressed the self-destruct button. The West Bengal unit of the party has always been deeply factionalized, trapped between an old guard with staunch RSS connections and a new order, which includes defectors from the TMC. The disarray became evident when the BJP included Pawan Singh, a Bhojpuri singer–actor, in the party's first list. Singh was to contest from Asansol against the TMC's actor–politician and former BJP MP Shatrughan Sinha, when his crude and vulgar music videos depicting Bengali women in an undignified manner were leaked, allegedly by a rival from within the party. Vociferous protests from women's groups, TMC MPs and even local BJP leaders forced Pawan to withdraw barely twenty-four hours after being announced as a party candidate. It was an early setback for the BJP in Bengal.

The Pawan Singh episode, which would normally be unthinkable in a well-organized party like the BJP, revealed unexpected cracks within the system. Apparently, the singer–actor was keen to contest from 'anywhere'. The idea to get him to take on 'Bihari Babu' Sinha was mooted in Delhi, in haste, without a background check or formal recommendation from the state unit. Home Minister Shah had left Bengal's ticket distribution to his trusted aide and the party's general secretary, Sunil Bansal, who in turn was reliant on BJP's Leader of the Opposition in Bengal Suvendu Adhikari's inputs. Adhikari, who had joined the party in 2020 from the TMC, was keen to establish his dominance in the BJP and was accused of sidelining the party's 'old guard'. Dilip Ghosh, former state party chief, was the sitting MP from East Medinipur but was shifted out to Durgapur against his wishes after a 'survey' indicated that he was losing ground. The BJP ended up losing both seats. 'We were all cut out from what was happening in Bengal by Adhikari and an all-powerful coterie around the high command,' complained a state BJP leader. Previously, the term 'high command' was used to define the Gandhi family's stranglehold over the Congress; now, in the Modi–Shah era, it appeared to have permeated into the BJP as well.

While the BJP was battling an internal power tussle, the TMC was pushing ahead with its campaign with a clear division of responsibility: Mamata Banerjee as the chief campaigner, nephew Abhishek Banerjee as the main organizational point person. The party, eager to gather a few star faces in its corner, spun a googly when it announced 2011 World Cup winner Yusuf Pathan as its candidate to take on five-time Congress MP Adhir Chowdhury from Berhampore. Banerjee was determined to defeat Chowdhury, who was continuously attacking and insulting her. 'We thought having a celebrity face from the Muslim community was the best path to victory,' said poll strategist Jain; Muslims made up another of the TMC's durable vote banks. The Vadodara-based Pathan had played for the Kolkata Knight Riders (KKR) in the Indian Premier League but had long retired from other formats of the game. 'I was on my way to Sri Lanka for a veterans' cricket event, when I was suddenly contacted by someone who said he was speaking from Didi and Abhishek's office and wanted to discuss the possibility of my contesting elections. My first reaction was to say a firm "no",' said Pathan. When the caller persisted, Pathan asked his brother, Irfan, also a former India star, for advice. Pathan had met the West Bengal chief minister a couple of times at KKR events. Irfan, along with a Bollywood star, persuaded an initially reluctant Pathan to take the plunge. The 'celebrity' strategy worked. Political debutant Pathan defeated the seasoned Chowdhury by more than 80,000 votes. An inclusive sporting hero on the cricket field was now a 'Muslim face' on the political pitch, and had successfully consolidated the Muslim vote behind him.

But the real battle within a battle in West Bengal in 2024 was fought in Krishnanagar. It was here, by the southern banks of the Jalangi river, that Mamata Banerjee kicked off her Bengal campaign and Prime Minister Modi took the unusual step of canvassing in the same constituency on two separate occasions. At stake was the future of the TMC's headline maker, the outspoken Mahua Moitra. Few first-time MPs have been on a dramatic roller-coaster ride like Moitra, who made an instant impact with her Parliament debut in 2019. Her impassioned maiden speech, in which she tore into the Modi government while warning of 'early signs of rising fascism', went viral on the internet. A star was born. 'Right from childhood, I have always loved to talk a lot, so oratory comes naturally to me. But I was surprised by the reaction to that speech because when even speaking the truth to power is seen as an act of courage, then you realize just how deep the fear is,' she said.

For India's left-liberal elite, the so-called 'Khan Market Gang', straining at the leash over the ascendancy of Hindutva politics, Moitra's emergence was a gust of fresh air. In a political universe where the discourse was being overwhelmingly shaped by right-wing ideologues, a well-spoken young woman offered a forceful counter-narrative. An articulate, English-speaking MP, educated at an elite American college, a former investment banker with no political family history, Moitra, with her chic saris, branded accessories and sharp intellect, was just the kind of urban sophisticate who would get under the skin of a conservative Hindu political establishment. 'I grew up on a tea estate in a typical Kolkata boxwallah family. I kept hearing that Indian politics is dirty, that you need hundreds of crores and family connections to enter politics, so I decided to take the plunge and prove the doubters wrong,' Moitra claimed.

And yet, just four years later, in December 2023, months before the 17th Lok Sabha's term ended, Moitra made front-page news, but this time for all the wrong reasons. She was expelled from Parliament, accused by an ethics committee of receiving bribes and sharing her Parliament log in and password details with a Dubai-based businessman. The line between fame and notoriety can be a thin one. A rising star suddenly found the lights abruptly turned off on her nascent parliamentary career. 'It is absolutely bizarre. The ethics committee was set up by the Lok Sabha speaker, the utterly execrable Om Birla, as a kangaroo court with a pre-decided agenda to get me out at all costs. I wasn't even allowed to cross-examine those who made these vile allegations,' fumed Moitra. In her brief tenure in Parliament, Moitra had already made several powerful enemies. She was known for targeting the Modi government repeatedly, in and outside Parliament, more specifically choosing to focus on business magnate Gautam Adani's foreign funding sources and his alleged links with the Prime Minister. She had accused BJP MP Nishikant Dubey of having faked his doctoral degree. Dubey was heckler-in-chief from the treasury benches every time Moitra spoke in Parliament. And there was no love lost between the MP and the speaker either. The duo often clashed over the Opposition being denied an equal opportunity to speak. Her critics argued that Moitra was carried away with the early adulation and was behaving like an 'attention-seeking diva'. 'If you stick to what you believe in, let people say whatever they want,' she retorted.

The chronology of Moitra's expulsion is revealing. In October 2023, Jai Anant Dehadrai, a young Delhi-based lawyer whom Moitra candidly referred to as her ex-boyfriend, rang up a few journalists, including me, to claim that he had 'explosive stuff' against a sitting TMC MP. I asked a colleague who covered the TMC beat to connect with him. But even before Dehadrai could spill the beans, Nishikant Dubey called a press conference and claimed that Moitra was guilty of receiving cash for questions. Dubey's charges would mirror those eventually made by Dehadrai, who was also engaged in a fierce custody battle with Moitra over their pet dog, a Rottweiler named Henry. Dehadrai and Dubey became the prime complainants against Moitra and were clearly acting in concert. Darshan Hiranandani, the Dubai-based businessman at the centre of the alleged 'bribes' issue, also submitted an affidavit admitting to having access to Moitra's password but, strangely enough, was not summoned to appear before the ethics committee. To add to the murky behind-the-scenes drama, Darshan's father, Niranjan Hiranandani, a leading Mumbai-based real estate magnate, was placed under the ED's scanner. 'Darshan is a friend who was forced to sign the affidavit under pressure from the Modi government. There was no cash involved; it was all a set-up carried out on behalf of Adani,' argued Moitra. Dubey maintained he was acting in 'public interest' in a 'cash for query' case. 'Her conduct was improper for an MP; she must pay a price,' he insisted.

Moitra said her 'lowest point' came in January 2024, when, having undergone a hysterectomy, she was served an eviction notice from the Estates department while still in hospital. She appealed to the Delhi High Court but to no avail. 'Here I am in bed, after a major surgery, with several stitches, and guess what, the government asks me to leave my MP house in two days. Would any MP be subject to this treatment unless the agenda was only to humiliate them?' she said.

In her darkest hour, Moitra found a staunch ally in the Bengal chief minister. Mamata Banerjee prides herself on siding with the underdog, and was enraged at the victimization of an MP elected by Bengal's voters. Launching the TMC campaign from Krishnanagar, Banerjee said, 'The BJP has targeted your MP by wrongly expelling her. Now you, the people, must restore her membership and our pride.' The 'people's court' became a recurring campaign theme in the battle between wounded Bengali pride and an imperiously hostile Delhi. Prime Minister Modi too plunged into the Krishnanagar battle. Not only did he address two meetings in the district, but he also held a video conference with the BJP candidate 'Rajmata' Amrita Roy, who traces her lineage to the royal family of the region. Where Moitra had been in the trenches of the constituency for over a decade, first as an MLA and then an MP, Roy was a political novice who was relying on Modi's appeal and the BJP machine to pull her through. 'We made many mistakes in ticket selection in Bengal; this was another one,' admitted a BJP office-bearer. An energized Moitra, with Banerjee firmly by her side, won by over 56,000 votes. 'My leader is a tigress to beat all tigresses … who can take on a dozen Modis if needed,' said the TMC MP.

Gender power is a double-edged sword in Indian politics. Patriarchal stereotypes are deep-rooted in an unequal gender battle. If a woman leader defiantly stands her ground, she is even more vulnerable to attack. As India's lone woman chief minister, Banerjee has often been a victim, targeted in shrill sexist tones like no male chief minister perhaps ever would. Moitra too was subject to an intimidating media and political trial, one where her character was called into question as much as the facts of the case. Moitra was unrepentant. 'I have absolutely no regrets. I wouldn't do any of this any other way, and I hope to inspire many others to live by a never-say-die spirit,' she said.

Moitra was one of twelve TMC women to win in 2024, the highest in terms of percentage for any party, winning 28 seats overall in West Bengal. The BJP was down to just 12 seats, far below survey predictions. 'Maybe the BJP needs to change its survey team—they keep getting Bengal wrong,' said TMC Rajya Sabha leader Derek O'Brien with a smirk. Once again, like in 2021, after projecting a big win for itself, the BJP was defeated in Bengal. Once again, the saffron army was badly served by pollsters who totally failed to read the mind of the politically alert Bengal voter. After Uttar Pradesh and Maharashtra, Bengal was another major setback for the BJP. But the surprises didn't end here. This time, even states that the BJP had swept in 2019 would prove difficult to conquer.

⸺

'I fear we are going to lose 25–0,' a senior Congressman from Rajasthan lamented in February 2024 at a meeting of party office-bearers in Delhi. Several Congress leaders at the meeting had also opted out of contesting the election themselves. The pessimistic outlook, bordering on near total surrender, was unsurprising. The BJP had swept Rajasthan's 25 seats in both 2014 and 2019 and had also just returned to power in Jaipur in the 2023 assembly polls. With the Ram temple seen as an emotive issue and with Prime Minister Modi's high ratings in the state, the BJP looked unbeatable. Amidst the despondence, one Congress leader was unwilling to give up so easily. The Rajasthan Congress president, fifty-nine-year-old

Govind Singh Dotasra, is a pugnacious leader who started his political journey as a village pradhan in the Sikar district. Often spotted wearing a traditional pink turban at public gatherings, the three-time MLA was a local Jat leader little known outside Rajasthan, until he was suddenly made the state party chief in 2020. The Congress party, split between the Ashok Gehlot and Sachin Pilot factions in the state, needed someone who could perform an effective holding operation. The blunt and rustic Dotasra had neither Pilot's erudition nor Gehlot's experience, but he did have one precious quality in politics: a tenacious attitude. 'When I heard one of my own leaders saying we would be wiped out in Rajasthan, I was incensed. Jo bhee ho, fight to dena hai. Yeh ab mooch ka sawaal hai (Whatever happens, we have to fight. This is a question of self-respect)!' he said.

In early March, Dotasra and the Congress received an unexpected boost. Rahul Kaswan, a two-time BJP MP from Churu with a sizeable following amongst the Jat community in the Shekhawati region, indicated that he was ready to jump ship and join the Congress, provided he was 'guaranteed' a Lok Sabha ticket. A young, ambitious leader, Kaswan, who was identified with the Vasundhara Raje camp in Rajasthan, was fretting over reports that the BJP would deny him a ticket for 'anti-party' activity. At the time, Kaswan was engaged in a power tussle with Rajendra Singh Rathore, a senior BJP leader who accused him of conspiring to defeat him in the assembly polls. His fellow Jat's willingness to switch sides enthused the Rajasthan Congress chief, who had a personal connection with the Kaswan family. The BJP MP was also related to Vice President Jagdeep Dhankhar and had approached him to mediate on his behalf with the top BJP leadership. Reluctant to get tangled in a state-level battle, Dhankhar reportedly told the Kaswan family, 'Keep me out of this.' On the day Kaswan was denied renomination—the final decision was taken in Delhi by Team Modi–Shah—Dotasra received a midnight knock. It was Kaswan's father, making a case for his son to be given the Congress ticket. 'At a time when everyone was leaving the Congress to join the BJP, this was just the tonic we needed to lift our morale,' said Dotasra. Within forty-eight hours, a joining ceremony was hastily organized in Delhi in the presence of Congress President Mallikarjun Kharge.

The messaging was not just about a BJP MP switching to the Congress days ahead of the Lok Sabha polls. It was also signalling to Rajasthan's influential Jat community that the Congress was now the only party with an effective home-grown Jat leadership. With the BJP having chosen a Brahmin in Bhajan Lal Sharma as their Rajasthan chief minister, the caste fault lines had widened further. 'We should have at least made a Jat our deputy chief minister; we had no Jat face in a senior government position to combat the Congress campaign,' admitted a Rajasthan BJP leader. In a caste-conscious state, the Congress had found their winning ticket.

The Jats voted overwhelmingly for the Congress across Rajasthan's Shekhawati belt. With Dalit groups also rallying behind the party on the 'Samvidhan khatre mein hai' plank and the Congress surging in the Gurjar-Meena pockets of eastern Rajasthan, the predicted wipeout was now turning in favour of the grand old party. In desperation, a senior BJP leader rang up Vasundhara Raje, hoping the former chief minister would shore up their sputtering campaign. Still seething at being passed over for the chief minister's post, Raje reportedly responded with a defiant message for the BJP leadership: 'I am now only an MLA, so I will campaign only in the Lok Sabha constituency of my son.'

In the first week of May, with polling in Rajasthan complete, an excited Dotasra rang me up. 'We will get at least 10 seats in Rajasthan; if we get even one less, I will give up politics,' he stated. I asked him if I could record his boast and use it on counting day if he was proven wrong. 'Please do, but don't forget to mention me if my numbers are right!' On 4 June, when the Congress won 11 seats in Rajasthan—a major turnaround from 2019— the state Congress chief was among the first people to call me. 'I think you should make me your pollster for Rajasthan next time,' he said, laughing. The BJP had paid the price for overconfidence and in-fighting in Rajasthan.

It wasn't just Rajasthan where the 'Jat factor' played a pivotal role. In neighbouring Haryana too, where Jats, at around 25 per cent of the population, are an even more dominant political group, the tide was gradually beginning to turn. As mentioned in previous chapters, the Jats were mobilizing in Haryana against the Modi government on a variety of issues. From the farmer agitation to protests by women wrestlers to demonstrations against the Agnipath scheme, community anger was mounting. The BJP had seized power in Haryana in 2014 on the back of a strong non-Jat caste consolidation and won all 10 seats in the 2019 Lok Sabha elections. Specifically, the Jat reservation agitation in 2016 had exploded in violence and created a sharp Jat-versus-non-Jat community divide on the ground, which the BJP had exploited politically. But after ten years in power, anti-incumbency was beginning to bite. Rising unemployment was a particular challenge. At 37.4 per cent, Haryana had the highest unemployment rate in the country in 2022 according to the Centre for Monitoring Indian Economy data. The BJP government's slogan in Haryana was 'Bina parchi, bina kharchi, naukri pakki' (Without recommendation, without bribery, employment is assured). Now, the slogan had come to haunt them amidst familiar charges of local corruption. Data discrepancies in online portals for availing government benefits had added to the long list of grievances. 'Of all the states I travelled through, the youth anger was maximum in Haryana. Many of the young are even turning to drugs in desperation, something previously unheard of in the state,' said Abhinav Pandey, a journalist with the Hindi news website Lallantop.

The BJP's chief minister in Haryana for the past decade, the seventy-year-old Manohar Lal Khattar, was a relative political lightweight. The dour and low-key Khattar had been a fellow RSS pracharak with Modi in the 1980s; the two had even shared a room for a while. 'He is personally honest and totally loyal to the Prime Minister,' remarked a BJP leader. But by early 2023, the party's surveys showed the chief minister becoming increasingly unpopular. The decision to replace Khattar was taken in principle but kept on hold for almost a year because Modi didn't want to alienate his old roommate and no one else in the party was willing to raise their voice. By the time Khattar was replaced in March 2024 by Nayab Singh Saini, an OBC face, there were just weeks to go for the general elections. 'We moved too late to effect a change in Haryana,' admitted a central BJP office-bearer.

By contrast, the Congress had sharpened up their act. A party notorious for factional battles in the state was putting up a united front; they had even agreed to give one seat to AAP, their INDIA alliance partner. Leading the charge were the Hoodas, the father–son duo who had been given almost total control of the Haryana Congress unit by the party's central leadership. A two-time former chief minister, Bhupinder Singh Hooda was part of the G-23 'rebellion' but had been mollified by the prospect of being made the face of the party in the state and his son, Deepender, being given a Rajya Sabha ticket. A seasoned politician who enjoys the occasional game of tennis at the Delhi Gymkhana and coffee at the India International Centre, Hooda is one of the few 'old guard' survivors in Rahul Gandhi's 'new' Congress. The canny Hooda knew that a strong showing in the 2024 Lok Sabha polls was the only way to boost his claims to be made chief minister once again. 'The road to Chandigarh runs through Delhi,' reiterated Deepender Hooda in every campaign speech.

When the Haryana results were declared, the Congress and BJP were locked in a neck and neck fight. Both had won 5 seats each, completely wiping out the region parties. Deepender won the Rohtak seat by 3.2 lakh votes, the highest margin in the state. A Jat–Dalit union, not too dissimilar to what was seen in Rajasthan, had propelled the Congress resurgence. Significantly, in both states, the Congress had proven that it could take on the BJP in direct fights in north India and win. In 2014 and 2019, these one-on-one contests had been wholly one-sided. For the BJP strategists, losing ground in their northern fortresses was an unimaginable prospect. In both states, flawed ticket distribution, shifting caste dynamics and an overbearing high-command culture had yet again damaged the party's chances. Pushed on the back foot, the BJP now desperately needed to discover new growth areas, including in the seemingly impenetrable deep south.

=

Here's a question: Which state did Prime Minister Modi visit the most in the first quarter of 2024 in the build-up to the Ram Mandir inauguration and then again in the run-up to the general elections?

The answer: Tamil Nadu.

From offering prayers at temples that had a Ramayana connection to invoking local cultural icons to leading glitzy roadshows, Modi made as many as seven trips to the southern state. The outreach was part of the BJP's concerted 'Mission South', aimed at increasing the party's support base and widening Modi's national acceptability. During Modi's first term, the southern states were not top of his agenda, his focus being almost entirely on consolidating gains across the Hindi heartland. But the big victory in 2019 changed the line of thinking. Secure of his dominant position north of the Vindhyas, Modi craved pan-Indian recognition.

Tamil Nadu and Kerala were the two main target states. In Kerala, the BJP was hoping to break the left-versus-Congress duopoly while wooing the Christian community. On Christmas Day in 2023, Modi met around seventy-five members from the Christian community, including clergy, educationists and influencers, at his residence, hoping to send out a 'Sabka saath' inclusive message. Former athlete Anju Bobby George and actor Dino Morea provided the 'celebrity quotient'. Among the organizers was Anil Antony, the son of A.K. Antony, a former Congress chief minister in the state. The Stanford-educated Anil had switched to the BJP in April 2023, when the party looked to project a few Christian faces in Kerala. The two-hour-long Christmas meeting over high tea was more about optics than substance. 'The PM was very polite but frankly, since it was a festive occasion, no one wanted to raise any contentious issue that would discomfit anyone,' said one attendee. 'We were all on our best behaviour.' In personal interactions, Modi can be a charmer, but breaking the ice with fearful minority groups needs more than just sharing a slice of Christmas cake.

Modi's charm offensive had a limited impact. Actor–politician Suresh Gopi became the party's first elected MP from Kerala, and the BJP's vote share rose to nearly 20 per cent in the state, but Kerala's large group of minority voters were still mistrustful of the saffron force. 'Gopi's win in Thrissur is because of his star appeal and anti-incumbency at a local level. Barring a couple of pockets, Christians by and large remained with the Congress,' said P.P. James, a senior Kochi-based journalist. Images of churches being burnt in Manipur, missionary schools being targeted in Chhattisgarh and Madhya Pradesh, and complaints of foreign funds being cut to Christian NGOs meant that the BJP could never fully overcome the trust deficit on the ground in Kerala. 'We can't expect things to change overnight, especially in a state like Kerala, where Congress and left cadres have deep roots, but we are making every effort to expand our social base,' said Anil Antony, who finished third in the Pathanamthitta constituency but received a decent 26 per cent vote share.

Tamil Nadu, one of the few states where Modi's popularity consistently lagged far behind Congress leader Rahul Gandhi's, was just as big a challenge for the BJP as Kerala was. 'When Modi ji came to Tamil Nadu earlier and was greeted by black flags and "Go back" slogans, it surely must have hurt him. He wanted to change that image desperately,' said G.C. Shekhar, a Chennai-based journalist.

The signs were there even a year ahead of the 2024 general elections, when, during the inauguration of the new Parliament building in May 2023, Modi opted for a Tamil cultural symbol as the defining image of the moment. Like with all Modi-led events, the inauguration was a well-choreographed exercise, planned weeks in advance. The 'adheenam' priests from different maths were flown in together on a plane specially chartered by the Centre and were guests of honour at the function. Photos and TV grabs of the Prime Minister being blessed by the saffron-robed priests and being presented with the Sengol, a sacred sceptre associated with Tamil kingdoms of the past, were splashed all over the media. A historical artefact from Tamil Nadu finding pride of place next to the Lok Sabha speaker's chair in the newly constructed Parliament—the symbolism was significant. Typically, the government gave its own twist to the Sengol tale, when it claimed that the sceptre was originally handed over to Jawaharlal Nehru on 14 August 1947 as a symbol of the transfer of power by the British to India but then was tucked away in a Nehru museum in Allahabad. Whether the Sengol was just a gift to Nehru or actually represented the moment of freedom at midnight is disputed by historians and the DMK–Congress Opposition. What is not in doubt is

Modi's attempt, as is his wont, to use the occasion for focused political benefit. As far as Modi was concerned, the Sengol was only an instrument to spread the Prime Minister's aura in Tamil Nadu, a big stick to wave over the heads of Tamil Nadu's voters, as if to say, 'Vote for me because I have brought your cultural symbol to Parliament.' 'The DMK–Congress objections to the Sengol only helped us; it gave us another talking point in Tamil Nadu,' emphasized a BJP office-bearer.

To make an impact in Tamil Nadu has been an unfulfilled BJP goal for decades. In a state defined by fiercely combative and well-organized Dravidian regional parties that are identified with a legacy of social justice movements, the BJP was typecast as a Brahminical Hindi-speaking, Hindutva-following 'outsider' from the Gangetic heartland. Interestingly, while the BJP remained diminished across the state, the Sangh Parivar, through affiliates like Hindu Munnani, was growing in pockets like Kanyakumari. In December 2022, the Modi government launched a month-long Kashi Sangamam in Varanasi, designed 'to promote historical and civilizational bonds between north and south India'. Several thousand people from Tamil Nadu were taken on a pilgrimage to Varanasi and Ayodhya, with the RSS playing a key behind-the-scenes role in the effort. 'We have always been deeply involved in Tamil Nadu society in religious and cultural events,' said an RSS leader. However, while the Sangh Parivar had karyakartas on the ground in Tamil Nadu, there was no effective leadership face. Ahead of the 2019 elections, the BJP made repeated efforts through intermediaries to get cinema superstar Rajinikanth to lead the charge. 'We came close on many occasions, but he kept backing away at the last moment,' claimed a Tamil Nadu BJP leader. Now, in 2024, the BJP was confident that they had found a future leader in Kuppusamy Annamalai, the aggressive, youthful, forty-year-old police-officer-turned-politician. Annamalai's rapid political ascent doesn't fit into any conventional mould. An engineer by training, he went to IIM, Lucknow, before joining the IPS cadre in Karnataka. Earning a reputation as a tough, no-nonsense officer, he eventually decided to quit the service because he felt constrained by 'rules' and 'protocol'. He resigned in

2019, when he was deputy commissioner of police in Bengaluru South. 'I wanted to do something meaningful for society, so I initially just took nine months off and helped set up an NGO—We The Leaders—in Coimbatore, to work with youth on various issues like skilling, rural rejuvenation and organic farming,' he said.

It is not clear whether the RSS–BJP 'discovered' Annamalai in this period or if he made the first move towards the Sangh Parivar. What is apparent is that the Sangh was looking for new leadership in Tamil Nadu and an ambitious Annamalai was the perfect fit. 'I was impressed by Narendra Modi ji's commitment to nation-building. For me, Hindutva is, above all else, about "Nation First",' he claimed. When he was appointed the Tamil Nadu BJP chief in 2021, Modi's mandate to him was to be a 'disruptor', to shake up the system by positioning the party as a national alternative to Dravidian politics.

It wasn't an easy ride. In 2021, Annamalai had contested the Tamil Nadu assembly elections and lost by a sizeable margin to the DMK candidate. Undeterred, in 2023, as a build-up to the general elections, Annamalai embarked on a statewide padyatra, during which he lashed out against corruption and the dynastical rule of both the ruling DMK and the opposing AIADMK, becoming an instant headline-grabber in Tamil Nadu's entrenched Dravidian politics. When DMK leader Udhayanidhi Stalin attacked 'sanatan dharma' and called for its 'eradication', likening it to malaria and HIV, Annamalai led the protests against these remarks. In the age of social media, his hard-hitting sound bites made him a digital sensation—every video of his went viral. For someone who had never won an election and whose party was an also-ran in Tamil Nadu, Annamalai was burning up the internet. 'I guess it's because I am a bit of a non-conformist politician who calls a spade a spade. I don't hold back, because I don't believe in political correctness like so many others,' asserted Annamalai. Fresh-faced and energetic, he is just the kind of media-friendly leader the Modi-led BJP hankers after. 'He was our "Singham", a young man who brought us the attention we were craving,' remarked a Tamil Nadu BJP office-bearer.

But headline-grabbing is very different from vote-catching. Despite his 2021 loss, in 2024 Annamalai was back in the electoral fray, this time contesting from Coimbatore, a constituency that the BJP was eyeing as potentially winnable. The original plan was for a statewide tie-up with the AIADMK, a party still struggling to recover from the demise of its stalwart leader J. Jayalalithaa in 2016. Backroom negotiations had begun between the two sides, but a self-assured Annamalai managed to convince Modi not to go ahead with it. 'Unless we fight on our own, how will we grow?' he contended. The state unit was keen on an alliance, but as their youthful leader who had Modi's ear was calling the shots, they didn't push for it beyond a point. The big spike in ratings for the party and Prime Minister in the BJP's poll surveys in March–April convinced the leadership that a 'historic' breakthrough was possible. Extra resources were pumped in to amplify the campaign. The Prime Minister even made it a point to pay homage to the victims of the 1998 serial blasts in the city, which were allegedly carried out by Al Umma, a local Islamist group, and claimed the lives of fifty-eight people. Later, when a visibly enthused Modi gave his first interview on the 2024 campaign trail to the Tamil channel Thanthi TV, wearing a veshti, the traditional Tamil attire, he began with a few words in Tamil before switching to Hindi, but kept reiterating his great love for the Tamil people throughout. 'After that interview and a Modi roadshow in Coimbatore, our surveys actually suggested that we could get 4–5 seats and more than 20 per cent vote share,' claimed a BJP poll strategist.

As in West Bengal, the Tamil Nadu surveys too would prove terribly misleading. Coimbatore, like the rest of the state, was never going to be an easy ride. Both the DMK and AIADMK have a strong organization in and around the industrial town. The communists too are influential; the CPI(M) candidate had won the seat in 2019. 'Modi was trying to revive the ghosts of 1998, but the fact is that people have moved on. Post-Covid Coimbatore needs to revive its small-scale industrial units, not play Hindu–Muslim politics,' said M. Raghu, who runs a micro enterprise in the city. When quizzed, Annamalai denied the charge of invoking past communal scars. 'We are talking of zero tolerance for terror; no one can have an issue with that, surely,' he responded.

What the DMK leadership did have an issue with is Annamalai's strident and repeated attacks on Dravidian politics. 'He speaks a language of arrogance that no self-respecting Tamilian will appreciate. He is disrespecting our icons, from Periyar to Annadurai to Karunanidhi; who will engage with him?' argued T.R.B. Rajaa, the DMK minister who was the party's Coimbatore in-charge. In what had become a prestige fight, the DMK and its INDIA alliance members pulled out all the stops to ensure victory. The concentrated effort worked. The DMK won Coimbatore, its candidate Ganapathy P. Rajkumar defeating Annamalai by over 1.18 lakh votes. Though Annamalai polled a substantial 4.5 lakh votes, it wasn't nearly enough. The BJP's much-anticipated breakthrough in Tamil Nadu also did not materialize. The DMK-led alliance, with Chief Minister M.K. Stalin leading the charge despite his indifferent health, swept all 39 seats, proving that the party's formidable cadre-based machine was intact and that the vote transfer between allies was near perfect. Annamalai, though, wasn't entirely despondent. 'This is the first time our vote share is in the double digits; it is a platform for us to build on for the future. One thing is certain, we are no longer a party of "outsiders" or of north India only,' he asserted.

What the future holds is uncertain, but in 2024 at least, Modi's Tamil Nadu campaign was built more on hype than reality. The southern state, with its distinctive political culture, remained resistant to the BJP's Hindutva ideology. The mighty Dravidian vote bank stood firm against the visitors from the north. Surprisingly, instead of Chennai, the winds of change were blowing in the BJP's favour in a less talked about region.

=

A 24/7 news cycle is unyielding, which means a television journalist can never switch off. In early March 2024, I was on my morning walk, relishing the all-too-rare crisp spring air in the national capital, when my mobile phone began ringing. It was the office asking me for a 'live' reaction.

'There is major breaking news: the BJP tie-up with the Biju Janata Dal [BJD] in Odisha is done!' exclaimed the voice from the news assignment desk. In a T-shirt and track pants, I reluctantly agreed to come on air, abandoning all thoughts of my morning exercise. Within an hour or so, as the news was still being flashed, I got a call from Sunil Bansal, the BJP's national general secretary, whose multiple assignments included election-in-charge for Odisha. 'This is wrong news; we have not entered into any alliance,' he insisted. A smart backroom nuts-and-bolts organizer and an Amit Shah loyalist, Bansal had moved from Uttar Pradesh to handle the party's east coast expansion. Any news break from him was usually spot on. Just forty-eight hours later, both the BJP and the BJD formally announced that they would fight the 2024 elections separately. It was a choice that would dramatically change the final national election picture.

So why was the 'almost' finalized tie-up suddenly dumped? After speaking to multiple sources in Delhi and Bhubaneswar, it is apparent that this alliance was being worked on at the highest level between the principal stakeholders, Prime Minister Modi and then Odisha Chief Minister Naveen Patnaik. Over the years, the two had built what one senior bureaucrat described as a 'personal bond of friendship': Patnaik, after all, was one of the longest-serving chief ministers in the country and Modi had now been in office, first in Gujarat and then at the Centre, for over two decades. 'I think the reason Modi liked Naveen babu is that he was not a threat to him in any way. Modi can't deal with chief ministers whom he feels threatened by,' said the bureaucrat. Which is why when Patnaik first raised the possibility of an election tie-up in late 2023, Modi did not baulk. Odisha chief minister since 2000, Patnaik, at seventy-seven, was keeping poor health and was keen to avoid another tough election battle. Modi too was keen to shore up his 'team' to counter the Opposition's INDIA alliance. It seemed a win-win for both. On 5 March, Modi attended an event celebrating the 108th birth anniversary of Biju Patnaik, Naveen's father and a swashbuckling grand figure in Odisha's politics. The event was held in Odisha's Jajpur, where Modi shared the stage with Naveen Patnaik. Both leaders lavished praise on each other, the Prime Minister referring to Patnaik as the 'lokpriya' (popular) chief minister of Odisha. As he was leaving, he whispered to Patnaik, 'Don't worry, jaldi kar denge (We will do it soon).' The tie-up had been green-lit by Modi and now bore the all-important imprimatur of the BJP's supremo.

What it didn't have, however, was the approval of the state BJP unit or the RSS, which exercised considerable clout in Odisha, especially in the tribal belt. The state BJP president, Manmohan Samal, in particular, was completely against the alliance. 'It will demoralize our cadres who have worked so hard in the last ten years to make us a fighting force in Odisha,' he wrote in a missive to the central leadership. The clincher came when, in the second week of March, the BJP's internal tracker survey showed the party not only moving ahead of the BJD in the Lok Sabha polls but also catching up in the Vidhan Sabha battle. (Simultaneous polls were to take place in Odisha for the assembly and Lok Sabha.) And while the BJP's surveyors would get states like Uttar Pradesh, Bengal and Tamil Nadu badly wrong, here they would be spot on. When Home Minister Shah received the survey feedback, he met the Prime Minister and suggested they rethink the alliance. Modi's initial response, reportedly, was, 'But I have given my word to Naveen babu.' Shah proposed a post-poll deal if required, and after some persuasion, Modi agreed to ditch a potential pre-poll ally. Modi's decision was proof of what many admirers consider his flexibility and what critics call his devious shiftiness. At crunch time, Modi puts victory above all else. While his admirers praise this as realpolitik, his critics see it as amoral politics in which there are no permanent friendships, only permanent interests.

Closely observing the unexpected shift in stance was V. Karthikeyan Pandian, widely regarded as the de facto chief minister of Odisha. A 2000-batch IAS officer, Pandian had worked in the chief minister's office for thirteen years and was Patnaik's constant shadow, following him everywhere. He was a keen advocate of an alliance with the BJP, which he felt was a win-win for both parties, and had been rushing between Delhi and Bhubaneswar to seal the deal. 'Naveen babu trusts him fully. This is not a usual neta–babu equation but a deeper relationship, like father and son,' said a former Odisha cadre officer. In November 2023, Pandian's special equation was formalized: he officially joined the BJD by touching Patnaik's feet at his residence, Naveen Niwas, in Bhubaneswar. With an ageing chief minister scarcely visible or accessible, Pandian was now regarded as the heir apparent, a growing perception that would come to haunt the BJD at election time. 'My joining the BJD was an emotional decision out of my love and affection for Naveen babu. I just wanted to reduce some of the burden on him in the belief that we still enjoyed the goodwill of the Odia people,' he said.

Pandian's conviction would prove to be misplaced. During his two decades in power, Patnaik and his team of bureaucrats led by the untiring Pandian had done some stellar work in boosting the development record of one of India's poorer states. From cyclone management to universal health initiatives, from women's self-help groups to world-class sports infrastructure, Odisha was taking rapid strides forward. Today Bhubaneswar is a city transformed, its wide roads, neat parks and modern shopfronts an example of Naveen Patnaik's commitment to efficient governance. But a strong development record doesn't always translate into guaranteed votes, especially not after two decades in power. Anti-incumbency, more likely fatigue, was gradually settling in. Even more crucially, Pandian's domineering presence now loomed large over the state's politics. A Tamil-born officer leading the BJD's campaign was seen as a slight to Odia pride. Rather swiftly, Pandian's Tamil identity and future role became the single biggest issue in the elections, his claims of being 'an Indian by birth and Odia by breath' notwithstanding. A slogan was now echoing in Odisha's towns and villages, one which mirrored a creeping public disquiet: 'Ame jadi vote deba Naveen ku, vote jiba Pandian ku (If we vote for Naveen, the vote will go to Pandian).' 'I think Pandian made the crucial mistake of taking centre stage at all party rallies. Had he stayed in the background, maybe nothing would have changed,' said Jajati Karan, editor of Ommcom News, an Odia news website. Pandian's unpopularity as a political figure became the BJD's Achilles heel.

The BJP sensed their breakthrough moment and were quick to seize it. As expected, the party targeted Pandian incessantly, but even Patnaik was not spared by an unrelenting BJP leadership. As the campaign heated up, the Modi–Patnaik bonhomie quickly became a thing of the past. At one rally, Modi dared the Odisha chief minister to name all the districts of the state, virtually challenging his knowledge of his home state. At another, the Prime Minister harped on Patnaik's health condition, wondering why his hand shook all the time and whether there was a 'conspiracy behind it'. A video of Patnaik's trembling hands being held up by Pandian was shared by BJP handles across social media. The chief minister issued a strong rebuttal: 'The Prime Minister says he is my good friend. All he had to do was pick up the telephone and ring me up about my health.' On the campaign trail, Team Modi–Shah have no friends. Unfeeling, coarse, rude, brazen, unabashed and willing to stoop to the lowest possible denominator, they are focused only on maximizing votes. Personal relationships have no place in their power playbook.

For Patnaik and the BJD, it was too late to make up lost ground. The BJP had taken control of the 'Odisha for Odias' narrative. Even so, the final results were a stunner. Not only did the BJP win 20 out of 21 seats in the Lok Sabha, but it also scored an impressive win in the Vidhan Sabha, winning 78 out of 147 seats. Even the BJP leadership was astounded by the scale of the triumph. Chastened by the verdict, Pandian announced that he was quitting politics. 'My only regret is that we were not able to counter the false propaganda of the BJP; we were simply too decent to hit the BJP below the belt like they did to us,' he remarked. At a time when the saffron army was losing steam in some of its original bastions, Odisha came to the BJP's rescue. It was the state's 20-seat bonanza that helped secure a third term as Prime Minister for the man from Gujarat. Not surprisingly, when Modi entered the NDA parliamentary party meeting after the elections to be formally confirmed as Prime Minister, the Central Hall echoed with chants of 'Jai Jagannath', not 'Jai Shri Ram'. The Prime Minister too opened his address with Jai Jagannath. Odisha's deeply revered god had helped Modi survive where other divinities had failed him.

=

Politics can be cruel to those out of power. In August 2023, Chandrababu Naidu invited senior journalists to a luncheon meeting in Delhi. Very few journalists turned up, even though preparations had been made for several dozen people to enjoy a lavish and delicious Andhra meal. Naidu was out of power and hardly a newsmaker at the time. Dressed in his trademark cream-coloured long-sleeved shirt, the former Andhra Pradesh chief minister appeared a trifle despondent. He was visiting the national capital to meet Home Minister Amit Shah and discuss a possible partnership between the TDP and the BJP for the 2024 elections. Shah kept him waiting for two days before finally granting an appointment but refused to commit to an alliance. 'Let the Telangana elections get over, then we can talk,' he said vaguely. The Telangana elections were scheduled for November, still three months away.

Just weeks after his brief Delhi stay, the Andhra leader made headlines. Naidu was arrested by the Andhra police on 9 September at 3 a.m. in a pre-dawn swoop while asleep in a bus in Nandyal, where he was camping as part of his pre-election campaign. He was accused of allegedly being involved in a scam that had reportedly taken place when he was chief minister in 2014. The timing and manner of Naidu's arrest brought back memories of former Tamil Nadu chief minister M. Karunanidhi being dragged out of his bed at 2 a.m. and arrested by the local police in 2001. At the time, AIADMK leader J. Jayalalithaa was accused of executing a vendetta; in 2023 it was the YSRCP leader and then Andhra Chief Minister Jagan Mohan Reddy who came under the lens for playing revenge politics. While Karunanidhi's political fortunes took a few years to recover, the seventy-four-year-old Naidu capitalized on events during the 2024 assembly and Lok Sabha elections and made an instant comeback. 'Arresting a senior leader in this manner was the biggest mistake Jagan could have made. Public sympathy swung entirely towards Naidu,' said Krishna Rao, a senior Andhra journalist.

The tracker poll findings bear this out. Till mid-September, Reddy was well ahead of his TDP counterpart in a weekly poll that was being conducted by his team. Just four weeks later, Naidu had edged ahead, a lead that would only grow in the ensuing months. The overnight decision to arrest his rival was typical of Reddy's autocratic style of functioning. He could be whimsical and pig-headed, refusing to listen to the advice of even his well-wishers at times. 'We tried to reach out to him, but he just wouldn't listen,' said a former YSRCP leader, now with the TDP. An obdurate Reddy was somehow convinced that Naidu had conspired with the Congress to put him in jail in 2012 for sixteen months. This was 'revenge'. A battle-weary Naidu spent fifty-three days in jail, during which his health took a turn for the worse. In his first week in prison, he was met by Pawan Kalyan, the popular actor and Jana Sena chief. Emerging from the meeting, Kalyan instantly announced a tie-up with the TDP for the Andhra elections. 'I was angry and moved by Naidu ji's plight. On the spur of the moment, I took the alliance decision. Enough is enough,' said the actor–politician.

Naidu was released to a rapturous welcome. The mood in Andhra Pradesh had decisively shifted in one direction. In early December, when Naidu was back in Delhi, there was a noticeable spring in his step. The BJP leadership had reportedly agreed to his alliance offer in principle, although a formal announcement was kept pending. The 17th Lok Sabha was still on, and the BJP needed the YSRCP's support to pass crucial legislation in the Rajya Sabha. True to form, Team Modi–Shah continued to practise their transactional, conniving and 'use and throw' brand of politics and alliance-building. (When Jagan Mohan Reddy would come to Delhi in July 2024 to protest against attacks on his party workers, neither the Prime Minister nor the home minister would give him an appointment. With just four Lok Sabha MPs, Reddy no longer mattered.)

There is another reason why this pact was finally sealed only in March 2024, days before the general elections were announced. Prime

Minister Modi and Chandrababu Naidu had had an on-off relationship through the years. In the aftermath of the 2002 Gujarat violence, the Andhra leader, then an ally of Vajpayee's NDA government, had called for Modi's resignation. After allying with the Modi-led BJP government, he had broken away in 2018, accusing the Prime Minister of betraying a promise of 'special status' for a divided Andhra. He even went so far as to call Modi a 'terrorist' at the time. When I asked him about the terrorist comment on the 2024 campaign trail, his aides requested it be deleted from the interview. So while Naidu was a useful ally for the BJP, which desperately wanted as many allies as possible to achieve its 'char sau paar' target, Modi hadn't forgotten the TDP leader's previous slights. The BJP's Big Boss has a long memory and is accused by his critics of a streak of vengefulness. Keeping Naidu waiting for a while was a gentle reminder of who was in charge.

Yet on the 2024 campaign trail, Modi was strategically warm and charming to his foe-turned-friend. At the new alliance's first 'Prajagalam' (voice of the people) joint rally, Modi and Naidu showered praise on each other. When Naidu passed on a chit of paper with a few suggestions for potential talking points, Modi instantly nodded in agreement and shook his hand firmly. A deal had been signed—now it was time to deliver the votes. Riding on the anti-incumbency wave against the Reddy government, the alliance swept both the Lok Sabha and Vidhan Sabha polls, winning 21 of the 25 seats. On the back of its Odisha success, the Andhra Pradesh victory was just about enough to ensure an NDA majority. The BJP itself had fallen well short of the 272 mark with 240 seats, but at least the alliance had weathered the storm.

Addressing his adoring supporters on verdict day, Modi kept referring to 2024 being the people's mandate for an NDA government, not a BJP-ruled one, for a third time. No speaker even mentioned 'char sau paar' in their less-than-euphoric speeches. Days later, when the NDA parliamentary party met, Modi was Prime Minister-elect once again, only this time he was sharing podium space with Naidu and Bihar Chief Minister Nitish Kumar. The 'N' factor—Nitish and Naidu—would now decide the fate of Modi 3.0. The once-dominating supremo who had dwarfed all others with his aura of invincibility and seeming permanence had been cut to size and was now dependent on those who had once repudiated him.

Intriguingly, I received a special invite for Modi's swearing-in ceremony at Rashtrapati Bhavan's forecourt. I normally stay away from official events—they tend to be deathly boring—but this time I saw this as an opportunity to observe the changing power axis from up close. To my surprise, I was seated in one of the front rows with New Delhi's 'new' political elite, including Naidu. Truly, 'hawa badal gayi thi'! India had boosted the opposition to Modi and voted for a coalition, for a government that would reflect the unique diversity of the nation. The voter had chosen many new MP faces, some of them real giant-killers, all of whom symbolized a renewal of hope in democratic pluralism. It is to those stories of hope and courage that we now turn.

THIRTEEN

'Democracy Zinda Hai': Stories of Hope

'Ai, babu, ye public hai public
Ye jo public hai ye sab jaanti hai …
Aji andar kya hai,
Aji bahar kya hai …
Ye sab kuch pehchanti hai'
(Roti, 1974)

THE Amethi headquarters of the Congress party mirrored the rickety condition of the grand old party in Uttar Pradesh. It's a rundown structure, with paint peeling off the walls, a few pieces of wobbly, dusty furniture strewn around and an open drain overflowing nearby. When I arrived on a warm summer evening in May 2024, I found a handful of Congress workers loitering about, arguing over cups of sugary tea, their voices rising with the soaring temperature. The power supply being erratic, an electrician had been summoned to check the generator. Sitting in a small room, the walls lined with sepia-tinted pictures of the Gandhi family, one man appeared strangely unfussed by the noise around him. The pint-sized sixty-three-year-old Kishori Lal Sharma resembles the perpetually bewildered 'common man' immortalized by R.K. Laxman. Not even twenty-four hours had passed since Sharma was given the biggest surprise of his political life: he had been named the Congress candidate from Amethi.

'When Kharge ji first rang me up and informed me that I had been chosen as the party nominee from Amethi, I thought someone was cracking a joke. Then, when Mrs Gandhi, Priyanka ji and Rahul ji rang up to congratulate me, I realized what had just happened. I am truly obliged to all of them; they are and always will be my leaders,' he said, a gentle smile peeping through his walrus moustache. For forty years, Sharma, originally from Ludhiana, had parked himself in Amethi, the Gandhi bastion in central Uttar Pradesh. From Rajiv Gandhi to Sonia Gandhi and now their children, he has always been a loyal follower of the family, and a permanent fixture in this small ramshackle town. 'Whether there is a marriage celebration or a death ceremony, be sure Kishori Lal will be there. He knows most people by their first name,' claimed a local Congress activist.

The quintessential backroom operator was now being pushed into a frontal role. Sharma admitted to being uncomfortable with the sudden media attention. 'I have never done an interview like this. I really don't know what to say,' he warned. But under the unassuming exterior there is a sharp political mind. Just before the interview began, he quickly put on his spotless white Gandhi topi and made sure that a Gandhi family portrait was suitably positioned in the backdrop. 'I am only where I am because of them,' he reiterated. Sharma's deferential attitude attracted BJP derision. Questioning his candidature from the high-profile Amethi seat, the BJP's nominee from the neighbouring Raebareli constituency disdainfully referred to him as a 'peon' and Priyanka Gandhi Vadra's 'clerk'.

Sharma's opponent in Amethi was the formidable Union minister and TV-star-turned-politician Smriti Irani, in many ways his polar opposite. Just five years earlier, in 2019, Irani had pulled off one of the biggest shock wins in Indian electoral history by defeating Rahul Gandhi by

55,000 votes. It was a victory that made her a national figure. A tireless go-getter, the ambitious Irani has all the attributes required to succeed in contemporary politics: she's energetic, telegenic, a fluent communicator and proficient in half a dozen languages. Having purchased a home in Amethi, she had been visiting the constituency at least once every month and claimed to be fully invested in its development. Rahul Gandhi, by contrast, had mostly been missing from Amethi since his 2019 loss, accused by the BJP of 'running away' from the area. 'I am not a member of any privileged dynasty that treats Amethi as a tourist spot; let my work for the people speak for itself,' proclaimed the star minister. Acerbic attacks on the Gandhi family were Irani's calling card. Fiery slurs against the Gandhis made her such an appealing figure for the BJP's rank and file. A spirited campaigner, Irani was criss-crossing Amethi's dirt tracks in a cavalcade of SUVs, her supporters raising familiar 'Bharat Mata ki jai' and 'Modi zindabad' slogans. The minister was banking on the BJP's well-oiled election machine to pull her through. Networks of village pradhans, deeply embedded in their local communities, were now all with the party. On the last day of the campaign, Home Minister Amit Shah led a noisy 'band baaja' roadshow through Amethi. This was then the archetypal battle between a faceless karyakarta and a larger-than-life shining star neta. On the face of it, this should have been a no-contest for the BJP.

The daunting presence of Irani made Amethi a prestige fight for the Gandhis. Till the last day of nominations, it was widely expected that Rahul Gandhi would contest from Amethi in addition to his more assured Kerala seat of Wayanad. This was billed as a sequel to the 2019 battle, an opportunity for him to settle the score as it were. Congress President Kharge said he had 'requested' Rahul Gandhi to contest from Amethi. 'I am very keen that Rahul ji fight from Amethi and Priyanka ji fight from Raebareli. That would really enthuse our cadres,' he claimed. The Gandhis, though, had other plans. At the last moment, Rahul was pitched as the Congress candidate from Raebareli, the other relatively safer 'family seat', while sister Priyanka opted out altogether. 'Why should we give Smriti Irani any importance?' asked Uttar Pradesh Congress leader

Pramod Tiwari. 'The Gandhis are national leaders who don't need to be confined to Amethi.'

Priyanka's role remained enigmatic: immersed in the hurly-burly of electoral politics as the star campaigner and yet staying away from contesting herself. Her brother's defeat in 2019 had stung her. She had taken it as a personal loss. Priyanka recalled a gloomy post-defeat journey back from Amethi, Sharma by her side. He was upset, almost tearful. 'Agli baar aisa nahi hone denge. Smriti Irani ko harayenge. Rahul bhaiya ko bhaari bahumat se jitayenge (We won't let this happen next time. We will defeat Smriti and ensure Rahul wins big),' he vowed. 'Nahi, agli baar Smriti Irani ko aap harayenge (No, next time you will defeat Smriti Irani)!' Priyanka replied. Sharma was perplexed as Priyanka explained: 'Agla chunav Amethi se aap ladenge, aur mera vaada hai: aap Smriti Irani ko harayenge (You will fight the next election from Amethi, and I promise: you will defeat Smriti Irani).' This was a revelation: the decision to field Sharma from Amethi was apparently taken in 2019 itself.

The Gandhi sister was on an avenging mission. Kishori Lal Sharma was the face on the ticket; Priyanka Vadra was the crowd-puller. She knew the area well, having first worked on her mother's Amethi campaign way back in 1999. Her assistant Sandeep Singh was also from the region. Together they planned a village-by-village interaction programme. A dozen meetings were scheduled every day across Amethi and Raebareli. On one occasion, during a power cut, she set aside the mic and addressed the crowd from the top of a jeep in an increasingly hoarse voice. Priyanka is an excellent campaigner, who easily struck a chord with Amethi's electorate. One emotional speech in which she invoked childhood memories of visiting Amethi with her father went viral.

An overconfident Irani, by contrast, faced one major impediment. There was a widely held perception that she was far too arrogant and inaccessible to those outside her charmed circle. Any trace of 'ahankar' (arrogance) can be a major hindrance at election time. Local journalists said they 'feared' approaching her. 'If we ask her any question that she doesn't like, she can be very rude to us,' claimed one. A section of the local BJP leadership too was indifferent towards her because of her condescending attitude towards some of them. Former MP Sanjay Singh, from the royal family of Amethi, stayed away from the campaign, still smarting from his defeat in the 2022 assembly elections. 'Woh badi neta hai, but hamara bhee samman rakhna chahiye (She is a big leader, but she should be respectful towards everyone),' complained a BJP district official. A coterie of local BJP leaders, including a certain Rajesh 'Masala', who ran a lucrative spice business from Amethi, were allegedly Irani's favoured few.

In Amethi's main market, 'mehngai' is always a topic of animated conversation. In her 2019 campaign, Irani had promised to make sugar available at Rs 13 per kilogram. Now, Congress workers were reminding voters of her broken promise by selling sugar at every street corner at a discounted price! Many locals admitted to being disappointed that Rahul 'bhaiya' wasn't in the fray. Amethi, after all, has been indelibly associated with the Congress's first family. 'If it were not for the Gandhis, who would even know of Amethi?' observed an elderly shopkeeper. There was almost a sense of regret among Congress voters about not having done enough to prevent Rahul bhaiya's defeat in 2019, a loss widely attributed to the 'Modi wave'. 'Iss baar koi lehar nahi hai; iss baar janata chunav lad rahi hai (This time there is no wave; this time the public is fighting the election),' insisted Raju, an unemployed graduate who was desperately in search of a government job and was eking out a living as a sugar cane juice seller. 'If Kishori Lal wins, you must interview me from your studio,' he pleaded.

On counting day, as the results began to trickle in, I kept an eye out for Amethi. The early trends showed Sharma in the lead. Could he really be pulling it off, I wondered. By noon, it was apparent that Sharma was moving ahead of Irani in the big fight, finally winning by a handsome margin of 1.67 lakh votes. When his victory was confirmed, I rang him up to join us for a live interview. 'Congratulations, you are now a giant-killer,' I reminded him. He unhesitatingly agreed this time, adding, 'When I come to Delhi, you must have dinner with me and my family. We can have butter chicken and naan together!' I couldn't connect with Raju to keep my promise of a studio appearance, but I visualized him selling extra glasses of sugar cane juice in a not-so-quiet celebration.

Pride goes before a fall, as the saying goes. Amethi revealed the limits of hubris and charisma in politics. Irani's imperious manner was in sharp contrast to Sharma's self-effacing nature. The same voters who had been carried away by the Modi wave of 2019 were now talking of 'badlaav' or change. The differences between them were stark: Sharma, soft-spoken, camera-shy, rooted son of the soil versus Irani, a flamboyant expert at sound bites and speeches, oozing celebrity razzle-dazzle and a high-flyer from Delhi. Sharma had none of Irani's captivating traits as a 'star' politician, but he did possess a precious, often underestimated winning quality: humility. When he went to meet the Gandhi family after his victory, he was given only one piece of advice. 'Jaise ho waise raho. Ghamand nahi karna hai ki aap MP ho gaye ho (Stay humble as you are. Don't be arrogant about being an MP).' His rivals may have ridiculed him as a 'family clerk' in television debates, but to the voters, Sharma was recognized as the friendly, reachable neighbour next door. And at election time, voters' perceptions matter more than idle studio chatter.

⸗

The rugged granite hills of Ramanagara, 45 kilometres outside Bengaluru, are part of Hindi cinema folklore. The panoramic landscape was the backdrop for *Sholay*, the 1970s blockbuster, its rocky terrain invoking memories of the infamous Gabbar Singh, the villainous dacoit on celluloid who became a household name for an entire generation of Indians. In 2024, the election battle in this sprawling rural Bengaluru constituency was not unlike a film script: a clash between hardened political toughies and a renowned doctor making his political debut.

The sitting MP was D.K. Suresh, the only Congress MP to win in the wake of a Modi-led BJP wave across Karnataka in 2019. Suresh is one half of Karnataka's all-powerful sibling duo: his brother, D.K. Shivakumar, is deputy chief minister and arguably one of the most resourceful politicians in the country. In 2023, the imposing Shivakumar, better known by his initials—DK, declared assets worth Rs 1,413 crore, officially making him the richest MLA in the country. DK's business interests vary from real estate to education to mining. 'By birth I am an agriculturalist, by profession I am a businessman, by choice I am an educationist, by passion I am a politician,' he said with his characteristic swagger.

The broad-shouldered Suresh, the lesser-known DK, isn't into punchy one-liners but is no less controversial. In February 2024, he stirred up a north–south divide. Accusing the Centre of diverting funds meant for the south to the Hindi heartland, Suresh warned: 'There is no other choice but to ask for a "separate country" as a result of the situation that the Hindi region has imposed on the rest of the country.' These were the kind of divisive, playing-to-the-gallery remarks that Suresh's election rival in rural Bengaluru, Dr C.N. Manjunath, would never make. Dr Manjunath, a celebrated cardiologist, had built one of the country's best heart centres in the Bengaluru Rural constituency, driven by the motto of 'treatment first, payment later'. His connection to politics is through marriage: he is the son-in-law of former Prime Minister and JD(S) supremo H.D. Deve Gowda. The BJP's decision to tie up with the JD(S) opened an election door for him. 'I am a doctor first and last; entering politics is only another way to serve the public,' he said about contesting on a BJP ticket with JD(S) support. Where the rough-edged Suresh was seen busily barking instructions to his supporters, looking every inch the practised politician, the soft-spoken Dr Manjunath in his jacket and tie appeared far removed from the campaign cacophony.

During the campaign, Shivakumar made headlines for the wrong reasons. In a viral video, he was seen warning the residents of an apartment complex not to expect occupancy certificates and regular water supply from the Cauvery unless they voted for his brother. Bengaluru Rural was in the midst of a serious drinking water crisis and the remarks were seen as 'blackmail' tactics. 'Arre, I was only joking,' clarified Shivakumar. 'I am assuring people that they will get water before the elections.' Yet his words struck the wrong note and made voters uncomfortable.

Politics in Karnataka is transactional, as it is increasingly across the country. In 2023, the Congress's 'guarantees' of welfare benefits for the poor had played a major role in an assembly election triumph. This time, both candidates were making a slew of promises but were also reportedly spending a lot of money on their campaigns. 'I know of cases where voters were offered Rs 2,000, even up to Rs 5,000 for their vote. You can't win an election in Karnataka unless you have at least 50 crore in the kitty to spend,' informed a senior journalist.

Money power is aligned to entrenched caste equations. Both Suresh and Dr Manjunath belong to the dominant Vokkaligas, a numerically strong land-owning caste across south Karnataka. For decades, Deve Gowda had been the tallest leader of the Vokkaligas, until the DK brothers challenged his supremacy and made Bengaluru Rural their citadel. Dr Manjunath brought a new dimension into the political caste calculus: a doctor with a stellar track record of medical service attracted voters across the caste divide. But Suresh was supremely confident. 'He may have done good work in medicine, but I know every nook and corner of this area. I will win by at least 3 lakh votes,' he insisted.

The three-time MP and political strongman was in for a surprise: he lost by over 2.6 lakh votes. The benefit of a BJP symbol, his father-in-law's caste base, a ground alliance of Vokkaliga and Lingayat voters, and his own personal goodwill and clean image all contributed to Dr Manjunath's win. The genial doctor had managed to convince voters to push for change.

The starkly different choices the Karnataka voters made in the Lok Sabha and assembly polls (which the Congress had swept) within the space of a year proved yet again how distinct every election fight can be. For Karnataka's domineering brothers-in-arms it was a sobering message: power can be ephemeral—and voters can never be taken for granted. Swag and flair grab headlines, but a more complex matrix of real issues determines the choices made in the quiet privacy of the polling booth.

'There is this young political activist who speaks really well. You must get him on your TV show!' enthused a friend. The year was 2015 and the topic up for a studio debate was the future of Dalit politics. It was to be my first encounter with Chandrashekhar Azad. Striding into the studio, the muscular, strapping Azad, with his luxuriant moustache and characteristic long blue scarf around his neck, cut an impressive figure. Leading a youthful group called the Bhim Army, he had added the moniker 'Ravan' to his name as a challenge to Hindu upper-caste supremacy. 'Next time you want to call me for a TV debate, don't get anyone else to join. I will only engage in a one-on-one interview with you,' he declared in his ringing baritone.

I was struck by the articulate Azad's self-assured demeanour. It reminded me of the late Kanshi Ram, the iconic BSP leader who transformed Dalit–Bahujan politics in the 1990s. Intriguingly, Kanshi Ram too had placed a similar condition when I first interviewed him for *The Times of India*. 'My interview must run on the front page, not in some corner at the back of the newspaper!' he had warned. Azad, who grew up in western Uttar Pradesh's Saharanpur district, claimed to draw inspiration from Kanshi Ram and Ambedkar. 'I want to be a true leader like them, not a "ghulam" (slave) of any party,' he claimed.

In 2017, I interviewed Azad again. This time, he was in hiding as the state police had issued an arrest warrant for him after caste violence had broken out in Saharanpur. 'I want you to know that I am not scared of going to jail; my popularity among the people is only going to increase now,' he said. Defiant. Daring. Different. Azad was determined to make an impact. He spent more than a year in jail under the National Security Act but remained unbending in his resolve to continue with his 'sangharsh' (agitation) against caste oppression. He would go to jail again in 2020, this time for agitating against the CAA. 'The police struck me with lathis, breaking four of my teeth, but I didn't succumb to their pressure,' he asserted. In 2021, he was featured in *TIME* magazine's annual list of '100 emerging leaders who are shaping the future'. 'Didn't I tell you that I will make a name for myself one day!' he boasted.

Evidently a man in a hurry to make a name for himself, Azad chose to contest the 2022 Uttar Pradesh assembly elections from Gorakhpur against Chief Minister Yogi Adityanath, only to forfeit his security deposit. Undeterred, he called it a 'symbolic fight' aimed at challenging the rise of political Hindutva. The timing, though, was significant. Three-time former Uttar Pradesh chief minister and BSP leader Mayawati and her party were in steep decline, accused of having struck a deal with the BJP. Young Dalits, especially, were looking for new leadership, and Azad was keen to fill the vacuum. By 2023, his Aazad Samaj Party had spread to over a dozen states and his public meetings were attracting sizeable crowds. But would the crowds translate into votes? 'I am offering a tie-up with the INDIA alliance for the 2024 elections, but they are keeping me hanging,' he claimed. He reportedly made the offer to Samajwadi Party leader Akhilesh Yadav, who promised to invite him over for a 'cup of chai'. The meeting never happened. 'I think they are all scared of me. Shane Warne once said that he would get nightmares just thinking of bowling to Sachin Tendulkar. I guess I am a bit like Sachin to them,' he said, laughing. Azad is a diehard Tendulkar fan.

The INDIA alliance leaders have a different take. With the Uttar Pradesh government providing special security to Azad, word quickly spread that he was being propped up as the BJP's 'B team'. 'The BJP wants to use him to divide the Dalit vote; how can we trust him?' said a Samajwadi Party leader. Azad, who was shot at and whose convoy was attacked by a group of armed men in June 2023, wasn't flustered by the allegation. 'These same people once called Kanshi Ram a CIA agent. They feel threatened by anyone who challenges their authority. I am telling you, I am a leader, not a ladder to be used by anyone,' he countered.

Instead of waiting for the INDIA alliance to accommodate him, Azad decided to fight the 2024 general elections on his own steam, announcing his candidature from Nagina in Uttar Pradesh's Bijnor district. The choice of Bijnor was interesting: Mayawati had first tasted electoral success here in 1989. Could Azad emulate the success of the state's first Dalit chief minister and Kanshi Ram's original political heir? 'I do not see myself as a Dalit leader only. I am representing all disadvantaged groups, Dalits, Muslims, backward castes—this is a coalition of the marginalized,' he emphasized. On the road in Nagina, it was apparent that Azad meant business. His street-corner meetings were a sea of blue, his kettle symbol staring down from every lamp-post. In a sure sign of his growing popularity, youngsters were queueing up to take selfies with him to make the image their mobile phone wallpaper. Azad has more than 4.4 million followers across different social media platforms, a whopping 2.2 million on Instagram alone.

In 2019, the Nagina seat was won by the BSP in alliance with the Samajwadi Party, the winning candidate polling more than 5.5 lakh votes. This time, the BSP ended up in fourth place, with just 13,272 votes. Azad, by contrast, got 5.12 lakh votes, winning by a comfortable margin of 1.51 lakh votes. In Kanshi Ram's electoral strategy for toppling the 'varna vyavastha' (caste system), the first election is fought to lose, the second to make others lose and the third to win. 'I guess I just skipped the second stage!' quipped Azad. The anti-establishment star had well and truly arrived.

In a political milieu where a disenchanted subaltern voter was looking for options beyond the tried and tested, a charismatic thirty-seven-year-old leader had shown that the power of agitational politics must never be discounted. At the grassroots there is a new energy: the power of personality can be effectively projected on social media and a lone challenger seen fighting against the odds can garner wildfire support among the young.

≡

Amongst the countless videos that went viral on counting day, one stood out. A young woman in a light-coloured sari dancing with her female companions while awestruck menfolk looked on from the sidelines. 'Hamare samaj mein khushi ke avsar par iss tarah se naachna parampara hai (In our community, it is tradition to dance like this on happy occasions)!' said Sanjna Jatav, the MP from Bharatpur in eastern

Rajasthan. Jatav had every reason to celebrate. The twenty-six-year-old mother of two from a poor Dalit family had created a slice of history by becoming the youngest-ever MP from Rajasthan. 'She is something else,' remarked Congress leader Sachin Pilot, who had previously held the record. 'She is a real fighter.' When campaigning for Jatav, Pilot was struck by just how effortlessly she mingled with people. 'She knew exactly what to say to whom, even which interaction could become an Instagram reel!' he said, laughing.

It was never going to be an easy fight. Bharatpur is part of Rajasthan Chief Minister Bhajan Lal Sharma's constituency, a reserved seat with sharp inter-caste rivalries. Jatav had contested the assembly elections from here in 2023 and lost by just 407 votes. Barely a month after her narrow defeat, her father passed away from a heart attack. She was distraught. But undeterred. When offered a Lok Sabha ticket by the Congress leadership in 2024, she took it up as a challenge, travelling from village to village to seek support with the limited resources at her disposal. Inspired by her spirit, state leaders like Jitender Singh and Vishvendra Singh, both from erstwhile royal families, contributed to her campaign. 'Main aapki beti hoon, pratyashi nahi (I am your daughter, not your candidate),' she said at every public meeting. It was just the kind of warm, touchy-feely reach-out that stood out in the din.

But more than her communication skills, it is Jatav's sheer grit that stands out. Married into a neighbouring village at the age of eighteen, she became a zilla parishad member two years later, a beneficiary of the pivotal reform of women's reservation in panchayats. Encouraged to complete her graduation and then pursue an LLB by her supportive husband, she didn't allow motherhood to hold her back. Her husband, Kaptan Singh, is a constable in the Rajasthan police, a government job that made him potentially vulnerable to political pressure to get his wife to back out from the contest. Reportedly, Singh did receive threatening calls from senior officials pushing him to withdraw his wife from the race, but he stood rock-like beside her, cheering her every step of the way. 'I am here because Kaptan Singh has been by my side all the way, always encouraging me to aim higher,' said Jatav. When his wife was elected an MP, winning by more than 50,000 votes, Kaptan Singh posted on Facebook: 'Aaj meri dharampatni, Sanjna Jatav, ne meri shaan badhayi!' (Today my wife, Sanjna Jatav, has raised my prestige.) A woman from a poor Dalit household, fighting an election in a conservative, male-dominated constituency, Sanjna Jatav's success reveals how subaltern role models are gradually reshaping the political map of the country. Away from flashy, high-decibel roadshows, there are lesser-known heroic figures who are creating their own soul-stirring storylines, often using social media's immense reach among communities—Jatav has over 63 thousand followers on Instagram—to build their campaigns. When I asked what drives her forward, she replieed, 'Ladki hoon; lad sakti hoon (I am a girl; I can fight).' That's the tagline Priyanka Gandhi Vadra first made popular in the 2022 Uttar Pradesh elections. The Congress leader is among those who pushed for Jatav to be given the ticket. Sachin Pilot was right: the young woman from Bhusawar village in Bharatpur is a natural people person with a keen appetite for competitive politics.

⹀

Thirty-two-year-old Rajkumar Roat sure knows how to make a splash. On the day he was taking his oath as an MP of the 18th Lok Sabha, the photogenic Roat entered Parliament on a camel, dressed in the colourful attire typical of the Bhil tribe of southern Rajasthan. 'I wanted to remind everyone that the Adivasis of this country have their own distinct culture, our special way of life, and no one can take it away from us,' he asserted. Roat had just won from Banswara–Dungarpur, a tribal-dominated constituency on the Rajasthan–Gujarat–Madhya Pradesh border, as a candidate from the newly formed Bharat Adivasi Party (BAP).

'Mujhme ladne ka keeda hamesha tha (I have always had the urge to fight),' said Roat, who started his political career as a student activist, setting up a Bhil Pradesh Vidyarthi Morcha in 2016. Although the Bhils have sizeable numbers in the tribal pockets of Rajasthan, they have never really influenced the power dynamics of the state. Growing up in a small village in Dungarpur, Roat became conscious of deeply embedded social inequalities early in life. 'I had friends in school whose homes I would never be invited to because they were upper-caste Rajputs who could not be seen eating with a tribal—khaan-paan nahi hoti hai (there is no inter-dining),' he disclosed.

These early experiences shaped Roat's political choices and made him keen to restore the dignity of his Adivasi community and fight for their rights. In 2018, he joined the Bharatiya Tribal Party (BTP), contested an assembly election from Chorasi and, at just twenty-six, became the youngest MLA in the Rajasthan assembly. The BTP is a Gujarat-based party formed by a local strongman, Chhotu Vasava, that advocates the cause of 'Bhilistan', a separate state for Bhils. When Vasava was looking to spread into neighbouring Rajasthan, he tapped Roat and his band of young tribal activists. But an ambitious Roat soon broke away from Vasava, saying he didn't want to be dictated to by a family-led party. 'The BTP was only about Vasava and his family. BAP, which we set up in 2023, is about the ideology of tribal people and our demands,' he declared.

While BAP made a breakthrough by winning 2 seats in Rajasthan and 1 seat in Madhya Pradesh in the 2023 assembly elections, the real test came in the 2024 Lok Sabha battle. Pitted against Roat was powerful BJP candidate Mahendrajeet Singh Malviya, a former Congress minister in the Ashok Gehlot government who had defected just before the Lok Sabha polls. Malviya is a veteran tribal leader and was one of the Congress's moneybags who reportedly switched to the BJP to 'protect his monetary interests'. In the elections, while Malviya travelled around the countryside in a large convoy of SUVs, Roat and his 'boys' sped through villages on their motorbikes, a symbol of youth power. In his T-shirt and jeans, with a gamcha wrapped around his head, Roat canvassing on his Hero Splendor across Banswara resembled a motorcycle gang leader. 'We call them the bikers of Banswara,' said Avinash Kalla, a Rajasthan-based journalist. 'They are a craze among young tribals.' With over 450,000 followers on Instagram, Roat's Instagram profile picture is of a dashing youth in a jaunty turban and the local Bhil dress. An affluent Malviya had unmatched financial muscle, but Roat had earned goodwill as a fighter for tribal causes. 'Do you know, when we held rallies, villagers would set up tents with their own money! You don't need crores to win elections, you need people power,' he said.

Interestingly, the Congress, which had initially given a ticket to Arvind Damor, a local leader, decided at the last minute to support Roat and BAP as part of the wider INDIA alliance. It was a decision pushed by state party chief Govind Singh Dotasra. 'For us in Rajasthan, 2024 was about winnability, and Roat with his youthful appeal was a winning candidate,' explained Dotasra. However, when the official Congress candidate refused to withdraw, it became a triangular fight. An undaunted Roat stuck to his 'land and development of tribals first' campaign theme. He won the election by an impressive 2.47 lakh votes. It was in Banswara that Modi had made his notorious 'mangalsutra' speech while villainizing Muslims as 'infiltrators'. His heavy-handed imposition of Hindutva across the land from on high spurred a million little mutinies on the ground. Roat's emphatic win was the perfect rejoinder. 'Abhi to yeh shuruat hai (This is only the beginning). We will soon spread to every tribal corner of this country. BAP will be the voice of Adivasis across India,' proclaimed Roat.

It's a voice that is increasingly a little strident too. In controversial remarks, the young MP claimed that tribals are not Hindus but 'mool nivasi', the original inhabitants of the land. When a Rajasthan BJP minister objected and asked Roat to undergo a DNA test to verify his religious identity, the angry BAP leader shot back: 'Not just me but every Adivasi will send you a blood sample. We are not part of your religion or your varna vyavastha. We have our own customs.' This brewing resentment is perhaps a reflection of just how tribal politics is gradually changing in India. The BJP has given the country its first tribal President, and the Congress was once the foremost national party in tribal areas, but a next-gen leadership among Adivasis is far more assertive and looking beyond traditional choices. 'We don't want Hindutva, we don't want sops, we want our land and our rights,' asserted Roat.

A national tribal-centric party may struggle to make an impact given the sharp intra-tribal differences that exist, but emerging young leaders from within tribal groups are no longer willing to be pawns in a larger power game. Roat with his passionate advocacy for Adivasi rights is a talisman for this new order. And yet, he does have a softer side too. When he got married a few years ago, he decided to have a pre-wedding photo shoot at the famed Dungarpur palace. 'In politics, I will always stand with my tribal brothers and sisters, but at a personal level, I have royal friends too!' he remarked. A tribal who stands up to the privileges of royalty but still takes pride in wedding photographs in the local palace, Roat is redefining the rules of power politics.

A young woman in her mid-twenties in London dreams of doing a PhD in political science at the prestigious School of Oriental and African Studies (SOAS), only to find herself navigating the sprawling sugar cane fields of Kairana in western Uttar Pradesh and seeking election to the Lok Sabha a few years later. The story of thirty-year-old Iqra Hasan is unusual: inspiring and disconcerting at the same time. Having completed her master's at SOAS, the academically inclined Hasan was planning on undertaking further studies, when the Covid pandemic forced her to return home in the summer of 2021. Her concerns didn't end there. Just a few months later, ahead of the 2022 Uttar Pradesh assembly elections, her brother, Nahid Hasan, a three-time Samajwadi Party MLA from Kairana, was arrested under the Uttar Pradesh Gangsters and Anti-Social Activities (Prevention) Act, 1986. 'It was like my whole world fell apart overnight. My father had passed away much earlier, my mother was unwell, my brother was in jail only because he had challenged the Yogi Adityanath government, our bank accounts were frozen, our properties placed under litigation. Forget about academics, I just had to stay focused to hold the family together,' said Hasan.

Her first challenge was to handle her brother's 2022 campaign. While she comes from a well-known family of politicians—her grandfather,

father and mother have all been MPs—organizing an election campaign was an entirely different ballgame for this shy young woman who until then had been engrossed in her political science books. 'I woke up to the world of difference that exists between theory and practice. Suddenly, I was dealing with caste and community politics in, dare I say, a very patriarchal set-up. I was a "bachhi" (little girl) for many senior leaders,' she recalled. Still, her diligent efforts paid off: Nahid was elected to the state assembly even while in jail. Soon after, when she was offered the chance to contest the Kairana Lok Sabha seat in 2024, she decided to take the plunge. 'I guess there was no option. We were fighting the Yogi government day and night in Uttar Pradesh, so I felt that it made sense for me to take the fight to the voter,' she said.

The Kairana Lok Sabha seat was a BJP bastion. In 2019, BJP MP Pradeep Choudhary had defeated Hasan's mother, Begum Tabassum Hasan, by 92,000 votes. Choudhary was again contesting on a BJP ticket, so Hasan had the added incentive of avenging her mother's loss. Kairana, a bustling agricultural town with a large Jat and Muslim population, had been at the epicentre of the 2013 Muzaffarnagar communal riots which had pitted the two communities, in direct conflict. Eleven years on, Hasan was faced with the seemingly insurmountable task of bridging the divide. She knew that to win the election she would need support from either side of the communal divide. Kairana has a roughly 40 per cent Muslim population, while Jats, Gujjars, Sainis, Rajputs and Dalits are the other key voting groups. 'From day one, I centred my campaign on issues cutting across "biradaris" (fraternities) that had nothing to do with religion. One of the major problems we face in Kairana is ensuring a remunerative and timely price to farmers for the cane crop from the sugar mills. The Yogi government promised to double farmer incomes, but they only doubled unemployment,' she said.

Dressed in a traditional salwar-kameez, she campaigned in the old-fashioned way. No big, splashy roadshows or noisy rallies but a sustained door-to-door campaign, where voters were instantly drawn to the quiet-voiced and sincere Iqra 'behen'. 'I don't think there is a single house in the constituency at whose door I did not knock. I wanted the people to know that I was one of them, someone who would be accessible to them at all times,' she remarked. The contrast with her BJP opponent who was accused of spending barely any time with the voters could not have been more glaring. Hasan's personal connection and hard work made an impact on the electorate. She won the Kairana seat by over 69,000 votes while polling more than 5.28 lakh votes. 'Kairana ki behen' was now an MP. Her base was not just a solid Muslim vote but also many Hindu caste groups, whose trust she had managed to gain. The fact that the BSP vote collapsed, as it did in most parts of Uttar Pradesh, was a bonus. But most importantly, her win was a sign that Kairana was finally exorcising the ghosts of the Muzaffarnagar riots.

A young Muslim woman, albeit from a political family, had defeated a strong BJP candidate who represented the dominant Hindutva lobby, which had been benefitting from communal polarization for years. Perhaps the sustained farm agitations of 2020–21 had finally convinced voters to look beyond religious identity and focus on livelihood issues. It was as if a divided society was slowly being healed by the victory of a fearless, tireless, educated woman.

The 18th Lok Sabha has just twenty-four Muslim MPs, the lowest share in Parliament ever, and Iqra Hasan is one of only three women Muslim MPs. 'I would love to see many more young women, Hindus and Muslims, enter politics. At the moment, politics is still a bit of a boys' club that needs a shake-up!' said the MP who has broken many stereotypes, and possibly inspired other young women to follow in her footsteps.

===

There is arguably no tougher task in Modi-era electoral politics than winning a Lok Sabha seat from the state of Gujarat as a non-BJP candidate. In 2014, the BJP, riding the crest of the Modi wave, won all 26 seats from Gujarat; 2019 was no different: if anything, the margins were even higher. Opposition candidates trying to go up against Modi, the symbol of Gujarati pride and the self-styled 'Gujarat ka sher', and the BJP's vast election machine have little chance to succeed. Unless the nominee happens to be Geniben Thakor, Congress MP and the only non-BJP candidate to win a Lok Sabha election in Gujarat since 2009.

'Geniben Thakor is the real giant-killer of 2024,' said Mahesh Langa, a senior Ahmedabad-based journalist. 'She was taking on not just her BJP rival but an entire political and economic system that can't see beyond the ruling party. Her achievement is stupendous.' Nor was her victory from Banaskantha a one-off. For nearly three decades now Thakor has been a serial election winner, contesting and quite incredibly winning her first election as a nineteen-year-old in 1995 with the introduction of women's reservation in panchayats. 'I won my first election to the taluka panchayat and became the taluka panchayat president. Since then, I have won district elections, assembly polls and now the Lok Sabha,' she pointed out.

It is an especially remarkable feat since her thirty-year-long political career has coincided with the rise of the BJP in Gujarat. The Congress is a pale shadow of its former self in Gujarat, struggling with a leadership deficit and organizational collapse. 'It is not easy to be a Congress leader in Gujarat at all. The BJP can do whatever it wants here. If any member of your family is in government, they will threaten you to switch sides or else lose your job. Yahan saam daam dand bhed ki rajneeti chalti hai, (Here the politics of persuasion, bribery, punishment and division works),' said the outspoken Thakor.

Banaskantha, a rural district in north Gujarat, is a particular challenge. At the heart of the area's political economy is the Banas Dairy, one of the largest co-operative dairies in the country, with an annual turnover of over Rs 15,000 crore. It is part of Gujarat's vast district-level milk union network that markets its products under the iconic Amul brand. Lakhs of farmers are members of the co-operative and fully dependent on it for their income. The BJP tightly controls the dairy network. Local strongman and Gujarat assembly speaker Shankar Chaudhary is the chairperson of Banas Dairy. At election time, the BJP has been accused by rivals of using its clout with the dairy management to influence farmer-voters. In 2024 too the BJP campaigned furiously to win the Banaskantha seat. It was at a rally here that Prime Minister Modi made the contentious speech warning voters that if they had two buffaloes, the Congress would take away one if it came to power.

So how did Thakor overcome the powerful forces ranged against her? Geniben Thakor was born into a middle-class family—the Thakors are an influential OBC Kshatriya community in north Gujarat—and her father was an old-style Gandhian social worker who inspired her to enter public life. 'I don't have personal wealth, but I have a lot of goodwill. People know that if they vote for Geniben, she will be there to serve them in good times and bad,' she said. As an MLA, she spent a large chunk of her allotted funds on girls' education, helping to set up schools and hostels. 'I have financed my elections through crowdfunding. People spontaneously give me donations ranging from Rs 100 to Rs 10,000. They give me money, I give my life for their service,' she said with a dramatic flourish.

In a sense, Thakor's success is a reminder that it is still possible to fight and win a Lok Sabha election without being dependent on a cash-rich party machine. Crowdfunding a campaign is a Gandhian approach to politics, showing that voters are willing to back a deserving candidate with their money as a form of political trusteeship. Raising contributions from the people is in a way an indicator of the people's commitment to invest in and claim ownership of politics. During the Independence movement Gandhi made collecting money and jewellery part of his political mobilization to transform political activity into a genuine people's movement, for, of and by the people. Can Geniben Thakor become a role model for others? 'All I know is that I will keep serving people. That is what makes me happy,' she responded. It's a back-to-basics approach that has made her defy the odds and script a historic win. The Mahatma would be proud.

—

In the 1990s, with militancy at its peak in the Kashmir Valley, a late-night knock on my hotel room door in Srinagar concerned me a little. Door firmly locked, I peered through the keyhole and saw a bald, unshaven man in a Pathan suit waving back. 'Don't worry, sir, I am not a terrorist!' he assured me, laughing. This was my first meeting with Sheikh Abdul Rashid, popularly known as Engineer Rashid. His nickname is a reminder that long before he was drawn into public life, he worked as an engineer in a Jammu and Kashmir construction company. 'Then I built bridges for people, now I am building bridges between people,' he pithily remarked. We struck up a friendship. Rashid is a plain-speaking political maverick from the town of Langate in north Kashmir. He opened a window for me into the turbulent and intensely complicated universe of the bloodied Valley.

Twice elected as an independent MLA, he was contesting the 2024 Lok Sabha elections from the Baramulla seat, but from the confines of Tihar Jail. Rashid was taken into custody in 2019, soon after Article 370 was revoked in Jammu and Kashmir by the Centre. He was charged under the UAPA and accused by the National Investigation Agency of working with separatists and Pakistani operatives in a terror-funding case. Rashid insisted the charges were trumped up and nothing he had said or done could be linked to terrorism. 'I am being victimized because of my politics, because I speak truth to those in power in Delhi and Srinagar,' he claimed. Rashid's politics were once described to me by a long-time Kashmir watcher as 'soft separatism with uncertain loyalties'. He's a firebrand leader who has always spoken out for the autonomy and rights of the Kashmiri people. But he has always advocated the cause through the ballot, not the bullet.

Now, he was back to proving a point by contesting from Baramulla against two of the Valley's biggest political faces: former chief minister and National Conference leader Omar Abdullah and People's Conference chief Sajjad Lone. On paper, it seemed an unequal fight. An independent candidate, contesting from jail, against two formidable adversaries backed by their party apparatus. And yet, his apparent weakness would prove to be his trump card. Being in jail, Engineer Rashid struck an emotional chord with voters. For many Kashmiris, prison bars are symbolic of an oppressive Indian state. For three decades, thousands of Kashmiris have been imprisoned, not all of them guilty as charged. 'Jail ka badla vote se (Avenge jailtime with the vote),' Rashid's twenty-two-year-old son, Abrar, shouted on the campaign trail.

Young Abrar, Rashid's campaign manager, canvassed across the mountainous terrain with limited resources. Raising funds through a volunteer network, he maintained that his main expense was a sum of Rs 27,000, which he spent on petrol money for a hired car. He also partly financed the campaign through the pension of his grandfather, a retired government teacher. The suggestion by political rivals that Rashid's election was being propped up by the security agencies to edge out the Valley's mainstream parties is rejected outright by his son. 'We didn't even have money for posters and banners; everything was done through volunteers. Even the loudspeakers were given to us through public donations, and when we couldn't find any, I just spoke without a mic!' said Abrar.

The common touch was unsurprising. Over his political career, Rashid had built a reputation for being a 'people's leader', a politician who defied the stereotype. He claimed to have spent his MLA fund money on providing free education to poor children in his district, often riding pillion on a motorbike or sipping kahwa with locals at street corners, at a distance from the trappings of power or security paraphernalia. 'When people have elected you, why do you need security? Their support is my biggest security,' he declared.

By contrast, Abdullah and Lone, both from renowned political families, were defined by their social status. Handsome, well-spoken and well-turned-out, they represented the Valley elite. Both were arrested in 2019 amidst a crackdown on political activity post the abrogation of Article 370 and were released only several months later. While Rashid has been in Tihar Jail for over five years, unable to even speak to his family, his rivals had at least got their freedom. 'Do you know that I have met my father only once in the last five years? They have barred him from speaking to us on the phone,' said Abrar. The cloak of victimhood was almost unknowingly conferred on Rashid by his jailors. In the eyes of many voters, supporting the independent candidate was a mark of protest.

It was an anti-establishment vote, even a form of public outrage against the excesses and injustices of the Indian state.

When the Baramulla result was finally declared, the 'protest vote' echoed loudly from every chinar tree. Rashid won from jail by more than 1 lakh votes. It was a real shock for those who had expected the contest to remain an Abdullah-versus-Lone battle. Against all odds, a UAPA detainee with limited resources had defeated his swanky rivals. The reaction of a humbled Omar Abdullah was heartening when he tweeted: 'I don't believe his victory will hasten his release from prison nor will the people of North Kashmir get the representation they have a right to but the voters have spoken and in a democracy that's all that matters.' Indeed. Rashid may have a long battle ahead to prove his innocence in a court of law, but in the court of his beloved Kashmiri people, he stands acquitted.

In September 2024, Rashid was granted three weeks bail to campaign in the Jammu and Kashmir assembly polls. Once again his opponents insisted that he had been set up by the Centre to divide votes in the Valley. 'One day I am called a terrorist sympathizer, next I am a vote cutter. How many conspiracy theories will be spun by my critics?' he asked. In jail or out, Engineer Rashid remains admirably defiant. And almost refreshingly idiosyncratic.

≡

With just 2 Lok Sabha seats, Manipur is a dot on the national election map. But in 2024, Manipur became a metaphor for a government in denial, blinded by a halo of political indestructability. More than 200 people had died and thousands had been rendered homeless by the ethnic violence that broke out in May 2023 between the Meitei and Kuki-Zo people. As armed militias took to the streets, the mighty Indian state strangely went missing. Security forces were struggling to bring the situation under control. Prime Minister Narendra Modi didn't visit the state even once after the fires erupted. Home Minister Amit Shah steadfastly refused to sack the chief minister, N. Biren Singh. It appeared as if Manipur was a festering sore that no one wanted to heal. It took the horrific visuals of two women being paraded naked, allegedly gang-raped, for the national conscience to be mildly awakened from an indifference created by the tyranny of distance.

Initially it wasn't even certain if elections would be held in Manipur. Amidst calls by Kuki-Zo groups to boycott the elections, a security advisory warned of candidates being targeted by militants. Fearing retribution, many potential political nominees chose to opt out. Stepping into this minefield was fifty-seven-year-old Bimol Akoijam, a social psychology professor at Jawaharlal Nehru University. A reputed academic and filmmaker, Akoijam had spent decades working on scholarly projects, including important field research on Partition. As a public intellectual–activist, he had written columns and had spoken eloquently about the Manipur violence on TV shows. 'I was angry and frustrated at the complete failure of the government to maintain law and order. The state had lost the moral and political authority to govern,' he said. When he was first approached by several parties to join politics in August 2023, Akoijam laughed it off. But when a concrete offer came from the Congress to contest the Inner Manipur seat in January 2024, he had a long discussion with his wife, Olivia, before deciding to take the plunge as a 'reluctant politician'. 'I felt that rather than just critiquing the state of our politics from the outside, I should try and make a difference for my people by entering the system,' he explained.

The shift was hardly easy. He was threatened physically, shots were fired at one of his campaign meetings, and just before the nomination withdrawal date, armed men entered his home in Imphal to force him to back off. 'I had to go underground for forty-eight hours and could surface only once the withdrawal date had passed. But these threats only strengthened my resolve not to give up,' declared Akoijam.

Pitted against him was the BJP's Thounaojam Basanta Kumar Singh, an influential state minister and former IPS officer with a wide network of backers. The BJP, in fact, has as many as twenty-nine MLAs in the thirty-two assembly segments of the Inner Manipur Lok Sabha seat. The entire state machinery was rallied against Akoijam and his limited resources.

'Idid have one thing going for me: the power of the common people. This was their election, not mine. You will be surprised how many young Manipuris spontaneously created WhatsApp groups endorsing me. We even had Manipuris flying in from across the country and the world, some from as far as Australia and Singapore, only to vote for me,' he claimed.

During a door-to-door campaign, an elderly vegetable vendor came and thrust Rs 100 into his hand as a mark of her support. During Akoijam's campaign, voters took a leading role. A year of unrelenting fear and violence had impacted the ordinary voter and their families. They wanted 'change'. Not change measured as anti-incumbency against the Biren Singh government's failures, but a complete break from the stultifying political culture of a scarred land. 'I think Akoijam was at the right place at the right time,' said veteran Imphal-based journalist Pradip Phanjoubam. 'He was a fresh face, an outsider to electoral politics at a time when people had begun to dislike the usual political faces.'

Interestingly, when Home Minister Shah campaigned in Imphal, he raked up Akoijam's JNU connection, branding him an 'anti-national' member of the 'tukde tukde gang'. But in a milieu where an anti-establishment mood had taken hold, the personal insult yielded no results. 'I guess we got a few thousand more votes as a result of these wild allegations,' remarked the professor–politician. In the final count, Akoijam won by more than 1 lakh votes, as the Congress wrested both the Manipur seats from the BJP.

Akoijam knows that his real test in public life has only just begun. Manipur remains sharply divided on ethnic lines with the Meiteis and Kukis still at daggers drawn. He is keen to appear all-inclusive. 'I am an MP for every Manipuri. Meiteis, Kukis, Nagas, Pangals, Marwaris—they are all my voters. I believe in citizen first, ethnicity later,' he asserted. Whether or not he succeeds in his mission to transform lives, his electoral triumph has demonstrated how voters often register their protest through the ballot box. 'Magic can happen when people speak up,' said Akoijam.

The people of the beautiful but traumatized state of Manipur have spoken out loud and clear. Will those in power listen to these voices from the periphery?

On the first Sunday of May 2024, Ayodhya was awash with saffron. Scores of Sangh Parivar activists from across Uttar Pradesh had poured into the town. Roads were being cleaned up, shops wore a festive look and temple lights were twinkling in the night sky. Prime Minister Modi was on an election roadshow. Thousands had lined up for a darshan of the self-styled 'god' of political Hindutva on his first visit to Ayodhya since the January Ram Mandir consecration ceremony. At every street corner, there were life-size cut-outs of the Prime Minister with posters thanking him for bringing Ram Lalla 'back home' and promising a 'char sau paar' victory as a return gift. When Modi climbed atop a gleaming yellow-hued van and brandished the BJP's lotus symbol in the direction of the crowd, the police struggled to hold back frenzied supporters showering rose petals and chanting 'Jai Shri Ram' and 'Bharat Mata ki jai'. Standing behind Modi was Uttar Pradesh Chief Minister Yogi Adityanath, consciously remaining a step away from the star attraction.

Caught between the two heavyweights was Lallu Singh, a sitting MP and five-time MLA from Ayodhya, which is part of the Faizabad Lok Sabha constituency. Singh waved to the crowd only occasionally, mostly basking in the afterglow of yet another Modi moment. The roadshow was streaming live across news channels, the on-air commentary breathlessly describing what the media projected as 'public euphoria'.

My crew and I had been filming all day in Ayodhya for an election programme. We debated a provocative question—'Ram ya Rozgaar' (Ram or jobs)—and heard a range of voices. The pilgrims from different parts of the country who had come to catch a glimpse of the Ram idol were mostly upbeat, applauding the Modi government for building the temple. The shopkeepers in and around the temple precincts seemed just as happy. The upsurge in tourist traffic had been good for business. We did hear a few locals complaining of rising LPG prices and civic corruption. But BJP supporters shut these discordant voices down. Then, just as we were about to switch off the camera, an auto driver stepped into the frame and insisted on having his say. 'Bhaisahab, na Mathura, na

Kashi, abki baar Awadhesh Pasi (This time, neither Mathura, nor Kashi, but Awadhesh Pasi)!' he emphatically declared.

My first reaction was, 'Awadhesh who?' Like many Delhi-based journalists who parachute into the election battleground, I hadn't really decoded Faizabad's complex web of caste and community politics. Our primary focus was on Ayodhya's apparent media-projected Modi mania and capturing the Ram temple's effect on voters. The rapturous roadshow was, in a sense, only an affirmation of the religious sentiments that appeared to overshadow any contrarian voices. And yet, the auto driver's slogan was compelling enough for us to explore the 'other side' of the Ayodhya story. The man whined about how big-ticket land deals were being struck between influential local BJP politicians and 'outsiders' for hotel complexes in the city, how municipal authorities were razing old houses only to widen roads for tourists and how those with 'connections' to mandir officials were profiting from rising property prices. 'Sab paise ka khel hai (It is all about money),' he insisted.

The morning after Modi's eye-catching roadshow, we were in the small tehsil town of Milkipur in the Ayodhya district. Unlike the temple hub, no tourists visited Milkipur. No cameras filmed its dingy dirt tracks, and no VVIPs posed for photo-ops here. But the lack of media attention hadn't stopped Awadhesh Prasad, the Samajwadi Party candidate for Faizabad, from kicking off his door-to-door campaign in the area.

The seventy-eight-year-old Prasad was a veteran politician and the sitting MLA from Milkipur, one of the five assembly segments that comprise the Faizabad Lok Sabha seat. Dressed in a crumpled kurta-pajama with the Samajwadi Party's distinctive red topi on his head, Prasad seemed pleased to see us. 'Koi toh national media humse bhi baat karne aaya hai (At least someone from the national media has come to meet us),' he said with a snigger. The grey-haired Prasad was no political novice but a nine-time MLA. He was jailed during the Emergency and won his first assembly election in 1977, the tumultuous year of the victory of the Janata Party. He was then a young political activist, a self-confessed 'chela' (follower) of the former Prime Minister and Lok Dal leader Chaudhary

Charan Singh. Such was his devotion to his mentor that he could not attend his father's last rites as he was away in Amethi during the 1981 by-polls in which Rajiv Gandhi made his electoral debut by defeating the Lok Dal's Sharad Yadav. Prasad was Yadav's campaign manager and had been instructed by Charan Singh not to leave the counting room till the last vote was counted. Prasad's staunch loyalty extended to 'Netaji' Mulayam Singh Yadav when the Samajwadi Party was formed in 1992. The Samajwadi Party in Uttar Pradesh was one of several regional parties that emerged when the Janata Dal fragmented across the country. A Dalit face from the Pasi subcaste in a Yadav-dominated party, Prasad was unwavering in his commitment to Netaji, even when the BSP became the preferred option for the majority of Dalit voters. 'Hamari rajneeti wafaddari ki hai, avsarwadi nahi (My politics is of loyalty, not opportunism),' he said. Which is why when Akhilesh Yadav offered him a ticket, he unhesitatingly agreed to take up the Faizabad challenge.

As I tracked his campaign, it was apparent that Prasad was not fazed by the Ram Mandir excitement around him. 'BJP Ram ke naam par apni politics karti hai; vote ka business karti hai. Asli Ram bhakt to hum hain; mere parivar mein kai logon ke naam Ram se jude hain (The BJP plays politics over Ram; the vote is a business for them. I am a true believer in Ram; many members of my family have Ram in their name),' he argued. And then came his punchline: 'BJP kehti hai, "Hum Ram ko laye hain." Sachchai hai ki yeh mehngai aur berozgaari laye hain (The BJP claims that they have brought Ram, but the truth is, they have brought inflation and unemployment)!' In the battle of narratives, a straight-talking, doughty salt-of-the-earth Prasad was taking on the BJP's Hindu nationalism plank in Ayodhya, the spiritual and cultural home of Hinduism. 'Please don't see me as a Dalit leader. I am a Samajwadi first and last,' was Prasad's parting shot to us.

Seen against the backdrop of the larger ongoing battle between the forces of 'kamandal' and Mandal, between the religious and caste identities that have shaped Uttar Pradesh's politics for three decades now, Akhilesh Yadav's choice of candidate was pitch perfect. Prasad is a Dalit in a constituency with a 26 per cent Dalit population, a 14 per cent Muslim population and substantial Yadav and Kurmi OBC pockets. On the other hand, the BJP's candidate, Lallu Singh, was a Thakur in a constituency where upper castes were comparatively fewer in number. Ayodhya–Faizabad was, in a sense, the ideal demographic profile for Yadav to project his PDA alliance as an alternative to Hindutva politics.

Although the canny septuagenarian politician appeared quietly confident of his chances, the overpowering media images of the Modi roadshow in Ayodhya kept swirling in the mind. Faizabad with its diverse population and local anti-incumbency wasn't a cakewalk for the BJP, but surely the Ram Mandir would deliver sufficient votes on its sacred home turf? Though my instincts kept telling me that the auto driver's catchy slogan might resonate beyond the shining lights of Ayodhya's temples, the fervour of Modi's supporters eventually swayed me to the other side.

When the Faizabad result came out, it was a bit of a shocker. Prasad had lived up to his claim of being an 'asli Ram bhakt'. He won by more than 50,000 votes, defeating not just his BJP opponent, Lallu Singh, but the entire Hindutva machine. Caste equations and local issues had trumped Hindu consolidation. Mandal had scored over kamandal. And I had been served a telling reminder of some of the oldest rules of election field journalism: one, never discount the opinion of a streetside chronicler—as in this case, an auto driver—who takes the trouble to quietly share a bucking-the-trend insight, and two, never get trapped in smug and hyper-partisan echo chambers.

Which leaves me with a critical question blowing in the election wind: How did we in the Indian media get the 2024 results so wrong? After the ten stories of hope highlighted in this chapter, it is time to turn the searchlight onto an abyss of darkness. An acute existential dilemma that wrenches the conscience. It is time to confront the elephant in the newsroom.

FOURTEEN

'You Are Godi Media': The Media Takeover

BBC: 'When you look back [at the Gujarat pogrom], do you think there is anything you would have done differently?'

Narendra Modi: 'Yes, one area where I was very, very weak, and that was how to handle the media.'

—*India: The Modi Question*, BBC, aired in 2023

'SIR, I think the Delhi police is coming to arrest you. Please take all necessary precautions!' The voice on the phone line sounded anxious. A colleague reporting from the home ministry had called me to say there were rumours in North Block that the Delhi police had received the go-ahead to arrest me on sedition charges. My initial reaction was one of utter disbelief. Arrest? Sedition? Imprisonment? Me? It all seemed a bit surreal, leaving me a little dazed and, frankly, fearful. Just a day earlier, on 28 January 2021, the Delhi police had filed an FIR against Congress MP Shashi Tharoor, senior journalists Mrinal Pande and Zafar Agha, and *Caravan* editors Vinod Jose and Anant Nath, and me, accusing us of having wilfully spread disinformation by tweeting about the death of a farmer during the Republic Day tractor rally taken out by agitating farmers in the national capital.

It wasn't just the Delhi police. Within hours, three near-identical FIRs had been filed by the Noida police in Uttar Pradesh, a police station in Madhya Pradesh and another one in Gurugram, Haryana. All three states had one thing in common: they were all BJP-ruled. 'Leave the house and just take a flight to a non-BJP-ruled state,' advised a lawyer friend. 'Just get out of Delhi.' My assistant, Surinder Nagar, was already busy lining up a ticket to Mumbai, where the Shiv Sena-led Maha Vikas Aghadi was in power. I was aghast and responded angrily, 'Are you seriously telling me to run away and go into hiding? Plus, if they arrest me, they will also have to arrest Shashi. Do you really think the government will arrest a leading Opposition voice who is globally recognized only because he tweeted about a farmer's death? And will they dare touch a woman journalist of the seniority and eminence of Mrinal ji? I think they are just trying to scare us with the threat of arrest. Nothing will happen.'

My seemingly nonchalant approach to a possible impending arrest didn't impress either my wife, Sagarika, or daughter, Tarini. In fact, Tarini, who had just completed her law degree and begun working from home for a leading corporate law firm—Covid social-distancing rules were still in place—was particularly incensed by my casual approach to the situation. 'How do you know they won't arrest you? You just can't take any chances with the law or the police,' she argued. My bravado at daring the police to arrest me had clearly enraged her sharp legal mind. Sagarika too was typically practical. 'Please don't grandstand. Just do what the lawyer says. Get your act together, pack your bags and spend a few days in a place where the cops can't track you. You know the Modi government has got you in its sights. Enough is enough!' she said with mounting irritation.

A compromise was arrived at. I wouldn't leave town, but I would go and stay with a friend who lived in Sainik Farm, a sprawling colony of bungalows, narrow lanes, green spaces and densely forested land, originally discovered by a few retired generals and their pals in real estate who were also very well-networked politically. Over the years, the area had been constantly encroached upon, widened and built upon, its legality under question. To avoid scrutiny, Sainik Farm even had its own electricity, water supply and private security. It was referred to jokingly as the 'Republic of Sainik Farm', where the writ of the all-powerful Indian state did not run, even though some of its occupants had once served the Government of India with distinction. In this vast, unregulated maze of farmhouses, it was possible to melt away from the bright city lights outside.

And so, on a cold winter evening, I slipped into the darkness of Sainik Farm, feeling like a fugitive on the run from the law and from a vindictive political system that was out to 'get' me. That night, as I snuggled under a warm blanket kindly provided by my friend, sipping a glass of Old Monk and Coke, the pervading sounds of silence around me began to clear the cobwebs of a cluttered mind. What criminal act had I committed to be labelled a seditionist? What does being branded 'anti-national' mean in the 'new' India we are living in? As I began to doze off, a flood of images from what had been a rather tumultuous week in my life replayed in my fatigued brain.

⚌

26 January. A day when the Indian state showcases its military might and cultural heritage. The ceremonies along the Rajpath boulevard—renamed 'Kartavya Path' by the Modi government—are designed to invoke patriotic fervour while showcasing the power and grandeur of the state. Whether a constitutional republic whose foundations were laid by heroic freedom fighters challenging a colonial empire needs a Soviet-style military ritual and tacky state-sponsored tableaux to keep the nationalistic testosterone pumping is debatable. But everyone loves a colourful parade, even if it's ultimately the VVIPs who get a ringside view of the show, while the rest of the country watches it on TV, awestruck, from their homes. In a sense, the parade symbolizes the national dominance of New

Delhi's Lutyens' elite, the very social class that Prime Minister Narendra Modi's government claims to despise.

Today, however, one elite has replaced another, the privileged Nehruvian charmed circle having given way to the torchbearers of Hindutva. The Lutyens' elite today is Team Modi.

The 2021 Republic Day parade, though, was very different. While the jawans marched on Rajpath, kisans agitating against the implementation of the farm laws enacted by the Modi government decided to undertake their own parallel tractor rally as a mark of protest. My reporter instincts suggested that the farmer protest was almost certain to be eventful and would be best covered in the field rather than the comfort of a television studio. And so, on the bitterly cold night of 25 January, with the city engulfed in dense fog, we drove cautiously with hazard lights blinking to the Singhu border near Haryana, ground zero of the farmer agitation. We found accommodation after midnight in a ramshackle bed-and-breakfast hotel along the highway and barely managed a few hours' sleep.

By 8 a.m. the next day, we were in the midst of a large crowd of slogan-shouting farmers wearing distinctive colourful turbans, most of them atop their tractors and a few riding horses and motorcycles. The mood was rebellious but festive, with patriotic songs blaring from loudspeakers. Posters of Bhagat Singh were held aloft. The tricolour fluttered in the skyline. Judging by the celebratory atmosphere, we could scarcely have foreseen the drama that was about to unfold. It was close to noon when we first got reports that the farmers' protest had turned violent in central Delhi.

A colleague shared images of the police clashing with farmers and using tear gas at the ITO metro station in the heart of the capital. The protestors had broken through the police barricades, some even using their tractors to ram through the police pickets, and engaged in pitched battles with the men in khaki. We, meanwhile, were struggling to make our way through the crowded streets. Mobile networks had been cut off and traffic was being diverted from the main road to restore law and order. We abandoned our vehicles and began to walk briskly towards central Delhi. It was almost 2 p.m. by the time we reached the ITO building, the epicentre of the violence. The police by then had regained control over the area, which looked somewhat like a war zone. Most of the protestors had been dispersed, the broken barricades, stones and tear gas shells littering the streets the only signs of the bedlam that had occurred just hours earlier. On the main thoroughfare, we noticed that a crowd had gathered and was refusing to leave the area.

Cutting through the police cordon, we saw a group of young protestors surrounding a body that lay motionless on the ground before them, wrapped in a white cloth. 'The police shot our friend when he was riding the tractor,' some of them shouted, pointing to the blood oozing from the forehead wounds of the dead man. 'We will not leave till we get justice,' insisted another. I was reporting live on the sights and sounds before me, the angry voices getting more enraged by the minute by my questions to them on just who was responsible for the violence.

'All of you are godi media who only put out the government version; get away from here,' a loud voice hollered even as another angry protestor tried to snatch our camera. 'Godi media' was a term being used with increased frequency to target journalists who were accused of being in the godi, or lap, of the Modi government. It was the first time anyone had called me a 'godi media' newsman. Aghast, I attempted to defend myself against the accusation, only to find that the situation was getting markedly hostile, and I was forced to walk away from the crowd that was closing in on us.

Soon after, I tweeted exactly what the victim's friends had said on camera to me: 'One person, 45-year-old Navneet Singh was killed allegedly in police firing. Farmers tell me the "sacrifice" will not go in vain.' A little later, the police claimed that the farmer–protestor had died when his tractor overturned while crashing through a barricade. Realizing that I may have been misled by the angry mob, I deleted the tweet and pointed out conflicting reports that were emerging from what was a rapidly evolving situation on the ground. Live news coverage in a highly charged atmosphere demands a high level of due diligence and sensitivity in reporting. However, in the heat of the moment and in a swiftly changing situation, it is practically impossible to verify every accusation being made. Reporters on the field are bound to report what they see and hear, and update their stories as events unfold. That is what I was attempting to do, although the tense environment made it even more difficult to navigate through the contradictory versions. I had no doubt erred in tweeting an unconfirmed, possibly misleading claim and putting out the unverified information on air in haste and in the heat of the moment. But was I guilty of sedition or indeed a 'mala fide act with the deliberate intention of inciting trouble'? Could a journalistic error of judgement in a crazed atmosphere be seen as evidence of seditious behaviour? Surely not.

At no stage had I tried to provoke the protestors. Ironically, it was the incensed crowd that shouted me down and drove me away from the site for questioning the farmers about their role in triggering the violence. I must confess to feeling hounded and targeted by the slew of FIRs that had been filed by the police in different BJP-ruled states accusing me of sedition. On 9 February 2021, the Supreme Court intervened to stay our arrest and protected us from any coercive action. During the hearing, then Chief Justice of India Justice S.A. Bobde asked Solicitor General Tushar Mehta whether the government intended to arrest us. Mehta, the government's legal voice, was non-committal, seeking more time to argue the matter instead. The hearing was taking place virtually over a Zoom link, so the tension was perhaps less palpable, but it was apparent that the government wanted to throw the book at us. That evening a minister friend called. 'Rajdeep, you need to be more careful. This is Modi raj and you are a marked man,' he warned.

My daughter's fears that the police could arbitrarily arrest anyone on sedition charges proved to be rather prescient. Days after my own tryst with the law, on 13 February, the Delhi police travelled to Bengaluru and arrested twenty-two-year-old climate change activist Disha Ravi for sedition, accusing her of sharing an online document supporting the farmers' protest. Ravi's 'crime' was that the document that she shared was a 'toolkit', containing details of the social media campaign and on-ground activities that had been planned by the protestors.

That this action by a young activist should have attracted charges of sedition and conspiracy and immediate arrest was prima facie absurd. After all, there are many such documents floating around in cyberspace. Besides, there seemed to be no direct connection between the information Ravi had shared and the violence at Red Fort, which was clearly fomented by extremist groups within the protesting farmers. The rebellious farmers from rural Punjab were hardly likely to follow a social media 'toolkit' prepared by youthful climate activists across the world. Ravi spent eight days in police custody before being granted bail. I met her months later at a media event, where she was a 'star' guest: a slight, soft-spoken young woman who appeared a little bewildered with all the attention she was suddenly getting. She told me how the arrest had scarred and shaken her. 'All I did was edit a couple of lines in a document and share it with fellow activists,' she pointed out.

Ravi became teary-eyed as she described the manner of her arrest and the way in which she was intimidated by the police. 'It's like a nightmare that I hope no one else has to go through,' she said. Sadly, Ravi is not alone. According to a database prepared by the website Article 14, more than 800 sedition cases were filed against 13,000 people under section 124A of the IPC between 2010 and 2021. Over these eleven years, 106 sedition cases were filed against people who posted allegedly 'anti-national' or 'pro-Pakistan' messages on social media; except one, all the other cases were filed after 2014. A staggering 96 per cent of the cases filed against 405 Indians for criticizing politicians and the government in this period—149 being accused of making 'critical' and/or 'derogatory' remarks against Prime Minister Narendra Modi and 144 for similar comments against Uttar Pradesh Chief Minister Yogi Adityanath—were registered after 2014. During the UPA-II years, sedition cases were mostly filed against those protesting a nuclear plant in Tamil Nadu and against Maoist groups. In the Modi years, as many as 519 cases were filed by the government between 2014 and 2020 against citizens' protest movements, journalists, activists and intellectuals. The data also shows that those accused of sedition spent an average of 50 days in prison until a trial court granted bail and up to 200 days when a high court did so. The conviction rate in sedition cases was found to be just 0.1 per cent.

Finally, in May 2022, the Supreme Court put sedition laws on hold, stayed all proceedings in sedition cases and directed the Centre and states not to register any fresh cases. Slamming the misuse of the law, then Chief Justice of India N.V. Ramana observed on 11 May 2022, 'The sedition law was used to silence Gandhi, Bal Gangadhar Tilak. Does the government want to retain a colonial law even seventy-five years after Independence? The sedition law is misused by the police to fix people who oppose the government. There is no accountability for slapping seditious charges. It's like giving a carpenter a saw to cut wood who then chops the entire forest.' The judicial intervention may have provided some relief to those charged with sedition, especially those languishing in jail for months without a trial, but not for long. In 2023, the Modi government passed a new 'indigenous' criminal code, the Bharatiya Nyaya Sanhita (BNS). Section 150 of the BNS Act revives the colonial law, only here 'sedition' is replaced by a vaguer but far broader term: 'subversive activities'. The sedition charges against me haven't been dropped yet, but I count myself lucky. In our sedition case, we had access to a fine legal team led by the redoubtable Kapil Sibal and several other top senior lawyers who quickly ensured protection from arrest. I am privileged in a way by my position as a recognized journalist. But what of the many unknown Indians who don't have the same advantages I do? When I look at the long list of citizens who have been charged with sedition—many of them from poor tribal communities—I almost feel as if wearing the 'anti-national' accusation is a badge of honour. Electoral majorities must be respected in a democracy where the ballot is ultimately decisive. But an election victory, however hard-fought and deserved, cannot mask a grim reality. In this 'new' India, dissent is often seen as a criminal act and asking inconvenient questions of the government can land you in jail. Especially if you are a journalist whom those in power do not like or approve of. The farmers may have misleadingly targeted me as 'godi media', but for the government and its cheerleaders I was and still am an 'anti-national'.

In August 2019, Dr Prannoy Roy and his wife, Radhika Roy, co-founders of New Delhi Television (NDTV)—a legacy brand that pioneered the private news TV revolution in the country—and a dozen or so family members were leaving for Kenya to celebrate Radhika Roy's seventieth birthday. The mood was understandably joyous. While the family members breezed through immigration, Dr and Mrs Roy were stopped at the counter. 'I am afraid we have orders not to allow you to travel abroad, sir,' the immigration official said in an apologetic tone. Frequent global travellers, the Roys were taken aback. When asked for an explanation, the official could not provide one. Nor could he furnish any formal written document prohibiting the Roys from travelling abroad. 'If you wish, the rest of your family can travel,' observed the official. It was an offer no self-respecting individual was ever going to accept. The entire family disconsolately returned home.

A couple of years later, while on a flight to Varanasi, I was seated next to a man who kept smiling at me. I guessed he might have recognized me. We got chatting. He mentioned that he was a government official who was working in the Customs and Immigration department. Seated next to him were his young daughter and wife. 'We are going for a holiday and for darshan at the Kashi Vishwanath temple,' he said. I wished him well and was about to get back to watching a Netflix video when the man interrupted me. 'You were the one on NDTV's *The Big Fight* also, no?' he asked. I nodded, and the gentleman's tone dropped. 'There is something I wish to confess. I was part of the team that stopped Dr Prannoy Roy from travelling abroad when I was at Mumbai airport. It was the worst day of my professional career. I knew what I was doing was wrong but I had no choice.' He sighed. And then came his parting shot: 'If you meet Mr Roy, please say sorry from my side!'

It was in June 2017 that the CBI filed a case against the NDTV promoters for allegedly causing losses to ICICI Bank by defaulting on a loan. The Roys argued the case in the Delhi High Court, pointing out that the loan was fully repaid with interest ahead of schedule. The same month, their home was raided by the CBI. A month later, the CBI 'investigation' became the basis for an ED probe. For the next couple of years, the matter made little headway. In fact, most government ministers the Roys spoke to admitted there was little merit in the case and that they had no reason to worry. Until, suddenly, they were stopped from boarding an international flight. 'It is utterly scandalous,' was eminent jurist Fali Nariman's first reaction at a solidarity meet organized at the Press Club. Post-Covid, in 2021, the ED was spurred into action. Over the next twelve months, Prannoy Roy had to appear at the directorate's headquarters for questioning on more than a dozen occasions. Radhika Roy too was summoned on at least four occasions, though the officials were reportedly far more courteous. Despite the prolonged questioning, no chargesheet was filed, either by the CBI or the ED. Meanwhile, Income Tax notices kept piling up, each requiring expensive litigation to be warded off. 'What happened to the Roys and NDTV is a textbook case of how governments can harass the media, where the process is the punishment,' concluded N. Ram, eminent editor and the Roys' family friend.

The Roys' crime had nothing to do with their financial dealings but almost wholly to do with their brand of journalism, which was seen to offer greater space to a more 'left-liberal' worldview. The Modi government saw the network as staunchly 'anti-BJP', or more specifically 'anti-Modi', a charge that dates back to NDTV's (then Star News) coverage of the 2002 Gujarat violence. I was stationed for weeks and months in Gujarat, covering the communal riots with a team of reporters who were fully committed to bringing every detail into the drawing rooms of millions of viewers. It was the first such instance of mass violence in the country in the age of 24/7 private news TV. More than 1,000 people, mainly Muslims, were killed in the communal riots that followed the burning of a train in Godhra in which fifty-nine Hindu karsevaks were burnt to death. The grisly images of death and horrifying stories of gang-rape and murder shocked the nation, leading to demands for punishment and accountability. Then Chief Minister Narendra Modi was the obvious target, with the Opposition Congress demanding his resignation. Even then Prime Minister Atal Bihari Vajpayee reminded the chief minister of the need to follow his 'raj-dharma' (duties of a king). No mass riot takes place without the complicity or incompetence, or both, of the state administration was the learning I had received from my late grandfather P.M. Pant, Gujarat's longest-serving inspector general of police in the 1970s. Not surprisingly, Modi was convinced that the media, especially NDTV, had been less than fair to him in its coverage of the riots. Once in command at the Centre, he had the power to exact 'revenge'. Vengeful and vindictive politics is an important part of Modi's playbook. He brazenly uses state power to fight his political battles. His ministerial colleagues, in Gandhinagar and in Delhi, fear getting on his wrong side.

The initial move was to deny NDTV any access to the power corridors. Most government ministers avoided being seen on the network. In June 2017, when news anchor Nidhi Razdan asked BJP spokesperson Sambit Patra to leave the show after a quarrelsome debate, a farmaan was issued to all party persons by the BJP media cell to boycott NDTV platforms. On one occasion, when another BJP spokesperson, Nalin Kohli, appeared on an NDTV programme on Independence Day, he received frantic SMSes and calls from the party headquarters to get off the channel right away. It didn't end there. The network was denied any government advertising or support. Even private companies were urged not to sponsor events on NDTV. Advertising, especially from the government, is integral to a channel's revenue model, making it even more challenging for NDTV to carry on.

In 2018, Prime Minister Modi met a group of senior journalists from Tamil Nadu at the Parliament House Annexe in New Delhi. He asked them about any complaints they might have. Among those who attended the informal meeting was N. Ram of *The Hindu*. The Prime Minister was extremely warm and affectionate to the senior editor. Sensing an opportunity to reach out to Modi, Ram asked to have a word with him after the media interaction was over. As the two walked towards the place where the other journalists had assembled for high tea, Ram inquired why the government was bent on finishing off NDTV, remarking that its actions had driven the media organization to 'the brink of collapse'. To this, Modi reportedly responded with the assertion, 'They have already collapsed!'

It would take another four years for NDTV to actually 'collapse'. The Roys were reportedly out of the country when they got the 'breaking news' on their mobiles. The company was the target of a hostile takeover bid by the Adani Group, promoted by India's richest billionaire, Gautam Adani. In an unexpected move, the Adani Group announced that they were acquiring a sizeable stake in NDTV through a little-known company called Vishvapradhan Commercial Private Limited (VCPL). VCPL, indirectly controlled by the country's other billionaire businessman Mukesh Ambani, had loaned the NDTV promoters Rs 350 crore in 2009 with the option of converting the loan into equity through convertible warrants. For more than a decade, Ambani had not interfered with NDTV's operations. Now, without informing the Roys, he had quietly chosen to transfer the VCPL equity conversion rights to Adani. While many business observers were stunned by the 'deal' between supposed corporate rivals, the political power elite in the capital were not. 'When Mukesh bhai hands over his stake to Gautam bhai, you can be sure there are other forces at play; in this case the matter was initiated at the very top,' a senior government minister told me.

'Gautam bhai wasn't initially keen to get into the media business, but as the government's most favoured businessman, he was the ideal choice to take over the one mainstream television media network that was seen to take an anti-government line,' claimed a leading business executive privy to the pre-agreement conversation. Four months later, in

December 2022, the takeover was complete. Adani had become the single largest shareholder of NDTV, acquiring most of the shares held by the founders. With this takeover, now two of India's biggest news networks were led by corporate barons close to the Modi government. (In 2014, Mukesh Ambani had taken over the TV18 network, including channels like CNN-IBN, which I had helped set up as editor-in-chief.)

'Trust me, the Roys wanted to fight to retain hold of their company,' said a senior lawyer, 'but they were advised it was best to let go. You can fight an individual, but you can't fight an entire system.' Prannoy and Radhika Roy, the founder–promoters, were reluctantly bidding adieu to a company they had started in 1988 from a small south Delhi colony basement and lovingly nurtured over three decades—while maintaining the highest possible professional standards—into one of India's most trusted and recognized media brands. Their growth was propelled by the post-1991 liberalization policies that allowed private broadcasters to break Doordarshan's monopoly. Along with other media barons like Aroon Purie, Raghav Bahl and Subhash Chandra, the Roys completely altered the news broadcasting landscape in India. 'It was brutal and devastating,' Radhika Roy would later tell a friend. She was not alone. A number of professionals who had worked with NDTV wistfully saw the takeover as the end of an era. I had joined NDTV in 1994, leaving the relatively stable world of print journalism at *The Times of India* in Mumbai—appropriately referred to as the Old Lady of Bori Bunder—for the more exciting but uncertain world of TV news. I was fortunate to be part of an incredible journey in which 24/7 news TV broke new ground. I spent eleven extremely fulfilling years at NDTV before moving on to take up fresh challenges. A mix of nostalgia and sadness swirled around me when the takeover led to a spate of exits from the network.

There was no doubt that Gautam Adani had financial muscle, but as a politically aligned business leader, could he really offer credibility to a news brand? The hostile takeover of NDTV spread fear within the news media industry. No one felt safe any longer. Journalists became fearful of doing stories that might attract the wrath of the Modi establishment.

Most news channels were openly partisan, reduced to government mouthpieces. During the peak of the second Covid wave, most news networks were reluctant to question the Modi government's handling of the pandemic or publicize opinion polls that showed a sharp dip in the Prime Minister's popularity. When Manipur was in flames, it required the horrific video of two women being paraded naked for the media to express outrage over the continuing violence. When enforcement agencies selectively targeted Opposition leaders, there was no 2011-like India Against Corruption media campaign to expose the misuse of power. Allegations of vast amounts of money changing hands when Opposition governments were being toppled were never followed up. Rare were the screaming headlines when electoral bond details revealed possible deal-making between corporates and political parties.

Individual legacy media brands who were ready to fight the good fight were somewhat protected by their longevity and public standing. A number of small media outlets and independent journalists faced far worse retribution. In October 2023, the homes of around eighty journalists and employees—including young trainees and probationers—linked to the online portal NewsClick were raided by the Delhi police's Special Cell. Its founder and editor-in-chief, Prabir Purkayastha, was arrested under the draconian anti-terror law UAPA, and its offices sealed. The Income Tax department also stepped in and froze its assets, confiscating Rs 4 crore and leaving just 40 paise in the bank account! The portal, run on a shoestring budget from a tiny office in the capital, was charged with receiving funding to push Chinese propaganda in India. The case against NewsClick was built on the basis of an article in *The New York Times*, which alleged that Shanghai-based American millionaire Neville Roy Singham was funding a slew of companies, including NewsClick, as part of a China-backed global information network. There was no evidence of criminality since the portal's foreign funds had got clearance from the Reserve Bank of India. While its editorial line was unabashedly anti-Modi government and supportive of left ideology, labelling NewsClick a 'Chinese-funded' propaganda site, jailing its editor and charging him under anti-terror laws was a tactic to send a chilling message to anyone who might raise a dissenting voice against the regime.

This was the second time the grey-bearded Purkayastha, a qualified engineer who studied at Jawaharlal Nehru University and has been a member of the CPI(M) for decades, was being incarcerated. He was also jailed during the Emergency in 1975. Then, it was a midnight knock; now, it was a morning alarm. Then, he spent a year behind bars; now, he got bail after seven arduous months. 'The one thing I learnt from my jail period in the Emergency is that you must take life one day at a time because there is no release date mentioned. Then, it was a declared Emergency; now it's undeclared!' said the seventy-five-year-old.

Among those raided was Abhisar Sharma, an ex-colleague and friend, who wasn't even a NewsClick employee but just a regular contributor of video content to the platform. Like many freelance independent journalists in the last decade, Sharma had started his own YouTube channel and received decent traction, especially during the 2020 farmer agitation. Policemen entered Sharma's house at 6.30 a.m. and took away his mobiles, recording equipment and laptop. 'I was taken to the Special Cell headquarters and interrogated over two days. The police told me that they were investigating my alleged terror links because I had covered the farmer agitation and the Shaheen Bagh protests. They even claimed that I had received Chinese funding while citing a *New York Times* article. When I asked them to show me the article, it turned out to be something written in OpIndia [a right-wing website], where my name was in the headline but not even in the copy!' he recalled, laughing. While Sharma was let off by an embarrassed law enforcement team, his costly equipment is still in police custody. More than 400 devices were seized by the police in the NewsClick raids. 'The cops were actually very polite and gentle. You could sense they were simply acting on orders from the top to send a message that anyone who covers anti-government stories will be treated as a criminal,' he remarked.

Also raided and interrogated for more than ten hours was veteran journalist Paranjoy Guha Thakurta, who has over the years done several investigative stories on the Adani Group. 'I guess there could be a connection since NewsClick has published several articles and videos on the Adani Group and how the oligarch has benefitted from his perceived proximity to the Prime Minister,' said Guha Thakurta. Like Sharma, Guha Thakurta too was not on the staff of NewsClick. Unlike many of the others, though, his mobile phone and SIM card were returned soon after the examination was complete. 'I was one of the privileged few whose phone was returned. I guess the cops instinctively realized that there was nothing incriminating in my mobile. They kept asking if I'd like tea, coffee or some fruit juice. They even offered chhole bhature, but I just didn't have an appetite for food and settled for a bottle of water instead,' he said.

This isn't Guha Thakurta's only brush with intrusive state scrutiny in recent years. In 2021, he was among several journalists, activists and Opposition politicians who claimed that their phones had been hacked by government agencies using the Israeli spyware Pegasus. Those reportedly under the Pegasus watch included journalists from websites like The Wire, another feisty news outlet taking an uncompromising anti-Modi stand. Siddharth Varadarajan, founder–editor at The Wire, recalled how a forensic examination of his phone had shown that he and his co-editor M.K. Venu were confirmed targets of Pegasus between 2019 and 2021. 'In 2023, I again got an alert from Apple, and once again a forensic examination confirmed a fresh Pegasus attack,' he said. 'Yes, I do feel targeted by the Modi government. Just look at the number of criminal cases that the police has filed against us in BJP-ruled states.'

The irrepressible Guha Thakurta, along with a group of eminent citizens, approached the Supreme Court, urging judicial intervention to declare the alleged snooping 'unconstitutional' and direct the Centre to set up a 'judicial oversight' mechanism to prevent any breach of citizens' privacy. The apex court appointed an expert committee to look into the charges, but the report was never made public. In August 2022, the Supreme Court said that the Modi government did not co-operate with the investigation into the Pegasus spyware cases. In Parliament, Union Information Technology Minister Ashwini Vaishnaw was dismissive of the Pegasus story, first published by The Wire. 'This is an attempt to malign Indian democracy and its well-established institutions. Many over-the-top, sensational allegations have been made,' Vaishnaw declared.

Interestingly, The Wire editor revealed that two of Vaishnaw's numbers were also found in the Pegasus database during their investigations, from when he was a businessman and had not yet joined the BJP and been made a minister. 'For Vaishnaw to admit to our investigation being valid would have meant admitting his own government had spied on him!' claimed Varadarajan. The Pegasus investigation was conducted across a dozen media organizations globally, and the sensational facts uncovered led to an international outcry over the misuse of surveillance powers. Yet in India, the Modi government stonewalled any scrutiny. Surely the accusation of public money being used to buy spyware from Israel was serious enough to order a thorough and transparent probe. In 1972, US President Richard Nixon was nearly impeached for a break-in at the offices of his Democratic Party rivals, whereas in India, the Pegasus report was kept in a sealed envelope despite the Chief Justice calling for parts of it to be uploaded to the court's website. Every action, rather inaction, points to the Modi government having much to hide in the Pegasus case.

The government's denials notwithstanding, a clear pattern is discernible. Anyone in the media who is critical of the government is vulnerable to coercive state action. In July 2021, the Dainik Bhaskar Group, which brings out a widely circulated Hindi newspaper, was raided by Income Tax inspectors. The raids came within weeks of the newspaper doing a series of exposés on the Modi government's mishandling of the second Covid wave, which included pictures of the dead bodies floating in the Ganges and details on the under-reporting of deaths. In February 2023, the BBC's offices were searched by the Income Tax authorities just weeks after the acclaimed global broadcaster aired a documentary critical of Prime Minister Modi's handling of the 2002 Gujarat riots. The documentary was blocked online after a government missive to YouTube and Twitter. In 2021, the Modi government refused to renew the broadcast licence for the Malayalam news channel

MediaOne due to concerns around 'national security', claiming that the channel promoters had links with the Jamaat-e-Islami Hind (JEIH), an Islamic organization. Two years later, the Centre's order was set aside by the Supreme Court, which found no evidence on record to show the channel shareholders were sympathizers of the JEIH, which in any case wasn't a banned group. 'National security claims cannot be made out of thin air,' warned the court. The entirely arbitrary home ministry order meant that dozens of journalists lost their jobs.

It is not just the media. Several activists, NGOs and policy research institutes have faced the wrath of 'agency power', be it the ED or the Income Tax department. Worse, the concerted attack on press freedom isn't restricted any longer to the Centre. Across Indian states, including those ruled by the Opposition, journalists who refuse to toe the official line are under threat. 'We are in an age where to do investigative journalism that exposes any government and their cronies is seen as a criminal act,' said Guha Thakurta.

In May 2023, India dropped from the 150th spot to the 161st on the Reporters Without Borders Press Freedom Index, which ranks 180 countries across the globe. The ranking merely indicates that there are challenges to reporting freely and fairly in the world's largest democracy, but it does not reveal the underlying human cost of being a professional journalist in an environment marked by fear, where there are fewer checks and balances than ever before. The 2024 report of the Committee to Protect Journalists, a global watchdog, stated that seven Indian journalists were in jail in 2023. Four of them were from Jammu and Kashmir, a troubled conflict zone where the Public Safety Act is a weapon to detain anyone without trial for up to two years.

In October 2020, Siddique Kappan, a Kerala-based journalist, was arrested and charged under the UAPA for alleged links to the PFI, a radical Islamist group subsequently banned by the Indian government. He was taken into custody while on his way to cover the murder and gang-rape case in Uttar Pradesh's Hathras district that was making national headlines. Just when he was about to be let off, the ED slapped money-laundering charges on him. There was scant evidence of any criminal activity and yet he struggled to get bail for more than two years. While Kappan was still in jail, his mother passed away, but he couldn't be there for her last moments. A group of Kerala journalists brought his wife, Raihana, to Delhi to meet a few editors. As I listened to the case, I could only empathize with the struggle of the young woman, a mother of three, as she waged a lonely battle against an unyielding police machinery. 'We have suffered a lot. All I can say is that my husband is a proud Indian citizen,' Raihana said tearfully. 'He is not a terrorist.'

I left the room feeling despondent, wondering whether being an Indian Muslim journalist in 'new' India makes an individual even more defenceless before state power. The future for independent media that dares to challenge the ruling establishment appeared grim. With a large part of the mainstream media's news coverage hopelessly one-sided, how could there be even a semblance of a level playing field in the 2024 elections, I wondered.

=

So, who is the third most powerful man in the Modi government? This was a googly question posed to me by a BJP MP in the run-up to the 2024 electoral battle. In a power axis that revolved around a supremo and his trusted No. 2, was there any place for a third person? Most Union ministers were seen as yes-men and -women, their departments closely monitored by officials in the all-powerful PMO. Enter fifty-four-year-old Hiren Joshi, the Prime Minister's communications in-charge, a qualified electronics engineer who taught briefly at a Bhilwara engineering college before making the transition to the chief minister's office in Gandhinagar in 2008. Joshi's initial task was to enhance Modi's digital footprint. Social media was still in its infancy; platforms like Facebook and Twitter had just entered the Indian media landscape. Amongst politicians, Modi was an early mover, with Joshi driving the outreach. When Modi was sworn in as Prime Minister in 2014, Joshi, along with the entire Gujarat team, moved into the PMO. From supervising the Prime Minister's social media profile, which included writing tweets and Facebook posts, Joshi was soon empowered to control the hydra-headed media and communications engine that drives the Modi juggernaut. When, for example, the Prime Minister conducts his monthly radio programme *Mann ki Baat*, state BJP leaders are expected to ensure that audiences are assembled in different parts of the country to listen to the broadcast. Videos and pictures of the ground event are then uploaded and sent in real time to the PM's media team. 'Hiren controls two of the most important elements in the Modi government: its media machine and access to the Supreme Leader. That is why I refer to him as the third most powerful person in the government,' said the BJP MP.

The stern-faced, moustachioed Joshi has certain qualities that endeared him to Prime Minister Modi. A workaholic who is fiercely loyal to his boss, he wasn't rushing to acquire a public profile for himself, preferring instead to play power games from behind closed doors. Previous Prime Ministers too had had media advisors, but they were usually senior journalists who were already recognized faces before they stepped into the role. Some of them saw it as a comfortable sinecure after a long journalistic career, others as an opportunity to shape a government's image and contribute to policymaking. The standard practice for these experienced journalists was to use their personal networks to maintain cosy relationships with fellow editors and reporters. This well-knit group was also part of a much smaller media ecosystem, one that could be controlled with a few phone calls or over extended lunches at the Delhi Gymkhana or India International Centre. On the other hand, as a digi-tech expert who was not a professional journalist, Joshi was an 'outsider' to the capital's media whirl. With no past obligations or individual relationships to build upon, he could exercise his clout with an unapologetically ruthless edge. He wasn't in this job to do journalists and journalism any favours but simply ensure, as Modi's image-maker, that Brand Modi was relentlessly built without any pushback from the media fraternity.

Stories abound about how the engineer-turned-communications-chief exercised his unbridled power to get the mainstream 'legacy' media, in particular, to fall in line. Heading a fairly large team within the PMO, Joshi created a watchlist by which every television show was monitored. Even tweets and Facebook posts of journalists would be constantly scrutinized by the PMO's media cell. Tweets, in particular, are an obsession for the Modi government. The Prime Minister is reportedly given a lowdown on all the important tweets concerning him every evening. An entire chain of Union ministers, BJP leaders, Modi supporters, celebrity influencers, surrogate handles and even journalists has been formed to ensure that the Prime Minister's 'achievements' are ceaselessly promoted. It isn't unusual for identically worded tweets to be put out in the public domain by this group. 'If we don't follow the suggested tweet format, we won't get access to news breaks,' admitted a PMO beat reporter.

By contrast, those mainstream media journalists who opined or tweeted against the government were singled out and targeted. While covering the Samajwadi Party during the 2017 Uttar Pradesh assembly elections, Rohini Singh, an investigative journalist working with a business newspaper, posted a few tweets suggesting that Akhilesh Yadav was ahead and that Modi's popularity may not translate into votes. A dossier of her 'offensive' tweets was sent to the newspaper's management, urging them to delete the tweets and take suitable action against her. The PMO, which already had issues with the newspaper's political reportage, then let it be known that neither Modi nor his ministers would attend the global business summit being organized by the newspaper. An unofficial boycott by the government meant a serious loss in revenue for a legacy brand with marquee sponsors for their annual money-spinner conclave. Soon after the BJP won the Uttar Pradesh elections, Singh was reprimanded and asked to do 'favourable' stories for the Modi government as a sign of 'atonement'. She chose to quit the job instead. 'They even spread rumours about how I had allegedly taken favours from the Akhilesh government. It was a brazen character assassination orchestrated by lead members of the BJP's IT cell,' she claimed.

Singh is not the only journalist who was in the firing line. A more egregious case involving a senior journalist with a leading English news channel occurred during the 2024 general elections. Diligently citing past precedent, the journalist reported on the failure of the ECI to send a notice to Modi on his contentious Banswara speech in a live broadcast. Almost instantly, the journalist was informed by his editorial leadership that he was being taken off air for the entire duration of the election campaign. The channel was apparently still waiting to get a Modi interview and didn't want to risk the PMO's ire. 'The decision to take the journalist off air was taken under orders from the "top",' claimed a senior editor at the network. Whether 'top' refers to timorous, self-censoring editors or a scary government media machine is unclear.

Over time, Joshi acquired a reputation for ringing up media owners directly to seek action whenever an article or tweet or news show went against the Modi government's interests. 'Who are we kidding here?' said Pawan Khera, the Congress's media head. 'Everyone in the media industry knows that news editors and godi media anchors are rung up by Joshi and his minions and told what topics to take up and what line to take in prime-time debates. They even decide the language to be used in the channel top bands and headlines.' The BJP media team remains unfazed by this criticism. 'Are you telling us that the likes of Ahmed Patel didn't ring up media owners to ensure that nothing negative was said about Sonia Gandhi? Who is the Congress to lecture us?' demanded a prominent BJP spokesperson.

Doubtless, 'managing' the media didn't begin in 2014. But now it was more brazen and intimidating—and perhaps also more effective. The Manmohan Singh government, especially during UPA-II, had almost ceded national space to prime-time news channels, which kept badgering it on charges of corruption and other failings. An authoritarian Modi regime had no intention of making the same mistake.

Modi's media strategy followed an unambiguous carrot-and-stick approach. Between 2017 and 2022, the Modi government spent an estimated Rs 526 crore on TV advertisements and Rs 1,829 crore on newspaper advertisements, as per a reply in Parliament. If the organizers of a media conclave or a special programme wanted to invite ministers and senior BJP leaders, they had to get in touch with the BJP's media in-charge, Anil Baluni. The soft-spoken Baluni, a former journalist and now a BJP MP from Uttarakhand, would give priority to those organizers who showcased the party and government 'appropriately'. The so-called 'godi' anchors who aligned themselves with the government's viewpoint were 'rewarded' with privileged access to the Prime Minister's inner circle; those who raised discomfiting questions were frozen out. I clearly fall into the latter category. When I asked Joshi for an interview for this book, his response was telling: 'In the interest of honesty I want to say the book will not be charitable to us. It will be, like your tweets, loaded with backhanded jabs, so I do not wish to legitimize this effort. But I wish you the best for it!' Unfailingly polite in our WhatsApp interactions but clearly hard-nosed in his professional goals, Joshi had perfected the art of speaking in his master's voice.

If Joshi was seen as the puppeteer in the PMO, the ultra-aggressive BJP IT cell chief, Amit Malviya, was accused by the Opposition of being the prime mover of viciously targeting on social media anyone who criticized the government. He and I had had run-ins on more than one occasion on TV. His nasty personal attacks are a standard ploy, but he didn't stop there. He would send offensive WhatsApp messages telling me to 'retire' and threatening to 'take me down'. Reluctantly, I blocked him on WhatsApp. He was a powerful member of the ruling party's media machine, someone who headed a large army of like-minded social media troll-warriors. Getting on his wrong side was an unpleasant experience, one that I hadn't really prepared myself for.

In 2021, during the West Bengal election campaign, I was asked by Home Minister Shah to join his cavalcade after he unexpectedly agreed to my request for an interview. 'We can do the interview on the chopper while I move to the next campaign stop,' said Shah. I was delighted. The home minister was a prized interviewee. We were travelling as part of the minister's convoy, when we were abruptly asked to get off by Malviya, who had apparently found out about the interview and was determined to scotch it. I was stunned by his sheer malice towards me. He was co-in-charge of the BJP's West Bengal campaign, but surely he didn't have veto powers over the country's all-powerful home minister? As it turned out, he did. A sheepish-looking Shah promised to do an interview 'some other time'.

Media 'management' isn't just limited to getting pesky journalists to fall in line. An entire ecosystem has been created by the Modi machine to amplify the noise around the Prime Minister. An illustrative example of how the government's well-orchestrated social media campaigns work is provided by the buzz generated around the 'Modi ka parivar' slogan. In early March 2024, days before the elections were announced, Opposition leader Lalu Prasad Yadav taunted the Prime Minister for not having a 'family of his own' in response to Modi's charge of dynastic politics. Within twenty-four hours, all BJP leaders and supporters had added 'Modi ka parivar' to their social media handles as a countermove and mark of solidarity with the Prime Minister. Though Malviya and the BJP IT cell were pushing the campaign online, the original idea was reportedly the brainchild of Joshi and his team in the PMO. 'We get the instruction directly from our party media cell, but we know where it actually comes from,' remarked a minister. The Modi cult is built around a high-decibel multimedia propaganda machine of a kind the country has never seen before. Capturing and dominating the media space is central to the Modi regime. Modi is, in many ways, a by-the-media, for-the-media and of-the-media personality. Every government advertisement, each promotional film, every photograph and all press statements made by the Prime Minister are always carefully curated to ensure maximum coverage. Joshi and his ilk are the artful choreographers, pulling the strings from the shadows, ensuring Modi's image is never dented by negative publicity. In the immediate aftermath of the 2002 Gujarat violence, Modi had been put through the wringer by the media. He was asked searching questions on his government's role. The journalistic interrogation of Modi post-2002 had culminated in his infamous walkout during a CNN-

IBN interview with Karan Thapar, an anchor known for his rigorous and tough questioning style. 'This cannot ever happen again,' Modi had told an aide at the time. The message was clear: Modi might do an occasional interview but only on his terms. Which might explain why, as Prime Minister, Modi has chosen not to do a single press conference in a decade of power. Nor has he answered a single question during Question Hour in Parliament. Instead, Modi's preferred modes of communication are tweets, speeches and his *Mann ki Baat* radio show. This type of top-down, one-way communication channel means that the narrative can be easily controlled—no unsettling questions could be asked.

But in the run-up to the 2024 elections, there was a distinct shift in strategy. Confident of winning another big majority, Modi decided to give a slew of interviews, as many as eighty-two according to one count, in a packed two-month period. After mostly staying away from the media while in government, this was an unforeseen windfall. 'The aim was to carpet-bomb and totally invisibilize the Opposition, to send out the message that there is only one leader in the country and that is Narendra Modi,' said a BJP political strategist. Fine optics mattered above all else, as they do with every Modi interaction. Each interview during the campaign was carefully designed by Joshi and his team to ensure the manufactured halo around the Prime Minister remained untouched and the viewer–voter felt diligently courted. National newspapers like *The Indian Express* and *The Hindu*, which had written the occasional critical story or editorial against the government, were denied access despite formal requests. The interviews played to a predetermined script: TV channels and interviewers were selected by Joshi keeping the election calendar in mind. For example, the first interview in late March was with the Tamil channel Thanthi TV only because Tamil Nadu was going to the polls in the first phase.

Before the polling began in mid-April, an interview was given to ANI, a government-friendly news agency subscribed to by all news channels, thereby ensuring wall-to-wall coverage across networks. In a first of sorts, most of the interviews were shot and edited by the PMO, which by now had its own in-house TV production team, complete with a camera crew, editors and sound recordists—a first for an Indian Prime Minister. 'This is like a show being produced and directed by the PMO with only one shining star; the anchors are simply there as sidekicks,' remarked a senior journalist. An analysis of the style and content of the interviews is revealing. Each interview was soft-focus and excessively deferential in tone. There were no raised voices, no arguments, no cross-questioning. The journalistic dictum 'ask the questions and question the answers' was given the go-by. The era of the hard-hitting, adversarial interview was well and truly buried.

Unsurprisingly, all questions to Modi during the campaign were now vetted, and the responses edited where necessary. Across the eighty-odd interviews, not one question was asked on the Manipur violence, in which more than 200 people had died, or on the standoff with China in Ladakh, which remained unresolved. One question was gently asked on Modi's equation with Adani but without any follow-up or fact-check. Instead, at least half a dozen interviewers asked about the secret of the Prime Minister's energy, more than one gushed that they 'had never seen a Prime Minister like Modi ji' and one introduced him as the 'leader without whom India couldn't dream of a "Viksit Bharat"'. The unending eulogistic pitch only seemed to reaffirm the mainstream media's conviction that a Modi-led BJP would score another landslide victory. One interview, in fact, was dedicated almost entirely to what Modi 3.0 would look like. A delighted Prime Minister proceeded to outline a 1,000-year vision as the anchor nodded admiringly!

By contrast, Rahul Gandhi refused to give even a single one-on-one interview to mainstream or digital media. During his Bharat Jodo Yatra, he had chosen to interact with YouTube influencers, which would attract a younger demographic. His YouTube interviews were mostly designed in an uncontroversial, feature-like format: Rahul's favourite food and marriage plans were among the light-hearted questions asked. Hard political questions were off the interview menu. But during the 2024 campaign, Rahul shut himself out completely from all interviews, preferring to hold press conferences and share personalized videos instead. A Team Rahul member recalled trying to persuade Rahul to give at least one or two interviews, but to little avail. 'Why should I engage with a media that has spent the last decade targeting me and the Congress party all the time? We don't need to give them any credibility,' he countered. The uneasy, fraught equation between Rahul and the legacy media reflects the Congress leader's sense of perpetual grievance against a media establishment that he remained convinced was playing to the BJP's tune.

Gandhi's headstrong stand mirrored that of a section of the Opposition. In September 2023, the Opposition INDIA alliance released a list of news anchors whose shows they would boycott. It was an unprecedented move, one that appeared prima facie anti-democratic and intolerant. Even if the Opposition was enraged by the hyper-partisan approach of a few anchors, why announce an 'official' boycott? 'This wasn't a boycott but an act of civil disobedience. For how long do you want us to engage with those whose single-point agenda is to defame the Opposition and persist with toxic narratives?' asked the Congress's Pawan Khera.

A media committee set up by the Opposition compiled a list of inflammatory headlines that they claimed proved their point that certain news channels were promoting a divisive anti-Opposition agenda. For example, one show ahead of the 2022 Uttar Pradesh elections screamed: 'Hinduon ke khilaaf Mahagathbandhan (An anti-Hindu grand alliance)?' The dangers of such hate propaganda became apparent when, in July 2023, a Railway Protection Force jawan shot and killed four passengers in a train. Roaming through the train he was meant to protect, he hunted for Muslim-looking people, asked for their names and pumped bullets into them. He justified his actions by claiming that his victims were operating from Pakistan, and later declared that the source of his unhinged information was the 'Indian media'. It was a tragic moment that should have called for introspection from the hatemonger channels masquerading as news networks. Sadly, neither did the offenders do any soul-searching nor was there an outcry from others in the news industry. While the watchdog News Broadcasting and Digital Standards Authority

(NBDSA) has occasionally stepped in to penalize offensive content, it is nowhere near enough to act as an effective deterrent.

Reportedly, a few Congress leaders, like Jairam Ramesh, had opposed the decision to boycott specific anchors. While the role played by a section of the media has been indefensible, such boycotts have limited utility, especially in the heat and dust of a charged election campaign. An intractable Rahul Gandhi's refusal to engage with the mainstream media when contrasted with the Prime Minister's umpteen interviews suggested that the Congress was only setting itself up to lose the perception war. After all, the BJP could now easily turn around and say that while a consummate communicator like Modi was opening himself to media interaction, his prime opponent was running away from being quizzed. In a normal political environment anywhere in the world, it would mean game, set and, in all likelihood, match to the media-friendly side.

Surprisingly, though, it didn't work out that way. Instead, the sycophantic nature of a majority of the Modi interviews and the Prime Minister's gloating, narcissistic responses boomeranged on him on more than one occasion. His assertion of being a 'non-biological messenger of God', for instance, made him an instant target of memes and jokes. Today Modi's claim of being 'non-biological' is often used by the Opposition to lampoon the self-glorifying Prime Minister. When Modi cackled, 'Kaun Rahul (Rahul who)?', it led to more spoofs than applause. Where even five years ago every Modi interview was a highly watched talking point, now the well-rehearsed, stilted, eulogistic conversations were falling flat before the spontaneity being shown by his rival's public interactions on the road. While the Prime Minister remained well ahead in terms of total followers and subscribers on his various platforms, Rahul Gandhi's social and digital media impressions, in terms of shares, likes and overall engagement, be it on Instagram or YouTube, edged ahead of Modi's for the first time ever. Maybe the audience's tastes had changed or, more likely, the credibility crisis of mainstream media, especially TV news, had finally caught up with it. With the traditional media being dismissed as 'godi' or 'durbari', depending on the viewers' political preferences, a space was opening up for alternative narratives to emerge. The 2024 election was the perfect stage for the long-awaited digital news revolution to take off.

It was in the town square of Hajipur, near Patna, that I received a reality check on the changing patterns of news consumption. I was engaged in a typically animated conversation with a group of first-time voters, when one of the young men launched into a diatribe against tanashahi, or dictatorship. I was impressed by his passion and spirited arguments. 'Looks like you are a political science student,' I remarked. 'Arre, main biology padhta hoon (I study biology). But I have been watching Dhruv Rathee's YouTube videos. I'm sure you have also!' he responded.

Yes, I had. Well, sort of. In February 2024, a Mumbai-based friend who doesn't like Modi sent me a WhatsApp forward of a YouTube video by Dhruv Rathee provocatively titled 'Is India Becoming a Dictatorship?' The video's thumbnail had a visual of Modi staring coldly with devilish-looking eyes. 'When will you guys on TV have the guts to do something like this!' my friend raged. Sensationalist headlines and arresting visuals are designed for YouTube virality. The lively and irreverent digital sphere made even tabloid TV look dull at times.

The twenty-nine-minute video gathered 2-million-plus views within hours. It was frenetically forwarded across scores of WhatsApp groups. Weeks later, Rathee was back with a sequel. About Arvind Kejriwal's arrest, this one crossed 5 million views within hours. By the time the election cycle began, just these two videos between them had crossed a whopping 50 million views on YouTube alone. Rathee, a twenty-nine-year-old Rohtak-born YouTuber, had well and truly arrived—on a mobile phone near you. As had India's first YouTube general election.

'Honestly, I didn't expect this kind of reaction; it was like people out there were just glad that someone was openly saying what they inwardly felt. It is a fact that democracy is under threat,' Rathee would tell me later. His success formula, as I saw it, was in the sheer simplicity and directness of his messaging. Open. Candid. Disruptive. Hard-hitting. But also, crucially, in Hindi. The credibility crisis facing TV news in general was especially aggravated on Hindi news channels, where most anchors were universally seen to toe a staunchly pro-BJP line. Worse, some were guilty of promoting the most vicious communal stereotyping and had become open purveyors of religious bigotry. Hindi is the ultimate mass-language medium, and the Modi government had its eyes and ears trained specifically on Hindi news narratives. With most Hindi TV news anchors noisily shouting down any dissenting views, Rathee was pitched as an anti-establishment counterpoint. Sure, he too was picking a side, but he was doing it in a style that was uninterrupted and unambiguous. There was no pretence of neutrality, no lofty preachiness. He wasn't even claiming to be a journalist; he was simply amplifying the primary data collected by on-ground journalists and then cutting through the noise to build a solid argument. One could disagree with his opinions, but there was no denying that the packaging and presentation were refreshingly different and attention-grabbing. It marked, in a sense, a generational shift. India's young and restless wanted their news and opinions to be freed from any conventional filters. They wanted journalists to be what the press is meant to be: anti-establishment and questioning.

The original 'dictatorship' video was triggered by the blatant rigging of the Chandigarh mayoral polls till a Supreme Court verdict righted a palpable wrong. 'I think all of us who saw what happened in Chandigarh were angry and wanted to vent. It wasn't just an isolated case. Arresting chief ministers, cornering electoral bonds, buying out MLAs—the fury was building up. I just felt that if I didn't speak up now, it would be a waste of a platform,' claimed Rathee. He insisted that he isn't left- or right- wing or even anti-Modi, but he is against the values Modi represents. 'I believe in the values of free speech, liberty and tolerance; those values were at stake in 2024,' he said. His viral videos, aimed at frontally challenging mainstream media narratives, were driven by a 'specific moment in time'.

Interestingly, prior to his 2024 tryst with fame, Rathee, a mechanical engineer by training, saw himself as a YouTube educator, breaking down complex topics of science and technology, society and culture. His first video in 2014 was a 'fun' travel blog. In 2020, he became a full-time YouTuber with a small team that has now grown to around fifteen people. Having obtained his engineering degree in Germany and set up residence 'somewhere in Europe', he is not sure of coming back home just yet. 'It's best that I don't reveal my exact address, even though I haven't received any threats as such beyond the usual trolling,' he said.

While Rathee is comfortably ensconced in Europe, there are other digital 'insurgents' closer home. In a country with close to 700 million (70 crore) mobile users and over 500 million (50 crore) active YouTube users, thousands of YouTubers and Instagrammers are creating their own band of devoted followers and communities, building online platforms that symbolize a rapid 'democratization' of news where traditional information monopolies can be challenged and alternative narratives can be set. Supporting an immense array of content creators, from established journalists to young influencers, from right-wing flag-bearers to left-wing radicals to Dalit–OBC community journalists, YouTube and Instagram are ideologically neutral spaces that remain mostly unregulated for now. At a time when a single directive from the information and broadcasting ministry could force India's 350-plus news channels to toe the line, these sites offer a precious platform for differing viewpoints to be heard.

The BJP and the Congress, and even regional parties, knew what was at stake in this digital boom, and allotted a substantial chunk of their 2024 political advertising funds to YouTube and Instagram campaigns. The Google Ads Transparency Center reported that in the crucial electioneering months between February and May, the Congress spent Rs 24.5 crore on Google ads for video content and the BJP Rs 50.4 crore and, reportedly, even more through surrogates with the sole aim of dominating the YouTube–Instagram space. And yet, unlike on TV, the BJP couldn't set a unidirectional agenda on social media. 'The growth of YouTube content is so organic that no single entity can control this revolution,' said a digital marketing executive.

One of the most visible faces of this revolution is forty-nine-year-old Ravish Kumar, a former NDTV anchor and winner of the prestigious Ramon Magsaysay Award for journalism in 2019. If Rathee had stepped into a digital news whirlwind almost by accident, Kumar was a mainstream journalist who adopted the YouTube universe because he was left with no other choice. The Adani takeover of NDTV in 2022 forced Kumar to resign after more than two decades at the network. For years, he had been the face of NDTV's Hindi channel, NDTV India, his unique presentation style and focus on people-centric issues like exam paper leaks, government job recruitment delays and collapsing urban infrastructure making him a celebrated standout figure in the din of breaking news. 'Look, Adani's takeover has absolutely nothing to do with journalism, and staying on at NDTV was simply not an option. It was like being asked to become a proofreader at the BJP headquarters!' insisted Kumar.

In a period of personal trauma—his mother in Patna was critically ill—Kumar found staunch supporters in the loyal viewers of his flagship NDTV show. Within ten days of his breaking into the YouTube universe, he acquired a staggering 2.3 million subscribers. By the time the 2024 election cycle began, the number had crossed 10 million. 'I think it was an act of rebellion by viewers who had registered the implications of the Adani takeover and decided to switch over from TV to my YouTube channel out of solidarity with an anchor speaking up for them!' he said. It was Kumar, after all, who had coined the term 'godi media' in 2016 to refer, in his words, to the 'total surrender of the media before one master'.

Despite international acclaim, the transition from prime-time TV to YouTube has not been easy, admitted Kumar. Getting up at 6 a.m. every morning to write his video scripts, meticulously researching stories and supervising the editing and production with a small team is a far cry from being part of a large newsroom and legacy media brand. Working from home without institutional support can be tough: 'freedom' comes at a price. Is his journalism now reduced to 'anti-Modi' rants as critics allege, I ask. 'If asking questions of the government, any government, by taking up pro-people topics makes me anti-Modi, then what is left to say?' he countered.

In a sense, Kumar's successful changeover from TV news anchor–reporter to YouTube opinion-maker reflects the rapidity with which mainstream media allowed itself to reach the point of no return by becoming a government cheerleader post-2014. The same media that in 2011 had spoken out in unison to support the Anna Hazare-led India Against Corruption movement and even hit the streets when a young woman in Delhi was brutally gang-raped and killed had sunk to disseminating one-sided and, at times, communally spiteful news narratives. This wasn't a normal left-versus-right binary ideological battle but a big media capitulation to state power. The digital disruption then, especially in the Hindi news media, was an inevitable outcome of a desperate urge to listen to alternative viewpoints. Crucially, unlike in 2019, it ensured at least a semblance of a level playing field in the 2024 'media war'.

And yet, while the YouTube explosion was an undeniable feature of the 2024 elections and after, it isn't certain just how long its growth can remain entirely uncontrolled. The Modi government's draft Broadcasting Services (Regulation) Bill, 2023 had sought to regulate online content and treat any individuals uploading videos, making podcasts or writing about current affairs as 'digital news broadcasters', and subject them to a government regulatory framework. 'Regulation' is often the first step towards control and censorship, terms that tend to be used interchangeably by a political leadership whose default mode has an inherently authoritarian and repressive streak. In response to a question in Parliament in December 2023, then Information and Broadcasting Minister Anurag Thakur admitted that 122 YouTube-based news channels had been blocked since December 2021 in the 'interest of sovereignty and integrity of India'. While the draft bill was withdrawn in August 2024 after criticism of its intent and content, those who had turned to YouTube to escape government censorship must now wonder if their turn too will come one day soon.

The larger questions, though, aren't centred on any specific platform but revolve around the media in general. For how long will the media choose the path where there is little to no resistance to overbearing state power? For how long will journalists self-censor and news organizations be fearful of speaking truth to power? Will media owners and journalists recollect that their primary duty is to their readers and viewers? That providing truth-telling, real journalism that serves the citizen is a far greater calling than simply trying to stay in the Modi government's good books? Maybe an exceptional election verdict has shown the way for a concerted pushback. If, despite a non-level playing field, and against all the odds, the humble voter could hold powerful politicians to account, can the Indian media not do the same now? Be fair and balanced to all sides? And perhaps a little courageous too?

Amidst the darkness of a 'managed' media, there are hopeful voices calling for change.

Phir subah hogi (Dawn will break again).

Modi vs Rahul: What Lies Ahead?

Frequently asked question: Is the Modi era drawing to a close?

THERE is a story, possibly apocryphal, about Narendra Modi's need to stay in power at all costs. Apparently, as a young man, when Modi worked briefly at his uncle's canteen in Ahmedabad, he would travel by a state transport bus from his home in the town of Vadnagar. He would leave his jhola, or bag, behind in the bus to reserve a seat since the same bus would take him back to Vadnagar. Moral of the story? Once Modi has sat on a chair, no one can snatch it away from him! This story was narrated to me by a Gujarat Congress leader, so it can be taken with more than a pinch of salt, but the underlying message is unmistakable. Instinctively domineering, narcissistic and bossy, Narendra Modi is uncomfortable without total control of his destiny. He has a Vladimir Putin-like desire for absolute power and a Recep Tayyip Erdoğan-like conviction that he is 'the Chosen One'.

In a newspaper column, Yogendra Yadav—the only political analyst who got the 2024 election numbers spot-on—described the verdict as a 'personal' and 'political' defeat for Modi.

Let there be no confusion about it. The election was about the Supreme Leader seeking post-facto public approval for the brick-by-brick dismantling of the republic and popular endorsement for the proposed mutilation of India's constitutional democracy. The Indian public refused to give him that authorization. If the contest was a shade more fair, he would have been sitting in the Opposition. Eventually, he managed to reclaim the chair he so desperately needed, but the public has denied him the 'iqbal' (prestige/legitimacy) that he so craved.

Yadav is quite correct to suggest that by blowing away the 'char sau paar' dream, the voter has cut Modi to size and seriously dented his moral and political authority. But in the end, India's electoral democracy is about who gets to be first past the post. After a decade, we are still in the BJP age of ethno-religious Hindutva nationalism that began in 2014, with the vast Hindu middle-class vote remaining with the party in large parts of the country. Modi's aura of invincibility has certainly diminished, and the 'Aayega toh Modi hi' or 'There is Modi only' sense of inevitability of outcome is slowly fading away, but Modi has also survived to fight another day. The BJP's 240 MPs are still more than twice the Congress's 99, that too in a period where incumbents across the world are being defeated.

Long-serving politicians have a survival instinct, honed into an art form over time. A number of such characters have popped in and out through the pages of this book: the Gandhis, Mallikarjun Kharge, Sharad Pawar, Mamata Banerjee, Nitish Kumar, Chandrababu Naidu, Siddaramaiah and, of course, the inseparable duo of Team Modi–Shah. Each of these seasoned politicians has one thing in common: a remarkable ability to stick around even in the most adverse circumstances. I am not a betting man nor a soothsayer, but I do believe that Modi 3.0 will eventually adjust to life in an NDA coalition. The swagger of a polarizing strongman will be increasingly tested by his opponents, but the fierce determination to cling to power hasn't been shaken by Verdict 2024. Not yet.

Will the Modi-led coalition complete a full five-year term? This is not a question this book, completed just a few months after the general election results, seeks to answer. This is a book of reportage and observation of a dramatic period in Indian politics and is not an exercise in crystal ball gazing. Especially not in a country like India, where, as the past decade has shown so demonstrably, even twenty-four hours can sometimes prove to be a long time in politics. But as a close observer of Modi's political career over three decades, I would never write him off just because he didn't get another massive mandate. As highlighted in this book, Team Modi–Shah's ruthless politics is matched by their readiness to do whatever it takes to stay in power. However, it does seem that the government's my-way-or-the-highway approach is now being tempered by the realities of coalition politics, and contentious legislation is being pushed on the backburner or sent for parliamentary scrutiny. For example, a proposed lateral-entry recruitment plan for mid-level bureaucrats was withdrawn within forty-eight hours of being advertised after protests from within and outside the government. Such a speedy rollback would have been inconceivable in the Modi-led government's previous avatars.

The BJP's key coalition partners are also settling into their new roles, taking full advantage of their increased bargaining power. A meeting with Chandrababu Naidu soon after the new government was sworn in was revelatory. There was renewed confidence in his body language, the kind that comes with electoral success. Naidu realizes he is in almost the same position that he was in during the Vajpayee years, when all roads led to Hyderabad. The Andhra leader's first target is to extract maximum financial support from the Centre for his 'rebuild Andhra' project. 'I am not interested in ministerships at the Centre. I want Andhra's interests to be put first,' he reiterated. When asked whether his 'secular' image was being compromised in the bargain, Naidu was emphatic that he would never tolerate 'communal' politics. 'We will abide by the Constitution at all times,' he said. A practised regional satrap, Naidu knows how to wield influence in the power corridors. Apparently, strict instructions have been issued by the Centre to senior bureaucrats that when Naidu comes calling in Delhi, appointments must be given instantly and can on no account be deferred. As Budget 2024 has already shown, Naidu is busily extracting his pound of flesh.

If there is one lurking challenge to Modi's continuity in office, it lies not with his allies or even the Opposition as much as it does with his own brotherhood in saffron. Throughout this book, I have highlighted numerous instances of the brutish and thuggishly transactional politics practised by Team Modi–Shah. It isn't just Opposition governments that have been toppled through inducements and the misuse of central agencies. BJP chief ministers have been replaced on a whim, many senior leaders sidelined, some even humiliated. Modi's authoritarian personality cult has cast even an organization like the Sangh Parivar into the shade, and many are now waiting patiently for their moment in the sun. A Union minister described Modi's first decade as an irresistible tidal wave that forced everyone else to just duck and hide. Today, after Verdict 2024, the minister smiles: 'We can finally see a glimpse of a calmer shore.'

While few in the BJP can challenge Modi's supremacy just yet, the RSS has already expressed its concerns over decision-making remaining a one-man show. In his first public reaction to the 2024 election results, RSS chief Mohan Bhagwat remarked, 'A true "sevak" (one who serves the people) never shows arrogance and always maintains decorum in public life.' It was a telling comment after an election campaign where Modi chose to project himself as a 'non-biological' god. Nor was it an isolated remark. In a speech in September 2024, the RSS head spoke out again: 'Through work, everyone can become a revered figure. But whether we have reached that level will be determined by others, not by ourselves. We should not proclaim that we have become God.' Bhagwat's words suggest that the RSS is trying to reclaim lost ground as the Sangh's paterfamilias from an unchallenged political supremo.

The Modi–RSS equation is the subject of much speculation. Modi, who cut his teeth as an RSS pracharak, is well aware of the Sangh's fervent desire to set the ideological agenda by realizing their vision of a 'Hindu Rashtra'. His decade of absolute power has given the RSS the opportunity to impose its footprint on Indian politics like never before. In July 2024, the Modi government lifted the forty-four-year-old ban on government employees joining the RSS, another step towards 'mainstreaming' a shadowy organization whose majoritarian outlook was once viewed with suspicion. The year 2025 marks a centenary of the RSS's existence, a landmark moment for the entire Sangh Parivar. A Bollywood producer revealed that the RSS leadership met a group of filmmakers and entertainment channel executives at a five-star hotel in Mumbai a few years ago and asked them to make movies and television serials on 'nationalist heroes' and 'Hindu icons' who they claimed were never given their due in previous Congress governments. 'We want to rewrite history from the right perspective,' the RSS senior leader had declared. These films were assured state patronage. This might explain why there has been a glut of 'saffronized' cinema in recent times, movies designed to showcase an RSS worldview of Indian history and culture.

Despite misgivings in some quarters, the RSS knows that Modi is their best bet for now. As the CSDS 2024 post-poll survey shows, Modi's popularity is still well above that of his party. One in every four BJP voters said they voted for the party only because of the Prime Minister's leadership; in 2019 it was approximately one in every three. Modi may no longer scale the same peaks of mass adulation as before, but his fall from the summit is unlikely to be as precipitous as his critics wish. More so because there is no visible challenger within the BJP just yet. The limitations of Amit Shah's election management skills have been shown up by the 2024 results. Even a hardline Hindutva mascot like Yogi Adityanath must rebuild his base after the party's 2024 Uttar Pradesh setback. None of the other frequently mentioned contenders—Nitin Gadkari, Rajnath Singh, Shivraj Singh Chouhan—can match Modi's pan-Indian appeal. Unless the RSS hierarchy chooses to assert itself more directly, which is still only in the realm of conjecture, Modi remains well-ensconced in his seat. He will turn seventy-five in September 2025 but for a hardened politician, age is just a number. As a global business summit in August 2024, Modi promised to return to address the gathering in 2029. 'Retirement', clearly, is not being contemplated anytime soon.

Frequently asked question: Has Rahul Gandhi finally arrived as a politician of substance?

For long lampooned as a non-serious politician, the reinvention of Rahul Gandhi, and his emergence as a leader who could set the election narrative, is unquestionably one of the bigger stories of the 2024 general election. By doggedly harping on the need to offer a cultural, moral and civilizational challenge to the RSS–BJP, he has undeniably provided an ideological compass to his politics. There was a moment when Modi and Rahul went head-to-head in the new Parliament in July 2024, in the first session of the 18th Lok Sabha, that signalled a marked shift in optics. The ageing, vituperative BJP supremo against a much younger and upbeat challenger radiating positive energy was now a genuine contest, forcing Modi to, at one stage, intervene and respond to charges made by the leader of the Opposition. In that face-to-face encounter, it almost seemed as if the much-needed political balance between the ruling party and the Opposition had been temporarily restored, and that the Opposition had finally begun to find its voice on a range of issues.

In my previous 2014 and 2019 election books, I wrote: 'Rahul Gandhi has never missed an opportunity to miss an opportunity.' The comment, which I would repeat at book events, would spark much laughter in audiences. Not any longer. A quote (wrongly attributed to Mahatma Gandhi) claims: 'First they ignore you, then they laugh at you, then they fight you, then you win.' Rahul Gandhi has never quite been ignored, since he belongs to India's most recognized political family. He has been mocked and nicknamed 'Pappu' by his rivals, principally because the BJP launched a well-orchestrated campaign—aided by a pliant media—to destroy his credibility, but he also did score his fair share of self-goals. Recall him tearing up an ordinance passed by the Manmohan Singh government in 2013. Over the years, he has fought on numerous fronts, personal and political. As an entitled fifth-generation dynast,

Gandhi carries some of the baggage from the Congress's not-so-glorious past. Perhaps his early exposure to political hypocrisy shaped his dislike for old-style, sycophantic netas. After all, the cabals and coteries that surrounded the Gandhi–Nehru family eventually diminished the Congress and its leadership. As a teenager, he experienced the trauma of his grandmother and father being cruelly assassinated by bullets and bombs. Certainly their violent deaths affected him deeply at a personal level and may even explain his seeming aversion to cut-throat politics. For years, it seemed as if the burden of the past weighed too heavily on him. He warned his party that 'power is poison', and yet he wasn't willing to entirely break away from the allurements of power.

The last few years, though, suggest that Rahul Gandhi has finally come to terms with his political identity. A former aide recalled asking the Congress leader what values he wanted to base his communication strategy upon. 'Love, empathy, truth and courage,' was Rahul's firm response. He is ready to lead from the front but without necessarily following the conventional routes to power. His stinging attack on 'crony capitalism'—the constant references to 'Adani–Ambani'—made many in his own party uneasy. In this age of oligarchs, taking on big business is risky politics. A senior Congress leader confessed that he did not know how to deal with his 'good friends' Gautam bhai and Mukesh bhai because of the mahaul being created against them. 'I actually didn't attend an Adani function because I wasn't sure how Rahul ji would react,' he claimed. As this book reveals, neither Adani nor Ambani donated any funds to the Congress's 2024 campaign. The Congress had cut itself off from its corporate benefactors. In fact, Rahul versus Adani became an unlikely proxy battle in the bigger political war.

An undeterred and determined Rahul Gandhi has marched to his own beat. Five years ago, that wasn't good enough. In 2024, though, the public seemed to see him with a new perspective. His Bharat Jodo Yatra was a landmark journey that helped extricate the Congress leader from an image trap. There was a realization that the path to political rejuvenation can only come through an unfiltered connection with common people.

This was the 'Mohabbat ki dukan' momentum he took into the 2024 campaign at a time when even most of his own party leaders were certain of impending defeat and unwilling to combat the BJP's election juggernaut. Rahul Gandhi's promise of 'khatakhat' cash guarantees was criticized as 'revadi' or 'freebie' populism by the BJP and his caste census push as potentially divisive, but in the 2024 war of narratives, the Congress leader set the pace and direction. His rousing 'Samvidhan khatre mein hai' slogan was a potential turning point, positioning him and the Congress party as unlikely anti-establishment social justice warriors for caste-based reservations. It certainly forced Prime Minister Modi to move away from his 'Viksit Bharat' plank to revive a more familiar pitch of incendiary communal dog whistles and, in desperation, again grab the religious hatred line.

There are sceptics who still wonder whether Rahul Gandhi has what it takes to remain consistent in his actions, whether his heart is still in competitive politics and whether he has the maturity to lead a disparate Opposition coalition. And whether a more conservative, business-friendly Congress party will adjust to a marked left-leaning thrust linked to social justice and economic inequality. Will the Congress leader's proposed cash handouts wreck fiscal health and undo the market-oriented reforms of the liberalization years? Will his caste reservation plank split society further and leave the aspirational middle class fearful of his ascent? Can the Congress, with its organizational limitations, mobilize support among lower castes, especially in the Hindi heartland, on a sustained basis? Or is Rahul Gandhi's social engineering experiment only a temporary disruption in the prevailing Hindutva-centric political order? These are questions that only Gandhi and his party can answer with future actions, but the key KBC (Kaun Banega Challenger) question has been pretty conclusively settled for now. Rahul Gandhi is the chosen face of the Opposition, leader of the INDIA charge in and outside Parliament. To some extent, Rahul has finally earned his inheritance.

However, any assessment of whether the 'Modi era' might give way to a future 'age of Rahul Gandhi' would be premature at this stage. Rahul's courtiers—just as obsequious as Modi's drum-beaters—have already anointed him as the next Prime Minister, when the inconvenient truth facing the grand old party is that he has led them to a third successive Lok Sabha defeat. Like Modi, Rahul too has been unable to break out of the us-versus-them hyper-polarization that afflicts Indian politics. Critiquing the RSS–BJP's Hindutva cannot be reduced to a certain contempt for anyone with divergent views. At a time when India's political centre is looking for viable options, Rahul needs to show that he can be a genuine bridge-builder and coalition leader and not get trapped in hubris and hereditary privilege. The Bharat Jodo concept needs to translate from vision to action on the ground. Ideas of social and economic justice and religious pluralism must go beyond catchy slogans and unformed agendas and be fleshed out into a constructive programme to effect meaningful change.

What is clear is that the 2024 mandate has given Gandhi and the Congress the foundation to build upon in states where the next big election battles will be fought. The effectiveness of Rahul Gandhi as a newly minted people-centric leader and the Congress as a resurgent vote-catching organization will depend upon the party's ability to capitalize on the 2024 momentum. If more assembly election results go their way, then the Lok Sabha upswing will not be seen as an aberration. Else the decades-old organizational atrophy that has plagued the party will make the Congress vulnerable yet again to the slightest switch in electoral fortunes.

Moreover, as the largest party in a non-cohesive INDIA alliance, a strong Congress party that willingly co-ordinates with regional forces remains a prerequisite for building a more effective and sustainable Opposition. 'Anti-Modi-ism' is the glue that brought these disparate parties together in 2024, but there is still no common purposeful identity. When a young female doctor was tragically raped and murdered in a Kolkata government hospital in August 2024, the state Congress hit the streets to protest against Mamata Banerjee's government. A proposed AAP–Congress alliance for the Haryana assembly elections fell through. When Arvind Kejriwal resigned as Delhi chief minister, the Congress distanced itself from the AAP leader.

Conflicting ambitions and personal rivalries won't evaporate overnight. Which is also why the Opposition needs to be more circumspect and not misread the 2024 verdict as heralding the beginning of the end of Modi raj. Putative elected autocrats do not go quietly into the shadows.

=

Frequently asked question: Will Indian democracy survive the Modi era?

This is an existential question perhaps best answered on the seminar circuit, where hand-wringing pontification and ideological positioning occasionally take over from an objective assessment of ground realities. I am not an academic but a newsman who observes the many twists in Indian politics with continuing interest. This book marks the completion of a trilogy that began in 2014, an election that changed India and triggered a tumultuous decade in Indian politics. As a political observer, there is much that troubles me about Indian democracy. The rampant use of money power, the merciless trampling upon of institutions, the weaponization of enforcement agencies, the hollowing out of ideology, caste and religion as divisive markers of identity, the pettiness, corruption and, at times, sheer venality of those meant to serve the citizen, the increasingly autocratic behaviour of leaders, the persecution of dissenting voices in civil society and the pathetic failure of large sections of the media to speak truth to power. Some of these cancerous ailments predate 2014 but are now spreading at an alarming rate and with cold-blooded remorselessness.

In the circumstances, any discussion over the future health of Indian democracy needs to look beyond just the 2024 verdict. While a wise voter may have arrested the 'democratic backsliding' of India's liberal democracy into an electoral autocracy by giving much-required oxygen to the under-siege Opposition, an election result by itself cannot address the multiple challenges confronting the Indian republic as it enters its seventy-fifth year.

The Modi decade has been good, bad and ugly. A stable government in times of global uncertainty has been reassuring. Few can deny that Modi's well-publicized persona has provided India with a more visible presence at the international high table and greater economic heft domestically. Autocrats like to stamp their presence on their surroundings, and the Modi years have seen rapid expansion in big-ticket infrastructure projects, banking sector reforms, a relatively effective Goods and Services Tax regime, scaled-up direct welfare benefits and a concerted digital push. These are standout aspects that surely will yield greater dividends over time to a growing economy. But a surging stock market, glistening highways and enterprising unicorns with their billion-dollar valuations cannot conceal the many patches of darkness that endure. Scarce quality jobs for India's large youth population pose a huge challenge, but there is no silver bullet to resolve the job crisis. India's reform agenda remains haltingly incremental. The regulatory mechanism, inspector raj and dysfunctional judicial system are still impediments to the ease of doing business. Small- and micro-enterprises and the informal sector have struggled in post-Covid times. Farmer suicides and rural distress remain a festering sore in several parts of the country. Almost half of India's population depends on agriculture, yet it accounts for only around one-sixth of the national income. The much-needed farm reforms failed because they didn't take stakeholders into confidence. The Smart Cities Mission launched by the Modi government in 2015 with typical bombast exposes the not-so-smart gap between ambition and actuality. Urban infrastructure, mired in municipal-level corruption, is still in varying stages of collapse. Amidst all the excitement of 'new' India being the fastest-growing economy and the fifth largest in the world, it is often conveniently forgotten that we ranked 125th in per capita GDP in 2024 and 111th out of 125 countries in the Global Hunger Index. A resurgent economy must build a more compassionate and egalitarian society based on equal opportunities, not a 'billionaire raj' that shines only for the well-connected while real wages for a vast number of Indians remain stagnant. The answer isn't unthinking economic populism, but a more inclusive reform agenda that focusses, above all else, on better education and health standards.

Troublingly, the Modi model has brought excessive centralization of power, a style of decision-making that is arbitrary, opaque and fundamentally undemocratic. It has led to the arrest of Opposition leaders, the downsizing of the only Muslim-majority state to a Union territory, sudden midnight lockdowns, charges of cronyism, the enfeebling of institutions and a general climate of fear and intimidation. As a result, the federal spirit, which is the cornerstone of Indian democracy, has taken a real blow. The concept of a 'double engine', trumpeted by the BJP during every election, is inherently flawed and discriminatory. What does 'double engine' really mean? Does it mean that Opposition-ruled states have no engines? Why should Opposition-ruled states be targeted and denied their due while BJP-ruled states are mollycoddled? A north–south divide looms, especially with a planned delimitation of seats after the next census threatening to further erode the political clout of the economically advanced southern states. A 'one nation, one election' trial balloon will only further undermine the federal compact. Hopefully, a coalition government and a strong Opposition will ensure a pushback against any further attempts at executive unilateralism.

It is the 'ugly' aspects of the Modi years that are the biggest stain on the republic. The divisiveness, name-calling and primeval hatreds unleashed periodically by Modi and his supporters in their quest for absolute power have wounded India grievously. His openly divisive, incendiary Banswara speech, which went unreproached, marked a new low in political rhetoric, and dredged up dark and evil prejudices. The 'normalization' of hate speech poses a challenge that must be met by decisive judicial and civil society intervention. 'Sabka saath, sabka vikas, sabka vishwas' (Together with all, development for all, trust of all) is a meaningless slogan when the reality is a ruling party that unabashedly promotes a Hindu majoritarian view and doesn't have a single Muslim MP in Parliament. The sinister minority-bashing and constant targeting of Muslims by various Sangh Parivar affiliates has attacked the very idea of India as a diverse, multi-religious society. And a shrilly communal 2024 election campaign did little to reassure anyone that the core liberal values of tolerance and mutual respect will be preserved in the days to come. A 'better' India must centre on the vision of our founding fathers and mothers and the constitutional values they embraced: Liberty, Equality and, yes, Fraternity. The battle between constitutionalism and Hindutva majoritarianism is far from over. The 'Samvidhan' debate may need reframing to ensure that it doesn't spill onto the streets and explode into discord and violence.

I, for one, remain heartened by aspects of the 2024 verdict that proved yet again that non-violent messaging is possible even in fraught times such as these, and that India's core diversity can still resist heavy-handed attempts to undermine our uniquely plural ethos. But there is no room for complacency. If constitutional responsibilities are abandoned, then the Indian public will have to, once again, show their resolve in holding their leaders to greater accountability and forcing them to shed their arrogance. As this book has emphasized repeatedly, there was no level playing field in the high-stakes 2024 electoral contest. And yet, millions of Indian citizens silently used the power given to us by the founders of our republic to ensure a triumph of the democratic spirit—the power of our votes. We must now move forward with that distinctly unshakeable Indian spirit and the eternal hope of a better India in our hearts.

ACKNOWLEDGEMENTS

As a part-time writer and a full-time newsman, the last few years have been a tough ride for me. I am truly indebted to those who willed me along to the finish line when I wondered if I had the stamina to complete an election book trilogy. A special thanks to the team at HarperCollins, especially Udayan Mitra and Ananth Padmanabhan, who have always been so encouraging. My editor, Shatarupa Ghoshal, is remarkably sound and diligent: her constant queries and suggestions have undoubtedly benefitted the manuscript. The team at A Suitable Agency, led by Hemali and Ranjana, have been very supportive. Kalli Purie at the India Today Group has given more space and freedom to me than today's mainstream news ecosystem might allow for and I am grateful for that. Praveen Shekhar has been meticulous with his research support and Surinder Nagar with his secretarial assistance. A special thanks to Shreyas Sardesai who is an encyclopedia on election data. I have many journalistic colleagues across the news industry to thank for their valuable insights, some of whom I have quoted in the book, and others who preferred to remain anonymous. I also wish to thank the politicians who shared their stories with me, both on and off record. We live in an age where fewer public figures are willing to speak freely so those who did are noteworthy.

Finally, a special word for my family. Sagarika Ghose has not just been wife, best friend and companion for over thirty years, but also an invaluable guide in the task of book writing. My wonderful children, Ishan and Tarini, give me so many reasons to hope and cheer even when the skies turn grey.

Over thirty-five years in journalism, my election travels have taken me across the length and breadth of this incredible country. To all those who have opened their hearts and homes to me during this journey, this book is for you.

APPENDIX

RESULTS

1: State/UT-wise result for major national parties and their allies in the 18th Lok Sabha election

State/Union Territory name	Total Seats	NDA (National Democratic Alliance)						INDIA (Indian National Developmental Inclusive Alliance)						Others	
		BJP		BJP Allies		NDA Separate		INC		INC Allies		INDIA Separate			
		Seats Won	Vote Share (%)	Seats Won	Vote Share (%)	Seats Won	Vote Share (%)	Seats Won	Vote Share (%)	Seats Won	Vote Share (%)	Seats Won	Vote Share (%)	Seats Won	Vote Share (%)
Andaman & Nicobar Islands	1	1	50.58	0	0.00	0	0.00	0	38.54	0	0.00	0	2.97	0	7.91
Andhra Pradesh	25	3	11.29	18	42.19	0	0.00	0	2.70	0	0.39	0	0.08	4	43.35
Arunachal Pradesh	2	2	48.53	0	0.00	0	0.00	0	30.40	0	0.00	0	0.00	0	21.07
Assam	14	9	37.43	2	8.91	0	0.07	3	37.44	0	2.07	0	1.80	0	12.28
Bihar	40	12	20.52	18	26.69	0	0.00	3	9.20	6	30.05	0	0.02	1	13.52
Chandigarh	1	0	47.67	0	0.00	0	0.00	1	48.22	0	0.00	0	0.00	0	4.11

State/Union Territory name	Total Seats	NDA (National Democratic Alliance)						INDIA (Indian National Developmental Inclusive Alliance)						Others	
		BJP		BJP Allies		NDA Separate		INC		INC Allies		INDIA Separate			
		Seats Won	Vote Share (%)	Seats Won	Vote Share (%)	Seats Won	Vote Share (%)	Seats Won	Vote Share (%)	Seats Won	Vote Share (%)	Seats Won	Vote Share (%)	Seats Won	Vote Share (%)
Chhattisgarh	11	10	52.65	0	0.00	0	0.00	1	41.05	0	0.00	0	0.24	0	6.06
Dadra & Nagar Haveli and Daman and Diu	2	1	52.81	0	0.00	0	0.00	0	25.08	0	0.00	0	0.00	1	22.11
Delhi	7	7	54.38	0	0.00	0	0.00	0	18.89	0	24.15	0	0.01	0	2.57
Goa	2	1	50.92	0	0.00	0	0.00	1	39.62	0	0.00	0	0.00	0	9.46
Gujarat	26	25	61.79	0	0.00	0	0.00	1	31.28	0	2.69	0	0.01	0	4.23
Haryana	10	5	46.10	0	0.00	0	0.00	5	43.68	0	3.93	0	0.22	0	6.07
Himachal Pradesh	4	4	56.43	0	0.00	0	0.00	0	41.68	0	0.00	0	0.00	0	1.89
Jammu & Kashmir	5	2	24.43	0	0.00	0	0.00	0	19.39	2	22.27	0	8.51	1	25.40
Jharkhand	14	8	44.55	1	2.62	0	0.00	2	19.25	3	19.79	0	0.53	0	13.26
Karnataka	28	17	46.09	2	5.60	0	0.00	9	45.39	0	0.00	0	0.01	0	2.91
Kerala	20	1	16.67	0	2.53	0	0.00	14	35.05	4	10.08	1	33.36	0	2.31

State/Union Territory name	Total Seats	NDA (National Democratic Alliance)						INDIA (Indian National Developmental Inclusive Alliance)						Others	
		BJP		BJP Allies		NDA Separate		INC		INC Allies		INDIA Separate			
		Seats Won	Vote Share (%)	Seats Won	Vote Share (%)	Seats Won	Vote Share (%)	Seats Won	Vote Share (%)	Seats Won	Vote Share (%)	Seats Won	Vote Share (%)	Seats Won	Vote Share (%)
Ladakh	1	0	23.58	0	0.00	0	0.00	0	27.59	0	0.00	0	0.00	1	48.83
Lakshadweep	1	0	0.00	0	0.41	0	0.00	1	52.29	0	0.00	0	46.91	0	0.39
Madhya Pradesh	29	29	59.28	0	0.00	0	0.00	0	32.44	0	0.13	0	0.14	0	8.01
Maharashtra	48	9	26.17	8	.17.36	0	0.00	13	16.92	17	26.99	0	0.06	1	12.50
Manipur	2	0	16.58	0	18.80	0	8.51	2	47.63	0	0.00	0	0.00	0	8.48
Meghalaya	2	0	0.00	0	24.25	0	2.60	1	34.06	0	0.00	0	2.85	1	36.24
Mizoram	1	0	6.82	0	0.00	0	0.00	0	20.07	0	0.00	0	0.00	1	73.11
Nagaland	1	0	0.00	0	46.13	0	0.00	1	52.83	0	0.00	0	0.00	0	1.04
Odisha	21	20	45.41	0	0.00	0	0.03	1	12.53	0	0.54	0	0.15	0	41.34
Puducherry	1	0	35.83	0	0.00	0	0.00	1	52.73	0	0.00	0	0.00	0	11.44
Punjab	13	0	18.56	0	0.00	0	0.02	7	26.31	0	0.00	3	26.24	3	28.87
Rajasthan	25	14	49.22	0	0.00	0	0.00	8	37.93	2	3.79	1	2.48	0	6.58
Sikkim	1	0	4.95	0	0.00	1	42.71	0	0.58	0	0.00	0	0.00	0	51.76

State/Union Territory name	Total Seats	NDA (National Democratic Alliance)						INDIA (Indian National Developmental Inclusive Alliance)						Others	
		BJP		BJP Allies		NDA Separate		INC		INC Allies		INDIA Separate			
		Seats Won	Vote Share (%)	Seats Won	Vote Share (%)	Seats Won	Vote Share (%)	Seats Won	Vote Share (%)	Seats Won	Vote Share (%)	Seats Won	Vote Share (%)	Seats Won	Vote Share (%)
Tamil Nadu	39	0	11.26	0	6.93	0	0.00	9	10.67	30	36.24	0	0.00	0	34.90
Telangana	17	8	35.19	0	0.00	0	0.01	8	40.10	0	0.00	0	0.36	1	24.34
Tripura	2	2	70.76	0	0.00	0	0.00	0	11.51	0	12.40	0	0.00	0	5.33
Uttar Pradesh	80	33	41.36	3	2.33	0	0.00	6	9.46	37	34.07	0	0.11	1	12.67
Uttarakhand	5	5	56.87	0	0.00	0	0.00	0	32.70	0	0.00	0	0.00	0	10.43
West Bengal	42	12	38.74	0	0.00	0	0.00	1	4.67	0	6.28	29	45.84	0	4.47
Grand Total	543	240	36.56	52	7.26	1	0.06	99	21.19	101	14.01	34	6.21	16	14.71

Source: Results available on the Election Commission of India (ECI) webpage (https://results.eci.gov.in/PcResultGenJune2024/index.htm)
Note: Vote shares have been rounded to two decimal points. NDA Separate and INDIA Separate include parties/candidates that were part of NDA and INDIA respectively but contested separately against the main/official NDA and INDIA candidates. An exception however has been made for Rajasthan's Banswara parliamentary constituency where the official INDIA candidate from Bharat Adivasi Party has been included in the INDIA Separate category as there was an INC 'rebel' candidate also in the fray who contested on the INC's election symbol.
BJP Allies include: Andhra Pradesh - JSP: Jana Sena Party, TDP: Telugu Desam Party; Assam - AGP: Asom Gana Parishad, UPPL: United People's Party, Liberal; Bihar - HAM (S): Hindustani Awam Morcha (Secular), JD (U): Janata Dal (United), LJP (RV): Lok Janshakti Party (Ram Vilas),

RLM: Rashtriya Lok Morcha; Jharkhand - AJSUP: All Jharkhand Students Union Party; Karnataka - JD (S): Janata Dal (Secular); Kerala - BDJS: Bharath Dharma Jana Sena; Lakshadweep - NCP: Nationalist Congress Party; Maharashtra – NCP, RSPS: Rashtriya Samaj Paksha, SHS: Shiv Sena; Manipur - NPF: Naga People's Front; Meghalaya - NPEP: National People's Party; Nagaland - NDPP: Nationalist Democratic Progressive Party; Tamil Nadu - AMMK: Amma Makkal Munnetra Kazhagam, PMK: Pattali Makkal Katchi, TMC (M): Tamil Maanila Congress (Moopanar), Independent supported by NDA; Uttar Pradesh - ADAL: Apna Dal, RLD: Rashtriya Lok Dal, SBSP: Suheldev Bharatiya Samaj Party.

NDA Separate includes: Andhra Pradesh - RPI (Athawale): Republican Party of India (Athawale); Assam - RPI (Athawale); Maharashtra – NPEP; Manipur - RPI (Athawale); Meghalaya - UDP: United Democratic Party; Odisha – AJSUP; Punjab - RPI (Athawale); Sikkim - SKM: Sikkim Krantikari Morcha; Telangana - RPI (Athawale).

INC Allies include: Andhra Pradesh - CPI: Communist Party of India, CPI (M): Communist Party of India (Marxist); Assam - AJP: Assam Jatiya Parishad; Bihar – CPI, CPI (M), CPI(M-L) (L): Communist Party of India (Marxist-Leninist) (Liberation), RJD: Rashtriya Janata Dal, VIP: Vikassheel Insaan Party; Delhi - AAP: Aam Aadmi Party; Gujarat – AAP; Haryana – AAP; Jammu and Kashmir - JKNC: Jammu & Kashmir National Conference; Jharkhand - CPI(M-L) (L), JMM: Jharkhand Mukti Morcha; Kerala - IUML: Indian Union Muslim League, KEC: Kerala Congress, RSP: Revolutionary Socialist Party; Madhya Pradesh – AIFB: All India Forward Bloc; Maharashtra - NCP (SP): Nationalist Congress Party (Sharadchandra Pawar), SHS (UBT): Shiv Sena (Uddhav Balasaheb Thackeray); Rajasthan – CPI (M), RLP: Rashtriya Loktantrik Party; Tamil Nadu - CPI, CPI (M), DMK: Dravida Munnetra Kazhagam, IUML, MDMK: Marumalarchi Dravida Munnetra Kazhagam, VCK: Viduthalai Chiruthaigal Katchi; Tripura – CPI(M); Uttar Pradesh – AITC: All India Trinamool Congress, SP: Samajwadi Party; West Bengal – AIFB, CPI, CPI (M), RSP.

INDIA Separate includes: Andaman and Nicobar – CPI (M); Andhra Pradesh: AIFB, CPI (M) (L), RSP, SP, VCK; Assam – AAP, AITC, CPI, CPI (M); Bihar – AIFB; Chhattisgarh – CPI; Delhi – AIFB; Gujarat – SP; Haryana - NCP (SP); Jammu and Kashmir – AIFB, JKPDP: Jammu & Kashmir Peoples Democratic Party; Jharkhand – CPI, CPI (M); Karnataka – CPI (M), VCK; Kerala – CPI, CPI (M), KC (M): Kerala Congress (Mani), VCK; Lakshadweep – NCP (SP); Madhya Pradesh – CPI; Maharashtra – AIFB, CPI, CPI (M); Meghalaya – AITC; Odisha – AIFB, CPI, CPI (M), CPI (M-L) (L), SP; Punjab – AAP, CPI, CPI (M), RSP; Rajasthan – Bharat Adivasi Party (BAP); Telangana – AIFB, CPI (M), RSP, VCK; Uttar Pradesh – AIFB, CPI; West Bengal – AIFB, AITC, CPI (M-L) (L).

Others include remaining parties, Independents and the None of the Above (NOTA) option.

2: Region-wise seats won by BJP, INC, their allies and others

East India was the only region where INC could not make any seat gains

	Total Seats	BJP			BJP Allies			INC			INC Allies			Others		
		2014	2019	2024	2014	2019	2024	2014	2019	2024	2014	2019	2024	2014	2019	2024
North West India	46	29	32	23	4	2	0	4	8	13	0	0	2	9	4	8
Northern Hindi States	174	145	131	88	11	25	21	6	3	17	5	0	45	7	15	3
Eastern and Tribal States	88	25	46	50	0	1	1	5	6	5	2	1	3	56	34	29
North East India	25	8	14	13	1	1	2	8	4	7	0	0	0	8	6	3
West India	78	53	51	36	19	18	8	2	2	15	4	4	17	0	3	2
South India	132	22	29	30	18	2	20	19	29	42	3	34	34	70	38	6

Source: Election results by ECI

Note: Composition of BJP Allies and INC Allies is not the same across the three elections. For example, unlike 2024, SP was not an ally of INC in 2014 and 2019.

North West India: Punjab, Haryana, Delhi, Uttarakhand, Himachal Pradesh, Jammu and Kashmir, Ladakh and Chandigarh

Northern Hindi States: Uttar Pradesh, Bihar, Madhya Pradesh and Rajasthan

Eastern and Tribal States: West Bengal, Odisha, Jharkhand and Chhattisgarh

North East India: Assam, Arunachal Pradesh, Manipur, Meghalaya, Tripura, Nagaland, Mizoram and Sikkim

West India: Maharashtra, Gujarat, Goa, Dadra and Nagar Haveli and Daman and Diu.

South India: Tamil Nadu, Karnataka, Andhra Pradesh, Kerala, Telangana, Andaman and Nicobar Islands, Lakshadweep and Puducherry

3: Region-wise vote share of BJP, INC, their allies and others

BJP suffered a major vote share loss in northwest and north India, gained the most in south India

	BJP (%)			BJP Allies (%)			INC (%)			INC Allies (%)			Others (%)		
	2014	2019	2024	2014	2019	2024	2014	2019	2024	2014	2019	2024	2014	2019	2024
North West India	32.1	44.1	39.8	9.6	7.9	0.0	26.9	31.1	30.9	0.9	0.0	7.6	30.5	17.0	21.8
Northern Hindi States	43.6	47.2	41.5	2.4	7.0	6.7	15.9	16.5	18.4	4.8	4.8	21.9	33.2	24.5	11.5
Eastern and Tribal States	24.9	42.6	42.8	0.0	0.6	0.4	17.2	13.1	13.1	1.4	2.5	6.2	56.4	41.2	37.5
North East India	28.1	33.7	35.0	4.2	9.5	10.2	29.8	33.6	35.1	1.1	0.0	2.5	36.8	23.3	17.2
West India	38.5	39.8	38.4	14.9	14.9	11.3	23.4	22.0	22.0	10.7	11.5	18.5	12.5	11.7	9.8
South India	15.6	17.5	23.9	5.8	8.7	12.5	18.6	20.4	24.8	1.1	14.9	11.3	58.9	38.5	27.5

Source: Election results by ECI

Note: Vote shares have been rounded to one decimal point.

Composition of BJP and INC allies is not the same across the three elections.

4: BJP and Congress vote shares, 2024 vs 2019

BJP's overall vote share fell by 0.8 percentage points despite the party contesting five seats more than 2019

Congress's overall vote share increased by 1.7 percentage points despite it contesting 93 fewer seats than 2019

BJP's contested vote share fell by 1.3 percentage points, Congress's increased by a whopping 10 points

	2019 LS (%)	2024 LS (%)	Change (% points)
Overall BJP Vote Share	37.4	36.6	-0.8
Contested BJP Vote Share*	46.1	44.8	-1.3
Overall INC Vote Share	19.5	21.2	+1.7
Contested INC Vote Share*	24.8	34.6	+9.8

Source: Election results by ECI

Note: Vote shares have been rounded to one decimal point
*Vote share only in seats contested by the party
BJP contested on 441 seats in 2024 and 436 in 2019. INC contested on 328 seats in 2024 and 421 in 2019.

5: BJP vs Congress contests

Congress's winning rate in its direct contests with BJP increased by nearly four times; it won 29 per cent of such contests as opposed to 8 per cent in 2019

Overall vote share gap between BJP and Congress in BJP vs Congress contests reduced to 10 percentage points from 21 points in 2019

	2019 LS	2024 LS
BJP vs INC Contest Seats*	190	215
Seats won by INC	15	62
Seats won by BJP	175	153
Vote Share of INC	35.3%	40.9%
Vote Share of BJP	56.5%	51.0%

Source: Election results by ECI

*Seats where the top two parties ended up being BJP and INC

SOME SLICES FROM CSDS SURVEY DATA

6: Narendra Modi and Rahul Gandhi as Prime Ministerial choices

Modi's popularity declined from 2019 high, Rahul Gandhi's increased further and doubled since 2014; gap between the two leaders reduced from 24 percentage points in 2019 to 14 points.

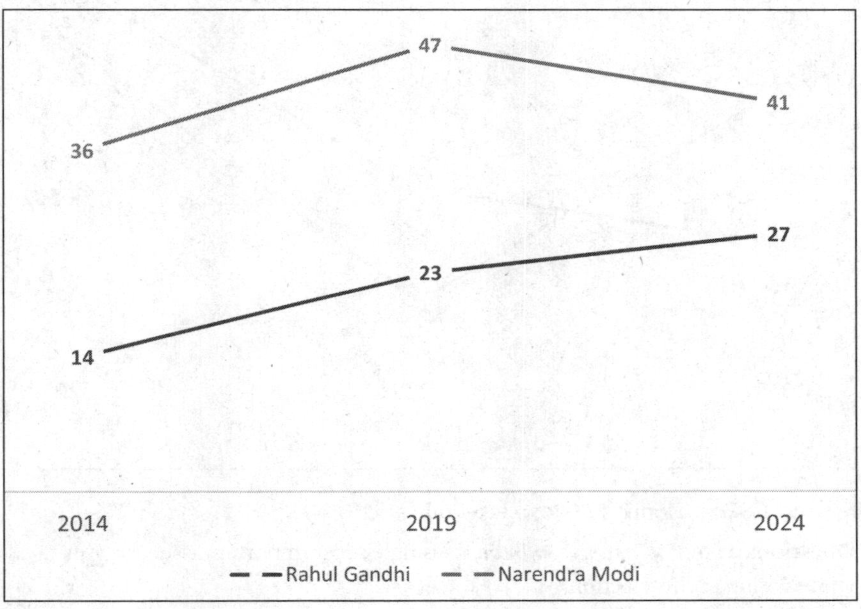

Source: CSDS-Lokniti NES Post Polls

Question asked by CSDS: Who do you want to see as the Prime Minister after this Lok Sabha election?

Figures are percentages.

Note: CSDS offered no names to the respondent while asking the question. The responses were spontaneous.

The rest of the respondents took other leaders' names or did not take any name.

7: Unemployment and Inflation as most important voting issues

50 per cent of the voters cited unemployment and inflation as the most important voting issues compared to just 16 per cent in 2019; those citing unemployment more than doubled in proportion compared to 2019 and those citing inflation increased by six times

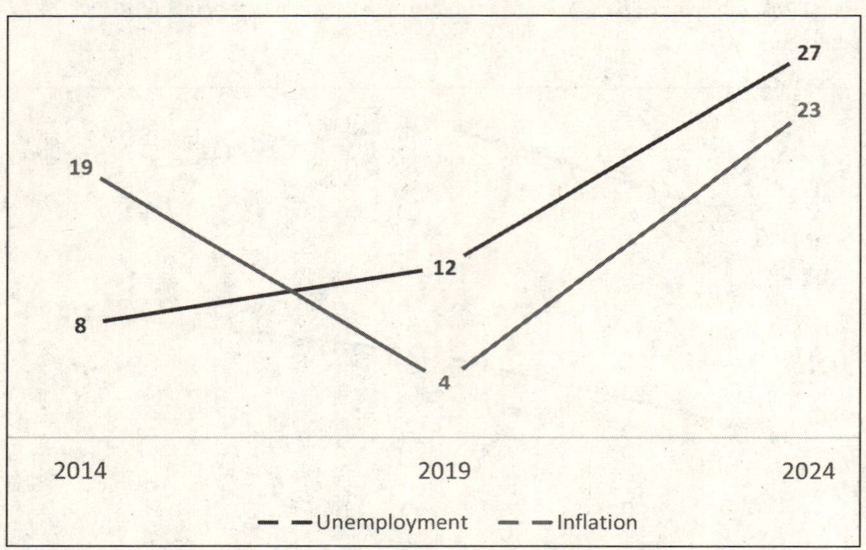

Source: CSDS-Lokniti NES Post/Pre-Polls

Questions asked: What was/will be the single most important issue for you while voting in this election?

Figures are percentages.

Note: CSDS offered no choices to the respondent while asking the question. The responses were spontaneous.

8: Modi effect on NDA voters

Modi's impact on BJP voters appears to have waned as only one in four of them voted for the party because of his being NDA's PM candidate; in 2019 one in every three BJP voters had cited Modi as a factor for voting for BJP. The Modi impact on BJP allies' voters, however, grew stronger.

	Would not have voted for NDA had Modi not been its PM candidate (%)		
	2014	2019	2024
BJP voters	27	32	25
BJP allies' voters	20	24	27

Source: CSDS-Lokniti NES Post Polls

Question asked by CSDS: If Narendra Modi was not the BJP's Prime Ministerial candidate, would you have still voted for the same party as you have done, or your decision would have changed?

9: Hindu Upper Caste Vote Choice, 2009-2024

Under Modi, Hindu upper castes have been the BJP–NDA's most loyal vote bank

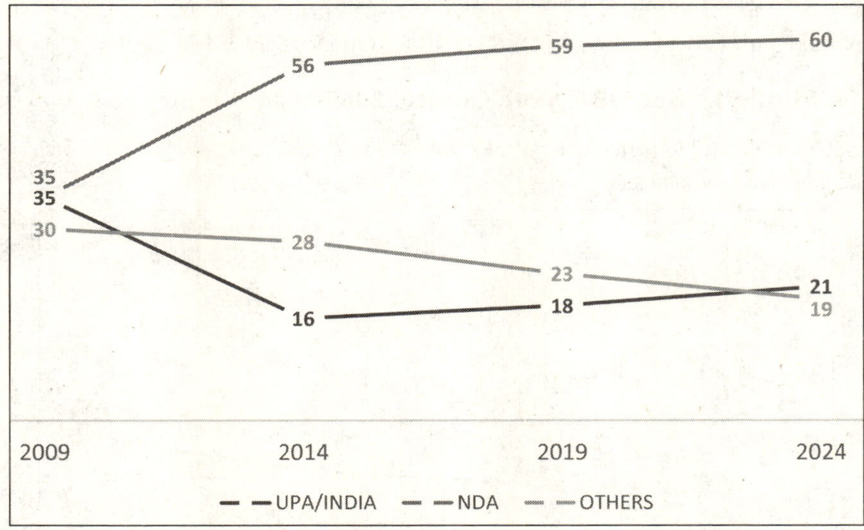

Source: CSDS-Lokniti NES Post Polls

Note: Figures are percentages

10: Hindu Upper OBC Vote Choice, 2009-2024

NDA lost some ground among Upper OBCs, Congress alliance gained tremendously among them registering its best performance since 2009

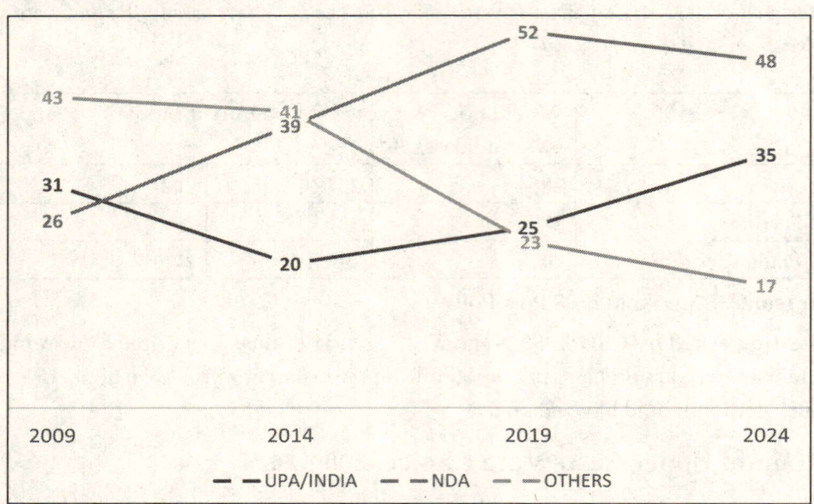

Source: CSDS-Lokniti NES Post Polls

Note: Figures are percentages; OBC stands for Other Backward Classes

11: Hindu Lower OBC Vote Choice, 2009-2024

NDA consolidated its performance among lower OBCs, Cong alliance also did much better than last time among them

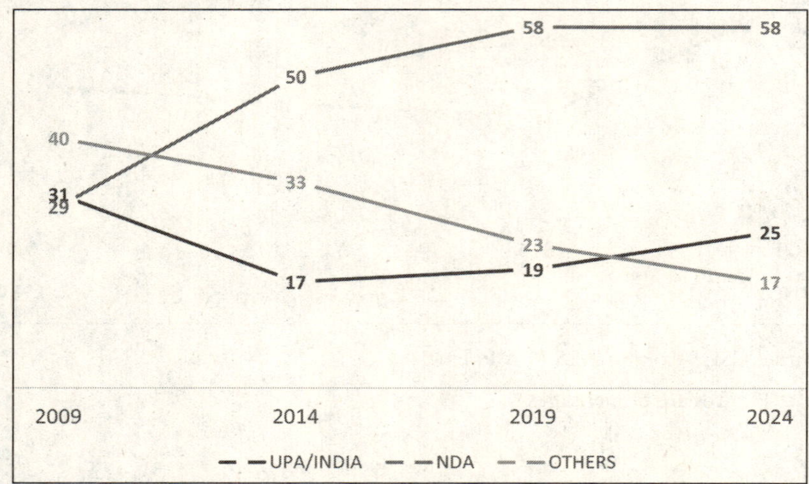

Source: CSDS-Lokniti NES Post Polls

Note: Figures are percentages

12: Hindu Dalit Vote Choice, 2009-2024

NDA's march among Dalits came to a halt; Congress and allies continued to regain lost ground, BSP's decline continued

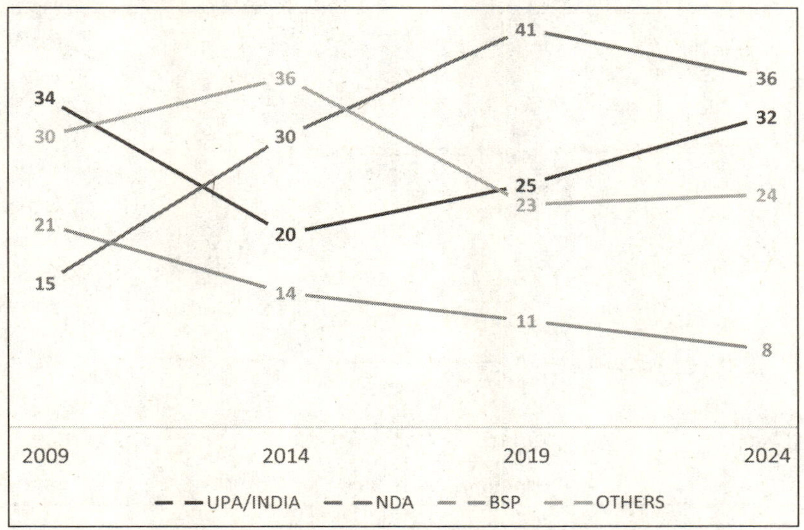

Source: CSDS-Lokniti NES Post Polls

Note: Figures are percentages

13: Hindu Adivasi Vote Choice, 2009-2024

Adivasi support for NDA consistently rising since 2014 and reached an all-time high nationally; Congress alliance performed poorly among them, on the whole.

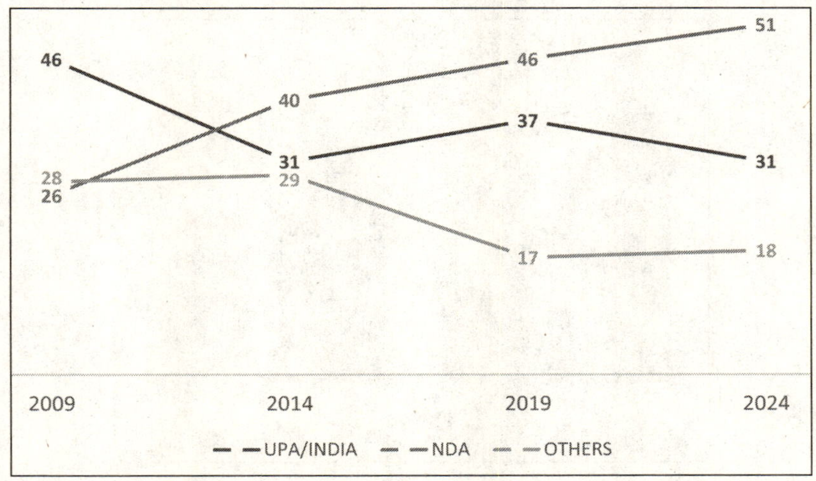

Source: CSDS-Lokniti NES Post Polls

Note: Figures are percentages

14: Muslim Vote Choice, 2009-2024

Muslims consolidated behind INDIA to defeat BJP, 20-point jump in Congress alliance's vote. Muslim support for non-aligned parties crashed

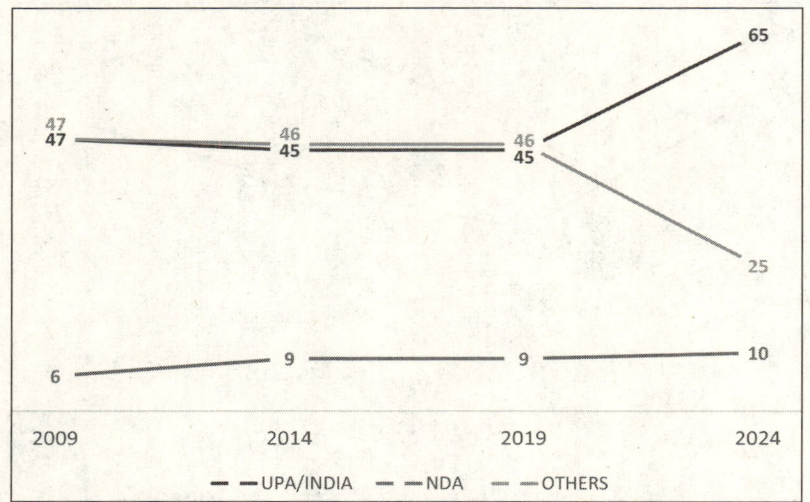

Source: CSDS-Lokniti NES Post Polls

Note: Figures are percentages

15: Vote for BJP and INC by Age Group, 2019 vs 2024

Even though young voters continued to be BJP's strongest supporters in 2024, support for party among them declined compared to 2019; support for Congress increased by around 2-3 points across all age groups

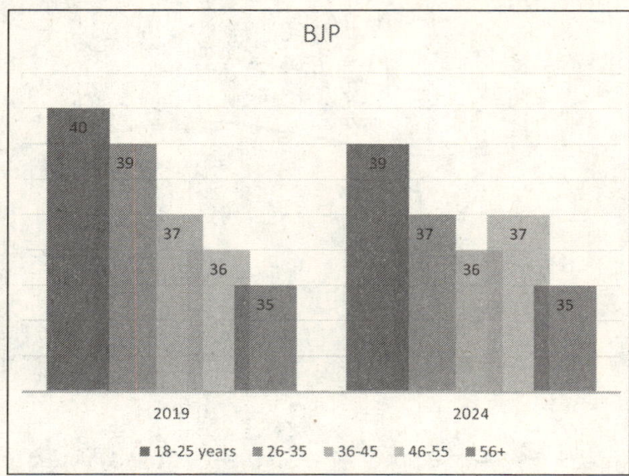

Source: CSDS-Lokniti NES Post Polls

Note: Figures are percentages

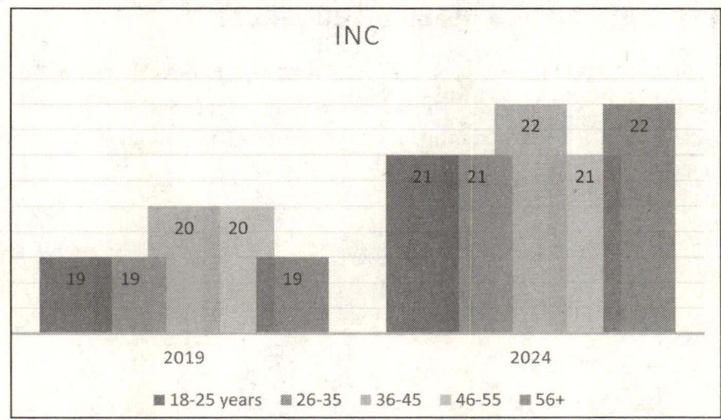

Source: CSDS-Lokniti NES Post Polls

Note: Figures are percentages

16: Vote for BJP among young voters in comparison to its overall vote share

Although the BJP's vote share declined among both 18-25-year-olds and 26-35-year-olds compared to 2019, the drop among the latter age group was greater than the decline among the former. Moreover, unlike 2014 and 2019, 26-35-year-olds were nearly as likely to vote for the BJP this time as the average BJP voter. 18-25-year-olds on the other hand continued to support the party significantly more than the average BJP voter, although among them too this tendency declined a bit.

	2014	2019	2024
Overall BJP Vote Share	31.0	37.4	36.6
BJP Vote Share among 18-25-year-olds	34	40	39
BJP Vote Share among 26-35-years-olds	33	39	37

Source: CSDS-Lokniti NES Post Polls

Note: Figures are percentages

17: Vote for BJP-NDA by Gender, 2009-2024

It's a myth that women are favoring the BJP more than men under Prime Minister Modi. At the all-India level, neither the BJP, nor the NDA have ever got a greater share of women's vote than men's vote according to CSDS post-poll data, although the gap has narrowed.

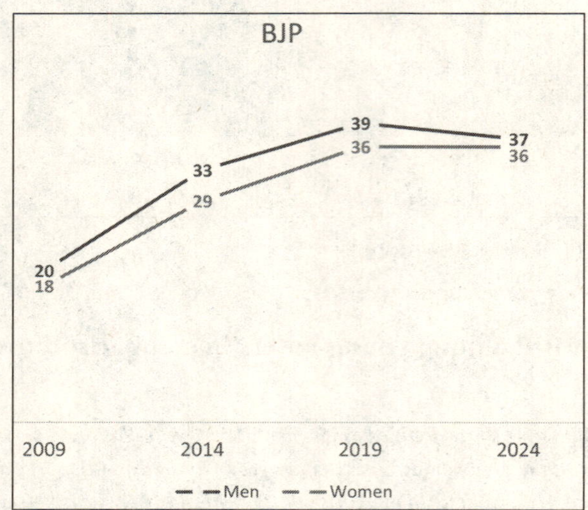

Source: CSDS-Lokniti NES Post Polls

Note: Figures are percentages

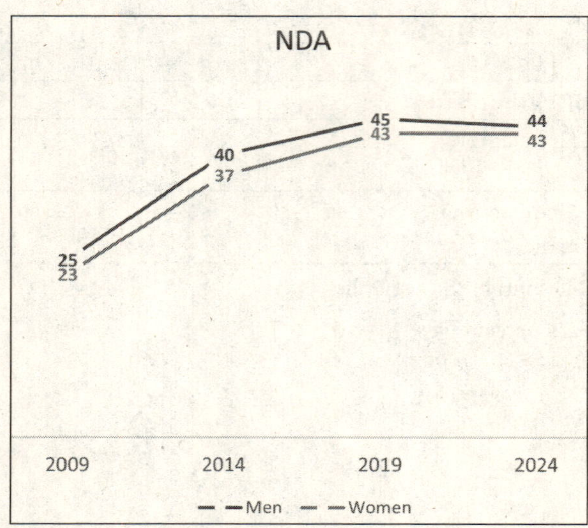

Source: CSDS-Lokniti NES Post Polls

Note: Figures are percentages

18: Vote for INC-UPA/INDIA by Gender, 2009-2024

INC has enjoyed a very slight advantage among women nationally in most Lok Sabha elections since 2009, however along with its allies there is no clear pattern

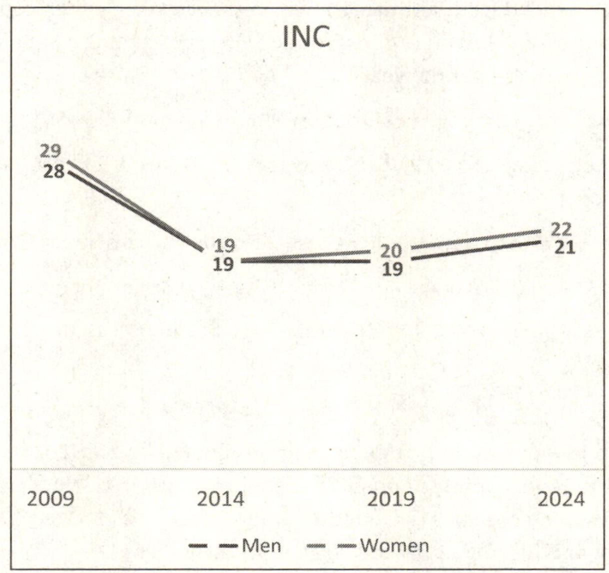

Source: CSDS-Lokniti NES Post Polls

Note: Figures are percentages

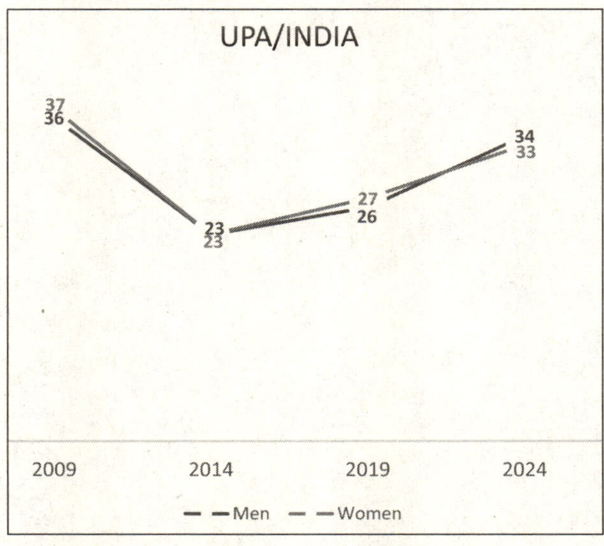

Source: CSDS-Lokniti NES Post Polls

Note: Figures are percentages

NOTE

Survey data shown is from National Election Studies (NES) 2019, 2014, 2009. All surveys were conducted by the Lokniti programme of the Centre for the Study of Developing Societies, Delhi. The data shown have been taken either from the CSDS-Lokniti website (www.lokniti.org) or from CSDS articles published in newspapers and academic journals over the years.

The sample size and coverage details of the surveys are as follows:

NES 2024: Sample size (N) – 19,663; Coverage – 23 States/UTs; 191 Parliamentary Constituencies

NES 2019: N - 24,236; Coverage - 26 States/UTs; 208 Parliamentary Constituencies

NES 2014: N - 22,295; Coverage - 26 States/UTs; 306 Parliamentary Constituencies

NES 2014 Pre-Poll: N - 20,957; Coverage - 21 States/UTs; 301 Parliamentary Constituencies

NES 2009: N - 36,169; Coverage - 29 States/UTs; 536 Parliamentary Constituencies

For detailed methodology and sampling method adopted for NES 2024, visit https://www.thehindu.com/opinion/op-ed/lokniti-programme-of-the-centre-for-the-study-of-developing-societies-csds-methodology/article68254913.ece; For detailed methodology of NES 2019, 2014 and 2009, visit www.lokniti.org

Index

ABOUT THE AUTHOR

RAJDEEP SARDESAI is an award-winning senior journalist, author and TV news presenter. Currently the consulting editor and lead news anchor of the India Today Group, he has over three decades of journalistic experience in print and television. He was the founder–editor of the IBN 18 network and before that was the managing editor of NDTV 24X7 and NDTV India. He has won more than fifty awards for journalistic excellence.

Rajdeep's previous books on the Indian elections, *2019: How Modi Won India* and *2014: The Election That Changed India*, have been national bestsellers. He is also the author of *Democracy's XI: The Great Indian Cricket Story*.